Since 1969, **Root & Branch** has published materials dealing with the efforts of social movements, past and present, here and abroad, to create a socialist society. We have focused on the problems for emerging movements posed by the development of contemporary society, as well as the insights to be gained from the experiences of earlier movements. Some of these movements we have participated in; others, occurring in other places or at other times, we have watched or studied. Our continuing involvement with these movements is informed by four perspectives: 1) that every social movement is, above all, a response of those who comprise it to the social conditions which they face. The development of socialism depends on their recognition that their needs can be met only when, collectively, they take control of their own activity; 2) that every social movement expresses the development of this recognition through its activities. It is such activities—foreshadowing the complete self-determination which is the hallmark of a socialist society—which we want to aid and encourage; 3) that the objective of a radical movement is the direct control of social institutions by those whose activities comprise them. The effort of any organization to substitute its control of society for this direct control is a distortion of this movement; 4) that attempts to impose intellectual orthodoxy, fixed ideas, or abstract slogans upon these social movements only serve to dissipate and hinder them.

Other Fawcett Crest and Premier Books of Interest:

# root & branch
# the rise of the workers' movements

edited by **root & branch**

A FAWCETT CREST BOOK

Fawcett Publications, Inc., Greenwich, Conn.

*ROOT & BRANCH: The Rise of the Workers' Movements*

A Fawcett Crest Original

Copyright © 1975 by Fawcett Publications, Inc.

Library of Congress Catalog Card Number: 75–607

Printed in the United States of America

First Printing: March 1975

1   2   3   4   5   6   7   8   9   10

---

The editor and publisher are grateful for permission to reprint the following selections:

"In the Heart of the Heart of the Country" by Peter Herman. Reprinted by permission of the author.

"The Working Class: A Break with the Past" by Stanley Aronowitz. Reprinted by permission of *Liberation* and the author.

"The United States and Indochina" by Paul Mattick. Reprinted by permission of the author.

"Soviets and Factory Committees in the Russian Revolution" by Peter Rachleff. Reprinted by permission of the author.

"The Origins of Job Structures in the Steel Industry" by Katherine Stone. Reprinted by permission of the author.

"Another View of the Working Class: Its Problems and Prospects" by Paul Mattick, Jr. Reprinted by permission of the author and *New Politics*.

this book was edited by:
jeremy brecher
rick burns
elizabeth long
paul mattick, jr.
peter rachleff

with the help of:
timothy costello
pat frost
peter herman
steven sapolsky
susan schweitzer
tom schweitzer
robert shapiro

**root & branch** would like to hear from all those interested in the ideas presented in this book. subscriptions to other **root & branch** publications are also available. write to **root & branch,** box 496, cambridge, mass. 02139.

this book is dedicated to **paul mattick**

# contents

**root & branch**
**the rise of the workers' movements**

# Introduction

## jeremy brecher

Most people have a healthy distrust of political statements and the people who make them, whether they come from Left, Right, or Center. Those of us who have worked on this book hope that they will treat the material in it with the same skeptical regard. For we believe the problems people face today cannot be solved simply by "correct ideas," or by following the "right people," but only by constantly criticizing present ways of thinking and acting and testing out new ones for ourselves.

Those of us who have worked on this book see it as one contribution to that process. It is an outgrowth of a magazine/pamphlet series, *Root & Branch*, we have published sporadically since 1969. *Root & Branch* developed in the context of the student and anti-war movements of the 1960s, in which its editors were active participants. From the beginning, our objective was a society in which decisions were controlled by those they affected. For that reason, we rejected both those who only wanted to change the policies of the present ruling élites, and those who wanted to replace those old élites with new ones. We found in the history of workers' councils concrete experience suggesting that such a transformation of society might be possible. We discovered in the little-known traditions of the libertarian left much to learn from, though also much to criticize. We found in the mass strikes in France, Italy, and Poland, and in the widespread wildcat strikes in England and the United States, an indication that through acting on their own to meet their needs, working people under certain circumstances would have to challenge the existing power relations of society. From a critical study of Marx, especially *Capital*, we gained much insight into the organization of capitalist society, the nature of its problems, and the process by which a society controlled by the producers might arise from it. We learned from a study of American labor history something about the

11

problems workers had met before in trying to organize themselves to gain more power over their conditions of life. Whatever sources we drew on however, we tried to bring to bear
on the situation we faced.

The concerns of *Root & Branch* are reflected in this book.
Section I presents four accounts of contemporary American
workers and their struggles. Section II analyzes several aspects of the social reality we face today in the United States.
Section III examines a number of important working-class
struggles of the past, with special emphasis on the attempts
by working people to take over and run society for themselves. Section IV presents a classic elucidation of that process. Section V discusses some of the issues facing those who
share such an objective.

While all of the selections in this book have contributed
to our own thinking, they are by no means intended as a complete expression of a unified "political position." Many questions of great importance are not dealt with at all—not
because we believe them insignificant, but because we had
little new light to shed on them. Further, individual editors
disagree with each other and with the pieces on various
points. Still less are the authors responsible for any views
besides their own. This diversity reflects our belief that what
is needed today is not a "correct line," but rather a serious
and open study of our society and how to change it. We see
our ideas as one contribution among many, which we hope
will come together in a ferment of thought and discussion
about these problems on the part of working people everywhere.

We share with most other people a basic problem: that we
have no control over the fundamental processes of our society. All modern societies claim that they represent the will
of the people. The ruling systems of our world, "Democracy"
and "Communism," proclaim in their speeches and in their
very names that they stand for equality and self-rule of the
majority. But this rhetoric only cloaks the control of real
social power by the few.

In capitalist societies, control over production and distribution is split up among a number of competing individuals and
businesses, but it is still tremendously concentrated. In the
United States, for example, 1.6 percent of the population
owns four-fifths of all privately held corporate stock.[1] These
corporations, in turn, own most of the factories, machines,

raw materials, offices, and other materials needed for production. Thus, directly or indirectly, the great majority of working Americans are working for these less than a million families who own society's most important means of production. Where 100 years ago most Americans were self-employed farmers, artisans, and small businessmen, today less than 10 percent are self-employed—the overwhelming majority, whether they wear a blue or white collar, are employees.[2] In "Communist" countries there is a single employer, the government, whose officials make the key decision; in capitalist countries, the key decisions are made by businessmen under the constraint of the forces of competition. But the great majority of the population, there as here, are in exactly the same predicament, forced to work for those who possess the means of production.

All of us who share that predicament are, however great the divergences in our immediate circumstances, members of the working class. It matters little whether the immediate boss represents corporate stockholders or self-perpetuating government bureaucrats; nor does it matter much whether the products we create are controlled individually by private capitalists or collectively by party functionaries. As long as our productive labor and its product are controlled by someone besides ourselves, we will be forced to serve their interests, not our own.[3]

Capitalists run their businesses with an eye to making profits, not to meeting the needs of those, their employees, who do the producing. This system has resulted in a tremendous expansion of production combined with chronic deprivation for the great majority of working people. Throughout its history, capitalism has had periods of considerable stability and growth, punctuated by periods of depression, war, and crisis.

During relatively prosperous periods, working people's social ideas have been directed largely toward how to better

1. Robert Lampman, *The Share of Top Wealth-Holders in National Wealth*, 1922-1956. A study by the National Bureau of Economic Research. Princeton University Press, Princeton, N. J. 1962.
2. *Statistical Abstract of the United States*, Bureau of Census, 1972 93rd edition Table No. 365.
3. For a further discussion of this and related points raised in this Introduction, see Jeremy Brecher, *Common Sense for Hard Times*. Straight Arrow Books, San Francisco, 1975.

their lives within the framework of their subordinate position. Such strategies can either be directed toward getting ahead individually, or toward improving conditions within capitalism generally, but in either case they require working people to participate in the system that subjugates them. This does not mean that they become remote-controlled robots or passive sheep; people go on pursuing their own apparent interests, rarely doubting that they can do so within the framework of existing power relations. During times of crisis, however, such strategies break down along with the social reality that gave rise to them, and workers have at times turned instead to actions which attempt to wrest control of their productive activity from their employers and wield it for themselves.

The two decades following World War II were among the lengthiest periods of growth and stability in the history of American capitalism. Punctuated by "small" wars in "remote" areas and by "recessions" of "minor" proportions, these years nonetheless saw a steady improvement of living conditions for most working people in America.[4] Given these conditions, there was no compelling reason for most working people not to try to find ways to fit into the existing organization of society.

Ever since the Great Depression of the 1930s, the United States government had been attempting by means of government spending policies to counteract the economic crisis cycle that has plagued capitalist society since its birth. Such "Keynsian" techniques considerably moderated the business recessions which continued periodically. A steadily growing government sector provided employment for millions who might otherwise have been jobless. This took the form above all of a continuous expansion of America's military power by means of what Charles Wilson (who moved from head of General Motors to U. S. Secretary of Defense) once hailed as the "permanent war economy."

This period of economic expansion was based in considerable part on the unique position in the world economy which the United States had achieved through World War II. With the economic and political power of capitalist competitors in Europe and Japan largely destroyed, American business found apparently limitless areas for investment. American

4. Much of the information which follows on changing living standards for various groups is drawn from "Living Conditions in the United States" below.

products dominated the markets of the world, and American business was free to supply the expanding domestic market as well, with little fear of foreign competition.

At the same time, some of the worst vicissitudes of working class life were eased by a variety of liberal reform measures. The social security system of unemployment compensation and old-age pensions provided an opportunity to subsist—albeit generally in poverty—to those aged, disabled, and "technologically obsolete" workers whom employers could no longer use profitably. Welfare payments allowed those never absorbed into regular employment, such as the steady stream of black and white migrants from the rural South, to survive, if barely. A constantly expanding educational system allowed most youngsters to receive more schooling than their parents and to aspire to a higher place in society.

From the days of Franklin Roosevelt, the Democratic Party made itself the vehicle for the impulse toward liberal reform, and won the support of a major part of the working class. Within it the union movement became a tremendous power, the backbone of the party organization. Many workers looked to its programs as an important prop to the "good life." Like the labor and social-democratic parties of Europe, the Democratic Party functioned as a means by which workers could pursue their needs within the framework of capitalism.

The development of trade unionism on a large scale allowed a substantial minority of workers—especially in industry— to find a better place for themselves in capitalist society. Legally protected by the federal government and fought for by workers in bloody struggles during the late 1930s, large-scale trade-unionism was actively fostered by the government during and after World War II, the period of greatest union growth. Union power kept workers' standards of living rising with economic growth, established a previously unknown security from arbitrary dismissal and demotion, and created a court of appeals for workers' grievances over working conditions. It created a channel through which workers could express their idealism, ambition, and sense of the need for organization—not to mention their anger—without threatening the ongoing processes of social life.

These developments created a markedly better position for most working people in American society. Compared to the terrors of the Great Depression, life seemed quite bearable. Many working people were able to buy (albeit on credit) suburban tract houses, new cars, and many other products they may never have expected to possess. The system was "delivering the goods"—ideas about how to change it were of little interest to most people. If the system provided for people's essential needs, then it seemed worthy of support, even at the cost of sending young men off to defend it periodically in foreign wars. Life might still be no bed of roses, but this year seemed better than last, and last year better than the year before.

The conditions of life in the post-World War II years, and the attitudes they fostered, were eagerly seized on by many social scientists as signs of a fundamental change in the nature of capitalist society. No longer was the "real issue" the conflict between the owners of the means of production and those who had to work for them. Indeed, they argued, class was no longer very important in a society where everyone lived well and workers seemed no more discontented than anybody else. The working class, they held, was now "integrated" into capitalism.

This comforting view had one flaw—it assumed that a unique historical situation would last forever. Indeed, every period of extended growth has fostered the illusion that capitalism has overcome its problems and has reached a "permanently high plateau" of "enduring prosperity," only to have this idea come crashing down amid the ruins of the expansion of which it was a part.

The specific conditions of the post-World War II period, which made American capitalism appear stable and the working class fully integrated into it, have now come to an end. Over the past quarter-century, Japanese and European capitalism have fully modernized their war-battered production plant and rapidly increased their industrial productivity, while the United States lagged behind. Only through massive devaluation, with its consequent increase in prices at home, has the American economy been able to remain internationally competitive. The real wages of American workers can no longer rise without threatening the international position of American business.

This international decline in turn resulted from economic stagnation at home, as Keynsian techniques ceased to ensure stable economic growth. No matter what mix of monetary and fiscal prescriptions the government has applied, the economy has produced both high unemployment and rapid inflation simultaneously for the past half-decade, an unheard of situation in the past. Professional economists, who in the past have proudly proclaimed the ability of their policies to control the course of the economy, admit their bafflement at this situation. As Nobel Prize winning economist Kenneth J. Arrow said recently, "The coexistence of inflation and unemployment is . . . an intellectual riddle and an uncomfortable fact."[5]

Current economic difficulties are essentially a return to the long-term pattern of capitalist boom and bust. The techniques which were believed to have made the capitalist economy subject to government management and control have evidently reached their limits. Government budget deficits and credit expansion now aggravate inflation without greatly increasing employment or economic growth. Likewise, deliberate government attempts to slow the economy and raise unemployment have had little success in preventing inflation. Once unemployment and inflation occur simultaneously, no solution can come from trying to shift from one horn of the dilemma to the other. Both hold us fast.

What this means for working men and women is all too clear. Inflation means that even those who managed to squeeze through last month have trouble meeting the bills for the most basic needs for food, shelter, and medical care this month. Anyone who predicted ten years ago that American workers would have a problem putting meat on the family table would have been considered hopelessly out of touch with reality; over the past two years, many families have had to cut back sharply on their meat consumption. Working people are forced into more and more inadequate housing as prices soar and construction falls to depression levels. Illness has become a financial disaster, even for those with health insurance, as benefits fall behind rising medical costs.[6]

As if the problems of inflation were not enough, simultaneous high unemployment poses another set of problems for working people. Hit hardest are those who are actually out of work or—even more common—employed only sporadically. In the event of layoffs, those who have been steadily employed in the past are likely to lose quickly whatever benefits of the "good life" they have been able to acquire—a home in the suburbs, consumer durables, and the other attributes

5. New York *Times,* March 26, 1973.
6. For further discussion of these points, see "Living Conditions in the United States" below.

of a mortgage-and-installment-payment way of life. For those who have never had even this, the "unemployment problem" is largely a problem of survival. Government studies show that undernourishment is already a severe problem for tens of millions of Americans, preventing healthy development for millions of children. Unemployment and underemployment are largely concentrated among young people, women, blacks, and other minorities, and those in depressed areas, aggravating the special problems of these groups.

But it is not only the unemployed themselves who are affected by unemployment. Employers have always viewed a long line of job applicants outside the gate as the best weapon to discipline their workforce. When the Nixon Administration took office in 1969, its top officials publicly portrayed rising unemployment as a way to pressure employed workers to limit wage demands. Furthermore, the unemployed are already being used directly to break down the established labor standards of employed workers—as in the employment of welfare recipients at low wages under the "workfare" program and the Talmadge Amendment. The rise of unemployment ensures the end of the era of steadily rising real wages that marked the two decades after World War II.

These new developments present working people with a set of pressing problems that can neither be escaped nor solved in the old ways. The conditions that made it easy to adapt to the status quo no longer exist. The unions and other institutions of reform by means of which people adapted, as we shall see, are no longer capable of dealing with the new situation.

Virtually from the moment unionism was established, in most industries there began a process of separation between union officials and the "rank and file." Workers have, of course, continued to support union efforts to achieve better wages and working conditions, but the feeling that "their" union constitutes an expression of their own ideas and activities has steadily eroded.

The most important reason for this is that union officials have taken over from management many of the functions of disciplining workers. It is the union that enforces the contract's no-strike clause.[7] When workers have a grievance and stop working, it is often a union representative who

---

7. "In the Heart of the Heart of the Country" and "Keep on Truckin'" illustrate this tellingly.

orders them back to work, saying "Cool down and let the grievance committee handle this." When there is a spontaneous strike it is the union which, by refusing to authorize it, gives the employer the right to fire participants. This situation is aggravated in many industries by the virtual collapse of grievance procedures. In some plants, thousands of grievances pile up; sometimes it takes years of going from one level of the grievance hierarchy to another for any kind of settlement to be reached.

This results neither from accident nor conspiracy; their specific context has led unions to develop interests separate from those of their members. U.S. business in the 1930s agreed to accept unionization if the unions would guarantee "management's right to manage" and prevent workers from disrupting production. Any union which permitted workers to strike when they wanted to or allowed them to "run wild in the plants" would not be fullfilling its side of the bargain with management and would meet immediate reprisals—lockouts, harassment, closing of plants, export of jobs, fomenting of challenges to union leadership, or even to the union itself. Further, any union victories which threatened an employer's competitive position would equally threaten the union's institutional survival—no industry, no union. Under these conditions, the path of least resistance for union officials—themselves not subject to their members' day-to-day problems—is cooperation with the employer.

Of course, unions must win something for their members and therefore must make demands on the employers and at times even fight them. But these fights proceed within a ritualized set of rules maintained by the government—rules which make most official strikes resemble a badminton game more than a boxing match. Far from trying to deliver each other a knockout blow, the objective of both union and management in many modern collective bargaining strikes is to get the workers back to work on terms they will accept. This mutual interest between employers and union officials is understood by both parties. As Richard C. Gerstenberg, Chairman of the Board of General Motors, put it recently, "We have come to a time when we can acknowledge that we have far more in common than in conflict, when we can jointly pay our respects to the buried animosities of the past even while we pay tribute to what we have jointly achieved despite them."[8] And as Steelworkers' Union President I. W. Abel said of the agreement by which his union voluntarily gave up the right to strike for four years, "The industry and the union had the mutual problem of self-preservation."[9]

The result of this complicity of union and management officials has been a rising level of wildcat strikes, job actions, and other movements by workers independent of "their" unions. We have included accounts of two such actions, the 1970 postal wildcat and a job action in the New York fuel oil industry. Of course, such actions independent of the union are nothing new. Workers have always developed their own ways of cooperating with each other to prevent the pace of work from getting too fast, to make a detested foreman or supervisor look bad in order to get him transferred, to establish some free time for themselves, and to make life more bearable for each other in any way possible. But in the past such actions often coincided with a genuine loyalty to the union, based on its defense of working conditions and its success at negotiating steady increases in real wages.

Several factors today are breaking down this lingering loyalty. The decline in America's economic position is undermining the strongest card in the unions' deck—the capacity of American business to raise wages and pass on the costs in higher prices. Employers can no longer raise wages without impairing profits. American companies now face increasing pressure to increase their productivity in response both to foreign competition and to low profit margins at home. The unions' top-down structure and their acceptance of "management's right to manage its own business" make them highly ineffective in combating speed-up attempts at the point of production. Indeed, the unions in many industries, dependent as they are on the health of their employers, are participating in the drives to increase productivity through the introduction of new machinery and reorganization, which inevitably mean speed-up, layoffs, and the breakdown of traditional work practices through which workers have secured improvements in life on the job. Rapid inflation turns union-negotiated wage increases into wage decreases for the great majority of workers not covered by full cost-of-living escalators. Thus during the rapid inflation of 1965-70, unions negotiated some of the largest wage increases in U.S. history,

8. New York *Times,* March 20, 1973.
9. Boston *Globe,* June 11, 1973.

but the real weekly take-home pay of production workers nevertheless declined—prices and taxes rose even faster than wages. The result was a wave of wildcat strikes, peaking in 1970, not only against employers but against union-negotiated contracts. As inflation becomes chronic, workers find themselves falling further and further behind and are forced to act on their own—union contracts, official exhortations, government wage policies, and no-strike clauses notwithstanding.

In the years 1961–68, the Kennedy and Johnson Administrations passed the greatest barrage of social legislation in American history. The entire liberal reform program of the postwar decades was enacted into law and funded at levels unprecedented in American history. Two civil rights acts, several education acts, a slew of housing acts, expanded Social Security, Medicare, urban development, War on Poverty, Aid to Depressed Areas—programs covering the entire list of social problems identified by liberalism.

Yet at the very time of its greatest "success," liberal social reform was losing its effectiveness as a channel for working-class aspirations. Indeed, the very institutions through which reform programs were carried out became objects of suspicion to those they were presumed to "help." Urban development programs came to be viewed as hostile attacks on poor and working-class neighborhoods; the welfare bureaucracy was recognized as an enemy of the welfare recipients, charged with "regulating the poor"; school administrators became the targets of attack for parents and students alike.

Liberal social reform programs came into disrepute because they failed to solve the problems they were presumably supposed to deal with. Education, housing, racism, poverty— these problems proved unresponsive to government programs. Indeed, as the bureaucracies that managed them grew, most of these programs were administered in such a way that little help ever reached those directly affected by the problems. The impact of the New Frontier–Great Society reforms on daily life was barely visible even before subsequent administrations began eliminating what little human services they provided in a "battle against inflation."

At the same time, loyalty to the main agent of liberal reform, the Democratic Party, rapidly eroded. The automatic assumption among industrial workers that the Democratic Party, the Party of Roosevelt, reflected their interests, has been severely shaken. There is a deep skepticism about all politicians, a feeling that they all are crooks, and that there are "no leaders you can trust." This attitude is reflected in the low level of participation in elections, especially among younger people. Few working people now view liberal reform through the electoral process as a solution to their problems.

* * *

In sum, we can see that the special conditions that led working people to accept their own subordination so willingly are at an end. The economic framework that made the status quo acceptable—America's world hegemony and steady domestic economic expansion—no longer exists. Without that framework the institutions through which workers have adapted to their position within American capitalism—trade unions and social reform through electoral politics—are losing their credibility as ways of solving the problems of daily life.

Working people are facing deteriorating conditions of life. No longer is it true that this year, whatever its hardships, is at least better than last. No one can tell how long the new circumstances we have described will last or how they will end. What we can say with confidence is that the special circumstances of the immediate postwar decades can never be restored, and that any new stabilization of society will have to rest on some new basis. Without it, the years ahead promise little but inflation, unemployment, international conflict, and general social crisis.

Each of us has an understanding of the society we live in which shapes the ways we meet the problems of daily life. When society stays the same for a long time it may be possible to go on living by the same understanding from year to year and even from generation to generation. But when, as now, the problems we face are changing, fixed ideas are no longer much help in dealing with them—indeed, they become a hinderance. In such situations, people have to develop new ideas and new ways of acting.

Such periods of continuing social crisis have throughout history called forth popular social movements. The recent years have been no exception. By the middle 1960s, radical movements had developed in the United States on quite a substantial scale, and by 1968 the atmosphere was so heated that leading historians were maintaining in the popular press that the level of social conflict was higher than at any time since the Civil War. Through the 1960s, a variety of social problems were growing, particularly for blacks, women, and students. But various facets of the crisis hit different special groups one by one, at a time when most working people could still hope that the former steady improvement of their conditions would soon be resumed. From their perspective, the noisy radical movements of the 1960s presented a threat to a stability they hoped to preserve. The "working-class conservatism" of the 1960s was grounded in the hope that the favorable conditions of the postwar era might continue indefinitely.

Minorities who were already reeling from the shocks of the new era could hardly count on this majority to bring about massive social change. This situation limited the possibilities and narrowed the perspectives of the radical movements of the 1960s. They developed in a period when there was no real possibility of challenging the power over working people's lives of those who own society's means of production. The most that could be hoped for was modest changes in government policies and moderate improvements in the status of discriminated-against groups. Consequently, the radical movements of the 1960s tended toward attempts at much-needed social reforms on the one hand (lunch-counter integration, legalization of abortion, and a new Vietnam policy, for example) and, on the other, cultivation of the internal life of the group, often glorified with an overlay of revolutionary rhetoric (communes, consciousness-raising, and black studies). None of these approaches could provide the basis for a challenge by working people to the power of their bosses. This helps explain why such movements are declining at the present time, when living conditions for most people are getting worse and their need to challenge the status quo is rising. In their time, these movements did much to raise the possibility of alternatives to the status quo and to demonstrate the power people can exercise through direct action. If their achievements were limited by the conditions in which they arose, their best aspirations may still contribute to the development of a new movement for power on the part of the great majority of working people.

One other radical tendency—it can hardly be called a movement—persists from the 1960s. This consists of the various sects and parties, each claiming to be the true vanguard of the revolution, who would "organize," "lead," and

"bring revolutionary consciousness" to the working class.[10]
They generally envision themselves leading a revolution in
America modelled after such revolutionary super-heroes as
Lenin, Mao, Castro, or even Stalin. In both theory and practice, these groups try to establish themselves as an alternative
leadership for the working class, and see themselves taking
power as a new, socialist government. For some of their
members, such groups reflect the power drives of individuals
who cannot find a place in the ruling class of this society,
or the need for social community which provides a sense of
meaning and purpose, emotional support, intense group life,
and absolute certainty of the truth of one's beliefs. To the
extent to which these groups reflect more general social conditions, they are a response to workers' acquiescence in their
position through much of the 1960s. Since workers were
clearly exploited, and yet seemed to accept their exploitation,
many radicals assumed that the radical's function was to bring
to workers an understanding of their oppression which the
workers could not achieve for themselves. These radicals saw
themselves as outside the working class, injecting radical
ideas into it. This whole approach, while natural to a period
of working-class quiescence, neglects the fact that what working people need to take control of society is not alternative
leaders with alternative programs, but the ability to think,
plan, decide, and act for themselves. The radical parties have
little chance of winning a mass following—most often they
are quickly sized up as just one more group of people looking
for power for themselves. But if they could win such a following, it would weaken rather than strengthen working people's capacity to act in response to their own needs.

* * *

What for the capitalist system is a crisis, is for those subjected to it both a scourge and, paradoxically, an opportunity.
Crisis makes it impossible for the routine of daily life to go
on. As we have seen, inflation and unemployment undermine
the established living standards for all workers, while concentrating misery among those in the weakest position. Employers
attempt to recoup their losses by speeding up production
and breaking down work standards. Meanwhile war and

10. This attitude is discussed further in "Old Left, New Left,
What's Left."

preparation for war not only lower living standards through taxation, but kill and maim those sent out to fight and threaten all with the possibility of nuclear devastation. Yet these very conditions create the possibility for a new kind of movement, based on the common interests of the great majority of working people—a movement to eliminate the power of those who cause such conditions by taking control of society for ourselves.

The working class is potentially powerful because it constitutes not only the great majority of the population, but the organized productive power of society. If workers refuse to cooperate with the existing set-up, it cannot function; if they do not work, production stops; if they refuse to produce for anyone but each other, capitalism will cease to exist. By such methods of direct action as strikes, mass demonstrations, general strikes, workplace occupations, and insurrections, workers have the means of parlaying this potential power into the real direction of society.

The difficulty is to find a mode of organization which joins together the entire power of the working population, yet at the same time does not become merely a new, separate bureaucracy, contesting with the old rulers for control over the workers' activity. This is the problem to which Anton Panekoek's *Workers' Councils* is directed. He proposes an approach, growing out of the present organization of society, which would let working people keep control of their activity in their own hands, while allowing them to coordinate their action on the widest possible basis.

The basic unit of social decision-making in Panekoek's conception is the assembly of all people who engage in face-to-face cooperative activity in a work-group, neighborhood, apartment building, school, or the like. What action a group will take is debated and decided within these assemblies. The decision of an assembly is not merely a poll of opinion for or against a proposal, but rather a decision on the participants' part of whether they will implement it. Where decisions must be made concerning groups too large to meet and discuss together face-to-face, the assemblies send delegates to more central coordinating bodies. These delegates are given binding mandates by those they represent. Delegates to central councils are vested with no authority of their own by virtue of their position. In this they differ completely from the elected officials of so-called "representative democracy," who exercise their own authority from election day to election day over the people they supposedly represent. Nor does any apparatus of coercion exist separate from the assemblies to enforce the delegates' decisions. The objective of this form of organization is to eliminate any separation of deciders and implementers and to prevent the formation of any special class of officials or bureaucrats.

This conception is far different from the usual idea of "an organization" to which individuals "belong." It is rather a *method* by which working people can direct and coordinate their own activity. In the struggle against the present rulers, it allows maximum local initiative at the same time that it permits the widest possible coordination. It has the added advantage of being far more resistant to repression; as long as people grasp the necessity for this kind of cooperation and control of their activity themselves, their "organization" cannot be broken by jailing or corrupting of leaders, or by court injunctions and other government attacks directed against formal organizational structures. As the basis for a new organization of society, it suggests a way in which production can be organized and all necessary social activities carried out, without the need for any class, bureaucracy, state, or other special group separate from the rest of us.

The idea that working people can create this kind of organization and use it to attempt solutions to their problems is no mere product of fantasy or theory. Indeed, they have done so repeatedly. But the history of workers' attempts to take over control of their labor and their society are little known. In this volume we have tried to present a few examples of that history. Older examples include the factory committees which took over much of Russian industry in 1917 and the Seattle General Strike of 1919. A more recent episode was the French general strike and occupation of factories of 1968.

Needless to say, all these attempts ended in failure—either through workers' domination by a new élite or through the restored power of the old one. Workers have been all too willing to give up their power to leaders who promised to solve their problems for them. Defeated in their bid for power, revolutionary workers' movements have often evolved into new institutions for workers' adaptation to their basic powerlessness—witness the Soviets in Russia and the Workers' Councils in West Germany today. The experiences of such movements reveal the great power of workers to act, but they require critical scrutiny if they are to be of any use to us in thinking about the future. Above all, we believe one lesson must be learned from them: working people can establish their control over society only if they keep direction of their own activity themselves, refusing to give it up to any other group, organization, or leadership, however much it may claim to represent the interests of the workers or the needs of society.

*   *   *

There are great obstacles to the process we envision. Working people are divided in myriad ways—by race, sex, age, nationality, residence, and job status.[11] We are taught from birth to "look out for number one" and to "get along by going along." It is always easier to let officials and leaders take responsibility for solving problems and making decisions than to do it ourselves. The risks involved are awesome, when challenging a ruling élite which is armed to the teeth.

But the alternatives are grimmer still. A continued deepening of the present crisis will mean a continued deterioration of living and working conditions. A continued intensification of international competition can only lead to war and more war. Perpetuation of the present system of social organization means mass misery and mass death on a scale to rival, and perhaps to exceed, what this system has produced for the past sixty years of war and crisis. To avoid such a fate, we must abolish all systems of power by which some people seek to control and exploit the activity of others. In doing so, we can open up the possibility of an entirely new kind of society, one in which we can direct our own activity to meeting our own needs and desires, and in which the free development of each can be the basis for the free development of all. If we can begin the process of taking control of our lives—through discussion and through action—in every place we work, live, study, and cooperate with other people, we can perhaps reduce the agony through which we will have to live in the years ahead.

11. These divisions are discussed further in "The American Working Class," "In the Heart of the Heart of the Country," "The Origins of Job Structures in the Steel Industry," and the "Introduction to 'Workers' Councils.'"

# I. On the Job

## The Postal Strike

### stanley aronowitz and jeremy brecher

I

A new labor movement is being born in America. It is the autonomous creation of the working class. It exists more potentially than actually, but its early seeds are appearing in wildcat strikes in the trucking, air-transport, and mail-communications industries. These wildcat strikes differ from most others in recent labor history. Unlike the sporadic outbreak of worker militancy outside union sanction in individual plants, the recent strikes have been national walkouts independent of the official labor movement. They have had a demonstrated capacity, moreover, to withstand invocations of union leadership for orderly procedure, government threats of legal reprisal, and apparent lack of national coordination except the universal idea of direct action to meet felt needs.

For years, most American workers and radicals within the labor movement were convinced of the absolute necessity of central organization on a national level to meet the corporations or the government on an equal footing. The local patterns of trade union organization predominant during the first sixty years after the Civil War were deemed inappropriate to the monopoly stage of capitalism, in which large national corporations with chains of plants dotting the country dominated the political economy.

The validity of this point of view was reinforced by the apparent success of the CIO and the AF of L which unionized multioccupationally most basic industries in the United States. The early successes of collective bargaining to achieve higher wages, fringe benefits, and some measure of worker control over the conditions of labor were attributed to the emergence of a bureaucracy which mirrored, in both scope and power, the structure of corporate capital.

Now, however, the central bureaucracies which control the trade unions have become an obstacle to the development of struggles centered on the elementary needs of workers. The strike of postal workers brought to the surface the sclerosis of the trade unions, exposed their alliance with the government against the workers, and ushered in nascent forms of workers' direct action independent of the trade unions.

## II

Several years ago, radicals in the United States and in Europe were proclaiming the end of deprivation as a central thread of working-class action. However cognizant of the need to understand class exploitation as primarily the exploitation of labor, its alienation at the point of production, radical theorists of neo-capitalism consistently underestimated the importance of understanding the crisis of contemporary capitalism as reflected in the antagonism between wages and profits. Nor have we fully understood the significance of state workers in the political economy.

The position that struggles for economic demands were eminently cooptable was a response to the specific conditions of U.S. capitalism in the '50s and early '60s. The familiar wage struggles consisted in the expiration of a contract, a union strike call, and a quick settlement with a mild wage increase, which was easily passed on by the corporations to the workers in higher prices. To radicals, this process looked hardly more revolutionary than any other business transaction.

The postal strike was completely different. From the first it was illegal. It did not play by the rules of the game. It fought national and local union leaderships tooth and nail. It was undeterred by appeals to patriotism and national interest. It based itself on the power of the workers, not on the goodwill of the bosses. Far from integrating the workers into the system, the postal struggle opposed its central institutions.

Nonetheless it was fundamentally a strike for higher incomes. Nor is it hard to understand why postmen should consider wage demands worth fighting for. Letter carriers make $6,176 to $8,442 annually. The Department of Labor considers $10,000 the minimum annual income for a family of four. Richard Nixon affirms that postal workers have been underpaid for twenty-three years.

An index of the potential explosiveness of wage issues is the fact that the weekly earnings of the average non-farm non-supervising worker in the private economy last year was approximately $2.00 less than the "grossly underpaid" postal worker.

This is not to say that wage demands are *more* important than others. In fact, it is wrong to oppose economic and non-economic demands. The real question is whether the struggle is conducted in a way which uses and increases the workers' power, their freedom of action.

The post office strike demonstrated that many groups now share the social position once reserved for blue collar industrial workers. The postal workers are underpaid and exploited in precisely the way the industrial workers are, and they clearly have a critical role in the functioning of society.

The use of troops and the application of the full legal powers of the state in both the mail and the rail struggles reveal the centrality of these functions to U.S. capitalism. Free movement of the mails and commodities are an absolute condition to the system's maintenance, much less its expansion. The government had no choice but to play out the alternatives to insure the resumption of rail and mail service. In the rail dispute, severe legal sanctions, such as congressional action to suspend the provisions of the rail labor act and invocation of compulsory arbitration, seemed sufficient, at first, to dissuade the workers from direct action in disregard of union leaders and state decree. But the frustrations of postal workers built up over thirty years could not be suppressed through legal means alone.

Federal workers are completely dependent on congress for wage and benefit improvements, however infrequently enacted. The strike ban has always been held sacrosanct, however, by union leaders and the government. But the dual pressures of inflation and tedious work conditions with no significant upgrading opportunities became too much for postal workers who were forced to hold two jobs or go on supplementary welfare to support themselves and their families.

One of the most interesting features of the strike was the fact that many signals had been flashed to postal officials and the federal government long before the wildcat broke out. Stories in the daily press reported that postal workers were receiving public assistance to meet basic needs. Demonstrations and intensive lobbying activities had reached their high point immediately prior to the strike. Yet congress and the administration seemed powerless to act decisively to meet the income demands of the workers.

The Vietnam war, the permanent war economy, and the production of waste subsidized by federal expenditures appear to be logical explanations for the slow pace of government action to meet the modest wage demands of postal union officials. Beyond the fiscal crisis of the public sector induced by the direction of state spending stands the absolute refusal of corporate capital to reduce profits in order to support the public sector. On the contrary. Public services exist to support business. (Witness the absolute need to resume mail service in order to guarantee the flow of information to the stock market.) But the use of the taxing powers of the state to redistribute income between workers and capitalists turns back on itself. The increasing inefficiency of the mails in comparison with the increasing volume (itself a concomitant of capital expansion) is a direct result of the pauperization of the traditional public services.

Business has been unwilling to finance even those social costs immediately beneficial to itself. Instead, it demands that public services be turned over to the private sector. One of the issues raised by the administration in response to the strike was the necessity of postal "reform" as a condition for pay increases. The proposed postal reform was to abandon public ownership of the mail service and create a government-owned corporation to run the mails. This corporation, similar to quasi-public transit corporations, would be self-sustaining; that is, it would not receive funds from the general treasury in order to subsidize the postal system. Instead, operating costs would have to be met by operating income, essentially the price of stamps. Such a corporation could issue bonds to finance capital improvements, but the debt service would have to be paid for from operating income.

### III

It is evident that as long as the war continues workers will bear its burden through lower real wages, higher taxes, unemployment, and inflation. In fact, real wages *cannot* be increased at the present time simply through strikes against one or another employer. This will have two effects on the labor movement. First, its actions will develop more and more into class actions, in response to the shifting of the burden of the war onto the workers. Second, its objectives will have to move beyond simple wage increases, which are impossible given present priorities. An end to the war and a shift in the tax burden will no doubt be two of the key demands. The program of the Alliance for Labor Action clearly reflects these tendencies. But the methods of struggle it proposes— union organizing and legislative lobbying—work only within a system which has sufficient resources to make concessions, not within a system which is already overextended and has its back against the wall.

The result is that the wildcat actions of the workers will more and more tend to become class actions and to become political. The pace of the process cannot be predicted— although a number of massive wildcat strikes for economic demands will probably be necessary before union leaderships are sufficiently discredited to permit workers to become aware of the need to engage in broader class and political actions independent of the trade unions.

The smell of general strike was in the air during the week-long postal strike. *The Wall Street Journal* explicitly warned of it; and even Rademacher, president of the letter carriers' union, threatened to ask George Meany [!] to call a general strike if the government refused to make concessions. The national administration and the corporate bourgeoisie experienced this nightmare for the first time since the great industrial union walkouts in 1946, when nearly three million workers in most basic industries left their jobs in order to counter the decline in real wages wrought by rising prices following the Second World War. There were differences however. In 1946 the "first round" wage strikes were officially sanctioned and controlled throughout by liberal industrial union hierarchies. At no time were the channels of collective bargaining in danger of being overrun. In the postal strike, the workers went outside the union framework. The national leadership opposed the walkout and was able to maintain the accountability of local union leadership to its command until the rank and file revolt pushed some local heads to support the strike.

A second feature of the mail strike was that it represented the first national wildcat in recent labor history. The strike spread from New York City to Nassau and Westchester counties, upstate New York, and nearby New Jersey and Connecticut almost immediately. Within a few days, the wildcat became national, as postal workers in Chicago, Detroit, Pittsburgh, Los Angeles, San Francisco, and other major centers took the initiative on their own despite the pleading, cajolery, and threats of local and national union chieftains. The day after the strike began, the press was already speculating about the possibilities of a general strike of federal employees. John Griner, president of the American Federation of Government Employees, was reported by the Washington *Star* to say "that he had to intervene personally to prevent several strikes by his locals." Nathan Wolkimir, president of the National Federation of Federal Employees, considered conservative by trade union standards, said that NFFE locals throughout the country had indicated they wanted to strike in support of the postal workers. Alan Whitney, executive vice-president of the unaffiliated National Association of Government Employees, gave a radio interview in which he reported:

> We have been receiving phone calls from our various local presidents in various agencies throughout the government and throughout the country. They have watched events of the past days and have seen postal workers striking with a degree of impunity, and their question to us is, if they can do it, why can't we?

Whitney, Griner, and other leaders of government employees' unions gave a standard answer to this question. "We advised them that it was against the law" (Nathan Wolkimir). Undoubtedly this advice served to dissuade those militants who were ready to strike, but were still under the hegemony of their union leadership. Whitney reported to the White House that "tremendous pressure" was being put on the national office of his union to authorize strikes, especially by "one of our biggest defense locals whose primary duty is to supply the war effort in Southeast Asia."

Simultaneously, municipal employees in San Francisco and Atlanta took to the streets. Similar demands informed their struggle. The up front public issue was the failure of Congress to enact a substantial postal pay increase. The spectre haunting local governments haunted the Nixon administration as well. Even if the postal demands could be met, suppose all municipal, state, and federal employees were to join in the struggle? Beyond this possibility was the danger that stalled teamster negotiations would result in a transportation wildcat, and perhaps trigger action by industrial workers. President Fitzsimmons of the Teamsters warned that "the natives are restless," an apparent attempt to force the trucking companies into a quick settlement, in order to forestall an event mutually undesirable to the unions, the companies, and the government.

There is little doubt that there was tremendous pressure from the ranks for widening the struggle beyond the postal strike, on the one hand, and various local disputes, on the other. National union leaders, taken aback by the temerity of the rank and file, recovered their composure. Simultaneously, they urged a back-to-work movement among the workers and attempted to force concessions from the Administration. The passivity of the AFL-CIO leaders was a clear indication of their fright at the implications of the postal walkout. They remained publicly mute throughout the one week strike, working "behind the scenes" to bring the Administration and congressional leaders to the bargaining table in order to settle the strike on the basis of a non-inflationary wage increase commensurate with cost of living increases since 1967. The postal settlement was in accord with the GE settlement. Union objectives were to recover lost ground, not to make substantial gains in real wages.

But the postal workers could not be herded back to work by peaceful means. Neither the promise of a piddling wage increase with a provision for achieving top rate after eight years instead of twenty years nor appeals to patriotism and the rule of the law was successful. The president was forced to resort to his ultimate weapon: the use of troops as strikebreakers in the most militant section of the 180,000-worker walkout—New York. Even though the troops were unarmed, the coercive implications of 25,000 of them in the post offices were not lost on the workers. Contrary to romantic leftist notions of impending bloodshed, most letter carriers were genuinely intimidated by the presence of the troops. They were unprepared, psychologically and militarily, to counter them effectively. The combination of congressional promises of a substantial wage increase and the massive presence of troops was sufficient to break the back of the strike for the time being.

But the end of the strike is not attributable merely to the show of state power and/or trade union constraint of the workers. More important than either of them was the failure of the strike to spread to other federal workers and beyond them to industrial workers. Short of a widening strike on generalized demands all struggles end in negotiated compromise. The material conditions existed for a wider strike. Conjuncturally, teamsters and auto workers face the most difficult negotiations in years. The current recession has produced stiffer corporate resistance to wage demands which would alter the relationship between profits and wages should international competition make it more difficult to offset wage increases by higher prices. Rank and file restlessness nevertheless has not reached the point of revolt against the trade unions and the employers in substantial parts of basic industry.

But the air controllers were ready and did strike. Workers in all public services, traditionally the least cohesive, are furious at the inability and unwillingness of the state to meet their needs. Implicit in their readiness to struggle for quantitative demands is their refusal to accept the sacrifices made necessary by the defense effort. The Vietnam war has lost its magic among workers who have been told they must subordinate their needs to national priorities—to militant anticommunism, that is, waged on their (the workers') backs. To be sure, there is no conscious rejection of these priorities. But the wildcat strikes evoked a decree of national emergency from the president amid arguments that vital services were being impaired. Most apparent was the inability of most workers to make an explicit connection between their strike and its ideological consequences not only in relation to the war, but more importantly, in relation to the legitimacy of the law as a determinant of social behavior. The workers *acted* subversively without bringing this subversion to consciousness. They had refused in practice to subordinate their own interests to the national interest, traditionally defined, but could not perceive it in its most general aspect, the struggle against state prerogative over them.

In some cities the union was able to maintain complete control. Postal workers in Washington, D.C., asked whether or not they were going to strike, often replied that they did not know. It was being decided for them by the officers; they were waiting, that is, for word from above. Meanwhile the president of the local announced on television that "the reason the D.C. workers are not out is that the local is doing everything possible to keep them from going out." When the membership arrived at the union hall for a meeting, which had been announced publicly, they found the hall locked and guarded. The leadership's attitude was we'll let you know when the national calls a strike. A general meeting of the local was not called until almost a week after the New York strike had begun. Wildcat advocates were not allowed to speak at the meeting. One of them had his union card torn up when he presented it to get in. (He never did get in.) A vote was announced. But what was being voted on was uncertain. The membership, it seems, was confused. The leadership, not at all. The meeting, it announced, had voted against a strike.

The wildcat forces met on the lawn in front of the main post office, but did not have sufficient strength to call a strike. They were weak, in part, because the strike nationally had peaked, and many other cities were going back to work. The local's stalling techniques had been successful. Two other conditions explain Washington's lack of militancy. First, the basic industry of the city is government, and government workers have no tradition of strikes; they have instead remnants of an ideology of "public service responsibility." Second, perhaps even more than elsewhere, D.C. postal workers are predominantly black, but D.C. has perhaps the most middle-class black community of any major city, based on access to government jobs and the security-consciousness which such jobs appeal to and generate. These same conditions were no doubt important in preventing the strike from spreading to other government workers in Washington. They will continue to retard as well such developments in the future.

In other major cities, however, black workers and young workers were the cutting edge of the walkout. In strikebound cities such as Detroit, Pittsburgh, Philadelphia, and New York, approximately 50% to 75% of the workers are black, many of them in their twenties and thirties. Black workers predominate because government employment, particularly in the post office, is one of the few opportunities for black men to get steady work at wages over $100 a week. Many black workers in the post office are college educated. Many of them have received two- or four-year college degrees. Still, a job in the post office represents an important means of gaining job security and a regular income.

The strike suggests further that new relations between the black and white movements impend. When the issue is access to a few hundred skilled construction jobs in one city, black workers have no choice but to attack white workers' privileges;

and the white workers, in turn, no choice but to defend their jobs. When the issue becomes a struggle by tens of thousands of workers against employers and the state, the need for solidarity becomes evident to everyone, and the special militancy of blacks becomes an extra force for unity, their special oppression an added fuel to the struggle against the common enemy. In a period of rising labor militancy, we may expect organizations with a specifically working-class base, like DRUM, to become increasingly significant in the black movement; and those with a bourgeois or street-culture base, to become relatively less significant. Race contradictions will feed, not counteract, class contradictions.

## IV

The fact that the struggle for immediate demands never grew into a struggle for more general political and social demands is not a function of the failure of radical political education to make the connections ideologically. It is rather the inability of the postal workers to spread the struggle to other workers—other federal workers, to begin with. One reason for this failure was the relatively short duration of the strike, itself a consequence of its narrowness. Another was the fact that the impulses to struggle among federal workers who wished to join the strike were effectively emasculated by union bureaucrats to whom militants turned for leadership. The reliance of federal workers on union leadership remained an internal barrier to a widened struggle. The trade union consciousness among federal workers reflects the relative newness of union organization among them.

If radicals had a role to play in the postal strike, it was not primarily to educate the postal workers, but to agitate for conditions which provide the soil of revolutionary education—to agitate, that is, for widened struggle. In most places, radicals contented themselves with organizing support demonstrations in town squares or with truncated attempts at "political education" without benefit of substantial contacts among postal workers. Most of the leaflets handed out to postal workers were politically "correct." They opposed the troop intervention; they connected the decline of real wages to the war and to corporate capitalist profit grabbing; and they tried to put forth a program of demands for postal workers, an incredible exercise in arrogance and abstract politics.

The brave attempts of organized radicals to be relevant to workers' struggles represents an advance over the situation several years ago. But radical consciousness still appears as an outside force. It still does not function as a tendency within the class. If radicals are to be relevant to workers, it is their vision, their description of alternatives to the modes of hierarchy which dominate the workers, which constitutes their primary contribution. Not their support for strikes at given levels. Nor their attempts to evolve demands or organizational strategies. The concrete aid radicals can render is to help widen the struggle to other industrial sectors, including those in which they are, themselves, employed.

# V

The postal strike makes vivid what state socialism means for workers—conditions identical to or worse than those in the private economy. The post office is, after all, a "nationalized" enterprise. Yet its workers are paid worse than those in the private sector, dominated just as thoroughly, deprived even more of such fundamentals as the right to strike, and enmeshed in bureaucracy. If socialism is viewed as a system in which "the government owns everything and everybody works for the government," it is hardly surprising that workers—and everybody else except potential government bureaucrats—shy away from it.

As the struggle of public workers becomes more important in the general movement of workers, the problem of redefining the socialist vision will become more acute for radicals. Clearly, the convergence of future state socialist solutions with contemporary state capitalism indicates the task for socialists. The socialist vision must be discussed as the control by the producers of their work and of all institutions of society. The wildcat strikes, directed against the corporations, the state, and their ideological apparatuses (e.g., the trade unions) imply an action critique of bureaucracy and hierarchy. Because state socialism preserves all the forms of capitalist domination and changes only the masters, it is not surprising that workers will have nothing to do with left wing alternatives which offer nothing better than a new bureaucracy.

In the postal workers strike, we can see a new labor movement struggling to free itself from the womb of the old one.

In the struggle between the wildcat movement and the

unions, we can see the struggle between two principles of workers' organization. Here, decision-making in free assembly, willingness to struggle within and without the law, mobilization of the workers' real power, spreading solidarity, intransigence, self-direction, action; there, obedience, division of the workers from each other, groveling before power (institutional and individual), authoritarianism.

In the postal strike and in the rising labor discontent, we can see the development of a new alignment of forces in America. During the 1960s the forces of movement in society were blacks and students. The middle and working classes opposed them both and looked to quasi-fascist solutions of increasing state dictatorship to protect their positions. But as the postal strike shows, in a non-expanding economy, the state must oppose even the day-to-day struggles of the workers. The convergence of radicalized workers with the student and black movements will be long and difficult, but it is pushed forward daily by developments within society. Only within the context of such realignment is serious struggle against fascism and repression, let alone revolutionary advance, possible.


# Keep on Truckin'

## mac brockway


Faced with the reality of making a living most people tend to establish a certain rhythm to their lives. This often means dividing one's life into compartments; for most people there is working and there is living. On the one hand, the worker is a producer who spends most of his waking hours doing dull monotonous work, who confronts the boss daily, who may engage in strikes, who is often willing to put aside abstract notions like "patriotism" or "the national interest" if they stand in his way. Off the job, on the other hand, he may be a perfectly respectable citizen, possibly a homeowner, who believes many of the myths about the "American Way." Off the job the worker is an atom, who probably does not socialize with the people he works with even if he knows them intimately, whose life revolves around his family and a small circle of friends, especially since the decline of neighborhoods in the big cities. As long as the job delivers enough in wages to maintain a relatively high standard of living, and as long as nothing off the job invades the little niches they have found for themselves, people seem willing to live around the contradictions in their lives and forget the price they must pay for material security.

If masses of people are going to act to change things, something must happen to shake them up on the level of their daily lives, forcing them to find new ways to satisfy their basic needs. Radical propaganda is not enough to convince people of the need for change. The combination of an established routine, a fairly high standard of living, and the constant exposure to the mass media is simply too strong to overcome with mere words. It seems to me that barring some kind of major political crisis, an economic crisis remains the only thing which will force people to act to change society. And yet it will not necessarily take a catastrophic crisis to prod people into action, since most people's standard of living hangs on the barest thread of credit which can snap at the first sign of unemployment. A few repossessions by banks and finance companies can have a sobering effect.

A crisis tends to unify a class by enabling people within it to see clearly the overriding interest they share with each other. A worker's whole life is disrupted by a depression. Speed-up, loss of overtime, lay-offs or partial lay-offs result in a sharp drop in the standard of living. A crisis also means further decay of the cities and a decline in the overall quality of life. This unification of the fragmented lives people live can be explosive.

In the past year the country has entered a mild crisis and already we have seen a reaction on the part of many workers. The Post Office strike and the Teamster wildcat are two dramatic examples showing that the workers are quite willing to put aside both the law and the unions to take direct action in their own interests. The concern shown by the auto companies that Reuther's death may spark "chaos in the plants" indicates that there is a fear in business circles that the wildcat might become a common tool of the workers.

But while the Teamsters' and the postal workers' strikes are dramatic examples of the rumblings in the working class, many less spectacular things are happening in industries across the country. A case in point is the New York fuel oil industry.

Until recently New York's oil drivers were not known for their militancy, but things have begun to change. While the shift in attitudes has translated itself into action on only one or two occasions, the general consensus of the men is that they have become more militant and that they will no longer be pushed around so easily. This change is worth discussing since it is fairly typical of what is happening in other places.

The 2,800 men of Teamster Union Local 553 drive for the numerous independent oil companies in New York. These companies are not attached to any of the national corporations and range in size from a few trucks to a few hundred. Together they deliver about 40% of the oil used in New York City. While there are a great many companies, there is a lot of interaction among the drivers at places like the large fuel terminals where trucks of many companies load. For most of the men the work is seasonal; they are bound by the contract to be available from October 15 to April 15 after which they can find work for the summer without losing their seniority. The amount of time a driver will actually work depends on the company and on his seniority. The average driver works about 20 weeks while the men with most seniority work most of the year.

The job consists of loading the truck and delivering the load. A driver is not required to make a set number of loads or stops if he is delivering house oil or oil used in small buildings. Instead he makes several stops with one load. The companies, often Neanderthal in their relations with the drivers, are continually after the men to work faster and sometimes play the drivers off against each other. ("Why did it take you two hours and him an hour and a half?") Besides the boss's harassment, the driver faces the everyday difficulties of the job: driving a trailer truck or large straight truck in heavy city traffic and on narrow residential streets in any weather, the anger of motorists if the driver has to block a street to make a delivery, or the freezing temperatures of the waterfront where he has to load his truck. There is also the continual danger of spilling the oil if too much is put into a tank—if a driver has too many spills he can be fired. The men must also work extremely long hours. During the peak of the season a driver does little else but work, often ten or twelve hours a day, six or seven days a week. The pay rate is $35 for an eight-hour day, time and a half for Saturday and double time for Sundays and holidays. In the middle of the season a man can take home $300 a week or better.

The continual company harassment (examples of which I will describe below) and the generally bad working conditions have been met with the opposition of some of the drivers for years. While the resistance takes several forms, the only type of organized opposition has been the insurgent coalitions, or slates of candidates which run against the local union leadership. These coalitions are not to be confused with rank-and-file caucuses since they are not open organizations but are composed primarily of candidates for the various positions in the local—president, vice-president, business agents, trustees, etc. During the last election one of the coalitions nearly defeated the incumbent leadership.

To get its message across, the coalition puts out a monthly newsletter pointing out the failures of the current officials and offering suggestions for reforms. Like insurgent groups in other locals that aim at capturing the union machinery, the coalition never transcends simple trade-unionism, nor does it ever advocate direct action. On the contrary, they constantly play down the potential for militance of the rank-and-file. Many of the opposition people have been driving for 10 or 20 years, have faced the day-to-day humiliation one faces and have seen the majority of the men passively accepting their fate. Predictably some of them have begun to feel a little anger and contempt at the passivity of the other men. What they don't realize is that their union militance is no real alternative and will generally be met with cynicism. The spirit of compromise inherent in trade unionism, the nature of bureaucracy which eventually sets itself apart and against the workers, and the temptation to sell out for money or status makes the unions a fraud. Most workers, I think, believe this even though, in lieu of an alternative, they wouldn't give the unions up. As one driver said of the coalition, "I'll vote for them because they might be good for one contract, but I've got no illusions—in two years they'll be under the hat."

When I talk about the passivity of the workers I am talking about passivity about day-to-day problems. When contract time comes around things are a little different. In December 1968, No. 553 went on strike for ten days when the men overwhelmingly rejected a contract negotiated by the union. The union's reaction was interesting: in spite of the fact that 2/3 of the men had voted against ratification, the local leadership called the strike a wildcat—at least until they

realized the depth of the feeling against the proposed contract. After 10 days the men won another ten dollars over
what had been negotiated. Even then the contract was ratified by a narrow margin.

The opposition coalition's increasing strength is one indication of a new militance on the part of the workers, but
there is at least one other kind of resistance to management
which is both widespread and common, that is individual
acts. Individual resistance to the companies grows out of the
particular type of relation the truck driver has with his boss.
Unlike the factory worker who confronts the boss with or in
front of other workers the driver has a much more personal
relation with the boss. For example, if a driver should get
on the bad side of a shipper, the person who gives out the
work, he may find that he is getting all the bad or difficult
jobs. The result is that the man feels he is being picked on
and has a personal reaction. He will often slow down and
say he was caught in traffic or held up in some other way.
He may sabotage the truck by getting a flat tire or pulling a
few wires. If he gets into a real fight he may just quit since
it is easy for a truck driver to find work. This is especially
true if he doesn't have much seniority. Clearly this type of
response, personal and not collective, won't get anyone any-
place since it serves to perpetuate the divisions among the
workers. Yet sabotage can become a very effective tool if it
is collectivized, that is, if the men as a group decide to respond to company provocations with slow-ups and similar
acts of sabotage. This collective sabotage can be a positive
action, an experiment in the regulation of work by the
workers themselves, adjusting the amount of work to the
drivers' comfort rather than the company's profits.

The men are more concerned about the conditions of work
than wages. In the mornings the men show up fifteen or
twenty minutes early to talk. Usually the conversation turns
to new outrages by the company, or to how they beat the
company in some way, or to what should be done to change
things and how. Recently the talk has become more militant
and while it is difficult to pinpoint the exact reasons for it
without describing what is happening in the country as a
whole, certain things stand out. First, the extensive media
coverage of the black and student movements has, to a certain extent, legitimated protest. One often hears, "We're not
going to take that, this is 1970, not 1930." To be sure, the
more active approach is not automatically a good thing as

the recent attack on demonstrating students by New York construction workers recently showed, yet hopefully objective conditions will force it in the right direction. A second factor responsible for the shift in attitudes at this company was the infusion of a number of younger workers with some new ideas who helped to crystallize much of the men's discontent and suggest new ways of dealing with problems. The episode I want to describe shows the nature of those new ideas.

On a Saturday last March one of the drivers was fired for taking too long on his coffee break. He had either been spotted or was followed by one of the company bosses who claimed he had taken an extra ten minutes. (Some companies, including this one, actually hire spies to occasionally put a tail on a driver to make sure he is not stopping anywhere.) There is nothing in the contract about coffee breaks but it is generally assumed in the industry, with the tacit consent of the companies, that the drivers are allowed fifteen minutes. After a discussion, the driver agreed to take a short lunch hour to make up the time. This was in spite of the fact that the boss was lying, for the driver knew he had not even taken fifteen minutes. The company man said he would let it pass with a warning. Later in the day, however, the boss returned to his office and found out that the man had had a previous run-in with the company some months earlier. Then he went back on his word and ordered the driver fired.

Monday morning there was another firing at the same company. This time a driver was fired for refusing to take out an unsafe vehicle. Throughout the season the man had been given either unsafe vehicles or ones that barely met minimum safety standards. Finally after a week in which he had at least one and sometimes two dangerous breakdowns every day, the driver refused to take out a truck which had leaks in the trailer, a broken window, bad tires, no windshield wipers, and a fuel tank which leaked through the vent (this drips fuel under the tractor wheels and causes poor traction). Some defects violated the contract. The defects had been reported numerous times but nothing had been done to repair them. The company told him that he would either have to take the truck out or punch out and go home since there were no other trucks available. The driver refused to do either since he felt he had a right to his day's pay even if the company did not have a decent truck for him. It is in the contract that if the company books a man and does not have

either work or a truck available the man must still be paid.
Instead, the company fired the man.

The two fired men then went to the Local headquarters on
the recommendation of the shop steward. They explained
what had happened to the vice-president who told them in
the manner of union officials the world over to "stay calm"
—even though the drivers had shown no signs of excitement.
He said a meeting would be set up with the business agent
who covered the area, where there would be a meeting with
the company and the men would have their jobs back.

The fired men had other ideas. First they made picket
signs and picketed the yard. They explained their cases to
the men, first verbally and then with a leaflet they wrote
which explained the circumstances of their being fired and
concluded with the following:

This harassment must stop—the time to fight is now. The
union tells us to keep calm and go to arbitration. But arbitration is a dead-end street. It is a trick used by the union and
management to prevent workers from taking real direct action
to settle their grievances. We pay union dues supposedly so
we will have some defense against the boss—why should the
union be able to get off the hook by passing the buck to an
arbitration board? We might as well forget the union and pay
our dues directly to the arbitration board. Going to arbitration means going without a pay check for weeks and it means
putting your fate into the hands of a board which is not im-
partial—few workers win in arbitration.

We are asking for action from the union now—today. If we
don't get action we are asking your support to help us get our
jobs back and to get the pay we have lost as a result of these
firings. We have heard a lot of talk from some of the men—
now is the time to put up or shut up. What happened to us
today will happen to you tomorrow. An injury to one should
be an injury to all. Let's get off our knees and stand up and
fight. We have the power to cage the animals that run this
company. Without us not a single gallon of oil moves, not a
single penny of profit is made. The choice is clear. Think it
over carefully. Who wants to live in a world of grovelers?

Picketing and distributing leaflets of this kind is unheard
of in the oil industry, yet the other men received them
enthusiastically. Men that the coalition militants had said
would never help came around offering encouragement and
asking what they could do to help. The women working in
the office promised to walk out with the men. The fired men

said that if the meetings scheduled with the company for the next day, Wednesday, did not come off in their favor, they wanted the men to walk off. In any event, the fired men and their supporters in the company—they felt they could actually count on a little less than half the forty or so men who drive from this particular yard—and even outsiders, would barricade the driveway and stop the trucks. The way it looked now the fired men would have the support of most of the other drivers. This was a big change from a few months earlier during another dispute when the thought of a wildcat was frightening.

The next morning, before the meeting, the drivers again picketed the driveway, walking back and forth slowly, which only let the trucks out one by one. This caused the trucks to back up in a long line under the office window. It was hoped that this would show the company that the men would not cross the picket line unless the picketers wanted them to.

The meeting the next day was really surreal. The participants were: the company man, known as "labor consultant" (what used to be called a goon)—he handles the labor difficulties of eleven independent companies, mostly in Brooklyn, and bills himself as a "hatchetman"; the union business agent; the shop steward, who firmly supported the men but who was forced to turn the cases over to the business agent because they involved firings; and the two drivers. Each driver met separately with the company. Each meeting followed essentially the same script. When one of the drivers explained his position and then said that the company did not care anything about the men, he was told that he was perfectly correct, the company was interested only in making money and didn't care about "little people who are nothing." What particularly enraged the labor consultant was that the drivers had distributed the leaflet. He claimed that the leaflet was grounds in itself for firing since it advocated ignoring arbitration, and because the contract specifies arbitration as the method of settling disputes the drivers were put outside the sphere of "protective activity." This is why workers can be fired for engaging in wildcats—they are breaking the union contract. When he was told that the company had broken the contract by assigning a truck that violated the contract because it had broken windows and no windshield wipers he snapped back that he did not care about contracts, the oil had to be moved. All the while the business agent sat there trying to calm the drivers down. It was finally agreed that, because the company feared trouble, the drivers would get their jobs back but not their lost pay (three days). The drivers decided to take the compromise settlement because they were not sure whether the men would act under the changed circumstances—and they felt it would be better to back down a little in order to be around to fight later.

The whole episode served a good purpose. First, the men were pushed to the point of walking out—something that had not happened before. Secondly, it clearly showed how bad the union was and that taking a militant stand might be the best way to fight the company. The two drivers and their supporters continued to hammer away at the need for direct action to handle disputes. There is more of a feeling of solidarity of the company, and not just among the younger workers who were already sympathetic.

Some of the men hope to put out a direct-action-oriented newspaper to spread the word. One of the men is also planning to run for shop steward when the present steward, who is running for local office on an opposition slate leaves. It is hoped that in this manner the actual *job* of a shop steward can be eliminated (except for the figure-head which is required by the union structure) and replaced by a committee made up of all the drivers who will meet regularly. This is a good first step in building an independent movement controlled by the drivers to fight for improved conditions without intermediaries. The meetings should serve, also, to eliminate many of the petty squabbles and divisions among the drivers. Most of the men think it is a very good idea. The way such a structure would relate to the union as a whole remains to be seen. The hard-core anti-union militants, of which there are only a few, feel that it is impossible to oppose the insurgent coalition and that it is best to merely point out that it will be powerless to do anything to really change things since the District Council or the International would crush it. At worst it will become just like the present leadership. Nevertheless, if people are going to vote, they should vote for the opposition.

It might be thought that the anti-union militants should have the same attitude towards the shop stewards as they do towards the local leadership. But these two levels of the union seem to be different. Often the shop steward has little to do with the union local; there is little contact and often genuine hostility. The shop steward is not considered by the men to be a union officer but as one of their own. After all, he's a worker on the job. But the fact remains that the steward functions as a mediator between the workers and the union structure. He is there and you have to get rid of him.

The men hope to run a shop steward who intends to stop being shop steward, and to function as no more than the moderator of meetings of the drivers. Many of the drivers feel that this action will serve notice on the companies and union that things should be different, and provide a concrete example for drivers in other yards. It should be noted that, while the events here are of little significance in themselves, confined to one yard, workers throughout the industry are in constant communication and the experience of this yard was known and discussed by workers throughout.

Perhaps this plan to abolish the shop stewardship by capturing it is a trojan horse. The men look upon it as an experiment. In any event, it is a step taken partially in recognition of the limits of the present fight. Many men still accept their fate as pawns between company and union. They are not willing to break with the union completely. The abolition of the steward's position will throw things in their laps, forcing them to confront their own problems on the job by relying on direct, collective action, rather than going with gripes to the steward.

The construction of a really independent workers move- ment will be a long-term process. Only when the idea of an independent workers' movement spreads to other workers can the drivers totally ignore the union and rely upon alternative forms of action in every instance.

# In the Heart of the Heart of the Country: The Strike at Lordstown

## peter herman

As you drive through the Ohio countryside on the turnpike between Youngstown and Cleveland, you suddenly pass an enormous factory, stretching for almost a mile along the

highway. This startling sight is the General Motors Lordstown installation, a major plant built for over $100 million
in 1966, and employing over 13,000 people. Comprising a
Fisher Body Fabricating plant, a Chevrolet Assembly plant
and a Chevrolet Truck plant, the Lordstown complex manu-
factures mainly the Chevrolet Vega subcompact. It is the
fastest and most highly automated assembly line in the world,
producing more than 100 cars per hour. Its construction
incorporated some of the most advanced technology for
production efficiency. All jobs were divided into small parts;
new computerized robot welders were installed. GM proudly
announced that Lordstown represented the plant of the
future. They little expected that within a few years Lordstown would have become a national symbol for blue-collar
discontent.[1]

When asked why they work at Lordstown, workers consistently reply: "the job's a drag, but you can't beat the
money." GM built the plant in an area where most workers
were used to working in the plants and mills of the Youngs-
town-Akron steel and rubber industries, where working conditions were poor and pay and benefits relatively low. GM
had no trouble recruiting workers; even older men gladly
gave up their accumulated years of seniority at the mills
to come to work at Lordstown, where physical working
conditions were better and the pay higher. Although GM
pays wages that are relatively high for unskilled labor (a
new worker will make about $11,000 a year), few workers
at Lordstown have any considerable savings or financial security. Many of them dream of quitting their jobs and
going into business for themselves, but most can't. One
worker explained that:

> GM has a way of capturing people in that a guy comes off
> the street and gets a job, and he's making more money there
> than he ever made in his life before, and so at first it's a real
> shock—you've got a lot of extra money. But you know, you
> watch TV, how they advertise, advertise—you've got to have
> this, you've got to have that—and pretty soon this dude's out
> spending like Mr. Millionaire. And then, if you work at
> Lordstown, that's instant credit. He's got credit and pretty

1. Among the articles on Lordstown, the best I have seen are:
   Emma Rothschild, "GM in More Trouble," *New York Review
   of Books,* March 23, 1972, and Barbara Garson, "Luddites in
   Lordstown," *Harper's,* June, 1972.

soon he's charging all kinds of stuff. I know a guy who works with me, he's been married for a year. He bought a $16,000 home, and with interest and everything on a thirty-year loan it's costing him $48,000. Then he had to borrow a thousand dollars for his car, and he had to buy his wife a washer and dryer, and he's got furniture payments, and then they got a little baby on top of all that, holy smoke, and they've got thirty-some fish too. He says he's got thirty-eight dependents, he's got to have all the money he can get.[2]

Such a worker, of course, is not really spending like "Mr. Millionaire." Most of his expenses are necessities for a young family, and in the inflationary economy of recent years, during which the real wages of industrial workers have declined, the wages at Lordstown are barely sufficient for a family to maintain itself without deprivation; many workers actually do not make enough money to pay their bills. To meet this dilemma many wives work, and since someone has to take care of the young children, the man often works the night shift and the woman works during the day. One worker described his family situation:

I never get to see my wife. When I'm going out the door she's coming in, and when I'm coming in, she's going out. We have little conferences to work things out and sometimes it runs into overtime. Last week, I got a reprimand for being late to work. I told my foreman that I needed to talk over a problem with my wife and he said, "Look, this is a business. We got no time for that. Up a tree with your marital problems."

Most workers are locked into their jobs at Lordstown, because they can't get better work or money elsewhere. It is this money which makes them bear the deadening monotony of the same operation performed over and over again, and the inexorable rate of the line which does not permit any variation in pacing. People at Lordstown often work a compulsory 50-hour week—10 hours a day doing the same job. A rate of 100 cars an hour means that the worker has to repeat his or her operation every 36 seconds. The Vega itself becomes a hated object. Few Lordstown workers drive

2. These quotes are based on interveiws wtth workers at Lordstown, which were taken by Peter Schlaifer and me in June, 1972, and which are available on videotape. Unfootnoted quotes are all from these interviews.

Vegas; most speak negatively of them. One worker described his feelings about working at Lordstown:

> You do it automatically, like a monkey or dog would do something by conditioning. You feel stagnant; everything is over and over and over. It seems like you're just going to work and your whole purpose in life is to do this operation, and you come home and you're so tired from working the hours, trying to keep up with the line, you feel you're not making any advancement whatsoever. This makes the average individual feel sort of like a vegetable.

The scene at the change of shifts is eloquent testimony to the workers' hatred of their working conditions. The shift going into work hangs around their cars in the parking lot or idles slowly toward the plant. In contrast, the workers coming off the shift dash out of the plant, leap into their cars and go racing away with horns blaring and tires squealing.

A few years ago, major magazines (such as *Life* and *Newsweek*) published feature articles about work on the assembly line. When they attempted to explain why workers were discontented at places like Lordstown, these media stressed the monotony and boredom of assembly-line work. The workers were treated with sympathy, but even so the interpretation is superficial. The real key to the dissatisfaction of the workers is the system of power relations in which they find themselves, a set of interlocking structures of power and authority of both management and unions which are designed to render them isolated and powerless and which enhances the boredom and monotony of the work itself. The first symptom of these relations is the climate of fear at the plant. One worker said:

> The whole plant runs on fear. The top guy in that plant is scared of somebody in Detroit. And the guy below him is scared of him and, man, it comes right down to the foremen, and the foremen are scared to death. And when they're scared to death they really put the heat on the people, and the people are scared to death 'cause they're afraid to lose their jobs. And they know if they don't do the work they will lose their jobs, 'cause the stupid union . . . . I'll tell you, them guys, they think they've got a great union, but, man, they don't do nothing.

Feelings of fear are endemic at all levels in the plant, but the distinction between a member of management and a worker, within the structure of power, is fundamental and extends to such apparently trivial matters as segregated parking lots, eating facilities, and separate dress codes. For a manager, however low in rank, the corporation is "us"; for a worker, GM is "them." When I asked a general foreman (a low-level job) how he handled a bad decision handed down from higher management, he made this distinction clear:

> A foreman, being a member of management, has to accept this decision, he is part of the decision, he cannot let the people know that he is in agreement with them. If he is in sympathy with the people, he's dead as a foreman, he's lost the ball game as far as conducting his job satisfactorily as a member of management. If he's in sympathy with the people he certainly cannot let it be known. There's been many a time when my heart's gone out to an individual I've had to discipline, when I've had to do something distasteful, but I had to do it, with the thought in mind that this is my job, that I am part of this decision, that this is the way it has to be.

To accept a promotion from assembly line worker to foreman is to cross the power line from "us" to "them." One worker, who had been a foreman at Lordstown till he quit in disgust, explained what it was like:

> After accepting a position of a management trainee, I came to really find out how underhanded the salaried personnel were in their dealings, 'cause they accepted me to go to their schools of what they wanted you to do and how to conduct these "brainless idiots" out on the line, these "people who function mechanically," you know, "anybody can do the job that these idiots we got down there do," you know, "train a monkey and we can send him down"—this type of talk they gave to show me that I was better than this guy that worked on the line. The school tried to show me how I could get somebody's goat and be cool about it. I couldn't believe this. Here were grown foremen teaching me Gestapo-type tactics.

Authoritarian control is a way of life at Lordstown. On entering the parking lot, one sees a huge sign announcing that this is Private Property, that GM disclaims all responsibility for any damages one experiences, and that the lot is under surveillance by closed-circuit TV. When I talked with one of the top Lordstown executives, I was only mildly astounded to see a portrait of Napoleon frowing at me off the wall over his desk. Workers at Lordstown need a written excuse if they miss work. If late to work, they may be given a disciplinary lay-off, ranging from the remainder of the shift to a week. A foreman can give a formal Direct Order, which must be obeyed, or the worker faces discipline for insubordination. A worker needs his or her supervisor's permission to leave the line to go to the bathroom, and the foreman can easily delay granting such permission. Lunch pails are regularly inspected to "prevent thievery." Armed security guards at the doors ask to see one's plastic identification card. One Lordstown worker justly remarked that by working at the plant he

came to find out that all dictators are not in communist countries. The Lordstown complex is its own individual dictatorship with their own little island, and everybody there falls under this dictatorship.

The union procedures aggravate the powerless situation of the worker on the line. If a worker has a grievance, say against a foreman, he does not make the complaint himself but must ask that very supervisor to call the union committeeman. This fact alone inhibits the filing of many grievances, since the offending foreman might well develop a grudge against the worker. Once the committeeman has been called, the aggrieved worker has nothing more to do with the case, which is handled through the highly bureaucratized and slow-moving grievance procedure. The case often takes several months to resolve, by which time the matter is often irrelevant. One worker said:

It's the worst feeling in the world when you call your committeeman and he comes and writes something on a piece of paper and goes away, and that's the last you ever hear of it —you're still left doing the job.

The roots of the present relationship between the company, the union, and the rank and file workers at Lordstown lie deep in the history of American labor.[3] In the great sit-down struggles of the Thirties, the union—in exchange for the right

3. See Jeremy Brecher, *Strike!* (San Francisco, 1972), Chapter 5.3, "Sitdown . . ." Much thanks to Jeremy for help on this article.

to be recognized as the bargaining representatives of the workers in contract and strike negotiations—agreed to discipline workers who engaged in unauthorized sit-down actions or who sought to exercise some control over the production process. This trade-off was unacceptable to many workers and there was a massive wave of sit-down strikes in the spring of 1937, right after the collective bargaining agreement was signed by GM and the union. For a time, the workers gained control of the speed of the line. The union actively struggled against these workers' actions and succeeded in controlling the situation. The measures taken were described by *The New York Times*:

1. As soon as an unauthorized strike occurs or impends, international officers or representatives of the UAW are rushed to the scene to end or prevent it, get the men back to work and bring about an orderly adjustment of the grievances.
2. Strict orders have been issued to all organizers and representatives that they will be dismissed if they authorize any stoppages of work without the consent of the international officers, and that local unions will not receive any money . . . from the international union for any unauthorized stoppage of, or interference with production.
3. The shop stewards are being educated in the procedure for settling grievances set up in the GM contract, and a system is being worked out which the union believes will convince the rank and file that strikes are unnecessary.[4]

Thus, from the very beginning, the union agreed to work hand in hand with GM in disciplining workers who acted on their own or who raised demands not recognized in the written contract, particularly the demand to have a say in the decisions about production.

During the long boom of the auto industry after the Second World War, the majority of the UAW members, who had experienced the deprivation of the Depression, acquiesed in bargaining for a larger share of the financial pie. Since the industry was expanding rapidly in those years, management could afford to make substantial increases in wages and benefits—especially since such wage costs could be passed along to the consumer in the form of price increases—and the UAW's role was grudgingly accepted. When a nationwide wildcat developed over "local issues" of working

4. *New York Times,* April 11, 1937.

conditions after the signing of the 1955 contract, the UAW disciplined the more militant locals and established a system that made working conditions issues part of the bargaining at the local level to help get rank and file demands more under control.

In the UAW "strike" against GM in 1970, company-union collusion was apparent. The long and costly strike was designed by GM and the union, according to the *Wall Street Journal*, "to help to wear down the expectations of members," "to create an escape valve for the frustrations of workers bitter about what they consider intolerable working conditions," and to "strengthen the position of union leaders."[5] GM in return expected the strike to stabilize the union's control over the men and to "buy peace in future years." When local negotiations lengthened the strike beyond the period planned by the union, GM actually lent the UAW $30 million to help them meet their strike insurance expenses, and engaged in secret talks to help the union leadership settle what threatened to become a "messy strike beyond the control of the top leaders."[6]

During the years 1970–72, the US auto industry, despite its great wealth, was operating under considerable pressure. Profit rates and sales were down; there was significant foreign competition on the domestic market. The entire industry was only operating at about 80 percent potential productive capacity. In these circumstances, when major capital investment was made reluctantly, there was great pressure to justify the $100 million already spent on Lordstown. In the fall of 1970, the plant was converted to manufacture the new Chevrolet Vega, a subcompact designed to meet the rising Japanese challenge (Toyota, Datsun) on the American market. The Lordstown complex—Fisher Body and Chevrolet Assembly—manufactured the Vega from start to finish and was supposed to be efficient enough to make all the Vegas for the entire USA.

Given the stagnation of the auto industry, the most obvious way that the corporations had of holding profit margins up was to increase the productive efficiency of the workers. The assembly line at Lordstown was designed with this kind of efficiency in mind. The goal was to reduce excess move-

5. *Wall Street Journal*, October 29, 1970. See also William Serrin, *The Company and the Union* (Alfred A. Knopf, Inc., New York, 1973) for a detailed account of the 1970 strike.
6. *Wall Street Journal*, October 5, 1970.

ments by workers to an absolute minimum and thus to shave seconds of waste time off each job. It has been estimated that if each Lordstown worker works 1 second per hour more for a year, GM would increase its profits for that year by $2 million.[7] The effect of the "advanced" technology at Lordstown is thus to increase the intensity and pace of work for the assembler. Lordstown represents the quintessence of Taylorism.

After the line was converted to make the Vega, GM tried to test the full productive capacities of the plant, and raised the speed of the assembly line from 60 cars per hour to an unprecedented 100 cars per hour. One worker said:

> We were already working hard, but it got ridiculous after they raised the speed of the line. The first day they brought out a sign—'First time in GM history, 100 cars/hour'— and some of the old-timers cheered, but I just thought we were fools to take it. Then they started getting competitive, and told us that the first shift ran 110 cars an hour. Pretty soon even the old-timers got sick of that shit and said, 'If first shift wants to put out 110 cars, fuck it, let 'em. We're not going to do it.'

During 1971 the situation became serious for GM at Lordstown. Absenteeism, already high, increased greatly, and many workers began letting cars go by on the line without doing their jobs. There were also cases of active sabotage. The repair lots quickly filled with Vegas, and the "Car of the Year" (according to *Motor Trend* magazine) became rapidly known to buyers as a repair-prone vehicle. Sales sagged badly, and the Vega not only failed to overtake Datsun and Toyota, but lagged behind Ford's Pinto. GM decided to get tough with the plant and in September, 1971, they announced that the entire plant was to be placed under the management of the General Motors Assembly Division (GMAD), a special team of managers, the following month.

GM's intense concern for worker efficiency explains the rapid rise within the corporation of GMAD, which, since its formation in 1965, has gained control of 18 GM plants and 75 percent of all GM car production. The essence of GMAD is the drive for production efficiency. They have instituted a competition among their 18 plants, which involves

7. See Emma Rothschild, "GM in More Trouble" mentioned above.

daily auditing of each plant's efficiency and quality by a centralized computer. Each plant's standing is publicly posted. Bonuses and promotions for GMAD officials are related to performance in this internal competition, and the pressures it generates on each plant's management are intense. These pressures have created an extremely tough disciplinary ethos in the management of GMAD plants.

The announcement of GMAD's impending takeover sparked a brief wildcat strike in the Lordstown Fisher Body plant. In October, GMAD's first move was to tighten even more the efficiency of the entire Lordstown complex. They laid off close to 300 men, and dispersed their work among the other workers. They also introduced severe new disciplinary measures to try to curb absenteeism and sabotage. Instead of controlling the workers, GMAD's repressive measures stiffened their determination not to buckle under. In the first few months of GMAD's tenure at the plant, over 5,000 formal grievances were filed. Conflict sharpened; absenteeism, sabotage, and work slowdowns mounted. *The New York Times* reported significantly that:

> "Both union and management were surprised by the depth of resistance . . . among the work force," and the President of the UAW local declared that, "a decision to work at their old pace to protest the change had come from the rank and file, not from the union leadership." [8]

The Vegas just weren't being made, or if they were—as one Lordstown worker put it—"I'd hate to buy one. If they last six months, I'll be amazed." Claiming that the workers' lack of discipline made production impossible, GMAD resorted to sending the men home early each day, in hopes of forcing them to obey by such *de facto* wage cuts, but this measure, too, failed to control the resistance. Instead, production fell so low that the situation became critical for management.

The union local through this period tried simultaneously to express and contain the discontent. The union leadership had not initiated the workers' resistance; they restricted themselves to generalized statements of support, promise of a strike, and insistence that the workers remain within the bounds of contractual legality. Here are some sample leaflets passed out by the union:

8. *New York Times,* January 23, 1972.

1) WE DO NOT CONDONE SABOTAGE:
   . . . both the International Union and your Local Union strongly urge that no matter what provocation is put forth by the Company that all members . . . maintain strong Union discipline and fight this battle with GM in a legitimate manner. Do not engage in any acts of sabotage. LET'S FIGHT TOGETHER & WIN TOGETHER.

2) WHAT IT'S ALL ABOUT:
   PROFITS:   GMAD doesn't care about your working conditions. They have always put profits before human values, that's why they have started a reign of terror in the plants.

   TERROR:    Using Hitler's method of terror GMAD hopes to scare the people into meeting their unfair standards. They hope to provoke a wildcat strike so they can get more hostages for their terror program. DO NOT BE PROVOKED INTO A WILDCAT STRIKE ! ! That is the Company game. The local Union is now preparing . . . a legal strike with the full support of the International Union . . . . Vote yes for strike action. Let's support the people who are fighting to make and keep this a decent place to work.
              RIGHT ON BROTHERS & SISTERS!
              RIGHT ON!!!

The workers realize that the union is entirely serious about its insistence that the people obey the "laws" set down in the written contract. One worker explained:

Our union is Miss Goody-shoes, see? We have a contract, and both GM and the union are supposed to keep it. The only trouble is, GM breaks the contract about twenty times a day, while the union sticks to the letter of the contract. Look, the fans broke down where I work the other week and the temperature went up to about 110. Our committee man threatened that we would take our shirts off—which is against the rules —if they didn't fix the fans. I told him: you can take your shirts off, you can take your pants off, but the cars are still being made and we're fools for doing it. Listen, if we want to get those fans fixed, let's all quit work and go sit down on the rail for an hour. That's 100 cars—they'll be going bananas in the top office. But the committeeman man said he didn't even want to hear about such an idea. So I went to the other guys and said, let's sit down for an hour, but they all said, is the union behind this? When I told them no, they said forget it.

See, the union won't back 20 or 30 guys who sit down. They'll
let them be fired, and it's nothing to GM—they can afford
to lose 20 guys. But for the guys, it's their job.

Such refusals by the union have an enormously inhibiting
effect on actions initiated by the workers. Why does the
union refuse to back such direct attempts by the workers to
affect their conditions? Union officials justify themselves by
pointing out that the grievance procedure is there to handle
small matters, and that the union can't strike a 10,000-man
plant over an issue that affects 30 people. They further note
that work stoppages force the union to bargain about the
disciplining of the men rather than the original issue. The
obvious rebuttal—that established procedures do not exhaust
all possible strategies—is beside the point. The real issue
concerns the nature of the union's power. Ever since the
collective bargaining agreement of the Thirties, the union
has been a kind of junior partner of the corporation. The
union's goal has been the health and well-being of the industry, its prosperity and smooth functioning. In exchange for
a wage and benefit package, the union agrees to be responsible for making sure that the workers do nothing to challenge
or disrupt the operations of the factories or such changes
in production as the corporation deems necessary to keep
up profitability. The union guarantees—as the contract puts
it—"management's right to manage." Unauthorized "spontaneous" actions by groups of workers are direct threats to
the union, and naturally it will not support such groups of
workers when the company moves against them. In many
cases the union will itself seek to impose sanctions on such
workers.

Local leadership is not really free to change these facts
of power. If a union local backed up a strike without clear-
ance from the International, they would be faced with
immediate cutoff of union funds and threats of Trustee-
ship, under which the International declares the local leadership dissolved, and appoints its own officers. And the International leadership, in turn, would be forced to see that locals
enforce work discipline, because GM can make some very
powerful threats to the UAW, such as refusing to cooperate
or help in national negotiations—as when GM loaned the
UAW $30 million in 1970—or moving assembly factories
out of the USA to lower-wage countries (as the president of
Mitsubishi Motor Company, noting that Japanese wages are

one-fourth those of the U.S., recently asked, "Would it not be more profitable for an American manufacturer to import compacts instead of spending vast sums on developing its own models?")[9]

It is no wonder that, by and large, union leaders are pleased to see unauthorized strikers fired by the corporation. Only if the causes of discontent are so widespread and acute that independent actions by workers threaten to lead to a spontaneous explosion of the entire plant, does the union find it necessary to act. By January 1972, it was evident that such a situation was at hand in Lordstown. Thousands of grievances had been filed, production had broken down and sabotage (damaged motors, slashed seat covers, ripped out wiring) was chronic. On February 1, the union held a strike vote. Despite the fact that many workers had lost their savings in the 1970 strike, and all were hard-pressed because of the money lost during the short work weeks of the last few months, 85 percent of the union's membership turned out to vote and 97 percent voted to strike. These numbers are overwhelming evidence of the mood at Lordstown; normally, there is much apathy about union votes, and a 40 percent turnout is considered good. This strike vote indicated that the workers were willing to risk making a considerable sacrifice to do something about working conditions. Many workers—most of them young and inexperienced about strikes—sincerely believed the union leaflets which claimed that the local and International were prepared to bargain seriously about working conditions. The local leadership was itself young and newly-elected. President Gary Bryner, only twenty-nine, was a hip character who quoted phrases out of *The Greening of America* while promising to struggle for "humanization" of working conditions. Workers had a real willingness to trust the local and go along with their strike strategy.

During the month of February, local leadership and International representatives, including UAW Vice President Irving Bluestone, negotiated with GMAD, while continuing to insist on strict "legality" from the workers—no wildcats or sabotage. GMAD continued sending the men home early, worsening their economic situation, since they were not, of course,

9. Takashi Oka, "American Made—in Japan," *New York Times*, June 13, 1971, Section 3. Cited in Noam Chomsky, *For Reasons of State* (N. Y.: 1973), pp. 279–280.

on strike and therefore received no strike funds from the union.

The union faced a dilemma. It was, no less than before, committed to remaining within its established sphere of power. GMAD was applying tremendous pressure on the union to get control of the men, because production was slipping. On the other hand, the union had to deal with a unified and angry local rank and file that had already absorbed a lot of punishment and were obviously not going to merely obey GMAD just because the union told them to.

The strategy the union developed was a short strike, in which the issues were defined narrowly and legalistically at the bargaining table, and generally and militantly in the union propaganda. With GMAD, the union merely asked for the restoration of the 300 men laid off or disciplined since October, as well as a few other small technical changes in rules. This would make it possible for GMAD to grant concessions which didn't mean much while the union claimed a "victory," which would be fine with GMAD if it meant regaining control over the plant's working force. In short, if the union "won," GMAD won.

In its propaganda to the workers, the union had repeatedly asked them to hold off acting on their own, because a legal strike was the way to handle their problems. It had promised that the strike would be a fight to humanize working conditions, break the "Hitler" power of GMAD, etc., etc. The union figured that the strike would drain the militant energies of the workers and possibly restore leadership to the union officials. The union evidently hoped to palm off the carefully planned opposition between their promises to the workers and their actual intentions, as the inevitable gap between "utopian" desires and "realistic" objectives.

The strike began on March 5. The next day *The New York Times* reported two salient facts:

> The international board of the union told local leaders when it authorized the strike that strike benefits would not be available for too long . . . . (and) Vega dealers would have a 30-day stock of Vegas.[10]

The basic orchestration of the strike on the highest level of GM and the UAW is evident. GM in effect said: we'll let you lift the lid to let the steam off, but only for a few weeks.

10. *New York Times,* March 6, 1972.

In any case the strike must not cut the supply line of Vegas to dealers. The UAW duly relayed this message to the local leadership.

One older worker—one of the few who voted against the strike—remarked:

> I've seen it before. The International is just giving them enough rope to hang themselves . . . . They see a kicky young local so they go along. They authorize the strike . . . but they don't give 'em no help. They don't give 'em no funds. They don't even let the other locals come out with them. So the strike drags on, it's lost, or they 'settle' in Detroit. Everybody says, "There, it didn't pay."[11]

The strike went off as planned. There were many eager volunteers for picket duty, ready to construct wood barricades and to build fires against the bitter cold weather, but the union only permitted "symbolic" small pickets and held long meetings (attendance compulsory if the worker wanted to receive strike benefits) in which they explained how valuable the UAW was to the workers, how many programs they offered, how they were winning at the bargaining table, etc. Tough questions from the rank and file were not answered, on the pretext that negotiations were at a delicate stage. Meanwhile, GMAD granted the rehiring of the 300 workers laid off in October. Apparently, they had been under some pressure to do this from GM. *The New York Times* reported:

> The Lordstown strike even caused dissension within management as to (GMAD's) policies—revolving around the . . . question as to whether these policies are not perhaps outweighed by the labor trouble.[12]

On March 25, settlement of the strike was announced, and the local held a return-to-work vote. Again, the numbers are eloquent. Only about 40 percent of the local voted, of whom only 70 percent voted to end the strike despite the severe economic pressure to return to work. Most workers, on returning to the job, found little if anything changed. The restored 300 jobs made little difference to the average assembler, and of course, the basic conditions of working at the plant were the same—they had never even been discussed,

11. Quoted in Barbara Garson, "Luddites in Lordstown," mentioned above, p. 73.
12. *New York Times*, April 16, 1972.

much less negotiated. Gary Bryner speaks of the strike as a "total victory" and one which "built union people." In a narrow sense, he is right about the victory. The union achieved what it set out to do. The only trouble is that it didn't set out to do anything to change conditions at the plant.

The strike certainly did not build union people. Two months after the strike, there was widespread feeling that the union had not dealt with the workers in good faith, that it had bargained—as one worker put it—"just to get us back to work." But in the absence of any other sense of power or organization, with the widespread feeling that they are help-less without the backing of the union, the majority of workers at Lordstown felt confused, cynical, apathetic and sold down the river. When the executive officers of the local ran for reelection during the summer of '72, there was no interest in the election; only about 30 percent of the union members showed up to vote. Bryner admits that now he is booed and greeted with catcalls by the workers every time he leaves his union office building and enters the plant.

When I asked Bryner how he squared his claim that the Lordstown strike achieved total victory with the evident general dissatisfaction with the settlement, he said:

Look, this is a very political union. If a guy is running for union office, he may make a lot of promises, and if a worker is naïve enough to take his statement at face value, I suppose he's going to be disappointed.

Of course, the politics of the union extend far beyond elections. In fact Bryner's words apply to his own strike propaganda, and to the entire union's goals and behavior. To believe the union's promises is indeed to be naïve. Bryner continued:

When you look at it realistically, we set out to change nothing in the strike. We said, let's return to the condition of October, '72, and we'll wait until 1973 to negotiate about all the other issues.

At the time of the strike, the local said—don't wildcat or commit sabotage, we'll deal with working conditions through our strike. Now, the local President, in effect, is saying, "Don't worry that the strike didn't do anything. We'll handle it all in the 1973 national negotiations."

Lordstown has become a symbol, but it is not qualitatively different from other auto plants. It is a slightly exaggerated version of conditions all over the country, and perhaps represents the future of many plants. It is interesting, therefore, to compare the Lordstown strike to another that began in April, 1972 at the GM plant in Norwood, Ohio. Norwood makes bigger GM cars, such as the Firebird and Nova. Its assembly line is slower than Lordstown's and its workers are not so young, but basic working conditions are the same. The Norwood strike developed over similar issues of lay-offs and disciplinary grievances, but the strategy of control by GM and the union differed from that at Lordstown.

Norwood is not the only GM plant which makes the Firebird and Nova, and there was a dealers' overstock of these cars. Hence, as *New York Times* reported,

> Unlike the Lordstown strike, where there was an outcry from the management of Chevrolet to settle quickly because the Vega was losing ground to the Ford Pinto, there was little pressure from within the company on the Norwood negotiations.[13]

The Norwood strike has aspects of a lockout; GM was glad to have the UAW pay the workers while they sold their overstock of cars. This time, however, there was no indication from the UAW International that there was a time limit on strike benefits, making it clear that the International's unwillingness to finance a long strike at Lordstown was not dictated by its economic situation but by the marketing considerations of the Vega. The Norwood strike dragged on for 172 days and was finally settled with GM making no concessions. One Norwood worker remarked, "the whole thing was a joke. But, yes, I voted (to go back to work). I need a job."[14]

The original justification of industry-wide unions such as the UAW was to coordinate and unify the power of workers at different plants. But despite the similarities of issues at Lordstown and Norwood and their overlap in time, the UAW never attempted to utilize GM's vulnerability at Lordstown to put pressure on GM for a Norwood settlement. Instead, the union kept the two strikes in watertight compartments.

13. *New York Times,* September 26, 1972.
14. *Ibid.,* September 28, 1972.

Lordstown workers were very interested in the situation at Norwood, but the union provided no information about it. Indeed, one could see things like, "How come we went back to work and Norwood's still out?" written on the bathroom walls at Lordstown.

In the fall of 1972, the International union adopted a familiar strategy by making strong but vague claims that a major effort to ease "workers' boredom and dissatisfaction would become one of the union's bargaining goals in the 1973 contract negotiations." [15] But later in the year, to no one's surprise, evidence began to mount that such was not in fact the case. In December, the *Wall Street Journal* indicated that "most demands [in the 1973 contract negotiations] will probably focus on escape from the job [i.e., more time off] . . . rather than on changes in the job itself," although —as Ford's director of industrial relations was candid enough to remark—"there is very little evidence—in fact, none that I'm aware of—to suggest that a reduction in working time will increase employee satisfaction while at work."[16]

While it is true that most workers would like more time off if it did not entail a loss of pay, proposals for "escape from the job" completely fail to come to terms with the issues of power relations in the plant, a failure which is, of course, perfectly intentional. In fact, some of the plans for "escape" are double-edged, and function as a bribe to help discipline the workers. For example, UAW President Leonard Woodcock praised as "very imaginative" a plan by UAW Vice-President Kenneth Bannon to reduce worker discontent by giving him "more paid time off, by crediting him with a percentage of the hours he works in a year."[17] Clearly, this plan seeks to control the growing problem of absenteeism in the plants, since management can deny a worker their paid time off if they fail to log their time on the job in the prescribed way. One can imagine GM very readily giving each worker an extra week paid vacation, if that would guarantee his or her regular, disciplined presence on the job for the rest of the year.

As for the organization of the assembly line, President Woodcock has bluntly stated that "this should not be a matter for confrontation in collective bargaining," because to make it a bargaining issue, the union "should have some

15. *Ibid.*, September 3, 1972.
16. *Wall Street Journal*, December 8, 1972.
17. *New York Times*, September 28, 1972 and December 27, 1972.

idea what the solution is. We don't."[18] The union is obviously not changing its ways in 1973, but will remain solidly integrated into the structures of power which preserve management control of the industry. This fact is the beginning of wisdom in understanding the auto workers' present situation, and constitutes the central conclusion to be drawn from an analysis of the strike at Lordstown.

Recently, there has been much discussion of "blue-collar blues" and such notions as "alienation" and "dehumanization" on the assembly line. *Work in America*, the HEW report, is a typical contribution to this discussion, and affords a good example of misleading ways in which the debate is carried on.[19] The report speaks of the sources of dissatisfaction among American workers—powerlessness, lack of opportunity, monotony, low self-esteem—and suggests seemingly practicable "humanizing" remedies: autonomous work groups, challenging jobs, job mobility, self-government for the plant community, etc., etc. Only in a two-page section, mildly entitled "Obstacles to the Redesign of Jobs," do they mention the little matter of corporate profits, and blithely suggest that, on the basis of their research, long-range productivity will go up if jobs are redesigned with such "humanization" in mind. Quite aside from the remarkably flimsy and superficial evidence they adduce in their appendix, the authors fudge the fact (admitted by UAW officials[20]) that reconversion of major industry along the lines suggested would be enormously costly and that immediate profits and productivity would sharply decline. This fact, by itself, makes nonsense of the Report, since nothing has convinced businessmen that they have anything to gain by such costly tinkering. The most one could expect is some trivial cosmetic exercises, analogous to the ecologically "clean" images being projected currently by the oil companies.

But these considerations do not get to the essence of the matter. American businessmen are deeply convinced that a business's ability to compete in the national and international market is directly related to management's strict control over the decisions affecting production. Hence, to relinquish serious decision-making powers to the workers (which, businessmen correctly perceive, is the real issue behind the talk of humanization and alienation) would be to agree to the eco-

18. *Ibid.*, January 28, 1973.
19. Published by M.I.T. Press, 1973.
20. *New York Times*, September 3, 1972.

nomic ruin of their companies. Given such attitudes, the
HEW Report must be understood as an exercise in public
relations, a deliberate attempt to confuse discussion of the
subject of workers' discontent in America, a subject which,
if considered seriously, raises fundamental questions of the
power relations between capital and labor.

Why don't the workers at Lordstown organize themselves
to do something about their working conditions? After all,
they build the cars; they could stop the line any time. Centrally important, of course, is the economic vulnerability of
each worker, and the atmosphere of fear and mistrust that
is generated by the carefully structured isolation and powerlessness of the individual worker. For another thing, after 8
or 10 hours on the job, workers usually don't have energy for
much besides their families, a little beer or pool, and whatever private interests they have. One of the workers I met
told me:

> Look, I get up at five, and don't get back till almost six. By
> the time I wash up, eat dinner and maybe play my guitar an
> hour, I'm through for the day. I suppose I should read my
> contract and go to union meetings, but I figure I'll leave it
> to my committeeman.

By the way, one can't blame anyone for not reading the
contract. The local Lordstown contract alone runs 166 pages
and is written in the most abstract bureaucratic language
which alone might justify in the workers' eyes a special caste
of officials who can read it.

Living conditions around Lordstown also inhibit organization and natural groups. GM built the plant out in the countryside of northeastern Ohio, and the workers live in the
50-odd towns and trailer parks within a 40-mile radius of
the plant. There is no common center to the workers' lives;
after work, each employee, much like a middle-class suburban commuter, drives to his own town and does not see his
fellow workers till the next day. They rarely get together to
talk about the plant, their lives, or shared concerns.

The heterogeneous character of the work force at Lordstown helps keep the workers divided. Only intermittently do
they perceive their common situation and, as elsewhere in
the United States, their animosities are often focused on
each other. The young "long hairs" distrust the older "hillbillies" (Appalachian people from West Virginia and Pennsylvania), whom they consider hard-core company men, or

"grits." The feelings are mutual, and hillbillies often do not like longhairs. The hillbillies are also often racists, and dislike the 10 percent black population as well as the small groups of Puerto Rican and Cuban workers. The blacks, accustomed to the smoldering racism among the older rank and file, patricularly resent the local union leadership, which they feel is a white clique intent on keeping blacks out of the union power structure and such élite jobs as the skilled trades.

Several years ago, a few blacks took over the leadership of the bankrupt Lordstown credit union, and by hard work turned it into a profit-making business. Now the UAW local is bidding to take over the credit union again, which the blacks naturally resent. The blacks at Lordstown have formed a non-union caucus, the only workers' organization at Lordstown not sponsored by the union. So far, the caucus has been quietly trying to build support and solidarity among the blacks at Lordstown, and has not initiated any major actions at the plant. The caucus is not anti-white in official ideology, but its leaders feel that for now the blacks must go it alone to improve their group situation at the plant.

Only three hundred women are employed in the thirteen-thousand-worker complex. Women are victims of sexism both from foremen and from their fellow workers. The male workers resent them, feel they get the easy jobs, and it is widely assumed that any woman working at Lordstown "makes money on the side," i.e., is a prostitute. Women are harassed by crude sexual propositions, sometimes from the foremen.

A woman of twenty described to me her isolated situation on the line. Resented by the older women for being young and pretty, she was constantly insulted and propositioned by the men. Her foreman mingled his sexual advances with threats of discipline. She wished to make an official case against this foreman but needed corroborative witnesses. The foreman had approached her openly, within hearing of the other workers on her part of the line, but they all refused to testify for her. "Look, I've got a wife and child. Do you think I'll risk my job for you?" she was told. There are no women union officials at the plant, and many women feel that the union is unconcerned with their problems. The privileges of a small, all-white group of skilled tradesmen further divides the workers. The "skills" involved are such things as repairing broken machinery, skills which only require a few weeks to learn, and which do not in themselves justify the existence of a special category of worker. One of the central functions of the skilled trades category is to create a special-interest group within the work force. Skilled tradesmen have much more variety and autonomy in their jobs than a worker chained to the assembly line. They consider themselves an élite—one skilled tradesman, a college dropout, referred to himself as a "technocrat"—and superior to the assembly line workers. Since skilled tradesmen traditionally hold a disproportionate number of official union positions, they are often a powerful group who look after their own interests first. Their loyalty to the union is correspondingly far greater than that of the assembly workers. As strong union supporters, the skilled tradesmen were highly visible during the strike at Lordstown, serving often as pickets. This visibility, which at first suggests militance, is in fact an indication of the essentially conservative role of the skilled tradesmen. Skilled tradesmen were not involved in sabotage and would be highly unlikely to initiate any unauthorized direct actions to slow down or gain control of production.

The union organization, as we have seen, actively contributes to the fragmentation of the workers by favoring special groups, making false promises, and by failing to provide a true picture of what is going on in the plant, at other GM plants, and in the automobile industry as a whole. The union also skillfully coopts other centers of potential organization by its committee system. There is a community committee, a black committee, a women's committee, and there was a pro-McGovern committee in 1972. These committees exist to try to convince groups that the union is concerned and looking out for them. They also defuse possibly explosive sources of organizational energy, as well as keeping union officials aware of the intensity of discontent among different groups.

Much at Lordstown resembles descriptions of U.S. auto workers two decades ago.[21] Workers hate their jobs and put up with them because "the money's good." They dream of escaping from the assembly line but few do. They expect and hope that their children will have a better life than theirs. But there is also an identifiable "new generation" of workers

21. See Charles Walker and Robert Guest, *The Man on the Assembly Line* (Cambridge, Mass., 1952); also Ely Chinoy, *Automobile Workers and the American Dream* (Garden City, New Jersey, 1955).

at Lordstown.[22] The average worker's age at the plant is about 26. These workers' parents experienced the Depression and never had expectations that work would be anything but hard and unpleasant. For the parents, the high pay and benefits at Lordstown and the modern plant conditions would seem highly desirable. Such older workers, favored as well by the union's seniority system, do not really understand why the young workers are so unhappy. But the young workers have had very different experiences. They have had more education and grew up in the Fifties and Sixties, a period of rising affluence for a large spectrum of the American people. From the promises of the general culture, the young workers have learned to expect a decent life, which includes pleasure and leisure, some meaning in their work, and some control of it. They are less willing than their parents to accept fifty or sixty hours of meaningless work for the sake of a large pay envelope.

The workers realize that many of them are at Lordstown for good. They are also beginning to understand that they can not expect the union to provide them with a better working life. Gary Bryner concedes that there is a growing demand for "instant justice," that young workers are fed up with the bureaucratic sclerosis of the union.

These young workers trusted the union during the strike of 1972 and were severely disappointed, but this experience can lead to a clearer insight into the function of the union. Next time the workers will believe the union's promises less readily and give up their own direct actions less easily.

Whether these workers' discontents will erupt into a major confrontation between the workers and the corporation depends on many factors. Now, as always, the workers have the potential power to regulate or to stop production. But to be able to utilize this potential, the workers must overcome the fear and isolation caused by the divisions within and between plants, and come to a politics of their own through their actions. The economic situation of GM and the US as a whole will influence the range of options open to the corporation and the union in response to serious pressure from the workers. We can not tell what the future will be. But analysis of the Lordstown situation can help to distinguish between possible futures and impossible ones.

22. See Stanley Aronowitz's article in this volume.

# A Break with the Past

### stanley aronowitz

### I

In the 1960s, during the New Left's apex of activity and influence, most radicals disdained the cornerstone of Marxist orthodoxy—the theory of the working class as revolutionary gravedigger. Having discovered its own limitation, the left is returning to this theory—albeit with a not inconsiderable dash of confusion and romanticism. Just as a section of the student left during the last decade deified the black movement as a result of its own guilt and sense of impotence, so a new generation (and a number of the older generation) has abstracted the proletariat in the same way. The loss of confidence in its own critical faculties is no less reprehensible today when the working class is uncritically embraced than it was in the bygone era when it was summarily dismissed. The underlying tendency to grasp at panaceas remains intact. If liberals have transformed George McGovern and the Kennedys from banal politicians into saviors, the workers have been equally objectified and falsified by some radicals. It is important to undertake a sober estimate of the history of and prospects for the working class in America. In undertaking this task, we must state at the outset that the working class is neither on the eve of revolutionary action, nor does it constitute the reactionary, racist mass which many infer from the huge Wallace constituency.

There are new currents in the working class, not the least of which is the rise of a generation of workers whose life experience has been radically different from all previous generations. Nor are the potentially revolutionary sectors of the working class sufficiently defined by Marx's famous concept of productive labor—that is, all those who own nothing but their labor power, but are engaged in the production of material commodities. The rise of corporate capitalism and its integration with the state, together with the rise of central

71

bureaucracies as a critical locus of economic and social power, have broadened the working class, both in size and composition.

The traditional industrial working class remains a necessary condition for expanded capitalist production, and its centrality in the production of capital in most industries has been essentially unaltered despite its numerical stagnation. But the rise of the mass of workers employed in the public bureaucracies, in the distributive trades and in the services is a striking feature of late capitalism, illustrating its parasitic character. Moreover, the relationship between mental and physical labor has altered dramatically since World War II within the production sector itself, so that in several key industries knowledge has become the critical productive force. This development has not been even in all mass production industries, however. The assembly line of the auto industry is still highly labor-intensive, and productivity is still measured in terms of the speedup of human labor. Despite recent technological advances in some giant corporations, the textile industry has barely scratched the surface of possible cybernetic technologies. But the oil and chemical industries, the electronics industry, and important branches of the paper industry are examples of dramatic shifts in the composition of the labor force. Here the absolute number of technically trained wage and salary workers has begun to approach the size of the unskilled and semi-skilled work force. In the oil industry, no newly hired production worker has lacked a high-school diploma for the past 20 years, and most of them aspire to college or technical school degrees so that they can work in the laboratories and as supervisors. Chemicals, oil, electronic equipment, synthetic fibers and some kinds of paper and food products are no longer produced by human physical labor, except for the maintenance workers who perform repair work. The production worker is a watcher of heat and volume gauges and his major task is to know the respective tolerances well enough to stop the flow of work when necessary. In the older plants, the production worker still adjusts some continuous flow operations by hand, but the recent expansion of the chemical and paper industries have made self-adjusting mechanisms more common. In plants where continuous-flow operations predominate, the key production workers are the chemist, the engineer, and the quality-control technician, not the machine watcher. It is not only the importance of the so-called research and development activities which define the growing importance of knowledge, but the production process itself.

Differences within the working class on the basis of race, nationality, sex, skill and industry are not obliterated by late capitalism. On the contrary, they constitute antagonisms which still act as a brake on the development of revolutionary consciousness within the working class. But the collective worker is emerging as the direct antagonist of the collective capitalist. What I shall describe in this article should be understood as tendencies in this direction, not accomplished historical changes. In my opinion, the direction is clear: the objective possibility for the emergence of a new revolutionary subject is in the process of formation. Not the old working class, which, as has been pointed out by Marcuse and others, was not a class in "radical chains" in America because it actually did become *of* society as well as in it. Nor is the new revolutionary subject only the controversial new technical and scientific worker. Knowledge has indeed become a productive force in our society, but it is widely disseminated among the whole new generation of workers, which is better educated than any in history. The new revolutionary subject is simply this generation of collective labor. It was created by the conjuncture of capital's own development and the struggles of previous generations of workers to limit the arbitrariness of capital. Its needs and aspirations are radically different from its ancestors. Its demands, not yet articulated, may be too far-reaching for capitalism to satisfy.

## II

The most important change from all previous generations is the emergence of a homogeneous working class in America, a country which, as Daniel Bell has noted, corresponds more exactly to Marx's classic model than any other capitalist nation except Britain. This homogeneity is a result of 1) the decline of ethnicity as a critical factor of American political and social life; 2) the common experience of this generation of workers of being separated from the gnawing poverty or the constant threat of it that suffused the consciousness of its elders; 3) the decline of commodity culture as a determining ideology among workers; 4) and the weakness of the fundamental institutions of authority, such as the family, schools, religion, and labor unions.

Among the most persistent demographic influences stultifying working-class consciousness has been the fact that a huge sector of the basic industrial working class in America was formed out of the waves of immigration between the end of the Civil War and the end of World War I. In the early days of trade union organizing, a frequent complaint of militants was that the task of bringing "unskilled" and semi-skilled workers into labor unions was made extremely difficult by ethnic splits within the working class. These splits were nearly all encompassing. Different nationalities were recruited into different industries: Italians and Jews into the garment industry; Italians and Portuguese into the New England textile industries, with a minority of Irish; Irish into the transport industry; Eastern Europeans into the steel industry. Within the same industrial plant, the technical division of labor was also organized along ethnic lines. Germans became foremen and skilled workers, closely followed by the Irish. Eastern and southern Europeans of all nationalities were relegated to the hottest, hardest and lowest-paid jobs, until the blacks occupied these positions after the First World War.

The tremendous growth of American capitalism between 1865 and 1920 was made possible by the agricultural crisis in Europe (and later within the U.S.) which forced millions of rural laborers to pour into European and American cities. The hierarchial organization of immigrant labor within our country, corresponding to the stratification of labor within the workplace, reinforced cultural and ethnic divisions. But the waves of immigration made possible some mobility within the working class itself. As long as the system kept expanding, the frontier myth could be sustained on the basis of the chance for upgrading as well as real and imagined opportunities for small-business ownership. Even if only a few workers ever left the shop or reached the exalted status of foreman, it was difficult to persuade workers that their own class solidarity was the best guarantee for change. The efforts of radicals to educate workers to the principle that they should rise *with* their class, rather than above it, were always counteracted by the differential access of different ethnic groups to opportunities within the system. The social division of industrial labor, combined with its ethnic divisions, was the core of the development of racist, chauvinist and egotistical ideologies within the working class.

Prior to the 1930s, success in the unionization of industrial workers was achieved among two groups: those who were native born, and those within industries where the bulk

of workers in the plant shared the same nationality. Among
native-born workers, for whom the entrance into industrial
occupations was often a defeat in comparison to their expectations of remaining on the land or owning a small business, the conditions of industrial labor were intolerable. During the first decades of the American industrial revolution
between the Civil War and the close of the century, the frequency and severity of strikes, food riots and other forms of
mass actions were of deep concern to the rising capitalist
class. The response of both employers and the government
was swift and sure. A national guard was mobilized to smash
protest movements, the courts were prepared to mete out
class justice on a mass scale, and, in some cases, the employers themselves retained private armies to deal with labor
violence.

Where mass unionism was successful among immigrants,
such as in the steel industry after World War I, organization could only proceed by taking ethnic differences into
account, that is, by organizing separately by nationality as
well as together by class. William Z. Foster, the chief organizer of the great steel strike of 1919, describes the immense
obstacles presented by ethnic divisions. Characteristically, after having achieved a degree of unity among the diverse
groups comprising the basic steel labor force, employers resorted to herding black scabs, an explicit admission of the
significance of race and nationality as an employer tool for
dividing the working class.

But the fact of cultural diversity was not sufficient to
explain the low level of class consciousness among immigrant
groups (except for skilled workers, many of whom shared
socialist and anarchist leanings or activities in the old country). Equally important was the exquisite sense of the promise of American life deeply embedded among the foreign
born. To the extent that historians have dealt with the impact of immigration on the development of social and political life, emphasis has been placed on the importance of the
frontier or Horatio Alger myths as determining the conservatism of the immigrants. But the ideology of social mobility
was more than a myth. It corresponded to the real opportunities for advancement within and from the ranks of the
unskilled made possible by the rapid expansion of American
capitalism at home and abroad.

My grandfather fled the Czarist military draft for the
war with Japan to come to America. His family were Jewish

peasants in Lithuania who were able to make a living on the land, but never had the security of daily life in the literal sense of the phrase. Most immigrants were victims of famines or other forms of agricultural crises, or were similarly victimized by repressive regimes. Many European peasants filled the cities of their native lands. For others, like my grandparents, there was no room in Amsterdam or London. The United States may not have been the promised land, but there was a chance to live.

Some immigrants had been imbued with the revolutionary traditions of the old country. When they came to America they sought out the labor and socialist movements. Others were attracted, after some years of life and labor in the United States, to the militant and idealist movements of immigrants and native born. Having fled from oppression, they were determined not to endure it all over again. But the majority saw a chance in America, if not for themselves, at least for their children. And this country did provide an opportunity for some of their children. Of course, the route of higher education was not available to most first- and second-generation children of the immigrants. But many of them found their way into the skilled trades or out of the lower-paid industrial jobs. America was not exactly the land of milk and honey, but it was certainly better than Sicily or County Cork.

The irony of the immigration was that its conservative influence was entirely misperceived by both radicals and the government. The rise of nativistic movements seeking to exclude immigrants from this country on the basis of their alleged radicalism and/or laziness was belied by the fact that American capitalism was built on the backs of black and white imported labor. Government suppression of immigration was prompted more by the slowing growth rate of the economy and the appearance of frequent economic crises after the turn of the century than by the clear and present danger of revolution. But it is important not to underestimate the significance of the anti-radical impulse behind nativist ideology. As with the emergence of the permanent war economy in the 1940s and 1950s, the "red menace" provided the rationale for government suppression of not only radicals but the entire working class as well. The most militant of the industrial workers' movements, the IWW, organized among immigrant groups as well as the native born. Although it never achieved a solid base of support among either group, its successful strikes were conducted as much among foreign-born workers in Lawrence, Massachusetts, as native Americans working in the lumber camps of the Northwest. The IWW did not disappear under the weight of its internal conflicts or the failure of its ideology or organizing tactics. It was defeated by a determined repressive state apparatus during the First World War when patriotism was rampant within liberal and socialist ranks, paralleling the jingoism rampant among large segments of the general population.

The last great waves of immigration came to our shores during the three years following World War I. In the wake of the Palmer raids against radicals, the government clamped down on immigrants and only permitted a trickle after 1921. Exceptions were to be made for the victims of the fascist terror in the late 1930s, the refugees of the Hungarian uprising in the late 1950s, and the Cubans after the rise of the socialist regime. Still, first-generation workers are often influenced by the attitudes of their parents, even though the mass culture of 20th-century America, together with the expansion of compulsory schooling, has created important differences between the generations. The rapid acculturation of new Americans was a key objective of the corporate-minded liberals at the turn of the century. Settlement houses, adult evening classes in English, the emphasis on public education, and the patriotic orientation of the ethnic social and fraternal clubs which sprang up to help immigrants make a successful adjustment to their new environment, were all assisted by large corporations and the government in the quest for a docile labor force.

Even though socialist-minded nationality groups were a powerful influence among some new arrivals and formed a significant part of the socialist and communist movements well into the 20th century, most foreign-born workers belonged to such organizations as the Polish Falcons or the Sons of Italy, which were strongly conservative, if not downright reactionary. These ethnic organizations preserved the contradictory goals of the American ruling class: on the one hand, homogenization seemed to be a strong preference of corporate and government planners; on the other, within industrial towns and plants, ethnicity was an important industrial-relations tool for the employers.

The Democratic party in the later 19th century developed into another powerful representative of ethnic interests.

Apart from its role in national politics, the party built its popular support on the basis of its links with the everyday needs of immigrants thrust into a hostile urban environment with few resources to deal with the bewildering welter of problems facing them. Because it often competed with socialist groups for the loyalty of the immigrant populations, it became a further factor in reducing the strength of radical movements among foreign-born workers.

It was not until the second and third generations of native-born workers that the process of homogenization was complete. Although many workers born in the 1920s were already well on their way to breaking from the hyphenated-American syndrome, a second important event in American life prevented the emergence of mass working-class consciousness.

## III

Among the most commonly held shibboleths of radical thought is the notion that misery brings revolutionary awakening. Unfortunately, this has long been proven false. There is convincing evidence that the leading forces in the rise of industrial unionism in this country were the native-born younger workers—who actually did not suffer as greatly from the Depression as their elders, but rather occupied the better semi-skilled jobs—the skilled trades workers within industrial plants, and the most stable of the older semi-skilled workers in the mines and the largest mass production shops. The skilled workers had suffered deterioration in their living conditions during the early years of the Depression, as did the basic work force in the mines. But none of the crucial elements in the general strikes in Minneapolis and San Francisco or in the Flint sit-down strike were the down-and-outers. The persons who were crushed by the Depression—older people thrown off the lines and out of their jobs—were part of the solid support for the New Deal, which offered them a life raft. The impulse behind industrial unionism was somewhat different. It was born of the resentment of workers who had suffered setbacks during the Depression, particularly as a result of the boldness of employers in cutting wages and speeding up the work. The workers who conducted the mass textile, mining and transportation strikes during the early years of the New Deal did not perceive the government as a friend, much less a savior. These mass strikes were genuine expressions of self-activity and remarkable class solidarity. It was the trade unions which tried to channel the explosive protest against blatant employer attempts to use New Deal institutions to make surplus profits into bureaucratic molds.

For the mass of Americans, the Depression was a deeply traumatic experience which resonated long after the economy resumed its upward movement. The fear of unemployment and outright starvation haunted the working class for at least another generation. My father reached his industrial coming-of-age in the late 1920s, on the eve of the Depression. He spent a year in college, but quit to work on a newspaper as a cub reporter. Since he was the son of immigrant parents, he always had one foot in the ghetto and the other in the American mainstream. The contradictory part of his Lower East Side childhood was his inheritance of a passion for social justice alongside a gnawing yearning for economic security. The gnarled, decrepit tenements of his childhood stamped themselves indelibly on his social consciousness. In his boyhood, he helped his father deliver cases of seltzer to customers living in fifth-floor walkup apartments.

Although my father resolved to escape the ghetto, first through sports and then through journalism, these avenues proved too risky in economic terms. After the newspaper he worked for folded in 1931, he worked briefly for the Associated Press, but he finally left the low-paid and extremely shaky newspaper business. After some time in a textile factory and in the WPA, he finally landed a clerical job with the city. Most of the rest of his life was spent in the choking confines of the civil service and, at the end, back in the factory. He died having worked and worried himself to death, but with some savings.

My father loved Walt Whitman's America, but lacked his recklessness. He respected the muckrakers and the radicals, but could not summon either the energy or courage to join their ranks. The spectre of the 1930s was never far from his nightmares and so he died an angry and frustrated man, unable and unwilling to take chances to realize his aspirations.

For the generation of workers reared in the first half of the 20th century, the quest for economic security dominated their lives. There was no way they could more than sentimentally respond to radical ideas, even when they were willing to accept the help of radicals in their struggle for social justice within the prevailing order.

Even the members of my own generation were too close to the scarcity mentality of the Depression to transcend it. I rebelled against my family's neurotic lust for upward mobility, so I remained a worker. My mother had been a member of the CIO retail union, having participated in the sit-down strikes in the 1930s. She was always more "class" conscious than my father. Her family was intimately tied to the labor and socialist wings of Jewish immigrants. Her father was a cutter in a men's clothing factory for much of his working life. He was an extremely unstable man, capable of blowing his whole pay on a pinochle game or his savings on an ill-fated venture into the candy-store business. Grandpa was a lousy businessman. He *gave* candy to the kids, and they robbed him blind besides. But momma always worked and fought for her union. She feared the bosses, but hated them more. I guess my propensity to take chances was learned from my mother and her family. My father's sisters married businessmen and that fact put a hell of a lot of pressure on him to match their achievement in some way. On the other hand, my mother was crazy enough, according to my father, to quit her department store job in the middle of the second depression in 1938, after the defeat of the strike. I was five years old then. And I didn't understand all this until recently. But looking at my childhood friends in the East Bronx and the second-generation workers I encountered in my years as a shopworker and union organizer, it seemed that few of them went much beyond the aspirations of their parents.

But most white kids born after 1940 never experienced real hunger. For them, the struggles for union security, health benefits and pensions were taken for granted. They could not get hot for welfare capitalism or the guarantee of a job, because they really had no sense of what it is like not to find a job for a good part of their lives. Instead, they were reared on the doctrines of infinite opportunity within an expanding economic system and the expectation that they would not starve, no matter what. Just as the workers of the 1930s often took factory or clerical jobs as a temporary cushion to ride out the storm of the Depression, so many high school and college graduates took these jobs in the 1960s as an aid to finishing college, technical or professional school. The relative freedom of this generation from the expectation that hard times are a permanent condition, interspersed with the opportunities provided by war, made the need for decent, satisfying jobs more important than the goals of decent income and job property rights guaranteed by a union contract.

The older generation was often grateful for the chance to work, even though it became necessary to rebel against the excesses of the companies, which took advantage of the plentiful labor supply to wring the last drop of profit out of the workers. But behind the gratitude was the eternal hope of escape into the middle class. The wartime and postwar expansion of U.S. capitalism, bringing steady work and rising wage levels, revived the expectation that some workers could escape the shop into their own tavern or small construction contracting business. Most of the postwar working class became quickly smitten (but also burdened) by huge mortgages, time payments for mechanical gadgets, and finally, college tuition for their children. Thus, steady work bringing regular paychecks helped to repress the realization that the distance between their rising educational levels or vocational aspirations and the routine character of their work was widening.

During the years immediately following the war, the idea of education as a rite of passage to better jobs was widely disseminated. Returning veterans were given the chance to go to college free of tuition and with government subsidies to defray living costs. The increasing reliance on schooling as a means of moving up the occupational ladder was prompted by the resumption of technical innovation within the production industries, particularly those which produced means of production, as well as the rapidly expanding public sector. Technicians and engineers were required by the war industries, particularly the aircraft companies which were not really dismantled after the war because of the decision to solve many of the economic problems of conversion by perpetuating the permanent war economy. And the baby boom following World War II created the need for teachers by the early 1950s.

Public employee unionism began to grow in the mid-Fifties as millions of new workers found jobs in state and local governments which were still offering salaries and fringe benefits appropriate to the prewar Depression decade. The public worker was a returning veteran who received his bachelor's degree under the GI bill of rights, a black worker able to get a job in the post office or in the sanitation department, or a woman leaving her home for a job because her husband was not taking home enough or had split. These workers were no longer grateful to be working. The more plentiful, but also higher credentialed, public service jobs were often taken at a sacrifice in comparison to better-paid industrial work. In this environment, weak, forgotten unions were able to revive. The nearly moribund State, County and Municipal Workers Union and the equally ineffectual American Federation of Teachers seized the opportunity provided by the restlessness and militancy of the public workers. During the late 1950s, the growth of public workers' unions was among the few bright spots in the already sclerotic labor movement.

The early impulses behind the mass migrations from factory labor to the colleges were prompted by the common perception that the need for new entrants into semi-skilled factory work was levelling off and, among the unskilled, actually declining. As technical and scientific labor expanded vastly in the 1950s, workers possessing administrative skills were in great demand.

Workers were still seeking jobs with more pay to offset their enormous debts, and the pay was more important than the quality of the job. The struggle for higher wages was a product of the inflationary spiral of the economy and the rise of consumerism as a way of life. In some instances in the 1950s, the speedup and stretchout in the shops were met with stiff worker resistance, but for most of the Depression babies who entered the labor force from 1945 to 1955, the emphasis was on higher pay, even if these monetary gains were purchased at the expense of the erosion of their hard-won right to limit the company's ability to displace labor with machines.

The fight for pension plans and health insurance also took place in the 1950s, but this was actually a sign of the aging of the industrial labor force owing to the restrictions on younger workers entering the shops. This situation was created by the two recessions of the 1950s and the rise of technical labor relative to manual labor. I remember entering a large steel fabricating plant in northern New Jersey as a trainee lathe operator in 1953 and finding most of the guys 30 years or younger breaking their asses on piecework, while the older guys who pretty much controlled the union were interested in retirement benefits. The few young (under 25) people in the plant who did not work on piecework jobs, particularly the black workers, were ready to fight for more money on the hourly rate. But the majority couldn't have cared less about "time workers." They fought the company's attempt to lower piece rates on new jobs. The family men were willing to work like hell, and even protested the so-called "small jobs" which required more skill and more time to set up, while yielding less money, because the only way to make out on a job was to have a long run.

Two years later I found a job in a small but technologically fairly advanced steel-making plant with about 1000 workers. The two strikes I participated in during the late Fifties had to do with protection of jobs against mechanization. This plant had a group bonus method of wage payment. Like piecework, workers were paid according to their output, but not on an individual piece. In the hot rolling mill, a gang produced a certain number of pounds of refined metal each day. Although everybody had different tasks, the work process was interdependent. We did not need bosses to push us. We pushed each other, since if one man fucked up, everybody's pay was affected. It was only when the company tried to bring in a machine which displaced 33 men and left three on the job to operate the push-button equipment that a wildcat strike became possible. The second strike was the 116-day steel strike of 1959, affecting 600,000 workers all over the country, over the issue of the company's right to alter the established work rules which stipulated that no changes in production methods could be introduced without prior consultation with the union. The strike was successful on paper, but the companies quickly disregarded the work-rule provision of the contract in succeeding years as output soared while employment remained the same. The result of the union's failure to stem the company onslaught against working conditions was rank-and-file revolt against the established leadership of the union. The new leadership was more careful for a while, but slowly sank back into the patterns of its predecessors.

It was not until the next generation of workers entered the shops and the public bureaucracies in the 1960s that the Depression-wrought issues of job security were pushed to the side of workers' struggles. In the service industries, particularly the public bureaucracies, workers possessing educational credentials entitling them (or so they thought) to work of genuine service to the community, or at least intellectually interesting to themselves, found that they had not succeeded in escaping the monotony of industrial labor—even if they were a little cleaner and less physically exhausted at the end of the day. But the expansion in the '60s generated by the Vietnam war, combined with the tremendous rate of retirement among those who had entered the labor force in the decade after the First World War, helped to build the CIO, and won the right to get out of the shop at 65, brought a relatively large number of young workers into industrial plants.

The new generation of workers was not prepared to endure a working life suffused with repetitive tasks performed with mindless submission. Neither the endearments of two cars in every garage, which had become a compulsion of their parents, nor the fears of plunging into the lower depths of poverty, which had propelled their grandparents, were sufficient to contain their resentment against the betrayal represented by highly rationalized factory or service work. Even those such as teachers or health workers, blessed with the chance to escape the most severe forms of rationalized labor, found the hierarchies of authority no less repressive.

Nearly all members of the present generation of wage and salary workers have jobs whose routinization bears no correspondence to the expectations generated by their educational experiences. This is not the place to argue that education prepares workers to accept routinized and boring labor. Everybody knows that the curriculum and authority relations in the schools breed submissiveness. But the dialectic of schooling consists in the tension between its socialization functions and its promise of deliverance from the banality of everyday life. It is too simplistic merely to assert that students stay in school in order to obtain the credentials needed for the shift from blue-collar to white-collar and gray-collar labor. This is true enough. But they are also motivated by powerful and persistent illusions—that school is a place of learning and that education is a means not only of escaping manual labor but of gaining access to interesting, meaningful jobs which will give them personal satisfaction and even, perhaps, enable them to make a social contribution.

Eighty percent of those entering high school now graduate. The number of college graduates exceeds the number of jobs available for which the degree is a prerequisite. The proliferation of youth who have successfully endured school has reached explosive proportions, and there is no room for

them either in the teaching profession or the public bureaucracies. These youth find themselves in factories, offices,
working as truck or cab drivers or as sales personnel in department stores. They are furious that they have wasted their
time and have been bullshitted about the importance of
school. The educational process for working-class young people is many-sided: it teaches a high tolerance for boredom,
but it is unable to pay off in jobs which are significantly
better than those of their parents.

The present generation of workers is qualitatively different
from any in the history of American capitalism. It has
shared the transcendence of ethnicity, the distance from
scarcity, the partial recognition that consumerism is insufficient to overcome the alienation of bureaucratically rationalized labor, and the experience of having been incompletely
socialized because of the loosening grip of the institutions
and ideologies upon which capitalism relies for its survival.

The satisfaction of old needs has created new ones. Many
young workers have begun to evolve new work patterns
to avoid having to do jobs which are essentially meaningless in terms other than bare survival. In many companies,
absenteeism is massive on Mondays and Fridays. The huge
turnover in auto plants mitigates the disruptive impact of the
refusal of many youth to work steadily. There is always a
new crop of students looking for summer jobs or those who
need money badly enough to work intensively for short
periods.

But in other industries, management has been forced to
consider, and in some cases introduce, shorter work weeks
with similar hours. The mass strikes in the postal industry,
among truck drivers and, more recently, in the Lordstown
plant of the GM company, were symptomatic of the refusal
of young workers to accept boredom and monotony for five
and six days a week, even at more than $4 an hour. Workers
who refused overtime work or Saturday work were given
disciplinary layoffs by the company.

In fairness to critics who maintain that wildcat strikes
against the company and the union are not new in the auto
industry or among youth, it should be stated that a similar
development occurred in the early 1950s in the auto plants;
however, there was no mass strike among the rest of the
workers, except for the big wage strikes in 1946 which could
be attributed to the pent-up rage against the wartime wage
freeze. Young workers, it is claimed, are always ready to

fight. But they get older, their debts grow, and so do their families.

The differences this time are substantial, I believe. The old mediations are losing their force. Neither the unions nor the anti-communist ideologies which were nurtured by immigrant fears are capable of containing the discontent.

On the other hand, this generation still shares the legacy of racism and sexism. This legacy is a force which counteracts the development of revolutionary consciousness. The division of labor according to race and sex remains a potent material force undercutting ideological struggles to overcome it. Despite the fact that American capitalism has brought women and blacks into the economic mainstream since the end of World War II, they occupy the lowest economic niches. In the productive sectors, women remain excluded except in the consumer-goods industries. Women and blacks have been massively employed in the emergent service sectors. For example, more than 75 percent of health workers are women, a large number of whom are from minority groups, especially in the large cities. But women and blacks are concentrated within clerical and skilled paraprofessional jobs, at best, and constitute the overwhelming majority of the semi-skilled and unskilled categories in such departments as housekeeping and dietary.

Black males found their way into the basic mass-production industries in large numbers during the War and again during the expansion of the 1960s. More than a third of auto and steel workers are black, many with substantial seniority, so that the old phrase "last hired and first fired" has been somewhat mitigated. Bue here again, few black workers are to be found in skilled trades or in the higher-paid semi-skilled occupations. They are the bulk of the low-paid semi-skilled and the unskilled in many important industrial plants.

A second brake on the development of genuine political consciousness is the persistence of the hierarchical division of labor in general. In recent years, the struggle of the black movement around workplace issues has been against discriminatory hiring, promotion and lateral transfer policies of employers and unions. Few blacks have been permitted to enter managerial ranks within corporations, although there has been a greater integration of blacks into middle management of government bureaucracies. Black workers remain excluded from the construction trades, and only a token number have been admitted to the traditional professions of law, medicine and engineering. But these struggles have been circumscribed by the prevailing occupational stratifications which are based as much on bureaucratically determined divisions as on the technical division of labor.

The social division of labor has been a source of persistent conflict within the working class. The division is not based simply on race, sex, or actual work requirements. The credential routes to higher occupations, the seniority system as a basis for promotion, the classification of jobs grounded in arbitrary distinctions which have no basis in job content or skill level, are important barriers to class solidarity. There are few industries where the levelling of status and skill is so complete as the automobile assembly line. The united action of the workers in Lordstown and other auto assembly plants in recent years is abetted by the relative uniformity of work assignments among the workers. There are distinctions between the grimy, heavy work for blacks in the body shop and the fast, but clean and light tasks, of final assembly. But the distinctions are not nearly as sharp as between foundry work and cold rolling in a steel mill or between the nurse's aide's job of emptying bedpans and the quasi-supervisory tasks of a registered nurse.

The minute division of labor, whose hierarchical structure is reinforced by the seniority and bidding system within union-organized industries, and by the system of educational credentials within both technical and human services' industries, provides the material roots for élitism within the working class. In many industries the so-called generation gap is produced as much by the relatively good jobs secured by older, high-seniority workers as by cultural differences. The unions have become representatives of the older workers and guardians of the prevailing occupational differentiations which produce higher pay and less onerous jobs for their constituency. Since the younger workers have taken for granted the real achievements of the unions, the union is increasingly judged not by its past record but by what it has done for the membership lately. Young workers find that the unions, like the school and the family, promise more than they are structurally able to deliver. The unions have all but abandoned the fight for decent working conditions and, insofar as they are perceived as staunch defenders of the status quo in terms of the organization of work, they are increasingly looked upon as enemies.

It would be a mistake to exaggerate the degree to which

young workers have liberated themselves from the institutions of socialization or the authoritarian structures and ideologies which accompany them. The internalization of arbitrary authority within consciousness cannot be rooted out in one generation. In fact, because the material supports within society for these structures remain powerful, without a convincing movement whose objectives are consciously anti-authoritarian, these structures of domination reassert themselves within the individual and the class. Although they have been weakened, the familiar subjective forms of labor's self-alienation still persist—workers "tune-out" on the content and implications of their work; production becomes nothing more than a means to consumption. The efforts of management to exceed the historically acceptable pace of work in a given location will be resisted by workers. But this is not the same as recognizing that deadening labor is immoral when the technological possibilities exist for its abolition. Young auto workers have neither challenged the object of their labor, the production of cars, nor have they transcended the inevitability of submitting to the old methods of production. Their struggle remains defensive even when they have an inkling of a different vision of life and labor.

Most young workers, whether in the factory or anywhere else, take their money and run. The idea is still to concentrate as little as possible on what actually happens on the job and to try to live as full a life as possible during leisure hours. But lacking the elements of an aesthetic culture, or an alternate concept of work, workers have been made manipulated objects of the productions of mass culture imposed from above. Here, the roles of the various spectacles of the capitalist marketplace are particularly relevant. Among these, especially for men, spectator sports play a unique part in replacing the traditional forms of folk or high culture.

The most significant characteristic of the capitalist division of labor is the transformation of the worker from an active producer to a spectator of his own labor. Workers who perform a set of discrete operations that are only a tiny part of the whole commodity and who have no real grasp of the object's destiny after it leaves the work station, tend to view the production process from the outside as if it actually emanated from the ingenuity and initiative of the company. The managerial function at the workplace is often regarded with awe. Workers have even made the reification of management part of their everyday self-deprecation: "If you're so smart, how come you ain't rich?"

Only in rare moments such as strikes does the understanding that workers themselves possess the real power over production make itself somewhat clear. The introjection of domination within the consciousness of the working class prevents this perception from being fully comprehended in ordinary life. To the extent that the real relations of power and initiative remain obscured in production, domination extends beyond the workplace to all aspects of existence.

Spectator sports retain the alienated character of labor, but create the aura of participation for the observer. Emotional catharsis is the mediation between the reality of the powerlessness of the fan over the events taking place on the playing field and the feeling of control which sustains personal involvement. The spectator appropriates the skills required to play the game symbolically. His involvement is energized by the passions of partisanship.

The sports arena has its own *élan* among spectators, who become strategists, generals and other substitutes for the authority they do not enjoy in their personal lives. In the workplace and in the home, sports is both a shared pleasure and a field of competition among observers. Like the movies, sports provides a way for total immersion in a manner that removes the observer from the banality of his own life, and creates the forms of manipulation which generate a sense of power and a vision of an alternative to the mundane.

Spectator sports is a way for men to establish contact with their children which is denied them at home. The father remains the supreme authority but his power does not have the appearance of arbitrary domination. If the son is willing to share the excitement and love of the games, he can get some love from his father, since most men can only express affection in a mediated way.

Everybody played the numbers in my plant. Every morning the numbers runner came around to collect the nickels and dimes from the guys at their machines. The numbers runner was usually a worker whose job assignment was bringing materials from machine to machine, so his illegal activities could be hidden behind legitimate work. Of course, everybody, including the foreman, knew who the runner was. But the identity of the "banker" was less obvious. I never knew who ran the numbers or the football pool until I hit the pool one week. You hit the number when you guessed the last three digits of the paramutual take for the daily double at a certain race track. It was a matter of pure chance. But the football, basketball and baseball pool required genuine skill. In football, you not only had to guess the winners of ten leading college games, but you had to guess the margins of victory. I rarely played the numbers except when I had a sentimental attachment to it, like my kid's birthday or some famous historical event. But I always played the football pool.

Discussions about football and baseball were serious shithouse conversation. Passions often ran pretty high, easily outdistancing raps about electoral politics or women. After all, you could not have much effect on these problems, but you could make money and earn prestige if you were lucky enough to hit the number or were smart enough to hit the pool. Workers daydreamed about sex while turning out thousands of parts on an automatic screw machine, but with sports, the sense of power was more concrete.

That Monday when I knew I had hit the jackpot, I immediately contacted the go-between. He told me that he did not give out the money (the odds were 150-1), so I had to wait until after work to meet the banker in the parking lot. I practically ran out of the washroom after work that day. A few minutes after I reached the parking lot, the runner came walking slowly towards me in the company of the vice president of the local union. I was a steward in my department at the time, so was well acquainted with "Tex," a long stringy Southerner who worked as a maintenance man. I'd always had him down for a pretty good guy. He was soft-spoken, sometimes downright taciturn, but he was an effective grievance man. Tex greeted me with a mumble and took out the bills to pay me off. I was stunned. It's one thing to play the numbers; it's another to be part of the apparatus.

Later that night it dawned on me that the company had to know about Tex. I began to wonder how many other union officials were operating similar businesses in the shop. Guys would come around all the time with watches, offers of cheap television sets and good buys on used cars. We all suspected that the merchandise was hot, but never begrudged a guy for trying to make a living. Almost everybody held down an extra job, sometimes even another full-time job. But at the time I thought it ought to be different for union officials: they should be free of that kind of vulnerability, especially illegal activity. This was going to be a field day for the company. The deal appeared simple. The union leader could operate his business, the company would shut its eyes, the men would get screwed.

It was not so simple. Tex was like a basketball player who scores 30 points a game instead of 40 and makes sure that his team only wins by 10 instead of 20 points, or a boxer who knocks his opponent to the canvas in the eighth round instead of the first. But how many other union officials were in similar positions? Later on I learned that in the large plants, few union leaders were so obviously corrupt, but in the medium-sized or smaller shops the union officer as businessman was the rule, not the exception. It was not so much that shop leaders take money from companies. It was more a matter of being tolerated for illegal behavior, or equally common, being allowed to roam the plant ostensibly on union business without having to work. It's hard to imagine a unionist selling the workers out for the price of freedom from being chained to a machine all day. But for many shop officials, that freedom is worth more than money.

More recently, many state governments have started lotteries, whose enormous appeal is comparable to the Irish Sweepstakes of a decade ago. The lottery, like sports, is a way to perpetuate the fantasies of many workers that there is a way out of the oppression of the routines of their labor. In the old days, becoming a fighter or baseball player was a universal dream of young boys for a way to escape having to go into the factory, just as becoming a movie star served the same function for Marilyn Monroe and the millions of girls who ended up in offices. For blacks and members of other minorities, the sports and entertainment industries still serve as the "impossible dream"—but not so impossible that it is completely discounted as a route to fame and fortune.

The sad thing is that many workers cling to gambling and sports as serious avocations even after the illusions of youth are shattered by the realization that they are not ever going to get out. Sports becomes the veil for the incapacity of workers to face the inevitability encompassing daily life. It is at once the protest against the worker's self-concept of her or his failure, and the means by which the ruling class is able to manipulate and channel discontent. As long as the workers can participate in the games through betting, and drain their passions in heated arguments about whether Mays or Mantle was the greatest all-around outfielder of all time, the system has a few years left.

But there are better ways for workers to structure their leisure. The typical working-class barroom of the first half of the century was the place where the fraternity could be asserted that was denied to workers in the isolating environment of the shop. Drinking itself had important rewards as a refuge from both the shop and the home. But it was more an excuse for entering social life. The tavern was the center of political discussions, gossip about the shop and the neighborhood, and some sports activities such as miniature bowling, pin ball and darts. The older working-class groups did their drinking in the ethnic fraternal clubs or veterans organizations. Later, the bowling alley and the union hall were added as places for workers to congregate.

The dispersal of industry to farmlands surrounded by nondescript housing developments or, worse, by no community or neighborhood center at all, has made it difficult for working-class people to enjoy any form of social contact. This generation of workers is often confronted by the absence of opportunities for communal ways to reaffirm their experience of anger against the quality of life, particularly of their work. The widespread practice of year-round daily overtime, robbing workers of time to meet other people, the long distance travelled from home to work (which also takes away any sense of common experience associated with a home town), the 24-hour shift, seven-day-week patterns of many plants and transportation industries, have helped defuse any sense of solidarity which arises from the emerging homogeneity of experience, language and culture.

We are witnessing the disappearance of daily life beyond the workplace in huge chunks of American society. The lack of social life has increased the capacity of bureaucratically organized cultural institutions to influence social consciousness, particularly through the media and mass sports. Moreover, under conditions of increasing isolation, workers reintegrate the protective function of the family which was eroded during the evolution of urban industrial society. Although Reich is right to describe the ways in which the authoritarian family structure reinforces the susceptibility of workers to the authority of the corporate and state institutions, the family is also experienced as a shield against the tyranny and the terror of the everyday world.

The conflict is played out among the young left in the search for new forms of family life; among young workers, there is a tendency to retreat into the nuclear or extended family when the whole idea of neighborhood has been rendered obsolete by the political economy.

Mass culture and mass politics developed on the ruins of the old ethnic and neighborhood ties associated with the large industrial city. Mass society, based on the fragmentation of the producers, buttressed by ideologies of consumerism, was challenged by a young generation which began to understand its objectification and develop a new subjectivity in the 1960s. The achievements of mass communications prevented the new sensibilities generated by the student protest from remaining class-specific or ensconced within the universities.

The fact that most young people reject the artificially stimulated ethnic revival and have refused to respond to the slowing of the economy in traditional ways, namely, by cooling their protest against the intolerability of the work world, is evidence that the working class is fundamentally altering its perspectives. Nor do they accept the old institutions as truly meeting their needs.

However, it is a long way from this point to significant movement for social change. There is absolutely no sign of emergent self-activity which transcends the ample evidence of defensive action against immediate injustices. What is clear is that as old needs have been satisfied for large numbers of workers, particularly the basic material requirements of survival, new needs are made. It is upon these new needs that the future will be fashioned.

# II. The Society We Face

## Living Conditions
## in the United States

### joe eyer

Why has social unrest grown in American society in the 1960s? What conditions is this unrest responding to, and what are the relations between these conditions and the forms of unrest? For some, the answer to these questions is obvious: the social movement arose when people looked around and discovered wrong and injustice everywhere, and decided to do something about it. But what made people aware of this injustice? Why didn't they do anything about it in the 1950s, when by all the standard indicators, poverty and oppression were worse in America than in the 1960s? Or have things gotten worse in the 1960s?

The main content of this article is a demonstration that in fact living conditions have deteriorated for several parts of the working class since the mid-1950s. These include youth, women, and blacks. In contrast, conditions for whites, now middle aged, male workers have improved, at least until very recently. These conclusions are reached by examining not only the standard wage and employment statistics, but vital and social statistics as well. Hence I argue that the unrest has grown out of a deterioration of living conditions.

Different conditions in different parts of the present and future working class have led to movements which are distinct in aims, rhetoric, and style of action; the student-youth revolution; the black and brown liberation movements; the wildcat strikes, led to a considerable extent by young workers; and the women's liberation movement. Since actual conditions have divided the workers, the people suffering the deterioration tend to see their problems not growing out of their social position as workers, but centering on their youth, sex, or race. The existence of a group of older white male workers, whose conditions continued to improve through the decade, reenforces these tendencies and provides the background for the concept that the "working class" has "become reactionary."

From this picture of the present, I try to discuss the conditions under which a general class movement might emerge. Without the growth of such a movement, the rulers will be able to divide and conquer as before, despite the deterioration of conditions and the rise of general but fragmented unrest. This discussion involves comparison with the statistics of past revolutionary situations. The present looks a lot like past revolutionary situations. But it has many of the same critical imbalances which made those situations abortive, the most important of which is the widening division within the working class.

What has produced these changes in living conditions? These changes are the inescapable results and the essential preconditions of the course of economic change. But by this I don't imply a mechanical relation, which is assumed by most leftists; deterioration of conditions comes only during depressions. For some parts of the working class, conditions get worse straight through the boom. This experience of depression within boom is now more widespread than in the earlier history of capitalism.

The treatment of economic movements here is just a sketch. What I try to describe are the relations between these movements and their social and biological consequences. I intend to develop an analysis of these economic movements themselves from their own proper perspective in greater detail in a future article.

## Conditions have improved
## for white, middle-aged, male workers.

To understand the position of white, middle-aged men now, we must go back to the end of the 'twenties and the Depression. At that time, young labor market entrants were few in number compared to the rest of the labor force, due to the cutoff of immigration and the long fall of the birth rate through the '30s. These young workers also had an educational advantage over the less literate older workers, due to the great upswing of high school education of the workforce which extended through the '20s and '30s. In the wave of unionization that emerged in response to the Depression, the young workers often led in the struggle and became more organized than the older.

This contrast between young and old is evident in the vital and social statistics. Going into the Depression, the older workers suffered a specially disastrous decline of living standards. Their suicide rates reached a huge peak as unemployment rose, and those admitted to mental hospitals, drug addiction- and alcoholism-treatment centers were primarily these older workers. Younger workers suffered a rather mild deterioration in the Depression. Their suicide rates rose to less than half the rate reached in the slowdown before the First World War, and other indicators of stress show only moderate rises. ....

As unemployment was sharply reduced by the Second World War, the young workers were in great demand, due to their superior education and their relatively small numbers, which were further reduced by the draft. This group is at the core of the great surge of unionization which made its greatest gains in membership during the 1940s. Unions then served to win gains for their members and the tight labor market made it easy to extend unionization widely.

After the war, young workers benefitted not only from unusually high wages, but from the lowering of interest rates and easy availability of credit which comes at the end of long cycle depressions. Many were veterans, and have benefitted through the postwar period from this fact, by VA mortgages and other benefits. Within this group, the inequality of income distribution has been reduced through the upswing and most of the postwar period, as income for the lowest ranks rises more rapidly than for the higher-paid workers.

Thus this group had an exceptionally favorable labor market position, due to its relative numbers, education, organization, and timing relative to demand for labor in reaching labor market and marriageable ages. As a result, they were able to marry younger, and their wives, after the war, could remain out of the labor force, at home having children. Many more young people married as well (1940–57), bringing proportions married at ages 20–24 back to levels reached in rural America before the impact of industrialization in delaying and breaking down marriage. The birth rate reversed its historical trend downward and peaked in the baby boom of the midfifties.

The conditions for reproduction improved rapidly, as the

infant mortality rate declined more swiftly than in any previous period, the fetal death rate fell, and the proportion of infants born at low birth weights and unfavorable gestational periods reached lows in the midfifties. Age-specific death rates, particularly death rates reflecting stress (suicide, cirrhosis of the liver, ulcers) fell rapidly for this group as well.

Higher wages and low mortgage interest rates enable the white workers of this age group to move out of the central cities to the fringes, powering the housing boom of the postwar period, which peaked in 1950. This movement contributed to the rapid fall of death rates from infectious diseases, as people escaped the crowded old central cities. But the conditions in the cities improved at this time as well, reflecting a great boom in hospital building, active public health programs, and the general upswing of production for people's needs. This is evident in the conditions of the blacks who migrated to the cities from the South at this time. In contrast to the second great period of massive black migration, the '60s, conditions improved in the late forties for urban blacks.

As political repression and a slowly rising trend of unemployment developed after the war, the unions became more and more organs for protecting the position of workers already organized, rather than aiming at great new gains in either standard of living or scope of organization. After the midfifties, the proportion of the labor force unionized levels off and declines, as new labor market entrants are not organized. This pattern repeats the experience of the First World War and the '20s.

We will discuss the slowdown of the economy, 1957–63, and the boom, 1965–69, more later, but here we must note that the conditions for the whites of this small, highly unionized group continue to be good through this whole period. Their real after-tax wages continue to rise, and the trend toward equalization of income within the group goes on, though at a slower pace. However, this improvement is won only at increasing costs. To keep ahead of inflation, higher costs of education for their children, rising medical expenses and finally taxation, the wives have been sent to work after having three or so children, increasing family income from this side. Death rates for this group, now aged 30–45, have leveled since the midfifties.

Against the background of these real conditions, the patriotism and lack of social or political consciousness among these workers is not hard to understand. Their conscious lives begin in the midst of a great collapse of the economy, but they have reaped a greater increase of standard of living on the upswing of the cycle than any other group of workers in the history of American capitalism. Because of their special position, they have been able to maintain or increase this standard until very recently. With homes and families already established, they are no longer free to try out new social arrangements to deal with new problems, and to them there seems to be no necessity for this innovation.

## Conditions for young people are deteriorating.

In sharp contrast with this favored group, however, younger workers entering the labor market and marriageable ages since the mid-fifties have suffered a deterioration of living conditions. This reversal grows out of the slump in the production of things for people's needs after the early '50s. There are definite reasons, as we shall see, why this slump affected young people more than older people.

Housing construction peaked in the early 1950s, and has declined, with cyclical variations, since then. The housing that has been constructed is more and more high-priced, responding to the demand of the middle-aged workers and the uppermost part of the young income distribution. Three quarters of the new housing priced under $15,000 is now mobile homes, recreating in a more affluent style the automobile camps of the Depression. Per capita protein, vitamin, and calorie consumption peaked during the Second World War or the late 1940s and have declined since then. Nutrition surveys show a rise of malnutrition in the postwar period, resulting in worse nutritional deficiencies among the American poor in the 1960s than in underdeveloped countries. The rapid expansion of medical facilities from the midthirties through the late forties slowed its pace thereafter and in many large cities, facilities have deteriorated to the present.

This decline in production for people's needs is part of the change in the composition of the social product which marks the fifties and the early sixties. The profit rate in productive investment declined steadily from the peak in the early fifties, slowing investment and producing a trend rise in unemployment rates. From 1957 to 1963, there was no net accumulation of capital in manufacturing. More and more of surplus went into military spending, consumption of the rich, advertising, and other forms of waste. These changes, punctuated by the rising trend of interest rates, speculation in stocks and land values, fit perfectly well into a classical model of the end of a long cycle. Had they continued without any compensating influences, the economy would have been in depression by the mid-1960's. As it was, the economy went through a slowdown similar in many respects to that just before the First World War, with unemployment averaging 6 percent, 1958–63.

But at this point, a number of influences came to operate which kept the economy from collapse. The returns of US imperialism abroad, including profits and cheapening of resources, were coming in at a greater rate, supporting profits here; a sharp upsurge of credit expansion in the private sector allowed new investment to proceed with increasing external financing, after the period of major reliance on profits for investments. After 1965, large government deficits resulting from the Vietnam War spending also stimulated the economy, as did redistribution of taxation through tax cuts on invested profits.

But perhaps most important of all in preventing the collapse of profits in production were certain labor market developments which have resulted in the deterioration of living conditions for youth, women, and blacks. For reasons which we will analyze, each of these groups has developed as an enlarging source of cheap labor for the capitalists, reducing labor costs and temporarily staving off the downtrend in the profit rate.

While the long decline of the birth rate up to 1935 resulted in proportionally declining numbers of workers coming to labor market entry ages through the midfifties, the sixties see the children of the baby boom, 1935–57, begin entering labor market and marriageable ages. The first flood of their numbers swells the ranks of teenagers in the midfifties, and this movement combined with the stagnation of the economy results in a sudden large jump of teenage unemployment rates after 1957. Thereafter, successively larger numbers of youth reach labor market ages, completely reversing the previous demographic history of American capitalism. The unemployment rate of young workers goes from very low in the late '40s and early '50s to consistently high, 1958–64.

While the slowdown of the economy resulted in a slowing of income rise for the highly-organized white group, for the majority of young labor market entrants, real after tax income falls from 1957 to 1964. Also, in contrast with the age group preceding it, inequality is growing rapidly in the young age group, reflecting the divergence of college-educated workers from high-school educated blacks and whites. The allocation of surplus to war and the running-out of the educational advantage for college-trained workers after 1967 have confronted recent BA, MA and PhD graduates with a growing glut of their labor market as well.

The special position of the favored labor group had allowed it to gain greater and greater proportions of the social product through struggle as it moved into prime working ages in the midfifties. Sharp recessions, following one on another with greater frequency and at higher unemployment levels, 1949–61, did not suffice to break this power. With the influx of unorganized young labor in the '60s, more effective competition was introduced onto the labor market. Whole new areas of employment were created outside union lines, reducing labor costs for the capitalists in some jobs to make up for the rising costs in others.

Although the repeated recessions and political repression did not suffice to achieve a cut in labor costs, these measures did serve to beat down the surge of unionization of new parts of the working class. By the midfifties, the union organization had been integrated into the lower levels of the control structure of the ruling class. With fewer gains possible, the leaders of the unions concentrated on getting job security for those already employed, against the risk of rising unemployment. Such security within the system depended on the creation of distinctions between different kinds of workers: middle aged against young (seniority), male against female, white against black, despite the performance of equal work. The other hierarchial structures of the workplace also took on this conservative, divisive character in the period of stagnation of the economy. This is a fundamental reason for the labor market weakness of new labor market entrants in the sixties.

These changes have also given a new lease of life to divide-and-rule tactics, as the eyes of new labor market entrants (especially blacks) are focused on the fact that a small part of the workforce is able to defend its position by excluding new members, rather than on the slowdown of job growth which lies behind this organizational change.

The drop in income and rise of unemployment for young workers resulted in a fall in proportions married among young people, which began for teenagers in the midfifties and extends to young adults in the '60s. Over age 30, proportions of women married are still increasing; under age 30, there is a decrease more rapid than in any previous depression. The decline in marriage is accomplished by the characteristic rise in illegitimacy, venereal disease, and even prostitution, again repeating the experience of past depressions. Birth rates come down at an accelerating pace from the peak reached in 1957, touching a point by 1969 well below the low of the 1930s.

Conditions for reproduction deteriorates as well, as evident in the rise of low-birth-weight infants, the shift of birth timing away from optimal periods of gestation, the rise of the fetal death rate, and the slowing of the decline of the infant mortality rate, from the midfifties through 1964. These changes come about both among whites and blacks, "middle-class" youth as well as the poor, although at a greater rate for the low-income workers.

Associated with the stagnation of the economy, 1957–63, infectious disease case rates rose from lows reached in the early '50s, peaking around 1963. At first, the incidence rises for all age groups, but increasingly in the '60s, as rates have come down for the middle-aged group, they have remained high for young people. This shift in age composition is also evident in mental hospital admissions and drug treatment center admissions rates, crime rates, imprisonment rates and death rates reflecting stress. For young people these rates are rising rapidly from low levels attained on the upswing of the long cycle; while for the relatively small, now middle-aged white male group, these rates remain low or have fallen recently.

The deterioration of conditions is evident in death rates as well. Since 1961, death rates in the age group 15–24 have turned up in trend, for both blacks and whites, after falling rapidly on the upswing of the long cycle. This upturn is more serious for males—a 25 percent increase to 1968—but occurs among females as well. War deaths and other deaths outside the United States are not included in this account. If they were, the upturn at 15–24 for males would be a 70 percent increase. This increase in death rate reflects the strong rise of suicide, homicide, accidents and some infectious diseases such as pneumonia and influenza. The level of the suicide rate for young people has now risen well above what it was for this age group in the Depression, and is approaching previous historical highs.

This deterioration of conditions is concentrated in the large cities, particularly in the areas of the country, such as the Northeast, which have not received great shares of military spending. In contrast, the situation in the South and Southwest has improved through this period, though relatively more slowly for young people, because of the large concentration of military spending in these areas.

The expansion of education and the draft have absorbed the numbers and delayed the entry of the baby-boom children to some extent. To this extent, the competition from this source has been less effective in sustaining the profit rate through depressing labor costs. But the political consequences of an even more rapid collapse of living conditions for a whole generation have been avoided by the rulers as well. The cost in taxation has been paid by the already employed workers.

Part-time and temporary employment have also risen, especially for the greater numbers of teenagers and young adults "kept off the streets" by high school and college. Again, this provides a convenient, flexible and cheap new addition to the labor force; but will there be full-time jobs for these youth when school is over? Young people are increasingly conscious of the fact that nothing special, and perhaps nothing at all, is waiting for them outside of school. The army trains them to kill and cannot guarantee a job when they get back. This growing uncertainty about their future combines with the industrialization of education and the proletarianization of their future work to make the schools an opening battleground for the struggle which is emerging from the conditions we have described.

## Women.

We have pointed out how in the boom of the long cycle, women in reproductive ages withdraw from the labor force and get married, stay at home and have children. As income rise slows, and as the burden of taxation increases, more wives past peak reproductive ages are sent to work to maintain the already established family's position. But as more and more women under age 30 are single, the labor force participation rate of young women has gone up even more rapidly. This rise reflects both the rise in single women and the increased competition in the young labor market as a whole, forcing young families to send the wife to work as well. Thus the economic forces of the evolving long cycle have resulted in a great upsurge of women's labor force participation in the 1960s.

Women workers have the advantage, from the capitalist point of view, of being a low wage group. In general, women receive little better than half what men do for the same work. The experience of the '60s repeats, on a larger scale, the experience of the twenties for women. Toward the end of the boom phase of the long cycle, women of all ages are brought into the labor force, while the labor force participation rate of men goes down. This trend continues right through the depression of the cycle, and is only reversed on the (postwar) upswing as women in reproductive ages withdraw from the labor market to have children. Like young people, women now serve to hold down labor costs and stave off a falling profit rate.

The present cycle has a unique twist in this aspect. The labor force participation rate of white, middle-aged men, the small group, has not fallen. The labor force participation of young men, black or white, has fallen rapidly since the late '50s; while the labor force participation rates of young women have gone shooting up. In addition to the effect of higher unemployment in depressing wages in the young labor market, increasingly sizable proportions of young men are without income altogether. Meanwhile, the influx of female labor of all ages has meant a rising trend of female unemployment rates. Like youth, women form an increasingly large proportion of total unemployment.

In contrast to the situation for men, there are only small differences in the deterioration of conditions for younger or middle-aged women. Suicide rates for women of all labor market ages have increased dramatically, the fall of age-specific birth rates is only a little more rapid at younger ages than at older, and the deterioration of birth conditions is similarly only a little more marked for young women than older women. Income has risen less rapidly, on the average, for full-time employed women than for men since the late fifties, and again there is increasing inequality of the female income distribution, growing out of greater labor market competition.

## Past capitalist experience is repeated in the 1960s.

If we put these trends into historical perspective, we find that they repeat—over a short time span—past capitalist experience. About 1830 death rates began to rise in the growing industrial cities, especially at labor market entry ages, and continued to do so until around 1875. The influx of immigrants—aged 20 to 30—depressed the labor market and prevented large cyclical increases in wages. Living standards deteriorated as cities grew without adequate sewer systems, water supply, transportation, or housing, and death rates from infectious diseases and stress deaths rose. The proportion of females married and the birth rate declined; the rise in women's participation in the industrial labor force begins at this time.

After 1880 this trend in urban areas is reversed. Death rates start to fall, particularly in childhood ages, as a result of immunization against specific diseases, installation of sewers, trash collection and other sanitary measures, purification of city water supplies, and a trend rise in real wages of city workers. After the depression of the 1890s this improvement of conditions becomes particularly marked. The proportion of women marrying at young ages rises, the birth rates in industrial areas go up, and the decline of infant mortality begins. These trends continue through the twentieth century, interrupted by the depression before the First World War and the great Depression of the 1930s, modified by the special factors affecting particular cohorts that we have discussed.

The changes of reproduction on the farm follow a different course. Through the 19th century, farm death rates were about half urban death rates; women married earlier and more women married than in the cities; birth rates were higher and infant survival better. The areas of most rapid rural settlement—the North Central—had higher incomes for people of migratory ages as well. Migration from the farm to the industrial cities did not become a large-scale phenomenon in America until the 20th century; up to that time the growth of the industrial labor force was largely supplied by increasing immigration and declining natural increase in the urban areas.[1]

---

[1]The immigrants most often came from countries where a past rise in natural increase had combined with agricultural depression and slow capital accumulation to make a large part of the emerging labor force superfluous.

Despite these favorable conditions, however, farm birth rates fall steadily through the nineteenth century. This reflects two things. First, land for expansion eventually got used up; the closing of the frontier comes gradually through the late nineteenth century, and with it, a change in the farmer's attitudes about how many sons he could produce with some hope of a good life. Also important was the creation of the national and international market for agricultural commodities. In the context of competition from ever-larger commercial farming and growing productivity, the family farm was squeezed out. In the initial phases of this process, more and more family income had to be spent on improving equipment and land, and less could thus be spent on children. Another way of seeing this same development is to note that the market moved in such a way as to extract a growing surplus from agriculture to support the growing industrial cities.

Up to 1910, per capita farm income generally rose, with cyclical fluctuations in response to the booms of urban demand for food and materials in the long cycles. But after that time, increased productivity and world competition caused it to fall, more or less steadily, through the teens and the twenties to the low reached in the depths of the Depression. This prolonged fall was accompanied by an even more rapid fall of farm birth rates. 1910 marks the cessation of net migration to the farm area in America: after that time, the rapid demise of the family farm supplies an ever-increasing internal source of industrial labor force growth. Responding as it does not just to the increase of employment and wages in the cities, but to the forces eliminating the family farm, this source of labor power also can be out of step with labor demand emerging from capital accumulation.

## Blacks have suffered
## the worst decline of living standard.

This is especially true of the blacks. They were first squeezed out of the South by the establishment of the racist system there in the late nineteenth century, and migrated to the Northern cities during the First World War and the 1920s, in response to the demand for labor. This is the period of rise of venereal disease and precipitous decline of the black birth rate. The Depression sees the beginning of the breakdown of black marriage as well. While for whites, the fluctuation of birth rates has a large component of planning, for blacks, the change in birth rates have been proportionally larger than for whites and much of this change has evidently been due to increase of sterility arising from disease and malnutrition.

Large government subsidies to agriculture and increasing prices on the upswing of the long cycle made farming once again profitable, and after the 1930s there was a large and continuing increase of agricultural productivity. But in the competition, both black and white small farmers were eliminated as viable units; and large capitalist farms increasingly reaped the benefits. Now less than 5 percent of the workforce is on farms. The people forced off farms supplied a big addition to city labor force growth on the boom. As we have pointed out, their conditions improved at this time, as is evident in the rapid decline of the black infant mortality rate, the upswing of black marriage and births, and the rapid decline of black death rates through this period, particularly for urban blacks.

But the early '50s mark the turning point to leveling or decline of conditions for the blacks, some five years before the turn for whites, and at a higher level of death rates. This is the point at which black infant mortality levels and in the Northern cities starts to rise. The proportion of infants of low birth weight rises continuously through the '50s and '60s for blacks, to the point where it is now comparable to the proportions prevalent in the colonies of the free world empire —15 percent as opposed to the suburban white rate of 6 percent. This rise is most serious in the Northern cities. The increase of death rates at labor market ages is also greater for blacks than whites since the early '60s, and has a larger component of infectious diseases. Black death rates are now comparable at most ages to the death rates of blacks in South Africa.

The fall of the black birth rate is as rapid as the white, and once again there is evidence that in many places, this is due to a rise in sterility. The breakdown of marriage and the rise of illegitimacy and venereal disease have accelerated for blacks in the '60s.

As among women, this deterioration of conditions is not confined to the young age group, although this is the group with the greatest deterioration. In many respects, conditions are now worse in many Northern cities for blacks than in the South. It is ironical that the only states in which black infant mortality has continued to decline rapidly are the states with development resulting from military spending.

After the '40s, when black labor made great advances, the flow of labor out of the South has continued, but in an economy not generating sufficient jobs to keep up with their rising numbers. The blacks now move into central cities in decay, where death rates are rising. They suffer unemployment at twice the white rate, and income in all occupations for blacks is little more than half what it is for whites. Welfare payments, taxed away from employed workers, allow some of them to exist, when in the South they might have starved for lack of work.

The welfare payments also sustain blacks as a large unemployed pool, and their emergence as a sizable low-wage urban labor force has made profitable the performance of many tasks that would have otherwise been eliminated or mechanized. To this extent they also serve to sustain the profit rate by counterbalancing with their losses the gains made by unionized white male workers. Much the same analysis applies to the Puerto Ricans that have immigrated to the big cities and the Mexican migrant workers whose importation was essential to the profitability of large agriculture until the latest wave of mechanization got under way.

## The boom of the '60s.

The result of this reduction of labor costs was a temporary reversal of the downtrend of the profit rate, and thus an extension of the long cycle beyond the point at which it would normally have collapsed into depression. While I have pointed out that this extension was at the expense of growing parts of the labor force, it is important to evaluate the achievements of this expansion, if only because they represent to many the evidence of the triumph of Keynesian economics in controlling the economy.

This expansion has two parts: before and after the beginning of heavy Vietnam war spending. From 1961–65, unemployment averaged 5.5 percent, and all the trends in living conditions that we have described worsened. From 1966–69, unemployment averaged 3.7 percent. (Unemployment came down most rapidly for the small, highly unionized age group, less rapidly for women and youth, and hardly at all for black teenagers.) But as unemployment fell, inflation and taxation rose, abolishing the normal wage gains made after 1965. The total unemployment rates achieved even with the huge government deficits of the Korean war (3.0 percent) or World War II (1.6 percent). Thus the Keynesian triumph has amounted to a moderate reduction in unemployment and a falling real wage.

The picture is vital and social statistics is equally equivocal. From 1965 to 1969, the infant mortality rate, the fetal death rate, and the infectious disease case rates (except for the young) have declined. The infant mortality rate remains above that in many other countries, for which the declines of mortality have been continuous through the '60s and at a greater rate. The proportion of infants of low birth weight stops increasing, but does not decline, in this second period. Housing production appears to be leveling through the '60s, but with the pricing shift I have referred to. Per capita nutrient consumption has moved up, but it would require the continuation of this trend for five or more years to reverse the effects of the previous downtrend.

However, the movement of age-specific birth rates, death rates, and marriage patterns continues the trends established in the late '50s. The major deterioration evident in vital and social statistics continued unbroken, with a slowing or reversal in a few indicators. When these indicators are looked at in various regions of the country, we find that in the parts that had the worst deterioration through the early sixties, there are no reversals.

The result of the saving in labor costs has been the extension of the long cycle beyond the point at which a depression would normally occur. Thus after the boom of the '60s, interest rates are higher, the profit rate lower, and the debt-dependence of capital expansion greater than before. The weaknessess of debt expansion are evident in the collapse of the Penn Central and the troubles of the Ling-Temco-Vought empire. In general, those parts of capital which expanded most rapidly through the '60s—those associated with war production—are now the most overextended and in danger financially. Special measures by the government, such as the proposed $750 million loan to ailing industries, may help to avert a general financial collapse. But these measures will further increase taxation and along with the unchecked development of the long cyclic trends, will more and more choke off production for people's needs.

Although a general depression will probably be averted, even government advisers project an economy limping along at unemployment rates above 5 percent for a year or more, with the inevitable worsening of all the trends of deterioration that I have discussed. It is this prospect, of depression for part of the working class, combined with slow decline of conditions for the rest, rather than full-scale depression, which should be the focus of attention.

This is especially true since the influx of youth, women and blacks will continue unbroken at least through the next decade, as past birth rate changes, decline of marriage, rising living costs for families and the elimination of blacks from the South continue to exert their effects on the labor market. As in the sixties, this will be a factor favorable to profits through continued cheapening of labor. But this means a more rapid decline of living standards for those who are the cheap laborers.

## Comparison to past revolutionary situations.

How do these prospects compare to the situations in the past when working people have organized themselves to do something about the capitalist system? Examination of the statistics for Germany and Italy during and after the First World War, and France during the revolution of 1848 and the Commune of 1871 reveals certain common characteristics of past revolutionary situations. The economy is generally in chaos, not producing for people's needs, because of a crisis: war, depression, or both. Stress has risen for a period of years to high levels, as evident in the rise of death rates and particularly suicide and other stress rates. In all of these situations, this deterioration is most concentrated on the younger age group of workers. While in all the situations referred to, the worsening of conditions was much more dramatic than what has happened in the last decade in America, there are evident similarities, which will probably develop further in the 1970s in the same direction.

This experience is in contrast to that of the Depression in America. Then, the older workers had the worst shock, while for younger workers, the worsening of conditions was only moderate and rapidly followed by the development of very favorable conditions. Now this picture is reversed. The part of the population—the young—which is most free to take an active part in struggle has already suffered a decline for over a decade, and if a depression occurs, will undergo an unprecedented increase of stress. If there is no depression, the same result will come more slowly.

There are other similarities as well. In all of these past revolutionary situations, the deterioration of conditions was less for middle-aged people than for the young. In Germany, for example, the death rates for middle-aged people rise only very little or fall, through the crisis, 1913–23; while for young people, death rates nearly double their prewar value through this period. This divergence corresponds to the widely different forms of political action taken by old and young at this time. The young swelled the ranks of the "crazy" left communists, against whom Lenin wrote his famous pamphlet, *Left Wing Communism, an Infantile Disorder*. They rejected all activity within the electoral machinery or the trade unions, and were ready in spirit, but not in numbers, organization, or means, to seize power immediately and proclaim the soviet republic. The middle-aged workers, on the other hand, followed the trade unions, which led general strikes against right-wing military takeover of the already existing parliamentary government. While they were ready to use the most powerful tactics, these aimed essentially at preserving the bourgeois system which they hoped could yield them further gains.

The depression within boom that has developed in America in the '60s has created a similar divergence, which is only thrown into higher relief by the impact of the draft on youth, particularly black youth. At various points, parts of the population feel themselves driven to rise against the system, unorganized, unprepared, and without any chance of success. The central question, for which there is no clearcut answer now, is whether the sluggish continuation of "growth" without depression will result in a sharp decline of living standards for the "protected" group of workers as well. If it does, the prospects of more unified class activity open up— prospects which may be suggested by the wildcat strike movement now developing.

# Problems and Prospects

## paul mattick, jr.

A cherished bit of trivia from the early '60s is the memory of a speech given by A.A. Berle, Jr., at Bryn Mawr College in 1962. Decrying those who were defensive about America's record, particularly in relation to Latin America, he observed that we had much to be proud of—in particular, that we were the first society in history to eliminate the working class. No doubt this would have surprised the building janitor already then, but today that halcyon era has gone even for the Berles and their children. On the one hand, the failures and collapse of the black and student movements of the '60s have broken hopes placed in new forces for progressive change in a period when the "middle Americans" seemed solidly for the status quo. On the other hand, the frequency and militance of strike movements throughout the capitalist world—particularly in Europe—and even in the state-controlled economies of the "East," have forced renewed attention to the proletariat as an active social force. Now "everyone" is worried about the blue-collar blues and the white-collar blahs; governmental commissions to studies on job alienation; academics and other intellectual racketeers get busy studying "industrial democracy" and "workers' control." Would-be revolutionaries, too, must think again about the working class and its relation to the problems and possibilities of communist revolution.

For Marx, the idea of communism had no real existence except as embodied in the actual practice of class struggle by the working class. In this he differed from his would-be disciples. Kautsky and Lenin, or whom the proletariat was rather the agency which by its numbers and key position in modern society could realize an idea worked out by middle-class intellectuals through their scientific critique of capitalism. Marx, in contrast, developed his concept of communism with his analysis of capitalism as an attempt to explain and give intellectual expression to the struggle of workers against the existing organization of society.

Marx defined "class" in terms of power over social decision-making. This means, essentially, the power of decision over the production of the goods—i.e., everything from butter and guns to books—that are the material basis of social life. This boils down to control over the means of production and so over the product they make possible. Capitalism began with the separation of the producers *en masse* from this control. This implied the transformation simultaneously of products and of the capacity to produce into commodities, goods for sale on a market. For when goods are available only when bought from the possessors of the productive apparatus, producers can exist only by selling their labor-power to the owners. Means of production become capital, then, insofar as their possessors are able to buy the labor-power necessary to operate them, an arrangement which permits them to keep the difference (surplus value or profit) between the amount produced and the amount demanded by the producers for their existence. The capitalist, possessing class comes into existence together with the working class.

At the same time, under this system (in which people do not produce for themselves directly) production as a physical process necessarily takes the form of a systematic interrelation between the producers, in which each person is dependent on the labor of vast networks of others for the means to live and to produce. This is true within the individual workplace, where now thousands may labor together, and between the various workplaces and departments of production. Nonetheless, since production is under private, capitalist control, it can appear to the producers as though their relation to each other exists only through their employment by their several masters.

Since the capitalists' profit consists entirely in the amount of social product withheld from the producers, there is bound to be conflict between the two classes over the division of the product, as well as over the conditions of work. Marx believed that this would lead to the growth, among the workers, of an understanding at once of their shared interest as exploited producers and of their ability to act together to protect that interest. The collective organization of work was expected to provide a natural framework for the development of conceptions and organizational forms of solidary struggle.

In addition, in Marx's view, the system's development over time is conditioned by capital's desire to maintain the existing class relations and individual positions of strength within these relations. The direction and rate of development of the system are determined, that is, by the need of each individual capital and so of capital as a whole to expand its value (and thus its economic and social power) by the production and accumulation of surplus value. But, Marx claimed to show, the private character of capital ownership conflicts over time with the needs of capital as a whole, threatening the stability of the social system. The process of capital expansion itself would create barriers to its continuation (in the form of a tendency for the rate of profit, and therefore of the rate of accumulation, to fall). The result would be a series of crises in the production of capital, each to be overcome only through a massive reorganization (primarily in the form of concentration) of capital structures, which would be paid for by enormous misery on the part of the working class.

In such a moment of crisis, Marx thought, the solidarity of the producers, developed in the long fight over wages, hours, etc., would come to the point of open struggle for control of the productive system, of society itself. The collective commonwealth of toil would liberate itself from the constraints on its well-being set by the private ownership of the means of production, to establish communism—the collective organization and direction of production by the producers themselves.

Capitalist society did not evolve in the direction of an obvious polarity between a small group of rich capitalists and a mass of impoverished proletarians. While control over capital has been continuously centralized, the small group of the very rich and powerful are at the top of a continuum of wealth and degree of privilege (of which the permanently unemployed are at the bottom). In addition, after a history of crises every ten or fifteen years the Second World War permitted a reorganization of world capitalism which made possible rising or stable incomes for large numbers of workers in the advanced countries. The result was twenty-odd years of a relatively high degree of social stability.

This situation allowed for a florescence of bourgeois theories of society in terms not of class but of status and income-level, linked in the association of status with amount of consumption. Residual problems—in general, "unfair" distribution of income and political and social power to the disadvantage of certain regional or racial groups—could be solved by "social engineering," possible within a pluralistic political democracy and an economy capable of infinite growth. The class war was over, in fact, and "ideology" had ended with it.

On the left, or what passed for the left, it was agreed that the working class, if not nonexistent, would no longer play a revolutionary role. In effect, the Marxian analysis was abandoned for or subordinated to the bourgeois interpretation of the situation, with class analysis giving way in analytical practice to status/income-distribution concepts. This pessimistic interpretation of bourgeois optimism was given a theoretical elaboration, for example, in the work of Herbert Marcuse, elevated by the press and the climate of the time into the "guru of the New Left." Technological advance, by making possible the continuous expansion of productive capacity and so the satisfaction of workers' demands, had effected the political integration of the proletariat into what therefore became a "one dimensional" system. With capitalism's material contradictions under control, opposition could arise only in the sphere of ideology—hence the concern with "alienation" or psychological malaise in a breadfull system —though Marcuse held that the ideological realm itself was largely absorbable in the pervasive one-dimensionality. Material opposition was thought restricted to developments outside the system proper; basically to the threat posed by the superior "rationality" of the so-called socialist systems, in which state control of production has taken the place of private capitalist control. Thus, to the extent that there was hope for change in the world at all, it lay not in the masses of "advanced industrial society" but among the peasants of the Third World, with—perhaps—stirrings in the developed countries among the disadvantaged minorities and the young intelligentsia, as represented by the civil rights and student anti-war movements. None of these groups could be identified with the revolutionary proletariat foretold by Marx.

On the other hand, it is clear that Marx's prediction of the proletarianization of the mass of the population has been fulfilled in all capitalist countries (and is a necessary corellate of the economic development which is the goal in the state-directed systems). The process which began with the expropriation of the peasantry, carried out in the West under private and in the East under state auspices, has continued, as is clear from a glance at occupational statistics. Capital units survive and prosper by expanding into the social and economic space occupied by precapitalist forms of life, or by competing capitals. As the labor-employing, profit-producing enterprise becomes the dominant form in goods production, all forms of work took on the characteristics of the industrial wage-laborer. The small farmer becomes an agricultural wage-worker under a "checkbook farmer." Nonproductive workers—occupied with distribution of goods, "services," or the handling of economic value (as in banking)—are wage-workers for firms who profit by the difference between what they must pay their employees and what they can extract from industrial capital for their services.

The concept of "middle class" is often used today by radicals—e.g., to describe themselves—who otherwise attempt to employ a Marxist terminology. The group thus referred to includes some members of what might be called a middle class—professionals like doctors, lawyers, and a few elite professors, as well as petty tradesmen—but it mostly includes people—managerial and supervisory personnel, engineers, technicians, teachers—who are workers in the Marxist sense: dependent for living on the sale of their labor power. Calling these people "middle class" only confuses class analysis with the bourgeois status/income categories. In the '50s we were told that "the workers" had become "middle class": in fact exactly the opposite was and is going on. As the development of labor productivity in manufacturing through technology and speedup has made for slow growth in the numbers of blue-collar workers, a major share in labor force increase has come precisely from the proletarianization of formerly middle-class occupations and people (particularly due to the vast expansion of government employment deriving from the growing role of the state in social and economic life). This period has also seen a steady growth in the use of women as (cheap) wage-workers, in addition to their role in the home as maintainers of labor power.

So much for the illusion of status. With respect to income, a worker remains a worker no matter how much he or she is paid. He must be exploited "be his wages high or low" because only on this basis can the employer realize the profit which allows him to continue in business as an employer. Still, as the left pessimists pointed out, the existence of class is not sufficient. Revolutionary activity requires a consciousness on the part of workers of their position in society—not just a consciousness of exploitation but an understanding that as the producers of all wealth they have the power to order production and social life in general to meet their own needs. In Marx's words, "the proletariat is revolutionary or it is nothing."

Among the ideas of the left pessimists, strangest of all, perhaps, was the view that the integration of the working class, its acceptance of the capitalist system, is a novel phenomenon, produced by a new (super-technologized) state of capitalism. The capitalist system consists of workers and capitalists together; one can speak of opposition to the *system*, as contrasted with opposition to some of its effects, only when the wages-system, the capital-labor relation itself is threatened. Such moments of revolution or near-revolution have been mighty few and far between in capitalism's history. The everyday struggle between employers and workers over the conditions and remuneration of wage labor, a necessary feature of a system in which the interests of the two groups are opposed, in itself threatened capitalism's existence no more yesterday than it does today, so long as demands could be kept at this level by their momentary and partial satisfaction.

What gave the appearance of a non-integration of the working class in the past was the existence of *ideologically* revolutionary organizations "of the working class"—the social democratic trade unions and parties, the Communist parties and unions of the Third International (and Soviet Russia itself in the age in which it was easier to believe in it as a bastion of world revolution). In fact these very organizations were, at their moments of strength, also instruments for the integration of the working class. Here three aspects of the development and functioning of the labor organizations, in America and Europe, may be noted. To begin with, until recently capitalism was in a period of growth (despite its interruption by periodical crisis). As the productive apparatus grew, raising the productivity of labor, capital was able to meet both its needs for profit and workers' demands for a better life. Thus the labor organizations, in government and at the workplace, could function as structures through which the power of the workers secured real gains. In America this effect was strengthened by the fact that the special conditions of this country until recently made movement upward, even—for a few—

into capitalist ranks, a real possibility for workers.

Second, the organizations which supervised the winning of demands, operating of necessity within a situation defined by the existence of the labor "market," channeled and controlled oppositional energies by institutionalizing the inevitable conflict of classes. This process was carried farthest in America in the modern collectively bargained contract, complete with grievance procedures and no-strike clauses. Finally, as the leaders of these organizations in their activity became de facto and then de jure part of the social and political structure of the capital-labor relationship and thus, whatever their (usually negligible) purity of heart, a part of the ruling apparatus, their immediate personal interest became tied to the maintenance of the status quo. This element of "corruption" is not, however, as important as the general effect of institutionalization of the struggle, which took not only the direction of the struggle but even in large part the activity itself out of the hands of what thus became the rank-and-file, substituting for their activity that of the union or party professionals. From the revolutionary point of view, the chain of labor's parliamentary and trade union victories made one long defeat.

The integration of the proletariat is the result, not of some new and peculiar circumstance but of a natural adaptation to the realities of its daily life. To speak crudely, we may say that we derive our ideas from our experience of the world. Growing up in capitalist society, with the lessons of daily life methodically reinforced by schools and media, it is hard to take seriously the possibility of some other way of living together, just as the idea of a slave-free society occurred to no Greek. And the desire for an alternative is bound to be weakened when things are improving or at least not getting much worse. In general, we are more likely to submit to bearable evils than to try to tear everything apart, destroying all our daily routines and personal security, for something we can hardly believe in.

Similarly, workers' understanding of their collective power to determine their own destiny comes only from experience of it. This means experience of solidarity, of their capacity to decide on and take action without the supervision of political or other "representatives." Such experiences are to be had in every strike, in every shop-floor struggle. But ordinarily they are experiences of joint action among only the workers in one department, one factory, one industry, against a particular capitalist, and not of something like the class as a whole against capital as a whole. Seemingly, these experiences develop the force to call into question the whole of the existing society only at moments of great social crisis. At such moments, the inability of the existing order to satisfy even minimal needs forces people to go beyond the ordinary boundaries of struggle to take class-wide action in organizing some alternative forms of social life. This was true, at any rate, for the European revolutionary wave of 1917–1923 (Russia, Germany, Italy) which arose out of the world crisis which took the form of world war. The Spanish Revolution of 1936 came out of years of turmoil, capped by the opening of the civil war.

While the mechanics of failure were different for each of these cases, each left capitalism able to reorganize itself economically and politically, and go on. However, the period between the two wars seems to have been a turning point in the history of the capitalist economy. Just as they misunderstood the character of working-class activity in the past, the left pessimists missed the novelties of the new situation. It is becoming clearer that pessimism about the possibility of proletarian revolution has been based on a too-ready acceptance of the bourgeoisie's self-satisfaction, though it has taken today's rocketing inflation, monetary difficulties, and mounting unemployment to draw people's attention to what amounts to a new stage in the unfolding of capitalism's contradictions.

Indeed, capitalism never rose from its Great Depression ashes as it had recovered from previous crises. That is to say, the reorganization of capitalism effected through the depression and World War II did not succeed in raising the rate of profit to a point where the system could continue to expand at the rate imposed by the previous level of development. As a result the measures of state interference in the economy introduced by the New Deal and its (fascist) equivalents in other countries, in the form of relief, public works, and war production, could not be abandoned after the war. Massive unemployment and social convulsion could be averted only by the state's utilization of capital value (insufficient for investment purposes) to take up the slack left by the low level of private capital investment. This procedure, hailed as the mechanism which had overcome the gloomy predictions of the Marxists, represented a confirmation of the theory of capitalist development laid out in *Capital*.

The steady growth of the "public" sector bears witness, that is, to the inability of the private sector—i.e., the capitalist economy proper—to achieve an adequate rate of growth.

The state-controlled sector of the economy is necessary to the continued existence of capitalism as a social system. In the first place it provides employment and therefore means of existence for the millions who would not otherwise be employed. In addition, it provides the materials—primarily weaponry—with which possibly a secure American empire can be built as a field for future investment to offset the decline of profitability of American capital at home and in Europe.

At the same time, the "public" sector is parasitic on the private property capitalist economy. Since the government is not an owner of capital, the funds disposed of in its projects must be taxed or borrowed from the private sector (i.e., from profits: either directly or by the sleight-of-hand of "taxes on wages," which in fact amounts to a reduction of wages since money never seen by the workers can hardly be considered a part of the wages-fund). Thus government transactions fall outside the market, i.e., out of the capitalist economy proper. For as the state pays for goods from a capitalist with money provided by the capitalists themselves, production on government account effects not the creation of new value and profit but merely the transfer of pre-existing value from the capitalist class as a whole to some favored members of it. Hence state-run production cannot offset the decline in the profit rate of the private economy.

Since the state sector is growing faster than the private sector (indeed it grows just because the private sector cannot) there must come a time when its further extension, while necessary to avert social crisis, would mean the pre-emption of economic space still open to private capital. State-controlled economy, fought under the name of socialism as incarnated in the Russian, Chinese, and allied regimes, is rightfully seen as a danger to corporate capitalism internally as well. For this reason, capital periodically attempts to slow down the expansion of the state sector, despite the leeway that still remains before the "public" sector enters into serious conflict with the private, offering the ruling class the choice between massive depression and the complete abandonment of the private property system.[1]

[1] For a detailed exposition of this argument, see Paul Mattick, *Marx and Keynes* (Boston: Porter Sargent, 1969).

The result is the situation of continuous tension suffered today by the working class. The attempt to raise the profit rate has meant longer hours of work, the intensification of labor on the job, and for some a steady fall in living standards since the end of the Second World War. State spending goes on at the cost of wage cuts, in the form of taxes and inflation, while the attempt to slow down state-sector growth means recession (i.e., conrolled depression). In the meantime, the use of state funds to secure the empire spells death and destruction for working-class youth. To this must be added the continuing destruction of the environment, which affects health and destroys sources of leisure-time pleasure; the degradation of the urban centers into which the population is crowded; and the inability of a stagnating system to offer any relief to masses of black people.

These pressures affect various sectors of the working class in different ways and to different degrees. On the one hand, large numbers of white, male workers, now middle-aged or over, have since the end of the Great Depression been in quite a stable position, with job security and a "reasonable" standard of living. On the other, black, young (of all colors) and the increasing number of female workers face low wages, high unemployment and steadily deteriorating conditions of life (as evidenced in high death rates, undernourishment, effects of psychological stress, etc.). As one researcher has put it, this part of the working population has been living in depression even while the first group experienced the boom of the '50s and '60s.[2] It is this which accounts for the apparently contradictory appearances both of a reactionary "working class" and of an increasing hostility to "the system" among young people, women, and blacks. The importance of phenomena like the present recession is the promise they hold of a worsening of conditions for the so-far favored group in the class—happening now even for high status and income technical and managerial people—with the potential of a class-wide opposition replacing the sectoral struggles of the last years.

Though isolated from the mass of the production processes of modern society, students have little social power, the problem of their relation to a future working-class movement must be taken seriously. In the age of mass education it is

2 Joe Eyer, "Living Conditions in the United States," this volume.

no longer possible to think of students as petty or just plain bourgeois "elements." At the same time, they are not workers; though they may toil and spin they receive no wages and produce no value. What they are—here I mean the vast majority, not the future board chairmen and/or politicians—is future workers, workers-in-training. This training is only partly in skills yielding a higher productivity; its function is largely to justify restricted access to certain jobs and salaries. In addition, much of collegiate (as of all school) education is purely ideological, teaching through both the content and the organization of school work a healthy passivity and intellectual respect for the status quo. Mass education exists because of the importance of all this training—both technical and attitudinal—for modern production. A large portion of the "knowledge" factory's product takes the form of teachers: expanded reproduction of channels for the transmission of skills and ideology. The schools also serve as research centers for industry and government. All these social functions of institutional education determine the existence of the student, forming the context within which the student movement can be understood.

The immediate interest of students is to remain students—i.e., first, not to work, and then, when a job is necessary, to get a good one. The first is obviously limited by time; the second less and less meaningful (objectively as the jobs available to an expanding number of degree-holders become scarcer; subjectively as the value-system fails to hold up in the face of reality). At school, students are simultaneously given great freedom of movement and subjected to bureaucratic administration, simultaneously urged to "develop their minds" and fed a lot of crap in preparation for stupid jobs. The results are the mysterious student malaise, conflict with authority, rejection of "professional" careers and life-styles, radicalization and—among the radicals—a tendency to accept the idea of "alliance" with the working class. In the absence of a radical working class this remains an attitude, or becomes a sterile ideology, reflecting the aims of sectarian groups rather than the development of the movement. But it acquires practical content as soon as it is possible (as in France, Italy, and on a few minor occasions in the U.S.). The students, as one formula has it, are not workers, but the workers' struggle is of necessity theirs.

The extent to which the submission of the working class to

capitalist conditions is the result of its internal division by formidable barriers of experience and special interest cannot be overemphasized. People work in the country and in the city; in big towns and small; in production, office work, education, and services; for private capital and for the state. With each of these divisions, within each workplace, we find a multitude of (generally spurious) skill grades and classifications, expressed as a hierarchy of wages and statuses. These divisions, which extend well into life off the job, hide the common position of exploited wage workers that unites the members of the class.

An important role in the maintenance of these barriers is played by numerous ideological and institutional factors (as well as by the general competition for jobs). Education or seniority is supposed to justify the hierarchy of grades and wages. The feeling that woman's place is in the home has made it difficult for men workers to support their women colleagues' struggles for equal pay, and for women themselves to be aggressive vis-à-vis their employers (or to support their husbands' fights with theirs). The most blatant of these factors at the present time is the racism which makes it nearly impossible for whites and blacks alike to view each other as class comrades.

These barriers, with the accompanying inhibitions of class solidarity and combativeness, have been particularly reinforced by the labor unions. These have functioned within the workplace to sanctify the hierarchy of position and wage, and through their craft or industrial structure to segregate and weaken the struggles of different groups. They have consciously attempted to exclude blacks, and indeed the majority of workers, from participation in their struggles and benefits won. To break through the divisions between workers will require rejection of the representative authority of the unions, and indeed, sooner or later, fighting against them. The restrictions which will undoubtedly be put on union activities by employers and the state must be met not by attempts to defend the unions but by efforts of the class to defend *itself* through the creation of forms of organization— presumably various sorts of workplace committees—over which the men and women on the job have direct control and which make possible the greatest unification of the class possible at any given time.

One of the most promising novelties of our situation is in fact the obsolescence of the traditional labor organizations, both political and syndical. In Europe, the mass Communist, Social Democratic and Labor parties are losing their proletarian mantles, while in the U.S. the Democratic Party has ceased to appear the workingman's friend. What remains of the workers' identification with the unions can only continue to decay. Of course, the new rank-and-file caucuses, committees, and networks of such can be expected, if the struggles thus organized are successful in winning demands, to become new structures of integration—most likely by their absorption into the existing unions (with the rise to syndical power of a new, militant leadership). But this depends on the ability of capitalism to achieve a new prosperity.

It is unlikely, if the past is any guide, that we will be able to participate in mass revolutionary action before a moment of real social collapse—though a period of resistance to increasing stress will doubtlessly help to ready the proletariat for such a time. The immediate prospect, indeed, is for a consolidation of capitalist forces to try to get by its impending squeeze, including severe repression of whatever left may exist. Yet the real possibility of a future reopening of working-class struggle on a large scale leaves radicals with both hope and the obligation to achieve the understanding of current realities necessary to taking active part in the development of that struggle.

# The Origin of Job Structures in the Steel Industry*

## katherine stone

In the 19th century, work in the steel industry was controlled by the skilled workers. Skilled workers decided how

*This article is an abridged version of a paper presented in March, 1973, at a conference on Labor Market Segmentation, Harvard University.

the work was done and how much was produced. Capitalists played a very small role in production, and there were very few foremen. In the last 80 years, the industry has transformed itself, so that today the steel management has a complex hierarchy of authority, and steelworkers are stratified amongst minute gradings along job ladders. Steelworkers no longer make any decisions about the process of producing steel.

The process by which the steel industry was transformed is the process by which steel employers tried to break down the basis for unity amongst steelworkers. Out of their efforts to gain control of their workers and prevent unified opposition, the steel employers set up the various structures that define work today. This paper traces that process in detail in order to demonstrate the class nature of existing job structures and the possibility for jobs to be structured differently.

## I: The Breakdown of the Traditional Labor System

In 1908 John Fitch, an American journalist who had interviewed hundreds of steelworkers and steel officials, described the labor system in the steel industry of his day.

> In every department of mill work, there is a more or less rigid line of promotion. Every man is in a training for the next position above. . . . The course would vary in the different styles of mills, as the positions vary in number and character, but the operating principle is everywhere the same. In the open-hearth department the line of promotion runs through common labor, metal wheelers, stock handlers, cinder-pit man, second helper and first helper, to melter foreman. In this way, the companies develop and train their own men. They seldom hire a stranger for a position as roller or heater. Thus the working force is pyramided and is held together by the ambition of the men lower down; and even a serious break in the ranks adjusts itself all but automatically.[1]

Anyone familiar with industry today will recognize this arrangement immediately. It is precisely the type of internal labor market, with orderly promotion hierarchies and limited ports of entry, which economists have only recently begun to analyze. When Fitch was writing, it was a new development in American history. Only 20 years earlier, the steel

1 Fitch, John, *The Steel Workers,* pp. 141–142.

industry had had a system for organizing production which appears very strange to us today.

Although steel had been produced in this country since colonial times, it was not until after the Civil War that the steel industry reached substantial size. In 1860, there were only 13 establishments producing steel, which employed a total of 748 men to produce less than 12,000 net tons of steel a year.[2] After the Civil War, the industry began to expand rapidly, so that by 1890, there were 110 Bessemer converters and 167 open hearth converters producing 4.8 million net tons of steel per year.[3] This expansion is generally attributed to the protective tariff for steel imports, the increased use of steel for railroads, and to changes in the technology of steel production.

The pivotal period for the U.S. steel industry were the years 1890–1910. During that period, steel replaced iron as the building block of industrial society, and the United States surpassed Great Britain as the world's prime steel producer. Also during the 1890s, Andrew Carnegie completed his vertically integrated empire, the Carnegie Corporation, and captured 25 percent of the nation's steel market. His activities lead to a wave of corporate mergers which finally culminated in the creation, in 1901, of the world's first billion dollar corporation, the U.S. Steel Corporation. U.S. Steel was built by the financier J. P. Morgan on the back of the Carnegie Corporation. At its inception, it controlled 80 percent of the United States output of steel.

In the 19th century, the steel industry, like the iron industry from which it grew, had a labor system in which the workers contracted with the steel companies to produce steel. In this labor system, there were two types of workers—"skilled" and "unskilled." Skilled workers did work that required training, experience, dexterity, and judgment; and unskilled workers performed the heavy manual labor—lifting, pushing, carrying, hoisting, and wheeling raw materials from one operation to the next. The skilled workers were highly skilled industrial craftsmen who enjoyed high prestige in their communities. Steel was made by teams of skilled workers with unskilled helpers, who used the companies' equipment and raw materials.

---

[2] Hogan, *Economics of Iron and Steel,* Vol. 1, p. 11.
[3] *Ibid.,* pp. 218, 224, 185.

The unskilled workers resembled what we call "workers" today. Some were hired directly by the steel companies, as they are today. The others were hired by the skilled workers, under what was known as the "contract system." Under the contract system, the skilled workers would hire helpers out of their own paychecks. Helpers earned between one-sixth and one-half of what the skilled workers earned.

The skilled steelworkers saw production as a cooperative endeavor, where labor and capital were equal partners. The partnership was reflected in the method of wage payment. Skilled workers were paid a certain sum for each ton of steel they produced. This sum, called the tonnage rate, was governed by the "sliding scale," which made the tonnage rate fluctuate with the market price of iron and steel, above a specified minimum rate below which wages could not fall. The sliding scale was introduced in the iron works of Pittsburgh as early as 1865, and in the 25 years that followed, it spread throughout the industry.

The sliding scale was actually an arrangement for sharing the profits between two partners in production, the skilled workers and the steel masters. It was based on the principle that the workers should share in the risks and the fruits of production, benefiting when prices were high and sacrificing when prices were low.

Another effect of the sliding scale was that by pegging tonnage rates directly to market prices, the role of the employer in wage determination was eliminated. Consider, for example, the following account, summarized by David Montgomery from the records of the Amalgamated Association of Iron, Steel and Tin Workers:

When the Columbus Rolling Mill Company contracted to reheat and roll some railroad tracks in January, 1874, for example, the union elected a committee of four to consult with the plant superintendent about the price the workmen were to receive for the work. They agreed on a scale of $1.13 per ton, which the committee brought back to the lodge for its approval.

There followed an intriguing process. The members soon accepted the company offer, then turned to the major task of dividing the $1.13 among themselves. Each member stated his own price. When they were added up, the total was 3¾ cents higher than the company offer. By a careful revision of the figures, each runback buggyman was cut 2 cents, and the gang buggyman given an extra ¼ of a cent to settle the bill.[4]

The employers had relatively little control over the skilled workers' incomes. Nor could they use the wage as an incentive to insure them a desired level of output. Employers could only contract for a job. The price was determined by the market, and the division of labor and the pace of work was decided by the workers themselves. Thus, the sliding scale and the contract system defined the relationship between capital and labor in the steel industry in the 19th century.

The skilled steel workers had a union, the Amalgamated Association of Iron, Steel and Tin Workers, which was the strongest union of its day. Formed in 1876 by a merger of the Heaters Union, the Roll Hands Union and the Sons of Vulcan, by 1891 the Amalgamated represented 25 percent of all steelworkers. Through their union, they were able to formalize their control over production. For example, at Carnegie's Homestead, Pennsylvania mill, a contract was won in 1889 that gave the skilled workers authority over every aspect of steel production there. A company historian described it this way:

The method of apportioning the work, of regulating the turns, of altering the machinery, in short, every detail of working the great plant, was subject to the interference of some busybody representing the Amalgamated Association. The heats of a turn were designated, as were the weights of the various charges constituting a heat. The product per worker was limited; the proportion of scrap that might be used in running a furnace was fixed; the quality of pig-iron was stated; the puddlers' use of brick and fire clay was forbidden, with exceptions; the labor of assistants was defined; the teaching of other workmen was prohibited, nor might one man lend his tools to another except as provided for.[5]

John Fitch confirmed this account of worker control at Homestead when he interviewed Homestead workers and managers in 1908. Fitch reported that:

A prominent official of the Carnegie Steel Company told me

[4] Montgomery, David, "Trade Union Practice and the Origins of Syndicalist Theory in the United States", pp. 3–4.
[5] Bridge, J. H., *History of Carnegie Steel Corporation,* pp. 201–202.

that before the strike of 1892, when the union was firmly
entrenched in Homestead, the men ran the mill and the foreman had little authority. There were innumerable vexations.
Incompetent men had to be retained in the employ of the
company, and changes for the improvement of the mill could
not be made without the consent of the mill committees. I
had opportunity to talk with a considerable number of men
employed at Homestead before 1892, among them several
prominent leaders of the strike. From these conversations I
gathered little that would contradict the statement of the official, and much that would corroborate it.[6]

The cooperative relationship between the skilled steelworkers and the steel employers became strained in the
1880s. The market for steel products began to expand rapidly. Domestically the railroads began to generate high
levels of demand for steel, and internationally the U.S.
steel industry began to compete successfully with the British and the German steel industry for the world market.
(In 1890, for the first time, U.S. steel exports surpassed
those of Great Britain.) The effect of this massive increase
in demand was to intensify competition in the U.S. industry.
What had been a stable market structure was disrupted by
the new markets opening up.

Firms competed for the new markets by trying to increase
their output and cut their costs. To do that they had to
increase the productivity of their workers—but the labor
system did not allow them to do that. For example, from
1880 on, the market price for iron and steel products was
falling drastically, so that the price for bar iron was below
the minimum specified in the union's sliding scale, *even
though* the negotiated minimum rates were also declining.[7]
This meant that employers were paying a higher percentage
of their income out in wages than they would have were the
sliding feature of the sliding scale operative, or had they
had the power to reduce wages unilaterally in the face of
declining prices.

At the same time that their labor costs as a percentage
of revenue were rising, the labor system also prevented employers from increasing their productivity through reorganizing or mechanizing their operations. The workers controlled
the plants and decided how the work was to be done. Em-

6 Fitch, *op. cit.*, p. 102.
7 Doeringer, Peter B., "Piece Rate Wage Structures in the Pittsburgh Iron and Steel Industry—1880–1900," pp. 266–67.

ployers had no way to speed up the workers, nor could they introduce new machinery that eliminated or redefined jobs.

In the past, employers had introduced new machinery, but not labor-saving machinery. The many innovations introduced between 1860 and 1890, of which the most notable was the Bessemer converter, increased the size and capacity of the furnaces and mills, but they generally did not replace men with machines. Lowthian Bell, a British innovator, who toured the U.S. steel industry in 1890, reported that: "Usually a large make of any commodity is accomplished by a saving of labor, but it may be questioned whether in the case of the modern blast furnace this holds good. To a limited, but a very limited, extent some economy might be effected, but if an account were taken of the weight of material moved in connection with one of our Cleveland furnaces, and the number of men by whom it is handled, much cannot, at all events with us, be hoped for."[8]

However, in the late 1880s and 1890s, the steel companies needed more than just bigger machines and better methods of metallurgy. Bottlenecks were developing in production, so that they needed to mechanize their entire operations. For example, the problem with pig-iron production—the first stage of steelmaking—was that with increased demand, the larger blast furnaces could produce pig iron faster than the men could load them, so that the use of manual labor became a serious hindrance to expanding output.

The steel masters needed to replace men with machines, which meant changing the methods of production. To do that, they needed to control production, unilaterally. The social relations of cooperation and partnership had to go if capitalist steel production was going to progress. The steel companies understood this well, and decided to break the union.

The strongest lodge of the Amalgamated Association was at Carnegie's Homestead mill; it is no wonder that the battle between capital and labor shaped up there. In 1892, just before the contract with the Amalgamated was to expire, Carnegie transferred managing authority of the mill to Henry

[8] Great Britain, Iron and Steel Institute, Special Proceedings, 1890, p. 173.

A further description of the non-labor-saving effects of the changing technology can be found in U.S. Department of Interior, Report on the Statistics of Wages in Manufacturing Industries in the Tenth Census, (1880), Vol. XX, 1886. p. 115.

Clay Frick. Frick was already notorious for his brutal treatment of strikers in the Connellsville coke regions, and he wasted no time making his intentions known at Homestead. He ordered a fence built, three miles long and topped with barbed wire, around the entire Homestead Works; he had platforms for sentinels constructed and holes for rifles put in along the fence; and he had barracks built inside it to house strikebreakers. Thus fortified, Frick ordered 300 guards from the Pinkerton National Detective Agency, closed down the Works, laid off the entire work force, and announced they would henceforth operate nonunion. The famous Homestead Strike began in 1892 as a lockout by the employers, with the explicit aim of breaking the union. Dozens of men were killed in the four months that followed, as the Homestead workers fought Pinkertons, scabs, the sheriff and the State Militia. In the end, the intervention of the state and federal governments on the side of the Carnegie Corporation beat the strikers. The Works were re-opened with strikebreakers, and Frick wrote to Carnegie, "Our victory is now complete and most gratifying. Do not think we will ever have any serious labor trouble again."[9]

The Homestead Strike was the turning point for the Amalgamated Association throughout the country. Other employers, newly invigorated by Frick's performance, took a hard line against the Union, and the morale of the members, their strongest local broken, was too low to fight back. Within two years of the Homestead defeat, the Amalgamated had lost 10,000 members. Lodge after lodge was lost in the following years, so that membership, having peaked at 25,000 in 1892, was down to 10,000 by 1898, and most of that was in the iron industry.[10] The union never recovered from these losses. The locals that remained were destroyed one-by-one by the U.S. Steel Corporation, so that by 1910 the steel industry was entirely non-union.

With the power of the Amalgamated broken, steel employers were left to mechanize as much as they needed. The decade that followed the Homestead defeat brought unprecedented developments in every stage of steel making. The rate of innovation in steel has never been equaled. Electric trolleys, the pig casting machine, the Jones mixer, and mechanical ladle cars transformed the blast furnace. Electric traveling cranes in the Bessemer converter, and the Wellman

9 Brecher, Jeremy, *Strike!*, p. 62.
10 Robinson, *Amalg. Assoc. of Iron, St. and Tin Workers*, p. 20.

charger in the open hearth did away with almost all the manual aspects of steel production proper. And electric cars and rising-and-falling tables made the rolling mills a continuous operation.[11] These developments led the British Iron and Steel Institute to conclude after its visit in 1903 that

> the (U. S.) steel industry had made considerable advances in the ten years ending with 1890. It is, however, mainly since that year that the steel manufacture has made its greatest strides in every direction, and it is wholly since that date that costs have been so far reduced as to enable the United States to compete with Great Britain and Germany in the leading markets of the world.[12]

One British economist, Frank Poppelwell, was particularly amazed by the degree to which new innovations were labor-saving. He concluded:

> Perhaps the greatest difference between English and American conditions in steel-works practice is the very conspicuous absence of labourers in the American mills. The large and growing employment of every kind of both propelling and directing machinery—electric-trolleys, rising and falling tables, live rollers, side-racks, shears, machine stamps, endless chain tables for charging on the cars, overhead travelling cranes—is responsible for this state of things. It is no exaggeration to say that in a mill rolling three thousand tons of rails a day, not a dozen men are to be seen on the mill floor.[13]

In this way, the steel masters succeeded in eliminating the bottlenecks in production by replacing men with machines at every opportunity. This mechanization would not have been possible without the employers' victory over the workers at Homestead. Thus we can see how the prize in the class struggle was control over the production process and the distribution of the benefits of technology. As David Brody summarizes it:

In the two decades after 1890, the furnace worker's pro-

---

[11] Brody, David, *The Steel Workers*, pp. 9–11.
[12] Jeans, J. Stephan, *American Industrial Conditions*, p. 121.
[13] Popplewell, Frank, *Some Modern Conditions and Recent Developments in Iron and Steel Production in America (1903)*, p. 103. See also: Jeans, *op. cit.* pp. 503, 551 and Bridge, *op. cit.*, p. 164.

ductivity tripled in exchange for an income rise of one-half; the steel workers output doubled in exchange for an income rise of one-fifth. . . . At bottom, the remarkable cost reduction of American steel manufacture rested on those figures.

The accomplishment was possible only with a labor force powerless to oppose the decisions of the steel men.[14]

The victory of the employers in 1892 allowed them to destroy the old labor system in the industry. They could then begin to create a new system, one that would reflect and help to perpetuate their ascendancy. Specifically, this meant that they had three separate tasks: to adapt the jobs to the new technology; to motivate workers to perform the new jobs efficiently; and to establish lasting control over the entire production process. The next three sections of this paper will deal with each one of these in turn.

## II: Effects of the New Technology on Job Structure

Unlike earlier innovations in steelmaking, the mechanization of the 1890s transformed the tasks involved in steel production. The traditional skills of heating, roughing, catching and rolling were built into the new machines. Machines also moved the raw materials and products through the plants. Thus the new process required neither the heavy laborers nor the highly skilled craftsmen of the past. Rather, they required workers to operate the machines, to feed them and tend them, to start them and stop them. A new class of workers was created to perform these tasks, a class of machine operators known by the label "semi-skilled."

The new machine operators were described by the British Iron and Steel Institute after their visit in 1903 as men who

have to be attentive to guiding operations, and quick in manipulating levers and similarly easy work . . . the various operations are so much simplified that an experienced man is not required to conduct any part of the process.[15]

Similarly, the U.S. Department of Labor noted the rise of this new type of steelworker in their report of 1910:

The semi-skilled among the production force consist for the

14 Brody, *op. cit.*, pp. 48-49.
   is not required to conduct any part of the process.[15]
15 Jeans, *op. cit.*, p. 561.

most part of workmen who have been taught to perform relatively complex functions, such as the operation of cranes and other mechanical appliances, but who possess little or no general mechanical or metallurgical knowledge . . . This class has been developed largely within recent years along with the growth in the use of machinery and electrical power in the industry. The whole tendency of the industry is to greatly increase the proportion of the production force formed by this semi-skilled class of workmen. They are displacing both the skilled and the unskilled workmen.[16]

The semi-skilled workers were created by the downgrading of the skilled workers and the upgrading of the unskilled. These shifts proceeded throughout the 1890s and early 1900s, as more and more plants were mechanized. Although there are no hard data on these shifts in job categories, they are reflected in the change in relative wage rates. Between 1890 and 1910, the hourly wages of the unskilled steelworkers rose by about 20 percent, while the daily earnings of the skilled workers fell by as much as 70 percent. Also after 1892, the wage differential between the various types of skilled workers narrowed substantially.[17] Thus, the British Iron-masters reported in 1903:

The tendency in the American steel industry is to reduce by every possible means the number of highly-skilled men employed and more and more to establish the general wage on the basis of common unskilled labour. This is not a new thing, but it becomes every year more accentuated as a result of the use of automatic appliances which unskilled labor is usually competent to control.[18]

The following table of wage rates for selected positions at the Homestead plant mill between 1892 and 1908 illustrates the fate of skilled workers throughout the industry. Bear in mind that during this interval, their productivity was multiplying and wages throughout the nation were ris-

[16] *Labor Conditions,* Vol. III. p. 81.
[17] Doeringer, *op. cit.* Doeringer attributes this shift purely to commodity market forces. He argues that shifts in demand for different kinds of steel products narrowed the wage differentials between steel workers. He mentions the decline of the Amalgamated after Homestead and the skilled workers' subsequent inability to hold their own against the employers, but does not relate this to the change in wage differentials.
[18] Jeans, *op. cit.,* p. 317.

ing. Also, their workday was increased from 8 hours to 12 hours, so that the decline in daily earnings understates their reduction in real wages.

These reductions were part of the steel companies' policy of reducing the wage differentials between the classes of workers to make them more consistent with differentials in skill requirements for the different jobs. An official of one Pittsburgh steel company put it this way:

". . . the daily earnings of some of the most highly paid men have been systematically brought down to a level consistent with the pay of other workers, having in mind skill and training required and a good many other factors."[19]

TABLE I: WAGES IN PLATE MILLS, HOMESTEAD, 1889–1908 [20]

| Position | Decline in Tonnage Rates | | | Decline in Daily Rates | | |
|---|---|---|---|---|---|---|
|  | 1889–92 | 1908 | % decl. | 1892 | 1907 | % decl. |
| Roller | $14.00 | $4.75 | 66.07 | $11.84 | $8.44 | 28.72 |
| Heater | 11.00 | 3.99 | 63.73 | 8.16 | 7.21 | 11.64 |
| Heater's Helper | 7.50 | 2.09 | 72.13 | 5.80 | 4.09 | 29.48 |
| Hooker | 8.50 | 2.40 | 71.76 | n.a. | n.a. | n.a. |
| Shearman | 13.00 | n.a. | n.a. | 9.49 | 5.58 | 41.20 |

The other side of the picture was the upgrading effect that the new technology had on the unskilled workers. Their wages were increased considerably during that same period. In part this was accomplished by a raise in the hourly rate for unskilled labor, from 14 cents per hour in 1892 to 17.5 cents in 1910, and in part it was the result of the steel companies putting more men on tonnage rates, enabling them to make higher daily earnings.[21]

Many unskilled workers were put in charge of expensive machinery and made responsible for operating it at full capacity. Fewer and fewer men were hired just to push wheelbarrows and load ingots, so that, as an official of the Pennsylvania Steel Company said, "While machinery may decrease the number of men, it demands a higher grade of workmen."[22] Thus, the effects of the new technology were to eliminate the distinction between skilled and unskilled workers and create a largely homogeneous workforce.

[19] Fitch, op. cit., p. 157.
[20] Fitch, op. cit., pp. 153, 156.
[21] Fitch, op. cit., p. 159.
[22] Quoted in Brody, op. cit., p. 32. From Labor Conditions, Chapter 9.

## III. Solving the Labor Problem

Having become the unilateral controllers of steel production, the employers created for themselves the problem of labor discipline. When the skilled workers had been partners in production, the problem of worker motivation did not arise. Skilled workers felt that they were working for themselves because they controlled the process of production. They set their own pace and work load without input from the bosses. When this system was broken, how hard workers worked became an issue of class struggle.

The introduction of the new technology introduced in the 1890s narrowed the skills differentials between the two grades of workers, producing a work force predominantly "semi-skilled." This homogenization of the work force produced another new "problem" for the employers. That is, without the old skilled/unskilled dichotomy and the exclusiveness of the craft unions, the possibility that workers might as a class unite to oppose them was greater than ever. Frederick Winslow Taylor, the renowned management theorist who began his career as a foreman in a steel plant, warned employers of this danger in 1905:

When employers herd their men together in classes, pay all of each class the same wages, and offer none of them inducements to work harder or do better than the average, the only remedy for the men comes in combination; and frequently the only posssible answer to encroachments on the part of their employers is a strike.[23]

Ultimately, however, both the problem of worker motivation and the problem of preventing unified opposition were the same problem. They both revolved around the question of controlling worker behavior. To do that, employers realized they had to control their perceptions of their self-interest. They had to give them the illusion that they had a stake in production, even though they no longer had any real stake in it. This problem was known as "the labor problem."

To solve the labor problem, employers developed strategies to break down the basis for a unity of interest amongst workers, and to convince them that, as individuals, their interests were identical with those of their company.

[23] Taylor, F. W., *Shop Management*, p. 186.

Out of these efforts, they developed new methods of wage payments and new advancement policies, which relied on stimulating individual ambition. They were designed to create psychological divisions among the workers, to make them perceive their interests as different from, indeed in conflict with, those of their co-workers. Employers also began to use paternalistic welfare policies in order to win the loyalty of their employees. The effect of all these new policies was to establish an internal labor market in the major steel companies, which has lasted, in its essentials, until today.

## 1. Development of Wage Incentive Schemes

With the defeat of the Amalgamated Association, the entire complex traditional system of wage payments collapsed. The sliding scale of wages for paying skilled workers and the contract system for paying their helpers rapidly declined. Employers considered them a vestige of worker power and rooted them out of shop after shop. Thus, the employers had the opportunity to establish unilaterally a new system of wage payment. Initially, they began to pay the new semi-skilled men day wages, as they had paid the unskilled workers. Soon, however, they switched to the system of piece work, paying a fixed sum for each unit the worker produced.

The most obvious function of piece work was, of course, to increase output by making each worker drive himself to work harder. Employers also contended that the system was in the workers' best interests because it allowed each one to raise his own wages. However, the employers soon found that straight piece work gave the workers too much control over their wages. That is, when it succeeded in stimulating workers to increase their output, their wages soared above the going rate. Employers would then cut the piece rates to keep the wages in line. Once they did that, however, they had reduced the piece rate system to simple speed-up—a way of getting more work for the same pay. Workers responded to the rate cuts by collectively slowing down their output, so that the system defeated itself, leaving employers back where they had started. "Wage payment Systems: How to Secure the Maximum Efficiency of Labor," gives an interesting account of this process:

It is in the administration of the piece work system that manufacturers, sooner or later, make their great mistake and over-reach themselves, with the result that the system becomes a mockery and the evil conditions of the old day work system reappears. Regardless of the continually increasing cost of living, the manufacturers decide among themselves, for example, that $1.50 for 10 hours is enough for a woman and that $2.50 a day is enough for the ordinary workingman and a family. The piece work prices are then adjusted so that the normal day's output will just bring about these wages . . . Immediately throughout the entire shop the news of the cuts is whispered about . . . with the result that there is a general slowing down of all producers.[24]

Thus, employers began to experiment with modifications of the piece rate. They developed several new methods of payment at this time, known as "premium" or "bonus" plans. These differed from piece work only in that they gave the workers smaller increments in pay for each additional piece.

The Halsey Premium Plan, developed in 1891, served as a model for most of the others. It called for establishing a base time period for a job, and setting one rate for workers who completed the job in that period. If a worker could finish the job faster, then he received a bonus in addition to the standard rate. The bonus was figured so that only a part of the money saved by the worker's extra productivity went to him, the rest going to the company. Different plans varied according to how they set the base time period and the base wage, and how they divided the more efficient workers' savings between the worker and the company. *Iron Age* recommended one particular variation, called the Half and Half Premium Plan, in which the rule was "to pay the more efficient workman only one-half what he saves by speeding up." The article described one example where, under the plan,

for every extra $1 the man earned by his extra effort, the manufacturers would gain $7. Not a bad investment, this premium system. It betters the workingman's condition materially, and, best of all, improves his frame of mind.[25]

Frederick Winslow Taylor's Differential Piece Rate is basically another variation of the Halsey Premium Plan. Under Taylor's system, the employer established two separate rates, a low day rate for the "average workman" and a high piece

[24] *Iron Age,* May 19, 1910, p. 1190.
[25] *Ibid.,* p. 1191.

rate for the "first class workman," with the stipulation that only the fast and efficient workmen were entitled to the higher rate. He suggests setting the high rate to give the worker about 60 percent increase in earnings, and for this, the employer would demand of him a 300–400 percent increase in output. Like the Halsey Plan, it was simply the piece rate system modified to give the worker diminishing returns for his extra effort.

In order for any of the output incentive plans to work, management had to be able to measure each worker's output separately. All of the premium plans stressed the importance of treating each worker individually, but only Taylor gave them a method for doing so. His great contribution was systematic time study—giving employers a yardstick against which to measure an individual's productivity. The emphasis on individual productivity measures reinforced the fragmenting effect of the plans. As Taylor said about his experience implementing the system at the Bethlehem Steel Works:

> Whenever it was practicable, each man's work was measured by itself . . . Only on a few occasions and then upon special permission (. . .) were more than two men allowed to work on gang work, dividing their earnings between them. Gang work almost invariably results in a falling off of earnings and consequent dissatisfaction.[26]

Output incentives were designed to increase individual worker output. Employers understood that to do that, they had to play upon individual worker's ambitions, which meant breaking down workers' collective identity. They gave each worker inducement to work harder, and also divided the workers into different groups, according to their output.

Thus, output incentives served as a lever to prevent workers from taking collective action. As one manufacturer explained in 1928, he had originally adopted output incentives

> To break up the flat rate for the various classes of workers. That is the surest preventative of strikes and discontent. When all are paid one rate, it is the simplest and almost inevitable thing for all to unite in the support of a common demand. When each worker is paid according to his record there is not the same community of interest. The good worker who is adequately paid does not consider himself aggrieved so will-

[26] Taylor, *Shop Management*, p. 52.

ingly nor will he so freely jeopardize his standing by joining with the so-called 'Marginal Worker.' There are not likely to be union strikes where there is no union of interest.[27]

Quite explicitly, then, the aim of the premium plans was to break up any community of interest that might lead workers to slow their pace (what employers call "restriction of output") or unite in other ways to oppose management. They were a weapon in the psychological war that employers were waging against their workers, and were, at least for a while, quite successful.

Between 1900 and World War I, piecework and premium plans became more and more prevalent in the steel industry.

Steelworkers opposed the new methods of payment, and the residual unions in the industry raised objections at every opportunity. In one instance, at Bethlehem Steel's South Bethlehem Works, opposition to the bonus system exploded into a major strike in February, 1910. Approximately 5,000 of the 7,000 workers there went out on strike spontaneously. The strike lasted several weeks, during which time one man was killed and many were injured. Strike demands were drawn up separately by each department or group of workers, and every single one called for uniform rates of pay *to be paid by the hour*, and time-and-a-half for overtime. Several added to that an explicit demand for the elimination of piecework and a return to the "day-work" system. A U.S. Senate investigation into the strike found that the " 'Time-Bonus' System in use was one of its major causes." [28]

However, worker opposition proved ineffective in preventing the use of output incentive schemes. Since 1892, the employers had held the upper hand in the industry, and they used it to perpetuate their power. The wage incentive schemes were aimed at doing just that.

## 2. New Promotion Policies
## & The Development of Job Ladders

As we saw above, the new technology diminished the skill requirements for virtually all the jobs involved in making

[27] *Systems of Wage Payment,* Nat'l Indus. Conf. Board, p. 25.
[28] "Report on Strike at Bethlehem Steel Works," Senate Document No. 521.

steel. Charles Schwab himself said in 1902 that he could "take a green hand—say a fairly intelligent agricultural labourer—and make a steel melter of him in six or eight weeks." [29] When we realize that the job of melter was the most highly skilled job in the open hearth department, we can see how narrow the skill range in the industry really was. The employers knew this, and put their knowledge to good use during strikes. For example, during a strike at the Hyde Park Mill in 1901

> it was resolved that the works should be continued with green hands, aided by one or two skilled men who remained loyal. The five mills thus manned were started on the 3rd of August, and up to the date of my visit, near the end of October, they had not lost a single turn.[30]

Around the turn of the century, employers began to recognize the dangers inherent in the homogenization of the work force. They formulated this problem as worker discontent caused by "dead-end" jobs. Meyer Bloomfield, an industrial manager who in 1918 wrote a textbook on factory management, summarized their discussion on this subject:

> A good deal of literature has been published within the last dozen years in which scathing criticism is made of what has come to be known as 'blind alley' or 'dead-end' jobs. By these phrases is meant work of a character which leads to nothing in the way of further interest, opportunity, acquisition of skill, experience, or anything else which makes an appeal to normal human intelligence and ambition. The work itself is not under attack as much as the lack of incentive and appeal in the scheme of management.[31]

Bloomfield says right off, then, that the problem of "dead-end" jobs need not be solved by changing the jobs themselves. The better solution is to change the arrangement of the jobs. To do this, he says,

> a liberal system of promotion and transfer has therefore become one of the most familiar features of a modern personnel plan, and some of the most interesting achievements of management may be traced to the workings of such a system.[32]

29  Jeans, *op. cit.*, p. 62.
30  *Ibid.*, p. 62.
31  Bloomfield, *Labor and Compensation*, p. 295.
32  *Ibid.*, p. 297.

The response of employers to the newly homogenized jobs was to create strictly demarcated job ladders, linking each job to one above and one below it in status and pay to make a chain along which workers could progress. As Bloomfield remarked, "what makes men restless is the inability to move, or to get ahead." [33]

The establishment of a job ladder had two advantages, from the employers' point of view. First, it gave workers a sense of vertical mobility, and was an incentive to workers to work harder. Secondly it gave the employers more leverage with which to maintain discipline. The system pitted each worker against all the others in rivalry for advancement and undercut any feeling of unity which might develop among them. Instead of acting in concert with other workers, workers had to learn to curry favor with their foremen and supervisors, to play by their rules, in order to get ahead. As one steelworker described the effect this had on workers during the 1919 organizing campaign, "Naw, they won't join no union; they're all after every other feller's job." [34] This competition also meant that workers on different ladder rungs had different vested interests, and that those higher up had something to lose by offending their bosses or disrupting production.

As early as 1900, *Iron Age* was advising employers to fill production work vacancies from inside the firm. They advocated a policy of hiring only at the lowest job levels and filling higher jobs by promotion—what contemporary economists refer to as limiting the ports of entry.

The principle of internal promotion was expounded by Judge Gary, the President of the U.S. Steel Corporation, in his dealings with the subsidiaries. For example, in a speech to the presidents of the subsidiary companies in 1922, Gary said:

We should give careful thought to the question as to who could be selected to satisfactorily fill any unoccupied place; and like suggestions should be made to the heads of all departments. Positions should be filled by promotions from the ranks, and if in any locations there are none competent, this fact should be given attention and men trained accordingly. It is only necessary to make and urge the point. You will

[33] *Ibid.,* p. 298.
[34] Williams, Whiting, *What's on the Workers Mind?* p. 152.

know what to do, if indeed any of you has not already well deliberated and acted upon it.[35]

These policies explain the rigid lines of promotion that John Fitch found in each department. He described the work force as "pyramided and . . . held together by the ambition of the men lower down." [36]

In this way, the steel companies opened up lines of promotion in the early years of the century by creating job ladders. Employers claimed that each rung of the ladder provided the necessary training for the job above it. But the skilled jobs in the steel industry had been virtually eliminated and production jobs were becoming more homogeneous in their content. If, as Charles Schwab said, one could learn to be a melter in six weeks, then certainly the training required for most jobs was so minimal that no job ladder and only the minimum of job tenure were needed to acquire the necessary skills.

While technological development made it possible to do away with distinctions between skilled and unskilled workers, employers introduced divisions to avoid the consequences of a uniform and homogeneous work force. The minutely graded job ladders were developed as a solution to the "labor problem," rather than a necessary input for production itself.

## IV: The Redivision of Labor

While employers were developing new systems for managing their work forces, they also altered the definition of jobs and the division of labor between workers and management. They did this by revising the training mechanism for skilled workers, retraining the foremen, and changing their methods of recruiting managers. The result of these changes was to take knowledge about production away from the skilled workers, thus separating "physical work" from "mental work." This further consolidated the employers' unilateral control over production, for once all knowledge about production was placed on the side of management, there would

[35] Gary, Elbert, *Addresses and Statements,* Volume 6, March 29, 1922.
[36] Fitch, *op. cit.,* p. 142.
    Note: The footnotes skip from 36 to 48 at this point. The missing footnotes refer to a section which has been deleted.

be no way for workers to carry on production without them.

Frederick Winslow Taylor was one of the first theorists to discuss the importance of taking all mental skills away from the worker. In his book *Principles of Scientific Management* (1905), he gives a description of the division of knowledge in the recent past:

> Now, in the best of the ordinary types of management, the managers recognize the fact that the 500 or 1000 workmen, included in the twenty or thirty trades, who are under them, possess this mass of traditional knowledge, a large part of which is not in the possession of the management. The management, of course, includes foremen and superintendents, who themselves have been in most cases first-class workers at their trades. And yet these foremen and superintendents know, better than anyone else, that their own knowledge and personal skill falls far short of the combined knowledge and dexterity of all the workmen under them.[48]

Taylor insists that employers must gain control over this knowledge. In his manual *Shop Management*, he says quite simply, "All possible brain work should be removed from the shop and centered in the planning or laying-out department." [49]

Taylor suggested several techniques for accomplishing this. They were all based on the notion that work was a precise science, that there was "one best way" to do every work task, and that the duty of the managers was to discover the best way and force all their workmen to follow it. Taylorites used films of men working to break down each job into its component motions, and used stop watches to find out which was the "one best way" to do them. Taylor also insisted that all work should be programmed in advance, and co-ordinated out of a "planning department." He gives elaborate details for how the planning department should function— using flow charts to program the entire production process and direction cards to communicate with foremen and workmen. These were called "routing" systems. One historian summarizes this aspect of scientific management thus:

> One of the most important general principles of Taylor's system was that the man who did the work could not derive or fully understand its science. The result was a radical sepa-

48 Quoted in Montgomery, *op. cit.*, p. 8.
49 Taylor, *Shop Management*, p. 99.

ration of thinking from doing. Those who understood were
to plan the work and set the procedures; the workmen were
simply to carry them into effect.[50]

Although most steel executives did not formulate the
problem as clearly as Taylor, they did try to follow his advice. Around 1910, they began to develop "dispatching
systems" to centralize their knowledge about production.
These systems consisted of a series of charts showing the
path of each piece of material as it made its progress through
the plant and how much time each operation took—enabling
the supervisors to know exactly where each item was at
any point in time.

At the same time that they systematized their own knowledge about production, the steel companies took that knowledge away from steelworkers. Previously, the skilled steelworkers, acting in teams, possessed all of the skills and know-
how necessary to make steel. They also had had authority
over their own methods of work. Now employers moved to
transfer that authority to the foremen and to transfer that
knowledge to a new strata of managers. This section will
describe and document that process, in order to show that
this redivision of labor was not a necessary outgrowth of
the new technology, but rather was an adaptation by employers to meet their own needs, as capitalists, to maintain
discipline and control.

## 1. The New Skilled Workers

As we have seen, the mechanization of production largely
eliminated the role of the traditional skilled worker. However,
the steel industry still needed skilled workers. Machines required skilled mechanics to perform maintenance and repair
work. Also, certain skills were needed for specialized production processes which had not yet been mechanized. However, these skilled workmen were very different from the
skilled workmen of the 19th century, who collectively possessed all of the skills necessary to produce steel. The new
skilled workers had skills of a specific nature that enabled
them to perform specific tasks, but did not have a general
knowledge of the process of production. This new type of
skilled worker had to be created by the employers.

One would think that finding skilled men should have been

[50] Haber, Samuel, *Efficiency and Uplift,* p. 24.

no problem because of the huge numbers of skilled workers who were displaced and down-graded in the 1890s. However, by 1905, employers' associations began to complain about the shortage of skilled men. The reason for this paradox is that when the employers destroyed the unions and the old social relations, they destroyed at the same time the mechanism through which men had received their training.

Previously, the selection, training, and promotion of future skilled steelworkers had been controlled by the skilled craftsmen and their unions. After the union was destroyed, the skilled workers were no longer able to hire and train their own helpers. Within a few years, employers, realizing that no new men were being trained, began to worry about their future supply of skilled workers.

In order to create new skilled workers, employers set up a training system that was an alternative to the union-controlled apprenticeship system of the past, known as the "short course." The "short course" involved a manager or superintendent taking a worker who had been in a department for long enough to get a feel for the process, and giving him individualized instruction in some specialized branch of the trade. By using the short course, employers could train men for specific skilled jobs in a limited period of time.

In this way, a new class of skilled workers was created during the first two decades of the 20th Century. These workers were selected by the employers, trained in a short period of time, and then set to work with their job-specific skill. These workers had skills which were only good for one job. They did not have the independence of the 19th Century skilled workmen, whose skills were transferable to other jobs and other plants. Nor did they have the generalized knowledge of the production process that skilled workers previously possessed. The knowledge they had was that which could serve their employer, but not that which could serve themselves. As *Iron Age* advertised in 1912:

Make your own mechanics. . . . The mechanics that you will teach will do the work your way. They will stay with you, as they are not sure they could hold jobs outside.[51]

## 2. Changing Role of the Foreman

As the employers expanded their control over the process

[51] *Iron Age,* November 28, 1912, p. 1263.

of production, they realized they had to develop an alternative means for exercising control on the shop floor. Just as they had taken knowledge about production away from the skilled workers, they also took away their authority over their own labor and that of their helpers. Now, the task of regulating production was transferred to the foremen, who previously only had authority over the pools of unskilled workers. Foremen were now seen as management's representatives on the shop floor. To do this, employers had to redefine the job of foreman and retrain the men who held those jobs.

In order to transfer authority to the foremen, the employers had to distinguish them from the skilled workers. This distinction had to be created; it did not evolve out of the new technology. Foremen were recruited from the ranks of the skilled workers—foremanship being the highest position to which a blue-collar worker could aspire. Once there, however, steel employers had to re-educate them as to their role in production. The re-education began with convincing them *not* to do manual work, which was no easy task. An editorial in *Iron Age* in 1905 quotes one superintendent lecturing an audience of foremen as saying:

'You men have no business to have your coats off when on duty in your shops unless you are warm. You have no business to take the tools out of a workman's hands to do his work. Your business is to secure results from other men's work.'

The editorial goes on to say why this is important:

A man cannot work with his hands and at the same time give intelligent supervision to a gang of men, and a foreman who does this is apt to lose the control of his men while he is weakening the confidence of his employers in his ability as a general.[52]

The foreman's job was to direct and correct the work, but never to do the work himself. His authority depended upon that. Foremen, as the lowest ranking "mind" workers, had to be made distinct from the manual workers. One steel company official likened the organization of authority to that of the "army, with the necessary distinction between the commissioned officers and the ranks." [53]

[52] *Iron Age*, July 6, 1905, p. 24.
[53] Fitch, *op. cit.*, p. 149, footnote.

The companies had to give their foremen special training courses in order to make them into bosses. These courses were designed to teach the foremen how to "manage" their men. One such course, at the American Steel and Wire Company, a U.S. Steel subsidiary, spent most of its time on that subject with only a few sessions on production techniques or economics.

This development was not unique to the steel industry. Throughout American industry, special foremen's training courses were becoming prevalent. Dr. Hollis Godfrey, President of the Drexel Institute in Philadelphia, the first private institution concerned solely with foremen's training, said that the purpose of foremen training was to

> make the skilled mind worker. The skilled mind worker is a little different proposition than the skilled hand worker, and a great many people are still wandering around in the differentiation between the two. . . . From the foreman to the president right straight through, you have got one body of mind workers, and they do but two things: they organize knowledge and then they use the knowledge as organized.[54]

Although foremen did little work, they also did little thinking. Most of their training was designed to teach them how to maintain discipline—techniques for handling men, developing "team work," deciding who to discharge and who to promote. They were the company's representative in the shop, and as the companies consolidated their power over the workers, the strategic importance of the foremen increased.

## 3. New Types of Managers

Just as the authority that the skilled workers had previously possessed was transferred to the foremen, their overall knowledge about production was transferred to a new class of managers, recruited from the public and private schools and their own special programs. These managers became the bottom rung of the management hierarchy.

Before 1900, most managers in the steel industry were men who had begun at the bottom and worked their way all the way up. Andrew Carnegie had insisted on using this method to select his junior executives. As he once said, boastingly, "Mr. Morgan buys his partners, I grow my

[54] *Ibid.*, pp. 9–10.

own." [55] Carnegie developed a whole partnership system for the management of his empire based on the principle of limitless upward mobility for every one of his employees.

Around the turn of the century, employers began to choose college graduates for their management positions. As one prominent steel official told a member of the British iron and steel institute in 1903: "We want young men who have not had time to wear themselves into a groove, young college men preferably . . . ." [56]

This was not mere philosophy; the British visitors found on their tour that, of the 21 blast furnaces they visited, "18 were managed by college graduates, the majority of whom were young men." [57]

Employers used publicly-funded technical colleges to train their new managers. Technical colleges were new, established with the support of the business community and over the protest of the labor movement. As Paul Douglas wrote in 1921:

> Employers early welcomed and supported the trade-school, both because they believed that it would provide a means of trade-training, and because they believed that it would remove the preparation for the trades from the potential or actual control of unions.[58]

Some steel employers also set up their own schools.

Technical training alone, however, was not sufficient to produce competent managers for steel factories. The young men also needed to know about steel-making. To meet this need, the steel companies developed a new on-the-job training program to supplement the formal learning of their young college graduates. This program consisted of short rotations in each mill department under the supervision of a foreman or superintendent, which gave the men experience in every aspect of mill work before they were put in managerial positions. This program was called an "apprenticeship," and although it trained managers instead of workers, it was an apprenticeship by the original meaning of the word. It gave the apprentices knowledge of each stage of the production process.

[55] Hendrick, *Life of Andrew Carnegie*, Vol. I, p. 297.
[56] Jeans, *op. cit.*, p. 500.
[57] *Ibid.*, p. 501.
[58] Douglas, *American Apprenticeship and Industrial Education*, p. 323.

By the 1920s, such methods were nearly universal throughout the industry. Charles Hook, the Vice President of the American Rolling Mill Company, a U.S. Steel subsidiary, described his method for selecting and training managers in a speech of 1927 to the International Management Congress:

> The condition as outlined respecting the selection of the 'skilled' employee is quite different from the condition governing the selection of the man with technical education. . . .
>
> Each year a few second- and third-year (college) men work during the summer vacation, and get a first-hand knowledge of mill conditions. This helps them reach a decision. If, after working with us for a summer, they return the next year, the chances are they will remain permanently . . . Some of our most important positions—positions of responsibility requiring men with exceptional technical knowledge—are filled by men selected in this manner.[59]

The prospective managers, in short, were increasingly recruited from the schools and colleges, not from the shops.

In these apprenticeship programs, a distinction was often made between different types of apprentices, distinguished by their years of schooling. Each type was to be trained for positions at different levels of responsibility. For example, at the Baldwin Works, there were three classes of apprentices, such that:

> The first class will include boys seventeen years of age, who have had a good common school (grammar school) education . . . The second class indenture is similar to that of the first class, except that the apprentice must have had an advance grammar school (high school) training, including the mathematical courses usual in such schools . . . The third class indenture is in the form of an agreement made with persons twenty-one years of age or over, who are graduates of colleges, technical schools, or scientific institutions. . . .[60]

Thus, formal education was beginning to become the criterion for separating different levels of the management hierarchy, as well as separating workers from employers.

During this period, employers redivided the tasks of labor. The knowledge expropriated from the skilled workers was

[59] Hook, *op. cit.*, pp. 15–16.
[60] Jeans, *op. cit.*, p. 351.

passed on to a new class of college-trained managers. This laid the basis for perpetuating class divisions in the society through the educational system. Recently several scholars have shown how the stratification of the educational system functions to reproduce society's class divisions. It is worth noting that the educational tracking system could not work to maintain the class structure were it not for the educational requirements that were set up at the point of production. These educational requirements came out of the need of employers to consolidate their control over production.

Within management, the discipline function was divided from the task of directing and coordinating the work. This is the basis for today's distinction between "staff" and "line" supervision. We must hypothesize that this division, too, had its origin in the desire of steel employers to maintain control over their low level managerial staff.

The effect of this redivision of labor on the worker was to make his job meaningless and repetitious. He was left with no official right to direct his own actions or his own thinking. In this way, skilled workers lost their status as partners, and became true workers, selling their labor and taking orders for all of their working hours.

## V. To the Present

The labor system set up by the steel employers early in the century has not changed significantly since 1920. The essentials of the system—wage incentives, job ladders, welfare schemes, and a division of labor that kept skills highly job-specific—have lasted to the present.

The only major change in the industry's labor relations has been the union organizing drive of the 1930s, culminating in the establishment of the United Steelworkers of America, affiliated with the Congress of Industrial Organizations (CIO). The union brought steelworkers job security and raised wages. For the first time, it gave workers a voice in the determination of working hours, working conditions, and fringe benefits. However, the presence of the union did not change the basic mechanisms of control that employers had established. Although the union was able to alter the manner in which employers exercised control, it never challenged the heart of this control as institutionalized in the labor system.

The effect of the union was to re-rationalize the wage

structure which employers had set up earlier. By the 1930s, small changes in the content of different jobs had eroded the earlier system and left the wage structure exceedingly complex and chaotic. What the union did, under the direction of the War Labor Board during the 1940s, was to work with the employers to streamline the old hierarchical system through a mammoth effort to re-evaluate and re-classify 50,000 job titles. The result was that they pegged every job to one of 30 job classifications, which they put in a strict order with a 3.5¢/hr. differential between them. This structure remains today, except the differential is now 7¢.

The impact of the union on promotion policies was to do away with favoritism and insist that seniority be used to regulate promotion and bumping. This also served to rationalize the old structure, by giving it a basis in fairness rather than the foreman's whim. However, it did not get rid of the divisive effects of the job ladders themselves.

Unionization failed to change the redivision of labor through which employers took knowledge about the production process away from the workers. The union did demand a say in the establishment and operation of training programs, but it did not question the content of the training courses.

In contrast, the American Federation of Labor, in 1940, adopted a position on training that insisted on the use of aprenticeship instead of skill-specific training. The difference between the steelworker's union and the AFL position on training no doubt stems from the fact that the AFL was composed of craft unions, who were ever conscious of the monopoly-power of their craft skills, while the former was composed of steelworkers whose craft skills had been taken from them long ago. The steelworkers probably did not consider the possibility that their skills could be other than job-specific. Such was the success of the earlier redivision of labor.

The other side of this coin, as we saw earlier, was the transferring of generalized knowledge to the managers, and the use of educational requirements to distinguish managers from workers. A study by the International Labour Organization in 1954 found that in the United States

More often than not, future supervisors are taken on by the companies as soon as they leave college and they start their careers with a spell of six months or a year as workmen in one of the departments in the plant.[61]

The International Labour Organization in another study found that the steel companies were still concerned with the problems of establishing status relations between supervisors and workers, and solved it by giving "supplementary training which is essential once supervisors have been appointed in order to raise and define their status in relation to their subordinates and to ensure that their activities and those of the management are fully coordinated." [62]

The presence of the union did, however, make some difference regarding the authority of the foremen in the steel industry. The establishment of formal grievance procedures and seniority as a basis for promotion undercut the power that foremen had held in the shop floor.

## VI. Conclusions

The period between 1890 and 1920 was a period of transition in the steel industry from a labor system controlled by the skilled workers to a labor system controlled by the steel employers. In that transition, the breaking of the skilled workers' union, which was the institutional expression of their control over the production process, was only the first step.

Once the union was destroyed, labor discipline became a problem for the employers. This was the two-fold problem of motivating workers to work for the employers' gain and preventing workers from uniting to take back control of production. In solving this problem, employers were creating a new labor system to replace the one they had destroyed.

All of the methods used to solve this problem were aimed at altering workers' ways of thinking and feeling—which they did by making workers' individual "objective" self-interests congruent with that of the employers and in conflict with workers' collective self-interest. The use of wage incentives and the new promotion policies had a double effect on this issue. First, they comprised a reward system,

[61] International Labour Organization, "Human Relations in the Iron and Steel Industry," p. 98.
[62] International Labour Organization, "Vocational Training and Promotion Practices in the Iron and Steel Industry," p. 37.

in which workers who played by the rules could receive concrete gains in terms of income and status. Second, they constituted a permanent job ladder so that over time this new reward system could become an accepted fact by new workers coming into the industry. New workers would not see the job ladders as a reward and incentive system at all, but rather as the natural way to organize work and one which offered them personal advancement. In fact, however, when the system was set up, it was neither obvious nor rational. The job ladders were created just when the skill requirements for jobs in the industry were diminishing as a result of the new technology, and jobs were becoming more and more equal as to the learning time and responsibility involved.

The steel companies' welfare policies were also directed at the attitudes and perceptions of the workers. The policies were designed to show the workers that it was to their advantage to stay with the company. This policy, too, had both short-term and long-term advantages for the steel employers. In the short run, it was designed to stablize the work force by lowering the turnover rate, thus cultivating a work force who were rooted in the community and who had much to lose by getting fired or causing trouble. In the long run, the policies were supposed to prevent workers from identifying with each other across company and industry lines, thus preventing the widening of strike movements into mass strikes.[63]

Employers also sought to institutionalize and perpetuate their newly-won control over production by redividing the tasks of production so as to take knowledge and authority away from the skilled workers and creating a management cadre able to direct production. This strategy was designed to separate workers from management permanently, by basing that separation on the distinction between physical and mental work, and by using the educational system to reinforce it. This deterred workers from seeing their potential to control the production process.

Although this paper has concentrated on the steel industry, the conclusions it reaches are applicable to many other industries in the United States. The development of the new la-

---

[63] The prevention of mass strikes continued to be a concern of employers well into this century. The provisions in the 1947 Taft-Hartley Law that outlaw sympathy strikes and secondary boycotts are some of the most repressive aspects of that law.

bor system in the steel industry was repeated throughout the economy in different industries. As in the steel industry, the core of these new labor systems were the creation of artificial job hierarchies and the transfer of skills away from workers to the managers.

Technological innovations in every major industry around the turn of the century had the effect of squeezing the skills levels of the work force, turning most workers into semi-skilled machine operators. Paul Douglas, writing in 1921, found that the skill requirements were practically negligible in most of the machine building and machine using industries, especially the steel, shoe, clothing, meat-packing, baking, canning, hardware, and tobacco industries.

While jobs were becoming more homogeneous, elaborate job hierarchies were being set up to stratify them. Management journals were filled with advice on doing away with "dead-end" jobs, filling positions by advancement from below, hiring only unskilled workers for the lowest positions, and separating men into different pay classes. This advice was directed at the problem of maintaining "worker satisfaction" and preventing them from "restricting output"—i.e., fragmenting discontent and making workers work harder. Thus, the creation of the internal labor market throughout American industry was the employers' answer to the problem of discipline inherent in their need to exert unilateral control over production. Were it not for that, a system of job rotation, or one in which the workers themselves allocated work, would have been just as rational and effective a way of organizing production.

At the same time, employers began a process which they called the "transfer of skill." [64] This meant giving managers the skills and knowledge that workers had previously possessed. They began to use technical colleges and set up their own programs to train managers in production techniques. This development was aided by the methodology of scientific management, as Paul Douglas pointed out:

> The amount of skill which the average worker must possess is still further decreased by the system of scientific management. The various constituent parts of the system, motion study, the standardization of tools and equipment, the setting

[64] For example, see L. P. Alford's speech to the American Society for Mechanical Engineers, 1922, titled "Ten Years Progress in Management," and the discussion that followed.

of the standard task, routing, and functional foremanship, all divest the individual operative of much of the skill and judgment formerly required, and concentrate it in the office and supervisory force.[65]

Likewise, Samuel Haber, a historian studying the progressive period, says

> The discovery of a science of work meant a transfer of skill from the worker to management and with it some transfer of power.[66]

Like the creation of job hierarchies, this transfer of skill was not a response to the necessities of production, but was, rather, a strategy to rob the workers of their power.

For the skills which were still needed on the shop floor, employers instituted changes in the methods for training workers that reduced their skills to narrow, job-specific ones. The basic social inefficiency of this policy should be obvious. In an era of rapidly changing products and production techniques, jobs and industries are constantly changing, causing major dislocations in the work force. Therefore, the rational job training policy would be to give people as broad a range of skills and understanding of modern technology as possible, so that they could be flexible enough to weather the shifts in technology and the economy through their capacity to change jobs. Instead, the system of job-specificity creates one aspect of what economists label "structural unemployment" by molding workers to single skill-specific occupations. This policy wastes both individual lives and socially-useful labor power.

To varying degrees, the labor movement was aware of these developments while they were occurring. Many unions in the American Federation of Labor developed an early opposition to piece rates, and especially to bonus systems of Halsey, Taylor, and others. In 1903, the International Association of Machinists expressed their opposition to "work by the piece, premium, merit, (or) task," and prohibited its members from accepting such work. In 1906, the Brotherhood of Locomotive Engineers successfully refused to accept the bonus system of the Sante Fe Railroad. In 1907, the Molders Union, the Boot and Shoe Workers, and the Garment Workers all resisted the bonus and premium systems.

[65] *Ibid.*, p. 120.
[66] Haber, Samuel, *Efficiency and Uplift*, pp. 24–25.

In general, unions opposed both the piece work and the bonus systems, although an opinion poll of union policies conducted in 1908–09 showed that "unions almost without exception prefer the straight piece system to premium or bonus systems." [67] In 1911, the Executive Council of the American Federation of Labor passed a resolution condemning "the premium or bonus system (because it would) drive the workmen beyond the point necessary to their safety." [68]

The growing opposition to scientific management in the labor movement went beyond a critique of the speed-up aspects of the bonus system. Samuel Gompers, founder and president of the AFL, was aware that Taylor's system meant the elimination of the role of the skilled craftsmen upon which the entire AFL was based. After reading Taylor's book *Shop Management*, he wrote to AFL Vice-President Duncan in 1911 that "I have no doubt that it would mean (the destruction of unionism) for it would reduce the number of skilled workers to the barest minimum and impose low wages upon those of the skilled who would be thrown into the army of the unskilled." [69]

The Machinists' Union was one of the more vocal in its fear of this aspect of scientific management. According to Milton Nadworny, in his book *Scientific Management and the Unions*, the IAM's "Official Circular No. 2"

revealed the craftsman's fear of a system which not only instituted a revolutionary approach to work, but which threatened to reduce his importance in the shop. The machinist, it contended, was no longer required to use his skilled judgment —the planning department provided full instructions; no longer was his 'honor' relied upon—the stop watch determined the time of his job. To complete the scheme, the possibility of organized retaliation against the system was prevented because only individual bargaining was permitted.[70]

The Industrial Workers of the World had an even deeper understanding of the new labor system that was emerging and the dangers it posed to the working class as a whole. In the Manifesto of 1905, announcing the IWW founding convention, they warned that

[67] Nadworny, Milton, *Scientific Management and the Unions*, pp. 25–26.
[68] *Ibid.*, p. 51.
[69] Quoted in Nadworny, *Ibid.*, p. 53.
[70] *Ibid.*, p. 56.

Laborers are no longer classified by difference in trade skill, but the employer assigns them according to the machine to which they are attached. These divisions, far from representing differences in skill or interests among the laborers, are imposed by the employers that workers may be pitted against one another and spurred to greater exertion in the shop, and that all resistance to capitalist tyranny may be weakened by artificial distinctions.[71]

The IWW understood the full implications of the developments of hierarchy at the point of production. However, they failed, as has every other labor organization in this century, to develop a successful strategy for countering it on the shop floor.

Under the old labor market system, the capitalists reaped profits from the production process but did not direct production themselves. The transition that this paper has described is the process by which capitalists inserted themselves into a central position of control over production. As Karl Marx, in writing about this transition, put it, "In the course of this development, the formal subjection is replaced by the real subjection of labour to capital." [72]

Labor market institutions are best understood in their historical context, as products of the relations between classes in capitalist society. Labor market institutions are both produced by and are weapons in the class struggle. Technology plays only a minor role in this process. Technological innovations by themselves do not generate particular labor market institutions—they only redefine the realm of possibilities. The dynamic element is the class struggle itself, the shifting power relations between workers and employers, out of which the institutions of work and the form of the labor market is determined.

The institutions of labor, then, are the institutions of capitalist control. They could only be established by breaking the traditional power of the industrial craftsmen. Any attempt to change these institutions must begin by breaking the power the capitalists now hold over production. For those whose objective is not merely to study but to change, breaking that power is the task of today. When that is done, we will face the further task of building new labor institutions, institutions of worker control.

[71] Quoted in Kornbluth, Joyce, *Rebel Voices*.
[72] Marx, Karl, *Capital*, Vol. I, Chapter XVI.

*I want to give special thanks to Jeremy Brecher, who helped
me sift through the evidence and piece together the ideas that
went into this article. Without his patience as an editor and his
enthusiasm for the project, this paper would not have been
possible.*

# Automatic Production

### joel stein

The benefits of industrial society under capitalism are purchased at a terrible cost: the regimentation and dehumanization of labor, the distortion of human needs, global war,
ecological unbalance. These facts are either denied by bourgeois writers, explained away as necessary evils, or glibly
accepted as temporary problems subject to amelioration. This
last group, so proud of its liberal willingness to admit to the
existence of social problems, is known for its boundless faith
in the ability of capitalism to solve problems.

Thus with what joy did they greet the "age of automation,"
"the new machine age," the "second industrial revolution."
The machine which had enslaved mankind would now liberate
it. With the same iron necessity with which the machine itself had supposedly ushered in the age of human mutilation,
it would usher in the new age of human freedom.

So the Museum of Modern Art held an exhibit on "The
machine as seen at the end of the mechanical age." John
Kenneth Galbraith wrote a widely heralded book on *The New
Industrial State* in which he promised the end of the class
struggle by means of the automation of the industrial working class out of existence. It was announced that "automation may be a reversal rather than an extension of the first
industrial revolution" because it would replace

large numbers of unskilled workers on drab, monotonous jobs
with highly trained technicians in challenging, responsible
assignments of keeping the fabulous machines running . . . .

The new technology may cure the evils of the old technology.[1]

can now be admitted. But behind the frankness there is a self-assured smile. Don't worry. What the machine hath taken away, as we told you all along, the machine giveth. Capitalist industry transformed the worker into a mutilated human being, the performer of repetitive dull operations, a complement, a part of the machine. Automation will now reverse this process, by eliminating these dull, boring operations through complete mechanization, demanding higher education levels of those who continue to work. It is contended that unemployment is not a problem but that, rather, there is, and for some unspecified reason, will always be, a dearth of skilled labor. Unemployment is said to result not from automation but from low growth rates, caused by wrong government policies, either of too much or too little, and by "structural unemployment" which is generally due to the undereducation of the work force.

## Two, Three, Many Industrial Revolutions

Automation is described as the second industrial revolution. According to Norbert Wiener, in *The Human Use of Human Beings,* the first industrial revolution was the replacement of human brawn whereas the second is the replacement of human intelligence in labor. Leaving aside the fact that, if this were the case it would make even more doubtful the increase of demand for intellectual labor (in fact Wiener was most pessimistic concerning, at least the immediate results of automation), this view is a serious misunderstanding. The first industrial revolution was also the automation of intellectual labor. It rested upon the transformation of skilled into unskilled labor, of the craftsman into a mere hand who no longer guided and instructed his tools but was instead guided and instructed by the machine. While it also eliminated many kinds of heavy labor, the machine in general was used to transform work into a purely physical task. It might be said then that the second industrial revolution actually is the final elimination of physical labor in contrast to the first which eliminated mental labor. In fact, both developments

[1] Frank K. Shallenberger, "Economics of Plant Automation," in E. M. Grabbe, ed. *Automation in Business and Industry.* N.Y. 1957.

occurred in each "revolution" insofar as they may be differentiated at all.

The tendency of capitalist industry is to displace human labor by the machine. All machines are automatic mechanisms operating to some degree without human guidance or control. From the point of view of the worker, automation is simply the total elimination of the human being from direct intervention in the production process. The means by which this total mechanization is effected, whether through cybernetic devices, computers, or other means, is irrelevant insofar as its effects upon the labor process and life conditions of the worker are concerned. From the historical viewpoint of the working-class movement, the introduction of new production techniques, such as cybernetic devices or new power sources, is not of decisive importance and does not warrant the title of a new industrial revolution. Rather, it continues the general effects of the first industrial revolution, that is to say, of the industrial revolution. This is of course hardly to say that these questions are of no importance, nor to deny the possibility of technical "revolutions"; it is merely to state the simple fact that automation and cybernation are continuances of the general tendency of capitalist industry.

The extent of automation is determined by the requirements of capital expansion and profit production which form its limit.[2] On the one hand, the goal of profit production, which is surplus-value, that is surplus labor, must ultimately conflict with the elimination of labor. On the other hand, the efficiency of automated processes is determined not in comparison with the total working-time but only with the necessary portion of the labor-time, that which the capitalist pays in wages.

> The history of technology shows that in many cases machines were ignored or abandoned for a time when manual labor remained more profitable for the industrialists, with no consideration of the difficulty of the tasks thus retained.[3]

In fact, automation is today still a rarity in production, affecting only a few industries fully, such as some chemical

[2] Paul Mattick, "The Economics of Cybernation." *New Politics*.
[3] Georges Friedmann. *Industrial Society*. N.Y. 1955. p. 174.

processes.[4] Labor is still cheaper than the gigantic investments required for fully automated processes. The limits of automation in the capitalist economy derive ultimately from the relative stagnation of that economy at the present time; a situation which seemingly cannot be overcome within the private property framework of the system as it exists.

The various spheres of industry are interdependent in the capitalist system. (This is, for instance, why a crisis and depression or a boom affects the economy as a whole.) In the long run, the transformation of one sphere of production through extensive new investment in automated equipment can proceed only to a limited extent unless this occurs in other spheres, throughout the economy as a whole. The piecemeal automation of the present time must eventually either come to an end or be accelerated throughout the system.

The situation is different in a state-controlled economy of the Russian type. In such a system, in which the ruling class, controlling the sum total of economic resources, can plan the allocation of capital for the system as a whole, automation could possibly continue indefinitely, while workers not needed for production could be kept employed in various forms of waste production. But in a mixed economy like that of the US, in which the government-directed sector is subservient to the private sector, this is impossible. Here the total capital can be dealt with practically only in the form of the private corporate capitals which make it up. There is no real planning of the economy as a whole; rather the individual corporations make investment decisions on the basis of their private profit requirements.

Given the stagnation of the capitalist economy at the present time, an acceleration of automation beyond its current limits would be possible only with the abolition of the mixed economy and the substitution of a state-controlled one. (Indeed, the technical developments of the post-war period in Western Europe and the United States are in general a function of State spending, mostly of the military kind.[5]) Such a change of the form of production by the ruling class is now imaginable only as a response to a deep-going social and

[4] For a full treatment of the limits of automation under capitalism see footnote three above and the chapter on "Technology and the Mixed Economy" in Paul Mattick's *Marx and Keynes*.
[5] See Michael Kidron *Western Capitalism Since the War;* London, 1968.

economic crisis from which genuinely revolutionary forces may also emerge.

## Part Machine, Part Human

As long as automated techniques are introduced piecemeal, workers must continue to supplement machine operations. Insofar as workers continue to produce directly with machines, no matter how otherwise automated, they suffer from increasing subordination to the machine, boredom, stupefication. As the machine takes over more and more of the intelligent functions of the producer, as of the physical activity—since mental and physical labor are always combined to some degree—the producer is more and more reduced to mindless activity.

> Automation has not reduced the drudgery of labor. The very opposite is true.[6]

Those who work with automated equipment do not enjoy the fact that, as Marcuse has said, their work is transformed into "psycho-technical rather than physical labor." [7] The worker is perhaps not exhausted physically. Instead he has no opportunity to use his body at all. In place of physical energy, he expends energy of tension. Both this lack of movement and constant tension contribute to disease and deterioration of mind and body.

Perhaps it is true in a few isolated cases that in the automated factory,

> The worker is swung along by the form and rhythm of his work; the satisfaction this gives him can be highly productive.[8]

In such instances, the worker would have to be a very incidental component of the plant. In general, the worker, as in all capitalist industry, is not swung but driven, and the feeling is anything but satisfying or productive. For example, it is said that,

> Petroleum refineries and chemical processing plants are so highly automated that everything is controlled by one or two operators, who certainly can also be replaced. If and when

[6] Charles Denby. "Workers' Battle Automation." Priscilla Long, ed. *The New Left*. Boston 1969.

[7] "Socialism in the Developed Countries." *International Socialist Journal*. April 1965. p. 147.

[8] Marcuse. *op. cit.* p. 148.

they are it will not be for reasons of cost but because they slow down the operation" [which is of course also a reason of cost].[9]

These workers, who form the upper limit of the speed of the production process must be under constant pressure to quicken their workpace.

It is highly instructive to examine the consequences of automation in one industry in some detail. Thanks to the US Department of Labor Bulletin No. 1437, it is possible to get a relatively complete picture of what is in store for the machine tool industry,[10] once consisting almost entirely of highly skilled tool and die makers and semi-skilled machine operators.

In this industry,

Numerical control permits automatic operation of machine tools by such means as a system of electronic devices (control units) and changeable tapes.[11]

Reductions in unit labor cost requirements in machining operations range generally from 25 to 80 percent, which more than compensates the increased costs of numerically controlled machine tools. Almost all new machine tools are therefore of this kind. At the same time, profit costs prevent the full automation of this industry. We may let the Department of Labor speak for itself in describing "Changes in Content of Machine-Tool Operator Jobs."

The machine operator working a conventional machine tool is required to set up a machine including indexing of table or workpiece, select the cutting speed and feed; and keep adjusting the machine settings to achieve part specifications. Under numerical control, these duties are automatically carried out by coded tape instructions. The operator of the numerically controlled machine tool is responsible for tending or watching a highly automatic, costly piece of equipment as it goes through a sequence of operations. He loads the control tape, fastens the part in the fixture, and verifies finished part dimensions. When finished part dimensions do not conform to speci-

[9] R.D. Hopper, "Cybernation, Marginality and Revolution" in Irving Louis Horowitz, ed. *The New Sociology.* p. 318.
[10] *Outlook for Numerical Control of Machine Tools.* 1965.
[11] *Ibid.,* p. 1.

fications, or an operating malfunction occurs, the operator of a numerical control machine is usually required to notify the supervisor or programmer rather than make the necessary adjustments himself.[12]

While the worker is thus reduced to this simple, dull activity, reduced from what was already a dull, mechanical job, companies demand highly skilled and trained workers, and perhaps even knowledge of programming techniques. In addition,

> Some companies prefer to use highly skilled and experienced machine-tool operators on numerically controlled tools.[13]

As the skill content of the jobs fall, the skill level of the worker is expected to rise. The high formal requirements asked by the companies are used in statistics pretending to show rising skill requirements of work, despite the actual fall.

But the machine operator is the least skilled producer in this industry. What are the consequences of automation for the most skilled, the tool designer and tool and die maker?

> Many of the decisions, judgments, shop practices, and precision machinery functions presently required of these highly skilled craftsmen will also be transferred to the planning and programming operations to be coded as instructions on a control tape . . . .
> The functions and skills of the draftsman and engineer-designer may be altered considerably as a result of various new methods of automating design being developed in conjunction with numerical control . . . . Techniques [which] produce a computer-captured model of the shape to be manufactured which can be converted readily into tape instructions for use on numerically controlled machine tools. When this occurs, it may affect the numbers of draftsmen required in the future. The principal duties of the engineer-designer will be the selection of design criteria and development of mathematical techniques for determining optimum design.[14]

Of course, these are not the limits of automation.

It is useful to briefly compare the changes of content in numerically controlled machine tool work in Soviet Russia. While Soviet sources make the same claims as US govern-

12 *Ibid*. p. 37–38.
13 *Ibid*. p. 38.
14 *Ibid*. p. 40.

ment and corporation officials concerning the enhancing effects of automation on work, the actual results also seem to belie the contentions. The machine operator, now liberated through automation, can

> tend several machines at the same time. Where a series of machines is controlled by one worker the manual operations on one machine may be carried out while the other machines are working automatically.[15]

But, in case this liberated worker has too much free time on his hands,

> On integrated automated lines the job of machine operator can be eliminated altogether, and the tool setter can perform the few operator functions that remain.[16]

In other words, as in US industry, a whole section of workers become mere tenders of "the fabulous machines." Rather than a deliberate policy of the elimination of the destructive hierarchical division of labor between skilled and unskilled workers, following, for example, the suggestions of Marx, Russian industry has reproduced the hierarchical division of labor which prevails in all capitalist industry. Like the US spokesmen, they contend that this will be changed through the technical uplifting of all job categories through automation. In fact automation tends to reduce rather than raise job categories.

Nor is this tendency confined to factory labor. In a study of the automation of office work, Michael Rose contends that,

> Computerization tends to reproduce the consequences—more repetitive, 'routinized' and 'machine-paced' work duties for employees and more standardized service to the customers— of mass-production factory mechanization.[17]

According to Donald N. Michael,

> While there is considerable feeling that cybernation is defi-

---

[15] *Labour and Automation*. Bulletin No. 3. Geneva 1966. "Technological Change and Manpower in a Centrally Planned Economy." International Labour Office. p. 24.
[16] *Ibid*. p. 27.
[17] *Computers, Managers and Society*. Baltimore 1969. p. 23.

nitely displacing the unskilled (and in some cases reducing what were skilled jobs to unskilled ones), only recently has there been a growing awareness that cybernation challenges the job security of many workers customarily classified as skilled. For example, numeric control, the technology of guiding the machine tool by computer, is just beginning to make inroads into the skilled blue-collar community of metal workers, welders . . . and the like . . . .[18]

Michael continues to list some of those who can expect to be replaced through cybernation: machine maintenance workers, clerical and office workers, middle management, engineers and others engaging in compiling information and issuing "expert" advice which can now be supplied through the computer and other cybernated equipment.

Michael notes that, due to automation,

White-collar workers are coming to recognize what blue-collar workers have long known: technological change introduces uncertainty. Many skilled persons will be subject to replacement by the latest cybernated device . . . . This means a continuing potential threat of downgrading or retraining for the skilled, and along with it the emotional difficulties of job insecurity which will be new to skilled workers.

Changes in organization within both plant and office, which are inevitable when computers and automatic production lines are introduced, change social relationships as well. Among other things, conversation on the job and other informal, social arrangements are often reduced during the working period because fewer people are needed to perform cybernated tasks and they may be physically separated. There are changes in the pathways to job promotion and the procedures by which efficiency is judged; these wipe out investments in time and experience which people have expected to be applied to their future careers. And with smaller work forces and fewer supervisory tasks, openings for job promotions are often sharply altered or reduced. These changes therefore destroy traditional expectancies about how things will be done and how people will be evaluated.[19]

In addition to the many other benefits which automation is bringing to the working population, a marked increase in shift work has been noted in recent years through the introduction

18 "The Impact of Cybernation." Kranzberg & Pursell, eds. *Technology in Western Civilization.* Vol. II. N. Y. 1967. p. 660.
19 Michael, *op. cit.* pp. 664–665.

of automation, as rising capital costs make the expense of idle machinery ever greater. In France, for example,

> the percentage of undertakings in the manufacturing industry which had introduced shift work rose from 8.7 in 1957 to 11.2 in 1959 and the percentage of workers in this sector who worked in shifts rose from 12 to 17 in the same period. . . .
> This increase is no doubt directly linked to the introduction of continuous processes, which are frequently automated, in a widening variety of operations.

In Britain as well,

> The installation of large-scale systems of automated data processing has led to some night shift working in certain offices. As yet this development affects only a very small number of employees, but the number is likely to grow, though not to any massive extent. The introduction of on-line computer-controlled systems of manufacture and material processing is likely to have a greater influence on the development of shift working in the future. There is, however, considerable resistance from workers and some trade unions to the spread of shift working.[20]

Attempts were expected to be made to exchange a four-day week for the introduction of shift work on week-ends and at night.

Thus for the majority of workers continuing to produce along-side of automated machines, automation promises no improvements, in fact the very contrary. It may be said that, despite all of this, the demand for highly skilled engineers, scientists and technicians will markedly increase with the development of automation.

## The Redundant Brain?

Even if this were true, while there is no doubt that the absolute and even the relative number of skilled technicians and scientists has increased with the post-World War II technological development, it must be remembered that the increased skill levels of some technicians develops on the basis of the general fall in knowledge requirements and applica-

[20] *Labour and Automation.* Geneva 1967. "Manpower Adjustment Programmes." I. France, Federal Republic of Germany, United Kingdom. pp. 61–62 & 184 respectively.

tions by workers in general. In every industry, scientific knowledge becomes the province of a small number of skilled workers while the majority is divorced from all intellectual activity. The computer industry is itself a recent example. Initially, in the immediate post-World War II period, all of those who worked with the machines' hardware were skilled maintenance men, capable of operating and repairing the equipment. As the industry became more developed, the technical training of these workers, and of all those who worked directly with the machines, was not kept up. Instead a new division of labor came into being with a handful of highly skilled computer repairers, and a large number of un- or semi-skilled workers who knew nothing of the operations of the machinery, and functioned merely as tape changers and in other mindless auxilliary capacities. Through the conscious policy of the creation of hierarchies, the machine which can replace skilled professional labor is serviced by full-time tape changers!

In general, automation continues the rising productivity of labor of the entire industrial development. This means that less labor is utilized to produce a greater quantity of goods. Included in the labor must be the education of the producers. While, for a truly free society, human beings must understand in order to control the scientific and technical processes at their disposal, a rising labor productivity which demanded increased labor time would be nonsense. It is precisely because rising labor productivity, including the development of technology, decreases the demands for training and for labor time in general that it is a potentially liberating force. Precisely this development under capitalism leads to the cheapening of labor which is the very goal of the capitalist process. The fact is that the computer has shown that intellectual labor is only labor and can be replaced by machinery as easily as any other kind of labor. Particularly under capitalist conditions where the skilled worker is assigned uncreative, restrictive tasks defined by the limited requirements of profits and war-making, mechanization of these jobs will continue. While the skilled workers' labor is differentiated from that of other workers often by only the degree of its boredom, the education factory is itself often only an element of hierarchy and discipline of the workers and technically trained. The university system also serves to cheapen brain work by mass production of students. In large part, the dissatisfaction of the "new working class" to which a numer of radicals a few years back looked for their "revolutionary constituency" stemmed from the fact that these workers feel slighted in production. After years of technical training, they are generally faced with the choice of performing mechanical, proletarianized functions or else joining management. The reality of their position stands in stark contrast to their belief in their own self-importance. Often, as frequently emerged in the May 1968 events in France, the demands of these workers for control in production stemmed from their desire to have greater control over the other workers (see *The Mass Strike in France,* this volume) to take what they felt was their rightful place as the technical masters of production. But a revolutionary movement of these workers, who are being unemployed today as well as proletarianized on the job, can develop only when they renounce any pretensions about their own importance in production and seek control as workers, that is, equally with all other workers.

As we noted, in order to actually control the machines and modern technology, human beings must understand them and a truly liberated humanity will require great knowledge and understanding. But these considerations do not define the requirements of capitalist technology. Production according to profit considers education to be merely a cost of production; education which can not be employed in the production of profits is sheer waste production and from this point of view is totally useless. Even if the absolute number of educated workers had to increase, it would not be great enough to compensate for the millions of unemployed and the denigration of those employed; but, in fact, there is even evidence that, just as automation may also lead to a general fall in the absolute numbers of productive workers, so will it lead to an actual fall in the absolute numbers of scientists and engineers. Cuts in armaments and space programs are actually leading to such results in the United States today.

Thus it has been said that

The control industry has 'closed the industrial loop' meaning that it has made intricate processes subject to computer control. It has now begun to close the 'intellectual loop', which will make the industrial operation subject to the control of management through a hierarchy of computers.[21]

21 New York *Times.*

Here is the dream world in which a few rulers' commands are transformed directly from will to reality without the intervention of human beings who look on as passive observers and recipients of the will of the gods. Under such conditions, however, as Paul Mattick has remarked,

> capital would feed labor instead of labor feeding capital. The conditions of capitalism would have been completely reversed. Value and surplus-value production would no longer be possible.[22]

As we have said, from the point of view of the working class, there have been not two, nor three, nor four industrial revolutions but only one continuous crisis-ridden process of capitalist development which has generally deteriorating effects for the working population. Automation does not reverse the results of the first industrial revolution, but continues the stupefication of labor, the insecurity of unemployment and work down-grading. "Giant robot brains" are not ironing out the "over-all complexities" of modern times but threaten rather to be instruments of human destruction. Automation is not eliminating the causes of class conflict but intensifying the crisis of class society. In short, automation, like industry in general, is not in itself a boon to humanity but is rather an instrument, an instrument which will be used against the workers until they seize control of it themselves. By seizing hold directly of production, the workers may abolish hierarchical and atomic divisions of labor and thus lay the groundwork for the abolition of labor itself.

The possibility of automation unfettered by capitalism is a real alternative now. This alternative holds up the spectre of the abolition of work, exposing the contradiction in the division of labor between managerial and managed functions; or between predominantly intellectual and predominantly physical work. Automation, while reifying these capitalist conditions, potentially exposes the absurdity of the fetishistic belief in the incompetence of the mass of producers and the special nature of those who perform intellectual and managerial functions. So long as the producer was required to perform definite productive functions within the machine process, even total workers' control and equality could not release him or her completely from the limitations of indus-

22 "Marxism and Monopoly Capital." *Progressive Labor*. p. 40.

trial work. Automation makes the whole basis of the wage system into an obvious obsolescent and absurd form. Like all technology, automation opens the basis for a restructuring and freedom of human life, opens up a wide variety of options for the greatest human freedom; and like all technology, used under capital production at its lowest common denominator, it becomes an instrument of human mutilation.

## Beyond Full Employment

Under capitalist conditions workers do not struggle first for the abolition of labor or even for the abolition of the wages system. First they fight to hold on to their jobs, or to defend their old positions in industry against the encroachments of capitalist technology. This they attempt to do through the old forms of "workers' organization" such as the labor parties and trade unions. However, these organizations are based upon an acceptance of the profit requirements of capital, while it is these requirements which demand the automation in the first place. At best, unions have managed to hold on to the jobs of members already employed, jobs which are closing up with retirement and workers leaving. At worst, as in the case of the United Mine Workers, the union receives actual payments to give the owners a free hand in automation. (In the case of the mine workers as well we see the destruction of health by virtue of the capitalist use of automation; through speed-up of the machines which kick up excessive amounts of dust. Here is the final irony, for potentially modern machinery could totally dispel the danger of work, and of mining, altogether.) In between are cases such as the West Coast Longshoremen. Here all "certified" workers were guaranteed pay for 35 hours work no matter how great automation. However, a great portion of workers are not certified and these suffer the full consequences of automation. But even this stratification of privileges will not serve to overcome the full effects of automation upon those who benefit from it now in the future.

The struggle, even to maintain jobs or to protect the given conditions can only take place through a movement which rejects the premises which make these demands appear realistic. That is to say, the demand to maintain the given conditions of wage-slavery can only be carried out through a movement which rejects the bases of the conditions of wage-slavery. Only through the seizure and running of plants and offices can workers force employers, even momentarily, to rescind those investment decisions which will displace the workers. What is at stake is not actually the demand to save jobs, or to retain the stupefying kinds of jobs presently carried out, but rather a rejection of the capitalist use of technology. Of course, workers today will and must fight for jobs, both to hold on to their own and to open up new ones. But as this need grows, the means by which it can be obtained can only be those which challenges the very bases of capitalist industry, posing the question of who determines production. A movement which could force full employment under capitalist conditions in violation of profit requirements is an impossibility. A movement around such a program might be capable of scaring, but not of destroying, the ruling powers. If the workers were prepared to implement such a program taking the full consequences into account, they would be fully revolutionary and therefore not interested in limiting themselves to the demand for full employment. Many socialists would for this very reason approve of this slogan, because they believe that programs consisting of demands of just this kind are needed to trick the workers into revolution. But a full understanding of the real conditions is precisely one of the things that a revolutionary workers' movement is about.

Thus the demand for full employment must give way to the demand for the abolition of the wage-system, for workers' control, for the abolition of the old division of labor, as means for the abolition of labor. The movement for jobs becomes the movement to abolish wage-labor through the means of class struggle which demands a practice which rejects the assumptions of the wage system and therefore of full employment. The means of factory seizures, general strikes, and operation of plants by the workers themselves which would have to be employed for a movement for full employment are not utilizable on a sustained basis by such a movement, for they demand a level of struggle which could be vigorously and consistently pursued only by a collectivity which has already gone beyond such limited demands. The workers must come to consciously reject the demand for full employment. Just as Engels noted that the demand "a fair day's pay for a day's work" must give way to the demand for "the abolition of the wages system," so we today must recognize that the movement for full employment must give way to the movement for the abolition of labor.

Automation will not naturally lead to the overcoming of the capitalist conditions; although it makes those conditions increasingly obsolete, it does so only as the consistent extension of those conditions. Only through the direct seizure of control of industry can the workers transpose the natural tendency of capitalist production by their conscious intervention, redetermining industry according to their own needs and knowledge. Automation can be used in a liberating way only by human beings who are themselves liberated.

# The United States and Indochina

## paul mattick

The origins of the war in Indochina are to be found in the results of the Second World War. Waged in Europe, Africa, and East Asia, World War II turned America into the strongest capitalist power in both the Atlantic and the Pacific areas of the world. The defeat of the imperialist ambitions of Germany and Japan promised the opening up of new imperialist opportunities for the United States, which emerged from the conflict not only unimpaired but enormously strengthened. America's opportunities were not limitless, however; concessions had to be made to the Russian wartime ally, which formed the basis for new imperialistic rivalries and for the ensuing "cold war." The postwar years were marked by the two great powers' attempts to consolidate their gains. This excluded further unilateral expansion that would destroy the new power relationships. To that end, America assisted in the reconstruction of the West European economies and the revival of their military capacities, as well as in the rebuilding of Japan under her tutelage.

The Second World War provided an opportunity for the colonial and semi-colonial nations of East Asia to gain their political independence. The British, French, Dutch, and Japanese colonizers lost their possessions. At first, the national liberation movement was welcomed by the Americans as an aid in the struggle against Japan, just as at first the Japanese had supported this movement as a means to destroy the European colonizers. Even after the Japanese defeat, the United States displayed no serious intentions to help the European nations to regain their colonies. The Americans were fully convinced that they would inherit what their European allies had lost, if not in the political then in an economic sense.

The Chinese revolution altered the whole situation, particularly because at that time it appeared as an extension of the power of the new Russian adversary and as the expansion of a socio-economic system no longer susceptible to foreign exploitation through the ruling world market relations. The needs of the American imperialists were clear: short of war, they would have to contain China in Asia, as they contained Russia in Europe. This necessitated a system of Asian alliances such as the Atlantic Pact provided for Europe.

## Capitalism and Imperialism

Capital is international. The fact that its historical development paralleled that of the nation state did not prevent the establishment of the capitalist world market. However, due to political interventions by which national bourgeoisies defend themselves against competitor nations, the concentration of capital was, and is, more difficult to achieve on an international than on a national scale. Even capitalist crises, world-embracing accelerators of the concentration process, needed the additional measures of imperialistic wars to extend the national concentration process to the international scene. The capitalistic organization of the world economy is thus a contradictory process. What it brings about is not the final accomplishment of capitalist world unity but capital entities competing more and more destructively for the control of always larger parts of the world economy.

This process is inherent in capital accumulation, which reproduces the fundamental capitalist contradictions on an always larger scale. With capital accumulation still the determining factor of social development, we re-experience more extensively and more intensely the experiences of the past with respect to both competition and the internationalization of capital. To regard the world as destined for private exploitation is what capitalism is all about. If, at the beginning, it was predominantly a question of exporting commodities and importing cheap raw materials, it soon turned into the export of capital for the direct exploitation of the labor power of other nations and therewith to colonization in order to monopolize the new profit sources.

The end of the colonial system did not remove the two-fold capitalist need to expand internationally and to concentrate the profits thereby gained into the hands of the dominant national capital entities. Because capitalism is both national and international it is by its very nature imperialistic. Imperialism serves as the instrumentality for bridging national limitations in the face of pressing international needs. It is therefore silly to assume the possibility of a capitalism which is not imperialistic.

Of course, there are small capitalist nations which flourish without directly engaging in imperialistic activities. But such nations, operating within the frame of the capitalistic world market, partake, albeit indirectly, in the imperialistic exploits of the larger capitalist nations, just as—on the domestic scale—many small subcontractors profit from business given to them by the large prime contractors producing for the war economy. Not all capitalist countries can expand imperialistically. They find themselves more or less under the control of those nations which can, even if this control is restricted to the economic sphere. It is for this reason that some European observers see a form of neo-colonialism in the recent expansion of American capital in Europe, and others press for a more integrated Europe able to act as a "third force" in a world dominated by imperialist powers.

The contradiction between the national form of capital and its need for expansion, which recognizes no boundaries, is intertwined with the contradiction between its competitive nature and its urge for monopolization. In theory, a competitive economy flourishes best in a free world market. Actually, however, competition leads to monopoly and monopolistic competition, and the free world market leads to protected markets monopolized by political means. Monopolistic competition implies imperialistic struggles to break existing monopolies in favor of new ones. The economic form of competition takes on political expressions and therefore ideological forms, which come to overshadow the economic pressures which are their source.

This transformation of economic into political-ideological issues has become still more confounded through the modifications of capital production brought about by way of social revolutions. The planned economies of Russia, China, and their satellites not only disturbed the monopolistically controlled world market but tended to prevent its further expansion under private-capitalist auspices. To be sure, there was not much capitalization in the underdeveloped parts of the world. International capital concentration resulted in the rapid development of existing capital at the expense of potential capital in subjugated countries. Lucrative markets, and cheap foodstuffs and raw materials, increased the profit rates in the manufacturing nations and therewith hastened their capital accumulation. Beyond that, however, it was expected that a time would come when further expansion of capital would include its intensified extension in the underdeveloped parts of the world.

Capital is not interested in the continued existence of industrially-underdeveloped nations per se. It is so interested only to the extent that this state of affairs proves to be the most profitable. If a further development of backward countries should be more profitable than, or equally as profitable as, investments in advanced nations, capitalists will not hesitate to foster their capitalist development just as they hastened it in their own countries. Whether or not this could ever become a reality under the conditions of private-capital production is a question the capitalists cannot raise, for their own continued existence is clearly bound up with the capitalization of the underdeveloped nations. They thus cannot help seeing in the formation and expansion of state-controlled systems a limitation of their own possibilities of expansion and a threat to their control of the world market. For them "communism" means the formation of super-monopolies which cannot be dealt with by way of monopolistic competition and have to be combatted by political-ideological means and, where opportune, by military measures.

In their opposition to "communism," the capitalists do not merely object to a different economic system. They also condemn it for political and ideological reasons, especially since, convinced as they are that the economic principles of capitalism are universal principles of economic behavior, their violation seems a violation of human nature itself. They do not and can not afford to understand the dynamics and limitations of their own social system. They see the reasons for its difficulties not in the system itself, but in causes external to it. From this point of view, it is the erroneous and depraved creed of communism which subverts society and robs it of the possibility of working itself out of whatever difficulties arise. It is thus not necessary that the capitalists, their apologists, and all the people who accept the capitalist ideology be aware of the fact that it is the ordinary business of profit-making which determines the national and international capitalist policies.

Neither is it necessary for the capitalist decisionmakers to comprehend all the implications of their activities in the defense of and, therefore, the expansion of their economic and political powers. They know in a general way that whatever lies outside their control endangers their interests and perhaps their existence and they react almost "instinctively" to any danger to their privileged positions. Because they are the ruling class, they determine the ruling ideology. They will thus explain all their actions in strictly ideological terms, taking their economic content for granted and as something not debatable. Indeed, they may never make a conscious connection between their political convictions and their underlying economic considerations, and may inadvertently violate the latter in satisfying their ideological notions.

The capitalists are not Marxists, which is to say that they must defend, not criticize, existing social relationships. Defense does not require a proper understanding of the system; it merely demands actions which support the status quo. Marxists, whose viewpoint includes criticism of existing conditions, often assume that all capitalistic activities are directly determined by capitalistic rationality, that is, by the immediate need to make profit and to accumulate capital. They will look for directly-observable economic motives behind the political activities of capitalist states, particularly in the international field. When such obvious reasons are not directly discernable, they are somewhat at a loss to account for imperialist aggression. In the case of Indochina, for example, the apparent absence of important economic incentives for American intervention has been a troublesome fact for Marxist war critics. This was seemingly mitigated only by the recent discovery of offshore oil potentials, which are supposed to explain, at least in part, the continued interest of big business in a victorious conclusion of the war. It is clear, however, that the Indochina war was there, and would be there, without this discovery and explanations must be found other than some definite but isolated capitalistic interests.

The apologists of capitalism utilize this situation to demonstrate that it is not the capitalist system as such which leads to imperialism, but some aberration thrust upon it by forces external to itself. They speak of a "military-industrial complex," conspiring within the system to serve its particularistic interests at the expense of society as a whole. In their view, it is one of the institutions of society, not capitalism itself, which is responsible for the war through its usurpation of the decision-making powers of government. Whereas the war—far from being waged for profits, current or expected —is an enormous expense to the American taxpayers and therefore senseless, it does directly benefit the particular group of war profiteers in control of government. Specific people, not the system, are to blame, for which reason all that is necessary to end the aberration is a change of government and the emasculation of the "industrial-military complex."

There is, of course, truth in both these assertions, namely, that imperialism is economically motivated and that it is spearheaded by groups particularly favored by war. But by failing to relate these explanations to the fundamental contradictions of capital production, they fail to do justice to the complexity of the problem of war and imperialism. Neither the production nor the accumulation of capital is a consciously-controlled process on the social level. Each capitalist entity, be it an entrepreneur, corporation, conglomerate, or multinational enterprise, necessarily limits its activities to the enlargement of its capital, without regard to or even the possibility of having regard for, social needs and the course of social development. They are blind to the national and international social consequences of their relentless need to enlarge their capital. The profit motive is their only motive. It is what determines the direction of their expansion. Their enormous weight within society determines social policies and therewith the policies of the government. This implies, however, that government and society itself operate just as blindly with respect to its development as each separate capital entity with regard to its profit needs. They know what they are doing, but not where it will actually lead them; they cannot comprehend all the consequences of their activities.

These consequences may include war and war may be initiated not because of some definite economic expectations, such as possession of specific raw materials, entry into new markets, or the export of capital, but because of past economic policies whose consequences were not foreseeable. This is quite clear, of course, in the case of imperialistic interventions in defense of capitalist property which stands in danger of being expropriated, or has been expropriated, in nations which try to gain, or regain, some measure of independence in economic as well as in political terms. This explains recent interventions such as those in Guatemala, Cuba, the Dominican Republic, the Congo and so forth. It is not clear with respect to the intervention in Indochina, where the United States' economic interests were minimal and their possible loss of no consequence to her economy. Yet this intervention, too, was the unforeseen outcome of past economic developments, even though it cannot be related to any immediate and specific economic needs or opportunity on the part of American capitalism.

## Imperialism and the "Mixed Economy"

Competition and the international capital concentration process leads to war between capitalist nations; and, indeed, *is* a form of international capital competition. But with this difference, that it involves not only economic interests of nationally-organized capital groups but also the defense, or destruction, of different social structures as, for instance, in the case of the transformation in Eastern Europe of hitherto private-property systems into systems characterized by state-ownership. A "civil-war" element thus enters the imperialist rivalries, even if this type of "civil-war" is carried on not within, but between, nations. "Communism" is to be fought internally as well as externally. The amalgam, "anti-communism," covers any and all movements and aspirations that threaten either the existence or the future of private capital.

This has been America's general policy since 1945, which no change in administration has altered. Although co-determined by specific capitalist interests able to influence government policies, the general policy springs directly from the expansion requirements of private capital accumulation and, short of the abolition of the market system itself, cannot be changed. A specific interest may be lost—like, for instance, the investments and the business of Cuba—while similar interests may be preserved by the occupation of the Dominican Republic, or the overthrow of the Guatamalan government. But the general policy must be directed toward the extension of America's role in the world economy and the simultaneous limitation of newly-arising state-capitalist systems of production.

The American economy is geared to the world market, of which it requires an increasingly larger share as U.S. capital expands. If this share contracts—and it is bound to contract, should more nations turn away from the American-dominated world market towards a kind of "second world market" which restricts, or excludes, the exploitation of less-developed nations by the developed ones—it will force the internal American development into isolation and in the direction of a state-controlled economy.

There is only one way to secure the capitalist market economy and that is through the continuous expansion of capital. It is this expansion which is the secret of its prosperous stages of development, just as lack of expansion results in its periods of depression. Capital development has been an alternation between prosperity and depression, the so-called business cycle. For American capital, however, the last big depression, that of 1929, did not lead to a new period of prosperity but to an era of relative stagnation and decline, which was overcome only through the transformation of the economy into a war economy, that is, the growth of production not by way of capital accumulation, but through the accumulation of the national debt and production for "public consumption" such as is required by war and preparation for war. But just like the Great Depression before, the war failed to restore a rate of capital expansion sufficient to assure the full utilization of productive resources and the available labor power. The government saw itself forced to continue its support of the economy by way of deficit-financed public expenditures which, given the nature of the capitalist system, are necessarily non-competitive with private capital and therefore largely arms expenditures. The "cold war" in the wake of the real war provided the rationale for this type of compensatory production.

Any significant decrease in government spending in the post-war world led to economic contraction which could be terminated only through the resumption and increase of government expenditures. The American economy, in other words, continued to stagnate, necessitating a relatively faster growth of the so-called "public sector" at the expense of the economy's "private sector." Unless a way should be found to reverse this development, it implies—in the long run—a slow transformation of private-enterprise capitalism into state-controlled capitalism, and a consequent shift of social power relations.

The dynamics and limitations of the "mixed economy" are too complex a problem to be discussed here.[1] It must suffice to say that waste-production and the accumulation of the national debt is not an accumulation of additional, *profit-yielding* means of production. It does expand production but not the production of profits, even if the favored contractors of government orders increase their profitability at the expense of the total social profits. That this type of production must be resorted to indicates a malfunctioning of the capitalist economy. It is a sign not of health but of sickness, and must be kept within definite bounds if it is not to destroy private capital production altogether. But to keep it within these definite bounds means to try to accomplish on a world scale what can no longer be sufficiently accomplished at home, namely, to increase the mass of profit in relation to the existing mass of capital. Just because of its "mixed character," the American economy is being forced more than before to augment an internal insufficiency of profit-production by an increase of profits from abroad. The American economy thus becomes increasingly more aggressive in its attempt to keep the world open to exploitation.

It has been said that "the familiar national aggregates—Gross National Product, national income, employment, etc. —are almost entirely irrelevant to the explanation of imperialist behavior," and that it makes no difference "whether the 'costs' of imperialism (in terms of military outlays, losses in wars, aid to client states, and the like) are greater or less than the 'returns,' for the simple reason that the costs are borne by the public at large while the returns accrue to that small, but usually dominant, section of the capitalist class which has extensive international interests." [2] Although this train of thought insists on the reality of imperialism even though it "doesn't pay" the nation, but merely those capitalists engaged in foreign business, it turns imperialism into the private domain of a segment of the capitalist class powerful enough to determine foreign policies to the detriment of the capitalist society as a whole.

In this theory the tail of imperialism seems to wag the dog of capitalism. And this despite the authors' discovery—contrary to traditional views, they believe—that imperialism is

[1] See: Paul Mattick, *Marx and Keynes, The Limits of the Mixed Economy,* Boston, 1969.
[2] P.A. Baran and P.M. Sweezy, *Notes on the Theory of Imperialism,* Monthly Review, March, 1966, p. 16.

not the result of a pressing need for capital exports but rather of the pleasures of capital imports, for the authors show convincingly that "for the United States as a whole the amount of income transferred to the United States on direct investment account far exceeded the direct capital outflow." [3] This, of course, is *the* point of capital exports as it is of all capitalist activity and is no argument against the idea that capital export dominates imperialist policy. While the relatively small amount of past capital exports points to the fact that, with the exception of the extraction industries, capital investments proved generally more profitable in developed than in underdeveloped countries, it is nonetheless expected that the future will reverse, or equalize, the situation. But in order to meet such a future, the world must remain open to private enterprise. Imperialism is thus a *precondition* for capital exports which, in turn, are preconditions for the exploitation of an increasing quantity of labor-power, and this, again, is a precondition for an enlarged international trade. On the other hand, of course, the capitalist concentration and centralization process prevents the homogenization of world economy, i.e., the capitalist development of underdeveloped countries, and divides the world, as it does the population in each nation, into haves and have-nots. But this general tendency of the capital accumulation process does not free the capitalists from the compulsive need to strive for an accelerated capital expansion on an international scale.

It is not just to safeguard the "returns" of special interests that the American government accepts the much larger "costs" of imperialism. It suffers the latter in order to increase the former in the hope of changing an over-all loss into an over-all gain. This might be a hopeless task—and in my opinion it is a hopeless task—so that, practically, the whole imperialistic effort might accomplish nothing more than safeguarding the "returns" of special interests, or not even that. In the Baran-Sweezy theory, however, imperialism appears not as a necessary product of capitalism but as the work of a special capitalist group looking for profits abroad even though their private gain implies a social loss. It follows from this that capitalist society would be better off without imperialism, i.e., without this particular capitalistic group. Actually, however, even a nonimperialist America would be forced to subsidize the dominant capital groups by

[3] *Ibid.,* p. 24.

way of government purchases, if only to avoid the depression conditions of a declining rate of capital expansion. These subsidies have to come out of total production; the "returns" of the subsidized capital imply the social "costs" of waste-production. This is precisely the dilemma in which capitalism finds itself and which it tries to overcome by external expansion.

The "national aggregates" of which the Baran-Sweezy theory speaks, and which it absolves from all responsibility for American imperialism, are a composition of profitable and non-profitable production, i.e., of market-production and government-induced production for which there is no market. The profits of market production are realized on the market and the "profits" of government-induced production are "realized" through government purchases with money borrowed from private capital. In other words, private capital "pays" itself by way of "government payments." As there is, in fact, no payment at all, the whole process is one of expropriation, and because capital and its government are an entity, it is a partial self-destruction of capital.

This "self-destruction" is, of course, a destruction in value, though not in material terms, for the productive apparatus is not altered thereby. Only it yields less in profits than it would if fully employed for private account; or, it yields no more than it would if there were no government-induced production. In other words, the yield through government-induced waste-production is illusory, and the larger the capital grows through government-induced production, the less the real yields, and the greater the illusory ones.

The illusion can be sustained, however, because of the fact that money, even in its noncommodity form, is considered a commodity-equivalent. Because all economic functions are money functions, it does not make any difference to the individual, or the individual corporation, whether they produce for the government or for the market, for in either case they realize their profits in money terms. Considering the national economy, however, it is clear that the money-value of total production—both market- and government-induced production—is necessarily larger than it would be in the absence of government-induced production. The whole production, whether profitable or not, is expressed in money terms as if there were no difference between profitable market-production and nonprofitable waste-production, as if production destined for destruction could be counted as an addition to the national wealth. Yet the real capitalist wealth is no greater than the money-values comprising the marketable part of production. It simply appears greater than it is, because the *expense* of waste-production is being counted as *income,* merely because of the government's power to inject money into the economy. But the borrowing of money cannot change an expense into an income, and the larger wealth in money terms represents a smaller capital in real terms.

The "false" character of a prosperity induced by government purchases is being betrayed by the steady devaluation of money and a continuous increase in the national debt. Both occurrences constitute, so to speak, the "price" of such a "prosperity"; it must be paid at the penalty of crisis, and this "price" is constantly increased, however slow at times, because the same conditions which make the "false" prosperity possible also make it increasingly more difficult to regain a "true" prosperity, i.e., an accelerated private capital expansion.

If we lift the money veil that covers all capitalistic activity, it is apparent that the "familiar national aggregates" are indeed able to explain imperialistic behavior. The increasing amount of waste-production which is required for an approximately full use of productive resources reduces the real mass of profits while maintaining or increasing its money-expression, a condition which can be altered only by an expansion of private capital relatively faster than that of waste-production. But the expansion of capital implies its extension in space. If waste-production in the form of war-expenditures were able to create conditions for an accelerated international capital expansion, it would not be waste-production from a capitalist point of view but merely an expense of exploitation. But even such a cynical notion would rest on the illusion that capitalism in general and American capital in particular, has no inherent limitations and no historical boundaries.

Capitalists and their government act, however, upon the optimistic hypothesis. Even if they should recognize the general trend of social development toward the dissolution of the market system, they still have to act as if the trend were non-existent, or as if it could be reversed. Their actions are determined by the trend, that is, these actions are devoted to the containment and destruction of socioeconomic systems not their own. Their imperialism is not an aberration but a necessity for securing the specific class relations of private-property capitalism. They are not making so many "mistakes" by rushing all over the world to secure the direct, or indirect, control of weaker countries, but they are living up to their capitalistic responsibilities which include imperialism. In the case of the United States the optimism is particularly prevalent because of its rapid development, aided by two world-wide wars, and its present overwhelming superiority vis-à-vis other nations. Precisely for this reason it is the most imperialistic power in the world today. It can afford more waste-production than any other nation and can, for that reason, assume that it is possible to turn its losses into future gains by dominating an increasing share of the world economy.

Even if the "mixed economy" has found acceptance as a probably unavoidable modification of the capitalist system, the "mix," that is, governmental interventions in the economy, are supposed to be only such as benefit private capital. To keep it that way, interferences in market relations must be limited on the national as well as on the international level. A general expansion of government production internally would spell the certain end of corporate capitalist property relations, just as the extension of a state-determined social system of production within the world economy points toward the contraction of the free-enterprise economies. The necessity of containing the spread of "communism," that is, of state-controlled systems, is thus related to the necessity of restricting governmental interventions in the economy within each private-capitalist nation. With more nations adopting the state-controlled form of capital production and thereby limiting the expansion of private capital, insufficient expansion of the latter calls forth more intensive government interventions in the private-capitalist nations. To halt the trend toward state-capitalism in the market economies requires the containment and possibly the "roll-back" of the already-established state-capitalist systems. But while at home the capitalists control their governments and thus determine the kind and degree of the latter's economic interventions, they can only halt the dreaded transformation abroad either by gaining control of the governments of other nations or by imperialistic military measures.

Capitalistically, war makes "sense" if it serves as an instrument for bringing forth conditions more favorable for a further expansion and extension of capital. War or no war, short of an accelerated rate of private capital expansion, there is only the choice between a deepening depression and the amelioration of conditions through the further extension of nonprofitable "public" expenditures. But whereas war may eventually yield the preconditions for an American penetration into other parts of the world, including East Asia, and its present expense be recompensed by future profits, public expenditures for other purposes do not have such effects. Experience shows that war does open up possibilities for further capital expansion. From a consistent capitalist standpoint a successfully waged war is more "rational" than a steady drift into economic decline.

There is, then, no special reason for America's intervention in Indochina, apart from her general policy of intervening anywhere in the world in order to prevent political and social changes that would be detrimental to the so-called "free world," and particularly to the power which dominates it. Like an octopus, America extends her tentacles into all the underdeveloped countries still under the sway of private-capitalist property relations to assure their continued adherence to the free enterprise principle or, at least, to the old world-market relations which make them into appendages of Western capitalism. She tries to rally all pro-capitalist forces into various regional alliances, arms and finances the most reactionary regimes, penetrates governments, and offers aid, all to halt any social movement which might strive for the illusory goal of political and economic self-determination. Because self-determination is not a real possibility, the United States recognizes that attempts to attain it could only result in nations' leaving the orbit of Western capitalism to fall into that of the Eastern powers. By fighting self-determination and national liberation, America is simply continuing her war against the Russian and Chinese adversaries.

## Nationalism and Self-Determination

Separately, none of the small nations which have experienced American intervention endangered the United States' hegemony in world affairs to any noticable extent. If they were hindered in their attempt to rid themselves of foreign domination and of their own collaborating ruling classes, this was because America recognizes that their revolutionary activities are not accidental phenomena, but so many expressions of an as yet weak but world-wide trend to challenge the capitalist monopolies of power and exploitation. They must, therefore, be suppressed wherever they arise and conditions that will prevent their return must be created, quite apart from all immediate profit considerations. In this respect, the present differs from the past in that while imperialist interventions used to serve to create empires within a world system, such interventions today serve the defense of capitalism itself.

At first glance, America's gains in Asia are quite impressive. She has not only regained the Philippines and destroyed Japan's "co-prosperity sphere," but found entry into nations that only a few years ago had been monopolized by European powers. With the aid of a reconstructed Japan, now allied to the United States, it seemed relatively easy to keep China out of Southeast Asia and secure this part of the globe for the "free world" in general and the United States in particular. But the "communist" enemy was to be found not only in China but to a greater or lesser extent in all the countries of the region, achieving by subversion what could ostensibly no longer be achieved by more direct procedures. Securing America's newly-won position in Southeast Asia thus required the destruction of native national forces which saw themselves also as communist movements and wished to emulate the Russian and Chinese examples rather than adapt themselves to the ways of Western capitalism.

Who are the people that the American government wants to keep "free" and "prosperous," and who so obstinately refuse—a large majority of them—to avail themselves of America's generosity? For a hundred years these people experienced enough of "the white man's burden" to know that "freedom" and "prosperity" can only be gained through their own efforts and the destruction of colonialism. World War II gave them the opportunity, and nationalism brought independence. But from the very beginning this nationalism was of a special kind; it involved not only opposition to foreign oppression but opposition to the native ruling classes as well. The national revolution was at once a social revolution. The nationalists, though united against foreign overlords and their native collaborators, were split on issues concerning the structure of the decolonized nation. There was a "right" and a "left" wing; the first, striving for no more than national liberation; the second, for combining it with social change. "Behind the seeming unity to nationalism there was a latent cleavage which was likely to come to the open after the attainment of the primary aim. Even during the nationalist struggle this conflict between the right and left was quite clearly distinguishable." [3]

Like the Far East as a whole, Southeast Asia is predominantly agricultural. Per capita income levels are abysmally low. "The combined gross national product of the Far East free world and Communist countries—containing more than one-half the world population—is only two-fifths that of the United States." [4] The level of consumption is lower than for any other region of the world. Plantation or estate agriculture is small when compared with that cultivated by peasants, but production in estate agriculture is market-oriented and nearly all of it destined for foreign trade. Peasant agriculture is subsistence-oriented—nearly all of production is consumed by the producers. Peasant holdings are generally limited to only a few acres whereas plantations frequently range up to several thousand acres in size. Family-farming characterizes the peasant holdings, while the plantations depend upon hired labor. To stay competitive, the plantations tend to displace labor through increased mechanization.

At the time of the European conquest, Southeast Asia represented a two-class system—a vast peasantry ruled over by an aristocracy. The Europeans availed themselves of the services of the latter to consolidate their own domination. The peasants' surplus-labor sustained the whole social edifice. The plantation system and the industries introduced by Europeans eroded the subsistence economy, and consumer goods manufactured in Europe displaced native handicrafts. Capitalist enterprises impoverished the peasantry by taking more out of the economy than it imported in return, and by the creation of an "agricultural proletariat" out of the local peasantry and through the importation of foreign laborers. Economic changes brought with them a new urban middle class which soon acquainted itself with European ideas of nationalism and with Marxism (in its ideologized Russian version). The new middle class began to envision independence and development not in the *laissez-faire* terms of the relatively unimportant native bourgeoisie, but in the direction of a state-capitalist, or state-socialist, system such as that which accounted for the rapid development of the Russian economy.

[3] W.F. Wertheim, *East-West Parallels*, Chicago, 1965, p. 98.
[4] An Economic Analysis of Far Eastern Agriculture. United States Department of Agriculture, Washington, D.C., 1961, p. 3.

The new socialistically-inclined middle class of professionals, intellectuals and bureaucrats, allied to urban working-class elements, must find support in the peasant population in order to be able to realize its concept of social development. The revolutionary program is thus, first of all, a peasant program, promising the abolition of their misery. Concretely, this implies that less must be taken away from them than had been customary. And this means lower taxes, the reduction or elimination of rent for tenant farmers, confiscation of large landholdings and their distribution among land-poor peasants, the availability of credit at less than the usual usurious rates of interest, and the elimination of trading monopolies —which are mostly in the hands of the Chinese—in favor of cooperative trading centers. On the other hand, of course, the long-run needs of the nation as a whole depend on an increase in agricultural productivity, on a larger agricultural surplus, and the setting free of agricultural labor to ensure industrial development which, in turn, will raise the productivity of agriculture through cheap fertilizers, irrigational systems, machines, electric power, and so forth. Still, the basis for this process is a greater surplus out of agricultural production, which involves the revolutionaries in the contradictory task of bettering the lot of the peasants only to increase their exploitation. But as first things come first, the immediate needs of the peasants are emphasized. Everything else had to await the taking of power and its consolidation by a new regime, which will then try, by force and persuasion to integrate agricultural and industrial policies in the interest of national development.

During and shortly after the years of colonial revolt, the Vietnamese revolutionaries were quite moderate in their agricultural policies as well as in their attitude toward private trade and industry. Only enterprises belonging to the old colonial administration were nationalized; only landowners opposing the Viet Minh were expropriated and their land given to the peasants. It was not until it had been in existence for ten years that the Democratic Republic of Vietnam spoke of the total nationalization of industry and the collectivization of agriculture as an ultimate goal. Meanwhile, there has been some "socialist" and some nonsocialist cooperative farming and there are still many private peasant holdings. Collectivization is largely inhibited by the expectation of North and South Vietnam's eventual unification and the need to keep this project attractive to the South Vietnamese peasants. All

newly-developed industries, however, are state-owned and
foreign trade and banking are government monopolies. A
complicated pricing system, partly manipulated and partly
left to market forces, assures some degree of economic control. There is free buying and selling and there are obligatory
deliveries, mainly with regard to rice and grain production,
which amount to between 12 and 24 percent of produced
quantities. Wages are partly fixed and partly left to bargaining. All in all, the economy as a whole is still closer to a
Western market economy than it is to the more rigid and
controlled systems such as prevail in Russia and China. The
conditions for a complete state-socialist system simply do
not exist as yet and this is more a political goal than a developing reality.

Since they are not as yet frozen into rigid social institutions such as prevail in the advanced state-capitalist systems,
the political regimes of the Southeast Asian nations, including
North Vietnam, appear to be still reversible; American agencies were operating to bring this about by internal subver
sion and external aggression. Given the weak social status
of the rising native bourgeoisie, it is clear that the political
structures of the emerging nominally-democratic nations will
be as authoritarian as they are in the nominally-communist
nations. Both "communism" and "democracy" are thus of a
purely ideological character, indicating no more than two
different development tendencies—the one toward state-capitalism and therewith away from Western domination, the
other towards a market economy to be incorporated into the
neo-colonial structure of Western capitalism.

Not only in Southeast Asia but quite generally, national
liberation for most underdeveloped countries does not alter
their economic dependency on other capitalist nations. Being
already inextricably "integrated" into the capitalist world
market, and being incapable of a self-sustaining existence,
they remain as a so-called "third world" an object of imperialistic competition. Their national-revolutionary exertions
are largely dissipated in internal political struggles instead
of being utilized in an actual reorganization of their socio-
economic structures. Their future appears to be bound up
with the changing fortunes of imperialist power relations,
which will find them either on one side or the other of the
warring social systems and imperialist powers.

The social revolutions against foreign and national exploitation are objectively limited by their national character and

by a general backwardness, which caused the social upheavals in the first place. Whatever else such revolutions may
accomplish, they cannot lead to socialism as an alternative to
modern capitalism. They are only one of many expressions
of the disintegration of the capitalist market economy as a
world system, but they cannot bring forth a social system
of the kind envisioned by Marxian socialism. It is only as
an element of disintegration that they support the general
need for a more rational social system of production than
that provided for by capitalism. Their own problems cannot
be solved apart from the problems that beset the advanced
part of the capitalist world. The solution lies in a revolutionary change in the capitalist world, which would prepare the
way for a socialist integration of the world economy. For
just as the underdeveloped countries cannot develop social-
istically in a world dominated by capital production, so they
could not develop capitalistically in a world dominated by
socialist systems of production. The *key* to the development
of the underdeveloped nations is the socialist transformation
of the advanced capitalist world.

But if this is the key, it does not seem to fit the real situation. While it is quite obvious that the industrially-advanced
parts of the world have the means to industrialize the underdeveloped regions of the world in a rather short time and
to eliminate hunger and poverty almost immediately merely
by diverting the world's waste-production, or even just the
expense of its arms production, into productive channels
where they can serve human needs, there are as yet no social
forces in sight willing to realize this opportunity and thus
bring peace and tranquility to the world. Instead, the destructive aspects of capital production take on an increasingly
more violent character; internally, by more and more waste
production; externally, by destroying territories occupied by
people unwilling to submit to the profit requirements of foreign powers, which can only spell their own doom.

## The Limits of Development

However, the impoverished people in the underdeveloped
countries cannot wait for a socialist transformation of the
capitalist world. Their needs are too urgent even to await
a possibly intensifying industrialization under the auspices
of private-enterprise and foreign capital. Although thus far
the Western world has done little to promote industrial de-

velopment in the non-industrial world, it is not, in principle, opposed to such a development wherever it might prove profitable. It does not prefer the exploitation of its own laboring population to that of other nations; quite the contrary. But capital flows where it is most profitable and lies idle where it cannot yield a definite rate of profit to its possessors. American companies have found that manufacturing profits in underdeveloped countries are not higher than in the United States and, more often than not, are even lower. All the government exhortions and guarantees intended to induce private capital to invest in backward nations are of little avail, so long as the productivity-gap between industries in advanced and underdeveloped countries nullifies the cheap-labor advantages of the latter. Where profits are exceptionally high, as in the oil and mining industries, capitalists will even fight for investment opportunities; but the huge profits made in these fields benefit the rich, not the poor countries. Nonetheless, there is some development, and it is this "creeping capitalization" itself which spurs in the backward countries the desire for a more rapid development that would benefit the nation instead of foreign capital.

There exists an apparent contradiction between the need to keep the world open for free enterprise and the refusal of free enterprise to avail itself of its opportunities. But this contradiction merely reflects the contradiction of capital production itself. It is not different from the contradiction that bursts into the open with any capitalist crisis, namely, that production comes to a halt in spite of the fact that the needs of the vast mass of the population are far from being satiated, and that there is a pressing need for an increased amount of production. Production is slowed down not because it is too abundant but because it has become unprofitable. But it would not enter the minds of the capitalists that their inability to increase production is reason enough to abdicate in favor of a social system capable of coordinating social production to actual social needs. Neither would it enter their minds that because they have not industrialized the world and are, apparently, not capable of doing so, they should leave the world to others who presumably can do so by employing a principle of capital production different from that of private capital accumulation. Just as they defend their control in each particular country irrespective of their own performances, so will they defend it in the world at large.

What the "communists" in the underdeveloped nations

aspire to do is what capitalism has failed to do—that is, to modernize their nations by way of industrialization and thus to overcome the increasing misery of a stagnating mode of production. But capitalism in its private-enterprise form was there before them and was able to determine that peculiar type of "development" which constantly widens the income-gap between the industrially-advanced countries and the colonized, or semi-colonized, regions. As elsewhere, so in Southeast Asia, capital investments were made exclusively for the production of raw materials and foodstuffs for the industries and consumption needs of the capitalist nations. The nations of Southeast Asia themselves were destined to remain markets for goods manufactured in the industrial countries. An unequal exchange played their surplus-labor, or profits, into the hands of Western capitalists. The inequality of exchange became even more pronounced because of a steady decline of the prices for primary products relative to those for manufactured commodities, and by capitalistic competition in the raw material sphere as, for instance, through the increasing use of synthetic rubber and America's rice exports. Ending this trend of increasing impoverishment means, first of all, to use the available surpluses for domestic development, to eliminate exploitation via a world-market dominated by Western capital, and thus to disturb the "international division of labor" as determined by private capital accumulation.

## The War in Indochina

The land area in the so-called "free" Asian nations is nearly double that of the "communist" nations but—leaving out Japan as a special case—there is a higher index of multiple cropping and greater irrigated area in the "communist" than in the "free" countries. In 1959 the latter had an aggregate population of 832 millions while the "communist" countries counted 692 millions. India and China alone contain over one-third of all the people in the world. (Mainland China is the largest Asian nation, exceeding the United States in size.) There are various degrees of economic development in the different nations. Apart from industrial Japan, the islands and the nations of the island archipelagos such as Indonesia, Malaya, and the Philippines—due to their access to the trade routes of the Pacific—show a higher degree of development than landlocked nations. In all nations, however, and in the absence of significant degrees of industrialization, the immediate economic problem appears as one of too many people and too little land.

The lack of usable land relative to the population does not prevent but rather encourages its unequal distribution. Landlordism characterizes the whole of the "free" Asian countries. Peasants are turned into tenants and the frightful exploitation of the latter enriches the land-owning class without necessitating any improvement in agricultural production. In South Vietnam, for instance, "40 percent of the land planted to rice in 1954 was owned by 2,500 persons—by a quarter of one percent of the rural population. Rent alone commonly took 50 percent of the tenant's crops and sometimes more; he either produced his own fertilizers, seeds, man- and draft-power, and equipment, or rented them at extra cost; he could be ejected from his leasehold at the landlord's whim." [5] There can be no doubt that the landowning class as well as the urban bourgeoisie, amassing fortunes in trade and industry, are anti-communist, that is, are vitally interested in the continued existence of their privileges and thus find themselves siding with the foreign powers in their defense of free enterprise.

The struggle for national liberation was thus at the same time a civil war. Its results would determine whether the liberated nations would have societies keeping them within the fold of Western capitalism. It became necessary to influence the outcome of the civil war by outside intervention. For the United States it was essential that whatever the results of the liberation movements they must not lead to new "communist" regimes willing to side with the Chinese adversary. America's politicians rightly surmised that notwithstanding the most exaggerated nationalism, which would tend to oppose a new Chinese domination as it had opposed that of the old colonial powers, China by sheer weight alone would dominate the smaller nations at her boundaries, disguised though this domination would be by ideological camouflage. The surge of nationalism was to be channeled into anti-communism, which meant the upholding or creation of governments and institutions friendly to the United States and Western capitalism.

It is on the traditional ruling classes that the American government must rely in its efforts to keep "free Asia" in the "free world." In the long run, this is quite a formidable

---

[5] J.P. Gittinger, *Studies on Land Tenure in Vietnam*, U.S. Operation Mission in Vietnam, 1959, pp. 1, 50.

undertaking, for the objective conditions in the nations of Asia produce a steady revolutionary ferment which is bound to explode sooner or later. To counteract these threatening social convulsions, the United States wants to combine political-military repression with social reforms designed to lead to general social acquiescence. But the decisive "reforms" necessary to alleviate the plight of the peasants and of the urban proletariat imply the destruction of existing class privileges, that is, the power of the only allies the United States can find, unless she wishes to ally herself to the "communists," the only group actually able to realize the "reforms." The programmatic "social reforms" largely serve, then, as an ideological cover for the repressive measures that have to be taken to avoid the spread of "communism" from China into the neighboring countries and from there to the whole of the Far East.

The Korean War indicated that, short of risking a new world war, already established "communist" regimes could not be detached from their protector states, Russia and China. In other respects, however, the situation was still fluid. Apart from North Vietnam, other Southeast Asian nations were either anti-communist, or declared themselves "neutralist" or "non-aligned," meaning that their civil wars, clandestine or open, were still undecided. In the case of Laos, this led to a tripartite arrangement, engineered by the great powers, with "neutralist"-, "communist"-, and "western"-oriented forces dividing the country between them. This too was thought of as a temporary solution which would perhaps be resolved at some future date. Cambodia maintained a precarious "independence" by catering to both sides of the overshadowing larger power conflict. Only in Thailand, where America had replaced Britain as the major foreign influence was the commitment to the West almost complete. Here the United States sent more than 30,000 troops and much aid to build this kingdom into a bastion of the "free world." (It became the most important American airbase for the Vietnam war.)

Because of the flexibility of the situation, it seemed essential to the United States to stop any further change in Southeast Asia by assisting all "anti-communist" forces in that region. This has been a consistent policy, from which none of the successive American administrations has deviated. Objecting to the Geneva Agreements of 1954, the American-installed regime of South Vietnam refused to consider the proposed elections, which were to decide the question of unification of South and North Vietnam. To assure the continued existence of South Vietnam, the United States poured money and soon troops into the country. The resumed civil war in the South received support from North Vietnam, turning the American intervention into a war against both the national liberation forces in the South and the North Vietnamese government. This intervention has often been found unjustified, because it concerned itself with a civil war instead of, as claimed, with the national independence of South Vietnam. However (as was pointed out above) in the context of Indochina no distinction can be made between international war and civil war, because here all wars for national liberation are at the same time civil wars for social change. It was precisely because of the civil-war character of the national liberation movements that the United States entered the fray.

America's determination to retain influence in Indochina at all costs did check a possible further extension of social transformations such as occurred in North Vietnam and in a part of Laos. As it became evident that neither Russia nor China would actively intervene in the Vietnamese war, the "anti-communist" forces in Southeast Asia were greatly strengthened and, aided by the United States, began to destroy their own "communist"-oriented movements, the most gruesome of these undertakings being that in Indonesia. But while neither Russia nor China was ready to risk war with the United States to drive the latter out of Southeast Asia, they tried to prevent the consolidation of American power in that region by enabling the Vietnamese to carry on the war. The military aid given to the Vietnamese by Russia and China could not lead to the defeat of the Americans, but promised a prolonged war which would deprive the United States of enjoying the spoils of an early victory. The immediate and growing expenses of the war would, instead, loom ever larger in comparison with its possible "positive" results, which would recede always further into the indeterminate future. By bleeding the people of Indochina America would, in increasing measure, bleed herself, and perhaps lose confidence in her ability to conclude the war on her own terms.

It seems quite clear that the Americans expected less resistance to their intervention than they actually came to face. They aspired to no more than a repetition of the outcome of the Korean conflict—a mutual retreat to previously demarcated frontiers, which meant halting the "communist" penetration at the Seventeenth Parallel in the case of Vietnam, and at the agreed-upon zones in Laos. As in Korea, in Vietnam too they had no desire to turn the war into a new world war by bringing Russia, China, or both into the conflict. A war of the great powers, possessing atomic weapons, could easily lead to mutual destruction. The fear of such a war has until now set limits to the war in Vietnam. It has prevented a concentrated, all-out American onslaught on North Vietnam to bring the war to a victorious conclusion, since neither Russia nor China, like the United States herself, can be expected to allow any territory already under their control or in their spheres of interest to be lost, without encouraging further encroachments on their power positions. It was for this reason that the Western powers did not intervene on the occasions of the Russian invasions of Hungary and Czechoslovakia, and that America has hesitated to attempt the complete destruction of North Vietnam.

Of course, a nation's determination to hold on to what it has, or has gained, is not absolute. The overriding fear of a possible atomic war, for instance, kept the United States from reconquering Cuba. Nations tend to avoid actions which have a very high probability of leading to undesired results. Uncertainty is the rule, however, and it is the presumed job of diplomacy to weigh the pros and cons of any particular policy with regard to long-run national and imperialistic interests. This may incorporate short-run decisions which need not have a direct logical connection with long-run goals. Since the dynamics of capitalism imply an ever-changing general situation which escapes political comprehension, long-run imperialist strategy put into practice remains a matter of blindly executed activity, in which all diplomatic expectations may come to naught. Actually, the political decision-makers can affect only immediate, short-run goals. They try to attain a definite and obvious objective. They may reach it or not; if they lose, it will be through the action of an adversary. Until stopped, they will see their course of action as the only "rational" one and will try to follow it up to the end. In the case of Indochina, the simple goal was to secure this part of the world for Western capitalism without initiating a new world war. The unexpectedly effective resistance of the adversaries led to a continuous escalation of the war effort and a growing discrepancy between the limited objectives and the costs involved in reaching it.

In one sense, to be sure, the American intervention proved successful, in that it not only prevented the unification of

South and North Vietnam but also sustained Western influence in Southeast Asia in general. Confidence in the ability to maintain this situation was reflected in new extensive direct investments in oil, timber, and mineral resources in Taiwan, Indochina, Thailand, and even South Vietnam. Still, the war went on, because the North Vietnamese and the National Liberation Front in the South were not willing to acknowledge defeat and to accept peace on American terms. Short of a successful invasion of the North or an internal collapse of the "communist regime" there was no reason to expect a change in this situation, though an apparent loss of offensive power on the part of the North Vietnamese and NLF forces allowed a reduction in the number of American troops in Vietnam.

## The Anti-War Movement

Political decisions are left to the decision-makers; so long as they are successful they find some kind of general support. Even if the decisions involve war, they will be accepted not only because of the generally-shared ideology, but also because of the practical inability on the part of the population to affect the decision-making process in any way. People will try to make the best of a bad situation—which also has its advantages. Certainly, the armaments producers will not object to the extra profits made through war. Neither will the arms production workers object to it, if it provides them with job security and steady incomes, which might be less certain under other circumstances. The military will see the war as a boon to their profession; war is their business and they will encourage business to make war. Because the mixed economy has become a war economy, many new professions have arisen which are tied to war conditions or to preparation for such conditions. A growing government bureaucracy relies for its existence on the perpetuation of the war machinery and of imperialistic activities. Widespread interests vested in war and imperialism ally themselves with those specific to the large corporations and their dependency on foreign exploitation.

While for some war and imperialism spell death, then for many more they constitute a way of life, not as an exceptional situation but as a permanent condition. Their existence is based on a form of cannibalism, which costs the lives of friend and foe alike. Once this state of affairs exists, it tends to reproduce itself and it becomes increasingly difficult to return to the "normal" state of capitalist production. War itself increases the propensity for war. The American decision-makers who decided to enter the Indochina conflict (or for that matter any other) were thus able to count on the consensus of a large part of the population, a consensus which was by no means purely ideological in nature.

Yet in time there developed an anti-war movement displaying a variety of motivations and gaining in strength with the deterioration of economic conditions. It was the long duration of the war, and the lack of recognizable advantages, which turned an increasing number of people against it. The moral opposition, based on pacifist and anti-imperialistic ideologies, found more general adherence—large enough to induce opportunistic politicians to enter the movement to further their personal aims and to keep it within the frame of existing political institutions. Although the anti-war protests were merely of a verbal nature, with an occasional fire-bomb thrown in, they contained the potential of more decisive future actions. Opposition to the war began to affect the military situation through an increasing demoralization of the armed forces. Even the noted apathy about the war on the part of the working population was apparently giving way to a more critical attitude. Among the bourgeoisie not directly favored by the war, dissatisfaction with its internal consequences was visibly rising. In any case, the Nixon Administration found itself obliged to placate the anti-war movement, even though it had no more to offer, at first, than demagogic promises, which masqueraded the continuing and intensifying war activities as so many attempts to reach an "honorable peace."

Still, the amorphous anti-war sentiment did not as yet constitute a real threat to the Administration's war policies. The developing polarization of pro- and anti-war forces pointed in the direction of civil strife rather than to the government's capitulation to the opposition. And in its broad majority this opposition directed itself not against the capitalist system, which is necessarily imperialistic, but only against this particular and apparently hopeless war, now viewed as a "mistake" which had to be undone. But there is no reason to doubt that at this juncture the United States preferred a negotiated peace, which would honor its main objective, to the prolongation of war, if only to stall the growing unrest at home. The war was to be "wound down" by way of

"Vietnamization" in accordance with the so-called Nixon Doctrine. This was seemingly substantiated by a partial withdrawal of American troops and the simultaneous increase of the South Vietnamese Army, as well as through the intensification of the American air war in Laos, Cambodia, North and South Vietnam. Withdrawal meant, in fact, the extension of the war into Cambodia and Laos to prepare the conditions under which the Asians themselves would be enabled to take care of all "communist aggression."

It seems indeed an "ideal situation," with many precedents, to have Asians fight Asians to secure Indochina for capitalist exploitation. However, the "ideal situation" is unrealizable, even though an approximation to it is a possibility, provided the enemy adapts itself to the American strategy. If it does not, then, of course, the Americans will have to return to defend their interests. The deterrent strategy of a large naval and air presence will be maintained in any case. This strategy assumes the continuation of an existing military stalemate, which favors the Americans, since it can be utilized for the systematic destruction of enemy forces within the areas under American control. It is hoped that a resurgence of resistance to the Americans and their Indochina allies will become increasingly more problematic, as ever greater masses of the population are driven into controlled "refugee" centers and as the countryside is laid waste. With Russia and China staying out of the conflict, the aid provided by them will, by itself, not enable North Vietnam and the NLF to win a war of attrition with the United States.

## The Cease-Fire Interval

The war could go on as long as the North Vietnamese continued to defy the American will, and as long as they received sufficient aid from either Russia, China, or both. In this sense, the war was also a war between the Eastern powers and the United States, even though the latter had to engage her own military forces due to the weakness of her Indochina allies, who were no match for the national-revolutionary forces they set out to combat.

The rift between Russia and China did not, at first, alter the situation of conflict between America and the state-controlled systems. Both Russia and China remain in opposition to the United States (and other capitalist countries) because of their different socio-economic structures and their own desires to make themselves secure by gaining greater power and more influence within the world economy. However, both the Stalin–Hitler pact and Russia's alliance with the anti-fascist powers during the Second World War show that different social systems can at times unite for a specific common goal without thereby losing their basic incompatibility.

The national form of the so-called socialist or state-controlled regimes sets them in conflict not only with the capitalist world, or with particular capitalist nations, but also with each other. In both the capitalist and "socialist" world, each nation tries first of all to safeguard its own special interests, or rather the interests of the privileged social strata whose existence and position is based on the control of the national state. There is then no real but only an opportunistic solidarity between the nations in the "socialist" as well as in the capitalist camp. Alliances are formed between nations of different social structures, and enmities arise between nations which had been expected to cooperate. This indicates, of course, that nationalism and imperialism are not opposites but imply each other, even though the national survival of some nations may depend on the imperialism of some other nations. Under these conditions, the so-called "third world" countries are not only objects of the rivalries between different capitalist nations, nor only of that between capitalism and "socialism" as such, but also of the rivalries between the "socialist" nations themselves. Not only has the end of colonialism led to neo-colonialism, through which the dominating powers exercise their control of dependent countries via their own governments, but this imperialism as neo-colonialism is no longer the exclusive privilege of the capitalist world but in a somewhat modified form appears also in the "socialist" part of the world, both as as an aspect of imperialist competition between different socio-economic systems and for its own sake. We are provided the spectacle of a "socialist" brand of imperialism and the threat of war between nominally socialist nations.

The imperialist imperative is more demanding than ever before, while, at the same time, anti-imperialist activities find their accentuation in a developing world-wide economic crisis. The recovery of European and Japanese capitalism implies the return of their imperialistic potentialities, and the diverging national interests between China and Russia are additional elements simmering in the caldron of contradictory capitalist, imperialist, and national aspirations. "Peace" is no longer secured by the "balance of terror," exercised by the two great atomic powers. National independence has proved to be no solution for the permanent crisis conditions of newly-formed national states. But national aspirations can assert themselves only through the rivalries of the great imperialist powers, just as these powers exercise their foreign policy options via the various national rivalries. Any small-scale war has thus the potentiality of issuing into a new world war. The explosive situations in India, the Middle East, Indochina, and elsewhere, involve issues at once nationalistic and imperialistic, affecting in one measure or another the economic interests of all nations. To avoid a new world conflagration, and yet to safeguard and expand the nationally-organized capitals and their profitability, brings about a feverish diplomatic activity in search for favorable political-military combinations as an additional aspect of capitalist competition.

Nixon's deliberations in Peking and Moscow revealed clearly that wars of national liberation can be waged only within the framework of overriding big-power interests, in which the latter are the decisive element. The situation in Indochina is what it is because neither Russia nor China have been willing to risk a world war in an attempt to drive the Americans out of Southeast Asia, just as they were equally unwilling to allow the United States to become the unchallenged power in the Pacific area. America's failure to subdue the Vietnamese, as well as the Vietnamese's failure to force the unification of their nation, left the situation at the time of the cease-fire arrangement as it was at the start of America's large-scale military intervention in 1964. As far as the American-Vietnamese military confrontation was concerned, there were neither victors nor vanquished, which allowed both sides to accept a temporary truce.

Of course, the stalemate remained unacknowledged. Both sides claimed some kind of limited victory; the one, by pointing to the fact of the continued independent existence of South-Vietnam, the other, by referring to the South-Vietnamese territory held by the Provisional Revolutionary Government and the expectation of a political victory should the Geneva Agreements of 1954 finally be honored. Actually, neither the South Vietnamese nor the North Vietnamese are satisified with the prevailing conditions and the civil-war aspects of the Vietnam war—which cannot find a compromise solution—goes on unabated, despite the cease-fire arrangement, which led to America's military departure from Vietnam. However, the truce remains precarious not only because of the unsettled civil war, but also because the current big-power understandings with respect to Indochina may dissolve on their own accord.

To some, of course, the fact that America, the militarily and economically strongest power in the world, was unable to defeat a small "third world" country, is reason enough to see in the truce a great triumph for the Vietnamese and the superiority of the revolutionary will over capitalistic technology. The stalemate is viewed as a great accomplishment and an encouragement for all national-revolutionary movements yet to come. Be this as it may, the fact remains that this struggle could be waged only so long as it found the support of imperialist powers in opposition to American imperialism. It found its temporary end through the involved powers' decisions to suspend for the time being the power struggle for the control of Southeast Asia and to regard the given as the best attainable conditions given the current balance of power.

To be sure, the Chinese-American rapprochement, as well as America's acceptance of Russia's long-standing offer of "peaceful coexistence," indicates, in a way, a change of policy on the part of the United States, forced upon her by changing conditions. Just as the capitalist world at large had finally to recognize the permanent existence of state-capitalist systems in Europe and their expansion by way of war, the United States also had finally to realize that the results of the Second World War in Asia as well as in Europe could not be undone and that the emerging state-capitalist systems were there to say. The desired "rollback" of "communism" was not attainable; but the freezing of the conditions resulting from the war—among other things, the elevation of the United States to the paramount power in Southeast Asia—was possible. This situation has not been altered but consolidated by the Indochina war. However, while Indochina seemingly lies secure in the American sphere of influence, it is only at the price of acceptance of the "communist" regimes as equal partners in the competitive world economy. The world economy will thus remain a "mixed economy," composed of "communist" and capitalist nations, just as in each capitalist nation the economy can only function as a "mixed economy," both situations indicating the ongoing decline of private property capitalism.

To become at least a temporary possibility, the "pacification" of world politics had to await an American readiness to come to terms with her "communist" adversaries and a willingness to do business with them. The "socialist" world had been ready for this for a long time, not only because it comprised the weaker imperialist powers, but also because it expected economic advantages through integration into the capitalist world market. Their national interests, overriding all ideological commitments, and their security needs, demanding an unprincipled opportunism, determine their foreign policies. They were quite ready to make concessions to the United States in exchange for their full recognition and for expanding business dealings. Moreover, the growing enmity between Russia and China, competing for spheres of influence in Asia; the rapid expansion of Japanese capitalism with its inevitable future imperialistic aspects; and the presence of American imperialism, turned the whole situation in Asia and Southeast Asia into a far more complex and more fluid problem than it appeared to be at the close of the Second World War.

A Chinese-American rapprochement, of course, has nothing to offer the Russians except the possibility of undoing such a "strange alliance" by way of accommodation with the Americans at the expense of Russian ambitions not only in the Pacific but on a global scale. With its overture to China, the American administration finds itself in a position to exploit the frictions between Russia and China for its own imperialist ends. It discourages a possible Russian attack on China by suggesting a possible Chinese-American alliance which could make such an attack a costly affair. It also prevents a weakening of America's position in Indochina, and therewith in the whole of Asia, by offsetting the Russian influence in these regions and by leaving the whole situation in Asia in an unresolved state. In brief, it allows for a postponement of the final struggle for the control of Asia, which, at this particular juncture, suited all the involved competing powers but still had to await the American initiative to become a reality.

That this initiative was taken indicates the present limits of American imperialism as determined by her deteriorating economic position within the world economy as well as at home. The Vietnamese war cost the United States approximately 150 billion dollars and was partly responsible for the inflationary trend, which, under the previously established international monetary arrangements, made it increasingly more difficult for the United States to retain its competitive position on the world market, threatened by the growing economic strength of Europe and Japan. It led first to an apparently permanent negative payments balance and finally to a negative trade balance reinforcing the unfavorable payments balance. To be sure, extensive capital exports share the responsibility for this situation, but this can be expected to be offset again by capital imports and the repatriation of profits which may reduce or eliminate the unfavorable payments balance, whereas the war expenditures are a sheer waste which cannot be recovered in the foreseeable future. The American ruling class, through its government, was induced to search for a way to liquidate the Indochina war in order to husband its resources not only in view of internal American conditions but also because of threatening conflicts in other parts of the world and its declining role in the world economy.

To say that the American ruling class was looking for a way to liquidate the Indochina war is not to disparage the anti-war movement, which had its own, independent, effect upon government policies regarding the execution of the war. Nonetheless, it was the government itself which tried to end the war on American terms with the aid of the "socialist" powers and by a shift of policy which turned the implacable enemies of yesterday into today's collaborators, and which were to restore the conditions in Indochina to what they had been at the time of the Geneva Agreements, which had been ratified by China and Russia but not by the United States. The precarious economic conditions in both Russia and China induced these powers to reach for the same breathing spell which the Americans tried to gain for themselves by way of a compromise solution which left the Indochina issue in abeyance.

Although such terms as "selling out" have no meaning with regard to policies determining national interests, that is, the interests of nationally-organized ruling classes, this inappropriate term describes nevertheless the procedures which led to the truce in Vietnam, however shortlived that truce may prove to be. It was made possible by ignoring the warring governments of both North and South Vietnam and their declared objectives, and was arranged by way of agreements between the great imperialist powers, which had also been responsible for the war and the course it took. The Vietnamese population, North and South, however heroic or un-heroic, merely served as cannon fodder in a war of willing or unwilling proxies for great power interests, to which their own governments subordinated themselves only to be sacrificed when this proved to be opportune. Contrary to all appearances, the age of nationalism lies in the past, in the nineteenth century; it has become an anachronism under the conditions of the twentieth century imperialism, of which the Indochina war provides only the most recent example.

"Peace in Indochina," according to the American spokesman, Kissinger, "requires the self-restraint of all the major countries, and especially of those countries which on all sides have supplied the wherewithal for the conflict. We on our part are prepared to exercise such restraint. We believe that the other countries—the Soviet Union and the People's Republic of China—can make a very major contribution to peace in Indochina by exercising similar restraints." China, being in the weakest competitive position and militarily most endangered pushed for an accord with the United States, if only to curb Moscow's influence by way of North Vietnam in Indochina, even though this implied the acceptance of America's continued presence and influence in that region. And for Russia, according to Brezhnev, "the struggle to end the war in Vietnam was one of the most important aspects of our foreign policy, of the peace program advanced by the 24th Congress of the Communist party of the Soviet Union. And now an end is made to the war. One of the most dangerous, to be more precise, the most dangerous seat of war in the world is being liquidated." But to reach this state of bliss, millions of Indochinese had first to die and whole countries had to be devastated only to produce, for the time being, a truce between the three competing imperialist powers in Southeast Asia.

At this writing, the war in Indochina has by no means been liquidated and even the Vietnamese cease-fire is being observed mostly in the breach. The bombs are still falling in Laos and Cambodia—which, however, did not prevent the Government of the Democratic Republic of Vietnam, the South Vietnam Liberation Front and the Provisional Revolutionary Government of the Republic of South Vietnam from solemnly declaring that they will strictly observe all the provisions of the Paris truce. It was reported that Kissinger and Le Duc Tho had entered into an explicit oral agreement that only when the principals in the civil wars in Laos and Cambodia agreed to a cease-fire in their respective countries would the United States and North Vietnam cease their own military activities in these nations. This common endorsement of diplomacy by way of murder, of the juggling of power positions of diverse ruling classes at the expense of uncounted human lives, shows clearly that in Vietnam, as in the world at large, it is not the will of the people but specific interests of their ruling classes which determine whether they shall live or die, and that the ruling classes themselves are subjected to the manipulations of the imperialist protectors who are also their masters. It also shows that the process of dividing up Indochina has not been completed and, perhaps, cannot be completed at all. In any case, this is not the end of the Asian upheavals but merely a pause to be utilized for a realignment of imperialist alliances in the hope of reaching a winning combination able to break the present stalemate and to determine the nature of Asia's further development by way of new power struggles.

# III. A Look at the Past

## The Seattle General Strike

An Account of what happened in Seattle
and especially in the Seattle Labor
Movement, during the General Strike,
February 6 to 11, 1919

### by the history committee
### of the general strike committee
### march, 1919

HISTORY COMMITTEE
Chairman, MAY YOUNG, Waitresses
JOHN McKELVEY, Boilermakers, Shipbuilders
and Helpers
FRED NELSON, Boilermakers
J. N. BELANGER, Steamfitters
Secretary, SAM FRAZIER, Carpenters 131
Historian, ANNA LOUISE STRONG

### Preface

From February 6 to February 11, 1919, nearly 100,000
Seattle workers participated in a general strike. What follows
is a history of the strike, written by the History Committee
of the General Strike Committee shortly after the end of the
strike. It was compiled by Anna Louise Strong, then a "progressive" reporter for the union-owned Seattle daily, *The
Union Record*. Before being published in final form, everything was submitted first to the history committee and then
published in *The Union Record*, where workers' comments
were invited.

We have included it in this book for several reasons. First, it provides a concrete account of one of the few general strikes in this country's history. Although conditions have changed considerably, it still gives a good idea of what happens during a general strike and what problems arise. Second, the Seattle general strike was the general strike in the USA that went farthest towards workers' management, both in concept and in practice. It was seen, by both participants and opponents, as part of a process through which workers were preparing themselves to run industry and society. Final authority in running the strike rested with a General Strike Committee, three members from each striking local, elected by the rank-and-file. The 300 members of the committee were mostly rank-and-filers with little previous leadership experience. During the strike, this committee or its Executive Committee of 15 virtually ran Seattle. The strike was not a simple shutdown of the city. Instead, workers in different trades organized themselves to provide essential services, such as doing hospital laundry, getting milk to babies, collecting wet garbage, and many other things.

Third, the idea of strikers providing partial services presented here can be useful not only in general but in more limited strikes. Such tactics can help to keep non-striking workers (i.e. workers outside the striking plant, industry, or service) on the side of the strikers and at the same time hit the capitalists more directly. For example, in the 1970 postal strike, letter carriers promised to deliver welfare checks even while on strike. In Cleveland, in 1944, streetcar workers threatened to refuse to collect fares in order to win a pay increase—the City Council gave in before they actually used the tactic. Another possible example would be if garbage workers picked up garbage everywhere but the wealthy and business sections. This type of action would in most cases have to be taken outside the union, since few union bureaucracies would use such a clearly class-directed tactic, and thus of necessity the workers would have to organize this themselves.

## HISTORICAL BACKGROUND OF THE STRIKE

The Seattle strike took place in a time of upheaval and crisis throughout the world. There had been a revolution in Russia, followed by revolts in Germany, Hungary and several other European countries. It was widely believed that workers in these countries were overthrowing capitalism and taking over management of production for themselves. The Russian Revolution was supported by large numbers of workers in the US as elsewhere. Late in 1919, longshoremen in both Seattle and San Francisco refused to load arms and munitions destined for Admiral Kolchak, leader of the counterrevolution in Siberia, and in Seattle they beat up the scabs who tried to load them onto the government-chartered ship. To many workers, the Russian revolution, as they conceived it (not realizing to what extent the Bolsheviks had already destroyed the power of the workers' own factory committees and soviets and instituted authoritarian rule), was something to be followed here.[1] As the leaflet "Russia Did It," circulated during the Seattle General Strike (referred to in the text but never quoted), put it:

> The Russians have shown you the way out. What are you going to do about it? You are doomed to wage slavery till you die unless you wake up, realize that you and the boss have nothing in common, that the employing class must be overthrown, and that you, the workers, must take over the control of your jobs, and through them, the control over your lives instead of offering yourself up to the masters as a sacrifice six days a week, so that they may coin profits out of your sweat and toil.

In this country also there was widespread labor turmoil.

[1] The idea of workers taking over production and society was in the air throughout the industrialized world in 1919. The autocratic kaisers, emperors, and tsars of Germany, Eastern and Central Europe, and Russia were overthrown in the wake of the war. In Russia, workers' factory committees in many places took over factories and ran them themselves, until ousted from control by the new Bolshevik government. In Germany, workers formed committees elected in the factory called "Workers Councils." While these councils actually accomplished little, their existence led the most militant workers to conceive of a society run by the councils. In Italy, the so-called "Internal Commisions" which had formed in Turin's factories during the war, were gradually being transformed into factory committees—organs of struggle representing all the workers in the factory (not just those in a certain union or party). These committees led several militant struggles, including a week-long general strike, and later, the occupation of most Turin factories to combat an employer lockout. During the occupation, many factories were run under the direction of the factory committees. A similar process was also occuring in the formation of the English Shop Stewards movement.

Vastly expanded production for World War I and the cut-off of immigration made labor scarce, and placed workers in a powerful position. To ensure steady production, under the changed conditions, business and government made a deal with the conservative American Federation of Labor. Government and management would give up union-breaking and allow the A.F.L. to organize; in return, the unions would prevent strikes. (This wartime experience of government-guaranteed unionization later became the model for containing workers' movements in the 1930s.) However, despite the appeals to patriotism, the promises of a "new era" after the war, and the opposition of Government, business, and the A.F.L., strikes mushroomed during the war: the war years 1916–1918 averaged 2.4 times as many workers on strike as 1915. Two factors were largely responsible for this. First, there was an enormous inflation associated with the war: the cost of living practically doubled from August 1915 to the end of 1919. Thus while real wages increased, they lagged far behind workers' expectations; meanwhile, the work week was greatly lengthened. Second, as one wartime labor mediator wrote, "the urgent need for production . . . gave the workers a realization of strength which before they had neither realized nor possessed."

Big strikes practically stopped spruce lumber production and closed down the most important copper areas early in the war. In Bridgeport, Conn., the most important munitions center in the US, workers repeatedly stopped production in defiance of the orders of both the National War Labor Board and their own national union leaders.

Increasing militance was accompanied by a growing spirit of solidarity. For example, shipyard workers on the Pacific Coast tied up the yards for several months in sympathy with the lumber strikers in the Northwest, refusing to handle "ten-hour lumber" in order to aid the lumberers' struggle for the eight-hour day. General strikes developed in Springfield, Ill., Kansas City, Mo., Waco, Texas, and Billings, Montana, all to support particular groups of striking workers.

When the war ended, the conflict increased. Now that the great war-time industrial expansion was over, capitalists widely felt it necessary to reduce wages relative to prices if profits were to be maintained. Thus, the Government simultaneously ended war-time price controls and allowed corporations to resume their traditional union-breaking policies. Between June 1919 and June 1920 the cost of living index (taking 1913 as 100) rose from 177 to 216. Unemployment increased considerably right after the end of the war. At the some time, workers were eager to receive the benefits that war propaganda had promised them. The "new era" they had been promised turned out to mean declining real incomes, growing unemployment, and the undermining of what little defense against arbitrary management authority they had won.

As a consequence, more workers participated in strikes in 1919 than in any other year in American history except 1946. There were large strikes in the New England and New Jersey textile districts, involving 120,000 workers, largely opposed by the unions. 350,000 steel workers walked out, crippling most of the industry. They were met with a reign of terror in the large steel districts in Western Pennsylvania, "red raids" and deportations from the Federal Government, and lukewarm support (and at times treachery) from the trade union movement. Since the A.F.L. unions had traditionally been all white, the employers had no trouble recruiting 30–40 thousand black workers as strikebreakers. The strikers held out for more than two months, but finally succumbed to the overwhelming power of the steel industry and the government.

There were several other large strikes, many of them "outlaw" or wildcat, heartily and openly opposed by the unions. The most important of these was the strike of the railroad workers, which spread across the country. It was eventually ended by the combined pressure of repression and some concessions. Most protracted was the mass upheaval in the coalfields, with sporadic strikes, national strikes, and armed battles running from 1919 into 1922. In the course of these struggles, the idea of workers' management of production often came to the fore. For example, in the course of a wildcat strike of Illinois miners, a mass-meeting of 2,000 from the Nigger Hollow Mines adopted a resolution which read:

In view of the fact that the presentday system of Society, known as the capitalist system, has completely broken down, and is no longer able to supply the material and spiritual needs of the workers of the land, and in further view of the fact that the apologists for and the beneficiaries of that system now try to placate the suffering masses by promises of reforms such as a shorter workday and increases in wages, and in further view of the futility of such reforms in the face of the world crisis that is facing the capitalist system; therefore be it . . .

Resolved, that the next National Convention of the UMWA issue a call to the workers of all industries to elect delegates to an industrial congress, there to demand of the capitalist class that all instruments of industries be turned over to the working class to guarantee that necessities, comforts, and luxuries be produced for the use of humanity instead of a parasitical class of stockholders, bondholders, and that the congress be called upon to pass an amendment to the Constitution of the United States legalizing all such action in the aforementioned Congress.

Similar forces were at work in Seattle. Radical sentiment had simmered there even during the war. When a socialist and former president of the Seattle A.F.L., Hulet Wells, was convicted for opposing the draft and then tortured in prison, the Seattle labor movement erupted with giant street rallies. Seattle union membership had increased from 15,000 in 1915 to 60,000 by the end of 1918. Most of the unions were affiliated with the A.F.L., but their ideas and actions differed greatly from A.F.L. policy; as Harry Ault, editor of *The Union Record*, and a moderate in the local labor movement, put it:

I believe that 95 per cent of us agree that the workers should control the industries. Nearly all of us agree on that but very strenuously disagree on the method. Some of us think we can get control through the Cooperative movement, some of us think through political action, and others think through industrial action. . . .

Right after the end of the war, the IWW (Industrial Workers of the World) and the A.F.L. Metal Trades Council cooperated in sponsoring a Soldiers', Sailors', and Workingmen's Council, taking the Soviets of the Russian revolution as their model.

If the Seattle General Strike was an aspect of the stormy conflicts throughout the US and the world in 1919, it also grew out of the specific historical conditions in Seattle. Partially because of its geographic isolation, the Seattle labor movement had developed a unique structure. Whereas most unions emphasize the relation of workers to others in their own industry or trade, the most important identification of Seattle workers was with the workers of Seattle as a whole.[2]

[2] In Seattle, an attack on one group of workers was felt as an attack on all.

This was reflected in and partially caused by the fact that most collective bargaining was coordinated through the Central Labor Council, in which all A.F.L. unions were represented. Such city-wide labor councils have been centers of radical activity in other countries, but in 20th century America they have been extremely weak. The very newness of most of the Seattle labor movement meant that there had been little time for a local union leadership with its own interests to separate itself off from the rank-and-file. Although the union leaders in Seattle certainly had their doubts about the general strike, they did not actively try to smash it—in marked contrast to union leaders' behavior in other general strikes, notably in San Francisco in 1934. Thus while the workers of Seattle had to create a new organ, the General Strike Committee, they did not come into direct conflict with the existing union structure—precisely because of the factors which made that structure unique.

## LIMITATIONS OF THE STRIKE AND OF THE HISTORY

There were many limitations both in the thought and actions of the participants in the Seattle General Strike and in this account of the Strike, which leaves many important questions open. Perhaps most striking in the pamphlet is the strong emphasis on the nonviolence of the strike, its peaceful intent, its maintenance of "law and order." To some extent, this stress can be explained by the fact that the History was written in part to serve as a defense for many radicals and other participants who were arrested after the strike was over. Also, it should be remembered that the author, who was one of those arrested, was a "progressive" newspaper writer and not a striking worker. However, it is true that the strike was entirely peaceful, that from the beginning it was conceived in a peaceful framework, and that this perspective shaped the development of the strike. Given the situation in Seattle, this made sense. The strike was almost completely effective and thus did not require mass picketing (which could lead to violence) to shut things down. There was no possibility of successful revolutionary action, which would have involved armed struggle, in as small and isolated a place as Seattle, whose workers were more radical than those in most other parts of the country—it would have been bloodily crushed by the much stronger forces of reaction. What is objectionable in the Strike History is the *emphasis* on peacefulness, its elevation to a principle rather than a tactic. To what extent this was shared by the participants we do not know.

Also strange is the attitude towards the Japanese workers expressed here. The Japanese workers had also gone on strike and were invited to send delegates to the General Strike Committee, *but with no vote*. It is unclear what the context of this decision was, but this might have been a serious and potentially destructive limitation in the class-consciousness of those who made the decision.

The history fails to give much information on what the Wobblies (the Industrial Workers of the World) and other radicals did during the strike, what role they played, or what had been the effect of their years of activity and propaganda (some of it about "The General Strike") on the participants. The Wobblies were especially active in the shipyards. But the general strike was by no means a Wobbly creation, as some people have portrayed it.

Because of its early date, the pamphlet does not tell much about what happened after the strike. The account Anna Louise Strong gives in her autobiography is discouraging, although apparently accurate. She notes that the economic crisis of 1920–21 came to Seattle a year before it came to other cities. The Seattle shipyards closed a year earlier than the yards of Hog Island and San Francisco which also worked on government orders; perhaps by accident, perhaps because of "shrewd men in the East who decided that 'red Seattle' must be tamed." She continues,

> . . . our shipyard workers drifted to other cities to look for work. The young, the daring, the best fighters went . . . The life died out of a dozen 'workers' enterprises' which were part of our 'inevitable road to socialism.' Overexpanded cooperatives went bankrupt in a storm of recriminations. . . . Workers fought each other for jobs and not the capitalists for power.

Would it have made any difference if the strike had gone farther, had lasted longer, managed more enterprises, been willing to resort to violence? Probably not. Of more significance is the question: to what extent was the decline of the workers' movement in Seattle (and in other places throughout the country) a direct result of the economic crisis, as Strong suggests, and to what extent were other factors involved?

One of the major problems of the workers in the strike was their leaders. This is recognized in the history and a fair amount of information is given concerning it, mostly about the attempts of the national unions to force their Seattle locals to break the strike. There is much that can be added from other sources as well. Seattle's union leadership was notoriously radical. Yet the decision to strike was made while most of the "labor leaders" were at a special conference in Chicago to organize a national general strike to free Tom Mooney.[3] According to one of them, Strong, the general strike would probably not have occurred if they had been in town. "They were terrified when they heard that a general strike had been voted. . . . It might easily smash something—us, perhaps, our well-organized labor movement." They went along with the General Strike because it was happening and in the hopes of controlling where it went and bringing it to a speedy conclusion. The established union leaders never did manage to gain control of the strike, but they had more and more influence as the strike went on. Strong also pointed out that:

> . . . as soon as any worker was made a leader he wanted to end that strike. A score of times in those 5 days I saw it happen. Workers in the ranks felt the thrill of massed power which they trusted their leaders to carry to victory. But as soon as one of these workers was put on a responsible committee, he also wished to stop 'before there is riot and blood.' The strike could produce no leaders willing to keep it going. All of us were red in the ranks and yellow as leaders.

This situation was dramatized when the Executive Committee voted 13 to 1 on Saturday (the third day of the strike) to recommend ending the strike that night. The 300 members of the General Strike Committee were almost persuaded until they took a supper break and talked with members of their own rank-and-file; they returned to the meeting and voted overwhelmingly to continue the strike. All of this suggests that the problem was not one of "bad" or "yellow" leaders, but was inherent in the division between "leaders"

---

[3] Tom Mooney was an A.F.L. organizer in San Francisco who had been convicted of throwing a bomb into a 1916 preparedness parade, despite the evidence of a photograph of him standing by a clock a mile away from the scene at exactly the time the bomb was thrown.

and "led". The strikers could continue only insofar as they kept decisions in their own hands.

For us, one of the most important questions in any strike is to what extent do the participating men and women take over direction of their activities themselves, and to what extent are they simply following the directives of an alternative élite. A strike committee, for example, can be only a means by which different groups of workers coordinate their activity; on the other hand, it can be a new directing authority. Many questions about decisionmaking in the Seattle strike are not answered by the Official History.[4] Who was on the General Strike Committee of 300 and the Executive Committee of 15? Were they rank-and-filers or leaders? If the former (as turned out to be the case) what was their position and level of activity in the A.F.L. unions? Did the rank-and-file ever meet during the strike? When did the delegates on the General Strike Committee consult them? From other books, we have gathered that there were union meetings during the strike and that these union meetings, unlike most today or even most A.F.L. union meetings outside Seattle at that time, did allow some kind of democracy and communication—the rank-and-file really could control what happened to a fair degree. Also it is probably true that the 30,000 rank-and-file workers a day who participated in the mass meals that had been arranged discussed the strike with each other at these meals. This was most likely the major way in which mass pressure was put on the Strike Committee members, many of whom came to these meals.

Exactly who ran these services that were run by "workers" during the strike? Were they the local union leaders? Were they workers elected from the rank-and-file? Were the decisions about how to run things made at mass meetings? If done by delegates, to what extent did they contact the rest of the workers about doing these things?

These are important questions to ask, about what for us was perhaps the most important aspect of the General Strike. Workers' management is the basis of the socialist society we hope to see created and to help create. But workers' management does not mean appointing leaders to make all the decisions, even if these leaders are workers. It means that workers make those decisions that affect them (in the area

---

[4] Most of these questions are not answered in any other accounts of the strike either.

of production, these decisions would be: what is produced, how is it produced, by whom, and how is it distributed). These decisions should be made directly when possible, by rotated and immediately recallable delegates when not, and then only after full discussion of the crucial issues by those to whom the delegate is responsible. It will also mean a drastic change in peoples' daily lives and relationships.

This brings us to another set of questions left unanswered by the pamphlet. What did the participants do with their time? To what extent did they just sit at home (except for the mass meals, which maybe half of them came to) or have a vacation, as some of the strike bulletins told them to do? How were their daily lives and relationships with friends, family, co-workers affected?

## GENERAL STRIKES TODAY

Finally, while it is useful for us today to study what happened during the Seattle General Strike, what problems the workers faced and how they tried to solve them, it is important also to point out the respects in which the situation and thus the problems are different today (and were different, in most places outside Seattle, in 1919 as well). As we have already pointed out, the Seattle union movement was uniquely democratic even for its own time. A general strike today would probably have to be wildcat, in opposition to, fought by, and out of the control of the union bureaucracy. This is because most unions are bureaucratic, hierarchical structures which allow little meaningful participation of rank-and-file members. Their function is to act as middlemen in the labor market: insuring employers a quiet and docile labor force between contracts, and at contract time making sure that both the demands and the methods used to win them, whether "collective bargaining" or strikes, do not threaten the system. These features seem to be inherent in the nature of modern trade unions.

A second difference is that the US Government would most likely play a more active and repressive role in fighting a general strike today. In fact it was very unusual for 1919 that there was not more repression and violence on the part of the employers and the government.

Third, a general strike now would probably require much more mass participation both in decision-making and in physical activity. The former because a general strike would be done in conflict with the union structures and workers would have to build new organizations to run the strike (which at the outset, at a minimum, would probably mean mass participation). The latter because most cities or areas now are not as isolated as Seattle was, and it would be necessary, even if the strike was totally effective within the city or area, to have mass picketing and related activities in order to stop shipments coming into the city or area from the outside and to prevent the use of troops as strikebreakers.

## THE SEATTLE GENERAL STRIKE
## INTRODUCTION

From coast to coast went the report that a revolution was imminent in Seattle. A General Strike had been called in sympathy with the shipyard workers, and no one knew what would come of it. Both before and after the strike, Government officials in Washington and other prominent persons, declared that Bolshevism had attempted to make its first appearance in the Northwest.

In Seattle itself the tension before the General Strike is difficult to describe. Business men took out riot insurance on their warehouses and purchased guns. The press appealed to the strikers not to ruin their home city. Later they changed their tone and became more threatening, appealing to the strikers to state "which flag they were under," and if under the American flag, to put down Bolshevism in their midst.

Many opponents of organized labor hoped to see the Labor Movement of Seattle broken by the attempt to handle a General Strike, and many old-timers in the Labor Movement feared that this would indeed happen.

Meantime the people of the city laid in supplies for a long siege. Grocery stores sold enormous quantities of goods. Hardware stores ransacked their storehouses for discarded supplies of lamps, of the sort used by last summer's resorters in beach camps, and sold them out at a substantial advance in price. A few of the wealthy families were reported in the press as having moved to Portland, to be out of the "upheaval."

And yet, when the strike occurred, never had there been less outward turmoil in the city of Seattle. Ordinary police court arrests sank below normal. Quiet reigned throughout the city. Even the ordinary meetings of radical groups were voluntarily suspended lest they give an opportunity to some one to start trouble. In short, as a reporter from a nearby town declared "while the authorities prepared for riots, labor organized for peace and order." And peace and order obtained.

Now that the strike has passed into history, it is the purpose of this account to gather up the information in scattered documents, in the press, and in the minutes of the strike committee and relate what happened during the strike in the labor world of Seattle. We do this because the General Strike is a new weapon to the workers of the United States. Before our strike occurred, we did not know how the weapon which we held in our hands would "go off." And we have gained an experience which we believe will be of use to the Labor Movement of our country.

In the uncertainty and tension before the strike occurred, when no one knew exactly what might come of it, the statement that "this is not a strike but a revolution" was first made by the mayor of Seattle. It was the morning paper, the *Post-Intelligencer*, which first publicly announced the alleged "Bolshevik" character of the strike, in a cartoon showing the red flag hoisted above the stars and stripes in the city of Seattle.

To what extent Revolution was or was not in the minds of workers participating in the strike, will be discussed later, after the actual happenings of the strike have been made clearer. But since an editorial published in the *Union Record* (the official daily organ of the Central Labor Council) the day before the strike, has been quoted in partial form from coast to coast, as a sign of revolutionary intentions, we give it here in full:

## On Thursday at 10 a.m.

There will be many cheering, and there will be some who fear.

Both these emotions are useful, but not too much of either.

We are undertaking the most tremendous move ever made by LABOR in this country, a move which will lead—NO ONE KNOWS WHERE!

We do not need hysteria.

We need the iron march of labor.

\* \* \* \*

LABOR WILL FEED THE PEOPLE.

Twelve great kitchens have been offered, and from them food will be distributed by the provision trades at low cost to all.

LABOR WILL CARE FOR THE BABIES AND THE SICK.

The milk-wagon drivers and the laundry drivers are arranging plans for supplying milk to babies, invalids, and hospitals, and taking care of the cleaning of linen for hospitals.

LABOR WILL PRESERVE ORDER.

The strike committee is arranging for guards, and it is expected that the stopping of the cars will keep people at home.

\* \* \* \*

A few hot-headed enthusiasts have complained that strikers only should be fed, and the general public left to endure severe discomfort. Aside from the inhumanitarian character of such suggestions, let them get this straight —

NOT THE WITHDRAWAL OF LABOR POWER, BUT THE POWER OF THE STRIKERS TO MANAGE WILL WIN THIS STRIKE.

What does Mr. Piez of the Shipping Board care about the closing down of Seattle's shipyards, or even of all the industries of the northwest? Will it not merely strengthen the yards at Hog Island, in which he is more interested?

When the shipyard owners of Seattle were on the point of agreeing with the workers, it was Mr. Piez who wired them that, if they so agreed —

HE WOULD NOT LET THEM HAVE STEEL.

Whether this is camouflage we have no means of knowing. But we do know that the great eastern combinations of capitalists COULD AFFORD to offer privately to Mr. Skinner, Mr. Ames, and Mr. Duthie a few millions apiece in eastern shipyard stock,

RATHER THAN LET THE WORKERS WIN.

The closing down of Seattle's industries, as a MERE SHUT-DOWN, will not affect these eastern gentlemen much. They could let the whole northwest go to pieces, as far as money alone is concerned.

BUT, the closing down of the capitalistically controlled industries of Seattle, while the WORKERS ORGANIZE to feed the people, to care for the babies and the sick, to preserve order—THIS will move them, for this looks too much like the taking over of POWER by the workers.

\* \* \* \*

Labor will not only SHUT DOWN the industries, but Labor

will REOPEN, under the management of the appropriate trades, such activities as are needed to preserve public health and public peace. If the strike continues, Labor may feel led to avoid public suffering by reopening more and more activities.

UNDER ITS OWN MANAGEMENT.

And that is why we say that we are starting on a road that leads—NO ONE KNOWS WHERE!

This editorial was perhaps more variously interpreted than any statement made during the strike. *The Post-Intelligencer* published it the next morning and made no further comment. And perhaps comment is needless, since each man will interpret it according to his own intentions.

It might be mentioned, however, that the editorial was submitted, as were all matters affecting the strike, to the members of the Conference Committee of the Metal Trades, before it was published. And at the very time when it was being held aloft as the banner of revolution, by the capitalist press of the country, members of Labor and other liberal-minded citizens of Seattle were declaring that here at last was, out of the turmoil, a suggestion of some truly constructive attainment that might come out of the General Strike.

For the mood of Labor, as the General Strike drew near, was one of deep seriousness. They knew that they were facing a situation as yet untried, and they did not know what would result from it, of good or bad, for the City of Seattle and the labor movement in that city.

What did come out of it, as will be seen as the story proceeds, was precisely what was hoped for in this editorial—"more and more activities under the management of labor." The stimulus to cooperative enterprise and to the enthusiastic working-together of unions was the most important, permanent and constructive result of the General Strike.

To supplement the editorial given above, we call attention to the two Anise verses printed as an appendix to this book, and also to an editorial printed in the *Union Record* some weeks after the strike, of which we quote only parts:

## Concerning Revolution

We are growing tired of explaining that we DIDN'T mean this and that; we are weary of seeming to take the negative, explanatory attitude in connection with a faith of which we are proud, a faith which adds meaning to our lives. We want to tell, in positive words, the glorious things we DO mean.

If by revolution is meant violence, forcible taking over of property, the killing or maiming of men, surely no group of workers dreamed of such action. But if by revolution is meant that a Great Change is coming over the face of the world, which will transform our method of carrying on industry, and will go deep into the very sources of our lives, to bring joy and freedom in place of heaviness and fear—then we do believe in such a Great Change and that our General Strike was one very definite step towards it.

We look about us today and see a world of industrial unrest, of owners set against workers, of strikes and lockouts, of mutual suspicions. We see a world of strife and insecurity, of unemployment, and hungry children. It it not a pleasant world to look upon. Surely no one desires that it should continue in this most painful unrest. * * *

We see but one way out. In place of two classes competing for the fruits of industry, there must be, eventually ONLY ONE CLASS sharing fairly the good things of the world. And this can only be done by THE WORKERS LEARNING TO MANAGE. * * *

When we saw in our General Strike:

The Milk Wagon Drivers consulting late into the night over the task of supplying milk for the city's babies;

The Provision Trades working twenty-four hours out of the twenty-four on the question of feeding 30,000 workers;

The Barbers planning a chain of co-operative barber shops;

The Steamfitters opening a profitless grocery store;

The Labor Guards facing, under severe provocation, the task of maintaining order by a new and kinder method;

When we saw union after union submitting its cherished desires to the will of the General Strike Committee:

THEN WE REJOICED.

For we knew it was worth the four or five days days' pay apiece to get this education in the problems of management. Whatever strength we found in ourselves, and whatever weakness, we knew we were learning the thing which it is necessary for us to know. * * *

Someday, when the workers have learned to manage, they will BEGIN MANAGING. * * *

And we, the workers of Seattle, have seen, in the midst of our General Strike, vaguely and across the storm, a glimpse of what the fellowship of that new day shall be.

## THE SHIPYARDS STRIKE

The General Strike in Seattle grew out of the strike of some 35,000 shipyard workers for higher wages.

The Seattle shipyards are on a basis of closed shop and collective bargaining between the various yard-owners and the Metal Trades Council of Seattle. The Council is composed of delegates from twenty-one different craft unions, (seventeen at the time of the first strike vote). These separate unions no longer make separate agreements with the yard-owners; a single blanket-agreement is made at intervals by the Metal Trades Council for all the crafts comprising it. This was the situation before the United States entered the war.

In August 1917 the workers had succeeded in establishing a uniform scale of wages for one-third of the Metal Trades men working in the city. Some of the shipyards were unable to reach an agreement on account of having clauses in their contracts with the Government preventing them from raising wages without the Government's consent. The Macy board came out on the Coast to adjust the wages and instead of bringing about uniformity in the wage scale through their system of applying the increased cost of living to wages received that had been brought about through collective bargaining, applied the increase to the wages received the year before and owing to some of the crafts having been in a disorganized condition at that period and others having been organized and in a position to maintain their standards, the application of the increase gave some crafts 60 cents per day more than they had requested and the great majority of basic ship yard trades 22 cents per day less than they were receiving in the other yards and shops. Making a difference of 82 cents per day between the crafts which created dissatisfaction from the very start.

There was bitter opposition to this among the Seattle workers, who saw themselves deprived of advantages gained by long years of organization and struggle. But the International Officers of various crafts involved had signed the memorandum creating the Macy Board, and the men, while protesting, refrained from striking for patriotic reasons, because of the war needs of the country.

The Seattle workers maintained that according to the constitution of the various craft unions, the International Officers of the various crafts had no authority thus to bind their locals, without a referendum vote. This was felt all the more keenly as the local crafts had themselves given over their rights to the Metal Trades Council, in order that they might bargain for the entire industry at once, and they felt that power was wrongfully taken from the instrument they had built for their own protection.

For more than a year they continued work, though under

constant protest against the fairness of the agreement, to which they constantly stated they had not been a party. Appeal after appeal was made, with no result. While continuing at work, the Seattle shipyard workers established world's records in the building of ships. So great was their efficiency that official records state that 26 percent of all ships built for the United States Shipping Board during the war were built in Seattle alone.

After the armistice was signed, and after repeated failure to get relief through appeals, the various crafts of the Metal Trades took a strike vote by referendum. According to the strong conviction of the Seattle unions, in voting on these matters each worker should count as one, no matter in which union he belongs. According to the constitution of the various international organizations and the Metal Trades Department of the American Federation of Labor, however, the vote is counted by crafts, and requires a majority of the crafts represented in order to settle an issue. Thus in Seattle, where the boilermakers and Shipbuilders' Union is about as large as the other twenty put together, it would have only one vote in twenty-one. The majority of men in the yards might be overwhelmingly one way and the majority of craft unions might be the other way.

In this particular case, however, the majority, counted either way, was in favor of the strike. Ten of the seventeen craft unions declared for the strike, each according to its own constitution, which in some cases required a two-thirds, in other cases a three-fourths vote. Of the remaining seven unions, only one failed to secure a majority vote for the strike. In counting the majority of workers the desire for the strike was even more noticeable, since it was precisely in the large unions that the vote went strong for the strike.

The vote was counted on December 10, 1918, and was announced and held by the Metal Trades Council to use whenever they decided the time had come.

Meantime attempts at negotiations were continued. Failing to secure satisfaction, on Thursday evening, January 16, the strike was called to take effect the following Tuesday morning. The Tacoma Metal Trades Council took the same action.

The demands of the men were $8.00 per day for mechanics, $7.00 for specialists or semi-skilled mechanics, $6.00 for helpers with a scale of $5.50 for laborers, eight hours per day, forty-four hours per week. This demand, however, was not final insofar as the vote was concerned and had there been a compromise offered affecting all men in the yards in the same proportion it would have been necessary to resubmit the vote to the membership for acceptance or rejection.

Many evidences point to the fact that it was the raise in pay for the lower-paid men which was most desired. Many of the skilled men were already getting more than the minimum asked under the new scale. They were, however, strong in their advocacy of the strike on account of the condition of the laborers. It is stated, on many good authorities, that Seattle business-men, and especially Seattle landlords, had taken occasion to profiteer to a greater degree than in other places along the coast, and that consequently the cost of living in Seattle had increased far above that in Los Angeles and other California points. This bore hardest on the lower paid men.

The Conference Committee which had conferred with the employers, reported that the yard owners were willing to grant an increase to the skilled mechanics but not to the lower paid helpers. The men stood together in their unwillingness to accept such an agreement, regarding this as a bribe to induce the skilled men to desert their brothers.

The shipyard workers came out and the yards closed down, making no attempt whatever to run.

Special reference must be made to the attitude of Charles Piez, Director General of the Emergency Fleet Corporation. During wartime, while ostensibly admitting the right of the workers to bargain collectively with their employers, he informed the Seattle yard-owners that if they gave in to the demands of their workers, he would not let them have steel.

When the appelate board, which reviewed the decision of the Macy Board, ended in a deadlock, Piez told James Taylor president of the Metal Trades Council and local representative of the Seattle workers with the Macy Board, that the men were free to deal directly with their employers. He later confirmed this statement by telegram to Mr. Skinner of Skinner & Eddy Corporation, and in an interview to Mr. Ashmun Brown, published in the *Post-Intelligencer* of January 24th.

But when the yard-owners and the workers took him at his word and entered into conference, he again threatened the yard-owners, this time with the withdrawal of contracts, in case they changed the wage scale.

This attitude continued throughout the strike. In a most perplexing manner one telegram from Mr. Piez stated that the yard-owners were free to make their own dealings with the men and that he had no power to prevent them; another stated that government contracts would be denied any yards which changed the rate of wages; still another stated that as far as he was concerned the government would not allow, even later, any raise in the war-time wages.

Throughout the strike, he seemed consistent only on one point—that he would have no dealings whatever with the men until they had returned to work.

## SYMPATHETIC STRIKE ASKED FOR.

The strike of the shipyard workers occurred on Tuesday morning, January 21st. On the following evening, at the meeting of the Central Labor Council, a delegate body composed of representatives from all the unions in the city, including the unions of the Metal Trades, a request was presented from the Metal Trades Council, asking for a General Strike throughout the city, in sympathy with the shipyard workers.

This request was approved by the Central Labor Council and went out to the various unions to vote on, as they hold the final authority in case of a strike of their members. On the following Sunday, a meeting of executive officers of local unions was held which recommended to the Central Labor Council that the General Strike, if it should be favorably voted upon, should be governed by a Strike Committee, composed of three delegates elected from each striking union, and that this General Strike Committee should be called to meet on the following Sunday.

By the next Wednesday meeting of the Central Labor Council, so many unions had declared their intention to strike, that the suggestion of the executive officers of unions was accepted and a General Strike Committee called to meet on Sunday morning, February 2nd, at 8 o'clock. This General Strike Committee, composed of delegates from 110 unions and from the Central Labor Council, held the ultimate authority on all strike matters during the time of the sympathetic strike.

## Some of the Striking Unions

The completeness with which the unions of Seattle voted for the General Strike came as a surprise to many unionists.

Union after union sacrificed cherished hopes, "in order to go out with the rest."

The Longshoremen's Union, in which, after many vicissitudes, the Truckers had at length combined with the Riggers and Stevedores, had just put through a closed-shop agreement for the waterfront of Seattle, which was seriously imperiled and in fact, broken down, by their participation in the General Strike.

The Street Car Men were 100 percent organized, after a long and bitter fight which had included a street car strike. They were looking forward at last, after a year of waiting, to some fruit from their labors. Poorly paid, and with long hours, they expected a decision to be handed down from the Supreme Court of the State, and on the very day after the date set for the General Strike, which would assure them a substantial advance in wages. All this seemed to them endangered. Yet a majority of them voted in favor of standing with the rest of labor. And although the Street Car Men were later among the first unions to go back, at the orders of their executive committee and an international officer, yet even the most radical union men, knowing the pressure under which they labored, were inclined to urge: "Don't be too hard on those boys; they've risked a great deal."

Many weak unions, knowing that they risked their jobs as individuals and their existence as unions, yet took this chance and went out with the rest. Among these were the Hotel Maids, the Cereal and Flour Mill Workers, the Renton Car Builders.

Over against these were the votes of the old and conservative unions, unused to indulging in sympathetic strikes or "in demonstrations." The most unusual was perhaps the vote of the Typographical Union, a union whose control of its own jobs has been for years so strong that strikes have fallen into disuse in its organization. Yet it gave a majority vote in favor of striking, although its strike was not allowed by its International, as it failed to get the required three fourths vote.

The Musicians' Union, another conservative union, took two votes. It was almost 5 to 1 against the idea of the General Strike, but 6 to 1 in favor of striking with the rest of organized labor, in case the others decided to go out. In other words, it stood for solidarity even against its own preferences.

The Carpenters' Union, 131, an old, conservative union,

which has become one of the "big businesses" of the city, due to its ownership of a very profitable building, voted for the strike by a majority of "better than 2 to 1." "There was no one down there haranguing us, either," said one of the members. "We wouldn't have stood for it. We took a secret ballot and decided to strike; and then we put our fate in the hands of the Strike Committee and stuck till the end."

The Teamsters' strike is remarkable because of the great pressure under which they labored. It is stated that 800 calls came into their office during the strike, from members of their own and other unions, complaining that fuel had given out and that they could not get any heat on account of the strike of the Teamsters. Many people realized for the first time how this union, which handles the transportation of freight in a modern city, is at the basis of all the city's activities.

These are only a few of the unions striking; others will be mentioned in connection with activities which they carried on. But these are sufficient to show the great variety of crafts which sank their own interests for the sake of the sympathetic strike in Seattle.

It is interesting to note, in passing, that among the few unions which did not go on strike were various groups of Government Employees. Workers in the Postoffice Department stated on the floor of the Central Labor Council that the regulations were such that they practically faced jail for striking. Thus for the first time, the Labor Movement in Seattle was brought face to face with the fact that Government ownership may mean, not greater freedom for the workers, but greater rigidity of regulations, and less freedom for the individuals employed than does even private ownership.

## ORGANIZING FOR THE STRIKE.

Four days before the strike actually took place, the meetings of the General Strike Committee began. With their first session on Sunday, February 2, 1919, authority over the strike passed from the Central Labor Council, which had sent out the call, and from the Metal Trades Council, which had asked for it, and was centered in a committee of over 300 members, elected from 110 local unions and the Central Labor Council, for the express purpose of managing the strike.

The first meeting was called to order at 8:35 in the morning, and continued in session until 9:35 that evening, with short intermissions for meals. From this time on until the close of the strike, there were meetings daily and at almost all hours of day and night, of either this General Strike Committee, or of the Executive Committee of Fifteen to which it delegated some of its authority. The volume of business transacted was tremendous; practically every aspect of the city's life came before the strike committee for some decision.

A general strike was seen, almost at once, to differ profoundly from any of the particular strikes with which the workers of Seattle were familiar. It was not enough, as some of the hasty enthusiasts declared, to "just walk out." The strikers were at once brought face to face with the way in which the whole community, including their own families, is inextricably tied together. If life was not to be made unbearable for the strikers themselves, problems of management, of selection and exemption, had to take the place of the much simpler problem of keeping everyone out of work.

The strikers had no quarrel with the city of Seattle or with its inhabitants, of whom they themselves and their families comprised perhaps half. They had no particular quarrel with the city government, and most of them took pride in the municipally owned light and water and garbage systems, the municipal car line and the public port. While they were doubtless deeply touched by that spirit of unrest and desire for a new world which is sweeping the world today, they had no definite revolutionary intentions.

Consequently the problems of what should be done about the water supply, the lighting system, the hospitals, the babies' milk supply, came before a committee of quiet working people whose stake in all these things was as great as that of any person in the city and who, while they intended to make a tremendous and solid demonstration of sympathy with their brothers in the shipyards, had at the same time no desire to wreck the city's life.

They realized that they were undertaking something new in the American labor movement; they were not quite certain where it would lead; but they felt themselves strong enough to handle whatever problems might arise.

## The Committee Organizes.

To make the problem harder, the General Strike Committee was not, like the Central Labor Council, composed of delegates who had experience in working together. They were a new group, a very large and unwieldy mass of unacquainted individuals, upon whom, almost at once, great and momentous questions descended.

The quantity of business transacted and the business-like attention to many aspects of complicated questions, is shown in the minutes of the committee, and indicates a much higher level of efficiency and business-like methods that could normally be expected from such a large governing group.

The morning session of the first day was taken up with passing on credentials. Eighty unions, in addition to the 21 unions of the Metal Trades, presented acceptable credentials at this meeting. A few other unions were added later, making 110 in all.

All unions which had voted to strike, or which belonged to a district council which was striking as a unit, were granted three delegates. A few of the officials of the labor movement were granted seats in the meeting by special vote. Several irregular credentials were turned down.

The first appearance of the inevitable problem of the relation of the strike to the city authorities occurred when the Garbage Wagon Drivers asked for permission to explain why they had voted against the strike. They stated that Dr. McBride, the health commissioner of Seattle, had told them that they must take care of the hospitals and sanitariums, subject to penalty under the law. They had not known whether the strike committee would make any exemption in favor of these emergency needs, and so had voted not to strike. Later the Garbage Wagon Drivers' delegates were seated and certain exemptions were made in the interests of health.

Another fundamental problem which raised its head in this first meeting was the opposition of officers of international unions. The stereotypers stated that one of their international officers was in the city and would probably try to force them back to work. They wanted to know what support the unions of Seattle could give them in case their international officers supplied men to fill their places and otherwise disciplined them. The committee declared that the sympathetic strike would not be called off until the stereotypers were reinstated in any positions lost as the result of striking.

The date on which the strike should be called came in for much discussion. It was finally decided to fix the following Thursday, February 6, at 10 a.m., and to ask Tacoma and Aberdeen to postpone the general strike, which they had ordered, until the time agreed on by Seattle.

An executive committee of fifteen was next appointed to work with the metal trades committee in formulating a plan of action, and to present this to the Central Labor Council on the following Wednesday evening. Almost at once other motions made this committee permanent and instructed it to consider all questions of exemption that might arise in the handling of the strike. The decisions of this committee were at all times subject to appeal by the General Strike Committee, but in practice, repeal was not found necessary.

Committees on publicity, on finance and on tactics were also appointed, and many other minor matters of business were disposed of. Among these were the forwarding of a resolution to Washington, D. C., demanding the removal of Mr. Piez of the shipping board, and the adoption of a resolution that no officer or committeeman should receive any salary during the strike.

Just at the close of the meeting two slogans were suggested. "We have nothing to lose but our chains and a whole world to gain" was rejected in favor of "Together We Win." The unions of Seattle were declaring in favor of labor's solidarity; they were not declaring in favor of the well-known phrases of the class war.

## Executive Committee Organizes.

Even while the first meeting of the General Strike Committee was going on, the newly appointed Executive Committee of Fifteen met and prepared for business. Brother Nauman, of the Hoisting Engineers, was elected chairman, and Brother Egan, of the Barbers, secretary. Three subcommittes were appointed to consider exemptions from the general strike order, under three main heads: Construction, Transportation, and Provisions.

Committees on miscellaneous exemptions, on grievances and on general welfare were also appointed.

The Cooks Union reported at this time that their arrangements for feeding the strikers and the public were well under way.

The executive committee decided upon daily meetings. As a matter of fact, so many and so important were the matters brought before them that they found themselves compelled to meet more than once a day.

## First Exemption Granted.

On the following day, Monday, the Committee of Fifteen met again. Before them came a delegation from the Firemen's Local 27, whom they had requested to appear. After some discussion the committee requested the firemen to stay on the job. This was the first exemption granted in the strike. It was followed by many more.

The transportation subcommittee was instructed to arrange for the necessary forms of permits and signs to designate the autos and trucks used by organized labor in carrying on the necessary activities of the strike. Here again the necessity of exemption was recognized.

C. R. Case, head of the department of streets of the city of Seattle, was the first department head to appear before the committee to state city needs. He pointed out the fact that the water supply of Queen Anne Hill and West Seattle depended on electrical help from the City Light and Power. He also stated that large quantities of food in cold storage would spoil if the power system did not run, and that without the sreet lights the city would be a prey to lawlessness and disorder and thuggery. He mentioned the needs of gas in hospitals and laboratories, and the need of transportation for the various city institutions.

The Committee of Fifteen realized what they were facing, if a strike were carried through without exemptions. They appointed a special hour on the following day at which they requested heads of city departments to appear and state their needs, and they expressed as the sense of the committee that they cooperate with these heads in every way possible.

## Organization of Laundry Workers.

One of the neatest little bits of team work between four different organizations came up for approval at this first meeting of the executive committee of 15. The Laundry Drivers' Union had at first voted not to strike, but later changed their vote. They had a great deal to lose in any strike, as they had built up laundry routes with much patience and the effort of many years. They were working under an agreement with the Laundrymen's Club, the organization of laundry owners.

There was also in Seattle a Mutual Laundry, owned by organized labor, and the question of its operation came to the fore. After consultation between the laundry drivers and inside laundry workers, it was proposed that hospital laundry only should be handled; that a certain number of wagons should be exempted and furnished with signs and permits to serve the hospitals; that one laundry should be agreed on as the one best qualified to handle hospital laundry and should be allowed to operate under a permit, with a sign, "Hospital Laundry Only, by Order of General Strike Committee." This laundry should not be the Mutual Laundry, which did not care to handle hospital work.

The laundry workers served notice to their employers to take no more laundry, as it could not be finished, and then requested the Committee of Fifteen to allow them to work a few hours past the time of the calling of the strike, in order that the clothes already in the plants should not mildew from dampness.

A note from the Laundry Owners Club, accepting the Washington Laundry as the one to be exempted, was also submitted, together with the rest of the requests from the laundry drivers and laundry workers. It was a well-thought out program, indicating complete agreement with the entire laundry industry, and it was accepted by the Committee of Fifteen.

## The Problem of the Butchers.

The meat cutters presented an entirely different problem from that of the laundries. Instead of a complete organization of the industry, they had a small and struggling union, organized in a few shops, but unable to gain an entrance into some of the big markets which were controlled by the representatives of the packers.

If they should strike, and withdraw their men from the little shops, which had dealt fairly with the union, were they not penalizing their friends and strengthening their enemies whose non-union shops would be running full blast?

The somewhat original and interesting solution proposed by

the Committee of Fifteen was that that the meat cutters should strike with the rest of labor, and should then contribute their time without charge to supply the public with meat through certain specified union shops, demanding only that the saving of their wages be deducted from the cost of the meat. In the end, the strike of the meat cutters was incomplete, due to the handicap they labored under.

## Law and Order Committee.

By Tuesday noon, still two days before the strike, the need of a law and order committee was felt to be pressing, and the Committee of Fifteen appointed a committee of three to handle this matter. An advertisement was placed in the *Union Record* asking that labor union men who had seen service in the United States army or navy come to a meeting to discuss important strike work. This was the beginning of the famous Labor's War Veteran Guards, who did such splendid service in preserving order during the strike.

## Demands for Exemptions.

Demands for exemptions came in thick and fast on Tuesday, now that the strike was actually looming near. The proposed meeting with heads of city departments never came off, but requests from several public officials came in formally for exemptions. These were referred to their appropriate committees, considered, returned with recommendations, and either granted or rejected. In some cases a conditional grant led the Committee of Fifteen into the position of actually prescribing the conduct of certain lines of activity.

Here are a few selections from Tuesday's minutes:

"King county commissioners ask for exemption of janitors to care for City-County building. Not granted.

"F. A. Rust asks for janitors for Labor Temple. Not granted. (This committee was playing no favorites. It is worth noting, however, that a few days later, when the Co-operative Market asked for additional janitor help because of the large amounts of food handlers for the strikers' kitchens, their request was allowed.)

"Teamsters' Union asks permission to carry oil for Swedish hospital during strike. Referred to transportation committee. Approved.

"Port of Seattle asks to be allowed men to load a governmental vessel, pointing out that no private profit is involved and that an emergency exists. Granted. (Note: This was on a later date.)

"Garbage Wagon Drivers ask for instructions. Referred to public welfare committee, which recommends that such garbage as tends to create an epidemic of disease be collected, but no ashes or papers. Garbage wagons were seen on the streets after this with the sign, 'Exempt by Strike Committee.'

## Drug Stores—Prescriptions Only.

"The retail drug clerks sent in statement of the health needs of the city. Referred to public welfare committee, which recommends that prescription counters only be left open, and that in front of every drug store which is thus allowed to open a sign be placed with the words, 'No goods sold during general strike, Orders for prescriptions only will be filled. Signed by general strike committee.'

"Communication from House of Good Sheperd. Permission granted by transportation committee to haul food and provisions only."

This is by no means all the business that came before the Committee of Fifteen in a single afternoon. An appointment of a committee of relief to look after destitute homes, the creation of a publicity bureau, an order that watchmen stay on the job until further notice, and many other matters were dealt with. And after this eventful afternoon there followed a night meeting at 10 p.m.

## To Fix an End for the Strike.

Should a final limit be fixed to the general strike? Or should it start to end—no one knew where? This was the question discussed on Tuesday evening by the executive meeting.

Many of the older members of the labor movement frankly dreaded the general strike. They saw in it even such possibilities as the complete disruption of Seattle's labor movement. They urged that a definite time limit be fixed to the sympathetic strike, with the threat to repeat it unless action was secured on the difficulties of the Metal Trades. Foremost among those urging this limit were James Duncan, secretary of the Central Labor Council, and E. B. Ault, editor of the *Union Record*.

The executive committee of the Metal Trades was at first reported as having approved such a time limit, but after they had conferred with their general conference committee, which refused to agree to the proposal, the Metal Trades Council sent word shortly after midnight that they had no request to make. They also stated that the mine workers of the state would be asked to strike and that the State Federation of Labor would be requested to co-operate with the strike.

The move to fix a time limit to the sympathetic strike consequently failed.

## Take Over Printing Plant.

On Wednesday the same grist of requests for exemptions and for directions came before the Committee of Fifteen. The Trade Printery asked for exemption on the ground that it was printed material needed by the various unions. The request was denied, and the Trade Printery was asked instead to turn over its plant to the strike committee, to be run by printers giving their services. To this the Trade Printery agreed.

The day before this offer was made the Equity Printing Co. offered to put its plant at the disposal of the strike committee, volunteering free labor. This offer was favorably considered by a sub-committee, but rejected by the Committee of Fifteen.

The auto drivers were given permission to carry "mail only" on the Des Moines road. They were also allowed to answer emergency calls for hospitals and funerals, provided those calls came through the Auto Drivers' Union.

## Ministers' Appeal.

The Ministerial Federation sent representatives to see the Committee of Fifteen on this day. After submitting the resolutions which they had already sent to Mr. Piez and Woodrow Wilson as evidence of their sympathy with labor's cause, they formally requested postponement of the general strike for one week to give a chance for peaceful settlement. They were given a rising vote of thanks for their interest, but their request was not granted.

The telephone girls were requested to stay on the job temporarily.

The school janitors' request to remain on the job was refused, and they were referred to the Engineers' Union, which on the following Saturday allowed them to return.

Bake ovens at Davidson's bakery were allowed to operate, all wages to go into the general strike fund. This was the usual policy adopted when union men were allowed to work for private employers in a matter of public emergency.

## THE QUESTION OF CITY LIGHT.

The eventful Thursday drew near. One most important matter was still unsettled—the question of city light. At the request of the Committee of Fifteen, Mayor Hanson came to the Labor Temple to a night meeting for conference on the subject. The meeting convened shortly before midnight, and the mayor arrived after midnight, remaining until 3:30 in the morning on Thursday.

The electrical workers had voted to strike without exemptions. On the day before the strike an interview purporting to be from Leon Green, their business agent, appeared in the morning paper, announcing that not a single light would burn in Seattle, and that the telephone system, the newspapers and every enterprise depending on "juice" would cease to run.

### "No Exemptions."

To the question, "How about hospitals, where people may die for want of light," Green was stated to have replied, "No exemptions." The same answer was made to the question of the automatic fire alarm system. More than any other one event during the entire strike, this front-page report of Green's intentions aroused both fear and resentment, not only among outsiders, but within the ranks of organized labor as well.

The mayor, who had previously taken no sides, announced that city light should run, even if he had to bring in soldiers to run it. Appeals were made to the public for volunteers to run the city light plant. And meanwhile the general public, uncertain of the outcome, laid in supplies of oil lamps and candles.

The electricians took the ground that a complete tie-up would shorten the duration of the strike. In answer to this the city authorities stated that the shutting down of city power would shut off the water supply in West Seattle and on Queen Anne Hill; would mean the spoiling of large quantities of food in the cold storage warehouses, while the darkening of the streets would inevitably lead to disorder, and the shutting off of lights from the hospitals might mean many deaths.

## All Committees Much Concerned.

The various committees dealing with the strike were all deeply concerned. The Committee of Fifteen requested the electricians to allow enough electricity to operate the fire alarm system; they also appointed a committee of three to formulate a solution of the electrical supply problem, and called for a late night meeting to make final decision.

At the same time the conference committee of the Metal Trades, charged with the conduct of the original strike of the shipyard workers, called into conference the three men who had been appointed by the electrical workers to handle their part in the strike. At first the committee of electrical workers stood firm for a complete shut-down, but when it was evident that the representatives of the Metal Trades were much opposed they finally consented to allow exemptions if a committee on exemptions could be installed in the city light plant, with authority to state what parts of the system should be allowed to run.

## First Conference With Mayor.

At this point A. E. Miller, chairman of the conference committee, called up Mayor Hanson on the telephone and asked him to join the conference. The mayor came over at once to the Collins building and announced that city light and city water should not be interfered with. He refused to recognize any committe on exemptions, but finally, after a long discussion, consented to meet such a committee and take up with them, section by section, the various parts of the lighting system, in an effort to prove to them that no part of the system should be shut down. A committee of three went over to the mayor's office, but a deadlock occurred at once on the question of street lighting, which the committee of three refused to allow.

Upon this the Engineer's Union announced to the mayor

that if the electricians left they would operate enough of the plant to supply hospitals and other public needs.

## Midnight Meeting With Mayor.

All the various pieces of consultation and planning on the subject of city light, which had started spontaneously in different quarters as soon as the Green interview appeared in the paper, came to a head in the midnight session of the Committee of Fifteen, called the night before the strike at the Labor Temple. The subject under consideration had been recognized all day as the most serious problem which had yet arisen, involving questions of relations with the city government, as well as the relations between individual unions and the general strike committee. In addition to the Committee of Fifteen, representatives of the electrical workers, the engineers and the conference committee of the Metal Trades were present.

The mayor, invited at a late hour by telephone, appeared shortly after midnight, and reiterated his statement that city water and city light must run. He said that he would prefer to run them with the union men, but that he would run them with soldiers from Camp Lewis or Bremerton if necessary. He added that he did not care about the other public utilities. The car line was not essential; in fact, he might even have the men given a lay-off so that they would not lose their civil service rating. But light and water, he stated, were needed for public health and public peace.

The mayor finally left at 3:30, and the Committee of Fifteen voted, after his withdrawal, to order the electricians back to run the city light plant, with the exception of the commercial service. A committee was appointed to announce this decision to the mayor, who, when called on the telephone, said he would be in his office at 8:30 in the morning.

In the end the city light plant ran without interruption, as far as was apparent to the citizens of Seattle. A month after the strike a member of the strike committtee of the electrical workers, when asked how this happened, made the following statement: "The matter of city light was a bluff between Green and Hanson. We had the operators in the sub-station only partially organized and could not have called them off if we had wanted to. We could and did call out the line men and meter men, who responded. But their absence made little immediate difference, and they went back before the strike was called off. The engineers were in a better position than we to close down city light, but this they declined to do, and only called off their men after it was sure that the city light could run anyway."

It was perhaps a rather inglorious explanation of a matter which caused so vital a stir. But, however much bluffing entered into it, a few facts stand out as interesting. First, that the executive committee of the srike, believing that it had the power to shut down city light, ordered that all city lights should run except the commercial power. This is important because it shows the temper of mind in the executive committee. Second, that up to the time when the strike was actually in full swing, Mayor Hanson was not the "revolution quelling strong man" that he has been announced as since, but a worried and busy mayor, not sufficiently familiar with the details of his light plant to call Green's bluff and endeavoring for many hours in midnight session to argue the strike committee into saving city light from serious inconvenience. It is perhaps not so thrilling a picture, but it is a more human one.

## ON THURSDAY AT 10 A.M.

The strike had been called for Thursday at 10 a.m. At that hour the street cars began to pull for the barns, the workers all over the town left their tasks, and the strike was on. Some crafts had stopped before the hour set. The cooks had been on strike all the morning, and were working hard preparing food for the strikers' kitchens.

According to the business press of the city, Seattle was "prostrate." According to an admission in the morning paper, "not a wheel turned in any of the industries employing organized labor or in many others which did not employ organized labor."

### Regular A. F. of L. Strike.

Some 60,000 men were out on strike. The strike was called, organized and carried through by the regular unions of the American Federation of Labor, acting regularly by votes of the rank and file. It was a strike in the calling and conduct of which, contrary to statements made widely throughout the country, no I. W. W. had any part.

Yet the strike affected more organizations than those in

the American Federation of Labor. Organizations of the I. W. W. also struck at once, and sent word that if any of their members proved unruly, they themselves would put them out of town and keep them out, as they intended to show the A. F. of L. that they could co-operate in a strike without causing disorder. Since no disorder of any kind occurred in Seattle in connection with the strike, it will be seen that they were as good as their word.

## Japanese Strike.

Among the other organizations striking were the Japanese barbers and restaurant workers. In fact, all the Japanese section of the city was closed up tight and remained closed. The response of the Japanese workers added greatly to the good feeling between them and the American workers, and they were invited to send delegates to the general strike committee, but without vote.

As has been said, the strike was from the beginning to the end under the firm control of duly elected representatives of regular A. F. of L. unions, and any other organizations which had also struck had no voice or vote in its conduct.[5]

## Many Individual Strikers.

How many individuals, unconnected with any organizations, struck just out of a feeling of fellowship for labor will never be known. But there were many of them. In the nature of the case, word is only heard of a few. An elevator boy in an office building of conservative business men, two laborers working for a landscape gardener, and hundreds of other sporadic cases of this type occurred. Persons of this kind had

[5] NOTE—The rumor that the I. W. W. had a leading part in the strike can be traced perhaps to the general desire on the part of the press to discredit the strikers, and partly to the fact that certain dodgers were published and distributed during the strike calling on the workers to emulate Russia, which seemed to be of I. W. W. origin. In the excited minds of business men untrained to discriminate in matters affecting labor, this was supposed to be part of the authorized "strike propaganda." It caused no excitement in the ranks of the workers, as they are accustomed to seeing such propaganda put forth by radical groups, and as they are also accustomed to distinguishing statements authorized by their organizations from totally unauthorized leaflets.

not even a union to protect them in securing their jobs again, yet they struck out of a feeling of sympathy, and a desire to be "a part of the general strike of Seattle's labor movement."

## Second Meeting of General Strike Committee.

Two hours after the strike began the general strike committee held its second full meeting, Thursday at noon. An avalance of business descended upon it. For three and a half days the Executive Committee of Fifteen had been the authority in strike matters. Now at last the strike was on and the general committee met to survey its handiwork.

The greater part of the first session was devoted to attempting to unwind the tangles of the city light situation, which is elsewhere described.

## Exemptions Referred to Executive Committee.

The regular grist of request for exemptions began to the general committee to come in to the general committee, but was soon found to be too burdensome for so large a body to deal with. It was finally directed that all exemptions should go first to the Committee of Fifteen.

A few typical instances of the type of exemption asked for from the general strike committee are as follows:

Seattle Renton Southern asks permission for transportation in carrying mail. All motions made on this were tabled.

Co-operative Market says that the milk supply is short, and the farmers have offered to deliver it if permission is granted. This was referred to the joint council of teamsters.

The longshoremen ask permission to handle government mails, custom and baggage. Permission is given for the mails and customs.

The postal clerks ask that enough taxi company's cars be exempted to give them transportation over the city. This was refused.

The icemen ask for exemption in transporting ice to hospitals and drug stores. This was referred to the joint council of teamsters.

Meanwhile words of greeting and help came from nearby towns. Tacoma had called her strike at the same time as Seattle. Various unions in Renton also struck. Everett sent a delegation to state that if any work was sent to Everett from Seattle they would call out their men. The mine workers from Taylor offered financial assistance.

The Renton mine workers, being affiliated with the Seattle Central Labor Council, struck. Other organizations of mine workers sent good wishes and the statement that they stood ready to strike if the movement was made statewide.

Meanwhile the Committee of Fifteen had been called upon for additional minor exemptions. They granted permission to the street car men to appoint six of their watchmen for the car barns. They gave permits to the plumbers and steamfitters for seven men to act in emergencies only under the direction of the Plumbers' Union. These details are of particular interest in showing the closeness with which the city was tied up, and the inevitable result in placing power in the hands of the strike committee over many aspects of the city's life.

## I. W. W. Cards Recognized for Meals.

On Friday morning a new issue came before the general strike committee. A committee from the Transport Workers, an I. W. W. organization, appeared to protest because their "red cards" were not recognized at the strikers' commissaries. At these eating houses the general public paid 35 cents, while men with union cards were admitted for 25.

The general strike committee voted that all union cards, regardless of affiliation, should be recognized in the eating places.

This instance of a tendency to cut across the barriers that existed before the strike also came out in discussion concerning the Japanese workers, who had struck in unison with the Americans. After much discussion between those who wished to offer the Japanese full representation on the general strike committee and those who wished only to send a committee to confer with them, it was finally decided to invite them to have seats in the general strike committee, but without vote.

## The Mayor Makes Demands.

Twenty-four hours after the strike began came the preemptory demand of the mayor that the strike be called off. It was perhaps the very completeness and success of the strike, together with the alarm of the business men, that brought him to take this aggressive attitude.

At all events, Mayor Hanson, who 36 hours before had

spent long hours conferring with the Committee of Fifteen regarding the city light, suddenly adopted a different position. He issued a proclamation to the people announcing that he had plenty of soldiers to maintain order; he sent word out by the United Press throughout the country that he was putting down an attempted Bolshevik revolution. And he sent word to the general strike committee that he wished at once to send their representatives.

To these representatives he declared that unless the strike was at once called off he would reopen all industries, using soldiers and declaring martial law if necessary. The time first fixed by the mayor was Friday at noon, but as it was noon before his communication finally reached the general strike committee he deferred the hour till 8 o'clock Saturday morning.

Already there were members of the committee who had been from the beginning in favor of a limited strike. But, according to the statements of committee members, this action of the mayor's solidified resistance. This view of the mayor's intrusion was given by Ben Nauman the following Wednesday at the Central Labor Council:

"Ole attempted to call the strike off at noon of Friday, and said that if we didn't do it he'd declare martial law. Then he said that unless we declared the strike off Saturday morning he'd declare martial law. We didn't declare it off, and Ole didn't declare martial law. Finally, he made many of the members of the committee so mad we couldn't declare it off ourselves."

## THE STRIKE CALLED OFF.

The picture of the calling off of the strike given by Mayor Hanson to the press of the country was dramatic enough. It is significant that it was not printed in the press of Seattle; it was not for "home consumption."

According to the accounts that went around the country, "the Central Labor Council, which is composed of the heads of the various unions, is controlled by the radicals.—Labor tried to run everything.

"We refused to ask exemptions from any one. The seat of government is at the City Hall. We organized 1,000 extra police, armed with rifles and shotguns, and told them to shoot on sight anyone causing disorder. We got ready for business.

"I issued a proclamation that all life and property would

be protected; that all business should go on as usual. And this morning our municipal street cars, light, power plants, water, etc., were running full blast.

"There was an attempted revolution. It never got to first base."

## Lost His Head.

This was the account of the Seattle strike sent out by the mayor of Seattle. Later, the president of the Port of Seattle said of Mayor Hanson, in a speech in Washington: "He is a pretty good fellow, and a mighty good advertiser, but he lost his head completely. He spent $50,000 of the taxpayers' money for extra policemen which was never needed. Tacoma spent no money and Tacoma had no trouble.

## How the Mayor Shifted His Ground.

It was not until the second day of the strike that Mayor Hanson under the pressure of business men finally took sides against the strikers.

Two days before the strike he took James Duncan, secretary of the Central Labor Council, and Charles Doyle, its business agent, out to lunch at Rippe's Cafe, paid for the dinner, and talked over the coming strike in a most friendly manner.

"Now boys," he said, "I want my street lights and my water, and the hospitals. That's all. I don't care about the car line or the other departments."

Perhaps it was the very completeness of the strike, or perhaps the pressure from meetings of business men. Or perhaps the tilt with Green over city light had angered and unnerved him. At any event, on Friday morning he issued a proclamation to the citizens, announcing that he had 1500 policemen and 1500 soldiers and calling upon the citizens to go about their business as usual.

He also called up James Duncan and said that the strike must close by noon. When Mr. Duncan replied that this was impossible, he asked that the Executive Committee of the Strike should come to his office at once. He was told that this message would be transmitted but that the committee was very busy and might be unable to come as a body.

The Executive Committee sent a sub-committee of six members to confer with the mayor. The mayor urged them to call off the strike, saying that if the matter could be settled locally they had won "hands down," but that Mr. Piez must be seen, and that "that group" had already double-crossed the city and were probably double-crossing the shipyard workers. He offered that if the strike were at once called off, to "lock up his desk and go to Washington with them, to try to get the wages of the lower men raised," a demand which he declared to be just.

In case the strike were not called off, he threatened martial law. The committee replied that they were not afraid of martial law, and if that was the mayor's next card, they had still other cards themselves. The gas workers had not been ordered out, and the mine workers of the state were ready to go out.

"If you want the strike to spread, declare martial law," they said. "And furthermore, you don't know how the boys in Camp Lewis will stand on the question of strikebreaking."

"By G——," said the mayor, "if they are not loyal I want to know it."

"If you want to see the streets of Seattle run with blood to satisfy your curiosity about loyalty, we don't," replied Mr. Duncan.

The committee suggested that if they could meet with representatives of the Conciliation Board, the latter might be able to present some offer that they could make to the men as a reason for going back. Consequently the mayor called J. W. Spangler, a banker, and Rev. M. A. Matthews, down to the office, as representing a group of business and civic organizations. Mr. Spangler said that he must report to "his people;" a further conference was then set for 8 o'clock in the evening.

## Tone Seems Changed.

When Mr. Spangler returned that evening, his tone had changed. Whereas in the afternoon he had called the labor men by their first names, he was now very short, stating that "his people" took the stand that this was a revolution and they would not deal with revolutionists. He admitted that he himself was "not fooled" and did not consider it a revolution, but that "his people" did; and that they refused to dicker in any way until the strike was called off.

"That's final, is it, Spangler?" said Hanson, and on being told that it was he said to the Strikers' Committee:

"Then that's all there is to it, boys."

From this time on the mayor definitely sided against the strikers. He threatened martial law; he issued his statement to the press of the country branding the strike a revolution.

The interpretation of his action given by the strikers since that time has been that he tried, like a good politician, to play both sides, but when it became necessary to choose, he sided with the business group.

After the strike was over, when employees of the city were being penalized for having taken part in it, and when officials of the Central Labor Council went to the mayor to intercede for the men, he remarked: "You think we couldn't run an open shop town here if we wanted to," clearly indicating that he had dropped his attitude of conciliation toward the Seattle labor movement for one of hostility.

## The Fateful Saturday Morning.

Many striking inaccuracies occur in the announcement made to the press of the country by Mayor Hanson. "We refused to ask exemptions from anyone" he proclaimed. The fact was that he had been conferring regarding exemptions for several days.

"I issued a proclamation and this morning all our municipal street cars, light, power plant, water, etc., were running full blast." The only effect of the mayor's proclamation was that seven cars began to run on the Municipal car line.

The water, power and lights had been running from the beginning. On Saturday morning, the time when the mayor called upon business to resume under his protection, business simply did not resume.

The main car lines of the city were not running. A picture taken of Second and Pike streets, one of the busiest corners of the city, at 9 o'clock on Saturday morning, shows a deserted city. Teamsters, trucks and autos were absent. The restaurants were closed.

## What Did Stop the Strike.

What did stop the strike, then, if the mayor's proclamation had so little effect. Pressure from international officers of unions, from executive committees of unions, from the "leaders" in the labor movement, even from those very leaders who are still called "Bolsheviki" by the undiscriminating press.

And, added to all these, the pressure upon the workers themselves, not of the loss of their own jobs, but of living in a city so tightly closed.

Saturday morning at 8 o'clock, the hour specified by the mayor for the reopening of industry, saw the General Strike still in full swing. The strike committees were still discussing exemptions, and sending delegates to other cities to explain the strike and ask for support.

But the Executive Committee of Fifteen was seriously considering a resolution for calling off the strike. It was realized that in some form or other the city would have to resume some activity soon. On Saturday afternoon this committee brought in to the General Strike Committee a resolution fixing Saturday night as the close of the strike. This had been passed by a vote of 13 to 1 in the Executive Committee, one member being absent and one voting against it.

The resolution follows:

WHEREAS; the unparalleled autocratic attitude of Charles E. Piez, General Manager of the Emergency Fleet Corporation, in refusing to permit the shipyard employers and employees of this community to enter into a mutually satisfactory agreement as to wages and working conditions (which would not add to the government cost one penny) so aroused the indignation of all unionists in Seattle as to cause them to express that indignation through the medium of a general strike; and

WHEREAS; it has been recognized that the objectives of such a strike would be extremely limited and consequently no good could be accomplished by continuing such strike indefinitely; and

WHEREAS; on the 7th day of February, 1919, the Executive Strike Committee was in session deliberating upon the advisability of calling off said strike on the ground that its object had been fully attained through the unprecedented demonstration of solidarity and the encouragement to the workers in other ship building centers to further co-operate; and

WHEREAS; the ill-advised, hysterical and inexcusable proclamation of Mayor Ole Hanson tremendously embarrassed the committee in carrying out its plans, by reason of the fact that it suggested coercion; and

WHEREAS; martial law having been suggested and threats made to throw the military forces of this nation in the balance on the side of the employing interests; and

WHEREAS; thirty thousand shipyard workers have been on strike for a period of sixteen days, and sixty-five thousand workers have been on strike for a period of three days with-

out so much as a fist fight or any other minor disturbance;
now, therefore be it

RESOLVED; that we recommend that the Executive Committee for the general strike, recommend that the general
strike, excepting the shipyard workers, be called off at 12
midnight, Saturday, February 8, with the understanding that
all persons, who went on strike return to their former positions, holding themselves in readiness to respond to another
call from the General Strike Committee in case of failure to
secure a satisfactory agreement of the Metal Trades' demands
within a reasonable length of time; and, be it further

RESOLVED; that Organized Labor of this community express to the Mayor, and all others, its deep regret at the
action taken, and announce as law abiding citizens they have
no fear of martial law or any other acts of intimidation used
by those presumed to represent the public, but who in reality
are representing only one class; and further be it

RESOLVED; that we take this opportunity of expressing
to the strikers our deep appreciation and admiration for the
splendid spirit and order maintained under the most trying
and aggravating circumstances.

## Not Yet Ready to Quit.

All afternoon and all night the discussion raged in the General Strike Committee.

Many of the most prominent men of the labor movement,
including the persons who have since been denounced by
Mayor Hanson as "leaders of revolution" argued most strongly in favor of ending the strike.

In spite of their arguments, however, after a discussion
which lasted until 4:12 in the morning, the voting of the
General Strike Committee showed such an overwhelming
defeat of the resolution that it was unanimously decided to
continue the strike. It was obvious that the Executive Committee of Fifteen and the old-timers in the labor movement
were more cautious than the larger committee just elected
from the rank and file.

But the break had already begun to appear. Whether the
recommendation of the Committee of Fifteen was merely a
wise forecast of what was about to happen, or whether their
action and the uncertainty about the closing of the strike gave
encouragement to the thought of returning, by Monday morning, when the General Strike Committee again met, several
unions had gone back to work, under orders from international officers or from their own executive committees, in

many cases hastily called and without full attendance. In no case is it recorded that this return was taken by the rank and file.

Most important of these unions were the Street Car Men and the Teamsters. The former reported that they had returned by order of their Executive Committee on recommendation of an international officer, but that they would come out again if called by the General Strike Committee.

The Teamsters had also returned on recommendation of the Joint Council of Teamsters, but the rank and file had called another meeting for Monday afternoon at which it was predicted that they would go out on strike again.

An incident in connection with the return of the Teamsters to work is enlightening, as it shows what results may happen through a minor personal friction. On Sunday evening Auditor Briggs, international officer of the Teamsters' Union, appeared before the Committee of Fifteen and stated that he had tried to gain the floor both in the Central Labor Council and at the General Strike Committee and had been denied admission. He stated that it was as a result of this attitude toward him (an A. F. of L. representative and an international officer) by the persons responsible for the strike that he had ordered the teamsters back, and that he might have acted differently if he had been treated by these bodies as the Committee of Fifteen had treated him.

## ROLL CALL ON MONDAY SHOWS SOME MISSING.

A few other scattering unions were found missing from their places when the General Strike Committee met on Monday morning. The Barbers had gone back, instructed thereto by a meeting of their Executive Committee.

At this meeting a member of the Lady Barbers was also present, arriving late, and through this fact some confusion arose, a few of the Lady Barbers going back to work without the knowledge of their officers. The majority, however, led by their own Executive Committee, remained out.

As a matter of fact all the women's unions showed a strong feeling of loyalty toward the strike, many of them outlasting the men of the same craft.

The Stereotypers were also back at work, reporting that they had been under severe pressure from their international officers, but had only gone back on the report made to them on Saturday night, that the strike was being called off.

The Auto Drivers, Bill Posters, Ice Cream Drivers, Milk Drivers were not present and were reported as having returned to work. Some of these organizations belonged to the Joint Council of Teamsters and were included in the general order that was issued by that body.

It was reported that the newsboys had been ordered back by a small meeting of their Executive Committee, at which not even a quorum was present, but that they were holding a general union meeting that evening to settle the question.

All other unions were still out on strike and many of them voted enthusiastically to remain "to the last ditch."

A few unions, while sticking to the strike, reported that it might involve them in great hardship. The Sailors' Union, for instance, felt that by striking they were placing the Seaman's bill in jeopardy. The Hotel Maids stated that, since they were a small union with much competition from non-union girls, they stood to lose their jobs.

At the end of the Monday morning session the Executive Committee of Fifteen again submitted a revised resolution, calling for all unions which had returned to work to go out on strike again, in order that all might return in a body the following day, Tuesday at noon. The resolution was passed almost at once by the General Strike Committee.

The voting was confined to the "allies" or sympathetic strikers, the shipyard workers not being granted a voice.

The text of the resolution was as follows:

WHEREAS, this strike committee now assembles in the midst of the general understanding of the true status of the general strike; and

WHEREAS, the Executive Committee is sufficiently satisfied that regardless of the ultimate action that the rank and file would take, the said committee is convinced that the rank and file did stand pat, and the stampede to return to work was not on the part of the rank and file, but rather on the part of their leaders.

(However, be it understood that this committee does not question the honesty of any of the representatives of the general movement.) Therefore, be it

RESOLVED, that the following action become effective at once, February 10, 1919:

That this strike committee advise all affiliated unions that have taken action to return their men to work, that said unions shall again call their men to respond immediately to the call of the rank and file until 12 noon February 11, 1919, and to then call this strike at a successful termination, and if developments should then make it necessary that the strike be continued, that further action should be referred to the rank and file exclusively.

In the evening the Teamsters reported that a meeting of the rank and file had unanimously voted to strike again till Tuesday noon in accordance with the recommendation of the General Strike Committee.

It was generally expected that the Street Car Men would also strike again, since they had reported on Sunday to the Committee of Fifteen that their Executive Committee had full power to call them out again, if it seemed needed in the interests of solidarity, and since they had reported on Monday to the General Strike Committee that they would go out again if called to do so by the General Strike Committee. It took, however, some hours to summon a meeting of the Street Car Men's Executive Committee, who were at work; and when they were called together, they stated that a meeting of the men to decide on the matter could not be held in time. Consequently the street car men did not come out again.

The meeting of Newsboys took a vote and decided to remain on strike till Tuesday noon. So also did the meeting of Auto Drivers.

It will be noticed that all cases in which the unions voted on the question were decided in favor of the request of the General Strike Committee, while all in which the Executive Committees or the International officers took action, were decided against the General Strike Committee.

This fact was apparent from the beginning of the strike to its close—that it was not a strike engineered by leaders, but one voted for, carried on, and kept up by that part of the rank and file that attends union meetings or takes part in referendum votes. The influence of recognized "leaders" was in every case on the side of greater caution and conservatism than was actually displayed.

## CONSTRUCTIVE ACTIVITIES OF STRIKE FEEDING THE PEOPLE.

Among the pieces of constructive organization carried on during the general strike were the supplying of milk to babies by the milk wagon drivers' union, the handling of hospital laundry by joint agreement between the laundry drivers, laundry workers, and laundry men; the feeding of strikers and many of the general public by the provision trades, and the maintaining of public peace by the Labor War Veteran Guard.

## Milk Stations for Babies.

The arrangements made by the laundry drivers and laundry workers for handling hospital laundry are related elsewhere. The milk wagon drivers at first attempted to make a similar type of agreement with the milk dealers or dairy owners. They worked out a plan for neighborhood milk stations all over the city, and for downtown depot stations from which delivery might be made to hospitals.

This plan was submitted to the employers. It was soon felt by the union that the employers were attempting to direct the operation of the plan in such a way as to gain credit themselves in relieving the milk situation of the city. Furthermore, the plan of the employers involved opening of downtown dairies only, which the union believed would leave thousands of babies, and especially of the poorer classes, unable to get milk.

The milk wagon drivers' union therefore withdrew from the attempt to work together with the employers and established through their own organization 35 neighborhood milk stations all over the city. The employers meantime combined together and operated one pasteurizing plant at which they themselves did the work, and from which they distributed milk to the various dairies in the city. For this distribution they applied for exemption of one truck, and the milk wagon drivers' union endorsed their request to the general strike committee. The hospitals were required to come to these dairies for their supply of milk.

## Arranged All Over Town.

The dairies thus supplied by the milk dealers were only eleven in number, so located that it would have been impossible for the mothers of Seattle to secure milk unless they owned automobiles. The milk wagon drivers therefore chose 35 locations properly spaced throughout the city, secured the use of space in stores, and proceeded to set up neighborhood milk stations.

The stations were announced as open from 9 to 2, but the milk was always gone before noon. The amount handled increased as the days went on until about 3,000 gallons were handled in the various stations The first day the supply ran noticeably short, especially in some parts of town, but by the third day of the strike the irregularities were ironed out and the supply was more adjusted to the need.

The milk was brought into town by the small private dairymen, whose dairies were near the city and had consequently been thoroughly inspected by the board of health. It was raw milk, pure, and authorized for babies. Each dairyman was given the address of a different milk station and made his deliveries direct. The over-supply at some and the under-supply at others was changed the second day by a small amount of delivery handled by the milk drivers' union between stations.

## Union Loses Money.

The men at the milk stations gave their services free, and as a result the union stood to make a small profit on their activities in spite of the loss in efficiency which always occurs when a new system is put into effect.

But this gain was more than offset by heavy losses in connection with the supply of milk to the strikers' eating places. The estimate of the number of people who would have to be fed was much heavier than the number of those who actually came, some 3,000 gallons of milk ordered for these kitchens were never required, and as the milk drivers' union had contracted for this with the farmers they stood the loss. The milk came from distant farms and could not have been transferred to the milk stations, because it was uninspected and not usable for babies. A loss of $700 was therefore sustained by the milk wagon drivers' union as part of their contribution toward meeting an emergency in the city of Seattle.

The union has, however, gained in an understanding of the milk problems of a large city, and in ability to do the teamwork of co-operation whenever, in the inevitable development of industry, it is seen desirable to handle the milk of the city as a co-operative unit.

## Feeding the Strikers.

The heaviest and most complicated job of organization fell to the provision trades, charged with feeding the strikers and such members of the general public as desired to patronize the strikers' commissaries.

The restaurants of Seattle are almost 100 per cent organized. When the vote of the cooks and assistants, the waiters and waitresses threatened to close them down the restaurant owners took the matter philosophically. Many of them offered their kitchens to the cooks for the preparation of food for the strikers and some offered their entire establishments to the unions for the duration of the strike.

It was realized that the feeding of people through a few large restaurants would be much simpler and less expensive than feeding them in specially arranged halls. But for various reasons the offer of the restaurant owners were refused. Chief among the reasons was the fact that to take a few restaurants and omit others would be unfair to the owners who were omitted.

One restaurant owner said to the union: "Sure, take my whole place and run it. When you boys get through I'll have some business." The truth behind this remark made it impractical to take some restaurants and leave others. In a few of the outlying districts, where it could be done without discrimination, an occasional restaurant was taken over in its entirety for the duration of the strike, with the consent of the owners.

## Open Twenty-one Eating Places.

Some 21 eating places were opened in various parts of the city. The food was cooked in large kitchens, the use of which was donated by various restaurants, and was then transported to various halls where it was served, cafeteria style. The original plan called for each person to bring his own "eating utensils," but this caused so much dissatisfaction that large quantities of paper plates and pasteboard cups were bought, together with small quantities of dishes, tin cups, knives, forks, and spoons.

The trials of the commissary department were many. It had to organize the supply of a large but quite unknown number of meals. It faced difficulties in securing provisions, in transporting cooked materials, in bringing the volunteer cooks to and from their homes. Each of these problems depended on the working together of people who had not had time to become welded into a complete organization.

Delay was experienced on the opening day from many

causes. Some of the kitchens promised were withdrawn at the last moment, and the cooks and provisions sent there had to be taken elsewhere. The arrangements for transporting cooked food from one place to another did not work perfectly. In many places the first meal of the day was not ready until 4 or 5 in the afternoon. When it arrived there was only the smallest possible supply of dishes, and the patrons had not noticed the order that each must bring his own. There was no corps of dishwashers to keep up the meager supply of dishes until the waitresses' union, assisted by patrons, leaped into the breach and organized this very necessary branch of service.

Many of the strikers had been without food all day, as the restaurants had not been open for breakfast. Consequently on the first day there was a certain amount of inevitable grumbling from hungry men. By the second day, however, the difficulties were much reduced and meals began to appear with regularity.

## Zeal and Sacrifice Under Difficulties.

The amount of zeal and sacrifice of many of the cooks deserves special mention. It was expected that they would be taken to and from their work by the auto drivers' union, but these arrangements did not always work at first, and men who had labored 12 to 14 hours at the hardest kind of work sometimes found themselves faced with a five-mile walk home, and another day on the morrow of the same kind of labor.

Through all these difficulties the commissary committee, consisting of William Hinkley, Bert Royce, William Wilkening, and Harry Nestor, with the special assistance of Fred Leandoys, business agent of the cooks, made persistent headway. They had greatly overestimated the number of people that would need to be fed, for many people stayed at home for one or all meals. In the end they were serving 30,000 meals a day with little trouble or friction. It was a task the magnitude of which only those can appreciate who have attempted to feed even a thousand people with a completely new organization of personnel and facilities.

There was some confusion as to the price of meals. It was at first reported that union men should pay 25 cents a meal, and the general public 35 cents. Different modifications took place in this order, sometimes without reaching all the eating houses. On the final day the price was 25 cents to everyone.

This covered a full and very substantial meal of beef stew, with large chunks of beef and whole potatoes and carrots, spaghetti with tomato sauce, bread and coffee. On some days the menu was varied by steak, or pot roast and gravy, in place of the stew. It will be seen that the diet chosen was by no means an inexpensive one, especially as every person was allowed as much as he could eat.

## Money Loss of Kitchens.

After the strike was over and the committee of the Metal Trades who had guaranteed the bills added up their accounts they found a loss of some $6,000 to $7,000.

Nearly $1,000 worth of bread was left on the last day and had to be given away. Over $1,000 had been spent on equipment, and $1,500 for trucks to haul the food from place to place. In addition to this the first day of the strike showed a loss, for this day alone, of over $5,000, due to the difficulties of getting started and the spoiling of so much food which soured before the next day. Much of this was due to over-estimating the number of meals that would be necessary, and much of it to the fact that a few hours was not long enough to get the machinery of transportation and operation into running order.

"If the strike had lasted four or five days more," states Bert Swain, secretary of the Metal Trades Council, "we would have come out even, and after that, reduced the price. Another time there should be some one caterer at the head for the buying of supplies, and some one person in charge of transportation. We did not realize how large a feature of the job the transportation work would be."

## PRESERVING THE PEACE.

It was the universal testimony that never had a strike been carried on so peacefully as the Seattle general strike. "Sixty thousand men out and not even a fist-fight" was the way one labor group expressed it.

The city was far more orderly than under ordinary conditions. The general police courts arrests sank to 32 on the first day of the strike, 18 on the second, and 30 on the Monday morning report for Saturday and Sunday. Not one of these arrests was due in any way to the strike.

Maj. Gen. Morrison, who came over from Camp Lewis

in charge of troops, told the strikers' committee which called upon him that in 40 years of military experience he had not seen so quiet and orderly a city.

## Reasons Given for Order.

What was the reason for this order? Mayor Hanson says it was secured by his extra police. "They knew we meant business and they started no trouble," he declared, in the pronouncement sent broadcast throughout the country.

"While the business men and the authorities prepared for riots, labor organized for peace." Such is the statement of a reporter from a nearby city, who came to get a first-hand view.

Robert Bridges, president of the port of Seattle, wrote a letter to the Central Labor Council in which he declared that "it was the members' of organized labor who kept order during the strike. To them and to no one else belongs the credit.

"It was a great spiritual victory for organized labor," he declares, "a victory that cannot be taken from you notwithstanding many assertions that others than yourselves were responsible for preserving that peace and order."

He alluded to the show of force and the calling in of the troops as "an aggravation" rather than a help, tending to give labor the impression that violence was expected from them. "Notwithstanding these extraordinary precautions, which were an extreme aggravation to them, the members of organized labor restrained themselves and went about their way quietly and peaceably. I sincerely hope that this will establish a precedent for future strikes."

## The View of the Business World.

There is no doubt that large numbers of business men in Seattle believed the view that has been sent broadcast throughout the nation, that it was the action of Mayor Hanson in bringing in machine guns, increasing the police force by six hundred men, and deputizing some 2,400 citizens of all varieties with the right to carry guns, that stopped a bloody and violent revolution in the Northwest. This is the time-honored method of the authorities, and the business world as a class believes in it, and expects machine guns to prevent violence.

## Bitterness Among Business Men.

Bitterness was great in the business world. Some reasons why it was greater among them than among the strikers may be touched upon later; here we will merely quote the statement made to the writer by a prominent public official who was mixing much with both sides: "It is only necessary to mix among the business men of this city and then among the strikers, and hear their remarks, or even watch their faces, to find out which ones have murder in their hearts!"

It was a commonly noticed fact that women on trains running into Seattle, or in clubs, or in gatherings of other kinds, expressed the view that those strikers ought to be stood up against a wall and shot down." Two weeks after the strike, a prominent business man remarked to friends: "If that strike had lasted a few days longer, there would have been some people hung." The expectation, even the desire, to see the streets run with blood, was heard constantly in business offices.

"I had four hundred requests for guns," said one proprietor of a hardware store, "and not one from a laboring man, as far as I could judge them."

Two thousand four hundred citizens, according to the mayor's statement, were given authority to use stars and guns. The process by which this authority was secured is thus described by two young men who were deputized:

"We went into an office and held up our hands and someone mumbled some oath or other and they pinned a star on us and turned us loose."

One responsible business man who secured a star in order to "protect his property" relates overhearing two "young kids" who had just been deputized, and who were openly exulting in the hope of "potting a striker."

## Soldiers Brought In.

In addition to the armed men thus turned loose somewhat irresponsibly in the city's streets, soldiers were brought over from Camp Lewis. These were, however, hardly seen at all by the citizens, as they did not appear on the streets in any numbers.

It was fortunate for the city of Seattle that the soldiers came under the charge of a man like Maj. General Morrison.

Vested, in the absence of President Wilson from our shores, with the right to declare martial law if he deemed it necessary, he appeared to wish to conduct himself in such a manner as to bring no censure from the president for hasty action. To a committee of strikers who called upon him to ask about the mayor's threat of martial law he replied that if any martial law was necessary, he himself would declare it, and it would be no bluff when he declared it.

Two facts deserve comment in connection with the calling in of the soldiers. One is that the high pile of "literature" about the strike which had been furnished Maj. Gen. Morrison to give him "information" contained not a single page of authentic statement from the strikers.

Denunciations in untempered language from small business sheets, together with unauthorized dodgers, some of which seemed to come from the I. W. W., were there in abundance. The whole collection tended to foster a belief in the revolutionary character of the strike. But not one single copy of the official announcements published by the strike committees; and not a copy of the *Union Record* or the strike bulletin, of which over 100,000 had been sent broadcast. The major general did not even know of the existence of the *Union Record*, the official organ of the Central Labor Council, and the paper which has the largest circulation of any newspaper in the Northwest. Who compiled the collection of "information" for him is not known, but its intent was obvious.

A second interesting fact is that when the writer of this history called upon the successor of Maj. Gen. Morrison, to secure information regarding the calling in of the troops such information was not available. The officer in charge stated that he was not authorized to inform the people of Seattle either the number of men sent over, nor at whose request or order they had been sent, nor for what purpose they were in the city, whether to guard government property or to give general aid in case of trouble. It thus appears that military authorities may be quartered in an American city, and the people of that city be denied the right to know at the time or afterward for what purpose or at whose request they have come and what they propose to do.

## Labor Organizes for Order.

Meanwhile the strikers "organized for peace and order." They realized that they had nothing to gain and everything to lose by a riot in the streets. The tone of the editorial comment in the Strike Bulletin and the *Union Record,* both before the strike and after, shows a marked absence of bitterness and a prevalence of good humor.

"A machine gun may be a good argument, but it does mighty little execution where there are no crowds" was one little squib intended to discourage the forming of large groups in the streets.

"Wild rumors are floating around. Be careful how you believe them. The worst of these tales yesterday was that the strikers had blown up the city water dam. Whoever started this is responsible for much unnecessary mental anguish. The strikers are not blowing up anything." So runs another of the "Strike Notes."

"Keep quiet. Let the other fellow do the quarreling," was another slogan passed around.

The Strike Bulletin commented favorably on the use of public libraries which had increased with a tremendous bound during the strike, and urged small community sings and recreational gatherings for the purpose of "making the most of your leisure time." And it ended: "This is fine weather for a vacation, anyway."

Editorials on "Keep Smiling" poked gentle fun at the self-important new youthful deputies who pushed their way through crowds at the Labor Temple, and urged the workers to remember that "when you were 18 you thought you ran the world," and not to grow angry at the youths.

## Labor's War Veterans.

In addition to this constant stream of propaganda in the interests of quietness and order, a group of some 300 union men who had seen service in the U. S. army or navy were organized into Labor's War Veterans. F. A. Rust, head of the Seattle Labor Temple Association, an old and tried and rather conservative member of organized labor, was at the head.

In an interview with the mayor before the strike, Mr. Rust was told that he could have his men deputized and given police authority if they would come down and be sworn in. He refused this suggestion.

"We think it will reassure the public to know," he said, "that we have no guns. We know that we can keep order in our own ranks without the use of force. If there is any shooting done, it will not be by us."

## "We Have No Guns"

Scrawled across the blackboard at one of the headquarters of the War Veterans Guard ran the words: "The purpose of this organization is to preserve law and order without the use of force. No volunteer will have any police power or be allowed to carry weapons of any sort, but to use persuasion only. Keep clear of arguments about the strike and discourage others from them."

The method of dispersing crowds was thus described by one of the volunteers: "I would just go in," he said, "and say: 'Brother workingmen, this is for your own good. We mustn't have crowds that can be used as an excuse to start any trouble.' And they would answer: 'You're right, brother,' and begin to scatter."

This was the method used in dispersing the crowd that gathered when the first unsuccessful attempt was made to start the municipal car line. One of the guards reporting on this stated that "the regular police didn't get in until we had the crowd moving, and then they came over swinging their sticks and saying 'get out of here.' "

## The "Shooting" Star.

One of the "aggravations" mentioned by Mr. Bridges as tending to provoke disturbance, but which failed to cause any trouble because of the methods used by the Labor's War Veterans Guard, was the action of the *Star*, a Scripps paper, which, until the advent of the *Union Record*, had been the largest paper in the Northwest. Its circulation by the time the strike occurred had been almost cut in two.

With the help of men who worked under the direct order of international officers, the *Star* published a small issue on the afternoon of the strike, and sent a boy to the postoffice corner to dispose of them. A large and somewhat irritated crowd gathered. A hurry call sent to the headquarters of the Labor Guard brought out several men who succeeded in quietly dispersing the crowd.

Then one of the Labor Guards talked to the boy, explaining what scabbing meant. The youth declared that he would stop if he could get back to the *Star* office, whereupon the

guard hailed a passing automobile belonging to a union man
and sent the boy with his papers to the paper that sent him
out.

On the following day the *Star* again printed its paper with
a cordon of police drawn up at both ends of the street. The
papers were passed out by police and were sent into the residence districts in machines full of armed guards. The strikers
made at no time any attempt to interfere. The episode seriously injured what remaining popularity the *Star* had with
the workers of Seattle. It has been alluded to in spontaneous
cartoon and comment, as the "shooting Star."

## A Permanent Gain.

The Labor War Veteran Guard was organized with two
headquarters, each with a chairman and secretary in charge
for eight-hour shifts day and night. The men in charge were
in every instance exceptional appearing individuals, the kind
one instinctively classes as "leaders of men." The groups acting under them were loyal labor men, most of whom could
have received from $5 to $6 a day as special police, if they
had acted under the police department instead of volunteering their service for labor. But they believed in the "big idea"
behind the Labor Guard, which one of them expressed thus:

"Instead of a police force with clubs, we need a department of public safety, whose officers will understand human
nature and use brains and not brawn in keeping order. The
people want to obey the law, if you explain it to them reasonably."

The Labor War Veteran Guard co-operated with the police
force and worked without friction with them. How long this
would have lasted cannot be estimated, since, of course, the
fundamental principles underlying the two groups are dis-
similar.

The Labor Guard is to become a permanent organization
in Seattle for the purpose of preserving order in labor's own
ranks, during strikes, parades, public meetings and similar
events.

## OUR OWN ACTIVITIES.

Some misunderstanding, intentional or otherwise, was
caused by the interpretation given by the daily press to the
editorial in the *Union Record* which spoke of "opening up

more and more activities under our own management." This was held to presage a violent overturning of government and a seizure by force of property in the city.

As a matter of fact, without disturbance or disorder, more and more activities in Seattle have opened under the management of labor; and the move in this direction seemed to be only a beginning. A month after the strike, when this was written, union after union is talking co-operative stores of various kinds.

These range from the simple desire to start a co-operative workshop in which members of the same union shall co-operate to produce—to more elaborate schemes for enlisting groups of unions in starting a department store. The barbers union is talking of a chain of co-operative barber shops. The jewelry workers have already opened a store on the Rochdale plan. The steamfitters and plumbers are carrying on a flourishing grocery business.

The interest in "our own activities" has been tremendously stimulated by the strike. Both money for starting movements and money for patronage come easily. The members of organized labor have had the experience of working together and they appear to want more of it.

Some of the unions, like the cooks, milk wagon drivers and laundry workers, have had the experience during the strike of co-operation on a large scale. These particular organizations are not announcing plans for co-operation at present, as their relations with their employers are satisfactory. But it is evident from the tone of discussion that the rank and file in these organizations feel a new sense of power to organize and manage activities of their own craft or industry. They are ready to use it, when occasion comes.

## Co-operative Markets Stimulated.

The Co-operative Meat Market grew greatly during the strike. It had three shifts of men working to supply the strikers' kitchens. On the first Friday in February, during the strike, this concern did a cash business of $6,257, including over $3,000 worth of meat bought by the strikers' kitchens. The contrast of this with the first Friday in January, when the cash business was $2,126, or with the entire month of January, when the business was $37,000, shows the big gain during the period of the strike.

How much of this gain will be permanent cannot be told.

Of course, the strikers' kitchens are no longer supplied, but the increase over the January sales, even after the strike terminated, is still noticeable. Some of this no doubt would have come through natural expansion, but the strike called attention more quickly.

The Co-operative Grocery (Rochdale plan) traces its sudden growth not only to the strike, but to a raid conducted on its office a week before the strike, during which the books were seized. Before that time, the business ranged from $250 to $500 a day; but the first Saturday after the raid a record of $1,100 was established. During the strike, the business was still nearly three times what it had been before the raid.

Membership in the grocery organization, which involves a $10 entrance fee, also increased 70 per cent during this period. Much interest started in outlying districts, and plans are now discussed for a large number of branch stores.

In Tacoma, the interest in Rochdale stores also reached a climax, resulting in the establishing of three such stores in a period of two weeks. At the same time, the Sheet Metal Workers' union opened a co-operative shop owned by their organization, and the auto-mechanics laid plans and raised money for an auto repair shop owned by the union, while the painters and decorators are getting a similar project under way.

## The Pipe Trades Grocery.

One of the most enthusiastic developments of the General Strike was the profitless grocery run by the steamfitters and plumbers. It was started to furnish provisions to strikers at wholesale cost plus the overhead cost of handling. Rent was secured free from the *Union Record*, striking steamfitters gave their time without charge, and the organization advanced a preliminary $1,500 to buy goods. On the first day the store was crowded with customers and has remained so ever since.

Then the steamfitters went into various unions and sold "grocery tickets," entitling the recipient to $5.00 worth of groceries. With receipts from these tickets, together with another $1,500 advanced from the organization treasury, and $2,100 from the plumbers, they had capital enough to buy out a $15,000 business on a prominent corner.

Already (a month after the strike) they are buying potatoes, eggs, butter, meats and milk direct from the farmers, and expect before long to get flour direct from the co-operative mill. They are doing a business of $1,800 per day. When the strike of the shipyard workers is over and the steamfitters and plumbers go back to work, those who are retained to care for the store will be paid wages. The plan is at present to pay $8.00 a day to everyone employed from the manager down, this being the wage demanded by their trades.

## Striking Against Their Own Plants.

Undoubtedly the business of the various union-owned activities in Seattle would have received a larger boost, if it had not been for the policy pursued by the strikers of "striking against their own plants." For when the capitalistically controlled industries of Seattle were shut down, no discrimination was shown by the strikers; the union-owned activities also took a vacation.

The underlying reasons for this were many. Among them is the fact that the workers, striking as crafts, were naturally in the position of employees, not owners, in each particular union-owned industry. To a janitor, the Labor Temple association was as much of an "employer of labor" as was the City-County building.

But the main reason was that the vast majority of the workers, not contemplating revolution, knew that after the strike they would still have to do business in a business world. And the standards of fairness in that world demanded that they should not unfairly favor one or two competing concerns, if they hoped to deal satisfactorily with both of them.

There was even talk of closing down the Co-operative Market, but the need for food prevailed over this idea. However, the Mutual Laundry shut down; the Labor Temple went without janitors, except for volunteers; and the *Union Record* stopped for a day and a half.

This shut-down caused more protest from the strikers than any other in the closing of industries. The *Union Record* was "their paper"; many of them hoped to see it sweep the others from the streets as the only paper issued. The craving for news, for printed matter of any kind connected with the strike, became very urgent. It was a need almost greater than for food.

The plant of the *Union Record*, under the direction of the Strike Committee with a volunteer force, published for free distribution a "Strike Bulletin," a small two-page sheet without advertisements, and with no telegraph news service except such as bore directly on the strike.

On the afternoon when it was given out, streets surrounding the *Union Record* office were jammed with a crowd of perhaps 5,000 people. Even the efforts of the Labor Guard were insufficient to keep them away.

But the Strike Bulletin served only to aggravate the desire for reading matter, and on Saturday, the third day of the strike, after the *Star* had disregarded the strike by sending out papers on wagons with armed police, and after the *Post-Intelligencer* had managed to issue a four-page sheet which was given away at its own doors, the General Strike Committee directed the *Union Record* to start printing again. At the same time, the General Strike Committee assumed full responsibility for the fact that the paper had not been published.

The grounds for closing down the *Union Record* are given by its editor, E. B. Ault, and board of directors, as follows:

"Since the strike was not revolutionary in intent, the conduct of the official organ of the Central Labor Council was a matter for careful consideration. The printing trades on the other papers had been asked and were expected to strike in concert with all the other trades. After the purposes of the general strike had been served these members expected to go back to work in the offices from which they had walked out, and the management of the *Union Record* felt that it would be unfair business practice to take advantage of their competitors by operating during the strike, and also felt that it would make it much harder for the printing trades to return to their work with continued amicable relations with their employers.

"Then, too, news is as much a part of public service as transportation, and since transportation was stopped news naturally should have been stopped in order that the community might know what labor solidarity really meant. The needs of the workers could be and were served by the issuance of a strike bulletin carrying all the essential developments of the day.

"The policy of the management of the paper was explained to the executive committee of the general strike committee and met with the aproval of that body. That it was justified has been proved by the fact that the circulation of the paper has increased tremendously since the strike, and by the further fact that the opponents of organized labor have not been able to point to any unfairness on our part in conducting the strike.

## THE AFTERMATH.

There were no arrests during the strike for any matters connected with the strike. There was, as the strikers liked to remark, "not even a fist-fight."

But no sooner was the strike over than the county authorities sent out and arrested thirty-nine members of the Industrial Workers of the World, on the charge of being "ringleaders of anarchy." Some of these arrests were accomplished by raiding the I. W. W. headquarters, and then stationing a plainclothesman in the office of the secretary to arrest all members as they came in to pay their dues. Most of the members were soon released, only a few of the more prominent being held.

The Socialist party headquarters was also raided and the Socialist candidate for the city council arrested. The Equity Printing Plant, a co-operative printing establishment, the stock of which is owned by various organizations of workers and many individual workers, was raided, its manager arrested and the plant closed down. Later the plant was allowed to reopen, for eight hours daily, under the constant surveillance of policemen. The policemen opened the plant in the morning, locked it up at night, and supervised its operation during the day. A marked falling off in business was stated to be the result.

The cause given for all these arrests was the passing out of leaflets during the strike, which were alleged to have been prepared by the I. W. W.s or radical Socialists and to have been printed at the Equity Printing Plant. Chief among these was a dodger entitled "Russia Did It," urging the workers to operate their own industries.

The arrested men had no connection with the Central Labor Council or with the General Strike. They claimed, however, that they were arrested because of a desire of the authorities to prosecute someone on account of the strike, and that they, being undefended by any union, were the easiest victims. They asked the Central Labor Council to come to their defense.

A committee of the Central Labor Council was appointed to investigate their case, and reported that in its opinion not one of the leaflets on which charges were passed gave any evidence of anarchy or desire for violence, but were rather socialistic in their teaching.

They alluded especially to the setting of a policeman in the Equity Printing Plant, together with the remark of the chief of police that he did this because "he got tired of what they were printing" and his further remark to a protesting committee that if any more committees came to see him he would close down the plant entirely.

Declaring that an "invasion of fundamental rights had taken place," through unlawful raids and arrests, they announced that "fundamental rights do not go by favor, and when they are denied to one they are denied to all."

While expressing their opposition to the I.W.W. as a dual organization, and urging workers everywhere, in the interests of solidarity, to join the regular labor movement, they yet recognized the existence in this case, of "one common enemy."

Their recommendation was adopted by a practically unanimous vote: "That the Central Labor Council immediately take up the defense of these men, in order that the fundamental rights involved in these cases which are necessary to our own existence, shall be preserved."

There the cases stand at present (March 6) with several workers, presumably members of the I.W.W., arrested on the charge of criminal anarchy in connection with the strike, and the Central Labor Council coming to their defense because "fundamental rights are involved."

## WON OR LOST?

From coast to coast the newspapers declared that the General Strike in Seattle was lost. The Seattle newspapers announced the same fact, declared that the workers were creeping back to work downcast, that they had lost their strike. The press then proceeded to offer them many bits of advice and admonition, chiefly that they must "clean house" at once, and get rid of their radical leaders.

But strange to say, except for an occasional note of regret, the workers of Seattle did not go back to work with the feeling that they had been beaten. They went smiling, like men who had gained something worth gaining, like men who had done a big job and done it well. The men went back, feeling that they had won the strike; although as yet there was no sign from Washington that Piez would relent on a single point.

They went back laughing at the suggestion that they "clean house of their radical leaders who had tried to make a Bolsheviki revolution." They knew quite well that these same leaders were the men who had counselled caution and moderation, who had urged them to fix a time limit, and had later urged a return before the individual unions should start back, one at a time. They knew that these "radical leaders" were really more conservative than the voting rank and file that goes to meetings; and they were amused at the attempts of the press to make them believe otherwise. They had chosen the strike themselves, and it had been a great experience.

Hardly a word of regret was heard from the men who had lost five days' pay for a cause. It was the men whose business had been hurt, the men who had expected riot and found none, who told them they had "failed."

So it is worth considering for a moment to what extent the Seattle General Strike was won—or lost?

## What Was the Strike For?

What did the workers expect to gain? What were they striking for?

It is easy once we have had an experience to analyze the complex motives that went into it. But reasoning and analysis cannot take place before there is an experience to learn from. There had never been a General Strike in this country. None of Seattle's workers had ever lived through one.

So it is not surprising that we should be able now to see the fact that many varied motives and reasons entered into the Seattle General Strike, and that we had not had the experience at the time to state to ourselves very clearly just what we wanted or expected.

Some were striking to gain a definite wage increase for their brother workers in the shipyards. Some few, a very few, were striking because they thought "The Revolution" was about to arrive. But the vast majority were striking "just for sympathy," just as a show of solidarity. The extent to which they were also moved, half-consciously, by the various forms of labor's upheaval going on throughout the world, cannot be estimated. Consciously perhaps, not very much;

but unconsciously and instinctively, a great deal. Strikes and upheavals were in the air.

## For a Definite Gain?

Those who struck for a definite aim—the raise of the wages in the shipyard, did not gain their aim. It is true that men were hurrying here from Washington, D. C., to look into matters. It is true that some gain may in the end be influenced by the strike. But the sympathetic strikers went back to work with Piez still interfering in the local situation.

Possibly one of the reasons they did not gain a definite end was that no end was stated quite definitely and simply enough. And perhaps one lesson that other cities may learn from the experience of Seattle is this: "If you are striking for a definite aim, and refusing to come back until you have gained it, make your aim so clear and simple that everyone in the city will know the one man on whom to bring pressure, and what one act to demand of him."

If the strikers had said: "We are remaining out until Mr. Piez definitely and publicly states that he will leave Seattle employers and employees alone to bargain together over their own affairs,"—if they had asked anything so simple as that it is quite possible that the worried business men and the general public of Seattle would have been led to concentrate their annoyance on Mr. Piez until he gave into this definite demand.

But what they were asking—a raise in wages in the shipyards—was not something which either Mr. Piez alone, or the Seattle shipyard owners alone, or the Seattle Chamber of Commerce alone could give them. It was something that demanded joint action by several different people.

And consequently the persons in the community who felt the ill effects of the general strike had no immediate outlet for their grievance. They felt that they were being annoyed and punished for something which was not their fault and about which they had the power to do nothing. This fact undoubtedly accentuated the feeling of bewildered bitterness in the business world.

They could see no constructive plan in the strike. They naturally jumped to thoughts of revolution and disorder.

## For Revolution?

Those workers, of whom there were probably few, who thought "the social revolution" was ready to start in Seattle, were also doomed to disappointment.

Probably hardly any of the so-called "leaders" accused by the press of trying to start Bolshevism in America, believed that the revolution was at hand. Such belief as there was occurred in isolated cases in the rank and file and was expressed by the disappointed youthful cry of the boy in the Newsboys' Union: "I thought we were going to get the industries."

The men who had been longer in Seattle's labor movement, even those among them who look forward to "the revolution" ultimately, were quite certain that it was not coming now. They knew that it was not coming because the majority of Seattle's workers did not have the intentions or the past experience on which revolution is built.

And yet, while no revolution occurred and none was intended, the workers of Seattle feel themselves, because of their experience, in the position of men who know the steps by which an industrial revolution occurs.

An editorial in the *Union Record*, two weeks after the strike, discusses the workers' government just arising in Belfast, and draws comparison with the Seattle general strike. "They are singularly alike in nature. Quiet mass action, the tying up of industry, the granting of exemptions, until gradually the main activities of the city are being handled by the strike committee.

"Apparently in all cases there is the same singular lack of violence which we noticed here. The violence comes, not with the shifting of power, but when the 'counter-revolutionaries' try to regain the power which inevitably and almost without their knowing it passed from their grasp. Violence would have come in Seattle, if it had come, not from the workers, but from attempts by armed opponents of the strike to break down the authority of the strike committee over its own members.

"We had no violence in Seattle and no revolution. That fact should prove that neither the strike committee nor the rank and file of the workers ever intended revolution.

"But our experience, meantime, will help us understand the way in which events are occurring in other communities all over the world, where a general strike, not being called off, slips gradually into the direction of more and more affairs by the strike committee, until the business group, feeling their old prestige slipping, turns suddenly to violence, and there comes the test of force."

## TO EXPRESS SOLIDARITY?

We come then to the last of the reasons entering into the general strike—the reason which was the simplest and the most important. The vast majority struck to express solidarity. And they succeeded beyond their expectations.

They saw the labor movement come out almost as one man and tie up the industries of the city. They saw the Japanese and the I.W.W.s and many individual workers join in the strike, and they responded with a glow of appreciation. They saw garbage wagons and laundry wagons going along the streets marked "exempt by strike committee." They saw the attention of the whole continent turned on Mr. Piez and the Seattle shipyards.

They learned a great deal more than they expected to learn—more than anyone in Seattle knew before. They learned how a city is taken apart and put together again. They learned what it meant to supply milk to the babies of the city; to feed 30,000 people with a brand-new organization. They came close for the first time in their lives "to the problems of management."

They went back proud of themselves for the way they had come out; proud of themselves for the way they had kept order under provocation; glad to have gained so much education with so little comparative suffering; glad to have worked shoulder to shoulder with their fellow unionists on a lot of big problems; and a bit relieved, to tell the truth, that no one had been raided, no one shot and that the labor movement of Seattle was still "going strong." For they were quite aware that they had held in their hands a weapon which might have exploded in any one of a dozen different directions. They were glad to find themselves able to use it, to examine it and to lay it down without any premature explosions.

And that is why they went back from the "glorious vacation" feeling that they had won. Not perhaps exactly the things they had set out to win, but something better.

At any event, whether this be the explanation or not, the

fact remains that the workers went back, most of them, not feeling defeated, but feeling quite reasonably successful, glad they had struck, equally glad to call it off, and especially glad to think that their experience would now be of use to the entire labor movement of the country as it makes its plans for the Mooney general strike, by giving the necessary information of just what happens in a community when a general strike occurs, what problems arise, and how one city met them.

And, for the giving of this needed knowledge and education, the labor movement of Seattle rejoices to know that both its successes and its mistakes will be of equal advantage to the labor movement of the country.

## THEY CAN'T UNDERSTAND
By Anise (in the *Seattle Union Record*, the Labor Daily.)

What scares them most is
That NOTHING HAPPENS!
They are ready
For DISTURBANCES.
They have machine guns
And soldiers,
But this SMILING SILENCE
Is uncanny.
The business men
Don't understand
That sort of weapon.
It comes
From a DIFFERENT WORLD
Than the world THEY live in.
It is really funny
And a bit pathetic
To see how worried
And MAD
The business men are getting.
What meetings they hold,
What WILD RUMORS
They use
To keep themselves
STIRRED UP.
Yet MOST of them
Might be real pleasant
HUMAN BEINGS
Except that life
Has separated them
Too much from common folks.
It is the SYSTEM

Of industry
That makes them sullen
And SUSPICIOUS of us,
Not any NATURAL depravity.
It is the system
That trains them to believe
In the words of our
Beloved Ole,
That they can bring in
Enough ARMED FORCE
To operate our industries.
But how many
MACHINE GUNS
Will it take to cook
ONE MEAL?
It is your SMILE
That is UPSETTING
Their reliance
On ARTILLERY, brother!
It is the garbage wagons
That go along the street
Marked "EXEMPT
By STRIKE COMMITTEE."
It is the milk stations
That are getting better daily,
And the three hundred
WAR Veterans of Labor
Handling the crowds
WITHOUT GUNS,
For these things speak
Of a NEW POWER.
And a NEW WORLD
That they do not feel
At HOME in.

# Soviets and Factory Committees in the Russian Revolution

### peter rachleff

The developmental possibilities of the Russian Revolution of 1917–1921 were determined not by the conceptions of contending political organizations, but by the aims and capacities of the social groups involved. While the entire population in revolt shared the political goal of the abolition of czarist despotism, the different social classes and groups within it had distinctly different economic wants. The tiny bourgeoisie was naturally interested in conditions making possible the expansion of Russian capital. The peasants, the overwhelming majority, forced to work the fields of the large landowners and to pay exorbitant rents for tiny plots of land, desired the expropriation of the large estates and the establishment of a system of small, privately owned farms. On the other hand, the workers, small in number and concentrated in the urban areas of European Russia, were confronted by low wages, economic insecurity, and terrible working conditions, problems which called for some form of socialization of industry and an ambiguous "workers' control" of production.

These goals were mutually incompatible. Aside from the obvious conflict between workers and bourgeoisie, a capitalistically organized agricultural sector could not coexist with a smaller socialized industrial sector. Because of the low level of agricultural productivity, not only would small-scale market agriculture provide an insufficient base for the development of industry, but violent fluctuations from year to year would preclude economic planning.

The political goals shared by the great social classes could be realized. But not only were their economic goals incompatible, none of them could serve as organizational principle for the whole society. A society regulated by the desires and needs of the workers was ruled out by their minority position, while a capitalist market economy was made impossible by the weakness of the bourgeoisie and their dependence on the state, the disorganization, poverty, and illiteracy of the peasantry,—and, finally, the political strength achieved by the Bolshevik Party after 1917.

"Politics" and "economics" are not separate phenomena, but different aspects of social power relations. The question of the political form to emerge from the revolutionary process was to be decided by the achievement of social and therefore economic power by one of the contending groups on the scene. As it turned out, this was accomplished by neither bourgeoisie, peasantry, nor proletariat, but by the fraction of the intelligentsia which made up the membership of the Communist Party. The feat of the Bolsheviks was to define a new social structure by the subordination of economics to the political sphere controlled by them, accomplished through their seizure of power as a ruling class over capitalists, peasants, and workers alike. Before they succeeded in this, by riding the waves of popular rebellion and organization, the Russian workers were able to evolve forms of struggle and social reconstruction which transcend in importance the limitations of the place and time in which they arose. The following article briefly traces the history of the two kinds of institutions—the soviets and the factory committees—which remain of greatest interest to revolutionaries today.

Capitalist development in Russia before the First World War had assumed a form quite similar to what exists in many underdeveloped countries today. Almost all industry was under the control of foreign capital and was located in a few urban areas. Although the working class was extremely small in relation to the total population (Trotsky's estimate of 10 percent is the highest of all accounts), industry—and, therefore, the working class—was very concentrated. Most factories were large and constructed along then-modern lines. The working class had grown rapidly in the three decades prior to the war, and a sense of class had been developing by leaps and bounds since the turn of the century.

Throughout the late 19th century, Russian industrial workers often spent only part of the year in the urban areas, earning their livings in factories. They also spent part of the year in their old villages, working the land, and their primary ties remained with their agricultural activities and village life. However, the rapid development of industry soon provided year-round employment to ever greater numbers of workers. They and their families moved to the urban areas, breaking their old rural and village ties. Between 1885 and 1897, the urban population grew by 33.8 percent, and Moscow, for example, grew by 123 percent.[1] These people began to think of themselves primarily as workers, not as peasants who worked part of the year in the factories. Their problems were no longer those of indebtedness, to landlords, or connected to agriculture, but became those of wages, working conditions, and the prices of the necessities of life. The lack of a craft tradition contributed to this growing new sense of belonging to a working class, as the divisions among the workers were few, and most

[1] Trotsky, *1905,* pp. 38–44.

faced similar problems. Concentrated together in huge factories, living together in rapidly growing urban areas, workers discovered that they shared a very specific set of problems quite unlike those of their previous rural existence. In this way, a new sense of class grew along with Russian industry.

The events of 1905 both were made possible by this developing sense of class and spurred it on. Over 100,000 factory workers in St. Petersburg had gone on strike in January of that year. A few days later, workers and their families, protesting both factory conditions and their lack of political representation, presented a petition to the czar, asking him to alleviate their problems and grant them a Constituent Assembly. The demonstration in front of palace was fired upon by czar's soldiers. Mass strikes spread throughout the industrial cities of the country, involving more than a million people over a period of two months, reaching at least 122 towns and localities.[2] Strikes, demonstrations and public meetings continued sporadically throughout the spring and summer months despite severe repression. Workers elected committees throughout the urban areas to organize the strikes.[3]

In mid-September, typesetters and printers in Moscow launched an industry-wide strike. Over fifty shops were shut down. Other industries in that city began to close in sympathy with the typesetters. At the beginning of October, typesetters in St. Petersburg went out on a three-day strike to show their solidarity with their Moscow fellow workers. At the end of the first week of October, the railway workers throughout European Russia decided to strike, and called for a national general strike, demanding the eight-hour day, civil liberties, amnesty, and a Constituent Assembly. The strike began to spread throughout the urban areas, succeeding in closing down all productive activities by the 12th, save those necessary for the success of the strike,

[2] *Ibid.*, p. 81.
[3] Oskar Anweiler, *Les Soviets en Russie, 1905–1921*, pp. 43–47. He writes: "The genesis of these councils during the revolution of 1905 irrefutably shows that these organs had for their original object the defense of the workers' interests on the basis of the factory. It is because the workers sought to unite their fragmented struggles and to give them a direction, not because they saw the conquest of power by political actions, that the first councils appeared." (p. 47)

such as print shops, trains carrying workers' delegates, etc.
The government responded with concessions and repression.

Beginning October 10, factories in St. Petersburg began
sending delegates to meetings of what was to become the
Soviet. At first, not more than thirty or forty delegates
attended. On October 13, they sent out a call for a political
general strike, i.e., for a Constituent Assembly and political
rights, and asked all the factories to send delegates. Workers
immediately understood the principles of such representation
on the basis of workplaces. There were the experiences of
sending factory representatives to the Shidlovski Commission
(which was studying factory conditions) and the strike
committees of the past nine months upon which to draw.
Anweiler writes:

> When the strike wave spread from Moscow to St. Petersburg,
> and when, on October 11, the first factories stopped work,
> the workers themselves felt the need to meet together in order
> to decide in common what path to follow. It was for this
> purpose that delegates were elected in several factories—
> the Putilov and Obukhov works, among others—of these
> delegates, more than one had been a member of the strike
> committee or a former representative to the Shidlovski Com-
> mission.[4]

More and more factories elected delegates. Within three
days, there were 226 delegates representing 96 factories
and workshops (the principle was usually one delegate for
every 100 workers in a factory). It was decided to admit
representatives of the socialist parties (Bolsheviks, Men-
cheviks, and Social-Revolutionaries). On October 17, this
group decided on the name "Soviet of Workers' Deputies"
and elected a provisional executive committee of 22 members
(two for each of the seven areas of the city, two for each
of the four most important unions) and decided to publish
its own newspaper, "News from the Soviet of Workers'
Deputies." The Soviet, at first performing no other task
than organizing and leading the strike, changed itself over
the course of several days into an organ of the general and
political representation of workers, in the center of the
revolutionary movement of the working class in the capital.

---

[4] *Ibid.*, p. 54–55. He notes that of the first forty delegates, only
fifteen had been neither delegates to the Shidlovski Commission
or members of the strike committees.

It quickly became a "workers' parliament," which it attempted to remain even after the strike ended at the end of October. According to Anweiler, "this change was neither deliberate or consciously expressed. After having at its peak engendered the Soviet, the revolutionary movement surged on, with greater impetuosity than ever, and the organ that it had created accompanied it on its path."[5] The Soviet had been formed out of necessity—that of organizing and maintaining the general strike. No one needed to convince the workers that such organization was crucial.

Similar organizations appeared amidst strikes in all the urban areas of European Russia (and in some larger villages as well). Between 40 and 50 came into existence in October. Although most only functioned for a short period, their importance should not be underestimated. This was the first experience of direct democracy for most of those involved. The Soviets were created from below, by the workers, peasants, and soldiers, and reflected their desires—which were expressed in non-sectarian resolutions. No political party dominated the Soviets, and many workers were opposed to allowing representation for political parties. At any rate, most of the Soviets were created by workers to solve their immediate problems—winning the strike, the eighthour day, and political rights. They concerned themselves with the daily problems confronting the workers.

The czar combined concessions (the granting of a parliament, the Duma) with selective repression and broke the strike and then destroyed the remaining Soviets. However, despite apparent failure, the revolution of 1905 paved the way for the events of 1917. Soviets had been formed on a factory basis and performed the functions of workers' parliaments, trade unions, and strike committees, and had provided the workers with a sense of self-government. These experiences would be relied upon in the face of the severe problems of early 1917, when workers found themselves in a situation of deep social crisis.

The problems facing the Russian population at the outset of 1917 were severe indeed. The effects of Russia's participation in the First World War began to become unbearable. Her dependence on Western Europe for raw materials crippled her. Inflation, usury, and shortages of food supplies reached crisis proportions. Production plummeted. The size

[5] *Ibid.*, p. 57.

of the draft led to a shortage of skilled labor in industry and a shortage of agricultural workers. Fuel became ever harder to obtain, both for personal use (heating) and for industrial production. There was no apparent hope for the masses of the Russian people, especially the industrial working-class. Voline writes from his personal experience:

In January 1917, the situation had become untenable. The economic chaos, the poverty of workers, and the social disorganization of Russia were so acute that the inhabitants of several large cities—notably Petrograd—began to lack not only fuel, clothing, meat, butter, and sugar, but even bread. February saw worse conditions, not only was the urban population doomed to famine, but the supplying of the army became entirely defective. And, at the same time, a complete military debacle was reached.[6]

Dissension appeared in the army and the navy as the war wore on. Peasants in the army began to rebel against the despotism of the officers and camaraderie developed among the draftees in the face of the ever-worsening military situation. Discussions between workers and peasants spread within the military. The beginning of 1917 saw the armed forces seething with revolt.

On February 23, a strike began among women textile workers in Petrograd (formerly St. Petersburg). Demonstrations, which were virtually bread riots, spread throughout the city. The troops who had crushed similar demonstrations in 1905 refused to put down the uprising, and many joined in. By the end of the month, after three days of spontaneous demonstrations and a general strike, Petrograd was in the hands of its working class. Victor Serge, a participant in the events, writes:

The revolution sprang up in the street, descended from the factories with thousands of striking workers, to cries of "Bread! Bread!" The authorities saw it coming, powerless; it was not in their power to overcome the crisis. The fraternization of the troops with workers' demonstrations in the streets of Petrograd consummated the fall of the aristocracy. The suddenness of the events surprised the revolutionary organizations . . .[7]

---

[6] *Nineteen-Seventeen*, p. 39.
[7] *L'An Un de la Revolution Russe*, pp. 55–56.

Even Trotsky goes so far as to admit that the revolutionary organizations acted in February as obstacles to the working-class:

> Thus, the fact is that the February Revolution was begun from below, overcoming the resistance of its own revolutionary organizations, the initiative being taken of their own accord by the most oppressed and downtrodden part of the proletariat—the women textile workers, among them no doubt many soldiers' wives.[8]

The revolution spread throughout Russia. Peasants seized land; discipline in the army collapsed; sailors seized their ships in the Kronstadt Harbor on the Baltic Coast and took over that city; the Soviet form of organization reappeared, first in industrial areas, then among soldiers, sailors, and peasants.

A Provisional Government came to power when the czar abdicated. Made up of members of the bourgeoisie and the aristocracy, this group at first sought the institution of a constitutional monarchy. They were soon to give up on this notion, but, regardless of their proclamations, laws, debates, etc., they failed to come up with solutions to the problems experienced by the bulk of the populations, both workers and peasants. The Soviets, which had sprung up across the country, were viewed as the legitimate government by workers, peasants, and soldiers, who came to them with their problems.

However, a close look at the formation and organization of the Soviets indicates that they were not mass organs that offered workers and peasants the means to exercise power over their daily activities. The most famous of all the Soviets—and a good example of their organizational structure and functioning—was the Petrograd Soviet. This organization was formed from the top down by a group of liberal and radical intellectuals who got together on February 27 and constituted themselves the "Executive Committee of the Petrograd Soviet."[9] They then called for elections to the Soviet itself. On February 28, in response to a proclamation from this "Executive Committee," elections were held in the factories. By one o'clock in the afternoon, over

[8] *The Russian Revolution*, p. 98.
[9] Anweiler, *op. cit.*, p. 128, reports that not one of these men was a factory delegate.

120 delegates assembled for the plenary meeting. However, this meeting—and most future ones—was chaotic: credentials could not be verified and little was accomplished. All essential decisions were made within the "strict intimacy" of the Executive Committee.[10] Some of these decisions, such as the one of March 2 stating that the Soviet would not co-operate with the Provisional Government, were submitted to the Soviet as a whole for ratification. Most decisions, however, were not.

Sukhanov, a journalist and a member of this Executive Committee, describes the functioning of this Soviet:

> To this day, I, a member of the Executive Committee of the Soviet, am completely ignorant of what the Soviet was doing in the course of the day. It never interested me, either then or later, because it was self-evident that all the practical pivotal work had fallen on the shoulders of the Executive Committee. As for the Soviet at that moment, in the given situation, with its quantitative and qualitative composition, it was clearly incapable of any work even as a Parliament, and performed merely moral functions.
>
> The Executive Committee had to accomplish by itself all the current work as well as bring into being a scheme of government. In the first place, to pass this programme through the Soviet was plainly a formality; secondly, this formality was not difficult and no one cared about it. . . .
>
> "And what's going on in the Soviet?" I remember asking someone who had come in from beyond the curtain. He waved his hand hopelessly: "A mass meeting! Anyone who wants to gets up and says whatever he likes!" [11]

The most interesting feature of this Soviet was the personal communication between delegates of both workers and soldiers in one body. The presence of so many soldiers' delegates gave the Executive Committee more actual power

[10] *Ibid.*, p. 129.
[11] Sukhanov, *The Russian Revolution 1917*, pp. 186–187, also quoted in Roger Rethybridge (ed.), *Witnesses to the Russian Revolution*, pp. 123–124. Sukhanov's recollections are corroborated by Anweiler, op. cit., and "The Political Ideology of the Petrograd Soviet in the Spring of 1917," in Richard Pipes (ed.), *Revolutionary Russia;* Chamberlin, *The Russian Revolution*, p. 109; Browder and Kerensky (eds.), *The Russian Provisional Government*, Volume I, p. 71; and Trotsky, *History of the Russian Revolution*, Volume I, pp. 216–217.

than the Provisional Government because it enjoyed the support of the local troops.

Over 3,000 delegates were members of the Soviet by the end of March: two-thirds of them were soldiers. The delegates were elected on the basis of one representative for 1,000 workers, and one for every factory with less than 1,000, and one delegate for every military unit. In mid-April, on the suggestion of the Executive Committee, the Soviet voted in favor of reorganization, as its size had become unwieldy. The new body had some 600 members, half soldiers and half workers. This reorganization was undertaken by a special committee, appointed by the Executive Committee, who pared the Soviet by excluding "occasional delegates" and those from groups which had been reduced in size. However, the power still remained in the hands of the Executive Committee. This had been the case from the start, and it continued to be the case throughout the spring and summer of 1917.[12]

The Executive Committee expanded its role. It created various committees to deal with different problems—publishing newspapers, overseeing various services, etc. As the number of these committees increased, the base of the Soviet lost more and more of its power. Meetings became less frequent and soon the Soviet itself became nothing but an open forum, where workers and soldiers could come together, air their views, meet others like themselves, and keep their constituencies informed about what was going on. It did offer people who had never had the chance to speak out to do so. But it did not represent the power of the working class. If anything, it represented its powerlessness.

This Soviet seems quite characteristic of the Soviets throughout Russia—both in the urban areas and in the countryside. Often, workers or peasants came into conflict with their Soviet. Neither this organ nor the Provisional Government can be considered as instruments of working-class power. However, the workers were able to create such an instrument—the factory committee.

Whereas the Soviets were primarily concerned with polit-

---

[12] Anweiler, *Les Soviets en Russie*, pp. 131–137, cf. also Chamberlin, *op. cit.*, p. 84; Irakli Tseretelli (a member of the Executive Committee), "Reminiscences of the February Revolution," *The Russian Review*, Vol. 14, Nos. 2, 3, and 4; George Katkov, Russia 1917: *The February Revolution*, p. 360.

ical issues, e.g., the structure of the government, the continuation of the war, the factory committees dealt solely with the problems of continuing production within their factories. Many sprang up in the face of lock-outs or attempted sabotage by the factory owners. It was through these committees that workers hoped to solve their initial problems—how to get production going again, how to provide for themselves and their families in the midst of economic chaos. Many workers were faced with the choice of taking over production themselves or starving. Other workers who were relatively assured of employment were influenced both by the burst of activity which characterized the revolution and the worsening economic situation. If they were to remain secure, they had to have a greater say in the management of their factories. They realized that they needed organizations on the shop level to protect their interests and improve their situations.

The trade unions could be of no help in these matters. Until the turn of the century, trade unions were illegal. The tradition of guilds, which had been an important precursor of trade-unionism in Western Europe, was lacking, due to the fact that industry was still rather young in Russia. Only the most politically-minded workers could be expected to be interested in trade-unionism under the repressive conditions and such workers were usually more apt to join the already existing radical political organizations. In 1905 the existing trade unions played an insignificant role in the upheaval. Many of them were crushed in the repression of the next few years. A select few were allowed to continue to function, but only under police supervision. By the time of the February 1917 uprising, several trade unions existed as national organizations, but few had any influence within the factories. Most of the trade union leaders were Mensheviks, who rejected the notion that workers should have any say about the internal affairs of a factory. During the first few months of 1917, trade unions, membership increased from a few scores of thousands to 1.5 million. Most of this increased membership was purely formal, i.e., it became a matter of principle for radical workers to belong to trade unions. The real activity was represented by the incredible proliferation of factory committees, organs consisting of and controlled by the workers within each factory. It was through these committees that most of the workers sought to solve their problems.

These committees were seen to provide the organizational structure through which workers could confront—and hopefully solve—their first problem: the taking over of production within their factory. Only through organs such as the factory committees, directly controlled by all the workers assembled within a factory, could the workers develop the organization, solidarity, and shared knowledge necessary to manage production. (As the Soviets were concerned primarily with "political" issues and because their meetings were usually chaotic, they offered little assistance for solving the pressing problems of the workers.) Such committees appeared in every industrial center throughout European Russia. The membership of a committee always consisted solely of workers who still worked in the factory. Most important decisions would be made by a general assembly of all the workers in the factory. The workers sought to maintain their own power within the factory in order to solve their pressing problems. No one else could do it for them. The committees were utilized by the workers in the early months of the revolution to present series of demands, and in some instances to begin to act to realize those demands. Paul Avrich describes the functioning of some factory committees in the first months of the uprising:

From the outset, the workers' committees did not limit their demands to higher wages and shorter hours, though these were at the top of every list; what they wanted in addition to material benefits, was a voice in management. On March 4, for example, the workers of the Skorokhod Shoe Factory in Petrograd did, to be sure, call upon their superiors to grant them an eight-hour day and a wage increase, including double pay for overtime work; but they also demanded official recognition of their factory committee and its right to control the hiring and firing of labor. In the Petrograd Radiotelegraph Factory, a workers' committee was organized expressly to "work out rules and norms for the internal life of the factory," while other factory committees were elected chiefly to control the activities of the directors, engineers, and foremen. Overnight, incipient forms of "workers' control" over production and distribution appeared in the large enterprises of Petrograd, particularly the state-owned metallurgical plants, devoted almost exclusively to the war effort and employing perhaps a quarter of the workers in the capital.[13]

As the economic situation became yet more severe following the February Revolution (inflation continued, production was only beginning to pick up, and then but sporadically), workers turned from making demands concerning wages, working conditions, and the principles of "workers' control," to actually taking over and operating an ever greater number of factories. Workers had to act if they were to find a way out of the deepening crisis. The immediate problem which confronted workers was experienced on the factory level—how to begin again (under their own direction) the production of their factories. Once this initial problem was confronted, and the workers, through their factory committees, began to solve it—by, in many cases, actually starting up production under their own management—a new and yet more difficult problem appeared.

No factory could be self-sufficient. Production required raw materials and continued production necessitated a structure of distribution. Many committees began to compete with the committees from other factories, both for the procurement of raw materials and the disposal of their products. Such a solution to the severe problems proved unsatisfactory. Not all the factories could acquire the needed raw materials. Competition drove the prices of raw materials up. More and more factories which had only recently recommended production found themselves threatened with being forced to close down due to their inability to get needed materials and new machinery. The necessity of federation became apparent. That is, workers realized—some more quickly than others—that they had to develop a means of cooperation and coordination with workers in other factories and regions: those that supplied them with raw materials, those that produced the same products, and those that needed their products. The "ownership" of a given factory by its own workers could not solve the pressing economic problems. Only a large-scale coordinated effort by the workers in many factories could do so. The isolation of workers within their own factories had to be transcended, and the workers turned to their factory committees to devise methods of industry-wide and regional coordination.

[13] Paul Avrich, *The Russian Anarchists*, p. 140–141.

At the same time, the Provisional Government sought to impose its own ideas about the management of production. It sought to undermine the activities of the factory committees, limiting them to overseeing health and safety conditions within the plants. All coordination should be under the supervision of the Provisional Government and its agencies. This provided another impetus for the factory committees to join together. Alone, they could be stripped of their power by the government. United, they could present a force that could not be destroyed—unless the government would be willing to stop all production, a rather unlikely action.

The first meeting of a group of factory committees appears to have taken place in mid-April in Petrograd. The major resolution of this conference was a strong re-affirmation of the workers' right to control the internal life of the factory, matters "such as length of the working day, wages, hiring and firing workers and employees, leaves of absence, etc."[14] However, there appears to have been no progress made as far as communications between factory committees for the purpose of organizing production on a city-wide level.

The Provisional Government also acted in April. On the 23rd of that month statutes were enacted which recognized the rights of the factory committees to represent the workers in bargaining with management and to oversee health conditions inside the factory. The principal goal of these statutes was "to restrain the importance and the role of factory committees and to limit their power."[15] But the Provisional Government had no power to enforce these statutes. Workers throughout Russia quickly recognized what it was that the Provisional Government sought to do, and they responded forcefully. According to Pankratova—a Bolshevik historian of the factory committee movement—every major factory and every large urban area was the scene of spontaneous activity in response to these statutes. Workers rejected the government's new regulations and took steps to strengthen

[14] Resolution quoted in Robert V. Daniels, *The Conscience of the Revolution*, p. 82, cf. also, Anna Pankratova, "Les Comités d' Usines en Russie à l'Epogue de la Révolution," originally written in Russian in 1923 and reprinted in French in *Autogestion*, #4, December 1967, pp. 8–10.

[15] Pankratova, *ibid.*, p. 12, cf. also Frederick Kaplan, *Bolshevik Ideology and the Ethics of Soviet Labor,* p. 48.

their own power within their factories. New attempts at communication and coordination between factories appeared. All this was not in response alone to the government's actions, but also because the economic situation continued to deteriorate.[16]

On May 29, there was a conference of factory committees in Kharkov, which resulted in a strong affirmation of the principles of workers' self-management, but failed to resolve the serious problems of the coordination of supply, production, and distribution. The next day, a conference of all the factory committees in Petrograd and its surrounding areas convened in the capital city. Some 400 representatives of the committees attended. A statement was adopted in the course of the conference which explained the progression of events up to that time—and indicated how these events were understood by the workers who were involved in them.

> From the beginning of the Revolution the administrative staffs of the factories have relinquished their posts. The workmen have practically become the masters. To keep the factories going, the workers' committees have had to take the management into their own hands. In the first days of the Revolution, in February and March, the workmen left the factories and went into the streets. The factories stopped work. About a fortnight later, the mass of workmen returned to their work. They found that many factories had been deserted. The managers, engineers, generals, mechanics, foremen had reason to believe that the workmen would wreak their vengeance on them, and they had disappeared. The workmen had to begin work with no administrative staff to guide them. They had to elect committees which gradually re-established a normal system of work. The committees had to find the necessary raw materials, and altogether to take upon themselves all kinds of unexpected and unaccustomed duties.[17]

The final resolution of the conference described the factory committees as "fighting organizations, elected on the basis of the widest democracy and with a collective

---

[16] Competition between factory committees and workers stealing everything that they could carry contributed, in many regions, to the economic chaos.

[17] Resolution adopted during May 30—June 5 Conference of Factory Committees in Petrograd, quoted in S.O. Zagorsky, *State Control of Russian Industry During the War*, p. 174.

leadership," whose objectives were "the creation of new conditions of work . . . the organization of thorough control by labor over production and distribution." Moreover, this resolutive also commented on "political" questions, demanding that there be a "proletarian majority in all institutions having executive power."[18]

The conference sought to go beyond a mere affirmation of the principles of workers' self-management to try to formulate tentative plans for greater coordination of production. Representatives at the conference turned to the trade unions for assistance. As we saw earlier in this essay, the trade unions, although weak and inconsequential as far as the course of events up to now, did have an existing pan-Russian (i.e., national) structure, which was based on relations between industries and regions. It was hoped at this conference that this structure could be made use of to co-ordinate the then rather disparate activities of the committees. Although qualms were expressed about turning to any other organization for assistance in coordination (be it political parties, trade unions, or anyone but the factory committees themselves), the severity of the economic crisis impressed upon the representatives the need for speedy action, and the adoption of an already existing structure appeared easier than the creation of a totally new one.

Beginning about this time (i.e., early June), the influence of the Bolshevik Party within the factory committees began to grow. They were a fairly small group of professional revolutionaries who argued, under Lenin's leadership, that a "socialist revolution" was possible in Russia. Until Lenin returned from exile in April, they had been fairly isolated from the events taking place. Lenin, however, quickly changed the orientation of the party. In the first months of the revolution, the Bolsheviks wavered on the question of workers' control of production, the division of land among the peasants, support for the Provisional Government, and the continuation of the war—all questions considered crucial by workers and peasants. Lenin, not without difficulty, brought the party around to clear positions on all these issues, and, in doing so, brought their program into line with the already articulated demands of the working class (e.g., control of production by the factory committees, political power to be exercised by the Soviets, the end of

[18] Fragments of resolution quoted in Maurice Brinton, *The Bolsheviks and Workers' Control*, p. 5.

participation in the World War) and the peasantry (e.g., the end of the war and the division of land among those who work it). No other political party placed itself openly in favor of the actions and demands of the Russian masses. Thus, in the face of attempts on the part of the Provisional Government to undermine their accomplishments and their attempts at expanding their power, many workers saw the Bolshevik Party as a welcome ally. According to most accounts, the Bolsheviks were a strong influence at this conference, favoring the uniting of the factory committees (to present a counterpower to the Menshevik-dominated Soviets).

Within several weeks, it became apparent that the factory committees could not rely on the trade unions for purposes of co-ordination. At the end of June, there was a trade union conference in Petrograd. Here it became clear that the unions desired to subordinate the existing factory committees to their control. Their conception of "coordination" was that the national organs should make all the fundamental decisions concerning production and distribution, and the factory committees (which would become institutionalized within the unions) would implement these decisions. In other words, "coordination" through the trade union would mean control by the trade unions.

By the end of June, a process of polarization appeared to be under way in Russia. The dividing lines were not sharply drawn, nor were they necessarily perceived by the participants. The most important line was that which separated the factory committees from all the other existing institutions—the Soviets, the trade unions, the political parties, and the Provisional Government—who were all trying in different ways to control the committees. There were also obvious differences within the latter group seeking to establish its hegemony over the others. (Only the Bolsheviks among the parties appeared to side with the committees.) The workers involved in the factory committees did not see the Soviets as enemies, but were disenchanted with their vacillations concerning the extension of control over all production by the committees and their unwillingness to openly confront the Provisional Government on the question of political power.

In early July, mass discontent with the Provisional Government and its policies (the continuation of the war, its attempts to undermine the factory committees) and with what the Soviets were doing (or, more exactly, not doing) surfaced in the form of violent mass demonstrations and peasant land seizures. On July 3, a group of soldiers and armed workers burst into the Petrograd Soviet (while a much larger group demonstrated outside) and assailed its members for compromising with the bourgeoisie and hesitating to take over power from the Provisional Government. They demanded that all power be taken by the Soviet, that all land be nationalized, that various bourgeois ministers be removed, and that participation in the war should end.[19] The entire month of July saw mass demonstrations and strikes throughout the urban areas of the country. The Provisional Government sought to blame the Bolsheviks for these disturbances. In fact, the Bolsheviks had tried to halt some of these demonstrations, arguing against them in their journals and demanding that party members not take part. As a result, they became viewed with suspicion by groups of workers, and some workers who belonged to the party tore up their party cards in disgust.

In early August, a general strike took place in Moscow, presenting mostly "political" demands—an end to the war, and that the Soviets should replace the Provisional Government. The Moscow Soviet was opposed to the strike, its leadership as yet unwilling to put itself forth as an alternative to the Provisional Government. Moreover, in the face of severe economic problems, the Soviet was becoming more and more concerned with the continuation of production. This strike was organized by the factory committees in the city, who quickly transformed themselves into strike committees, "informing and educating the workers, collecting money, giving out subsidies," and raising the demand for control of production by the producers themselves, exercised through the factory committees.[20] Polarization between the workers and the existing Soviet sharpened.

On August 7–12, the second conference of factory committees of Petrograd and surrounding areas took place. This conference

. . . made a definite attempt to construct an efficiently working center of united factory committees by resolving that ¼ of one per cent of the wages of the workers represented by factory committees was to be put aside for the support of a Central Soviet of Factory Committees. This was to give the

[19] Trotsky, *History of the Russian Revolution*, Vol. II, p. 19.
[20] Pankratova, *op. cit.*, p. 30.

Central Soviet a means for support, independent of the state
and the trade unions.[21]

There was a consensus that the trade unions could not be
used for organizing and coordinating production. The Bolsheviks, who made up a majority of the delegates at this
conference, clearly saw this Central Soviet as a body with
a very different function than mere coordination. It should,
in their view, have considerable power to make decisions
concerning production and distribution, decisions which
would be binding on the factory committees.[22] Many of
the other delegates saw that such a body could undermine
the already existing (and expanding) control of the process
of production by the producers themselves, taking important
decisions out of their hands. There was thus considerable
ambivalence about creating this Central Soviet, which would
solve the problem of coordination only by weakening the
power of the producers themselves and their factory committees. The final resolution, which stated that "all decrees
of the factory committees were ultimately dependent on
the sanctions of the Central Council, and the Council could
abolish any decree of the factory committees,"[23] represented
a real defeat for those who opposed control of the committees by any body constituted above them. At about the
same time—early August—there was an all-city conference
of factory committees in Moscow. Here, too, there was an
attempt made to devise a structure of coordination, but
again in the form of a "centralization" under the control
of a regional council.

While these attempts at coordination were being made,
the factory committees continued to try to solve their initial
problems—the taking over of productive apparatus and its
operation by the producers themselves. The necessity of
doing so was becoming ever greater as the prices of necessities (e.g., food, clothing, and shoes) rose two to three

[21] Kaplan, *op. cit.*, p. 66.
[22] According to Kaplan, the Bolsheviks were interested in the creation of this Central Soviet for reasons other than the smoother
functioning of production. He writes: "The Bolsheviks seem to
have wanted to strengthen the Central Council so that they could
manipulate a workers' organization capable of taking a place
alongside the trade unions and in opposition to other non-labor
organizations," *ibid.*, p. 67.
[23] *Ibid.*, p. 75.

times faster than wages, and more and more factory owners attempted to shut down production.[24] The Provisional Government was alarmed by the activities of the factory committees and launched an all-out legal attack on them. The extent to which the Government felt it necessary to destroy the committees gives us an indication of how much these committees must have been doing. On August 22, Skobelev, the Minister of Labor, issued a circular letter which stated that:

> The right of hiring and firing of all other employees belongs to the owners of these plants . . . Coercive measures on the part of workers for the purpose of dismissal or employment of certain persons are regarded as actions to be criminally punished.[25]

Another circular letter of August 28 forbid the holding of factory committee meetings during working hours. However, as the government lacked the power to enforce these new laws, they were generally disregarded by the workers. The factory committees offered the workers the best means of maintaining production and controlling it for their own benefit. Thus, the workers were unwilling to yield to the unenforceable decrees of the Provisional Government. Into the fall of 1917 this struggle continued, a struggle which could only end with the destruction of one protagonist or the other. Pankratova takes note of the logic of this struggle:

> The passage from passive to active control had been dictated by the logic of preservation. Intervention of workers' committees in hiring and firing was the first stage toward the direct intervention of the workers in the production process

[24] Many workers understood the alternatives and the tasks confronting them. Pankratova cites a resolution adopted at a conference of textile industry factory committees in late summer. The delegates there saw that their choices were "to submit to the reduction of production or to risk being fired by intervening actively in production and taking over control and the normalization of work in the firm." They resolved: "It is neither by the bureaucratic path, i.e., by the creation of a predominantly capitalist institution, nor by the protection of capitalist profits and their power over production that we can save ourselves from catastrophe. The path to escape rests solely in the establishment of real workers' control." *Op. cit.,* p. 40.

[25] Quoted in Browder and Kerensky, *op. cit.,* Vol. II, p. 722.

. . . Later, the passage toward higher forms of technical and
financial control became inevitable.
This placed the proletariat before a new problem: taking
power, establishing new production relations.[26]

However, the workers and their factory committees failed
to see the importance of their fighting for social power.
Their efforts remained within the sphere of "the economy."
"Political power" was a problem for the Soviets. The workers
hoped that the Soviets would soon wrest "political power"
away from the Provisional Government and allow the
factory committees and their expanding regional organizations
to manage industrial production. By October, such councils
of factory committees existed in many parts of Russia:
Northwest: Petrograd, Pskov, Nevel; Central Industrial
Region: Moscow, Ivanovo-Vosnesensk; Volga Provinces:
Saratob, Kazan, Tsaritsyn; Ukraine: (Southern Mining District): Karkhov, Kiev, Odessa, Iuzovka; Southwest and
Caucasus: Rostov, Nakhichevan-on-the-Dan, Ekaterinodar;
Urals and Siberia: Irkutsk.[27] Conferences of local factory
committees in Petrograd and Moscow in late September
and early October reaffirmed the necessity of proceeding
with their role in production-managing the entire productive process—and in developing ever better methods of
coordination.

A short time later, the first "All-Russian Conference of
Factory Committees" was convened. ("All-Russian" is a
bit misleading because the committees only existed in the
industrialized urban areas.) Members of the Bolshevik Party
made up 62 percent of the delegates and were the dominant
force. By now, the Party was in firm control of the recently
created Central Council of factory committees and used
it for its own purposes. According to one account

. . . the work of the Council proved to be very limited. The
Bolsheviks, who entered the Central Council in a considerable
number and who, as a matter of fact, controlled it, apparently deliberately obstructed the work of the Central Council
as a center of economic struggle on the part of the workers.
They used the Council chiefly for political purposes in order
to strengthen the campaign to win the unions.[28]

26 Pankratova, *op. cit.*, p. 48.
27 Kaplan, *op. cit.*, p. 81.
28 Browder and Kerensky, *op. cit.*, p. 726.

The Bolsheviks at this conference succeeded in passing a resolution creating a national organizational structure for the committees. However, this structure explicitly limited the factory committees to activity within the sphere of production and suggested a method of struggle which embodied a rigid division of activities—the factory committees, under the supervision of their organization, would continue their activities at the point of production; the Soviets (now under Bolshevik control—many members of the Soviets saw the Bolsheviks as supporting the demands of the workers and the peasants and many other members, particularly soldiers, who had supported the more liberal parties, had left the cities to return to their villages; thus, they achieved majority) would contest the political power of the Provisional Government; and the Bolsheviks would bring together the activities of these bodies, as well as the disparate struggles of the working class and the peasantry. The non-Bolshevik delegates—and the workers they represented—did not reject this new plan. Few realized the necessity of uniting the "economic" and the "political" aspects of the class struggle.

The Bolsheviks, now on the verge of seizing "state power," began laying the foundations for the consolidation of their control over the working class. No longer did they encourage increased activity by the factory committees. Most workers and their committees accepted this about-face, believing that the new strategy was only temporary and that once the Bolsheviks had captured "political" power they would be given free reign in the economic sphere.

Shortly thereafter, the Bolsheviks successfully seized state power, replacing the Provisional Government with their tightly-controlled Soviets. The effect on the workers was tremendous. They believed that this new revolution gave them the green light to expand their activities, to expropriate the remaining capitalists and to establish strong structures of coordination. E. H. Carr describes what happened immediately after the seizure of power:

> The spontaneous inclination of the workers to organize factory committees and to intervene in the management of the factories was inevitably encouraged by a revolution which led the workers to believe that the productive machinery of the country belonged to them and could be operated by them at their own discretion and to their own advantage. What had begun to happen before the October revolution now happened

more frequently and more openly; and for the moment, nothing would have dammed the tide of revolt.[29]

Out of this burst of activity came the first attempt of the factory committees to create a national organization of their own, independent of all parties and institutions. Such an organization posed an implicit threat to the new Bolshevik State, although those involved still saw their organization as relating only to the "economy."

The Bolsheviks, seeking to strengthen their position, realized that they had to destroy the factory committees. They now had available to them the means to do so—something which the Provisional Government had lacked. By controlling the Soviets, the Bolsheviks controlled the troops. Their domination of the regional and national councils of factory committees gave them the power to isolate and destroy any factory committee through denying them raw materials, for example. The trade unions, now an appendage to the Bolshevik State, were used to suppress the power of the factory committees. Isaac Deutscher describes how the Bolsheviks used the trade unions to emasculate the committees within months after the revolution.

The Bolsheviks now called upon the trade unions to render a special service to the nascent Soviet State and to discipline the factory committees. The unions came out against the attempt of the factory committees to form a national organization of their own. They prevented the convocation of a planned all-Russian Congress of factory committees and demanded total subordination on the part of the committees. The committees, however, were too strong to surrender altogether. Towards the end of 1917 a compromise was reached, under which the factory committees accepted a new status: They were to form the primary organizations upon which the trade unions based themselves; but, by the same token, of course, they were incorporated in the unions. Gradually they gave up the ambition to act, either locally or nationally, in opposition to the trade unions or independently of them. The unions now became the main channels through which the Government was assuming control over industry.[30]

[29] E.H. Carr, *The Bolshevik Revolution*, Vol. II, p. 69. Cf. also Paul Avrich, *"The Bolshevik Revolution and Workers' Control in Russian Industry,"* in *Slavic Review,* March, 1963.
[30] Deutscher, *Soviet Trade Unions*, p. 17.

Groups of workers fought back in various factories and localities (the Kronstadt revolt was the most famous of these battles), but they were labeled "counter-revolutionaries" and crushed by the Bolshevik-controlled forces of order. Soon, even the trade unions were to be destroyed, as the Bolsheviks moved to eliminate any possible opposition to their power. Space prohibits my going into detail about how the Bolsheviks consolidated their position, but numerous accounts exist and most are fairly readily available.[31]

Looking back over the course of events, several features stand out. The revolution was determined—if only passively —by the vast peasant population. The factory committees represented only a small portion of the population and could never have successfully managed all of Russian production. The inability of the workers to break out of the blinders that led them to see their role in the narrow terms of the "economy" was to be expected. However, it confined their activities and allowed their accomplishments to be destroyed by the wielders of "political" power.

On the other hand, the Russian events clearly show that, under certain circumstances, working people are capable of creating their own organizations of struggle, organizations which can function as the means by which the producers can directly control the process of production within their factories. But "workers' control" over the production process in individual workplaces is insufficient. The next stage, the coordination of these organizations, i.e., the attempt of the working class to manage all the production of society, is much more difficult. Various other groups will invariably put themselves forward to do this *for* the working class, and if they are accepted they will try to control the activities of the workers. Such organizations are potential new ruling classes and must be opposed as such. As Karl Marx wrote as the first premise of the *Rules* of the First International Workingmen's Association: "the emancipation of the working classes must be conquered by the working classes themselves."

---

[31] The best are: Brinton, *op. cit.*; Avrich, article *op. cit.*; Daniels, *op. cit.*; Leonard Schapiro, *The Origin of the Communist Autocracy;* James Bunyan, *The Origin of Forced Labor in the Soviet Union, 1917–1921;* Alexandra Kollontai, *The Workers' Opposition;* Marya Gordon, *Workers Before and After Lenin;* and many others.

# The Mass Strike in France:
# May–June 1968

## informations correspondance ouvriere
## translated by root & branch

*Informations Correspondance Ouvriere* (ICO) is a group of people who meet to compare their experiences and to discuss larger problems with the end of a clarification of ideas. This pamphlet is the result of one such collective discussion: written by a number of manual and intellectual workers, it was discussed by all those who took part in ICO's meetings in Paris during May and June, 1968.

## Introduction

The Mass Strike in France *is unique among the mass of print devoted to its subject. It is neither a chronology of events, nor a record of the "leadership" role of one or another political sect, nor yet the discovery of some fashionable new dynamic of revolt in "neo-" or even "post-capitalism." Instead, it looks at the activities of the workers and students in May and June 1968 to discover in what way they were a response to the conditions of capitalist life today; what were their strengths and limitations; and in what way they point to the possibilities of a new kind of society.*

*French capitalism is of course different from the American version. The old-fashioned nature of the French university system is just one aspect of a general backwardness. Yet the May-June strike holds lessons for us as well as for our comrades in France. Capitalism today, despite national rivalries and unevenness of development, is more of a world system than ever before. This is true not only on the level of economic ties—the dollar-dominated money system, the world market, the multinational corporations—but in the necessity for each national economy to develop the most modern forms and structures of social and economic organization in order to compete with the advanced sectors of the global economy. It is for this reason that the central phenomena discernable in the French "events" are to be found operating in the US, as well as in all other capitalist nations.*

*Young people today are subjected to special stress, as their increased number comes up against an economy less able to provide satisfying jobs, in an economy whose basic irrationality and unpleasantness is more and more visible. Young people necessarily have had less time than their elders to habituate themselves to the kind of life capitalism imposes on them. They are therefore quicker to respond to possibilities of change that suggest themselves in a period of social flux or crisis. It is also easier for them to challenge the institutions which seek to control and contain their rebellion, like the trade unions or political sects.*

*The student movement of the 1960s must be understood within this context. The university is as central a part of modern capitalism as it is due to the fact that students have become for the most part workers-in-training. It is to a great extent against the ideological rather than the technical aspect of their training that students rebel. Their rebellion, however, does not stay on the plane of ideas. It acquires form (occupation of campuses) and content (disruption of the training process) by reference to the university's function as a point of production of labor-power.*

*One of the serious limitations of the American student movement was its failure to deal with the source of its radical energies in the oppression of students. Instead, radicalism meant devotion to redressing the wrongs of others. The result is that student radicals appeared as outsiders in other people's struggles, rather than as members of a group whose own interests require joint activity with other groups.*

*In this regard the French students presented a valuable example. The students who wrote the leaflet reprinted in the text consciously rebelled against their utilization by capital in the exploitation of labor, a role in which they themselves were to be exploited. As* The Mass Strike *shows, students and workers acted together not to meet the demands* of a radical political program but because the development of students' and workers' struggles in the schools and in the shops led to a point where "all the productive workers found themselves up against the same problems, with identical perspectives of action." Indeed the active union of workers and students turns out to be a special case—one today of the greatest importance—of that necessity for any important working-class movement: class solidarity. Thus the first real student-worker conjuncture (soon followed by similar experiences in Italy) was echoed in a hitherto unexperienced degree of solidarity between French workers and the many foreigners working in France who are usually, like American blacks, both super-exploited and denied participation in trade union struggles.

(Secondly,) the French events only illustrate in a spectacular fashion what is visible as well in every workers' struggle: the reactionary role of the trade unions at the present time. Here the work which follows is correct to point out the uselessness of an analysis of this role in terms of "treason" and "misleadership." It is foolish to imagine that such organs, whose function is the negotiation of the terms at which wage-labor sells itself to capital, can serve as a means to the overthrow of the wages system.

This puts the accent of analysis and practice alike where it ought to be: on the problems and progress of the self-organization of the proletariat through organs of struggle deriving directly from the concrete antagonism of capital and labor at the workplace and in the community (strike committees, action committees, workers' councils, neighborhood councils). As long as the economic and social situation is reasonably stable, the workers allow control of their struggles to pass into the hands of permanent organizations with officials to handle the workers' affairs. When they are striking, on the other hand, particularly when their strike goes outside regular channels, there is no one else to do their thinking and their acting for them.

The spread of the wildcat strike as the form of militant struggle in the workplace throughout the capitalist world, indicating the obsolescence of the trade union, is the sign of a period in which capital is less able to make the concessions which sustained the labor unions in the past. The dream of the "militant" trade union is thus, hopefully, an empty one, not just because of the historically determined characteristics of this form of organization, but because of

*its growing uselessness for the working class even from the
point of view of purely ameliorative demands at the present
time.*

*Similar considerations apply to the mass "left" parties,
like the CP, whose behavior in May 1968 should have
surprised no one. The CP has no interest in seriously rock-
ing a boat which gives its officials a place among the major
domos of capital; a parliamentary and trade union-oriented
organization is hardly likely to support a movement struggling to break out of all bourgeois channels. But the problem is not one of "revisionism" and lack of revolutionary
purity. The May-June strike allows us to junk, along with
the "revolutionary trade union," the rubbish about the revolutionary Marxist-Leninist vanguard party. The real question is: why do such groups—unlike the mass parties, which
are part of the general apparatus of repression—play no
significant roles at all in political events of this magnitude?
Organizations—like the Marxist-Leninist sects—who see the
whole point of social revolution in terms of their accession
to positions of power, obviously fall out of the picture when
large numbers of people discover their capacity to run their
own affairs.*

*The error of the sects is made as well by those comrades,
who, while not Leninists, ascribe the "failure of the revolution" to lack of initiative on the part of the militants,
or even their failure to occupy government ministries.[1] The
general point is, not to deny the importance of decisive and
imaginative action by "militant minorities" in the triggering
of mass action, but only to recognize that the limits and
general character of a social movement are set by the spirit of
the masses and not by that of revolutionary groups.*

*The meaning of events like the 1968 mass strike is to be
looked for not in the continuing existence either of permanent leftist parties or of forms of organization based in
and tied to a period of active struggle (like the comités
d'action). Evidence of the importance of May-June in the
development of the French workers' movement appears
rather in the rise in the number of wildcats and factory
occupations since 1968, in an increasing militancy and imagination with which workers have been confronting the powers
that be.*

[1] *See D. and G. Cohn-Bendit,* Obsolete Communism, The Leftwing
Alternative *(McGraw-Hill, 1970), and F. Perlman and R. Gregoire,*
Student-Worker Action Committees *(Black and Red, Detroit).*

The question of the role of violence—in the sense of streetfighting, terrorism, sabotage—in the process of radicalization has recently come to the fore within the radical movement here as in France. Much has been made of the effect of the barricaded streetfighting against the police in setting off the French mass strike. As the comrades of ICO point out, power lies not in the streets but in the workplaces where workers have, if they wish to exercise it, the power to decide what is to be produced, how, and for whom. The strength of the students' battles with the cops lay not in their violence per se—necessary as that was—but in the exhibition of a determination to fight for control of their workplace, the Sorbonne. It was this character of the fighting which linked the solidarity of students and young workers at the Latin Quarter barricades to the united front of students and workers against the cops for control of the factory at Flins.

The heart of revolutionary violence, indeed, lies not in battling the protectors or symbols of the bourgeois order but in battling that order itself: in the refusal to submit to the definition of man as capitalist or worker through the seizure of control over the points of production—factory, office, school—which are the centers of social power. As long as capitalism exists, this seizure of social decision-making power can in general only consist in the exercise of direct control over the class struggle itself, in opposition to the claims of parties, trade unions, or press-appointed spokesmen.[2] With the social revolution that will grow out of this struggle the problem will be posed at a new level, that of the organization and direction of production by the producers. One of the virtues of this pamphlet is that it makes intelligible the dynamic link between the struggle as it exists and its imaginable extension into revolution. This link is what the authors discovered in the French workers and students as "the will to assume responsibilities," the felt need, imposed upon us by the capitalist system itself, to take control of our existence into our own hands.

I believe that the present work is mistaken in placing the idea of social labor-time, as a measure of production and consumption, at the center of communist economic calculation. For one thing, individuals' needs are not directly related to their contribution to production—young children

[2] See P. Mattick, "Workers Control," in P. Long, ed., The New Left (Porter Sargent, Boston, 1969).

*and old people are obvious examples—and indeed the con-
cept of "average social labor-time" may be appropriate only to
a society geared to value-production. For another, the problem may well be obsolete; given the immense productive
power of modern technology, the realization of the slogan
"From each according to his ability, to each according to
his needs" seems closer to a practical possibility than to a
distant goal.*

*This is, however, a question which can be resolved
theoretically only by a wide-ranging and serious discussion
which must be carried on; and practically, only in the
process of revolution itself.[3] The great virtue of* The Mass
Strike in France *is to show how such a discussion is meaningful by locating through an analysis of the events of
1968 those characteristics of the class struggle at the present
time that point to the emerging reality of its revolutionary
goal.*

Paul Mattick, Jr. July 1970

# I   IL S'EST PASSE QUELQUE CHOSE

What was the situation in France as 1968 began?

At this time, as for a very long time now, the class
struggle consisted in more or less short-lived and scattered
actions. Now and then sudden outbreaks of resistance,
tough but quickly broken by order of the union bigshots,
made it possible to think that other forms of struggle could
appear—then everything would collapse back again into
apathy.

The chiefs and chieflings of the parties and the trade
unions loudly deplored this apathy, without permitting anyone to inquire in public whether this apathy was not itself
at once the basis of their position as bureaucrats and the
consequence of their dirty work—legal, patriotic, electoral,
and so forth. And then there were the little political groups,
the *groupuscules,* preaching in the desert conceptions a
half-century old and more. Their isolation engendered the
idea that modern capitalism was able to manipulate the

---

[3] *The study of these questions on which the comrades of ICO
base their thinking has recently been republished:* Grundprinzipien
kommunistischer Produktion und Verteilung *(Institut fur Praxis
und Theorie des Ratekommunismus, Rudiger Blankertz Verlag,
Berlin: 1970)*

workers, as producers and as consumers, at it pleased. And solemn sociologists went on and on about a working class stupefied with cheap cars and TVs, bourgeoisified, they said, as if they were talking about a sick man, indifferent to revolt and passive before the iniquity of his condition.

In the face of all that, it was necessary first of all to discover other words, other ideas.

If something had to change, it had to be first of all in men's minds. If something changed a little, it was above all among the young. They were *blousons noirs, yes-yes, cheveux longs*——hoods, rock'n'rollers, long-hairs—one didn't really know what, nothing very precise but yet enough to plunge the bourgeois into fear and incomprehension. The young could no longer be completely controlled; they lived differently, had no longer the old feeling for property, work, and the family. People generally tried to reassure themselves with formulas like "Youth will have its fling!" but it didn't turn out like that.

For, in the end, the weakest link of French capitalism is the youth and the problems it raises for itself and for ruling classes incapable even of perceiving them, imprisoned as they are in a style of politics in which promises take the place of acts and immobility and respect for the moneyed powers that be are decked out with dynamic formulas. These classes are caught up almost relentlessly in rigid and sclerotic institutions like the University, a prey to insurmountable contradictions beween the interests of the old teachers and administrators (not always a question of physiological age) preserved in obsolete conceptions and out-of-date relations of domination as well as in pontificating stupidity, and the interests of an industry which needs technicians at the lowest possible cost of production. Contradictions of this type, setting the old against the (at least relatively) new, are to be found in every level of the society of the Fifth Republic. Even greedier, more limited, and more self-satisfied than the others, the French employers as a class—and their lieutenants in the parties and labor unions made in their own image—yield only to great popular movements, in the colonies as well as at home.

There is no need to dwell here on the sequence of events, on the repression effected by police and by ideology which made the action of the young people—students and workers together—a detonator setting off an immense and spontaneous movement, without an apparent goal but of a breadth not experienced in France since the Commune and, moreover, spreading this time over the whole country. "We did not suspect the importance of the unorganized . . . There was a climate of apathy in the unions. They had been built in the image of the power of the bosses in the enterprise." This declaration of a CFDT bureaucrat, after fifteen days of general strike, is most significant."[1]

Not a train or a subway on the rails, not a letter or a telegram carried, not a car or a ton of coal moving—and everywhere, from the smallest enterprise to the biggest, occupation, following that of the universities, of the factories, the offices, the schools, all the cells of economic and social life. One even saw (indicating the depth of the movement), soccer footballers occupying the seat of their Federation, managerial staff occupying the headquarters of an employers' federation and schoolteachers that of their union. Only the organs of political life were ignored, as on that day when 40,000 students passed by the National Assembly, where the deputies were in session, without according it even a hostile cry. The unions, the parties, all the frameworks within which the workers are organized were overflowed and emptied of all real power.

On the surface, the only force still at the disposal of the State was that of the police and the army. But, it must be said, at no moment was this force obliged to intervene with all its means. The police were brutal, but they did not shoot. As for the army, it served at the very most as a dissuasive force, an implicit threat. A ruling class which feels the situation getting out of its control doesn't use tear-gas grenades: in May-June 1968 there was not a truly revolutionary situation in France.

However, just as the strike arose spontaneously, in the wake of the student revolt, without precise demands, new forms of workplace organization were considered nearly everywhere. Impassioned and utterly novel discussions took place; people asked themselves about forms of society in which it would no longer be necessary to put things off forever. Now it was possible to talk about everything with everyone; in thousands and thousands of production units, for the first time, people started to put their heads together, on the job, about their condition—about the problems of real life. All of this went on, not in opposition to but outside of

[1] *Le Monde*, 2-3 June.

the old organizations (like the State) and, for the same reason, the latter more or less sat out the game. Consciously or not, they acted as though they were fully aware that the strikers were not able, from one day to the next, to coordinate their action without going through the old network, and they waited for the movement to fall back, putting their shoulders to the wheel and pushing in this direction with all their still considerable strength. And nevertheless the strikers, if they didn't succeed in setting up even the embryonic form of a new organization of society, thought no longer of joining up again en masse with political organizations just like the old ones. Thus, when the "militants" —Trotskyites, Maoists, or other—tried to recruit a vanguard within the student movement, it turned out that the overwhelming majority of the unorganized intended to stay that way, without there being in that intent for a single minute a sign of apathy.

Whether it was a matter of the Grenelle agreements or of shop agreements, of "popular government" or of "revolutionary party," the largest number of the producers in struggle felt that this was not the right response, that something else was necessary, even if this something else was indistinct in appearance and unformulated. Here is how this feeling was expressed in brief by a worker who spoke during a meeting of a strike committee in answer to the union leaders and the managerial staff of his place of work. The latter controlled the committee and were astonished to see that after fifteen days a gulf had opened between the workers on strike, who came each day to get the good word at the general assembly, and the strike committee, who took it upon itself to hand it out to them:

> It was not the unions who started the strike. It was people who violently wanted something. The unions afterwards took the strike in hand and proposed the usual demands. They broke a working mechanism, and that explains the chasm which separates the strike committee from the employees on strike.

"Il s'est passe quelque chose"—something real happened, even if one could at no time speak of revolution. Everyone felt that this was not 1936, but something else again. What burst into the concrete universe of the worker, something which was formerly at best only literature for a *groupuscule*, or ritual formula, was the explicit will for responsibilities in production, for exercise of control of production, the birth in the struggle of a feeling of lived interdependence, of fraternity even, between the different categories of producers in a word, the rough sketch of a response of workers and students to a sudden crisis of society.

Without doubt, there are few real and particularly significant examples—at least so far as we know of factories started up again by the strikers themselves. But everything depends on this. It is true that in certain cases, for instance, at Nantes, the unions tried to take care of provisioning; elsewhere, students sought to get agricultural products to factories, to establish with the truckers a liaison between peasants and striking workers. In other cases, going by the letter of the CFDT's slogans, workers demanded management of the factories by themselves. Yet elsewhere, there was only discussion, the words—radical at first—becoming more and more timorous as the return to work progressed and the traditional power-relationships were reestablished.

The great mass of the workers entered into struggle under the impulsive desire to somehow change the system exploiting them. But at the same time, the ideas and concepts born of all the attempts to integrate them into the system remained: the great majority of workers did not believe that it was possible for them to run their workplaces and the society themselves. This is why the various attempts which got underway in this direction remained vague and isolated; and this is also why the traditional organizations could get the movement back into their hands. In what follows, we will try to take inventory and discuss these attempts, though they remained isolated and could not succeed in really taking shape and becoming general.

But it is useful also to go beyond this. As soon as a mass strike clears the way for the organization of production by the producers, the problem of who has power at the level of the enterprise, of the state, of the whole world, is posed. Social power lies in the hands of the workers when they are in control of their own activity on the job; but the survival of organs of political power disposing of an apparatus of repression (police, union marshalls, political parties, etc.) sooner or later provokes a conflict. It is not by chance that the directors of the economy and of politics, the CRS, the unions, do the same work, each in his own way. They have the same vocation of dominating and repressing the workers in a State in which they hold political power or which they make their servant. In the same way, on the international scale, no capitalist state (of either the Western or the Eastern branch) can tolerate the development —even in the universities—of workers' control of the enterprises and of society.

These problems are not new. The dictatorship of Capital, Leninism, Stalinism, and fascisms of all types, the Second World War—all these have succeeded in wiping out even the memory of everything which in the Russia of 1917, the Germany of 1918–1921, the Spain of 1936–37, the Hungary of 1956, could attest to the existence of a continuing movement for emancipation which looked to the organization of production and consumption by the producers themselves. Beyond the problem of power, this new society—which we now know to be wholly other than a comforting myth— will have to resolve economic problems, those of communist production and distribution. We have tried to sketch these problems in the light of this past.

## II  CAPITALIST SOCIETY

Modern capitalist society is characterized by a technical development without precedent. At least in the advanced countries, the means of production have attained a fantastic level. At the same time, the system has become quite complicated and appears almost incomprehensible to all observers. This complexity has brought with it a great erection of barriers between men.

All this is not the effect of chance but results rather from the capitalist system's need to continually realize more profits. Pushed by the very dynamic of its development, this system could no longer remain that of laissez-faire which reigned in the 19th century, with its corresponding organization of society based on a large number of individual small capitalists fighting each other through the intermediary of the market. Its continued existence necessitated raising the productivity of labor, since it is from labor that its profits are drawn. Every worker, every employee knows perfectly well that his employer tries continually to raise the rate and the output of work, a tendency which, moreover, every worker continually fights. To raise productivity, capitalism has employed machines increasingly complex and increasingly numerous, and has made increasing use of scientific discoveries to improve the system of production.

Capital has concentrated and continues to concentrate. Small businesses disappear, and the formation of great monopolies has been realized in the course of the last decades.

The fundamental reason for this concentration lies in the fact that, to augment productivity, in a given sector it is necessary to utilize larger and larger masses of capital to set up the necessary technology. To obtain these masses of capital, it is necessary to set greater and greater masses of laborers to work to extract from them greater and greater masses of profit.

This development of the system makes necessary organs of coordination more structured than before. Every large enterprise has developed an enormous managerial corps in order to make it work. Of necessity, the State itself has been forced to interfere more massively in the economy. It has taken charge of entire sectors, indispensable to the working of the system, but of which the private capitalists, even at the level of highly concentrated trusts, are now no longer able or willing to take charge—no longer willing, because these sectors are no longer directly profitable; no longer able, because running them requires too great masses of capital. The State, through the medium of taxes, can distribute these enormous investments (e.g., in France, electricity, transports) among the population as a whole.

In societies of the Western type a mixed capitalist economy has developed, in which a "private" and a "public" sector coexist, permanently reacting on each other in a state of often unstable equilibrium.

In societies of the Eastern type (USSR, China, Cuba, the Eastern European countries) the State has entirely taken charge of the economy, putting into effect a state capitalism in which a new exploiting class decides for everyone the orientation and the volume of production and extracts benefits from it in the form of high salaries and social advantages.

To maintain a high level of profit for part of capital, the capitalist system does not hesitate to destroy the rest of capital, that is to say, to engage in activities not productive of wealth. This is the role, for example, of advertising, scientific research (which to a great extent is pointless: for instance, space research), armaments production, etc. Here again, the whole population, through the intermediary of taxes or the market, bears the cost of the achievement of objectives not attainable by individual capitalists.

Concurrently with this transformation of capitalism's economic structure, a corresponding transformation of social classes has come about. Far from having ended up as a sharply contrasting division between a handful of exploiters and a large mass of exploited, the complexity of the capitalist system has brought about a pyramidal social structure, in principle based on criteria of technical competence, which rises without discontinuity from the worker to the PDG (*President Directeur General*, or Chairman of the Board). The old bourgeois class has been transformed. Doubtless, in the West, there are some bourgeois who live exclusively on their private means, but the most general case is one of integration into the system of production and managerial control from which they profit by high salaries and all sorts of advantages.

This hierarchal structure presents the advantage of opening up possibilities for integration of all strata of society into the system. In principle, access to different levels of the social system depends on the education and abilities of the individual. Official propaganda doesn't fail to stress this point. It tries to create a real cult of the educated man, of the Nobel prize-winner for example, which ranks with the love affairs of princesses and the infidelities of pop-singers. "Culture" is extolled as the means of moving from the position of controlled to that of controller.

The population as a whole falls for this propaganda. It does not question the idea of a society hierarchized on the basis of knowledge and aptitudes, a hierarchy expressed in terms of wage-differentials.

That the social pyramid rises on the criteria—true or false —of education and ability, and that there is a continuity linking the base with the summit doesn't at all change the exploitative character of modern Capital, the existence of a ruling class. There exists in fact such a class, which (individually or collectively) owns the means of production, which determines the orientation and the volume of production, which finally reaps the benefits of the exploitation of lower levels.

Since the end of the last war, western capitalism has known a new era of prosperity. Thanks to this, it has been able to furnish generally higher wages to the population as a whole. It could do this for two main reasons: first, as a result of the rapid growth of productivity; second, because a certain number of unskilled jobs, in which productivity could not be increased, have been left to certain strata like the blacks in the United States or the North Africans and foreign workers in Europe, systematically excluded from the process of enrichment.

This rise in the general standard of living is expressed by an increased consumption—cars, refrigerators, television, etc.—which has bound the various strata yet more closely to the status quo. This rise in the standard of living can be seen again in social benefits, like social security, paid vacations, etc., which are further means of integration into the system. Another consequence of this rise is the possibility for larger sections of society of having their children accepted into the educational system which had until then been closed to them. This is especially true of the middle classes which consist of the lower-level managers, highly skilled workers, and petty tradesmen of all sorts. For them, sending their children to the University is a luxury which they can now afford, just like the purchase of a color television.

In doing this the middle classes are responding to two attractions. To begin with, they dream that their children may escape the mediocrity of their condition: either disappearing, like the small businessman, or else imprisoned in a cretinizing system, without hope of a way out, as subordinate managers and employees, always submitting to the moods of an office head.

Further, these middle classes see possibilities for their children of entering a higher level in society, which as a result of the accelerated development of the system, has need of more and more cadres—decision-making personnel: managerial and technical staff—of every sort.

The influx of young people into the University is thus one of the byproducts of the period of post-war capitalist prosperity.

For several years, however, the system has shown signs of being out of breath. There is no longer as great a need of managerial staff as before. Even technicians no longer enjoy the same job security. There are often changes in methods of production and accumulated knowledge is no help in adapting to new techniques. Technological unemployment has appeared. It is a matter not only (as it still was yesterday), of shutting down certain non-profitable enterprises and transferring the staff to employment elsewhere, leaving the workers to find new jobs themselves as best they can (thus creating a permanent unemployment which keeps wages down), but of effecting in numerous areas important transformations which require new knowledge, inaccessible to the old staff. The classical openings for students become constricted, on the one hand by the recession in capitalist development, and on the other by the existence of unemployed cadres competing on the market.

In this lies the profound economic reason for the student "malaise" apparent throughout the world. Students question a system which can no longer offer them their traditional opportunities. They discover on this occasion the existence of unemployment and the idiocy of the system of production.

Without a real economic crisis in capitalism, which at present halts its progress at most only temporarily, there exist premonitory symptoms of a social crisis which in favorable cases—that is to say, if it occurs together with possibilities of crises in the world of labor—can provoke an explosion.

In this respect, France in 1968 has furnished a good example. This strongly traditional, chauvinist country has experienced profound and rapid tranformations during the last few decades. Formerly—since the revolution of 1789—France was the land of petty property in both the industrial and the agricultural domains. Following the Second World War, the reconstruction of French capital, which permitted it to reenter the concert of nations, was effected in a way which led to an ever more accentuated concentration. The Marshall Plan and the resulting importation of American production techniques have turned the conservative capitalism of pre-war France upside down. This did not occur without conflicts and risks. Those bound to the old system have resisted and continue to resist. The struggle was carried on for a long time on the terrain of the colonial Empire, one of the pillars of the earlier regime but one about which the new capitalists cared little, or rather, to which they preferred another type of exploitation. Finally, monopoly capital, "modern" capital, had to prevail and, with this victory, to reduce to impotence the old system's supporters, of which the army is a striking example.

The concentration of capital here as everywhere is accompanied by a transformation of social classes, in particular by a great reduction of the peasantry. Concentration proceeds also in the agricultural domain, because mechanization is profitable only for sufficiently large properties. The peasant population of France has fallen from 30 percent to 10 percent since the end of the war and the decrease continues. The peasants thus "liberated" have gone to enlarge the masses of workers, putting greater strain on the labor market, a tension being all the more serious as France has had to accept, since 1962, 1,500,000 *Pieds-Noirs,* colonists dispossessed by the Algerian revolution.

At the same time industrial development, while it permitted and required the creation of new types of manpower, had to take place within a society little ready to accommodate it, the French bourgeoisie being one of the most conservative and obtuse in the world. Until the last few years, the training of industrial managers was accomplished through the channel of the *grandes ecoles,* a sclerotic system, entered through a very difficult competitive exam; little professional skill was taught but one obtained the degree necessary to enter the higher social strata. On the other hand, the University remained a medieval island within the modern world, desiring only to reproduce itself. In contrast to the *grandes ecoles,* one enters the University upon obtaining the *baccalaureat* degree which marks the end of secondary school. This system worked smoothly as long as only the most fortunate sections of the bourgeoisie could pay for the studies of their children. With the rise in the standard of living and the demographic pressure of the post-war period, the University has been invaded by a whole younger generation. These young people prefer the mediocrity of student life, which offers a semblance of freedom and which permits them to put off for a while their entrance into the detestable world of production, even if they know that in all probability they will fail their exams and not get the really privileged jobs. With this influx, the University was condemned to death. There has been no lack of well-intentioned men to propose reforms for it. All of these tend towards adaptation to the outside world, that is to say, to the laws of the capitalist market. Their ultimate expression is to be found both in the recommendations of the Caen colloquium and in the Fouchet reform. In both these cases, it was a matter of organizing a system of selection among the students to direct them towards a carefully graded hierarchy of channels permitting the formation of more or less specialized technicians.

This policy in the long run was bound to run up against two oppositions: on the one hand, that of the faculty, the majority of whom remained ferocious partisans of the mandarinate; on the other hand, that of the students, who did not wish to enter the selection system. It was almost inevitable that violent cleavages would appear inside the world of the University.

The liquidation of the old French capitalism and its evolution towards a concentrated capitalism necessitated a transformation of methods of government. The bonapartist regime installed by the gaullists fills this need. As in all countries, an almost total effacement of parliament is experienced. Parliament used to serve, in effect, as a place for discussion between different interest groups, as a process of compromise by which the policy of the ruling class was decided. It no longer has this raison d'être in a more concentrated economy in which the State has a more essential role to play.

Authoritarian decisions have to be made to accelerate the process of concentration and the transformation of the country, especially when they express the necessity of adaptation to a vaster economy on the European scale. The gaullists have not wronged themselves in stressing the authoritarian and arbitrary character of their regime, all the more easily accomplished as the evolution of the system required that entire strata of the middle classes (little enterprises, little businesses, etc.) be transformed, causing the traditional left to lose much of its social power. However, if the gaullist regime answers well to a necessity of "modern" capitalism, it presents a character of rigidity, which it has inherited without doubt from its leader, but which results also from the conditions of the struggle against the Algerian revolution and the O.A.S. For ten years, the gaullist government has ignored those capitalist groups which could not adapt themselves to the evolution in progress, except to shut them up brutally. It has found itself in a delicate position for resolving the university problem because it would have been necessary to attack directly the old University and because it considered other questions more urgent. Its attitude has been to let the situation putrify, hoping that in five years a generation smaller in numbers would furnish an automatic solution to the problem.

However, problems are not solved by denying their existence, or by treating them with scorn. They become aggravated and lead to situations which can be overcome only with brutality. Faced with student movements like the *22 March,* the government was caught defenceless. At first the government left it alone, sure of its rapid extinction. After that, it tried to render the Movement's "leaders" harmless, for from the bureaucratic viewpoint of the ruling class all action is necessarily directed by an apparatus. The police action at the Sorbonne on May 4th had probably no other aim than the decapitation of the movement by getting the names of and arresting its leaders, unknown till then.

But the Movement was precisely not one of leaders, and the attempt made by the bourgeois press to transform Danny Cohn-Bendit into a leader and an idol failed completely. What characterized the Movement was precisely that a larger number than was believed felt themselves directly implicated both as individuals and as a group, that it first set itself to question the university structures and then, progressively, as a result of the streetfighting against the police, came to question bourgeois society as a whole.

This attitude set a double example, first because it showed that direct action can pay, that it can force opposing power to retreat (only for a moment, doubtless, in this case), but especially because it showed that in action consciousness of the problems posed grows rapidly.

This example was not lost on the masses of workers. They were profoundly struck by it. They saw something completely different from the routine of union struggles for almost automatic amelioration of the standard of living. Without doubt, the latter are not without interest in the Common Market country with the lowest wages except for Italy, but, confusedly, the masses put forward other types of demands which, timidly, called into question the very form of society. Here also the role of the young was particularly important. Not yet caught up in the system of modern life, feeling solidarity with other young people of neighboring social strata, not having known the war or the "victories of 1936," more than most workers threatened by unemployment, they felt themselves less inclined to obey blindly the union's commands, to which their elders have become accustomed, and often joined the students in their combats in the street and in their desires for self-determination and for responsibility.

Something new, which quite proves that the movement

of May, 1968 went far beyond simple wage demands: the
cadres participated and, in certain cases, even set it off,
demanding non-hierarchial wages or calling into question
the direction of the enterprise by insisting themselves that
all social strata must have responsibility. One can no doubt
maintain that the participation of cadres in the movement
was in fact only an attempt at its bureaucratic or technocratic recapture. But that is to see only one side of this
activity. Every attempt at self-management, every self-
determined movement which does not end in total overthrow
of the bourgeois order of things is always recapturable by
bureaucrats or technocrats. But attempts at self-management—and it is these which we are trying to distinguish,
analyse, and criticise in this pamphlet—contain something
else: the promise of a society in which, finally, the exploitation of man by man will come to an end.

## III   THE STUDENT MOVEMENT

One cannot overemphasize the role of crucible played,
with respect to the general action, by the student demonstrations which the young workers came to join in ever increasing numbers; and with respect to thought, by that
extraordinary marketplace of ideas, experiences, and contacts that was the Sorbonne, become the symbol itself of the
movement, and after it the other faculties. This was so
because all productive workers found themselves up against
the same problems, with identical perspectives of action.
Similarly, it was in the faculties that the idea of self-management, which flowed naturally from the occupation of the
university centers, necessarily came into general circulation,
though its significance there was not the same as in the
factories or offices.

Starting from the Nanterre campus, the student movement very quickly won the other centers. It is evidently
impossible to examine here everything that was done and said.
We give only four examples: the Nanterre movement and
its extensions on the ground of political organization, the
Faculty of Sciences, the establishment of liaisons with the
workers and with the peasants.

### 1 The Movement at Nanterre

In the first trimester a strike launched outside of traditional political or union organizations united 10,000 of the 12,000 students on the campus around problems of improving working conditions. The result: the establishment of commissions drawing members equally from each department, which very quickly showed their sterility.

This was followed in the second trimester by a series of sporadic incidents, expressing a diffused malaise: a demonstration of solidarity with a student threatened with expulsion ended in a scuffle with the cops called by the Dean; some courses were disrupted, and so on. Incidentally, the activity of *Cite Universitaire* (University housing) residents in February provided the University with an excuse for the abrogation of internally set rules.

At the end of March a new phase took shape:
* psychology students boycotted their preliminary exams;
* four students distributed a paper questioning the teaching and uses of sociology ("Why sociologists?");
* On Friday, March 22, following the arrest of six anti-imperialist militants, a protest meeting was organized which ended by voting for the occupation of the administration building that very evening. 150 students, gathered in the faculty-council room, debated numerous political problems until 2 A.M. A day of unrestricted political debates on various themes was set for Friday, March 29.

The university authorities were upset by this turn of events (intensive preparation for the 29th: leaflets, speeches, inscriptions on the campus walls, and a poster campaign) and drew up the personnel to oppose the students with closure of the library and a strike of classroom attendants. On Thursday the 28th, Dean Grappin ordered the suspension of classes and lab sessions until the following Monday. A meeting of 300 students decided to continue the previous day's action but as a day of preparation for the political discussions, which were postponed until April 2.

On Friday the 29th, while a large force of police surrounded the campus, 500 students participated in an opening meeting held in a commonroom of the *Cite,* and constituted themselves as a commission to discuss the themes set for debate.

Monday, April 1, a majority of second-year sociology students decided to boycott their exams. They then voted to endorse a text denouncing sociology as ideology. Meanwhile, among the professors, dissensions appeared between the liberal departments (human sciences and letters), favorable to granting premises for the next day's meeting, and the reactionaries (history), who demanded the arrest of the "ringleaders."

Tuesday, April 2, was a success: the administration did not succeed in preventing the occupation of a lecture hall by 1,500 people for a preliminary meeting, nor were the corporatists (adherents of a "pure", "nonpolitical" university) and fascists able to stop commissions from meeting in another building. The final plenary assembly, attended by 800 students and some lecturers, decided to continue the movement.

## The Nature of the Movement

The Nanterre movement was clearly political. Unlike the November strike, which was "corporatist" in spirit, it stressed nonunion issues such as "Down with police repression," "Critical university," "The right of political expression and action on campus." At the same time it revealed its minority character and its consciousness of this fact: several orators denounced the illusion of the slogan, "Defence of the common interests of all students." At Nanterre it is clear that many students accepted higher education as an initiation into the management of bourgeois business. One thus saw the disengagement of a core of 300 "extremists" capable of mobilizing 1,000 of the Faculty's 12,000 students.

The actions carried out accelerated the emergence of consciousness in some people: it was a matter not so much of "provocations" as of *obliging latent authoritarianism to manifest itself* (such as the truckloads of CRS ready to interfere) by showing *the true face of the proposed "dialogues"* between students and administration. As soon as certain problems appeared, dialogue gave place to clubbing. The result was political consciousness, but also active participation on the part of all those who had until then been paralyzed by the inefficacy of the *groupuscules* and the routine of traditional demands by means of petitions and silent marches. Finally, students and professors had to drop their traditional political labels when the apparatus of repression got going. With interest we saw the UEC call for the proper functioning of a bourgeois university or certain "leftist" or even "Marxist" professors terrified to see their status questioned.

We must insist on *the novelty of the movement set in motion,* novelty at least in the French context. First of all, *work had been done in common,* transcending the oppositions between *groupuscules:* it's a matter not of decreeing the inanity of these groups because we feel like it, but of a process in the course of which divergences rose out of theoretic and practical confrontation with reality rather than out of verbal quarrels between sects. Terminological peculiarities were questioned as rigid and unchanged perceptions of reality which *groupuscules* use to distinguish themselves from each other and not as instruments of scientific analysis. On the other hand, we resolved not to fall under the control of particular political groups or of the administration and the liberal teachers, adepts of "dialogue" and of confrontation in closed rooms.

New problems arose, in particular those of more direct and effective rejection of the class university, of a denunciation of the concept of neutral and objective knowledge as well as of its specialization, of an inquiry on the place which we are destined to occupy in the current division of labor, of joining the workers in struggle, etc.

Simultaneously, original forms of action were developed: meetings improvised on campus, occupation of classrooms to hold our debates, interruptions of lectures, boycotts of exams, posting of bulletins and posters in the halls, taking possession of the microphone monopolized by the administration, etc.

*The Problems of the University*

It appeared to the March 22 Movement (M22M) that the problems of the university had to be settled rapidly in order that the students might devote themselves to studying the basic problems.

With respect to exams, the Movement wished to see to it, on the one hand, that the student revolt and the many problems which it raised would not be stifled by the mass of good boys and girls looking out for their immediate personal interests: to pass their exams (which excluded simply postponing them); on the other hand, that the most disadvantaged students would not suffer from the decisions taken (which excluded a pure and simple boycott). This is why we proposed a transitional solution, pending the elaboration of a new mode of control of knowledge, which must lead to a practice of teaching renovated in its content as much as in its methods. This examination of a particular type would be given three weeks after the acceptance of the movement's conditions, the granting of amnesty for all the demonstrators and the obtaining of information on those students who had "disappeared."[2]

All those wounded in demonstrations, wage-earning students, scholarship students, and those on term leave were to be automatically passed.

All the students whose university records for 1967–1968 were satisfactory were to be passed.

The others were to go before a commission representing both students and faculty which would judge them on a subject freely chosen by themselves. The exam would be written or oral, given individually or to a group.

Profiting from the current situation and from our position of power we will use whatever structure is set up to impose:

• the opening of the dormitories and university restaurants to young apprentices, unemployed, and workers.

• the opening of the campus to workers of Hauts-de-Seine, the area northwest of Paris within which lies Nanterre.

Regarding the autonomy of the Faculties and the universities, the M 22 M is conscious that an island of socialism cannot exist in a society which continues the capitalist profit system. When the State controls the funds and the bosses corral the students as they leave the campus, simple university autonomy is a utopian notion and a reformist illusion. The M 22 M, opposed anyway to the university authorities' attempts to coopt the student movement, would therefore come out against this idea, if we did not see in it a means of achieving our ultimate objectives. In fact, the realization of autonomy was accompanied by the institution of student power in the university, with right of veto over every decision taken and if the students utilized this power not to do the work of management that we don't accept but to continue to act in confrontation, then autonomy would appear desirable to us.

All these rearrangements of the established order within

---

2 These proposals were made during the second week of May, when the movement was very little radicalized. Events made the majority of M 22 M afterwards lose interest in the problem.

the university structure are not justified in the eyes of M 22 M unless they are elements of a revolutionary process seeking to transform capitalist society into a classless society. This transformation of society cannot be realized by the students alone, who find *natural* allies in the workers: we refuse to be the watchdogs, they, to be the servants of the bourgeoisie. Alliance with the working class has always been one of our objectives.

## Joining with the Working Class

We occupy the Faculties, you occupy the factories. Are we fighting for the same thing?

Workers' sons make up only 10 percent of the students in higher education. Are we fighting for there to be more, for a democratic reform of the university? That would be an improvement, but it isn't what is most important. These workers' sons will become students like the others. That a worker's son can become a Director is not our program. We want to suppress the separation between workers and directors.

There are students who on leaving the university cannot find work. Are we fighting for there to be more work for them to find? For a just employment policy for graduates? That would be an improvement but it isn't the essential point. These graduates in psychology or sociology will become career planners, personnel directors, psycho-technicians who will try to arrange your working conditions; graduates in mathematics will become the engineers who put into operation machines more productive and more unsupportable for you. Why do we, students deriving from the bourgeoisie, criticize capitalist society? For a worker's son to become a student is to leave his class. For a bourgeois' son it can be the occasion of his getting to know the true nature of his class, of questioning himself on the social function for which he is destined, on the organization of society, on the place you occupy in it.

We refuse to be scholars cut off from social reality.

We refuse to be used for the profit of the ruling class.

We wish to abolish the distinction between the labor of production and the labor of thinking and organization. We wish to construct a classless society; we struggle in the same direction.

You demand a minimum wage of 1,000 F. in the Parisian region, retirement at 60, a 40-hour week with 48 hours pay. These are honorable and venerable demands. They appear, however, to be unrelated to our objectives, but in fact you occupy the factories, you take the bosses as hostages, you are striking without warning. These forms of struggle have been made possible by long actions carried out with perseverance in the enterprises and also thanks to the recent fight of the students.

These struggles are more radical than our legitimate demands, because they not only seek an improvement of the workers' condition in the capitalist system, but imply the destruction of that system. They are political in the true sense of the word; you fight not for a new prime minister but for an end to the boss's power in the shop and in society. The form of your struggle offers to us, students, the model of a truly socialist activity; the appropriation of the means of production and of decision-making power by the workers.

Your struggle and ours converge. We must destroy everything which isolates us from each other (habits, newspapers, etc.). There must be a joining together of the occupied shops and Faculties.[3]

## The Organization of the March 22 Movement

The Movement is composed of base groups of ten people:
• who discuss all the political problems with which we are confronted.
• who delegate someone to report their discussions to each of the special commissions dealing with various political problems: autonomy, exams and action on campus, action towards the working class, anti-imperialist struggle, self-defense, etc.
• who delegate one person to report their discussions, participate in emergency meetings of the coordinating committee which will also contain a delegate from each special commission.
• who take charge of the distribution of leaflets, discussions, and, in general, of dealings with several factories and with a specific geographic sector.
• who take charge of their own security in propaganda work and their self-defense in general.
• who take charge of their transportation: each group is supposed to have at least one car available to them.

It is not necessary that a group's delegates to the different commissions be fixed from the time the group delegates someone to a given meeting.

On the other hand, to the extent that we are joined by new militants, new groups will be formed so that each

[3] Leaflet issued by M 22 M on May 24, published in *Partisans*, no. 42, pp. 107-8; *Ce n'est qu'un début . . . (Cahiers Libres, no. 124)*, pp. 49-57, parts of the latter were translated in *Cawl*, issue no. 3.

group has no more than 12 members.

The special commissions serve to make syntheses of the group · discussions on various themes. One is created each time a new political problem appears. They coordinate the actions and the activity of the neighborhood committees and each delegate someone to the coordinating committee. They take charge of the *concrete* application of political decisions and make sure to be close to the technical applications committee.

*The Coordinating Commitee* includes the delegates from base groups and committee delegates. It is the structure responsible for decisions and the organization of movement activity in normal times. However, in case of conflict between delegates from a base group and a commission on some problem, a general assembly will be called to settle it.

A certain number of executive commissions depend directly on the coordinating committee:

• collection of money from personalities and synthesis of various purchases

• relations with the outside: sending militants to explain our activity wherever we are asked—answering journalists' interviews, etc.


• coordination with the rest of the movement (other than M 22 M) that is to say, CAL, May 3rd Action Committee, student-worker committees at Censier, Halle-aux-Vins, UNEF, and SNESup, the union central bureaus, and eventually other structures.

• editorial committees: coordination of work on pamphlets and stuff people want to write about (like *Action*, etc.)

• press review

• propaganda, printing tracts, posters, etc.

• health: medicine, advice, etc.

• legal: counsel in case of arrest, legal defense, etc.

• foreigners, because of special legal problems; and everything else subsequently thought useful.

A newsletter for information and discussion is written by the militants. All write in it under any form at all: three lines of information, ten lines of political poetry, theoretical sketch, analysis, etc. In it the commissions circulate their reports, and the communiques of the movement are published. When a piece of work is carried out somewhere, when information arrives from the provinces, a text is written.

*Principles of Action*

A certain number of principles inspire our actions:

• the recognition of the plurality and diversity of tendencies in the revolutionary movement

• the revocability of representatives and the effective power of the collectives

• the permanent circulation of ideas and the struggle against the monopolizing of information and understanding

• the struggle against hierarchization

• the abolition in practice of the division of labor (to fight the barriers between manual and intellectual work).

• the rejection of the mystifications exemplified by the motions for censure, referendum, electoral coalitions, round tables, delegated power

• refusal of dialogue with the bosses

• destruction of the myth of the State as arbiter, in the service of the general interest

• the direction by the workers themselves of their shops, a form of action which can for the moment only be spontaneous but which we must advocate as one of the revolutionary possibilities

*Activities—Four axes:*

• information
• provisioning
• self-defense
• organization of demonstrations

*Information* has a double aim:

• to fight against the poison campaign of the bosses and the government which gives false information on the work places.

• to institute direct links beween the different strike committees and between the inhabitants of a neighborhood. Neighborhood meetings, attended by workers in various enterprises have, in fact, taken place.

For that, daily bulletins are put out using information given by the strikers (on the Parisian level and for certain neighborhoods). These bulletins are put together in liaison with the different action committees.

On the other hand, leaflets produced by the strikers are mimeographed and distributed. In the neighborhoods, meetings for political agitation and information are held in the street.

*Provisioning:* Collections of money and food are organized every day. Contacts are established between striking workers and peasants. Workers make their trucks available for looking for supplies in the provinces. Stocks of food are centralized in the workplaces which offer their space. It is in this way possible to distribute tons of food.

*Self-defense:* groups of militants are at the disposition of the workers for reinforcement of strike pickets, and resistance to the attacks of UNR commandos, fascists, the cops.

*Demonstrations:* Demonstrations of support–physical and political–for the workers are organized in the neighborhoods of Paris, in the suburbs, at Flins. After May 10, numerous demonstrations were proposed to the UNEF and the SNESup, notably that of Friday the 10th, first night of the barricades.[4]

## 2 Faculty of Sciences, University of Paris at Halle-aux-Vins

Unlike Nanterre, the Faculty of Sciences had not experienced important protest movements before the disorders in the Latin Quarter. But, there was here as everywhere a latent uneasiness among the students (35,000 enrolled) about Dean Zamansky's projects of setting up a selective system and the Fouchet reform whose realization must involve an increase in the students' problems. The students' reactions were at that time limited to purely reformist demands: accelerated construction of the new campus at Villetaneuse and creation of new teaching jobs. These demands were taken up by the lecturers who saw there a means of penetrating the professorial ranks. In return, no criticism was directed against the teaching methods, except in respect to the desire of the university authority to raise the productivity of studies and to increase the selection procedure.

However, from May 3 on, courses were stopped in certain *advanced* sections, under the direction of professors with "advanced ideas" like Monod. These stoppages were only a visceral reaction to the police brutalities, but the situation rapidly evolved towards calling into question the situation of the students within the University. For the first time,

---

[4] In fact this was the Movement's form only for a short period; if it was abandoned, it nonetheless made possible the creation of several Action Committees.

direct discussions between teachers and students took place
in each department, often in the crowded lecture halls
(500 to 600 people). Of course, the discussions bore at
first on the examinations which were to begin May 15,
but they opened up quickly enough to general political
questions.

In other sections, where the professors are particularly
reactionary, courses continued to meet. The students already
mobilized, organized themselves spontaneously to go to
these courses, to interrupt them, and to describe the discussions which were going on elsewhere. Whereas during
the year it was impossible to get a whole lecture hall to
participate in whatever discussions there were, whereas
before people would whistle whenever someone talked about
politics, about capitalism, now the majority of the students
listened and took part, even if it was to express their opposition to the movement. In everyone appeared the desire
to take an active part in running things but, on the whole,
these sentiments were hardly expressed outside the halls
and the department.

On the other hand, a student strike committee of about ten
people wished to pose more general problems. This committee set itself up on May 10. It charged itself with
organizing life in the occupied buildings, with having everything under its control, with preventing courses still being
given from meeting. This committee was formed spontaneously, of its own free will; in no way elected by students,
it also didn't derive in any direct way from the UNEF
(not very strong here, and controlled by the stalinist UEC),
which had been left behind by the movement, together with
all the political groups who stood apart or obstructed
(with the exception of the trotskyite FER). The mass of
students thus found themselves faced with the *fait accompli*
of a strike committee which existed, functioned, made decisions, created organizations.

After the night of the barricades, a faculty strike committee was formed, uniting members of the SNESup and,
almost exclusively, junior faculty (lecturers). (It contained
only four professors and junior professors.) It also was
not elected.

The two strike committees at first met separately but
soon merged. From the beginning, the two committees
pushed for the creation of rank-and-file committees in the students' lecture halls, and for laboratory councils in the

research units attached to the Faculty. While the laboratory councils constituted themselves very rapidly, the strike committee was opposed to immediate elections of student rank-and-file committees because the Dean had organized the students who had been absent from the Faculty and had not participated in the movement. Ten days later, after many political discussions, the rank-and-file committees were set up. To the great annoyance of the Dean and the professors who wanted to play the mass of the strikers against the committee, the rank-and-file committees supported the action of the strike committee, though it was first strongly criticized for not having been an elected body.

More than the students in the strike committee, the teachers tried to set up representative structures to replace the old government of the Faculty (the Faculty assembly which consisted only of professors and lecturers and the Dean it elects), a desire shared by the laboratory researchers and technicians. A provisional representative commission, consisting of 18 students, 9 professors, 9 lecturers or master-lecturers, and delegates from the technicians, research scientists, and administrators, was created, which settled the question of examinations by postponing them to October, and which was to prepare for the establishment of a representative central committee to replace the old university power structure.

Thus there was within the Faculty a tangle of parallel authorities: (1) the laboratory councils, revocable by the lab personnel, and leading a life separate from the rest of the Faculty; (2) the rank-and-file committees of the students, revocable at any time by the lecture halls and meeting in general assembly to make their decisions; (3) the General Assembly of the instructors, containing master-lecturers and lecturers as well as those professors who wished to participate; (4) the strike committee; (5) the provisional representative commission composed of student delegates chosen by the strike committee and revocable at any time by the committee and by the general assembly of the rank-and-file committees, and of teacher delegates, revocable at any time by the teachers' general assembly (the Dean himself picked the professors sitting on this committee); (6) finally, the old Faculty government.

All these centers of power coexisted more or less well during the ascending period of the movement, in the course of which the ranks of professors and the Dean were in no position to oppose the decisions of the strike committee. The decision to put off the exams until October led a large number of students to leave for their vacation—and after de Gaulle's speech on May 30, the professors hardened and refused to sit on the representative commission.

This decision contributed to reinforcing the unity between students, researchers, and master-lecturers, who then organized elections to the representative central committee. This move put the professors and the Dean in an awkward position, and serious cracks appeared within the professors' ranks; the reformists, sensing that the hour had come to attempt to coopt the movement, asked the Dean to have the elections of the professors' delegates proceed. The entry of the police into the Faculty was perhaps not unrelated to this situation.

The strike committee for its part came out for the creation of a Summer University, as the other Faculties were planning; the more radical of its members wanted in effect to establish contact with the workers and to open the Faculty up to the outside. A central bureau for the Summer University was elected by the assembly of the student rank-and-file committees. This office centralized the different initiatives which were making themselves seen: (a) in the various departments, experiments in new teaching methods were made with the cooperation of the most dynamic part of the professoral corps; (b) political activities: seminars enlivened by a certain number of mandarins (from the Faculties of Letters and of Law) and also, and above all, working groups in which students and workers rubbed shoulders and in which very fruitful discussions took place; (c) artistic activities (cinema, sale of books, etc.), which had the advantage of attracting many people.

The experiment of the Summer University, difficult to realize and assuredly with many faults, was without doubt one of the most attractive projects of the Faculty of Sciences, and the strike committee devoted a large part of its efforts to maintaining the occupation of the classrooms so that it could go on.[5] It goes without saying that the gaullist government could not allow it to develop, and the first

[5] The Faculty also sheltered a certain number of commissions, including the "eyewitness" commission, which collected depositions concerning police brutality, the student-worker action committees, and a poster studio similar to the popular studio of the Beaux-Arts (School of Fine Arts).

cops who invaded the campus, in the early morning of July 5, admitted that they came to stop it.

## 3 Flins: Student-Worker Solidarity

One of the slogans the students stressed in their demonstrations was: "Power is in the street!" This phenomenon is not without a touch of the 19th century (not by far the only one one might have observed); in reality the power of the future is to be found in that place where the producers are concentrated, where they work. But the street remains no less an unavoidable preliminary to the emergence of consciousness and, besides, an inevitable experience. It was at Flins that workers of the Sorbonne shop and workers of the Renault shop united in practical action, and it was there also (unlike at Billancourt or Cleon, for example) that in fact more than half of the personnel was to come out, despite all the pressures, against the return to work.

At Flins, the workforce is composed largely of young people, not yet very well habituated to the ways of the unions; the strike was spontaneous (breaking out here before at Billancourt) and the rank-and-file had rather tight control over the strike committee; likewise, participation in the picket line was higher than elsewhere.

On the night between Thursday and Friday, June 7,[6] half-tracks broke through the factory gates, allowing the CRS (there were about 4,000 of them in this sector) to enter, which forced the strike pickets to evacuate the plant. In the morning, under police protection, scabs came to take the strikers' places at work (or at least were supposed to do this) so that the management could announce an "effective resumption of work." However, despite an enormous deployment of police, young workers and those students who succeeded in escaping the roadblocks set up by the police met together before the factory gates and explained to the workers, deceived with false information (which the CGT made no attempt to refute), that no decision to resume work had been made. Thenceforth the workers refrained from reentering the factory. During this time, the CGT and the CFDT organized a meeting 4 miles away from the plant, which was attended by at most fifty or so

[6] See the *Tribune of March 22,* reprinted in I.C.O. No. 72, in *Partisans,* No. 42, etc.; translation in *Caw!,* No. 3, pp. 33-35.

union officials. These then returned to the factory gates where 2,000 to 3,000 demonstrators were assembled. The union delegates issued their slogans: "No provocations! Disperse! Do not reenter the factory!" But the workers insisted that the students speak. A union bigshot seized the mike again: "Disperse!" But the pressure of the ranks forced the mike to be given to Geismar (leader of the SNESup). He reported that at Paris the students had met the CRS head on and that students and workers united could reoccupy the factory. At this moment the police attacked. The students showed the workers how to fight—it didn't take too long! And the free-for-all went on for several days, through the fields, over a pretty wide area.

An attempt of several thousand demonstrators, assembled before the Saint-Lazare station, to go to Flins by train ran up against the obstruction of the CGT and the lack of solidarity on the part of the railwaymen. At Billancourt, the 30,000 workers of Renault did not for an instant try to break the union vise and make contact with Flins. Under these conditions, the struggle at Flins, after hard skirmishes, was bound to meet defeat. It remained the only one of its type, at least in the seriousness which it took on at certain moments, a seriousness however quite modest in the context of the apparently gigantic dimensions of the strike, even taking into account the fact that the most active elements were held up in the shops by urgent tasks. And yet, with all the limitations one can think of, a struggle of this type, such a witness to lived solidarity, remains a rare fact in the whole history of the workers' movement. On the spot, it developed the fighting spirit of the workers, sowing a seed which must some day bear fruit.[7]

## 4 Other Forms of Solidarity

Another aspect of worker-student solidarity, less spec-

[7] One saw this very well the day after the strike, when the management decided, despite the formal agreements, to speed up the line and to fire two foreign workers. After a daylong work stoppage, a meeting of workers on the evening of Wednesday, June 19, voted with raised hands for an unlimited strike. Officially, the CFDT was at the head of this movement; but the CGT would not hear of this "provocation": it opposed the strike and the CFDT finally fell into step with it, all the while denouncing very loudly (of course!) the "treason" of the other union (the elections to the CE would soon be held . . .).

tacular than the preceding but perhaps even more important, was the creation of Action Committees (CA), based either on the neighborhood or on the workplace, with the active cooperation of students most of whom belonged to no organized group. These committees directed at the workers a simply enormous quantity of leaflets. By their actions of various sorts they contributed to laying the foundations of a new form of consciousness. With the reflux of the movement, these committees receded, but nothing is more natural since they are the expression of the movement, in its highest and its lowest levels. An outstanding fact nonetheless, the CA's as a whole took on the task of "transcending union and political structures" through the creation of a "multitude of political cells" which must someday unite but "without organizational pushing," as a function of the real struggle and not of abstract demands.[8]

The CLEOP (*Comites de liaison etudiants-ouvriers-paysans*) performed an activity no less important: they assured the provisioning of the strikers, especially in the small enterprises, which, not being supported by workplace organizations (like canteens), had need of aid. Some arose in the agricultural schools, others had a less definite origin. They established relations between themselves and cooperatives or certain unions of agricultural workers (CNJA, FNJA). They went particularly to Brittany (because of its proximity), where they were most welcome (for reasons stemming from the surplus of produce due to the lack of transports and from the open hostility to the existing circuits of transportation; in effect, transactions were made directly).

Likewise, students and peasants carried on discussions, which made up for the purposeful deficiencies of the official system of information. In this area, the CLEOP effectively fulfilled a task analogous to that of the Action Committees. The important thing was that meeting places appeared, in the Faculties, that a network of information and clarification of ideas was set up, with the CA's, that the solidarity between the various categories of producers in struggle did not always remain at the level of declarations of intention but took a tangible form, in the battles with the police in the streets or at Flins, and in the matter of provisioning.

[8] Leaflet: "How to go on?" (CA Sorbonne)

## IV THE WORKERS' MOVEMENT

For reasons of space, we will be able to examine only a limited number of events, choosing then from among those which are in our opinion most significant. In any case, it would be pointless to retell here the history of the general strike. Among the mass of works dedicated to it, the reader will be able to find documents and a useful chronology.[9]

In the beginning, then, the student movement. It brought to light the virtues of direct and spontaneous mass action. The students came down into the streets: *they dared*, and in so doing brought many people together to hold their own, united, against the power that faced them. Faced with that other unity which is that of the bourgeois class and its police, in coalition with the parties and the unions, they showed strength. More than this, they proved that it was possible to occupy the workplaces; and while people might have known that, no one yet risked doing it.

However, the day after the night of the barricades (May 10 to 11) there was no spontaneous reaction on the part of the workers; everything appeared destined to be canalized by the national day of strike, controlled by the unions. But on Tuesday the 14th, late in the evening, it was learned that the Sud-Aviation factory at Nantes was occupied, that the workers had welded shut the factory gates and imprisoned the directors in an office. Then, from May 14 to 17, other strikes broke out, all with occupation of the premises: at the *Messageries de Presse*, the newspaper-distribution monopoly, at Paris; at the Renault plant at Cleon; and the movement, always spontaneous, spread everywhere. Friday, May 17, the SNCF (*Societe Nationale de Chemins de Fer Francais*, the nationalized railroad company) began to shut down, and in several hours everything stopped in the pretty train stations of France. The union leaderships profited by the weekend of May 18-19 to "recapture" the movement: without issuing the call for a general strike, interunion strike committees were set up almost everywhere, charged with directing the strike as soon as it broke out.

Among the rank-and-file, there is in fact no precise demand. Everyone, obviously, is for a wage-increase, a shorter work week, and so on. But the strikers, or at least the

[9] A useful chronology with documents may be found in *Partisans*, no. 42, June-July 1968, *"Ouvriers, etudiants, un seul combat!"*

majority of them, are not unaware that these are precarious advantages. The best proof of this is that they have never resolved on an action like this one (though this was also, it is true, because they did not know that they would be so numerous). The real reason, a very simple one, is given clearly by the signs hung from the doors of the little factories of the Parisian suburbs: "We have had enough!" Enough of low wages, yes, but above all enough, enough of this colorless life in which the annoyances themselves are so shabby that one doesn't even dream of complaining about them, and less yet of fighting them. As for the young, they have had enough, enough in advance of this life which is going to make of you, as of everyone, a poor bastard, the spitting image of your father, of his father before him, and so on, in a somewhat more comfortable frame.

And this wild feeling, which no one teaches you at school, is so strong, so deeply rooted, that it is going to resist for days and days, holding out against the masters of the State, the threats of the bosses, the coaxings of the union bigshots. These last don't at all, in general, hide their objectives, and it is exactly these objectives which the working masses would scorn for two, three weeks and in some cases much more.

As early as Friday, May 17, the CGT distributed everywhere a leaflet which stated precisely the limits it wished to put on its action. To accuse it afterwards of treason makes hardly any sense; it put its cards on the table at the start: on the one hand, traditional demands coupled with the conclusion of agreements like the Matignon accords,[10] guaranteeing the existence of union locals in the shops; on the other hand, a change of government, that is to say, elections. This leaflet contained not one proposal outside this framework, and, significantly, it didn't in six pages once mention the word *strike* (let it be said once more: the CGT, no more than the FO or the CFDT, will declare neither a general strike nor a strike in some particular branch of activity). From then on, the policy of the CGT (and, with variation, of the other unions) was clear and simple: the Grenelle agreements (made by the unions and Pompidou on May 15, but rejected by the workers) give

[10] Agreements signed with Leon Blum in 1936, ending the strike, legalizing the unions, guaranteeing 15 days vacation per year, creating social security, etc.

satisfaction to the need for reforms; the strikers must therefore go back to work.

It was the policy of loyal opposition, which has been for a long time the politics of the unions in France as throughout the western branch of capitalism, and it was this that the workers were going to reject with a determination never seen in history, but nevertheless without going on to the very end: the definite leap beyond legality, the starting up again of the great majority of production units (occupied to extremely varying degrees, in general rather low). Also, since the strikers, at that stage, had not succeeded in solidly taking the offensive, the State and the bosses, uniting in a perfectly natural way with the country's various political and union forces, would themselves take the offensive, and finish by carrying the day.

It remains no less evident that a phenomenon of an extraordinary breadth occurred: an immense movement, a level of consciousness which was uneven but often high, and sometimes exemplary, and everywhere the discussion that went on, everywhere. Only on the basis of some abstract schema could one imagine that consciousness can develop without a confusion of ideas, mixed-up in the beginning, without groping, without visible incapacities and returns to old ways looking at things. But what was happening, was the consciousness that one was doing something, and, for the moment, the projects (rarely thought up by the rank-and-file itself) into which all that was translated mattered little. Such a phenomenon, in some way one of men's minds, is hard to encompass by an analysis. However, it is useful to report certain practical experiences in order to try to distinguish in them features pregnant with the future, the far-reaching tendencies.

# 1 Assurances Générales de France

The *Assurances Générales de France*, second largest insurance company in France, is a nationalized enterprise which in four years has experienced a double concentration: first, the merger of seven companies in one group and then of this new group with three others, and on the other hand an accelerated automation and centralization. Neither the unions nor the cadres ever talked about workers' control but confined themselves to denouncing the arbitrary character of the management, which left them out of every decision (and which, in addition, had been taken over by a gaullist clique).

It was a tiny minority of employees who on Friday, May 17 (before the strike which was to go into effect May 20) raised the question of control in clear and brutal terms in a leaflet distributed by students of the March 22 Movement in all the companies of the group, and of which this is the essential part:

*Like the students:* Proposals for discussion in a general assembly of all the employees and cadres of the *Groupe des Assurances Générales de France.*

1. *The Assurances Générales de France* continue to function normally, managed under the autonomous control of all those working here at the present time.

2. All the directors, cadres, and AM are deprived of their former functions. Each department will designate one or several representatives chosen solely for their human qualities and their competence.

3. The department representative will have a double role:

• to coordinate the operation of the department under the control of the employees;

• to organize with the other department representatives a Management Council which, under the control of the employees, will assure the functioning of the enterprise.

4. The department representatives must be able to explain their conduct at any time before the employees and will be revocable at any time by those who have chosen them.

5. The hierarchy of wages is abolished. Every employee, cadre, or director, will receive provisionally a uniform salary equal to the average May wage (total wages divided by the number of employees present).

6. The personal dossiers of the employees will be returned to them; they will be able to remove everything not a purely administrative document.

7. All the property and materials of the *Assurances Générales de France* becoming the goods of all, administered by all, each person engages himself to ensure its protection in every circumstance.

8. To meet every threat, a volunteer protection squad under the control of the Management Council assures the protection of the enterprise day and night alike.

Monday, May 20, a new leaflet was distributed, stressing the following points:

• how social conquests had been rapidly won back in the past;

• let us be suspicious of our friends and have confidence only in ourselves;
• election of strike committees;
• control of the management of the enterprise, recalling the preceding leaflet;
• finally, going beyond the strike itself:

We are beyond the strike, we must get everything going again by and for ourselves, without waiting for others to give us the order, but with Management Councils elected by all. Where then will the disorder be: it will be those who defend their property, their interests as rulers and as enjoyers of privilege by oppression, violence, poverty, and war. . . . It is at the place where you work that everything can be decided. And there, with all the workers together, there can be the collapse of a whole world in which you are nothing and at the same time the construction of a whole world in which you are everything.

In the beginning, at the central office, the strike involved only a minority of the employees (500 out of 3,000, because of the transport strikes); it was the deed of a minority of young workers, union and nonunion; the unions followed, controlling but not urging on. From the start the militants affirmed the desire that what would be obtained be irreversible. The list of demands is impressive; it is preceded by four preconditions (notably, payment for hours on strike) that the management was to accept without discussion; one of the preconditions concerned the maintenance of a commission of the strike committee supposed to take care of structural reforms and participation in decision-making. The entrance of cadres into the strike of May 22, (130 for the strike out of 250 voting and 500 total), a majority of them young technocrats, modified the style of the strike: cadres and union leaders came together again to dominate all the bodies of the strike committee and, notable in the case of the CFDT, to talk about control, each from its own point of view. Several divisions appeared in the discussions which cut into everything that could be said on these questions:
• There was a violent altercation with the CFDT after a critique of this union's idea, managerial control "by the union," made before the General Assembly of the employees, with repercussions in the strike committee.
• There was a split in the commission dealing with

structures, a subcommission of the strike committee supposed to deal with control. Members of one of these subcommissions, young technocrats, principally CGC members, saw in the strike a chance to put forth their ideas about how the enterprise should be organized in opposition to those of the management; the plan of operation they proposed leaves intact the powers of the head of the enterprise and the hierarchy and is only an application of certain modern theories of management in an attempt to restructure jobs so as to integrate the employee into his work and to obtain his active "participation." The other sub-commission, on the contrary, tended to put forth the principle of a participation in decisions that is to say a system of co-management or joint control (on the Yugoslav model, for example).

• These latter discussions were interesting because they afforded an opportunity to develop a concrete and very strong critique of all forms of participation and to raise the most theoretical questions in a manner accessible to all. It is not only that this critique was listened to and understood, notably by the young (at the very least those whom such discussions didn't alienate) who realized, on the basis of their experience, that since the power of decision was still out of the hands of the employees, they were dealing only with half-measures which lead in the end to the system's having a firmer hold on them through the intermediary of the cadres and managerial apparatus. But also, those who discussed were brought to admit that even co-management, if one wanted it to be genuine, leads to the calling into question of established structures like the hierarchy of functions and of wages, authority, the system of grading and advancement, access to information, etc. and that in the measure to which these structures are maintained or only modified, the whole system set up will be rapidly corrupted and will lose all meaning. Conflicts with the directors, if they are resolved by the directors, will be resolved in their interest—that is to say, in that of capitalism—and it will be, as it is now, the criteria of profitability and profit which finally determine everything. This is why the debate on the participation of the employees in decisions rapidly became constricted when things became more concrete: in discussing on what level the rank-and-file's power of decision must stop and where could the decision-making power of the heads impose a decision, with due respect for form, of course.

Even this formula of co-management is at any rate
thought of by the unions (including the CFDT) and the
cadres as utopian at the present stage. The real world
doesn't work that way: in the terms in which the issue is
raised, co-management leads to the elimination of an important part of the power of the unions and the cadres; it
tends to promote a direct representation of the workers or
even a direct decision-making power. To understand this,
observe what this commission envisaged:

• Every decision without exception will be made collectively by the rank and file unit (12 employees) and the
person in charge (subchief).

• In case of agreement, the decision is to be put in force.
In case of conflict, the matter is carried before a representative commission presided over by the department chief
and formed of equal numbers of representatives of the
cadres and of the employees, at the rate of one per rank-
and-file cell. These delegates are non-permanent, revocable,
and chosen by the base specifically for the problem to be
discussed. This commission has no power of decision; it
reexamines the whole problem, suggests solutions, and passes
it back for a decision to the rank-and-file unit where conflict
arose.

• If the conflict remains, everything goes before a permanent commission at the department level, equally representative, formed of permanent delegates elected by two
colleges in the framework of the department (one-year
terms; the possibility of their revocability was suggested)
which decides by majority vote, the department head having
a deciding voice. The decision must be accepted without
appeal.

• Two things are evident: the cadres are reduced to their
technical function, and the union delegates are eliminated
up to the level of the department. This explains the position
of the cadres and unions formulated thus: "It is necessary
to know exactly what this signifies concretely for us. We are
not yet ready for that, but the trail has been blazed."[11]

The most striking fact is, in addition, that the unions
and the cadres decided in no way to *impose* a mode of
operations on these bases, but to have it *granted* them in
negotiations with the management once the strike was over.
This was to recognize that all power of decision lies with

[11] Declaration of the unions of the *Assurances Générales, Le
Monde,* June 2-3, 1968.

the management. It is important to state also that the principle of co-management or of participation did not even figure in the preconditions for discussion, but only the creation of a commission concerned with "structures," a term which we have seen to have very different meanings for different interested parties. It is evident that all this will result at best in consultative bodies in which unions and cadres will divide the positions, and which will have no real power.

The principle by which the commission on structures was to be maintained also ran into opposition from the unions. Autonomous or under the aegis of the workplace committees? It was this latter solution which prevailed, showing clearly that everything, even if it is laughable, which would escape the power of the unions in the enterprise is opposed by the unions' desire to block any direct representation of the workers.

All these facts were perceived by the young people, who thought of the strike a little as theirs, not in an abstract way but as a function of one or another of the discussions which they brought back immediately to their particular situation in the enterprise. So that they rapidly discovered what was wrong with all those speeches whose language repelled them more than it attracted them.

The persistance of this language represented besides in their eyes a rupture with everything that the strike offered them as a starting point for communication and the breaking down of barriers. If the operation of the strike committee could appear a model—work done on the basis of equal participation by 150 members, without a permanent office and with commissions dividing up the tasks, in a coordinated way—in reality the unions and cadres took such an important part in it that one could see in it the possibility of a new bureaucracy, within an enterprise placed under the system of co-management. Without a doubt, the strike committee was forced to allow the presence of nonunion men in the negotiations with the management, in discussions with the students after long refusing them, and in discussions with the striking employees as a whole after recognizing that the daily meeting was becoming a pure formality. But that hardly breached the bureaucrats' hold on the strike committee, all the more as the young, wearied by so many efforts always opposed, so much incomprehension, participated less in the discussions so as to devote themelves to the practical tasks of the strike, and shut themselves up in their own world of young people. If the unions did not succeed in breaking the spirit of which we spoke above, they succeeded nonetheless in preventing it from expressing itself openly. Thus the strike rapidly led back—a clear sign that it didn't open up the way to a revolutionary trans-formation—to a modified reproduction of the hierarchized structures of capitalist society, put to use by the same people who deem that they have a vocation to run this society, from the position that they presently occupy in it.

## 2 Compagnie Generale de Telegraphie sans Fil (CSF), Brest

Several years ago the CSF (General Radio Co., a great electronics trust) set up a factory at Brest, in the frame-work of the plan, for the industrialization of Brittany, and in this way benefitting from the government subsidies granted to enterprises which decentralize. Cadres were imported from Paris and 1,100 workers recruited on the spot, the majority of them unskilled laborers. The management—doubtless in order to continue to collect the subsidy—offered at Brest only the least interesting jobs, which permitted it to counter every wage demand with the fact—real, but deliberately brought about—that the factory was not profit-able and always operated at a deficit. This didn't go on without causing a certain frustration among the personnel, notably the cadres, who feared to find themselves one day out of work again, with a reduced level of qualification.

There has been only one union in the Brest plant, the CFDT, every member of the CGT being rapidly fired. At the time of the CSF-Thomson merger, the difficulties of the factory at Brest increased even more. "We had used that," said a CFDT delegate,[12] "to explain to the personnel the workings of the economy, of capitalist society, of the banks, etc. Our union activity has had an important influence on the minds not only of the workers but also of the engineers and the cadres."

On May 20, the groups which made up work-units (shops, offices, laboratories) first elected a strike committee, then made a study of reform of the hierarchy in the enterprise. 70 engineers participated in this work. The personnel also set up "workers' tribunals" to judge cadres for incompe-

[12] *Le Monde,* May 29, 1968.

tence in their work and their relations with their subordinates; dossiers were assembled and transmitted to the management by the delegates. Summing up these proceedings, the CFDT representatives declared:[13] "We think that the workers' commissions and the factory committee that we have set up consitute irreversible choices. The strike committee has all powers of decision in a democratic enterprise. Workers' commissions will be set up in each production-unit. They are to deal with everything that directly affects the wage-earners in their work (methods of work, definition of jobs, hiring, promotion, etc)." A leaflet, put out and distributed right at the plant, demanded the "democratization of the enterprise with a view towards self-management" in requiring, notably: "workers' control of professional training, with a budget equivalent at least to 2 percent of the annual rise in the total amount of wages; contractual policy for promotions; definition of each job and its sphere of competence; a plan for development of the numbers and qualification of the personnel; control of hiring; financial control of the factory and of the business."

On June 18, after 6 days of fruitless discussions with the management, the personnel decided to continue the strike, by a vote of 607 to 357. The negotiations stumbled against the problems of control, among others the setting up of representative commissions. The management invoked the illegal character of these structures to justify its refusal of them; the CFDT delegates then presented, without any more success, a plan for a commission integrated into the workplace committee, which could have played the same role as the bodies projected in the first place.

Finally, work resumed on Friday, May 21 (551 votes for resumption, 152 against). The conversations of the CFDT delegates from the Brest factory with the central office in Paris have led to the creation of a commission within the factory committee, consisting of 5 representatives of the management and twelve of the personnel, it will be charged with studying the renovation of the structures of the enterprise and will take an interest more particularly in the planning of work, in the "production time," and in the conditions of work. This measure concerns only the factory at Brest. The commission is only qualified to set down

[13] *Syndicalisme* (organ of the CFDT), no. 1191, June 10, 1968, p. 24.

its "conclusions," before the end of the year.

A significant feature, this progressive whittling down of demands: in the beginning it was a matter of creating rank-and-file committees assuring the workers' control of important aspects of the life of the enterprise; then, it changed to representative commissions, chosen from out of the workplace committee; and it finished by being content with a simple study commission which will put forth "conclusions," of which the management will or will not take account, depending on its interest or even its whim.

One saw such a process at work, though generally in less clear a form, in many medium-sized (and even large) enterprises on strike. It must be stressed, however, that in case of the movement's revival, institutions of this type however ridiculous their authority may be, would be able to set up—at least as a beginning—as spokesmen for the will of the workers against the management; in the opposite case, of the definitive "return to normalcy," they must be reduced at best to functioning as auxiliaries to the management, sharing with it certain not very popular administrative tasks, or—most likely—to nothing at all.

## 3 Commissariat a l'Energie Atomique (CEA), Saclay

The CEA (Atomic Energy Commission) employs a total of 6,000 to 7,000 people at Saclay. Of this number about 4,500, of which a quarter are engineers, work under a "collective agreement"; the rest work for "outside enterprises" (cleaning women, secretaries, draughtsmen, skilled workers, technicians, building workers, etc.); in addition, there are graduate students on fellowships and foreigners working there for a term. The CGT has 625 members, with a nucleus formed by the oldest agents of the CEA, hired between 1946 and 1950, under the reign of the Stalinist Joliot-Curie. The CFDT, which at Saclay has made a specialty of leftist one-upmanship, has 300 members and the FO the same. The house union is supposed to have about a hundred members. The CGC, very recently set up, has "made a killing" in the last elections of cadre delegates.

The strike was carried out with effective occupation of the work sites. (83 percent of the personnel remained at the sites throughout the strike; even on holidays [Ascension, Pentecost, weekends] there were at least 500 people at the center).

The time was entirely occupied by discussion—general or in committee—bearing either on fundamental problems or on the reorganization of the CEA, a question which interested many of the personnel, since the future of the Commission appeared to be in jeopardy. The strike itself started with a small nucleus of people doing experimental and theoretical research in pure physics; particularly well-paid agents, unconnected with production, often young and always tied professionally to the Universities; these personnel, union and nonunion, acted outside of and, when necessary, against the union controls. For the first time one could observe a real solidarity with the workers employed by the outside enterprises.

The strike was of short duration, 15 days, officially. In fact, the general discussions, with an almost total stoppage of work, had preceded the actual strike vote by almost a week. The return to work took place under pressure from the administration, which promised full payment for hours missed if work began again before June 4. Nonetheless, the discussions within the enterprise had been carried far enough for a certain number of structural demands to be presented to, and, after being emasculated, accepted by the administration.

In this way, a whole "pyramid" of representative commissions was set up. At each echelon (division, department, management) a unit council was constituted, presided over by the head of the unit and playing a *consultative* role. The unit council is elected outside of any union routine, on the ratio of one delegate to 10 people, and with representation of all the professional categories in the division, but the election is made by a single college; the delegates are in principle revocable at all times. At first it had been required that the head of the division (or of the unit) be open to challenge by the unit. Of course this demand was not satisfied. Nevertheless, certain units went on to vote for or against their division head. Certain unanimous "confrontations" made a stir for the moment. Then, it appeared that the "confronted" continued to go on as before . . .

In addition, a national committee has been created representing both employees and management, but it is presided over by an administrator general delegated by the government, who has a decisive voice. This committee discusses programs, the budget, and the general organization of the Commission. It is informed of nominations to the staff of the CEA. The same device is found in all the centers depending on the CEA, including the DAM (*Direction des Applications Militaires*–Office of Military Application). Contrary to the unit councils, this committee is exclusively composed, on the personnel side, of union delegates. (At the DAM, where the union representation came up against an in principle prohibition, the latter requirement was lifted.)

One sees thus that as far as effective control goes, the famous "pyramid of committees" has in the end no power. Its only utility could have been to keep the personnel informed; but even in this sphere, its possibilities are narrowly limited. The old strike committee, formed spontaneously, has been re-elected almost as a whole, under the name of "coordinating committee," with the mission of facilitating the circulation of information horizontally, that is to say, between unit councils. Although the majority of its members are union men (but not union delegates) this committee is just barely tolerated (and this thanks only to the pressures exerted by the rank-and-file), by the administration of the Center and by the unions. A number of division heads have already succeeded in injecting into the unit council a bureaucratic mentality, by making it a "privileged interlocutor"; that is to say, in blocking in fact the diffusion of information among the rank-and-file, the coordinating committee is beginning to chase its own tail. Its last notice posted (at the beginning of July) proposes that the meetings of the unit councils be public, like the municipal councils. But in the current context of discouragement, it doesn't look as though this suggestion will meet with many echoes.

## 4 Sud-Aviation, Nantes

For a month, half-hour work stoppages followed one after another. On May 7, two days before a full day of strike, the director, one Duvochel, was chased by 35 workers; he succeeded in saving himself. During the night of May 13, at the instigation of militants of a trotskyite group (OCI)[14],

---

[14] As in the student movement, one finds here, though to a much more limited degree, the role of detonator which certain "activist" minorities had in favorable circumstances (in 1936 as well, there were several cases of this type when the strikes began). Of course, these minorities couldn't furnish the "material basis" of the strike (general conditions, state of consciousness, etc.) any more than its direction.

300 to 400 workers stopped work again; in the morning of the next day there were three half-hour stoppages, while the union delegates were received by the said Duvochel. But in the afternoon, according to an inquiry carried out on the spot by three students from Nanterre:[15]

> Three union delegates decided to throw people on monthly salary out of their offices and to shut the boss up in his office. Several cadres joined the imprisoned director. A guard post was installed before his door. So that the boss wouldn't get bored, a loud-speaker was installed before the door and bellowed revolutionary songs at an earsplitting level, a device which permits a boss to learn the *International* by heart without any ideological effort . . .

At Flins and in certain factories of Elbeuf, directors found themselves imprisoned in the same way. This action, perfectly illegal (as was not the case with the strike, at least in itself), was of course condemned by the unions with all their strength. It thus bore witness to the autonomous character of the struggle carried on by the workers; an index of their combativity, it helped to further heighten it.

Here as everywhere, it was the young people from 25 to 30 who showed themselves the most determined to continue the struggle, and the return to work, as a comrade said to us, came "with discouragement and disgust."

## 5 Electricité de France (EDF)—Central Plant at Cheviré

The EDF-GDF (nationalized electric and gas company) on strike continued to furnish current and gas under the direction of the strike committees (CGT members greatly predominating). Decreasing the flow of current had the effect of stopping a great number of machines that were still running; thus, at the Faculty of Sciences at Orsay the computer had to stop and the technicians, thenceforth, joined the strike. However, the conditions under which the activity was carried out at the EDF (just as in the hospitals, for example) are not well known to us. Here is what the inquiry of the three from Nanterre said about the Cheviré center, near Nantes:

> When the 293 workers had occupied the plant, on Saturday, May 18, they chose a strike committee composed of delegates

[15] *Action*, No. 6, 10, June 7, 11; reprinted in *Cahiers de Mai*, No. 1, June 15, p. 4.

from each union (90% at the EDF were unionized). But it was necessary, even while diminishing the current flow (which helped to paralyze the local industries), to maintain a minimum of electricity to assure safety services: hospitals, etc. The strike committee thus asked the strikers to "take on their responsibilities" in this matter. Actually, the elected Committee held, for 15 days, . . . all authority in the plant. It made sure that uninterrupted operation was assured by the workers. It organized the search for supplies of combustibles (natural gas). For the provisioning of the strikers, it had arranged an active, but somewhat confused, solidarity with the surrounding population. The militants with which I spoke were very conscious (even the CGT delegate!) of the political meaning of this experience, and one of them explained: "We wished to show our capacity, and thus our right, as producers, to manage the means of production which we use. We proved it."

On the radio, a union delegate from the Savings Bank (nationalized) expressed himself in analogous terms at the time of the limited reopening of the bank windows. It is beyond doubt, for anyone who sticks his head out the window, that this was one of the most widespread feelings, and that it remains. If but lately it was latent among a large part of the workers, when they came to have a "confrontation" with some cadre, it is today readily expressed. And yet (we will return to this) this remains a sentiment, not an objective fact from which the consequences need only be drawn.

## 6 The Situation at Nantes, at the End of May

Nantes is of all the cities of France that in which the union seems to have had the greatest control at the local level. According to the inquiry which we have already cited twice,[16] a central Strike Committee took (or intended to take) a certain number of initiatives, especially as regards provisioning—such as distribution of permits and vouchers for gasoline, which does not in any case appear to have been very seriously carried out; organization of transports with

[16] An inquiry confirmed in its own way by the *Figaro*, which wrote (5/30/68): 'The unions in reality have laid an iron hand on the Loire-Atlantic region . . . On the market, new inspectors, but this time union men, control prices following the official government guidelines. From the metalworker to the fisherman, everyone waits for the union's decision," etc.

the co-operation of the FO truckers, the municipality then putting cars at the disposition of the Committee.

To the families of strikers, who found themselves in the worst financial situation, the union organizations distributed vouchers for foodstuffs. These vouchers are equivalent to a certain quantity of food. For each child under three years: one voucher for 1 F. of milk, and for each person over three, a voucher for 500 grams of bread and one voucher for 1 F.

On the roads, the FO truckers set up roadblocks (there were also roadblocks around Caen, but for only one day). In the neighborhoods:

The three workers' familial organizations (AS, APF, UPF) made contact with the peasant unions of the nearest village, La Chapelle-sur-Erdre. A meeting attended by 15 unionized peasants and a delegation of workers and students decided to assure a permanent liaison to organize a network for distribution without middlemen. . . . Every morning, the union men came to check the prices at the markets. . . . Notices are put up in the stores authorized to open, with the following words: "Taking care of the provisioning of the population, the unions authorize this little store (the big ones were forced to close) to open its doors on condition that it respect the standard prices.

The correspondent for *Figaro* expressed himself in analogous terms:

As the prefecture could not take care of the most urgent problems, an "Interunion Strike Committee" installed itself in the city hall. Little by little, it substituted itself for the administration. It is thus that it issued the traffic vouchers, permits to ambulances and to the trucks of the bakers and the market-gardeners; it is thus that the shopkeepers had to place on their shop-fronts these notices: "This store is authorized to open. Its prices are controlled permanently under the responsibility of the unions." Signed: CGT, CFDT, FO'

How much of this, exactly, is fact? According to another student traveller, the inquiry of the Nanterre three was "partial in both senses." Thus, they wrote that two delegates from the UNEF appeared in the Central Strike Committee; in fact, the trotskyite and FO members of the Committee, having demanded their admission, would have been in the position of opposing a categorical refusal by the delegates from the other unions, of workers as well as of peasants, who always accepted—but only for a short time—the presence of student delegates in the capacity of observers. On the other hand it is possible that the following lines had, at one time, described something actually going on:

> The Central Strike Committee is suspicious of the neighborhood committees and reproaches them for not having worked through it at the beginning. In fact, the neighborhood committees will turn out to be much more effective in the organizing of provisioning, and their action will be of much greater import than that of the unions. Starting from the creation of a direct market for produce, they are going to become the cells of the politization of the workingclass neighborhoods.[17]

But, with the general reflux of the movement, and thus the shift in the balance of power in favor of the unions, the situation was obviously modified. Here is what *Action,* the newspaper of the "leftist" students, said about it:[18]

> As for the strike and neighborhood committees of Nantes, they have been the object of a recapture operation that they are not about to forget.

Be that as it may, we see clearly here how, given the bankruptcy of the old authorities (prefecture, municipality), but also with their active support, the united unions use their respective organizations and related associations to set up a new structure of authority. Far from forcing the great modern shopping centers, whose personnel were on strike, to reopen—which would have been to attack the rule of private property and take "risks"—they relied on the shopowners and small peasants. Wedged between this "base" and the old administrative (and police) apparatus, the interunion Committee was to be obliged to manoeuvre shabbily until the day of the "return to normalcy."

When in its course it encounters organs arising directly from the people, which tries in this way to meet its immediate needs, it is suspicious and invokes, in a typically bureaucratic way, its self-styled representative character, which gives it the right to run the life of society. At a new stage, if there is one, there will be two possibilities: either the masses will submit to this transitional union power just as they submit to the power of Capital; or else they

[17] *Cahiers de Mai,* art. cit., p. 10.
[18] *"La revelation de Mai: les CA dans les enterprises,* "No. 18, June 27, 1968.

will enter into conflict with it through the intermediary of their own organs of struggle and control (rank-and-file, neighborhood, and other committees). Thus one sees concretely that to support the Action and Neighborhood Committees in a period of social crisis is not a question of rhetoric, or even of simple "politicization." This is what matters, more than the point of knowing to what extent the Central Strike Committee at Nantes exercized the functions which it arrogated with the blessing of the old class society.[19]

## 7 Rank-and-File Committees, Direct Action

With a number of exceptions, the strike committees were in general controlled by the union centrals (as was, nearly as often, the composition of the picket lines). In a certain number of factories, however, especially in the Parisian region, rank-and-file (or action) committees were created. Thus, at the Rhone-Poulenc factory at Vitry, rank-and-file committees existed in each sector; the rate of effective participation in the occupation of the work sites was particularly high: 1,500 took part out of a personnel totaling 3,500 workers. Elsewhere, in a large printing works:

A Strike Committee got set up which succeeded, for a while, in going beyond, outflanking, and finally neutralizing the powerful college of union delegates. The members of this committee were union men (of necessity, since at our plant the union is in control of hiring). But there was here no question of infiltration: the men deliberately and openly set up in their factory a "parallel power," parallel to that of the CGT . . . In the electronics section, a rank-and-file committee was created on a proposal of the CGT, which hoped in this way to "sink" the two rival unions.[20] Result: the CGT was "sunk" itself, and from the union rank-and-file committee a true revolutionary organization emerged, which included

[19] "When they have a demand to make, they come to make it before the city hall (of Nantes), that is to say before the strike committee, but finally they appeal to it as in other circumstances they appealed to the Mayor"—said a guy of the March 22 Movement. *Ce n'est qu'un debut* . . . pp. 94-95.
[20] This was also the origin of the rank-and-file committees at RP-Vitry, an experience about which a participant notes that it showed "in an obvious way the reasons for the 'depoliticization' and the 'apathy' of the workers: for the latter, when they feel themselves concerned, participate actively and massively, in a

more than 50% of the workers as active members and considered itself perfectly capable of running the factory.[21]

At the *Assurances Générales de France,* following the denuciation of a part of the agreement relating to the payment for strike hours, it was proposed to the strike committee that an action committee elected on the ratio of one delegate per section be set up and that modes of action be envisaged which would be acceptable to all, consisting in making decisions in the areas reserved for the management on certain points (clocking in and out, making up for hours lost, determination of pay, etc.). Although it met with a favorable response, this project fell through essentially because of the formal veto of the CGT and the falling into line of the CFDT, which would not admit the existence of a committee which could constantly and directly translate the will of the rank and file and make the control of the factory a matter for struggle—to be exercised and imposed—and not a demand for which one awaits satisfaction from the management or the State.

Of course, the fate of these committees was strictly determined by the general course of events and, likewise, their attitude towards the unions varied as a function of conditions specific to each shop; some went so far as to consider themselves potential little unions, only, it goes without saying, to be blown away by the wind. These instruments had, in fact, meaning only for the struggle; that ended, their active role has ended also, or, more exactly, they can continue to exist (sometimes good, sometimes bad) only thanks to a new form of activity: discussion, the comparison of experiences. To wish to act differently, to wish to substitute themselves in isolation for the old organizations, while maintaining their modes of action, is to move in the direction of certain and complete dissolution. There have been enough attempts of this type in the history of the international labor movement, for one to be categorical on this subject.

---

direct way. In a decision in which the decisions are made in their name by someone else the disinterest is almost total." *(Cahiers de Mai,)* No. 2, 1-15 July, p. 11.
[21] *Action, ibid.*
   See, for example, J-J Servar-Schreiber, *Le Reveil* de la *France,* Paris, 1968; an idiotic book which is interesting for its presentation of May-June events entirely from this point of view.

In the newspaper presses, at the *Aurore* the linotypists threw out certain headlines; at the *Parisien libéré* the personnel unanimously refused on one occasion to put out the paper because of an outrageously lying headline on the front page; at the *Nation* the printers refused to put out this gaullist rag. But there was no coordination of action and no attempt to establish this on the part of the rank-and-file: they were content to swallow the tall tales of the obligatory union CGT which wished L '*Humanité* (but not the weeklies or the leaflets) to appear at any cost.

In a host of enterprises, the strike committee took care of the payment of wages, or of money paid on account (to be regularized after the strike), or even (as at the SNECMA) cashed checks with petty cash taken from the company cash-desk; sometimes, the canteen continued to function, where canned goods were distributed, etc. These things occur in every strike of such extent, but it must be stressed that the initiative came from the workers themselves, these tasks being often carried out outside of the usual rules, and that the orders came from the strike committee, acting to meet immediate necessities and not on instructions from the management.

Finally, at the moment of the return to work, wildcat demonstrations took place, the initiative for which often came from activist minorities. This was the case among the bookprinters of the Boulevard Blanqui; at the labor exchange for the employees of the RATP, the demonstrators came to the headquarters of certain union organizations to get some explanations and to protest just as if they were up against heads of personnel, and were thrown out by the union marshalls. Several hundred shoolteachers briefly occupied the office of the SNI, with an analogous result.

# V   PARTICIPATION AND STRUCTURAL REFORMS

If one demand appeared clearly in the course of the general strike, especially among the tens of thousands of young people, students and workers alike, it was the desire to take responsibilities. In one sense, that is related to the fact that the mentality of the heads of French business still considerably retards the scope of the productive forces (technology, equipment, level of qualification, attitudes of the producers, etc.); this backwardness—incompetence, really—is recognized by certain theoreticians friendly to the bosses.

Why does this advanced section of the ruling class love to talk about "participation"?

Given the level reached by the concentration of capital, its degree of rationalization and of automation, the exploitative society has trouble functioning without some participation by the workers. Decisions are made at such a high level, tasks are so highly divided, that the immediate producer cannot catch the sense of directives which are worked out without his participation and which fail to take account of the methods of practical application; in short, he no longer understands the direction of his work. So he tends to be completely detached from it; whereas the very structure of the enterprise (this distance separating directors and directed) requires that the producer "participate" for the directors plan to work properly. Therefore, those who *speak* of participation are the very ones who don't want and can't create a worker-controlled management because that would destroy all meaning both of the apparatus of domination which they represent and the functions they exercise within it. On the other hand, those who through their autonomous struggles spontaneously create, even if on an embryonic level, new forms and organizations of management and of struggle, realize in deeds a participation of all; but they not only do not talk about it but even often doubt that it can be realized.

## The Power of the State and the Bosses: Participation as Slogan and Scale Model of Society

That "participation" is only a matter of "rendering social structures flexible" in the words of one high functionary (C. Gruson), is shown clearly by the June 7, 1968 declaration of the President of the Republic:

That implies that the law assign to each person a part of what the business earns and of what it reinvests in itself. That implies also that everyone be adequately informed how the enterprise is going and can, through their freely chosen representatives, participate in the company and in its deliberations so that their interests, their points of view, and their proposals may be honored therein . . . . In a participative society, where everyone has an interest in its continuing to function, there is no reason at all for anyone not to wish the management to exert itself with vigor. Deliberation is the work of many and taking action is the work of one alone.

In fact, it is nearly a quarter-century since "the law" created workplace committees designed "to honor the interests" of the rank and file, which, in reality, have at best served to save the bosses the trouble of managing certain branches of social security and to take his place in communicating disagreeable news to the personnel.[22] As for "profit sharing," another worn out joke, it has long been notorious bunk, and the fate of the "Vallon-Amendment,"[23] latest of these pleasantries, has just confirmed it last year.

Frivolous as they may be, even these proposals are rejected by the bosses of the medium-sized and small businesses, who feel no need to "associate the workers with the management," under any form at all despite the legal text in many cases. The big employers find that participation has already been realized.

> The French structures permit the development of a true participation on the level of the national economy, in particular in the planning commissions and in the Economic Council, where the viewpoints of all partners in society are expressed, confront each other, and most often harmonize . . . . Participation in the enterprise can be a factor of efficiency only if it is founded on the enforcement of the structures and the managerial hierarchy, which it must help to assume all its responsibilities but whose authority it must not undermine . . . . It is essential that the representatives of the personnel and the unions take up their responsibilities in this regard, that is to say, agree to take account of the economic data which demand attention from the enterprise.[24]

Perhaps the big employers will consent, under the circumstances, to cease their habitual bullying and come to see a "valuable go-between" in the unions if the latter admit to pushing for the interests of the business as such before those of its constituents, the rank and file (something impossible in the long run, as we just saw in May-June). In fact, if some decisions are effectively made, they will lead without doubt in the direction of the creation of a system of collective bargaining at fixed times, the State reserving a power of arbitration, as is the practice in most of the great industrialized countries. The gaullist "participation" would

[22] "Les Comités d'enterprise," ICO, no. 51, July 1966, p. 11.
[23] Vallon, a left gaullist deputy, proposed a law instituting profit-sharing.
[24] "L'assemblée générale de CNPF," Le Monde 10/7/68.

then remain one of those magic words that the eminent men of France like to wave around, like the "resistance," the "familial virtues," and, now, "alienation" and "revolution." And distinguished professors, high functionaries in retirement, young Christian bosses and modernists of the CFDT will continue to expound virtuously on this theme . . . .

## The CGT: Living by Bread Alone

The French bosses declare themselves in favor of "a constructive social dialogue, sheltered from destructive demagoguery, rooted in the realities of work and life, not in fantasy."[25]

This is as well—they have declared it a thousand times— the essential aim of the CGT. On both sides, it is a matter of showing that they are realists, that is to say, of limiting themselves to discussing purely bread-and-butter demands, of not going beyond existing laws, at least when one cannot avoid them; and, for the unions, of placing confidence in dialogue, particularly in the parliamentary system. Both sides' vision of the world has the same foundations: the enterprise can be governed only by a hierarchy of competent men, just as is society as a whole on the model of Western and Eastern capitalism alike. The unions' disputes with the employers bear on the necessity of readjusting wages[26] and giving free rein to union propaganda within the enterprise, as is the case in most of the enterprises all over the world. On a more general level, the CGT envisages a change in government, accomplished through elections, which would permit it to consolidate by means of the law, its position in society and in the enterprises.

Forced to talk about self-management, because everyone talks about it, the CGT, through Séguy, its general secretary, declared its position in these terms:

> The movement guarded by the workers is much too powerful to be stopped by the hollow phrases, "self-management," "reform of civilization," "planned social and university reforms,"

[25] ibid.
[26] Which is evident when one knows that with a higher hourly productivity and labor-time, the hourly earnings of French workers were in general lower than wages in the same branches within other countries in the Common Market—except Italy, and even then not always. (Cf. J. Servant in *Economic et politique* —theoretical journal of the PC—No. 168.)

and other inventions which all end up in relegating to the background the immediate demands . . . . We propose solutions and we refuse to stand surely for a vague formula.[27]

Under the pen of Salini, *Humanité-Dimanche* (6/2/68) set out the intentions of the PC:

> The far-reaching structural reforms which our country needs, are nationalizations . . . of only those sectors of the economy in the hands of the great capitalists . . . . Ten years of authoritarianism have made urgent the participation of all Frenchmen in the management of their own affairs. By the vote. By the extension of union freedoms in the enterprise . . . . We hope that the structural reforms and the full bloom of democracy will open the road to socialism, a socialism conforming to our traditions, our experience, our French political methods.

The theoreticians of the PC have elaborated certain models of management for the use of future nationalized enterprises.[28] To discuss them would be superfluous. These plans are not to be taken seriously; the Party hatches a few at every great social crisis; one could have read similar ones 25 years ago, which have never been applied (the fault doubtless of a parliamentary majority!). History has confirmed the just objection that the CGT itself makes about the "self-managementarians," modernists of the CFDT and others, that we can be sure that a system of partial control in a society which remains set on capitalist foundations is condemned to employ capitalist methods and to preserve a capitalist content, and that changing the style of management doesn't change very much. The idea of the CGT leaders is really very simple: it is the ideal of a bureaucratic society in which a class of technocrats rule by planning on all the problems of production and consumption; it suffices that an apparat calculate the needs of men and everything else follows. No place for workers' control in such a framework, except perhaps to draft at, the rank-and-file level certain rules,[29] decided upon by the higher-ups

[27] *L'Humanité,* May 22, 1968.
[28] For example: J. Brieve, *"La gestion démocratique des enterprises du secteur public et nationalisé," Economie et Politique.* No. 166-67.
[29] *Cf. ibid.*: "These decisions (of the General Management), which must conform to the line set by the Administrative Council (in function of a policy set by the National Assembly [sic!])

and concerning the execution of tasks and the distribution
of products; something which is always done somehow or
another anyway.

## The CFDT: Self-management, the Magic Word

For a long time now, the CFDT has wielded a language
in which modernist accents occasionally came to give some
uplift to a speech identical, in the end, to those made by
other union central bureaus. Last to enter the market, thus
with leaders often younger and more inclined to take initiatives, the CFDT or a part of its directors, was certainly
not unaware of the principle current in advertising, according to which the consumer, placed before two products
of like quality, will choose the one presented most at-
tractively, the "brand image" at once most original and
most conforming to traditions. Besides, the monopoly on
pure bread-and-butter demands belongs to the CGT.

In the end—with formal variations, of course—the CFDT
joins hands with the CGT: only "reforms of the economic
structure," a "process of democratization of the enterprise"
can guarantee that wage increases will not be reduced to
nothing in the near future.[30] How to attain these objectives?
By parliamentary means, of course! However, what the
CGT proclaims with loud yaps, designed to sound reas-
suring to the bourgeoisie and imperative to the rank-and-
file, the CFDT suggests with a quite jesuitical caution:

> The movement is of such depth that we don't see how the
> parties can today absorb the new forces and their demands,
> which are not only quantitative but also call for profound
> reforms of the structures of society. . . . As of the CFTD,
> we have decided to assume all our responsibility.[31]

But, of course, one must know how to be "realistic" and
several days after these fine words, on the eve of the
election, the headquarters distributed a leaflet in which it
invited the workers to vote for the candidates which "appear
to them the most apt to constitute that left majority on

---

can be at all times controlled by the latter and by the personnel,
within the bounds of its rights." Longwinded on these "rights," the
author is absolutely silent on these "bounds": one would have bet
on it.

[30] Leaflet put out 5/27/68.

[31] Special edition of *Syndicalisme*. May 30, 1968.

which the future of democracy depends . . . . Above all we put forward our objectives of union recognition, of the development of 'union power,' the expression of "worker power" in the enterprise, of structural reforms in the economy."[32]

What this means is clear, but it gives the CFDT only half of its brand name, the traditional side. That is not enough for the modernists of the central bureau who have pounced on the occasion to again launch a conception, at first sight advanced, extremist even in certain respects, in the measure to which the role of rank-and-file discussion and the idea of self-management is set in relief:

> Self-management, participation: something readymade?
> No. It must be defined by the workers!
> The idea which we support—and of which the first prerequisite is union recognition in the enterprise—is an act of the working masses.
> What counts for us, is that in the factories, the administrations, the workers discuss these problems and that they profit from the time of strength which the strike represents for workers to really discuss their place and the responsibilities they wish to assume in the enterprise and the economy.
> If these discussions are carried on throughout the country, then, quite naturally, the content of what we want will be made precise, will be enriched with a whole working-class experience which we don't perceive completely but which is extremely rich.
> Words take on meaning only when they take possession of the masses because it is the masses who nourish the content of the formulas that we put forward. Isn't self-management the final form of socio-economic life?[33]

For workers "bread and butter" issues are a response to an immediate reality, to a need that the unions translate with more or less success in their negotiations with the representatives of the State and the employers. Likewise, the passage we have just cited expresses a desire widespread among the workers, above all among the young—students, workers, salaried employees, peasant—a desire which gave the days of May-June 1968 their unique coloration: a profound demand, originating in a desire for individual self-affirmation, through at last responsible and meaningful action, and in

[32] Supplement to *Syndicalisme*, 6/13/68.
[33] *Syndicalisme*, 5/25/68.

the feeling of collective interdependence born in confused fashion during the struggle. These producers, unable to realize that profound demand at once envisaged its realization through organs like the rank-and-file committees, action committees, etc., which corresponded to the struggle that they were carrying on at the time, and not to ancient phrases of general cretinization and social harmony. This, and nothing else, is the extremist point of view.

But the CFDT, following its vocation, ties this new content to obsolete practices which constituted a restraining force in the struggle—though not the only one and perhaps not the most important. These old practices are based on dialogue, between union and management within the enterprise, in parliament on the level of the society as a whole, and the inanity of which is recognized by a great part of those who give it their votes for lack of anything better. Self-management, workers' control, for the CFDT, is no more and no less than the means for its implanting itself in the enterprises, since every union central bureau makes "worker power" and "union power" synonymous expressions. The following quotation without doubt does not express the position of the ex-Christian Confederation as such;[34] it has at least the merit of saying things crudely; while the usual proclamations live in a prudent *clair-obscur*

> The meaning of workers' control has all its value in a planned economy oriented towards need and controlled by union organizations. . . . But we want to pursue the construction of a union apparatus powerful and controlled at all levels . . . Without this reinforcement of unionism, everything we have said above is just literature.[35]

In the light of its action in May and June, it would appear that the CFDT has always had in view only legal, parliamentary consecration of the movement's "gains," that is to say, of nothing at all, apart from the (promised) recognition of the union section in the enterprise. In general a minority in the shops, it preserved a certain freedom in speech, but where it had a majority—for example, at the

[34] Another CFDT bigshot limits himself to demanding an increase in the "powers of parties other than the possessors of capital," a system "assuring the workers and their union organizations the full exercise of their rights." (R. Bonéty, *Le Monde. 7/9/68*).
[35] Declerq, "Pour une planification démocratique," report to the 30th Congress of the CFTC, June 19-21, 1959.

Assurances Générales de France—it aligned its attitude with that of the CGT minority, thinking to make it take the blame in case the personnel contested the agreements made with the management. At any rate, the old guard sprung from the CFTC has the apparatus in its hands, and it is only a younger and more active nucleus which here plays the role played by the "activist minorities" in the *Force Ouvrier*.

## FO: In the Image of the Traditional Left

The FO was hardly mentioned in the course of events, except in a few specific cases. Nearly a trifle, it was as imperceptible as the fragments of the traditional left, and for the same reasons: these groups bring together only dignitaries looking for government jobs and a circle of gaping strollers who are all washed up from the viewpoint of the powers that be in French society. These people are still into the individualism dear to the nineteenth century. This perhaps explains why at least two of the leaders of the FO, Hébert at Nantes and Labi at the *Fédéchimie* (chemical workers' union), could take leading positions without even dreaming of breaking with a visibly exhausted headquarters and, at least until now, without being expelled for it.

FO appeared to come out for important reforms "to humanize hierarchical relations," through union recognition in the enterprises and to the participation of its high officials in the elaboration of the Plan and in the "Economic and Social Council, in its consultative form."[36] In short, to furnish specialists, eminent but not responsible, and thus to mitigate its absence at the rank-and-file level by a presence at the summit. As far as action proper goes, a leaflet distributed by the FO after the strike limits itself to endless boasting about the reinforcement of the central and the "incontestable advantages" acquired, and so forth and so on. Entirely different, it is true, was the behavior of the *Fédéchimie* and of several other local or shop sections both FO and CFDT), which did not hesitate to demonstrate its active sympathy to the student movement. What is more:

Keeping the pledge made at Charlety [to make no agreements with the bosses; Charlety was the site of a mass meeting organized by the UNEF and the SNESup among others], the *Fédéchimie* CGT-FO has signed no agreement with the employers in any of the chemical industries: chemicals,

[36] *Le Monde*, 7/9/68.

petroleum, glass, rubber, plastics. It has authorized the agreement of its National Union in the Atomic Energy Commission to the protocol which is the only one in France to anticipate the institution of organs of workers' control.[37]

And, in an attitude rather rare today among union officials, its secretary, Maurice Labi, came out against the elections:

> The solution can be found only in the collective appropriation of the principal means of production, the democratic control of the enterprises, the reform of existing organs or the setting up of new institutions permitting the regulation of production and the harmonizing of social life. . . . In every factory, neighborhood, village and town, united committees of workers, peasants, students, and high school students should be set up; the Estates General of the new France will meet to give our country a look young and modern, joyous and happy, socialist and free.[38]

O.K. Only when one proposes to abandon parliamentary methods, one must accept the consequences and, for example, continually keep up the pressure in favor of the organs charged with carrying on dialogue with the directors at all levels. We have seen above what came of the organs of the CEA one month after their legalization. Doubtless, since nothing has changed in other respects, they have hardly any chance to survive—but has the FO made an effort to support them by all the means of its propaganda? No. More generally, can the appeal to these "Estates General" come from an organization whose bigshots intend at the same time to play a consultative role in the various institutions of gaullist power? Is it simply a matter of replacing, as at Nantes, a mayor who called in sick? Labi bears witness to the old revolutionary syndicalist tradition, former glory of the French labor movement, but what does that mean now? At Rhone-Poulenc, a part of the workers has already answered: they joined up with the rank-and-file committees, seeing clearly that the old structure had no value for the unity of the movement.

## The CGC: The Cadres have their Right Place

We must put aside the critique of the hierarchy as such

[37] *Contre le piege a c . . . des elections,"* Combat. 6/17/68.
[38] *Ibid.*

and of the concept of competence, not because these are unimportant questions—quite the opposite—but because their discussion would require a pamphlet the size of this one. We limit ourselves to calling attention to a very significant position.

In a leaflet of May 24, 1968 (*Cadres CGC de l'Assurance*) it is stated that "our desire to obtain a participatory structure doesn't date from today."

At the time of the last congress of the union of insurance cadres belonging to the CGC (March 13, 1968) this "desire" was thus defined:

> We must be conscious of the role which we can play: we must realize that in the enterprises "capital" in the sense it used to have plays a less and less evident part, for the ownership of concerns is divided up between a large number of shareholders; finally at the head of the latter are various boards of directors and high level managers, who in the end play a much more important role than all the owners of capital. But we ourselves, to a different degree, have salaried status like the directors for, in the end, these directors are only, in relation to the proprietors of these concerns, neither more or less than cadres; they are very high up, but their situation depends finally, despite everything, on these "corporate capitals" (even if the expression is losing meaning).
>
> Consequently, one can say that the team of cadres which stands outside of the board of directors ought in its turn to have a chance to participate in making decisions; and it is this that we must absolutely demand in all circumstances. It is on the basis of these ideas that it is good to repeat whenever one has the chance that we must structure our activity in such a way as to install in the course of years a true representation of cadres with power in the enterprise.

The May crisis set in relief the narrow spirit of the French bourgeoisie: its inconceivable distance from the real, its generic blinders. There is nothing astonishing about a group of cadres wishing to lean on the movement in order to curtail some few of the powers of its immediate superiors who, all shook up as they are, have a more than slight resemblance to idle royalty (without going on to ask themselves if they, the cadres, aren't in the same position). In the commissions that sprung up during the strike, the cadres frequently proposed two bases for reflection: (a) to define new structures capable of conferring a greater power to the cadre position, relaxing the old system of

command and entrusting to the rank-and-file part of the
regulation of its working conditions, in order to avoid the
usual conflicts about "everything and nothing;" (b) to contest the role played in the working of the enterprise by
factors both exterior (banks, the State) and interior (administrative council, board of directors), with a view to
imposing—in the name of the "correctly understood interests"
of all—the legal participation of "cadre power" in decision-
making.

There was also a convergence between the situation of
the cadres on the job and that of the future cadres, the
students. The rapid evolution of the techniques and materials
of production and control (until very recently) has engendered a technological unemployment, and thus a limitation of job openings, coupled with a tendential devaluation
of their intellectual function. But when the students' action
transcended itself to go as far as to confront the existing
order ("We do not want to be the watchdogs of capitalism"),
the great majority of cadres limited themselves to expressing
the demands of which we have just spoken and whose
success remains doubtful, under present conditions, since
it is left to the discretion of the bosses' power.

Nevertheless, during the strike certain cadres advocated a
non-hierarchal raise in wages and participated in the
strike committees (with rank-and-file—cadre equality). This
happened most often in the most modern industries, where
the cadres are young, well payed, and severed from administrative tasks; it is a matter of a minority of the whole,
but it is important that this occurred, and not only in a
few isolated cases. It took a lot for the cadres, *qua* social
stratum, to renounce, even on paper, what there is of authority in their functions (and only in very rare cases were
they asked to).

To a great extent, the sympathies of the cadres toward
the student movement expressed a sort of solidarity with the
future members of their social class. This was also the source
of the workers' distrust of both the students and the
cadres. Even while supporting the cadres' demands of the
sort mentioned above, the CGT exploited this suspicion to
maintain a barrier between workers and students; to do this
it did not hesitate to preach an "anti-intellectual" attitude,
which is neither more nor less than a form of racism and
is due entirely to imbecility and not at all to a reasoned
critique.

## Unions and Workers

The May movement permitted many to discover what a restraining force the unions represent. For, if spontaneity sufficed to lift the movement to great heights, it was not enough to keep it there, especially since the fight took on a sharp character only in exceptional cases. People became conscious of the function of the unions in the modern world: to participate in the administration of the labor force in the interest of society as it is, that is to say, to submit a certain number of demands to a series of specialized bargaining sessions, all while trying to reinforce their position within the apparatus of domination (the differences between union centrals turning solely on modes of realizing this last objective). But the unions could not function, thus they did not receive the approbation, passive in general, of the greatest mass of workers; in other words, the strength of the unions has produced only the weakness and the division of the workers.

When we see these powerful organizations, with hundreds of thousands of members, with a machinery run and guided by teams of experienced professionals, come to shabby results, the first reaction is to reproach them for their lack of efficiency (an inefficiency evident in France: the American union bosses are often gangsters or legal professionals but are at least relatively efficient in negotiations). After this, they are often accused of corruption, even of treason, and the means which comes to mind to remedy this situation is apparently simple: create another organization, this time pure and tough. To which the old centrals answer, with reason, that this would be to accentuate the division of workers even more. To which one could furthermore add that the history of the labor movement has showed for a century that these "new" organizations have been destined either to lose themselves in sectarian behavior and to wither on the stalk, or else, if they escape this fate, to model themselves on the old forms (as is demonstrated by the evolution of the various sections of the communist movement). Clearly: it is an impasse.

But why are the workers the only ones who don't talk about workers' control? Is it that they don't feel it would concern them? No, on the contrary: in their actions they already utilize spontaneous forms of organization and struggle which move in this direction. Even more, in his mentality and in his daily attitudes, in disobeying orders, in criticizing the cadre who confronts him directly, the worker contests in fact the principle and the practice of hierarchical control, the very basis of the capitalist system of management. But, just as in daily life this confrontation remains at a very individualized level, likewise at the first stages of collective action it doesn't succeed in generalizing itself. Although the spontaneous reactions, as we saw in May, often go quite far, they retain a passive adhesion to norms considered unbreakable. Thus, when at the *Assurances Générales* a CFDT militant, opposing the creation of a struggle committee elected by the workers, declared before 3,000 employees: "I am for it, but it can't be done . . . perhaps in 50 or 100 years," no one reacted. A call to the same employees to organize by themselves a referendum on the question of strike pay found practically no response. And no one dreamed of reacting to arguments like, "The employees within one section will never succeed in coming to an understanding with each other," even after an extraordinary strike!

It is the capitalist mode of production which continually secretes such passive reactions among almost all of those who are under it. The established order appears to be the natural one in virtue of the consciousness which it in some spontaneous way engenders, according to which appearances correspond to reality, everyone receiving more or less his just share of the social product and finding himself in his just place. Of course, there are variants of this consciousness, a crowd of variants, but they are only phrases and ideas heard a thousand times since childhood in the family, at school, at work, and out of work: respect for authority, the cult of the leader, idolatry of knowledge–and the dogma that one's rank in the hierarchy naturally reflects a level of competence sanctioned in general by the diploma.

During the days of May and June, this thick blindfold was cracked; but the crack was neither deep nor lasting– at least at first sight. The fundamental reason for this was stated in the course of another great social crisis: "No proletariat in the world can from one day to the next reduce to smoke the traces of a century of slavery" (Rosa Luxemburg). And only the revival of the movement, with greater determination, can overthrow from top to bottom the mentality of the exploited masses.

## VI THE ORGANIZATION OF PRODUCTION AND DISTRIBUTION BY THE PRODUCERS THEMSELVES

A ruling class allows itself to be dispossessed of its power only by violence. Every working class struggle important enough to contest the social power (and not only, by troubling public order, the political power) of this class must expect to face the most pitiless repression to the extent that this contestation takes form in deeds and action.

The workers, as we have said, don't talk about control and think themselves incapable of managing an enterprise or society, if they so much as pose such questions or are asked them. The attempts at management we have spoken of should be considered from two points of view, contradictory in tendency:

• they are a response to a profound necessity of capitalist society which has reached a certain level of development and concentration: the notion of workers' control arises spontaneously from the conditions of the modern factory, the modern enterprise.

• this is also evident to the ruling class, which perceives this fact from within the framework of exploitative society and tries to respond to it in terms of this framework. To integrate the worker into the enterprise by various recipes is fine for it and appears to the most "advanced" technocrats to be absolutely necessary for the survival of the capitalist enterprise. But this is to try to square the circle, because one can never integrate a worker into an activity the decisions about which and final control of which are totally out of his hands, decisions aiming above all to maintain the dominance of one class.

This very contradiction lies at the center of all the questions which we have brought up. Everyone in the various milieus—economic, political, union, technocratic—talks about "management," "control" because it is in this that the problem lies; but the solutions they propose succeed only in showing that they are no answer to the central problem of our society.

This question may now come to mind: "How may this problem be resoved?" But to pose it in this form expresses the viewpoint of a conscious and activist minority, and thereby reintroduces the division between minority and masses which appears to us to generate a new class system.

Only the workers in struggle can give the answer–and all that we can do is to explicate situations in which the workers realize more or less rapidly that nothing fundamental has been changed.

This answer of the workers will be forthcoming only out of the struggle itself through the very development of this struggle. It is not conscious and formulated as a demand: it is the activity of struggle itself.

It is ultimately the only answer to the profound necessity for a system of production which gives total satisfaction to human needs and for a society in which the individual is not constantly frustrated in his activity. We think that this is the fundamental way to look at it: in terms of a system of management, control that flows from the struggle itself.

A struggle for material demands (wages, hours, vacations, retirement), if it is not content with partial satisfactions, if it is carried on with determination, if like this strike it extends to the whole country, if it is general, soon poses other problems than those of the strike itself, although they are the direct consequence of the strike and of its continuation with the same combative spirit.

First, all activities cannot come to a total stop: provisioning, medical care, transports, etc. pose problems which must be solved immediately, even if only for the strikers and their families. The longer the strike is prolonged, the more these problems of getting certain sectors going again become acute and important, till they extend to the country as a whole. Special questions (furnishing current to a hospital, delivering milk, etc.) at first, they come to be posed at the local level (provisioning of a city) or at the national level (assuring the transmission of information, for example).

At the same time, the struggle of the ruling class against the strike acquires definite form and becomes more violent to the extent that the strike, precisely in lasting so long, changes in nature and seeks to *control* and *manage* instead of make demands. For then the social balance of power tips suddenly to the side of the workers in virtue of the simple fact that the activity of production and distribution is gotten on the road again and that they do it to serve themselves. As the repression develops, the struggle itself again transforms itself giving rise now also to the necessity of getting certain services functioning again, simply for the conduct of the strike: radio, the mails, transports.

These two domains of renewed activity—which appear distinct—interact and make the need for liaisons and co-ordinating organs clear. This very necessity leads thus to replacing the apparatus of administration, of the police, by organs of workers' control of a local or national, or inter-professional, or other scale. In this way, the structures of a new society are set up under the initiative and the control of rank-and-file organs in the shops.

This reactivation of the economy can be accomplished in several ways. Let us set aside the case where this minimum functioning which preserves society from asphyxiation is assumed under the aegis of the existing power: either by scabs, or by the army, or by agreements made between unions controlling the strike and the "authorities" at whatever level. It is quite clear that power in such cases has not changed hands and that the workers do not control the strike themselves.

Likewise, some organization or other formed in the course of the struggle could take over management, if it could get control of the struggle and play a coordinating and organizational role that the workers would not have assumed themselves. The role of such an organization—party, union, revolutionary committee, etc.—would be the same as that played by the interunion organization at Nantes. It would exercise a power distinct from that of the workers in struggle: the latter either would submit to it in the same way that they submit to the current power—or would enter into conflict with it, through their own organs of struggle (strike committees, for example) or through those which they would create at that moment.

If at some point in the strike, the workers themselves set up an elected strike committee of which they kept control, everything would be turn out differently. The reactivation of the enterprises, the creation of liaisons and coordinating organs, everything is done by the workers themselves, for it is they who must solve the material problems posed by the strike, its maintenance, and its development, and it is they themselves who do solve them. The management of production and distribution becomes the work of the workers. They did not think previously that they would run the enterprise, and if one had told them they could would not have believed it. But the very necessities of the strike force them to solve a practical problem and in doing this they seize social power.

It is certain that the ruling classes will do everything, absolutely everything, to prevent power from being taken by associated, free, and equal producers. Beyond measures of intimidation and violent repression, they will try to interest the masses in *their* politics of exploitation by organizing agitation in favor of the various tendencies among *them* which are supposed to be representative, those installed in power or those hoping to exercise it: electoral campaigns, a referendum, change of government, diversionary campaigns, etc. Then, or perhaps at the same time, the rulers will stress the risks of disaster and chaos that a prolonged struggle will bring to *their* economy. If the producers persist as a mass in remaining relatively indifferent to the politics and the economics of the ruling classes and continue their struggle, getting the enterprises going again under their own direction, then the ruling classes, all united, will decide to recapture, arms in hand, that of which they have always dispossessed the immediate producers: they will unleash civil war.

As early as May, when the forms of real worker power existed only in rough outline, the different ruling groups were unanimous in flourishing this menace: the right by speaking of it openly, the left, knowing themselves incapable of reacting, speaking only of the risk of military dictatorship. To the old reflexes of passivity among the producers were added reflexes of fear, also quite old.

The workers entered into struggle not only because they saw the students occupy their workplaces and open them to all but also and above all because they saw the most resolute portion of the youth go down into the street and meet the forces of repression head on; they were "ready to fight to the finish," people said, and this opposition in its turn made everyone "ready to fight to the finish." There was much of this feeling in the greeting the strikers gave the union officials who had obtained at best a readjustment of French wages to the levels practiced in the other countries of the Common Market. But afterwards the workers had either to submit to the rod of the State, the employers, and the unions, that is to say, to the laws of the market, or really to go to the finish, to the reactivation of the occupied enterprises. And that no one dared to do; everyone knew what that would mean; fear paralyzed everything.

And now? Since nothing has changed, since there was

no victory, but no defeat either, the alternatives remain the same: either to submit or to take up the fight again. Without doubt there will be groups or individuals capable of sweeping away the difficulties with a phrase, of rigorously working out a perspective to accommodate a strategy of dreams; and others, more numerous assuredly, to explain that all that happened had for origin "impatience raised to the level of a theory,"[39] or will have no future. In fact, it is clear, the question of a renewal of the struggle clearly may not be settled in the domain of reflection but, to begin with, depends on the success of exemplary actions. All one can say is that the shock has been felt profoundly by the masses, that a new mentality has begun to emerge, that the pressures of authority restored and the arrogance of the bosses are not likely to diminish.

Consequently, at some time relatively near, the struggle will be able to begin again, on condition that it beats the ferocious opposition that it will meet at the hands of the union centrals. It will be a matter of wildcat strikes and demonstrations, carried on by organs arising directly from the struggle. When the struggle extends and is prolonged and these committees will have to take in hand the task which the ruling classes are from that moment on incapable of carrying out: they will have to administer production and distribution on the local, then on the national level. Faced by a State power already today deprived of all other support among the masses but that of the ballot—less than nothing in a period of social crisis—and one which can count only on the meager police forces, they will organize self-defense. They will transform themselves into councils of producers—workers, professionals, students, and peasants—instrument for the struggle and for the direct organization of production and society by the producers themselves.[40]

We think of ourselves as contributing, in our position within the movement,[41] to pushing the event in its natural

[39] L. Figuéres, *"Le Gauchisme," Cahiers du Communisme.* No. 6; 1968.

[40] See Appendix I, Thesis 3.

[41] That is to say, in participating in organs which are in principle non-exclusionary, with all its disadvantages on the side of visible efficiency, and not based upon a principle of discrimination, which must, whatever the supposed justification, obey the principle of class society and can in consequence never engender the slightest real efficiency but only produce a sect.

direction. That means among other things to propose for discussion certain general ideas; not a plan preconceived by a few people, not a program which, under present conditions, can be tied only to organizations of the old type, by all the evidence maladapted to periods of social crisis.

These general ideas relate above all to the principles on which societies do or might function. Capitalist society without doubt still functions in the way Stone-Age societies did, at least in one fundamental aspect: the subordination of men to an order over which they have little or no control. It is, however, possible to reduce capitalism's special mode of functioning to several basic principles, for example the extraction, the realization, and the accumulation of surplus value, the search (private or carried on by particular social categories) for profit. Likewise, the appearance of the new society, born of the old, is dependent on the diffusion and the realization of new social principles, applied on local, national and finally—else the new world is condemned to disappear—international levels. Assuredly, this application can only be empirical, can only take on forms varying to fit different places and times, and it would be pointless to wish to predict these practical forms today in detail. However, the permanent existence of producers' councils presupposes the appearance in the course of the struggle, indeed because of the class struggle, faced with the failures of capitalism and the ruling classes, of new economic foundations of society as a whole.

At a certain point, during the crisis, the problems of the organization of production and of the return for labor will ineluctably pose themselves. On the local level, then on the national level, the councils will have to organize production and distribution as a function of a plan whose data will be made available to everyone and which will be decided by everyone. In the present state of technique, in view especially of the progress of economic calculating techniques and of the computer industry, which makes it possible for anyone who wants to check up at any time on how things are going, this no longer appears to pose fundamentally insoluble problems, although a profound change of mentality is necessary.

There now exists a plan in each of the two great branches of the world capitalist system but, although what takes the place of a plan here is quite different from the plan in the East, these two forms of planning have at least the common characteristic of resting on the system of prices or of credit allocations, which rests in turn on the system of wage-labor, that is to say, on the exploitation of man by man. Producers who have learned to *direct their struggles themselves,* under conditions of equality for all and collective effort, will tend in a natural way to make the planned production and distribution of goods rest on new foundations. First, as we have seen, because this follows the natural tendency of the struggle, and also because, the value of money having been reduced to zero by inflation, it will be necessary to choose a new unit of account; but also because contemporary history has shown that the abolition of the private ownership of the means of production, though an evident necessity, does not absolutely coincide with the end of exploitation.

In the capitalist economy the system of prices more or less determined by the market (or credit allocations more or less "determined" by the divisions of the plan) constantly creates the illusion that exploitation is a problem of the market (or of planning), whose conditions need but be modified—generally, in the more or less democratic countries, by a "dialogue" between the classes in parliament and within other so-called representative structures—to effect a real and lasting transformation of the human condition. In the same way, the wages system only hides the reality of exploitation and divides the producers from each other by attaching the level of remuneration to levels of qualification which are basically imaginary. In fact, all the products of human labor, and thus the labor-time of various categories of producers materialized in these products, have qualitative value, since they are all the crystallization of a certain quantity of labor, immediate and mediated: immediate in the factories and the fields, mediated by means of knowledge socially accumulated, transmitted, and applied.

In the capitalist system, the measure of the value of commodities is always money, which itself hides this fundamental reality: the producer is and can't be other than an article of commerce, himself a thing with a value. In other words, the producer cannot see himself otherwise than as an object who functions either as director or as directed to the extent to which he is considered and considers himself as gifted with competence or with rights; judged by criteria of differentiated value, he is linked to others by an abstract relation. He does not appear as he really is, a producer linked to other producers like himself by their sharing equally the quality of social labor. The abstract relation between things with values is incarnated in money, another abstract power, incarnating in turn the play of laws which essentially escape the will of men in general; the visible source of all baseness and all unhappiness, money is one of the properties of Capital. By contrast, labor-power is one of the properties common to all men. The measure of the time which each producer devotes to work is the hour of labor. And the measure which permits the calculation of the labor-time crystallized in the products of human activity (with some near exceptions: scientific research and other creative works) is the hour of average social labor, basis of the communist production and distribution of goods.

But, it will be said, what is the difference between value-money and the "consumption voucher" calculated on the basis of the average social hour of labor? In a capitalist system, exchange expresses a fundamental fact: the immediate producer is not master of the means of production and social labor is the property of the ruling classes. The latter divide up the products of social labor as a function of "property rights," of "degrees of competence," of the laws of the market and other laws, of a lot of factors and rules, sometimes corresponding to reality but always falsified by the division of society into classes—of which the old union organizations constitute one expression. On the other hand, when the hour of average social labor serves as the basis for calculation of production and consumption, there is no more need for a "wages policy"; the productive forces, supposing the will of the producers and the existing capacities of production, determine automatically the volume of consumption, of the society of the whole and of the individual.

Henceforth, the producers themselves regulate production, but this regulation is no longer effected more or less blindly and always arbitrarily, as it is today. The social relations run no longer vertically, from top to bottom, from director to executor, but horizontally, between associated producers. It is no longer factors escaping human control or expressing the division of society into classes that fix the objectives of production, but the free producers themselves. And the measure that serves to regulate production is a quality distributed equally among men. But association, liberty, and equality of producers may not properly be said to flow from the realization of moral aspirations; in one sense, they are the consequence of the natural tendency to self-emancipation to which the old organizations and the old ideas are opposed; in another sense, each enterprise remains a cell of that immense economic body which is society and whose vital metabolism, the system of exchange, necessitates and produces organic unity. The various cells are integrated into one whole which rests on a radically egalitarian basis, and which can be no other than this: labor time taken as sole unit of calculation of production and consumption, a standard controllable by all.

All this is doubtless far from the immediate facts: a general strike which derived above all from a spontaneous explosion and propagation: a movement which really deepened only in a certain sector, that of the production of the higher levels of producers; new forms of organization which here and there appeared in embryonic state and as a function of specific situations; discussions of a qualitative and quantitative extent the like of which have never been seen in the history of human societies and which in the absence of their extension into action—the reactivation of the economy by associated, free, and equal producers—rapidly fell to chasing round in circles. Months and months of inaction are going to follow weeks of action. But just as the initiatives of some served to unleash the initiative of the greater number, the reflections of some may serve to awaken those of the great number. And this awakening to reflection is itself a first condition of the struggle.

## List of Abbreviations

| | |
|---|---|
| AM | *Agents de maîtrise*—junior executives (not an organization) |
| CA | *Comités d'Action*—Action Committees (see text) |
| CAL | *Comités d'Action Lycéens*—High school Action Committees |
| CFDT | *Confédération Française Démocratique du Travail*—French Democratic Confederation of Labor, created from the CFTC. While the latter admitted only Catholics, the CFDT is open. It is unattached to any political party. |
| CFTC | *Confédération Française des Travailleurs Chrétiens*—French Confederation of Christian Workers, maintained by a few members of the old CFTC when the mass of the union was transformed into the CFDT |
| CGC | *Confédération Générale des Cadres*—General Confederation of Cadres |
| CGT | *Confédération Générale du Travail*—General Confederation of Labor; the largest union in France, in principle independent of the PC but in fact directed by it: its secretary general Séguy is also a member of the PC politburo, as are all the most important leaders. |

CLEOP    *Comités de Liaison Etudiants-Ouvriers—Paysans*—Student-Worker-Peasant Liaison Committees (see text)

CNJA    *Centre National des Jeunes Agriculteurs*—union of young peasants and farmworkers

CNPF    *Centre National du Patronat Français*—National French Employers Association

CRS    *Compagnies Republicaines de Sécurité*—special police force ("riot police") created by the gaullist provisional government after World War II to maintain "order"

FER    *Fédération des Etudiants Révolutionnaires*—Revolutionary Students' Federation; one of several trotskyist groups; very dogmatic

FNJA    *Fédération Nationale des Jeunes Agriculteurs*—union of young peasants and farmworkers

FO    *Force Ouvrière*—Workers' Strength; more correctly CGT-FO, a union resulting from a split in the CGT after the war on the issue of PC control and pro-Russian policy; FO has links with American unions, has been suspected of CIA financing; has a mostly white-collar membership

PC    *Parti Communiste*—Communist Party

RATP    *Régie Autonome des Transports Parisiens*—nationalized company running all public transportation in Paris

SNCF    *Société Nationale des Chemins de Fer Français*—French National Railway Company, nationalized after the war

SNECMA    *Société Nationale d'Etudes et Construction de Moteurs d'Avion*—National Airplane Motor Research and Construction Co., one of the first companies to be nationalized after the war

SNESup    *Syndicat Nationale de l'Enseignement Supérieur*—National Union of Higher Education; union theoretically of all university faculty, in fact mostly junior faculty; very leftwing

SNI    *Syndicat Nationale des Instituteurs*—National Union of Primary School Teachers

UEC    *Union des Etudiants Communistes*—Union of Communist Students, official student organization of the PC

UNEF    *Union Nationale des Etudiants de France*—National Union of French Students; the main student union, with leftist tendencies

UNR    *Union pour la Nouvelle République*—Union for the New Republic, one of the changing names of the gaullist party

# IV. Workers' Councils

## Introduction to **Workers' Councils**

### peter rachleff

The following text, Anton Pannekoek's *Workers' Councils*, attempts to present the dynamics of the revolutionary process, and a general picture of the socialist society which may result from revolution. Pannekoek's conception of socialism differs fundamentally from the notions of the future society that have dominated official "Marxist" discussions in the 20th century. Social-Democratic and Leninist theories of revolution have shared the assumption that the working class cannot emancipate itself and manage a future society by itself, without the leadership of professional revolutionary politicians. From this point of view, the Party was to educate the workers to the virtue of socialism, until with the workers' backing it could seize state power and reorganize production and distribution in the "interest" of the workers. *Workers' Councils*, however, is little concerned with the role professional revolutionaries can play in the class struggle. Instead, it concentrates on the working class' attempts to organize itself, first of all in its conflict with the employers and then, with the development of the struggle, in the construction of a system of social production run by the workers themselves.

The entirely new social, economic, and political system which is here projected differs fundamentally from both of the systems which divide up the world today—from capitalism on the one hand, and from state-controlled systems (like those of Russia, China, Cuba, etc.) on the other. In capitalism,

[1] Cf. Paul Mattick, "Anton Pannekoek," *New Politics* I: 2 (1961), and Serge Bricianer, *Pannekoek at les Conseils Ouvriers* (Paris: 1969), a selection of texts with historical and critical commentary.

decisions as to what is produced, how much, and how are made by the owners of businesses, as they compete with each other for profit. The actual producers, whose labor is the source of business's profits, have no say over the production system either as a whole or in their places of work.

In the state-run system, centralized planning takes the place of competition between economic units. But since the planning process is monopolized by the Party bureaucrat-controlled state, the workers again have no control over production or distribution. They are exploited by one employer, the state, who appropriates their surplus labor-time to use as it sees fit. In contrast, Pannekoek conceived of socialism as a regime of direct control over production by those who actually do the work, unmediated by any organizations or institutions with an independent power (army, police) of their own. There must of course be organized co-ordination linking units of production (and other areas of social life), but these must be assured by organizations such as factory committees and councils which are directly controlled by all who work together.

Far from being dreamed up in the realms of utopian theory, these ideas are based on an analysis of workers' struggles in the first half of this century, struggles in which the author took an active part. The wide gap between Social Democratic and Leninist theories and the ideas presented in *Workers Councils* developed in the course of Pannekoek's participation in both forms of organization. Born in a rural town in Holland in 1873, Anton Pennekoek studied mathematics at the University of Leyden and earned a doctorate in astronomy there in 1902. He made good use of his scientific training in his approach to society and the revolutionary process; in his approach, he attempted to think on the basis of real events and their dynamics, and not to force them into *à priori* frameworks.

In 1901, Pannekoek joined the Dutch Social Democratic Party (SDAP), and immediately became a member of a small left-wing group within the Party, which included Hermann Gorter and Henriette Roland-Holst. The SDAP was tightly controlled by its leadership, and Pannekoek's group frequently came into conflict with the party chieftan, Troelstra. More seriously, the Party leadership time and time again acted to restrain the militance of groups of workers. Pannekoek and his comrades were both impressed with the ability of the workers to organize themselves and act on their own, and dismayed by the Party's opposition to such attempts, In 1907, the group set up its own journal, *De Tribune,* and in 1909 left the SDAP to form their own party.

Pannekoek had left Holland in 1906 to teach Marxist theory at the school run by the German Social Democratic Party (SPD) in Berlin, although he remained in close contact with his Dutch comrades and often contributed to *De Tribune.* Threatened with deportation by the Prussian police, he left Berlin after one semester and traveled around Germany as a journalist, until 1909 when he settled in Bremen, where he worked with a left splinter group within the SPD. In Bremen he came into contact with a large industrial working class which was extremely active politically; but here again he saw the dominant organization (the SPD) function to hold back radical workers. He realized that for these "socialist" parties independent working class activity was a threat to their own existence, so that they acted to protect the Party rather than to further the development of the revolutionary consciousness which, Pannekoek argued, can only grow out of the experience of the class struggle itself. He began to develop the idea that it is through mass direct actions in pursuit of their interests that workers could develop the solidarity and understanding necessary to transform society, without having formulated the goal of socialism beforehand. But despite his stress on mass actions rather than on the parliamentary activity of the Party, Pannekoek remained an active member of the SPD, expressing his views in debates with Kautsky and Bernstein in the Party journals. He still believed that socialism meant putting "the power of the state . . . at the disposal of the working class. . . ."[2]

The failure of the international working class movement to prevent the outbreak of the First World War caused Pannekoek to reconsider many of his earlier ideas. In a series of articles rewritten between 1914 and 1917, he undertook to criticize the weaknesses of the old form of organization embodied in the social democratic parties of the Second International, and sought to lay the theoretical foundations of a new form of organization which would be based on mass action and be willing to undertake and support rev-

---

[2] *New Review,* 16 January 1913. At this time Pannekoek was an important influence on the American socialist movement, contributing many articles to the socialist *New Review.*

olutionary struggle. By 1917, in calling for the formation of a new International, Pannekoek found himself allied with Lenin and the Zimmerwald leftists, who sought to "turn the imperialist war into civil war."

In February of that year the Russian Revolution broke out and organs of working-class self-emancipation appeared in Russia in the form of Soviets and factory committees.[3] Like revolutionaries throughout Europe, Pannekoek was an immediate supporter of the revolution and an avid student of the soviet (council) and factory committee movement. He saw these organs both as instruments of struggle against the old society and as the basis for the construction of the new. The German revolution of 1918 confirmed the central importance of workers' committees and councils for proletarian revolution. In Germany, workers' councils functioned primarily as a means of political expression for the war-weary working class, who used the social power to end the war and replace the monarchy with a Republic. That the workers then gave up their power to an alliance of liberal and socialist parties, who were ony too willing to oversee the restoration of bourgeois power, did not detract from the significance of workers' councils as a means of geniune self-organization and self-expression, although its role as organs of self-emancipation was limited by the German working class's failure to move politically beyond support for an SPD-led government.

Initially, Pannekoek and his comrades (Herman Gorter, H, Canne Meijer, Henriette Roland-Holst, and others) supported the Bolsheviks in Russia, overlooking the authoritarianism of Lenin's *What is to be Done?* in the face of the new slogan of "All Power to the Soviets." In early 1920 Pannekoek published a book (*Weltrevolution und Kommunistiche Taktic*) in which he suggested that communist revolutions would first appear in underdeveloped countries, and supported Lenin against Rosa Luxemburg on the question of national self-determination. Pannekoek and his comrades joined with the Bolsheviks in stressing the necessity of forming a third, Communist International.

Disillusionment quickly developed among the leftists, however. Events within Russia—e.g. the destruction of the factory committees—along with Bolshevik manipulation of the new International pushed the leftists to a more critical

[3] See "Soviets and Factory Commitees in the Russian Revolution," this volume.

stance vis-à-vis the new Russian regime. Surrounded by hostile capitalist powers, the Bolsheviks sought to gather immediate support for their new state wherever possible. While entering into diplomatic negotiations with capitalist states, they urged the western European Communist parties to adopt methods of activity (parliamentarism and trade unionism) that many militants had already learned to reject, in order to gain as massive a following as they could. In 1920 Lenin published his *Left-Wing Communism: an Infantile Disorder,* which chastised the leftist militants, and effectively threw them out of the International. The leftists replied as splits appeared within the European parties over the question of adherence to the ideological and organizational requirements of the Russian-controlled International. Behind the tactical questions lay the fundamental issue, whether the need for social revolution in Europe could be subordinated to the national interests of the new Bolshevik state.

In the process of renewed analysis of the Russian Revolution, Pannekoek rejected his earlier optimistic evaluation of the possibilities for communist revolutions in underdeveloped countries. He recognized the limitations resulting from Russia's economic backwardness; for a revolution with a working class minority could not lead to a society controlled by workers. The course of events in Russia, demonstrated once again both the tendency of a party which saw its own domination of society as the heart of the revolution, to restrain the revolutionary activity of the workers; and the ability of working people to evolve their own organs of struggle. Much of the remainder of Pannekoek's work, and that of his comrades, was devoted to deepening and elaborating these two lessons.

Pannekoek's thought on these matters is summed up in this book, which was largely written during the German occupation of Holland in World War II. Although its political reference is specifically to post-war Europe, its breadth of vision makes it relevant to all industrialized countries today. The value of the general analysis has been borne out by such subsequent events as the development of workers' struggles in Hungary in 1956, France in 1968, and the wave of wildcat strikes in the United States and every country of Europe in the late 1960s and early 1970s. In our view, *Workers' Councils* represents the best available starting-point for thinking about the problems of transforming present-day society. But on some important questions, of course, *Workers' Councils* has little to say, and in other areas the analysis is weak or incorrect.

Pannekoek's entire analysis is based on the circumstance that capitalism as a system is prone to periods of severe crisis. His own explanation of this phenomenon is open to a good deal of question. As Karl Marx showed, the cause of crisis must be looked for in the inability of the system to produce sufficient profit for continuous expansion, and not in a difficulty in realizing profit due to a lack of effective demand as Pannekoek thought. This question, at any rate, has little significance for Pannekoek's analysis of the actual development of the class struggle. Whatever the causes of the business depressions which give capitalism its cyclical character, *Workers' Councils* helps us understand the social forces which may be set in motion in a crisis situation.

There are weaknesses in Pannekoek's discussion of the revolutionary process. He utilized the notion of a relatively homogeneous working class, a category perhaps more applicable to the Western Europe of his day than to the United States. In reality there are important differences of condition and experience within the working class—among the races, between the sexes, between unionized and non-unionized workers, and among the various levels of job hierarchies. Similarly, there is a division between those who have jobs and those who are unemployed, which has led for instance to the antagonism felt by employed workers to welfare recipients. The problems raised by the necessity for those who under present conditions lead relatively isolated existences, e.g., housewives who do not work outside the home, to participate in the collective transformation of society should not be ignored.

The discussion of the new society is also overly abstract. Pannekoek focuses on the positive features of the various revolutionary upsurges of the first half of the twentieth century and the negative role played by organized parties. He gives only a sketch of the means by which workers could coordinate society. The problems of carrying on regional, national, and international planning through democratic structures in a complex, technologically advanced, and highly interdependent society have yet to be seriously dealt with.

Problems of space have limited us to including only Parts I and II of the original text, which contain Pannekoek's theory of workers' self-organization. The last three parts, applying this theory to the wartime and postwar periods, while valuable are of less general importance. We hope that it will be possible to publish the integral work in the near future. The translation is by the author; we have thought it best to leave Pannekoek's occasionally eccentric use of English as he wrote it, with the exception of some outright solecisms (e.g. "wild strike" for "wildcat strike") and needlessly obscure constructions. Material in brackets is by the editors.

# Preface

### (As it appeared in the original Dutch Edition)

This book was written in the war years 1941-42 under the occupation of Holland by the Germans. The author, who during many years attentively observed and sometimes actively took part in the workers' movement, gives here a summary of what from these experiences and study may be derived as to methods and aims of the workers' fight for freedom. What a century of workers' struggles presents to us is neither a series of ever-again failing attempts at liberalism, nor a steadfast forward march of the workers following a fixed plan of old well-tried tactics. With the development of society we see arise new forms of struggle, and this development imposed by the growth of capitalism and the growth of the working class, must go on in ever mightier display.

The first part of the book shows the task which the workers have to perform and the fight they have to wage. The following parts treat the social and spiritual trends arising in the bourgeoisie that determine the conditions under which the workers had and have to fight. The whole discussion is based on the deep connection between production system and class-fight elucidated in Marxian theory.

—The Editor.

# Workers' Councils

## anton pannekoek

## 1. THE TASK

### 1. Labor

In the present and coming times, now that Europe is devastated and mankind is impoverished by world war, it impends upon the workers of the world to organize industry, in order to free themselves from want and exploitation. It will be their task to take into their own hands the management of the production of goods. To accomplish this great and difficult work, it will be necessary to fully recognise the present character of labor. The better their knowledge of society and of the position of labor in it, the less difficulties, disappointments and setbacks they will encounter in this striving.

The basis of society is the production of all goods necessary to life. This production, for the most important part, takes place by using means of highly developed technics in large factories and plants using complicated machines. This development of technics, from small tools that could be handled by one man, to big machines handled by large collectives of workers of different kind, took place in the last centuries. Though small tools are still used as accessories, and small shops are still numerous, they hardly play a role in the bulk of the production.

Each factory is an organisation carefully adapted to its aims; an organisation of dead as well as of living forces, of instruments and workers. The forms and the character of this organisation are determined by the aims it has to serve. What are these aims?

In the present time, production is dominated by capital. The capitalist, possessor of money, funds the factory, buys the machines and the raw materials, hires the workers and makes them produce goods that can be sold. That is, he buys the labor power of the workers, to be spent in their daily task, and he pays to them its value, the wages by which they can procure what they need to live and to continually restore their labor power. The value a worker creates in his daily work in adding it to the value of the raw materials, is larger than what he needs for his living and receives for his labor power. The difference that the capitalist gets in his hands when the product is sold, the surplus-value, forms his profit, which, in so far as it is not consumed, is accumulated into new capital. The labor power of the working class thus may be compared with an ore mine, that in exploitation gives out a produce exceeding the cost bestowed on it. Hence the term exploitation of labor by capital. Capital itself is the product of labor; its bulk is accumulated surplus-value.

Capital is master of production; it has the factory, the machines, the produced goods; the workers work at its command; its aims dominate the work and determine the character of the organization. The aim of capital is to make profit. The capitalist is not driven by the desire to provide his fellow-men with the necessities of life; he is driven by the necessity of making money. If he has a shoe factory he is not animated by compassion for the painful feet of other people; he is animated by the knowledge that his enterprise must yield profit and that he will go bankrupt if his profits are insufficient. Of course, the normal way to make profit is to produce goods that can be sold at a good price, and they can be sold, normally, only when they are necessary and practical consumption-goods for the buyers. So the shoemaker, to produce profits for himself, has to produce well-fitting shoes, better or cheaper shoes than others make. Thus, normally, capitalist production succeeds in what should be the aim of production, to provide mankind with its life necessities. But the many cases, where it is more profitable to produce superfluous luxuries for the rich or trash for the poor, or to sell the whole plant to a competitor who may close it, show that the primary object of present production is profit for the capital.

This object determines the character of the organisation of the work in the shop. First it establishes the command by one absolute master. If he is the owner himself, he has to take care that he does not lose his capital; on the contrary he must increase it. His interest dominates the work; the workers are his "hands," and they have to obey. It determines his part and his function in the work. Should the workers complain of their long hours and fatiguing work, he points to his task and his solicitudes that keep him busy till late in the night after they have gone home without concerning themselves any more. He forgets to tell, what he hardly understands himself, that all his often strenuous work, all his worry that keeps him awake at night, serves only the profit, not the production itself. It deals with the problems of how to sell his products, how to outrival his competitors, how to bring the largest possible part of the total surplus-value into his own coffers. His work is not a productive work; his exertions in fighting his competitors are useless for society. But he is the master and his aims direct the shop.

If he is an appointed director he knows that he is appointed to produce profit for the shareholders. If he does not manage to do so, he is dismissed and replaced by another man. Of course, he must be a good expert, he must understand the technics of his branch, to be able to direct the work of production. But still more he must be expert in profit-making. In the first place he must understand the technics of increasing the net-profit, by finding out how to produce at least cost, how to sell with most success and how to beat his rivals. This every director knows. It determines the management or business. It also determines the organisation within the shop.

The organisation of the production within the shop is conducted along two lines, of technical and of commercial organisation. The rapid development of technics in the last century, based upon a wonderful growth of science, has improved the methods of work in every branch. Better technics is the best weapon in competition, because it secures extra profit at the cost of the rivals. This development increased the productivity of labor, it made the goods for use and consumption cheaper, more abundant and more varied, it increased the means of comfort, and, by lowering the cost of living, i.e., the value of labor power, enormously raised the profit of capital. This high stage of technical development brought into the factory a rapidly increasing number of experts, engineers, chemists, physicists, well versed by their training at universities and laboratories in science. They are necessary to direct the intricate technical processes, and to improve them by regular application of new scientific discoveries. Under their supervision act skilled technicians and workers. So the technical organisation shows a carefully regulated collaboration of various kinds of workers, a small number of university-trained specialists, a larger number of qualified professionals and skilled workers, besides a great mass of unskilled workers to do the manual work. Their combined efforts are needed to run the machines and to produce the goods.

The commercial organisation has to conduct the sale of the product. It studies markets and prices, it advertises, it trains agents to stimulate buying. It includes the so-called scientific management, to cut down costs by distributing men and means; it devises incentives to stimulate the workers to more strenuous efforts; it turns advertising into a kind of science taught even at universities. It is not less, it is even more important than technics to the capitalist masters; it is the chief weapon in their mutual fight. From the viewpoint of providing society with its life necessities, however, it is an entirely useless waste of capacities.

But also the forms of technical organisation are determined by the same motive of profit. Hence the strict limitation of the better paid scientific experts to a small number, combined with a mass of cheap unskilled labor. Hence the structure of society at large, with its low pay and poor education for the masses, with its higher pay—so much as higher education demands for the constant filling of the ranks—for a scientifically trained minority.

These technical officials have not only the care of the technical processes of production. Under capitalism they have also to act as taskmasters of the workers. Because under capitalism production of goods is inseparably connected with production of profit, both being one and the same action, the two characters of the shop-officials, of a scientific leader of production and of a commanding helper of exploitation, are intimately combined. So their position is ambiguous. On the one hand they are the collaborators of the manual workers, by their scientific knowledge directing the process of transformation of the materials, by their skill increasing the profits, they also are exploited by capital. On the other hand they are the underlings of capital, appointed to hustle the workers and to assist the capitalist in exploiting them.

It may seem that not everywhere the workers are thus exploited by capital. In public-utility enterprises, for instance, or in cooperative factories. Even if we leave aside the fact that the former, by their profit, often must contribute to the public funds, thus relieving the taxes of the propertied class, the difference with other business is not essential. As a rule co-operatives have to compete with private enterprises; and public utilities are controlled by the capitalist public by attentive criticism. The usually borrowed capital needed in the business demands its interest, out of the profits. As in other enterprises there is the personal command of a director and the forcing up of the tempo of the work. There is the same exploitation as in every capitalist enterprise. There may be a difference in degree; part of what otherwise is profit may be used to increase the wages and to improve the conditions of labor. But a limit is soon reached. In this respect they may be compared with private model enterprises where sensible broad-minded directors try to attach the workers by better treatment, by giving them the impression of a privileged position, and so are rewarded by a better output and increased profit. But it is out of the question that the workers here, or in public utilities or co-operatives, should consider themselves as servants of a community, to which to devote all their energy. Directors and workers are living in the social surroundings and the feelings of their respective classes. Labor has here the same capitalist character as elsewhere; it maintains its deeper essential nature despite the superficial differences of somewhat better or worse conditions.

Labor under capitalism in its essential nature is a system of squeezing. The workers must be driven to the utmost exertion of their powers, either by hard constraint or by the kinder arts of persuasion. Capital itself is in a constraint; if it cannot compete, if the profits are inadequate, the business will collapse. Against this pressure the workers defend themselves by a continual instinctive resistance. If not, if they willingly should give way, more than their daily labor power would be taken from them. It would be an encroaching upon their funds of bodily power, their vital power would be exhausted before its time, as to some extent is the case now; degeneration, annihilation of health and strength, of themselves and their offspring, would be the result. So resist they must. Thus every shop, every enterprise, even outside the times of sharp conflict, of strikes or wage reductions, is the scene of a constant silent war, of a perpetual struggle, of pressure and counter-pressure. Rising and falling under its influence, a certain norm of wages, hours and tempo of labor establishes itself, keeping them just at the limit of what is tolerable and intolerable [if intolerable the total of production is effected]. Hence the two classes, workers and capitalists, while having to put up with each other in the daily course of work, in deepest essence, by their opposite interests, are implacable foes, living, when not fighting, in a land of armed peace.

Labor in itself is not repulsive. Labor for the supplying of his needs is a necessity imposed on man by nature. Like all other living beings, man has to exert his forces to provide for his food. Nature has given them bodily organs and mental powers, muscles, nerves and brains, to conform to this necessity. Their wants and their means are harmoniously adapted to one another in the regular living of their life. So labor, as the normal use of their limbs and capacities, is a normal impulse for man and animal alike. In the necessity of providing food and shelter there is, to be sure, an element of constraint. Free spontaneousness in the use of muscles and nerves, all in their turn, in following every whim, in work or play, lies at the bottom of human nature. The constraint of his needs compels man to regular work, to suppression of the impulse of the moment, to exertion of his powers, to patient perseverance and self-restraint. But this self-restraint, necessary as it is for the preservation of oneself, of the family, of the community, affords the satisfaction of vanquishing impediments in himself or the surrounding world, and gives the proud feeling of reaching self-imposed aims. Fixed by its social character, by practice and custom in family, tribe or village, the habit of regular work grows into a new nature itself, into a natural mode of life, a harmonious unity of needs and powers, of duties and disposition. Thus in farming the surrounding nature is transformed into a safe home through a lifelong heavy or placid toil. Thus in every people, each in its individual way, the old handicraft gave to the artisans the joy of applying their skill and phantasy in the making of good and beautiful things for use.

All this has perished since capital became master of labor. In production for the market, for sale, the goods are commodities which besides their utility for the buyer, have exchange-value, embodying the labor implemented; this exchange-value determines the money they bring. Formerly a worker in moderate hours—leaving room for occasional strong exertion—could produce enough for his living. But the profit of capital consists in what the worker can produce in surplus to his living. The more value he produces and the less the value of what he consumes, the larger is the surplus-value seized by capital. Hence his life-necessities are reduced, his standard of life is lowered as much as possible, his hours are increased, the tempo of his work is accelerated. Now labor loses entirely its old character of pleasant use of body and limbs. Now labor turns into a curse and an outrage. And this remains its true character, however mitigated by social laws and by trade-union action, both results of the desperate resistance of the workers against their unbearable degradation. What they may attain is to turn capitalism from a rude abuse into a normal exploitation. Still then labor, being labor under capitalism, keeps its innermost character of inhuman toil: the workers, compelled by the threat of hunger to strain their forces at foreign command, for foreign profit, without genuine interest, in the monotonous fabrication of uninteresting or bad things, driven to the utmost of what the overworked body can sustain, are used up at an early age. Ignorant economists, unacquainted with the nature of capitalism, seeing the strong aversion of the workers from their work, conclude that productive work, by its very nature, is repulsive to man, and must be imposed on unwilling mankind by strong means of constraint.

Of course, this character of their work is not always consciously felt by the workers. Sometimes the original nature of work, as an impulsive eagerness of action, giving contentment, asserts itself. Especially in young people, kept ignorant of capitalism and full of ambition to show their capacities as first-rate workers, feeling themselves moreover possessor of an inexhaustible labor-power. Capitalism has its well-advised ways of exploiting this disposition. Afterwards, with the growing solicitudes and duties for the family, the worker feels caught between the pressure of the constraint and the limit of his powers, as in tightening fetters he is unable to throw off. And at last, feeling his forces decay at an age that for middle-class man is the time of full and matured power, he has to suffer exploitation in tacit resignation, in continuous fear of being thrown away as a worn-out tool.

Bad and damnable as work under capitalism may be, still worse is the lack of work. Like every commodity, labor-power sometimes finds no buyer. The problematic liberty of the worker to choose his master goes hand in hand with the liberty of the capitalist to engage or to dismiss his workers. In the continuous development of capitalism, in the founding of new enterprises and the decline or collapse of old ones, the workers are driven to and fro, are accumulated here, dismissed there. So they must consider it good luck even, when they are allowed to let themselves be exploited. Then they perceive that they are at the mercy of capital. That only with the consent of the masters they have access to the machines that wait for their handling.

Unemployment is the worst scourge of the working class under capitalism. It is inherent in capitalism. As an ever returning feature it accompanies the periodical crises and depressions, which during the entire reign of capitalism have ravaged society at regular intervals. They are a consequence of the anarchy of capitalist production. Each capitalist as an independent master of his enterprise is free to manage it at his will, to produce what he thinks profitable or to close the shop when profits are failing. Contrary to the careful organisation within the factory there is a complete lack of organisation in the totality of social production. The rapid increase of capital through the accumulated profits, the necessity to find profits also for the new capital, urges a rapid increase of production flooding the market with unsaleable goods. Then comes the collapse, reducing not only the profits and destroying the superfluous capital, but also turning the accumulated hosts of workers out of the factories, throwing them upon their own resources or on meagre charity. Then wages are lowered, strikes are ineffective, the mass of the unemployed presses as a heavy weight upon the working conditions. What has been gained by hard fight in times of prosperity is often lost in times of depression. Unemployment was always the chief impediment to a continuous raising of the life standard of the working class.

There have been economists alleging that by the modern development of big business this pernicious alternation of crises and prosperity would disappear. They expected that cartels and trusts, monopolising as they do large branches of industry, would bring a certain amount of organisation into the anarchy of production and smooth its irregularities. They did not take into account that the primary cause, the yearning for profit, remains, driving the organised groups into a fiercer competition, now with mightier forces. The incapacity of modern capitalism to cope with its anarchy was shown in a grim light by the world crisis of 1930.

During a number of long years production seemed to have definitely collapsed. Over the whole world millions of workers, of farmers, even of intellectuals were reduced to living on the doles, which the governments by necessity, had to provide: From this crisis of production the present war crisis took its origin.

In this crisis the true character of capitalism and the impossibility to maintain it, was shown to mankind as in a searchlight. There were the millions of people lacking the means to provide for their life necessities. There were the millions of workers with strong arms, eager to work; there were the machines in thousands of shops, ready to whirl and to produce an abundance of goods. But it was not allowed. The capitalist ownership of the means of production stood between the workers and the machines. This ownership, affirmed if necessary by the power of police and State, forbade the workers to touch the machines and to produce all that they themselves and society needed for their existence. The machines had to stand and rust, the workers had to hang around and suffer want. Why? Because capitalism is unable to manage the mighty technical and productive powers of mankind to conform to their original aim, to provide for the needs of society.

To be sure, capitalism now is trying to introduce some sort of organisation and planned production. Its insatiable profit-hunger cannot be satisfied within the old realms; it is driven to expand over the world, to seize the riches, to open the markets, to subject the people of other continents. In a fierce competition each of the capitalist groups must try to conquer or to keep to themselves the richest portions of the world. Whereas the capitalist class in England, France, Holland made easy profits by the exploitation of rich colonies, conquered in former wars, German capitalism with its energy, its capacities, its rapid development, that had come too late in the division of the colonial world, could only get its share by striving for world-power, by preparing for world war. It had to be the aggressor, the others were the defenders. So it was the first to put into action and to organise all the powers of society for this purpose; and then the others had to follow its example.

In this struggle for life between the big capitalist powers the inefficiency of private capitalism could no longer be allowed to persist. Unemployment now was a foolish, nay, a criminal waste of badly needed manpower. A strict and careful organisation had to secure the full use of all the labor power and the fighting power of the nation. Now the untenability of capitalism showed itself just as grimly from another side. Unemployment was now turned into its opposite, into compulsory labor. Compulsory toil and fighting at the frontiers where the millions of strong young men, by the most refined means of destruction mutilate, kill, exterminate, "wipe out" each other, for the world-power of their capitalist masters. Compulsory labor in the factories where all the rest, women and children included, are assiduously producing ever more of these engines of murder, whereas the production of the life necessities is constricted to the utmost minimum. Shortage and want in everything needed for life and the falling back to the poorest and ugliest barbarism is the outcome of the highest development of science and technics, is the glorious fruit of the thinking and working of so many generations! Why? Because notwithstanding all delusive talk about community and fellowship, organised capitalism, too, is unable to handle the rich productive powers of mankind to their true purpose, using them instead for destruction.

Thus the working class is confronted with the necessity of itself taking the production in hand. The mastery over the machines, over the means of production, must be taken out of the unworthy hands that abuse them. This is the common cause of all producers, of all who do the real productive work in society, the workers, the technicians, the farmers. But it is the workers, chief and permanent sufferers from the capitalist system, and, moreover, majority of the population, on whom it impends to free themselves and the world from this scourge. They must [manage] the means of production. They must be masters of the factories, masters of their own labor, to conduct it at their own mill. Then the machines will be put to their true use, the production of abundance of goods to provide for the life necessities of all.

This is the task of the workers in the days to come. This is the only road to freedom, this is the revolution for which society is ripening. By such a revolution the character of production is entirely reversed; new principles will form the basis of society. First, because the exploitation ceases. The produce of the common labor [will belong to] all those who take part in the work. No surplus-value to capital any more; ended is the claim of superfluous capitalists to a part of the produce.

More important still than the cessation of their share in the produce is the cessation of their command over the production. Once the workers are masters over the shops, the capitalists lose their power of leaving in disuse the machines, these riches of mankind, precious product of the mental and manual exertion of so many generations of workers and thinkers. With the capitalists disappears their power to dictate what superfluous luxuries or what rubbish shall be produced. When the workers have command over the machines they will apply them for the production of all that the life of society requires.

This will be possible only by combining all the factories, as the separate members of one body, into a well organized system of production. The connection that under capitalism is the fortuitous outcome of blind competition and marketing, depending on purchase and sale, is then the object of conscious planning. Then, instead of the partial and imperfect attempts at organisation of modern capitalism, that only lead to fiercer fight and destruction, comes the perfect organisation of production, growing into a world-wide system of collaboration. For the producing classes cannot be competitors, only collaborators.

These three characteristics of the new production mean a new world. The cessation of the profit for capital, the cessation of unemployment of machines and men, the conscious adequate regulation of production, the increase of the produce through efficient organisation, give to each worker a larger quantity of product with less labor. Now the way is opened for a further development of productivity. By the application of all technical progress the produce will increase in such a degree that abundance for all will be joined to the disappearance of toil.

## 2. Law and Property

Such a change in the system of labor implies a change of Law. Not, of course, that new laws must first be enacted by Parliament or Congress. It concerns changes in the depth of society [in the customs and practice of society], far beyond the reach of such temporary things as parliamentary acts. It relates to the fundamental laws, not of one country only, but of human society, founded on man's convictions of Right and Justice.

These laws are not immutable. To be sure, the ruling classes at all times have tried to perpetuate the existing Law by proclaiming that it is based on nature, founded on the eternal rights of man, or sanctified by religion. This, for the sake of upholding their prerogatives and dooming the exploited classes to perpetual slavery. Historical evidence, on the contrary, shows that law continually changed in line with the changing feelings of right and wrong.

The sense of right and wrong, the consciousness of justice in men, is not accidental. It grows up, irresistibly, by nature, out of what they experience as the fundamental conditions of their life. Society must live; so the relations of men must be regulated in such a way—it is this that law provides for—that the production of life-necessities may go on unimpeded. Right is what is essentially good and necessary for life. Not only useful for the moment, but needed generally; not for the life of single individuals, but for people at large, for the community; not for personal or temporal interests, but for the common and lasting weal. If the life-conditions change, if the system of production develops into new forms, the relations between men change, their feeling of what is right or wrong changes with them, and the law has to be altered.

This is seen most clearly in the laws regulating the right of property. In the original savage and barbarian state the land was considered as belonging to the tribe that lived on it, hunting or pasturing. Expressed in our terms, we should say that the land was common property of the tribe that used it for its living and defended it against other tribes. The self-made weapons and tools were accessories of the individual, hence were a kind of private property, though not in our conscious and exclusive sense of this word, in consequence of the strong mutual bonds amongst the tribesmen. Not laws, but use and custom regulated their mutual relations. Such primitive peoples, even agricultural peoples in later times (as the Russian peasants of before 1860) could not conceive the idea of private ownership of a tract of land, just as we cannot conceive the idea of private ownership of a quantum of air.

These regulations had to change when the tribes settled and expanded, cleared the forests and dissolved into separate individuals (i.e., *families*), each working a separate lot. They

changed still more when handicraft separated from agriculture, when from the casual work of all, it became the
continual work of some; when the products became commodities, to be sold in regular commerce and to be consumed by others than the producers. It is quite natural
that the farmer who worked a piece of land, who improved
it, who did his work at his own will, without interference
from others, had the free disposal of the land and the tools;
that the produce was his; that land and produce were his
property. Restrictions might be needed for defence, in
mediaeval times, in the form of possible feudal obligations.
It is quite natural that the artisan, as the only one who
handled his tools, had the exclusive disposal of them, as
well as of the things he made; that he was the sole owner.

Thus private ownership became the fundamental law of
a society founded on small-scale working-units. Without
being expressly formulated it was felt as a necessary right
that whoever exclusively handled the tools, the land, the
product, must be master of them, must have the free disposal of them. Private ownership of the means of production
belongs as its necessary juridical attribute to small trade.

It remained so, when capitalism came to be master of
industry. It was even more consciously expressed, and the
French Revolution proclaimed liberty, equality and property
the fundamental Rights of the citizen. It was private ownership of the means of production simply applied, when,
instead of some apprentices, the master-craftsman hired a
larger number of servants to assist him, to work with his
tools and to make products for him to sell. By means of
exploiting the labor-power of the workers, the factories
and machines, as private property of the capitalist, became
the source of an immense and ever growing increase of
capital. Here private ownership performed a new function
in society. As capitalist ownership, it ascertained power and
increasing wealth to the new ruling class, the capitalists,
and enabled them strongly to develop the productivity of
labor and to expand their rule over the earth. So this
juridical institute, notwithstanding the degradation and misery
of the exploited workers, was felt as a good and beneficent,
even necessary institution, promising an unlimited progress
of society.

This development, however, gradually changed the inner
character of the social system. And thereby again the function of private ownership changed. With the joint-stock com-

panies the twofold character of the capitalist factory-owner, that of directing the production and that of pocketing the surplus-value, is splitting up. Labor and property, in olden times intimately connected, are now separated. Owners are the shareholders, living outside the process of production, idling in distant country-houses and maybe gambling at the exchange. A shareholder has no direct connection with the work. His property does not consist in tools for him to work with. His property consists simply in pieces of paper, in shares of enterprises of which he does not even know the whereabouts. His function in society is that of a parasite. His ownership does not mean that he commands and directs the machines; this is the sole right of the director. It means only that he may claim a certain amount of money without having to work for it. The property in hand, his shares, are certificates showing his right—guaranteed by law and government, by courts and police—to participate in the profits; titles of companionship in that large Society for Exploitation of the World, that is capitalism.

The work in the factories goes on quite apart from the shareholders. Here the director and the staff have the care all day, to regulate, to run about, to think of everything, the workers are working and toiling from morning till evening, hurried and abused. Everybody has to exert himself to the utmost to render the output as large as possible. But the product of their common work is not for those who did the work. Just as in olden times burgesses were ransacked by gangs of wayside robbers, so now people entirely foreign to the production come forward and, on the credit of their papers [as registered owners of share scrip], seize the chief part of the produce. Not violently; without having to move as much as a finger they find it put on their banking account, automatically. Only a poor wage or a moderate salary is left for those who together did the work of production; all the rest is dividend taken by the shareholders. Is this madness? It is the new function of private ownership of the means of production. It is simply the praxis of old inherited law, applied to the new forms of labor to which it does no longer fit.

Here we see how the social function of a juridical institute, in consequence of the gradual change of the forms of production, turns into the very reverse of its original aim. Private ownership, orginally a means to give everybody the possibility of productive work, now has turned into the means to prevent the workers from the free use of the instruments of production. Originally a means to secure for the workers the fruits of their labor, it now turned into a means to deprive the workers of the fruits of their labor, for the benefit of a class of useless parasites.

How is it, then, that such obsolete law still holds sway over society? First, because the numerous middle-class and small-business people, the farmers and independent artisans cling to it, in the belief that it assures them their small property and their living; but with the result that often, with their mortgaged holdings, they are the victims of usury and bank-capital. When saying: I am my own master, they mean: I have not to obey a foreign master; community in work as collaborating equals lies far outside their imagination. Secondly and chiefly, however, because the power of the State, with its police and military force, upholds old law for the benefit of the ruling class, the capitalists.

In the working class, now, the consciousness of this contradiction is arising as a new sense of Right and Justice. The old right, through the development of small trade into big business, has turned into wrong, and it is felt as a wrong. It contradicts the obvious rule that those who do the work and handle the equipment must dispose of it in order to arrange and execute the work in the best way. The small tool, the small lot could be handled and worked by a single person with his family. So that the person who had the disposal of it, was the owner. The big machines, the factories, the large enterprises can only be handled and worked by an organized body of workers, a community of collaborating forces. So this body, the community, must have the disposal of it, in order to arrange the work according to their common will. This common ownership does not mean an ownership in the old sense of the word, as the right of using or misusing at will. Each enterprise is but part of the total productive apparatus of society; so the right of each body or community of producers is limited by the superior right of society, and has to be carried out in regular connection with the others.

Common ownership must not be confounded with public ownership. In public ownership, often advocated by notable social reformers, the State or another political body is master of the production. The workers are not masters of their work, they are commanded by the State officials, who are leading and directing the production. Whatever may be the conditions of labor, however human and considerate the treatment, the fundamental fact is that not the workers themselves, but the officials dispose of the means of production, dispose of the product, manage the entire process, decide what part of the produce shall be reserved for innovations, for wear, for improvements, for social expenses, what part has to fall to the workers, what part to themselves. In short, the workers still receive wages, a share of the product determined by the masters. Under public ownership of the means of production, the workers are still subjected to and exploited by a ruling class. Public ownership is a middle-class program of a modernized and disguised form of capitalism. Common ownership by the producers can be the only goal of the working class.

Thus the revolution of the system of production is intimately bound up with a revolution of Law. It is based on a change in the deepest convictions of Right and Justice. Each production-system consists of the application of a certain technique, combined with a certain Law regulating the relations of men in their work, fixing their rights and duties. The technics of small tools combined with private ownership means a society of free and equal competing small producers. The technics of big machines, combined with private ownership, means capitalism. The technics of big machines, combined with common ownership, means a free collaborating humanity. Thus capitalism is an intermediate system, a transitional form resulting from the application of the old Law to the new technics. While the technical development enormously increased the powers of man, the inherited law that regulated the use of these powers subsisted nearly unchanged. No wonder that it proved inadequate, and that society fell to such distress. This is the deepest sense of the present world crisis. Mankind simply neglected in time to adapt its old law to its new technical powers. Therefore it now suffers ruin and destruction.

Technique is a given power. To be sure, its rapid development is the work of man, the natural result of thinking over the work, of experience and experiment, of exertion and competition. But once established, its application is automatic, outside our free choice, imposed like a given force of nature. We cannot go back, as poets have wished, to the general use of the small tools of our forefathers. Law, on the other hand, must be instituted by man with conscious design. Such as it is established, it determines freedom or slavery of man towards man and towards his technical equipment.

When inherited law, in consequence of the silent growth of technics, has turned into a means of exploitation and oppression, it becomes an object of contest between the social classes, the exploiting and the exploited class. So long as the exploited class dutifully acknowledges existing law as Right and Justice, its exploitation remains lawful and unchallenged. When then a growing consciousness of their exploitation gradually arises in the masses, at the same time new conceptions of Right awaken in them. With the growing feeling that existing law is contrary of justice, their will is roused to change it and to make their convictions of right and justice the law of society. This means that the sense of being wronged is not sufficient. Only when in great masses of the workers this sense grows into such clear and deep convictions of Right that they permeate the entire being, filling it with a firm determination and a fiery enthusiasm, will they be able to develop the powers needed for overturning the social structure. Even then this will be only the preliminary condition. A heavy and lengthy struggle to overcome the resistance of the capitalist class defending its rule with the utmost power, will be needed to establish the new order.

## 3.  Shop Organisation

Thus the idea of their common ownership of the means of production is beginning to take hold of the minds of the workers. Once they feel the new order, their own mastery over labor to be a matter of necessity and of justice, all their thoughts and all their actions will be consecrated to its realisation. They know that it cannot be done at once; a long period of fight will be unavoidable. To break the stubborn resistance of the ruling classes the workers will have to exert their utmost forces. All the powers of mind and character, of organisation and knowledge, which they are capable of mustering must be developed. And first of all they have to make clear to themselves what it is they aim at, what this new order means.

Man, when he has some work to do, first conceives it in his mind as a plan, as a more or less conscious design. This distinguishes the actions of man from the instinctive actions of animals. This also holds, in principle, for the common struggles, the revolutionary actions of social classes. Not entirely, to be sure; there is a great deal of unpremeditated spontaneous impulse in their outbursts of passionate revolt. The fighting workers are not an army conducted after a neatly conceived plan of action by a staff of able leaders. They are a people gradually rising out of submissiveness and ignorance, gradually coming to consciousness of their exploitation, again and again driven to fight for better living conditions, by degrees developing their powers. New feelings spring up in their hearts, new thoughts arise in their heads, how the world might and should be. New wishes, new ideals, new aims fill their mind and direct their will and action. Their aims gradually take a more concise shape. From the simple strife for better working conditions, in the beginning, they grow into the idea of a fundamental reorganisation of society. For several generations already the ideal of a world without exploitation and oppression has taken hold of the minds of the workers. Nowadays the conception of the workers themselves master of the means of production, themselves directing their labor, arises ever more strongly in their minds.

This new organisation of labor we have to investigate and clarify to ourselves and to one another, devoting to it the best powers of our minds. We cannot devise it as a fantasy; we derive it from the real conditions and needs of present work and present workers. It cannot, of course, be depicted in detail; we do not know the future conditions that will determine its precise forms. Those forms will take shape in the minds of the workers then facing the task. We must content ourselves for the present to trace the general outlines only, the leading ideas that will direct the actions of the working class. They will be as the guiding stars that in all the vicissitudes of victory and adversity in fight, of success and failure in organisation, keep the eyes steadily directed towards the great goal. They must be elucidated not by minute descriptions of detail, but chiefly by comparing the principles of the new world with the known forms of existing organisations.

When the workers seize the factories to organize the work an immensity of new and difficult problems arises before them. But they dispose of an immensity of new powers also. A new system of production never is an artificial structure erected at will. It arises as an irresistible process of nature, as a convulsion moving society in its deepest entrails, evoking the mightiest forces and passions in man. It is the result of a tenacious and probably long class struggle. The forces required for construction can develop and grow up in this fight only.

What are the foundations of the new society? They are the social forces of fellowship and solidarity, of discipline and enthusiasm, the moral forces of self-sacrifice and devotion to the community, the spiritual forces of knowledge, of courage and perseverance, the firm organisation that binds all these forces into a unity of purpose, all of them are the outcome of the class fight. They cannot purposely be prepared in advance. Their first traces arise spontaneously in the workers out of their common exploitation; and then they grow incessantly through the necessities of the fight, under the influence of experience and of mutual inducement and instruction. They must grow because their fulness brings victory, their deficiency defeat. But even after a success in fighting attempts at new construction must fail, so long as the social forces are insufficient, so long as the new principles do not entirely occupy the workers' hearts and minds. And in that case, since mankind must live, since production must go on, other powers, powers of constraint, dominating and suppressing forces, will take the production in their hands. So the fight has to be taken up ever anew, till the social forces in the working class have reached such a height as to render them capable of being the self-governing masters of society.

The great task of the workers is the organisation of production on a new basis. It has to begin with the organisation within the shop. Capitalism, too, had a carefully planned shop-organisation; but the principles of the new organisation are entirely different. The technical basis is the same in both cases; it is the discipline of work imposed by the regular running of the machines. But the social basis, the mutual relations of men, are the very opposite of what they were. Collaboration of equal companions replaces the command of masters and the obedience of servants. The sense of duty, the devotion to the community, the praise or blame of the comrades according to efforts and achievements, as incentives take the place of fear for hunger and perpetual risk of losing the job. Instead of the passive utensils and victims of capital, the workers are now the self-reliant masters and organizers of production, exalted by the proud feeling of being active co-operators in the rise of a new humanity.

The ruling body in this shop-organisation is the entirety of the collaborating workers. They assemble to discuss matters and in assembly take their decisions. So everybody who takes part in the work takes part in the regulation of the common work. This is all self-evident and normal, and the method seems to be identical to that followed when under capitalism groups or unions of workers had to decide by vote on the common affairs. But there are essential differences. In the unions there was usually a division of labor between the officials and the members; the officials prepared and devised the proposals and the members voted. With their fatigued bodies and weary minds the workers had to leave the conceiving to others; it was only in part or in appearance that they managed their own affairs. In the common management of the shop, however, they have to do everything themselves, the conceiving, the devising, as well as the deciding. Devotion and emulation not only play their role in everybody's work-task, but are still more essential in the common task of regulating the whole. First, because it is the all-important common cause, which they cannot leave to others. Secondly, because it deals with the mutual relations in their own work, in which they are all interested and all competent, which therefore commands their profound considerations, and which thorough discussion must settle. So it is not only the bodily, but still more the mental effort bestowed by each in his participation in the general regulation that is the object of competition and appreciation. The discussion, moreover, must bear another character than in societies and unions under capitalism, where there are always differences of personal interest. There in his deeper consciousness everybody is concerned with his own safeguarding, and discussions have to adjust and to smooth out these differences in the common action. Here, however, in the new community of labor, all the interests are essentially the same, and all thoughts are directed to the common aim of effective co-operative organisation.

In great factories and plants the number of workers is too large to gather in one meeting, and far too large for a real and thorough discussion. Here decisions can only be taken in two steps, by the combined action of assemblies of the separate sections of the plant, and assemblies of central committees of delegates. The functions and the practice of these committees cannot exactly be ascertained in advance now; they are entirely new, an essential part of the new economic structure. When facing the practical needs the workers will develop the practical structure. Yet something of their character may, in general lines, be derived by comparing them with bodies and organisations known to us.

In the old capitalist world central committees of delegates are a well-known institution. We have them in parliaments, in all kinds of political bodies and in leading boards of societies and unions. They are invested with authority over their constituents, or even rule over them as their masters. As such it is in line with a social system in which a working mass of people is exploited and commanded by a ruling minority. Now, however, the task is to build up a form of organisation for a body of collaborating free producers, actually and mentally controlling their common productive action, regulating it as equals after their own will—a quite different social system. Again in the old world we have union councils administering the current affairs after the membership, assembling at greater intervals, have fixed the general policy. What these councils then have to deal with are the trifles of the day, not vital questions. Now, however, basis and essence of life itself are concerned, the productive work, that occupies and has to occupy everybody's mind continually, as the one and greatest object of their thoughts.

The new conditions of labor make these shop-committees something quite different from everything we know in the capitalist world. They are central, but not ruling bodies, they are no governing board. The delegates constituting them have been sent by sectional assemblies with special instructions; they return to these assemblies to report on the discussion and its result, and after further deliberation the same or other delegates may go up with new instructions. In such a way they act as the connecting links between the personnel of the separate sections. Neither are the shop-committees bodies of experts to provide the directing regulations for the non-expert multitude. Of course, experts will be necessary, single or in bodies, to deal with the special technical and scientific problems. The shop-committees, however, have to deal with the daily proceedings, the mutual relations, the regulation of the work, where everybody is expert and at the same time an interested party. Among other items it is up to them to put into practice what special experts suggest. Nor are the shop-committees the responsible bodies for the good management of the whole, with the consequence that every member could shift his part of responsibility upon the impersonal collectivity. On the contrary, whereas this management is incumbent upon all in common, single persons may be consigned special tasks to fulfill with their entire capacity, for which they take full responsibility, while they carry all the honours for the achievement.

All members of the personnel, men and women, younger and older, who take part in the work, as equal companions take their part in this shop-organisation, in the actual work as well as in the general regulation. Of course, there will be much difference in the personal tasks, easier or more difficult according to force and capacities, different in character according to inclination and abilities. And, of course, the differences in general insight will give a preponderance to the advice of the most intelligent. At first, when as an inheritance of capitalism there are large differences in education and training, the lack of good technical and general knowledge in the masses will be felt as a heavy deficiency. Then the small number of highly trained professional technicians and scientists must act as technical leaders, without thereby acquiring a commanding or socially leading position, without gaining privileges other than the estimation of their companions and the moral authority that always attaches to capacity and knowledge.

The organisation of a shop is the conscious arrangement and connection of all the separate procedures into one whole. All these interconnections of mutually adapted operations may be represented in a well-ordered scheme, a mental image of the actual process. As such it was present in the first planning and in the later improvements and enlargements. This image must be present in the minds of all the collaborating workers; they all must have a thorough acquaintance with what is their own common affair. Just as a map or a graph fixes and shows in a plain, intelligible picture the connections of a complicated totality, so here the state of the total enterprise, at every moment, in all its developments must be rendered visible by adequate representations. In numerical form this is done by bookkeeping. Bookkeeping registers and fixes all that happens in the process of production: what raw materials enter the shop, what machines are procured, what product they yield, how much labor is bestowed upon the products, how many hours of work are given by every worker, what products are delivered. It follows and describes the flow of materials through the process of production. It allows the continuous comparison in comprehensive accounts, of the results with the previous estimates in planning. So the production in the shop is made into a mentally controlled process.

Capitalist management of enterprises also knows mental control of the production. Here, too, the proceedings are represented by calculation and bookkeeping. But there is this fundamental difference that capitalist calculation is adapted entirely to the viewpoint of production of profit. It deals with prices and costs as its fundamental data; work and wages are only factors in the calculation of the resulting profit on the yearly balance account. In the new system of production, on the other hand, hours of work is the fundamental datum, whether they are still expressed, in the beginning, in money units, or in their own true form. In capitalist production calculation and bookkeeping is a secret of the direction, the office. It is no concern of the workers; they are objects of exploitation, they are only factors in the calculation of cost and produce, accessories to the machines. In the production under common ownership the bookkeeping is a public matter; it lies open to all. The workers have always a complete view of the course of the whole process. Only in this way they are able to discuss matters in the sectional assemblies and in the shop-committees, and to decide on what has to be done. The numerical results are made visible, moreover, by statistical tables, by graphs and pictures that display the situation at a glance. This information is not restricted to the personnel of the shop; it is a public matter, open to all outsiders. Every shop is only a member in the social production, and also the connection of its doings with the work outside is expressed in the bookkeeping. Thus insight in the production going on in every enterprise is a piece of common knowledge for all the producers.

## 4.  Social Organisation

Labor is a social process. Each enterprise is part of the productive body of society. The total social production is formed by their connection and collaboration. Like the cells that constitute a living organism, they cannot exist isolated and cut off from the body. So the organisation of the work inside the shop is only one-half of the task of the workers. Over it, a still more important task, stands the joining of the separate enterprises, their combination into a social organisation.

Whereas organisation within the shop already existed under capitalism, and had only to be replaced by another, based on a new foundation, social organisation of all the shops into one whole is, or was until recent years, something entirely new, without precedent. So utterly new, that during the entire nineteenth century the establishing of this organisation, under the name of "socialism" was considered the main task of the working class. Capitalism consisted of an unorganised mass of independent enterprises —"a jostling crowd of separate private employers," as the program of the Labor Party expresses it—connected only by the chance relations of market and competition, resulting in bankruptcies, overproduction and crisis, unemployment and an enormous waste of materials and labor power. To abolish it, the working class should conquer the political power and use it to organise industry and production. This State-socialism was considered, then, as the first step into a new development.

In the last years the situation has changed in so far that capitalism itself has made a beginning with State-run organisation. It is driven not only by the simple wish to increase productivity and profits through a rational planning of production. In Russia there was the necessity of making up for the backwardness of economic development by means of a deliberate rapid organisation of industry by the bolshevist government. In Germany it was the fight for world power that drove [the National Socialist government] to State control of production and State-organisation of industry. This fight was so heavy a task that only by concentrating into the hands of the State the power over all productive forces could the German capitalist class have a chance of success. In national-socialist organisation property and profit—though strongly cut for State needs—remain with the private capitalist, but the disposal over the means of production, their direction and management has been taken over by the State officials. By an efficient organisation the unimpaired production of profits is secured for capital and for the State. This organisation of the production at large is founded on the same principles as the organisation within the factory, on the personal command of the general director of society, the Leader, the head of the State. Wherever Government takes control over industry, authority and constraint take the place of the former freedom of the capitalist producers. The political power of the State officials is greatly strengthened by their economic power, by their command over the means of production, the foundation of society.

The principle of the working class is in every respect the exact opposite. The organisation of production by the workers is founded on free collaboration: no masters, no servants. The combination of all the enterprises into one social organisation takes place after the same principle. The mechanism for this purpose must be built up by the workers.

Given the impossibility to collect the workers of all the factories into one meeting, they can only express their will by means of delegates. For such bodies of delegates in recent times the name of workers' councils has come into use. Every collaborating group of personnel designates the members who in the council assemblies have to express its opinion and its wishes. These representatives take an active part themselves in the deliberations of this group, they come to the front as able defenders of the views that carried the majority. Now they are sent as the spokesmen of the group to confront these views with those of other groups in order to come to a collective decision. Though their personal abilities play a role in persuading the colleagues and in clearing problems, their weight does not lie in their individual strength, but in the strength of the community that delegated them. What carries weight are not simple opinions, but still more the will and the readiness of the group to act accordingly. Different persons will act as delegates according to the different questions raised and the forthcoming problems.

The chief problem, the basis of all the rest, is the production itself. Its organisation has two sides, the establishment of general rules and norms and the practical work itself. Norms and rules must be established for the mutual relations in the work, for the rights and duties. Under capitalism the norm consisted in the command of the master, the director. Under State-capitalism it consisted in the mightier command of the Leader, the central government. Now, however, all producers are free and equal. Now in the economic field of labor the same change takes place as occurred in former centuries in the political field, with the rise of the middle class. When the rule of the citizens came in place of the rule of the absolute monarch, this could not mean that for his arbitrary will the arbitrary will of everybody was substituted. It meant that, henceforward, laws established by the common will should regulate the public rights and duties. So now, in the realm of labor, the command of the master gives way to rules fixed in common, to regulate the social rights and duties, in production and consumption. To formulate them will be the first task of the workers' councils. This is not a difficult task, not a matter of profound study or serious discordance. For every worker these rules will immediately spring up in his consciousness as the natural basis of the new society: everyone's duty to take part in the production in accordance with his forces and capacities, everyone's right to enjoy his adequate part of the collective product.

How will the quantities of labor spent and the quantities of product to which he is entitled be measured? In a society where the goods are produced directly for consumption there is no market to exchange them; and no value, as expression of the labor contained in them establishes itself automatically out of the processes of buying and selling. Here the labor spent must be expressed in a direct way by the number of hours. The administration keeps book [records] of the hours of labor contained in every piece or unit quantity of product, as well as of the hours spent by each of the workers. In the averages over all the workers of a factory, and finally, over all the factories of the same category, the personal differences are smoothed out and the personal results are intercompared.

In the first times of transition when there is much devastation to be repaired, the first problem is to build up the production apparatus and to keep people alive. It is quite possible that the habit, imposed by war and famine, of having the indispensable foodstuffs distributed without distinction is simply continued. It is most probable that, in those times of reconstruction, when all the forces must be exerted to the utmost, when, moreover, the new moral principles of common labor are only gradually forming, the right of consumption will be coupled to the performance of work. The old popular saying that whoever does not work shall not eat, expresses an instinctive feeling of justice. Here it is not only the recognition that labor is the basis of all human life, but also the proclamation that now there is an end to capitalist exploitation and to the appopriation of the fruits of others labor by the property titles of an idle class.

This does not mean, of course, that now the total produce is distributed among the producers, according to the time given by each. Or, expressed in another way, that every worker receives, in the form of products, just the quantity of hours of labor spent in working. A considerable part of the work must be spent on the common property, on the perfection and enlargement of the productive apparatus. Under capitalism part of the surplus-value served this purpose; the capitalist had to use part of his profit, accumulated into new capital, to innovate, expand and modernize his technical equipment, in his case driven by the necessity not to be outflanked by his competitors. So the progress in technics took place in forms of exploitation. Now, in the new form of production, this progress is the common concern of the workers. Keeping themselves alive is the most immediate, but building the basis of future production is the most glorious part of their task. They will have to settle what part of their total labor shall be spent on the making of better machines and more efficient tools, on research and experiment, for facilitating the work and improving the production.

Moreover, part of the total time and labor of society must be spent on non-productive, though necessary activities, on general administration, on education, on medical service. Children and old people will receive their share of the produce without corresponding achievements. People incapable of work must be sustained; and especially in the first time there will be a large number of human wrecks left by the former capitalist world. Probably the rule will prevail that the productive work is the task of the younger part of the adults; or, in other words, is the task of everybody during that period of his life when both the tendency and the capacity for vigorous activity are greatest. By the rapid increase of the productivity of labor, the time needed to produce all the life necessities, will continually decrease, and an increasing part of life will be available for other purposes and activities.

The basis of the social organisation of production consists in a careful administration, in the form of statistics and bookkeeping. Statistics of the consumption of all the different goods, statistics of the capacity of the industrial plants, of the machines, of the soil, of the mines, of the means of transport, statistics of the population and the resources of towns, districts and countries, all these present the foundation of the entire economic process in well ordered rows of numerical data. Statistics of economic processes were already known under capitalism; but they remained imperfect because of the independence and the limited view of the private business men, and they found only a limited application. Now they are the starting point in the organisation of production; to produce the right quantity of goods, the quantity used or wanted must be known. At the same time statistics as the compressed result of the numerical registration of the process of production, the comprehensive summary of the bookkeeping, expresses the course of development.

The general bookkeeping, comprehending and encompassing the administrations of the separate enterprises, combines them all into a representation of the economic process of society. In different degrees of range it registers the entire process of transformation of matter, following it from the raw materials at their origin, through all the factories, through all the hands, down to the goods ready for consumption. In uniting the results of co-operating enterprises of a sort into one whole it compares their efficiency, it averages the hours of labor needed and directs the attention to the ways open for progress. Once the organisation of production has been carried out the administration is the comparatively simple task of a network of interconnected computing offices. Every enterprise, every contingent group of enterprises, every branch of production, every township or district, for production and for consumption, has its office, to take care of the administration, to collect, to treat and to discuss the figures and to put them into a perspicuous form easy to survey. Their combined work makes the material basis of life a mentally dominated process. As a plain and intelligible numerical image the process of production is laid open to everybody's views. Here mankind views and controls its own life. What the workers and their councils devise and plan in organised collaboration is shown in character and results in the figures of bookkeeping. Only because they are perpetually before the eyes of every worker the direction of social production by the producers themselves is rendered possible.

This organisation of economic life is entirely different from the forms of organisation developed under capitalism; it is more perfect and more simple. The intricacies and difficulties in capitalist organisation, for which the much glorified genius of big business men was needed, always dealt with their mutual struggle, with the arts and tricks of capitalist warfare to subdue or annihilate the competitors. All this has disappeared now. The plain aim, the providing for the life necessities of mankind, makes the entire structure plain and direct. Administration of large quantities, fundamentally, is hardly more difficult or more complicated than that of small quantities; only a couple of cyphers has to be put behind the figures. The rich and multiform diversity of wants and wishes that in small groups of people is hardly less than in large masses, now, by their massal character, can be secured more easily and more completely.

The function and the place numerical administration occupies in society depends on the character of this society. Financial administration of States was always necessary as part of the central government, and the computing officials were subordinate servants of the kings or other rulers. Where in modern capitalism production is subjected to an encompassing central organisation, those who have the central administration in their hands will be the leading directors of economy and develop into a ruling bureaucracy. When in Russia the revolution of 1917 led to a rapid expansion of industry and hosts of workers still permeated by the barbarous ignorance of the villages crowded into the new factories they lacked the power to check the rising dominance of the bureaucracy then organising into a new ruling class. When in Germany, 1933, a sternly organised party conquered the State power, as organ of its central administration it took in hand the organisation of all the forces of capitalism.

Conditions are entirely different when the workers as masters of their labor and as free producers organise production. The administration by means of bookkeeping and computing is a special task of certain persons, just as hammering steel or baking bread is a special task of other persons, all equally useful and necessary. The workers in the computing offices are neither servants nor rulers. They are not officials in the service of the workers' councils, obediently having to perform their orders. They are groups of workers, like other groups collectively regulating their work themselves, disposing of their implements, performing their duties, as does every group, in continual connection with the needs of the whole. They are the experts who have to provide the basic data of the discussions and decisions in the assemblies of workers and of councils. They have to collect the data, to present them in an easily intelligible form of tables, of graphs, of pictures, so that every worker at every moment has a clear image of the state of things. Their knowledge is not a private property giving them power; they are not a body with exclusive administrative knowledge that thereby somehow could exert a deciding influence. The product of their labor, the numerical insight needed for the work's progress, is available to all. This general knowledge is the foundation of all the discussions and decisions of the workers and their councils by which the organisation of labor is performed.

For the first time in history economic life, in general and in detail, lies as an open book before the eyes of mankind. The foundations of society, under capitalism a huge mass hidden in the dark depths, dimly lighted here and there by statistics on commerce and production, now has entered into the full daylight and shows its detailed structure. Here we dispose of a science of society consisting of a well-ordered knowledge of facts, out of which leading causal relations are readily grasped. It forms the basis of the social organisation of labor, just as the knowledge of the facts of nature, also condensed into causal relations, forms the basis of the technical organisation of labor. As a body of knowledge of the common simple facts of daily life it is available to everyone and enables each person to survey and grasp the necessities of the whole as well as his own part in it. It forms the spiritual equipment through which the producers are able to direct the production and to control their world.

## 5.  Objections

The principles of the new structure of society appear so natural and self-evident, that there may seem to be little room for doubts or objections. The doubts come from the old traditions that fill people's minds with cobwebs, so long as the fresh storm wind of social activity does not blow through them. The objections are raised by the other classes that up till now are leading society. So first we have to consider the objections of the bourgeoisie, the ruling class of capitalists.

One might say that the objections of the members of the capitalist class do not matter. We cannot convince them, nor is this necessary. Their ideas and convictions, as well as our own, are class ideas, determined by class conditions different from ours by the difference in life conditions and in social function. We have not to convince them by reasoning, but to beat them by power.

But, we should not forget that capitalist power to a great extent is spiritual power, power over the minds of the workers. The ideas of the ruling class dominate society and permeate the minds of the exploited classes. They are fixed there, fundamentally, by the inner strength and necessity of the system of production; they are actually implanted there by education and propaganda, by the influence of school, church, press, literature, broadcasting and film. As long as this holds, the working class, lacking consciousness of its class position, acquiescing in exploitation as the normal condition of life, does not think of revolt and cannot fight. Minds submissive to the doctrines of the masters cannot hope to win freedom. They must overcome the spiritual sway of capitalism over their minds before they actually can throw off its yoke. Capitalism must be beaten theoretically before it can be beaten materially. Because only then can the absolute certainty of the truth of their opinions as well as of the justice of their aims give such confidence to the workers as is needed for victory. Because then only hesitation and misgivings will lame the forces of the foe. Because then only the wavering middle groups, instead of fighting for capitalism, may to a certain degree conceive the necessity of social transformation and the benefit of the new order.

So we have to face the objections raised from the side of the capitalist class. They proceed directly from its view of the world. For the bourgeoisie, capitalism is the only possible and natural system of society, or at least, since more primitive forms preceded it, its most developed final form. Hence all the phenomena presented by capitalism are not considered as temporary but as natural phenomena, founded on the eternal nature of man. The capitalist class sees the deep aversion of the workers against their daily labor; and how they only resign themselves to it by dire necessity. It concludes that man in the great mass is naturally averse to regular productive work and for that reason is bound to remain poor—with the exception of the energetic, industrious and capable minority, who love work and so become leaders, directors and capitalists. Then it follows that, if the workers should be collectively masters of the production, without the competitive principle of personal reward for personal exertion, the lazy majority will do as little as possible, trying to live upon what a more industrious minority performs; and universal poverty would inevitably be the result. All the wonderful progress, all the abundance capitalism has brought in the last century will then be lost, when the stimulus of personal interest is removed; and mankind will sink back into barbarism.

To refute such objections it is sufficient to point out that they form the natural viewpoint from the other side of society, from the side of the exploiting class. Never in history were the old rulers able to acknowledge the capability of a new rising class; they expected an inevitable failure as soon as it should try to manage the affairs; and the new class, conscious of its forces, could show these only in conquering and after having conquered power. Thus now the workers grow conscious of the inner strength of their class; their superior knowledge of the structure of society, of the character of productive labor shows them the futility of the capitalist point of view. They will have to prove their capacities, certainly. But not in the form of being tested beforehand. Their test will be their fight and victory.

This argument is not directed to the capitalist class, but to my fellow workers. The middle class ideas still permeating large masses of them consist chiefly in doubt and disbelief in their own forces. As long as a class does not believe in itself, it cannot expect that other groups should believe in it. This lack of self-confidence, the chief weakness now, cannot be entirely removed under capitalism with its many degrading and exhausting influences. In times of emergency, however, world crisis and impending ruin, compelling the working class to revolt and fight, will also, once it has won, compel it to take control of production. Then the command of dire need treads under foot the implanted lack of confidence in its own forces, and the imposed task rouses unexpected energies. Whatever hesitation or doubt may be in their minds this one thing the workers know for certain: that they, better than the idle people of property, know what work is, that they can work, and that they will work.

The futile objections of the capitalist class will collapse
with this class itself.

More serious objections are raised from other sides.
From such as consider themselves and are considered as
friends, as allies or spokesmen of the working class. In
later capitalism there is a widespread opinion, among intellectuals and social reformers, among trade union leaders
and social democrats, that capitalist production for profit
is bad and has to disappear, and that it has to make place
for some kind of socialist system of production. Organisation of production, they say, is the means of producing
abundance for all. The capitalist anarchy of the totality
of production must be abolished by imitating the organised
order within the factory. Just as in a well-directed enterprise the perfect running of every detail and the highest
efficiency of the whole is secured by the central authority
of the director and the staff, so in the still more complicated
social structure the right interaction and connection of all
its parts can only be secured by a central leading power.

The lack of such a ruling power, they say, is what must
be objected to the system of organisation by means of
workers' councils. They argue that nowadays production
is not the handling of simple tools, easily to survey by
everybody, as in the bygone days of our ancestors, but
the application of the most abstract sciences, accessible
only to capable and well instructed minds. They say
that a clear-sighted view of the intricate structure and its
capable management demand talents that only few are
gifted with; that it fails to see that the majority of people are
dominated by narrow selfishness, and that they lack the
capacities and even the interest to take up these large responsibilities. And should the workers in stupid presumption
reject the leadership of the most capable, and try to direct
production and society by their own masses, then, however industrious they may be, their failure would be inevitable; every factory would soon be a chaos, and decline would
be the result. They must fail because they cannot muster a
leading power of sufficient authority to impose obedience
and thus to secure a smooth running of the complicated
organisation.

Where to find such a central power? They argue, we
have it already in State government. Till now Government
restricted its functions to political affairs; it will have to
extend them to economic affairs—as already it is com-

pelled to do in some minor cases—to the general management of production and distribution. For is not war against hunger and misery equally, and even more important than war against foreign enemies?

If the State directs the economic activities it acts as the central body of the community. The producers are master of the production, not in small groups separately, but in such a way that in their totality, as the entire class, as the whole people they are master. Public ownership of the means of production, for their most important part, means State ownership, the totality of the people being represented by the State. By the democratic State, of course, where people choose their rulers. A social and political organisation where the masses choose their leaders, everywhere, in the factories, in the unions, in the State, may be called universal democracy. Once chosen, these leaders of course must be strictly obeyed. For only in this way, by obedience to the commandment of able leaders of production, the organisation, can work smoothly and satisfactorily.

Such is the point of the spokesmen of State socialism. It is clear that this plan of social organisation is entirely different from a true disposal by the producers over the production. Only in name are the workers masters of their labor, just as only in name are the people masters of the State. In the so-called democracies, so-called because parliaments are chosen by universal suffrage, the governments are not at all delegates designated by the population as executors of its will. Everybody knows that in every country the government is in the hands of small, often hereditary or aristocratic groups of politicians and high officials. The parliamentarians, their body of supporters, are not selected by the constituents as mandataries to perfom their will. The voters, practically, have only to choose between two sets of politicians, selected, presented and advertised to them by the two main political parties, whose leaders, according to the result, either form the ruling cabinet, or as "loyal opposition" stand in abeyance for their turn. The State officials, who manage the affairs, are not selected by the people either; they are appointed from above, by the government. Even if shrewd advertising calls them servants of the people, in reality they are its rulers, its masters. In the system of State socialism it is this bureaucracy of officials that, considerably enlarged, directs production. They dispose of the means of production, they have the upper command of labor. They have to take care that every-thing runs well, they administrate the process of production and determine the partition of the produce. Thus the workers have got new masters, who assign to them their wages and keep at their own disposal the remainder of the produce. This means that the workers are still exploited; State socialism may quite as well be called State capitalism, according to the emphasis laid on its different sides, and to the greater or smaller share of influence of the workers.

State socialism is a design for reconstructing society on the basis of a working class such as the middle class sees it and knows it under capitalism. In what is called a socialistic system of production the basic fabric of capital-ism is preserved, the workers running the machines at the command of the leaders; but it is provided with a new improved upper story, a ruling class of humane reformers instead of profit-hungry capitalists. Reformers who as true benefactors of mankind apply their capacities to the ideal task of liberating the working masses from want and misery.

It is easily understood that during the 19th century, when the workers only began to resist and to fight, but were not yet able to win power over society, this socialist ideal found many adherents. Not only among socially minded of the middle class who sympathised with the suffering masses, but also among the workers themselves. For here loomed up before them a vision of liberation from their yoke by the simple expression of their opinion in voting, by the use of the political power of their ballot to put into government their redeemers instead of their oppressors. And certainly, if it were only a matter of placid discussion and free choice between capitalism and socialism on the part of the masses, then socialism would have a good chance.

But reality is different. Capitalism is in power and it de-fends its power. Can anybody have the illusion that the capitalist class would give up its rule, its domination, its profit, the very basis of its existence, hence its existence itself, at the result of a vote? Or still more, to a campaign of publicity arguments, of public opinion demonstrated in mass meetings or street processions? Of course it will fight, convinced of its right. We know that even for reforms, for every minor reform in capitalism there had to be fighting. Not to the utmost, to be sure; not or seldom by civil war and bloodshed. Because public opinion, in the bulk of the middle class, aroused by the determined resistance of the workers, saw that in their demands capitalism itself, in its essence, was not engaged, that profit as such was not endangered. Because it was felt that, on the contrary, capitalism would be consolidated rather, reform appeasing the workers and attaching them more firmly to the existing system.

If, however, the existence of the capitalist class itself, as a ruling and exploiting class is at stake, the entire middle class stands behind it. If its mastery, its exploitation, its profit is threatened, not by a sham revolution of outward appearances, but by a real revolution of the foundations of society, then we may be sure that it will resist with all its powers. Where, then, is the power to defeat it? The irrefutable arguments and the good intentions of noble-minded reformers, all these are not able to curb, still less to destroy its solid force. There is only one power in the world capable of vanquishing capitalism: the power of the working class. The working class can not be freed by others; it can only be freed by itself.

But the fight will be long and difficult. For the power of the capitalist class is enormous. It is firmly entrenched in the fabric of State and government, having all their institutions and resources at its disposal, their moral authority as well as their physical means of suppression. It disposes of all the treasures of the earth, and can spend unlimited amounts of money to recruit, pay and organise defenders, and to carry away public opinion. Its ideas and opinions pervade the entire society, fill up books and papers and dominate the minds of even the workers. Here lies the chief weakness of the masses. Against it the working class, certainly, has its numbers, already forming the majority of the population in capitalist countries. It has its momentous economic function, its direct hold over the machines, its power to run or stop them. But they are of no avail as long as their minds are dependent on and filled by the masters' ideas, as long as the workers are separate, selfish, narrow-minded, competing individuals. Number and economic importance alone are as the powers of a sleeping giant; they must first be awakened and activated by practical fight. Knowledge and unity must make them active power. Through the fight for existence, against exploitation and misery, against the power of the capitalist class and the State, through the fight for mastery over the means of production, the workers must acquire the consciousness of their position, the independence of thought, the knowledge of society, the solidarity and devotion to their community, the strong unity of class that will enable them to defeat capitalist power.

We cannot forsee what whirls of world politics will arouse them. But we can be sure that it is not a matter of years only, of a short revolutionary fight. It is a historical process that requires an entire epoch of ups and downs, or fights and lulls, but yet of unceasing progress. It is an intrinsic transformation of society, not only because the power relations of the classes are reversed, because property relations are changed, because production is reorganised on a new basis, but chiefly—decisive basis of all these things—because the working class itself in its deepest character is transformed. From obedient subjects they are changed into free and self-reliant masters of their fate, capable of building and managing their new world.

It was the great socialist humanitarian Robert Owen who has taught us that for a true socialist society the character of man must change; and that it is changed by environment and education. It was the great communist scientist Karl Marx who, completing the theory of his predecessor, has taught us that mankind itself has to change its environment and has to educate itself, by fighting, by the class-fight against exploitation and oppression. The theory of State socialism by reform is an arid mechanical doctrine in its belief that for social revolution a change of political institutions, of outer conditions of life is sufficient, without the inner transformation of man that turns submissive slaves into proud and spirited fighters. State socialism was the political program of social-democracy, utopian, because it pretended to bring about a new system of production by simply converting people through propaganda to new political opinions. Social-democracy was not able, nor was it willing to lead the working class into a real revolutionary fight. So it went down when the modern development of big capitalism made socialism won by the ballot an obsolete illusion.

Yet socialist ideas still have their importance, though in a different way now. They are widespread all over society, among socially feeling middle-class people as well as among the masses of the workers. They express the longing for a world without exploitation, combined, in the workers, with the lack of confidence in their own power. This state of mind will not disappear at once after the first successes have been won; for it is then that the workers will perceive the immensity of their task, the still formidable powers of capital, and how all the traditions and institutions of the old world are barring their way. When thus they stand hesitating, socialism will point to what appears to be an easier road, not beset with such insurmountable difficulties and endless sacrifices. For just then, in consequence of their success, numbers of socially-minded reformers will join their ranks as capable allies and friends, putting their capacities in the service of the rising class, claiming, of course, important positions, to act and to lead the movement after their ideas. If the workers put them in office, if they install or support a socialist government, then the powerful existing machinery of the State is available for the new purpose and can be used to abolish capitalist exploitation and establish freedom by law. How far more attractive this mode of action than implacable class war! Yes, indeed; with the same result as what happened in revolutionary movements in the 19th century, when the masses who fought down the old regime in the streets, were thereupon invited to go home, to return to their work and put their trust in the self-appointed "provisional government" of politicians that was prepared to take matters in hand.

The propaganda of the socialist doctrine has the tendency to throw doubts into the minds of the workers, to raise or to strengthen distrust in their own powers, and to dim the consciousness of their task and their potentialities. That is the social function of socialism now, and at every moment of workers' success in the coming struggles. From the hard fight for freedom brilliant ahead, the workers are to be lured by the soft shine of a mild new servitude. Especially when capitalism should receive a severe blow, all who distrust and fear the unrestricted freedom of the masses, all who wish to preserve the distinction of masters and servants, of higher and lower, will rally round this banner. The appropriate catchwords will readily be framed: "order" and "authority" against "chaos," "socialism" and "organisation" against "anarchy." Indeed, an economic system where the workers are themselves masters and leaders of their work, to middle-class thinking is identical with anarchy and chaos. Thus the only role socialism can play in future will be to act as an impediment standing in the way of the workers' fight for freedom.

To summarize: the socialist plan of reconstruction, brought

forward by reformers, must fail, first because they have
no means to produce the forces to vanquish the power of
capitalism. Second, because only the workers themselves
can do that. Exclusively by their own fight they can develop into the mighty power needed for such a task. It
is this fight that socialism tries to forestall. And once the
workers have beaten down capitalist power and won freedom, why should they give it up and submit to new masters?

There is a theory to explain why indeed they should and
they must. The theory of actual inequality of men. It points
out that nature itself makes them different: a capable,
talented and energetic minority rises out of an incapable,
stupid and slow majority. Notwithstanding all theories and
decrees instituting formal and legal equality, the talented
energetic minority takes the lead and the incapable majority
follows and obeys.

It is not for the first time that a ruling class tries to explain, and so to perpetuate, its rule as the consequences of
an inborn difference between two kinds of people, one
destined by nature to ride, the other to be ridden. The
landowning aristocracy of former centuries defended their
privileged position by boasting their extraction from a nobler
race of conquerors that had subdued the lower race of
common people. Big capitalists explain their dominating
place by the assertion that they have brains and other
people have none. In the same way now especially the
intellectuals, considering themselves the rightful rulers of
tomorrow, claim their spiritual superiority. They form the
rapidly increasing class of university-trained officials and
free professions, specialized in mental work, in study of
books and of science, and they consider themselves as the
people most gifted with intellect. Hence they are destined
to be leaders of the production, whereas the ungifted mass
shall execute the manual work, for which no brains are
needed. They are no defenders of capitalism; not capital,
but intellect should direct labor. The more so, since now
society is such a complicated structure, based on abstract
and difficult sciences, that only the highest intellectual
acumen is capable of embracing, grasping and handling it.
Should the working masses, from lack of insight, fail to
acknowledge this need of superior intellectual lead, should
they stupidly try to take the direction into their own hands,
chaos and ruin will be the inevitable consequence.

Now it must be remarked that the term intellectual here

does not mean possessor of intellect. Intellectuals is the name for a class with special functions in social and economic life, for which mostly university training is needed. Intellect, good understanding, is found in people of all classes, among capitalists and artisans, among farmers and workers. What is found in the 'intellectuals" is not a superior intelligence, but a special capacity of dealing with scientific abstractions and formulas, often merely of memorizing them, and combined, usually, with a limited notion of other realms of life. In their self-complacency appears a narrow intellectualism ignorant of the many other qualities that play an important role in all human activities. A rich and varied multitude of dispositions, different in character and in degree, exists in man: here theoretical power of abstraction, there practical skill, here acute understanding, there rich fantasy, here rapidity of grasping, there deep brooding, here patient perseverance of purpose, there rash spontaniety, here indomitable courage in action and fight, there all-embracing ethical philanthropy. All of them are necessary in social life; in turns, according to circumstances, they occupy the foremost place in the exigencies of practice and labor. It is silly to distinguish some of them as superior, others as inferior. Their difference implies the predilection and qualification of people for the most varied kinds of activity. Among them the capacity for abstract or scientific studies, under capitalism often degenerated to a limited training, takes its important place in attending to and directing the technical processes: but only as one among many other capacities. Certainly for these people there is no reason to look down upon the non-intellectual masses. Has not the historian Trevalyan, treating the times of nearly three centuries ago, spoken of "the wealth of imagination, the depth of emotion, the vigour and variety of intellect that were to be found among the poor . . . once awakened to the use of their minds"?

Of course in all of these qualities some people are more gifted than others; men and women of talent or genius excel their fellow-beings. Probably they are even more numerous than it appears now under capitalism, with its neglect, misuse and exploitation of human qualities. Free humanity will employ their talents to the best use; and the consciousness to promote with their greater force the common cause, will give them a greater satisfaction than any material privilege in a world of exploitation could do.

Let us consider the claim of the intellectual class, the domination of spiritual over manual work. Must not the mind rule over the body, the bodily activities? Certainly. Human mind is the highest product of nature; his spiritual capacities elevate man above the animals. Mind is the most valuable asset of man; it makes him lord of the world. What distinguishes human work from the activities of the animals is this very rule of the mind, the thinking out, the meditating and planning before the performing. This domination of theory, of the powers of the mind over practical work grows ever stronger, through the increasing complication of the process of production and its increasing dependence on science.

This does not mean, however, that mental workers should hold sway over manual workers. The contradistinction between mental and manual work is not founded in nature, but in society; it is an artificial class-distinction. All work, even the most simple, is mental as well as manual. For all kinds of work, till by repetition it has become automatic, thinking is necessary; this combination of thinking and acting is the charm of all human activity. Also under the natural division of labor, as a consequence of differences in predilection and capacity, this charm remains. Capitalism, however, has vitiated these natural conditions. To increase profit it has exaggerated the division of labor to the extreme of one-sided specialising. Three centuries ago already, in the beginning of the manufactury-system, the endless repetition of always the same limited manipulations turned labor into a monotonous routine where, through undue training of some limbs and faculties at the cost of others, body and mind were crippled. In the same way capitalism now, in order to increase productivity and profit, has separated the mental and the manual part of work and made each of them the object of specialized training at the cost of other capacities. It made the two sides that together constitute natural labor, the exclusive task of separate trades and different social classes. The manual workers, fatigued by long hours of spiritless work in dirty surroundings, are not able to develop the capacities of their minds. The intellectuals, on the other hand, through their theoretical training, kept aloof from the practical work and the natural activity of the body, must resort to artificial substitutes. In both groups full human endowment is crippled. Assuming this capitalistic degeneration to be permanent human nature, one of these classes now claims superiority and domination over the other.

By yet another line of argument the claim of the intellectual class for spiritual and, hence, social leadership is supported. Learned writers have pointed out that the entire progress of humanity is due to some few geniuses. It was this limited number of discoverers, of inventors, of thinkers, that built up science, that improved technics, that conceived new ideas and opened new ways, where then the masses of their fellow-men followed and imitated them. All civilisation is founded upon this small number of eminent brains. So the future of mankind, the further progress of culture depends on the breeding and selection of such superior people and would be endangered by a general levelling.

Suppose the assertion to be true, the retort, with becoming irony, could be that the result of these superior brains, this pitiful world of ours, is indeed in keeping with such a narrow basis, and nothing to boast of. Could those great precursors witness what has been made of their discoveries they would not be very proud. Were we not able to do better, we should despair of humanity.

But the assertion is not true. Whoever makes a detailed study of any of the great discoveries in science, technics or what else is surprised by the great number of names associated with it. In the later popular and abridged historical text books, however, the source of so many superficial misconceptions, only a few prominent names are preserved and exalted, as if theirs alone was the credit. So these people were declared exceptional geniuses. In reality every great progress proceeded from a social surrounding pregnant with it, where from all sides the new ideas, the suggestions, the glimpses of insight sprang up. None of the great men, extolled in history, because they took the decisive and salient steps, could have done so but for the work of a large number of precursors on whose achievements his are based. And besides, these most talented thinkers, praised in later centuries as the authors of the world's progress, were not at all the spiritual leaders of their time. They were often unknown to their contemporaries, quietly working in retirement; they mostly belonged to the subjected class, sometimes even they were persecuted by the rulers. Their present-day equivalents are not those noisy claimants for intellectual leadership, but silent workers again, hardly known, derided perhaps or persecuted. Only in a society of free producers, who are able to appreciate the importance of spiritual achievements and eager to apply them to the well-being of all, the creative genius will be recognised and estimated by his fellow-men at the full value.

Why is it that from the life work of all these men of genius in the past nothing better than present capitalism could result? What they were able to do was to lay the scientific and technical foundations of high productivity of labor. Because of causes beyond their control, it became the source of immense power and riches for the ruling minority that succeeded in monopolizing the fruits of this progress. A society of freedom and abundance for all, however, cannot be brought about by any superiority of some few eminent individuals whatever. It does not depend on the brains of the few, but on the character of the many. As far as it depends on science and technics to create abundance, they are already sufficient. What is lacking is the social forces that bind the masses of the workers into a strong unity of organisation. The basis of the new society is not what knowledge they can adopt and what technics they can imitate from others, but what community feeling and organized activity they can raise in themselves. This new character cannot be infused by others, it cannot proceed from obedience to any masters. It can only sprout from independent action, from the fight for freedom, from revolt against the masters. All the genius of superior individuals is of no avail here.

The great decisive step in the progress of mankind, the impending transformation of society, is essentially a transformation of the working masses. It can be accomplished only by the action, by the revolt, by the effort of the masses themselves; its essential nature is self-liberation of mankind. From this viewpoint it is clear that here no able leadership of an intellectual elite can be helpful. Any attempt to impose it could only be obnoxious, retarding as it does the necessary progress, hence acting as a reactionary force. Objections from the side of the intellectuals, based on the present inadequateness of the working class, in practice will find their refutation when world conditions compel the masses to take up the fight for world revolution.

# 6.  Difficulties

More essential difficulties in the reconstruction of society arise out of the differences in outlook that accompany differences in development and size of the enterprises.

Technically and economically society is dominated by big enterprise, by big capital. The big capitalists themselves, however, are only a small minority of the propertied class. They have behind them, to be sure, the entire class of rentiers and shareholders. But these, as mere parasites, cannot give a solid support in the struggle of the classes. So big capital would be in an awkward position were it not backed by the small bourgeoisie, by the entire class of smaller business men. In its domination of society it takes advantage of the ideas and the moods growing out of the world of small trade, occupying the minds of masters and workers in these trades alike. The working class has to give ample consideration to these ideas, because its task and its goal, conceived on the basis of the developments of big capitalism, are conceived and judged in these circles after the familiar conditions of small trade.

In small capitalistic business the boss as a rule is the owner, sometimes the sole owner; or if not, the shareholders are some few friends or relatives. He is his own director and usually the best technical expert. In his person the two functions of technical leader and profit-making capitalist are not separated and can hardly be distinguished. His profit seems to proceed not from his capital, but from his labor, not from exploitation of the workers, but from the technical capacities of the employer. His workers, engaged either as a few skilled assistants or as unskilled hands, are quite well aware of the generally larger experience and expertness of the boss. What in large enterprise, with its technical leadership by salaried officials, is an obvious measure of practical efficiency—the exclusion of all property interests—would here take the retrogressive form of the removal of the best technical expert and of leaving the work to the less expert or incompetent.

It must be clear that here there is no question of a real difficulty impeding the technical organisation of industry. It is hardly to be imagined that the workers in the small shop should want to expel the best expert, even the former boss, if he is honestly willing with all his skill to co-operate in their work, on the foot of equality. Is not this contrary to basis and doctrine of the new world, the exclusion of the capitalist? The working class, when reorganizing society on a new basis, is not bound to apply some theoretical doctrine; but, to direct its practical measures, it possesses a great leading principle. The principle, living touchstone of practicability to the clear-sighted minds, proclaims that those who do the work must regulate the work, and that all who collaborate practically in the production dispose of the means of production, with the exclusion of all property or capital interests. It is on the basis of this principle that the workers will face all problems and difficulties in the organisation of production and will find a solution.

Surely the technically backward branches of production exercised in small trade will present special, but not essential difficulties. The problem of how to organize them by means of self-governing associations, and to connect them with the main body of social organisation must be solved mainly by the workers engaged in these branches, though collaboration from other sides may come to their aid. Once political and social power is firmly in the hands of the working class and its ideas of reconstruction dominate everyone's minds, it seems obvious that everybody who is willing to co-operate in the community of labor will be welcome and will find the place and the task appropriate to his capacities. Besides, in consequence of the increasing community feeling and the desire for efficiency in work, the units of production will not remain the isolated dwarfish shops of former times.

The essential difficulties are situated in the spiritual disposition, the mode of thinking produced by the conditions of small trade in all who are engaged here, masters as well as artisans and workers. It prevents them from seeing the problem of big capitalism and big enterprise as the real and main issue. It is easily understood, however, that the conditions of small trade, the basis of their ideas, cannot determine a transformation of society that takes its origin and its driving force from big capitalism. But it is equally clear that such a disparity of general outlook may be an ample source of discord and strife, of misunderstandings and difficulties. Difficulties in the fight, and difficulties in the constructive work. In small-trade circumstances social and moral qualities develop in another way than in big enterprises; organisation does not dominate the minds in the same degree. Whereas the workers may be more headstrong and less submissive, the impulses of fellowship and solidarity are less also. So propaganda has to play a greater role here; not in the sense of impressing a theoretical doctrine, but in its pure sense of exposing wider views of society in general, so that the ideas are determined not by the narrow experience of their own conditions but by the wider and essential conditions of capitalist labor at large.

This holds good still more for agriculture, because of the larger number and greater importance of small enterprises. There is a material difference, besides, because here the limited amount of soil brought into being one more parasite. The absolute necessity for living space and food-stuff production enables the owners of the soil to levy tribute from all who want to use it; what in political economy is called rent. So here we have from olden times an ownership not based on labor, and protected by State power and law; an ownership consisting only in certificates, in titles, assuring claims on an often big part of the produce of society. The farmer paying rent to the landowner or interest to the real-estate bank, the citizen, whether capitalist or worker, paying in his house-rent high prices for barren soil, they are all exploited by landed property. A century ago, in the time of small capitalism, the difference between the two forms of income, the idle income of the landowner as contrasted with the hard-won earnings of business man, worker and artisan, was so strongly felt as undue robbery, that repeatedly projects were proposed to abolish it, by nationalisation of the soil. Later on, when capitalist property ever more took on the same form of certificates commanding income without labor, land reform became silent. The antagonism between capitalist and landowner, between profit and rent disappeared; landed property is now simply one of the many forms of capitalist property.

The farmer tilling his own soil combines the character of three social classes, and his earnings are indiscriminately composed of wages for his own labor, profit from directing his farm and exploiting the farm hands, and rent from his ownership. Under the original conditions, partially still living as tradition of an idealised past, the farmer produced nearly all the necessities for himself and his family on his own or on rented soil. In modern times agriculture has to provide foodstuffs for the industrial population also, which

gradually everywhere, and increasingly in the capitalist
countries, forms the majority. In return the rural classes
receive the products of industry, which they need for ever
more purposes. This is not entirely a home affair. The bulk
of the world's need of grain is supplied by large enterprises,
on virgin soil in the new continents, on capitalist lines;
while it exhausted the untouched fertility of those vast
plains, it depressed by its cheap competition the rent of
European landed property, causing agrarian crises. But also
in the old European lands agrarian production nowadays
is production of commodities, for the market; the farmers sell
the chief part of their products and buy what they need for
living. So they are subject to the vicissitudes of capitalist
competition, now pressed down by low prices, mortgaged
or ruined, now profiteering by favorable conditions. Since
every increase of rent tends to be petrified in higher land
prices, rising product prices make the former owner a rentier,
whereas the next owner, starting with heavier expenses, suffers
ruin in the case of falling prices. So the economic position
of the agricultural class in general is weakened. On the whole
their condition and their outlook on modern society is
similar in a way to that of small capitalists or independent
business people in industry.

There are differences, however, due to the limited amount
of soil. Whereas in industry or commerce whoever has a
small amount of capital can venture to start a business and
fight against competitors, the farmer cannot enter the lists
when others occupy the land he needs. To be able to
produce he must first have the soil. In capitalist society
free disposal of the soil is only possible as ownership; if
he is not a landowner he can only work and apply his
knowledge and capacity by suffering himself to be exploited
by the possessor of the soil. So ownership and labor are
intimately connected in his mind; this lies at the root of
the often criticised property-fanaticism of the farmers. Ownership enables him to gain his living during all his years by
heavy toiling. By letting or selling his property, hence living
on the idle landowner's rent, ownership also enables him in
his old age to enjoy the substance which every worker should
be entitled to after a life of toil. The continuous struggle
against the variable forces of nature and climate, with
technics only just beginning to be directed by modern
science, hence strongly dependent on traditional methods
and personal capacity, is aggravated by the pressure from

capitalist conditions. This struggle has created a strong stubborn individualism, that makes the farmers a special class with a special mentality and outlook, foreign to the ideas and aims of the working class.

Still, modern development has worked a considerable change here also. The tyrannical power of the great capitalist concerns, of landed estate banks and railway magnates on whom the farmers depend for credit and for transport, squeezed and ruined them, and sometimes brought them to the verge of rebellion. On the other hand, the necessity of securing some of the advantages of large enterprise for small-scale business did much to enforce co-operation, for the buying of fertilizers and materials as well as for procuring the necessary foodstuffs for the accumulated city population. Here the demand for a uniform standardized product, in dairy production for instance, exacts rigid standards and controls, to which the individual farms have to submit. So the farmers are taught a bit of community feeling, and their rugged individualism has to make many concessions. But this inclusion of their work into a social entirety assumes the capitalist form of subjection to a foreign master-power, thus stinging their feelings of independence.

All these conditions determine the attitude of the rural class to the workers' reorganisation of society. The farmers, though as independent managers of their own enterprises comparable to industrial capitalists, usually take part themselves in the productive work, which depends in a high degree on their professional skill and knowledge. Though pocketing rent as landowners, their existence is bound up with their strenuous productive activity. Their management and control over the soil in their character of producers, of workers, in common with the laborers, is entirely in accordance with the principles of the new order. Their control over the soil in their character of landowners is entirely contrary to these principles. They never learnt, though, to distinguish between these totally different sides of their position. Moreover, the disposal over the soil as producers, according to the new principle, is a social function, a mandate of society, a service to provide their fellow-people with foodstuffs and raw materials, whereas old tradition and capitalist egotism tend to consider it an exclusive personal right.

Such differences in outlook may give rise to many dissensions and difficulties between the producing classes of industry and of agriculture. The workers must adhere with absolute strictness to the principle of exclusion of all the exploitation-interests of ownership; they admit only interests based on productive work. Moreover, for the industrial workers, the majority of the population, being cut off from the agrarian produce means starvation, which they cannot tolerate. For the highly industrial countries of Europe, certainly, the transoceanic traffic, the interchange with other food-producing continents, here plays an important role. But there is no doubt that in some way a common organisation of the industrial and the agricultural production in each country must be established.

The point is that between the industrial workers and the farmers, beween the city and the country, there are considerable differences in outlook and ideas, but no real differences or conflicts of interest. Hence there will be many difficulties and misunderstandings, sources of dissent and strife, but there will be no war to the knife as between working class and capital. Though so far the farmers, led by traditional political and narrow social slogans, as defenders of property interests have mostly stood on the side of capital against the workers—and this may still be so in future—the logic of their own real interests must finally place them over against capital. This, however, is not sufficient. As small business men they may be satisfied to be freed from pressure and exploitation through a victory of the workers with or without their help. But then, according to their ideas, it will be a revolution that makes them absolute and free private possessors of soil, similar to former middle-class revolutions. Against this tendency the workers in intensive propaganda have to oppose the new principles: production a social function, the community of all the producers master of their work; as well as their firm will to establish this community of industrial and agricultural production. Whereas the rural producers will be their own masters in regulating and directing their work on their own responsibility, its interlocking with the industrial part of production will be a common cause of all the workers and their central councils. Their continual mutual intercourse will provide agriculture with all technical and scientific means and methods of organisation available, to increase the efficiency and productivity of the work.

The problems met with in the organisation of agricultural production are partly of the same kind as in industry. In big enterprises, such as the large estates for corn, wheat, and other cases of mass production with the aid of motorized machines, the regulation of the work is made by the community of the workers and their councils. Where, for careful treatment in detail, small production units are necessary, co-operation will play an important role. The number and diversity of small-scale farms will offer the same kind of problems as small-scale industry, and their managing will be the task of their self-governing associations. Such local communities of similar and yet individually different farms will probably be necessary to relieve social management as a whole from dealing and reckoning with every small unit separately. All these forms of organisation cannot be imagined beforehand; they will be devised and built by the producers when they stand before the necessities of practice.

## 7.  Council Organisation

The social system considered here might be called a form of communism, only that name, by the world-wide propaganda of the "Communist Party" is used for its system of State socialism under party dictatorship. But what is a name? Names are ever misused to fool the masses, the familiar sounds preventing them from critically using their brains and clearly recognising reality. More expedient, therefore, than looking for the right name will it be to examine more closely the chief characteristic of the system, the council organisation.

The workers' councils are the form of self-government which in the times to come will replace the forms of government of the old world. Of course not for all future; no such form is for eternity. When life and work in community are natural habit, when mankind entirely controls its own life, necessity gives way to freedom and the strict rules of justice established before dissolve into spontaneous behaviour. Workers' Councils are the form of organisation during the transition period in which the working class is fighting for dominance, is destroying capitalism and is organising social production. In order to know their true character it will be expedient to compare them with the existing forms of organisation and government as fixed by custom as self-evident in the minds of the people.

Communities too large to assemble in one meeting always regulate their affairs by means of representatives, of delegates.

So the burgesses of free medieval towns governed themselves by town councils, and the middle class of all modern countries, following the example of England, have their Parliaments. When speaking of management of affairs by chosen delegates we always think of parliaments; so it is with parliaments especially that we have to compare the workers' councils in order to discern their predominant features. It stands to reason that with the large differences between the classes and between their aims, also their representative bodies must be essentially different.

At once this difference strikes the eye: workers' councils deal with labor, have to regulate production, whereas parliaments are political bodies, discussing and deciding laws and State affairs. Politics and economy, however, are not entirely unrelated fields. Under capitalism State and Parliament took the measures and enacted the laws needed for the smooth course of production; such as the providing for safety in traffic and dealings, for protection of commerce and industry, of business and travel at home and abroad, for administration of justice, for coinage and uniform weights and measures. And its political work, too, not at first sight connected with economic activity, dealt with general conditions in society, with the relations between the different classes, constituting the foundation of the system of production. So politics, the activity of Parliaments may, in a wider sense, be called an auxiliary for production.

What, then, under capitalism, is the distinction between politics and economy? They compare together as the general regulation compares with the actual practice. The task of politics is to establish the social and legal conditions under which productive work may run smoothly; the productive work itself is the task of the citizens. Thus there is a division of labor. The general regulations, though necessary foundations, constitute only a minor part of social activity, accessory to the work proper, and can be left to a minority of ruling politicians. The productive work itself, basis and content of social life, consists in the separate activities of numerous producers, completely filling their lives. The essential part of social activity is the personal task. If everybody takes care of his own business and performs his task well, society as a whole runs well. Now and then, at regular intervals, on the days of parliamentary election, the citizens have to pay attention to the general regulations. Only in times of social crisis, of fundamental decisions and severe contests, of civil strife and revolution, has the mass of the citizens had to devote their entire time and forces to these general regulations. Once the fundamentals have been decided, they could return to their private business and once more leave these general affairs to the minority of experts, to lawyers and politicians, to Parliament and Government.

Entirely different is the organisation of common production by means of workers' councils. Social production is not divided up into a number of separate enterprises each the restricted life-task of one person or group; now it forms one connected entirety, object of care for the entirety of workers, occupying their minds as the common task of all. The general regulation is not an accessory matter, left to a small group of specialists; it is the principal matter, demanding the attention of all in conjunction. There is no separation between politics and economy as life activities of a body of specialists and of the bulk of producers. For the one community of producers politics and economy have now coalesced into the unity of general regulation and practical productive labor. Their entirety is the essential object for all.

This character is reflected in the practice of all proceedings. The councils are no politicians, no government. They are messengers, carrying and interchanging the opinions, the intentions, the will of the groups of workers. Not, indeed, as indifferent messenger boys passively carrying letters or messages of which they themselves know nothing. They took part in the discussions, they stood out as spirited spokesmen of the prevailing opinions. So now, as delegates of the group, they are not only able to defend them in the council meeting, but at the same time they are sufficiently unbiassed to be accessible to other arguments and to report to their group opinions more largely adhered to. Thus they are the organs of social intercourse and discussion.

The practice of parliaments is exactly the contrary. Here the delegates have to decide without asking instructions from their voters, without binding mandate. Though the M.P., to keep their allegiance, may deign to speak to them and to expound his line of conduct, he does so as the master of his own deeds. He votes as honor and conscience direct him, according to his own opinions. Of course; for he is the expert in politics, the specialist in legislative matters and cannot let himself be directed by instructions from ignorant people. Their task is production, private business, his task is politics, the general regulations. He has to be guided by high political principles and must not be influenced by the narrow selfishness of their private interests. In this way it is made possible that in democratic capitalism politicians, elected by a majority of workers, can serve the interests of the capitalist class.

In the labor movement also the principles of parliamentarism took a footing. In the mass organisations of the unions, or in such gigantic political organisations as the German Social-Democratic Party, the officials on the boards as a kind of government got power over the members, and their annual congresses assumed the character of parliaments. The leaders proudly called them so, parliaments of labor, to emphasize their importance; and critical observers pointed to the strife of factions, to the demagogy of leaders, and to the intrigue behind the scenes as indications of the same degeneration as appeared in the real parliaments. Indeed, they were parliaments in their fundamental character. Not in the beginning, when the unions were small, and devoted members did all the work themselves, mostly gratuitously. But with the increase of membership there came the same division of labor as in society at large. The working masses had to give all their attention to their separate personal interests, how to find and keep their jobs, the chief contents of their lives and their minds; only in a most general way, moreover, could they decide by vote their common class and group interests. It was to the experts, the union officials and party leaders, who knew how to deal with capitalist bosses and State secretaries, that the detailed practice was left. And only a minority of local leaders was sufficiently acquainted with these general interests to be sent as delegates to the congresses, where notwithstanding the often binding mandates, they actually had to vote after their own judgment.

In the council organisation the dominance of delegates over the constituents disappears because its basis, the division of labor, disappears. Now the social organisation of labor compels every worker to give his entire attention to the common cause, the totality of production. The production of the necessaries for life as the basis of life, as before, of every worker, but entirely occupies the mind, not in the form, now, as care for his own enterprise, his own job, in competition with others. Life and production now can be secured only by collaboration, by collective work with his companions. So this collective work is uppermost in the thoughts of everybody. Consciousness of community is the background, the basis of all feeling and thinking.

This means a total revolution in the spiritual life of man. He has now learnt to see society, to know community. In former times, under capitalism, his view was concentrated on the small part related with his business, his job, himself and his family. This was imperative, for his life, his existence. As a dim, unknown background society hovered behind his small visible world. To be sure, he experienced its mighty forces that determined luck or failure as the outcome of his labor; but guided by religion he saw them as the working of supernatural Supreme Powers. Now, on the contrary, society comes into the full light, transparent and knowable; now the structure of the social process of labor lies open before man's eyes. Now his view is directed to the entirety of production; this is imperative, for his life, his existence. Social production is now the object of conscious regulation. Society is now a thing handled, manipulated by man, hence understood in its essential character. Thus the world of the workers' councils transforms the mind.

To parliamentarism, the political system of the separate business, the people were a multitude of separate persons; at the best, in democratic theory, each proclaimed to be endowed with the same natural rights. For the election of delegates they were grouped according to residence in constituencies. In the times of petty-capitalism a certain community of interests might be assumed for neighbours living in the same town or village. In later capitalism this assumption became an ever-more senseless fiction. Artisans, shopkeepers, capitalists, workers living in the same quarter of a town have different and opposed interests; they usually give their vote to different parties, and chance majorities win. Though parliamentary theory considers the man elected as the representative of the constituency, it is clear that all these voters do not belong together as a group that sends him as its delegate to represent its wishes.

Council organisation, in this respect, is quite the contrary of parliamentarism. Here the natural groups, the collaborating workers, the personnels of the factories act as unities and designate their delegates. Because they have common interests and belong together in the praxis of daily life, they can send some of them as real representatives and spokesmen. Complete democracy is realized here by the equal rights

of everyone who takes part in the work. Of course, whoever
stands outside the work does not have a voice in its regulation. It cannot be deemed a lack of democracy that in
this world of self-rule of the collaborating groups all that
have no concern with the work—such as remained in plenty
from capitalism: exploiters, parasites, rentiers—do not
take part in the decisions.

Seventy years ago Marx pointed out that between the
rule of capitalism and the final organisation of a free
humanity there will be a time of transition in which the
working class is master of society but in which the bourgeoisie
has not yet disappeared. He called this state of things the
dictatorship of the proletariat. At that time this word had
not yet the ominous sound of modern systems of despotism,
nor could it be misused for the dictatorship of a ruling
party, as in later Russia. It meant simply that the dominant
power over society was transferred from the capitalist to
the working class. Afterwards people, entirely confined within
the ideas of parliamentarism, tried to materialize this conception by taking away the franchise for political bodies
from the propertied classes. It is clear that, violating as it
did the instinctive feeling of equal rights, it was in contrast
to democracy. We see now that council organisation puts into
practice what Marx theoretically anticipated but for what
at that time the practical form could not yet be imagined.
When production is regulated by the producers themselves,
the formerly exploiting class automatically is excluded from
taking part in the decisions, without any artificial stipulation.
Marx's conception of the dictatorship of the proletariat now
appears to be identical with the labor democracy of council
organisation.

This labor democracy is entirely different from political
democracy of the former social system. The so-called political
democracy under capitalism was a mock democracy, an
artful system conceived to mask the real domination of the
people by a ruling minority. Council organisation is a real
democracy, the democracy of labor, making the working
people master of their work. Under council organisation
political democracy disappears, because politics itself disappears and gives way to social economy. The activity of
the councils, put in action by the workers as the organs
of collaboration, guided by perpetual study and strained attention to circumstances and needs, covers the entire field
of society. All measures are taken in constant intercourse,

by deliberation in the councils and discussion in the groups
and the shops, by actions in the shops and decisions in the
councils. What is done under such conditions could never
be commanded from above and proclaimed by the will of a
government. It proceeds from the common will of all concerned; because it is founded on the labor experience and
knowledge of all, and because it deeply influences the life
of all. Measures can be executed only in such a way that
the masses put them into practice as their own resolve and
will; foreign constraint cannot enforce them, simply because such a force is lacking. The councils are no government; not even the most central councils bear a governmental
character. For they have no means to impose their will
upon the masses; they have no organs of power. All social
power is vested in the hands of the workers themselves.
Wherever the use of power is needed against disturbances
or attacks upon the existing order, it proceeds from the
collectivities of the workers in the shops and stands under
their control.

Governments were necessary, during the entire period
of civilisation up to now, as instruments of the ruling class
to keep down the exploited masses. They also assumed
administrative functions in increasing measure; but their
chief character as power structures was determined by the
necessity of upholding class domination. Now [with councilist
organization] that the necessity has vanished, the instrument,
too, has disappeared. What remains is administration, one of
the many kinds of work, the task of special kinds of workers;
what comes in its stead, the life spirit of organisation, is
the constant deliberation of the workers, in common thinking
attending to their common cause. What enforces the accomplishment of the decisions of the councils is their moral
authority. But moral authority in such a society has a more
stringent power than any command or constraint from a
government.

When in the preceding time of governments over the
people political power had to be conceded to the people and
their parliaments a separation was made between the legislative and the executive part of government, sometimes completed by the judicial as a third independent power. Law-
making was the task of parliaments, but the application,
the execution, the daily governing was reserved to a small
privileged group of rulers. In the labor community of the
new society this distinction has disappeared. Deciding and

performing are intimately connected; those who have to do the work have to decide, and what they decide in common they themselves have to execute in common. In the case of great masses, the councils are their organs of deciding. Where the executive task was entrusted to central bodies these must have the power of command, they must be governments; where the executive task falls to the masses themselves this character is lacking in the councils. Moreover, according to the varied problems and objects of regulation and decision, different persons in different combinations will be sent out and will gather [in councils to make the necessary decisions.] In the field of production itself every plant has not only to organise carefully its own extensive range of activities, it has also to connect itself horizontally with similar enterprises, vertically with those who provide it with materials or use its products. In the mutual dependence and interconnection of enterprises, in their conjunction to branches of production, discussing and deciding councils will cover ever wider realms, up to the central organisation of the entire production. On the other hand the organisation of consumption, the distribution of all necessaries to the consumer, will need its own councils of delegates of all involved, and will have a more local or regional character.

Besides this organisation of the material life of mankind there is the wide realm of cultural activities, and of those not directly productive which are of primary necessity for society, such as education of the children, or care for the health of all. Here the same principle holds, the principle of self-regulation of these fields of work by those who do the work. It seems altogether natural that in the care for universal health, as well as in the organisation of education, all who take part actively, here the physicians, there the teachers, by means of their associations regulate and organise the entire service. Under capitalism, where they had to make a job and a living out of the human disease or out of drilling children, their connection with society at large had the form either of competitive business or of regulation and command by Government. In the new society, in consequence of the much more intimate connection of health with labor, and of education with labor, they will regulate their tasks in close touch and steady collaboration of their organs of intercourse, their councils, with the other workers' councils.

It must be remarked here that cultural life, the domain

of arts and sciences, by its very nature is so intimately
bound up with individual inclination and effort, that only
the free initiative of people not pressed down by the weight
of incessant toil can secure its flowering. This truth is not
refuted by the fact that during the past centuries of class
society princes and governments protected and directed
arts and sciences, aiming of course to use them as utensils
for their glory and the preservation of their domination.
Generally speaking, there is a fundamental disparity for the
cultural as well as for all the non-productive and productive
activities, between organisation imposed from above by a
ruling body and organisation by the free collaboration of
colleagues and comrades. Centrally directed organisation
consists in regulation as much as possible uniform all over
the realm; else it could not be surveyed and conducted from
one centre. In the self-regulation by all concerned the inia-
tive of numerous experts, all poring over their work, per-
fecting it by emulating, imitating, consulting each other
in constant intercourse, must result in a rich diversity of ways
and means. Dependent on the central command of a government, spiritual life must fall into dull monotony; inspired
by the free spontaniety of massal human impulse it must
unfold into brilliant variety. The council principle affords
the possibility of finding the appropriate forms of organisation.

Thus council organisation weaves a variegated net of
collaborating bodies through society, regulating its life and
progress according to their own free initiative. And all
that in the councils is discussed and decided draws its
actual power from the understanding, the will, the action
of working mankind itself.

## 8.    Growth

When in the difficult fight against capital, in which the
workers' councils have appeared and developed, victory
is won by the working class, it takes up its task, the organisation of production.

We know, of course, that victory will not be one event,
finishing the fight and introducing a then following period
of reconstruction. We know that social struggle and economic
construction will not be separated, but will be associated
as a series of successes in the fight and beginnings of new
organisation, interrupted perhaps by periods of stagnation

or social reaction. The workers' councils growing up as organs of fight will at the same time be organs of reconstruction. For clear understanding, however, we will distinguish these two tasks, as if they were separate things, coming one after another. In order to see the true character of the transformation of society we must treat it, in a schematical way, as a uniform, continuous process starting "the day after the victory."

As soon as the workers are master of the factories, master of society, they will set the machines running. They know that this cannot wait; to live is the first necessity, and their own life, the life of society depends on their labor. Out of the chaos of crumbling capitalism the first working order must be created by means of the councils. Endless difficulties will stand in their way; resistance of all kinds must be overcome, resistance by hostility, by misunderstanding, by ignorance. But new unsuspected forces have come into being, the forces of enthusiasm, of devotion, of insight. Hostility must be beaten down by resolute action, misunderstanding must be taken away by patient persuading, ignorance must be overcome by incessant propaganda and teaching. By making the connection between the shops ever stronger, by including ever wider realms of production, by making ever more precise accounts and estimates in the plans the regulation of the process of production continually progresses. In this way step by step social economy is growing into a consciously dominated organisation able to secure life necessities to all.

With the realisation of this program the task of the workers' councils is not finished. On the contrary, this is only the introduction to their real, more extensive and important work. A period of rapid development now sets in. As soon as the workers feel themselves master of their labor, free to unfold their forces, their first impulse will be the determinate will to do away with all the misery and ugliness, to finish with the shortcomings and abuses, to destroy all poverty and barbarism that as inheritances of capitalism disgrace the earth. An enormous backwardness must be made up for; what the masses got lagged far behind what they might and should get under existing conditions. With the possibility of fulfilling them, their wants will be raised to higher standards; the height of culture of a people is measured by the extent and the quality of its life exigencies. By simply using the available means and methods of working, quantity and quality of homes, of food, of clothing for all can be raised to a level corresponding to the existing productivity of labor. All productive force that in the former society was wasted or used for luxury of the rulers can now be used to satisfy the higher wants of the masses. Thus, first innovation of society, a general prosperity will arise.

But also the backwardness in the methods of production will from the beginning have the attention of the workers. They will refuse to be harrowed and fatigued with primitive tools and obsolete working methods. If the technical methods and the machines are improved by the systematic application of all known inventions of technics and discoveries of science, the productivity of labor can be increased considerably. This better technics will be made accessible to all; the including in productive work of the many who before had to waste their forces in the bungling of petty trade, because capitalism had no use for them, or in personal service of the propertied class, now helps to lower the necessary hours of labor for all. So this will be a time of supreme creative activity. It has to proceed from the initiative of the expert producers in the enterprises; but it can take place only by continual deliberation, by collaboration, by mutual inspiration and emulation. So the organs of collaboration, the councils, are put into [unceasing] action. In this new construction and organisation of an ever more excellent productive apparatus the workers' councils, as the nerve fibers of society, will rise to the full height of their faculties. Whereas the abundance of life necessities, the universal prosperity, represents the passive side of the new life, the innovation of labor itself as its active side makes life a delight of glorious creative experience.

The entire aspect of social life changes, even in its outer appearance, in surroundings and utensils, showing in their increasing harmony and beauty the nobleness of the work that shaped them anew. What William Morris said, speaking of the crafts of olden times with their simple tools: that the beauty of their products was due to work being a joy for man—hence it was extinguished in the ugliness of capitalism—again asserts itself; but now on the higher stage of mastery over the most perfect technics. William Morris loved the tool of the craftsman and hated the machine of the capitalist. For the free worker of the future the handling of the perfectly constructed machine, providing a tension of acuteness, will be a source of mental exaltation, of spiritual rejoicing, of intellectual beauty.

Technics makes man a free master of his own life and destiny. Technics, in a painful process of growth during many thousands of years of labor and fight developed to the present height, puts an end to all hunger and poverty, to all toiling and slavery. Technics puts all the forces of nature at the service of mankind and its needs. The growth of the science of nature opens to man new forms and new possibilities of life so rich and manifold that they far surpass what we can imagine to-day. But technics alone cannot perform that, but only technics in the hands of a humanity that has bound itself consciously by strong ties of brotherhood into a working community controlling its own life. Together, indissolvably connected, technics as material basis and visible power, the community as ethical basis and consciousness, they determine the entire renovation of labor.

And now, with his work, man himself is changing. A new feeling is taking hold of him, the feeling of security. Now at last the gnawing solicitude for life falls away from mankind. During all the past centuries, from original savagery till modern civilisation, life was not secure. Man was not master over his subsistence. Always, also in times of prosperity, and even for the wealthiest, even behind the illusion of perpetual welfare, in the subconsciousness lurked a silent solicitude for the future. As a permanent oppression this anxiety was sunk in the hearts, weighed heavily upon the brain and hampered the unfolding of free thinking. For us, who ourselves live under this pressure, it is impossible to imagine what a deep change in outlook, in world vision, in character, the disappearance of all anxiety about life will bring about. Old delusions and superstitions that in past times had to uphold mankind in its spiritual helplessness, now are dropped. Now that man feels certain that he truly is master of his life, their place is taken by knowledge accessible to all, by the intellectual beauty of an all-encompassing scientific world view.

Even more than in labor itself, the innovation of life will appear in the preparing of future labor, in the education and training of the next generation. It is clear that, since every organisation of society has its special system of education adapted to its needs, this fundamental change in the system of production must be accompanied immediately by a fundamental change in education. In the original small-trade economy, in the farmer and artisan world, the family with its natural division of labor was the basic element of society and of production. Here the children grew up and learned the methods of working by gradually taking their part in the work. Afterwards, under capitalism, the family lost its economic basis, because productive labor was transferred more and more to the factories. Labor became a social process with broader theoretical basis; so a broader knowledge and a more intellectual education was necessary for all. Hence schools were founded, as we know them: masses of children, educated in the isolated small homes without any organic connection with labor, flocking into the schools to learn such abstract knowledge as is needed for society, here again without direct connection with living labor. And different of course according to social classes. For the children of the bourgeoisie, for the future officials and intellectuals a good theoretical and scientific training, enabling them to direct and rule society. For the children of the farmers and the working class an indispensable minimum: reading, writing, computing, needed for their work, completed by history and religion, to keep them obedient and respectful towards their masters and rulers. Learned writers of academic text books, unacquainted with the capitalistic basis of these conditions which they assume to be lasting, vainly try to explain and to smooth out the conflicts proceeding from this separation of productive labor and education, from the contradiction between narrow family isolation and the social character of production.

In the new world of collaborate production these contradictions have disappeared, and harmony between life and labor is restored, now on the wide base of society at large. Now again education of the youth consists in learning the working methods and their foundation by gradually taking part in the productive process. Not in family isolation; now that the material provision of life necessities has been taken over by the community, besides its function as productive units, the family loses that of consumption unit. Community life, corresponding to the strongest impulses within the children themselves, will take much larger place; out of small homes they enter into the wide air of society. The hybridical combination of home and school gives way to communities of children, for a large part regulating their own life under careful guidance of adult educators. Education, instead of passively imbibing teachings from above, is chiefly personal activity, directed towards and connected with social labor. Now the social feelings, as an inheritance of primeval times living in all, but extremely strong in children, can develop without being suppressed by the need of egotism of the capitalist struggle for life.

Whereas the forms of education are determined by community and self-activity, its contents are given by the character of the production system, towards which it prepares. This production system was ever more, especially in the last century, based upon the application of science to technics. Science gave man mastery over the forces of nature; this mastery has made possible the social revolution and affords the basis of the new society. The producers can be master of their labor, of production, only if they master these sciences. Hence the growing generation must be instructed in the first place in the science of nature and its application. No longer, as under capitalism, will science be a monopoly of a small minority of intellectuals, and the uninstructed masses be restricted to subordinate activities. Science in its full extent will be open to all. Instead of the division between one-sided manual and one-sided mental work as specialities of two classes, now comes the harmonious combination of manual and mental work for everybody. This will be necessary also for the further development of the productivity of labor, depending as it does on the further progress of its foundations, science and technics. Now it is not merely a minority of trained intellectuals, but it is all the good brains of the entire people, all prepared by the most careful education, that occupy themselves with the creation of knowledge and its application in labor. Then may be expected a tempo of progress in the development of science and technics, compared to which the much praised progress under capitalism is only a poor commencement.

Under capitalism there is a distinctive difference between the tasks of the young and of the adults. Youth has to learn, the adults have to work. It is clear that as long as labor is toiling at the command of others to produce the highest profit for capital, every capacity, once acquired, must be used up to the limits of time and force. No time of a worker could be wasted for learning ever new things. Only an exceptional adult had the possibility, and still less had the duty regularly to instruct himself during his further life. In the new society this difference disappears. Now in youth the learning consists in taking part, in increasing rate with the years, in the productive work. And now with the increase of productivity and the absence of exploitation ever more leisure is available to the adults for spiritual activities. It enables them to keep apace with the rapid development of the methods of work. This indeed is necessary for them. To take part in the discussions and decisions is only possible if they can study the problems of technics that continually incite and stimulate their attention. The grand development of society through the unfolding of technics and science, of security and abundance, of power over nature and life, can only be ascertained by the growth of capability and knowledge of all the partners. It gives new contents of thrilling activity to their life, it elevates existence and makes it a conscious delight of eager participation in the spiritual and practical progress of the new world.

Added to these sciences of nature are now the new sciences of society that were lacking under capitalism. The special feature of the new system of production is that man now dominates the social forces which determine his ideas and impulses. Practical domination must find its expression in theoretical domination, in knowledge of the phenomena and the determining forces of human action and life, of thinking and feeling. In former times, when through ignorance about society their social origin was unknown, their power was ascribed to the supernatural character of spirit, to a mysterious power of the mind, and the disciplines dealing with them were labelled spiritual sciences: psychology, philosophy, ethics, history, sociology, aesthetics. As with all science their beginnings were full of primitive mysticism and tradition; but contrary to the sciences of nature their rise to real scientific height was obstructed by capitalism. They could not find a solid footing because under capitalism they proceeded from the isolated human being with its individual mind, because in those times of individualism it was not known that man is essentially a social being, that all his faculties emanate from society and are determined by society. Now, however, that society lies open to the view of man, as an organism of mutually connected human beings, and that the human mind is understood as their main organ of interconnection, now they can develop into real sciences.

And the practical importance of these sciences for the

new community is no less than that of the sciences of nature. They deal with the forces lying in man, determining his relations to his fellow men and to the world, instigating his actions in social life, appearing in the events of history past and present. As mighty passions and blind impulses they worked in the great social fights of mankind, now elating man to powerful deeds, then by equally blind traditions keeping him in apathetic submissivity, always spontaneous, ungoverned, unknown. The new science of man and society discloses these forces and so enables man to control them by conscious knowledge. From masters driving him through passive instincts they become servants, ruled by self-restraint, directed by him towards his well-conceived purposes.

The instruction of the growing generation in the knowledge of these social and spiritual forces, and its training in consciously directing them will be one of the chief educational tasks of the new society. Thus the young will be enabled to develop all endowments of passion and will-power, of intelligence and enthusiasm, and to apply them in efficient activity. It is an education of character as well as of knowledge. This careful education of the new generation, theoretical and practical, in natural science and in social consciousness, will form a most essential element in the new system of production. Only in this way an unhampered progression of social life will be secured. And in this way, too, the system of production will develop to ever higher forms. Thus by theoretical mastery of the sciences of nature and society, and by their practical application in labor and life, the workers will make the earth into a happy abode of free mankind.

## II. THE FIGHT

### 1. Trade Unionism

The task of the working class, to take production in its own hand and to organise it, first has to be dealt with. In order to carry on the fight it is necessary to see the goal in clear and distinct lines before us. But the fight, the conquest of power over production is the chief and most difficult part of the work. It is in this fight that the workers' councils will be created.

We cannot exactly foresee the future forms of the workers'

fight for freedom. They depend on social conditions and must change along with the increasing power of the working class. It will be necessary, therefore, to survey how, so far, it has fought its way upward, adapting its modes of action to the varying circumstances. Only by learning from the experience of our predecessors and by considering it critically will we be able in our turn to meet the demands of the hour.

In every society depending on the exploitation of a working class by a ruling class there is a continuous struggle over the division of the total produce of labor, or in other words: over the degree of exploitation. Thus medieval times, as well as later centuries, are full of incessant struggles and furious fights between the landowners and the farmers. At the same time we see the fight of the rising burgher class against nobility and monarchy, for power over society. This is a different kind of class struggle, associated with the rise of a new system of production, proceeding from the development of technics, industry and commerce. It was waged between the masters of the land and the masters of capital, between the declining feudal and the rising capitalist system. In a series of social convulsions, of political revolutions and wars, in England, in France and in other countries consecutively, the capitalist class has gained complete mastery over society.

The working class under capitalism has to carry on both kinds of fight against capital. It has to keep up a continual struggle to mitigate the heavy pressure of exploitation, to increase wages, to enlarge or keep up its share in the total produce. Besides, with the growth of its strength, it has to gain mastery over society in order to overthrow capitalism and bring about a new system of production.

When for the first time, in the beginning of the Industrial Revolution in England, spinning and then weaving machines were introduced, we hear of revolting workers destroying the machines. They were not workers in the modern sense, not wage earners. They were small artisans, independent before, now starved by the competition of cheaply producing machines, and trying in vain to remove the cause of their misery. Afterwards, when they or their children became wage workers, themselves handling the machines, their position was different. It was the same for the hosts from the countryside, who, during the entire 19th century of growing industry, flocked into the towns, lured by what to them appeared good wages. In modern times it is ever more the offspring of the workers themselves that fill the factories.

For all of them the struggle for better working conditions is of immediate necessity. The employers, under the pressure of competition, to enlarge their profits, try to lower the wages and to increase the hours as much as possible. At first the workers, powerless by the constraint of hunger, have to submit in silence. Then resistance bursts forth, in the only possible form, in the refusal to work, in the strike. In the strike for the first time the workers discover their strength, in the strike arises their fighting power. From the strike springs up the association of all the workers of the factory, of the branch, of the country. Out of the strike sprouts the solidarity, the feeling of fraternity with the comrades in work, of unity with the entire class: the first dawn of what some day will be the life-giving sun of the new society. This mutual aid, at first appearing in spontaneous and casual money collections, soon takes the lasting form of the trade union.

For a sound development of trade-unionism certain conditions are necessary. The rough ground of lawlessness, of police arbitrariness and prohibitions, mostly inherited from pre-capitalistic times, must be smoothed before solid buildings may be erected. Usually the workers themselves had to secure these conditions. In England it was the revolutionary campaign of Chartism; in Germany, half a century later, it was the fight of Social Democracy that, by enforcing social acknowledgment for the workers, laid the foundations for the growth of the unions.

Now strong organisations are built up, comprising the workers of the same trade all over the country, forming connections with other trades, and internationally with unions all over the world. The regular paying of high dues provides the considerable funds from which strikers are supported, when unwilling capitalists must be forced to grant decent working conditions. The ablest among the colleagues, sometimes victims of the foe's wrath from former fights, are appointed as salaried officials, who, as independent and expert spokesmen of the workers, can negotiate with the capitalist employers. By strike at the right moment, supported by the entire power of the union, and by ensuing negotiations, agreements can be reached about better and more uniform wages and about fair working hours, in so far as the latter are not yet fixed by law.

So the workers are no longer powerless individuals, forced by hunger to sell their labor-power at any price. They are now protected by their union, protected by the power of their own solidarity and co-operation; for every member not only gives part of his earnings for the colleagues, but is ready also to risk his job in defending the organisation, their community. Thus a certain equilibrium is reached between the power of the employers and the power of the workers. The working conditions are no longer dictated by all-powerful capitalist interests. The unions are recognised gradually as representatives of the workers' interests; though ever again fighting is necessary, they become a power that takes part in the decisions. Not in all trades surely, and not at once everywhere. Usually skilled craftsmen are the first in building their unions. The unskilled masses in the great factories, standing against more powerful employers, mostly come later; their unions often started from sudden outbursts of great fights. And against the monopolistic owners of giant enterprises the unions have little chance; these all-powerful capitalists wish to be absolute master, and in their haughtiness they hardly allow even servile yellow shop unions.

Apart from this restriction, and even assuming trade unionism to be fully developed and in control of all industry, this does not mean that exploitation is abolished, that capitalism is repressed. What is repressed is the arbitrariness of the single capitalist; abolished are the worst abuses of exploitation. And this is in the interest of the fellow-capitalists, too—to guard them against unfair competition—and in the interest of capitalism at large. By the power of the unions capitalism is normalised; a certain norm of exploitation is universally established. A norm of wages, allowing for the most modest life exigencies, so that the workers are not driven again and again into hunger revolts, is necessary for uninterrupted production. A norm of working hours, not quite exhausting the vitality of the working class—though reduction of hours is largely neutralised by acceleration of tempo and more intense exertion—is necessary for capitalism itself, to preserve a usable working class as the basis of future exploitation. It was the working class that by its fight against the narrowness of capitalist greed had to establish the conditions of normal capitalism. And ever again it has to fight, to preserve the uncertain equilibrium. In this fight the trade unions are the instruments; thus the unions perform an indispensable function in capitalism. Narrow-minded employers do not see this, but their broader-minded political leaders know quite well that trade unions are an essential element of capitalism, that without the workers' unions as normalising power capitalism is not complete. Though products of the workers' fight, kept up by their pains and efforts, trade unions are at the same time organs of capitalist society.

With the development of capitalism, however, conditions gradually grow more unfavorable for the workers. Big capital grows, feels its power, and wishes to be master at home. Capitalists also have learnt to understand the power of association; they organise into employers' unions. So instead of the equality of forces arises a new ascendency of capital. Strikes are countered by lock-outs that drain the funds of the trade unions. The money of the workers cannot compete with the money of the capitalists. In the bargaining about wages and working conditions the unions are more than ever the weaker party, because they have to fear, and hence must try to avoid great battles that exhaust the reserves and thereby endanger the secured existence of the organisation and its officials. In the negotiations the union officials often have to accept a lowering of conditions in order to avoid fighting. To them this is unavoidable and self-evident, because they realise that by the changed conditions the relative fighting power of their organisation has diminished.

For the workers, however, it is not self-evident that they are silently to accept harder working and living conditions. They want to fight. So a contradiction of viewpoints arises. The officials seem to have common sense on their side; they know that the union's are at a disadvantage and that fight must result in defeat. But the workers feel by instinct that great fighting powers still lie hidden in their masses; if only they knew how to use them. They rightly realise that by yielding, again and again, their position must grow worse, and that this can be prevented only by fighting. So conflicts must arise in the unions between the officials and the members. The members protest against the new settlements favorable to the employers; the officials defend the agreements reached by long and difficult negotiations and try to have them ratified. So they often have to act as spokesmen of capital interests against workers' interests. And because they are the influential rulers of the unions, throwing all the weight of power and authority on this side, the unions in their hands may be said to develop into organs of capital.

The growth of capitalism, the increase of the number of workers, the urgent necessity of association, make the trade unions giant organisations, needing an ever increasing staff of officials and leaders. These develop into a bureaucracy administering all business, a ruling power over the members, because all the power factors are in their hands. As the experts they prepare and manage all affairs; they administer the finances and the spending of money for different purposes; they are editors of the union papers, by which they can force their own ideas and points of view upon the members. Formal democracy prevails; the members in their assemblies, the chosen delegates in the congresses have to decide, just as the people decide politics in Parliament and State. But the same influences that render Parliament and Government lords over the people are operative in these Parliaments of Labor. They turn the alert bureaucracy of expert officials into a kind of union government, over the members absorbed by their daily work and cares. Not solidarity, the proletarian virtue, but discipline, obedience to the decisions is asked from them. Thus there arises a difference in viewpoint, a contrast in opinions on the various questions. It is enhanced by the difference in life conditions: the insecurity of the workers' job, always threatened by forces of depression and unemployment as contrasted to the security that is necessary for officials to manage the union affairs well.

It was the task and the function of trade unionism, by their joint united fight to raise the workers out of their helpless misery, and to gain for them an acknowledged place in capitalist society. It had to defend the workers against the ever increasing exploitation of capital. Now that big capital consolidates more than ever into a monopolistic power of banks and industrial concerns, trade unionism can no longer perform these functions effectively. Its power falls short compared to the formidable power of capital. The unions are now giant organisations, with their acknowledged place in society; their position is regulated by law, and their bargaining agreements are given legally binding force for the entire industry. Their leaders aspire at forming part of the power ruling industrial conditions. They are the apparatus by means of which monopolistic capital imposes its conditions upon the entire working class. To this now all-powerful capital it is, normally, far more preferable to disguise its rule in democratic and constitutional forms than to show it in the naked brutality of dictatorship. The working conditions which it thinks suitable to the workers will be accepted and obeyed much more easily in the form of agreements concluded by the unions than in the form of dictates arrogantly imposed. Firstly, because to the workers the illusion is left that they are masters of their own interests. Secondly, because all the bonds of attachment, which as their own creation, the creation of their sacrifices, their fight, their elation, render the unions dear to the workers, now are subservient to the masters. Thus under modern conditions trade unions more than ever are turned into organs of the domination of monopolist capital over the working class.

## 2.   Direct Action

As an instrument for the working class struggle against capital the trade unions are losing their importance. But the fight itself cannot cease. The tendencies towards depression grow stronger under big capitalism and so the resistance of the workers must grow stronger, too. Economic crises grow more and more destructive and undermine apparently secured progress. The exploitation is intensified to retard the lowering of the profit rate for the rapidly increasing capital. So again and again the workers are provoked to resistance. But against the strongly increased power of capital the old methods of fight no longer can serve. New methods are needed, and before long their beginnings present themselves. They spring up spontaneously in the wildcat strike, in the direct action.

Direct action means action of the workers themselves without the intermediary of trade union officials. Such a strike is called a wildcat as contrasted to the strike proclaimed by the union according to the rules and regulations. The workers know that the latter is without effect, when the officials are made to proclaim it against their own will and insight, perhaps thinking a defeat a healthy lesson for the foolish workers, and in every case trying to finish it as soon as possible. Thus, when the pressure is too heavy, when negotiations with the directors drag along without effect, at last in smaller or larger groups the exasperation breaks loose in a wildcat strike.

The fight of the workers against capital is not possible without organisation. And organisation springs up spontaneously, immediately. Not of course in such form that a new union is founded, with a board chosen and regulations formulated in ordered paragraphs. Sometimes, to be sure, it was done in this way; attributing the inefficiency to personal shortcomings of the old leaders, and embittered against the old trade union, they [the workers] founded a new one, with their most able and energetic men at the head. Then indeed in the beginning all was energy and strong action; but in the long run the new union, if it remains small, lacks power notwithstanding its activity, and if it grows large, of necessity develops the same characteristics as the old one. After such experiences the workers at last will follow the other way, of keeping the direction of their fight entirely in their own hands.

Direction in their own hands, also called their own leadership, means that all initiative and all decisions proceed from the workers themselves. Though there is a strike committee, because all cannot be always together, everything is done by the strikers; continually in touch with one another they distribute the work, they devise all measures and decide on all actions directly. Decision and action, both collective, are one.

The first and most important task is the propaganda to expand the strike. The pressure upon capital must be intensified. Against the enormous power of capital not only the individual workers, but also the separate groups are powerless. The sole power that is a match for capital is the firm unity of the entire working class. Capitalists know or feel this quite well, and so the only inducement to concessions is the fear that the strike might spread universally. The more manifestly determinate the will of the strikers, the greater the numbers taking part in it, the more the chance of success.

Such an extension is possible because it is not the strike of a tardy group, in worse conditions than others, trying to raise itself to the general level. Under the new circumstances discontent is universal; all the workers feel depressed under capitalist superiority; fuel for explosions has accumulated everywhere. It is not for others, it is for themselves if they join the fight. As long as they feel isolated, afraid to lose their job, uncertain what the comrades will do, without firm unity, they shrink from action. Once, however, they take up the fight, they are changed into new personalities; selfish fear recedes to the background and forth spring the forces of community, solidarity and devotion, rousing courage and perseverance. These are contagious; the example of fighting activity rouses in others, who feel in themselves the same forces awakening, the spirit of mutual and of self-confidence. Thus the wildcat strike as a prairie fire may spring over to other enterprises and involve ever greater masses.

Such cannot be the work of a small number of leaders, either union officials or self-imposed new spokesmen, though, of course, the push of some few intrepid comrades may give strong impulses. It must be the will and the work of all, in common initiative. The workers have not only to do, but also to contrive, to think out, to decide everything themselves. They cannot shift decision and responsibility to a body, a union, that takes care of them. They are entirely responsible for their fight, success or failure depends on themselves. From passive they have turned into active beings, determinedly taking their destiny into their own hands. From separate individuals each caring for himself, they have become a solid, firmly cemented unity.

Such spontaneous strikes present yet another important side; the division of the workers into different separate unions is effaced. In the trade union world, traditions from former petty-capitalist times play an important role in separating the workers in often competing, jealous and bickering corporations; in some countries religious and political differences act as partition fences in establishing separate liberal, catholic, socialist and other unions. In the workshop the members of different unions stand beside one another. But even in strikes they are often kept apart, so that they will not be infected with too many ideas of unity, and the unification in action and negotiation is solely kept up by the boards and officials. Now, however, in direct actions, these differences of union membership become unreal as outside labels. For such spontaneous fights unity is the first need; and unity there is, else there could be no fight. All who stand together in the shop, in the very same position, as direct associates, subject to the same exploitation, against the same master, stand together in common action. Their real community is the shop; personnel of the same enterprise, they form a natural union of common work, common lot and common interests. Like spectres from the past the old distinctions of different membership fall back, almost forgotten in the new living reality of fellowship in common fight. The vivid consciousness of new unity enhances the enthusiasm and the feeling of power.

Thus in the wildcat strikes some characteristics of the coming forms of struggle make their appearance: first the self-action, the self-initiative, keeping all activity and decision in their own hands; and then the unity, irrespective of old memberships, according to the natural grouping of the enterprises. These forms come up, not through shrewd planning, but spontaneously, irresistibly, urged by the heavy superior power of capital against which the old organisations cannot fight seriously any more. Hence it does not mean that now the scales have turned, that now the workers win. Also wildcat strikes mostly bring defeat; their extent is too narrow. Only in some favorable cases they have success in preventing a lowering in working conditions. Their importance is that they demonstrate a fresh fighting spirit that cannot be suppressed. Out of the deepest instincts of self-preservation, of duty towards family and comrades, the will to assert oneself ever again springs up. There is a gain of increasing self-reliance and class-feeling. They are the harbingers of future greater fights, when great social emergencies, with heavier pressure and deeper distress, drive the masses into stronger action.

When wildcat strikes break out on a larger scale, comprising great masses, entire branches of industry, towns or districts, the organisation has to assume new forms. Deliberation in one assembly is impossible; but more than ever mutual understanding is necessary for common action. Strike committees are formed out of the delegates of all the personnel, for continual discussion of circumstances. Such strike committees are entirely different from union boards of officials; they show the characteristics already of workers' councils. They come up out of the fight, to give it unity of direction. But they are no leaders in the old sense, they have no direct power. The delegates, often different persons, come to express the opinion and the will of the groups that sent them. For these groups stand for the action in which the will manifests itself. Yet the delegates are no simple messengers of their mandatory groups; they took a foremost part in the discussion, they embody the prevalent convictions. In the committee assemblies the opinions are discussed and put to the test of momentary circumstances; the results and the resolutions are brought back by the delegates into the group assemblies. Through these intermediaries the shop personnel themselves take part in the deliberations and decisions. Thus unity of action for great masses is secured.

Not, to be sure, in such a way that every group bows obediently to the decisions of the committee. There are no paragraphs to confer such power on it. Unity in collective fighting is not the outcome of judicious regulation of competencies but of spontaneous necessities in a sphere of passionate action. The workers themselves decide, not because such a right is given to them in accepted rules, but because they actually decide, by their actions. It may happen that a group cannot convince other groups by arguments, but then by its action and example it carries them away. The self-determination of the workers over their fighting action is not a demand put up by theory, by arguments of practicability, but the statement of a fact evolving from practice. Often in great social movements it occurred—and doubtless will occur again—that the actions did not comply with the decisions. Sometimes central committees made an appeal for universal strike, and only small groups here and there followed; elsewhere the committees weighed scrupulously, without venturing a decision, and the workers broke loose in massal fight. It may be possible even that the same workers who enthusiastically resolved to strike shrink back when standing before the deed. Or, conversely, that prudent hesitation governs the decisions and yet, driven by inner forces, a non-resolved strike irresistibly breaks out. Whereas in their conscious thinking old watchwords and theories play a role and determine arguments and opinions, at the moment of decision on which weal and woe depend, strong intuition of real conditions breaks forth, determining the actions. This does not mean that such intuition always guides right; people may be mistaken in their impression of outer conditions. But it decides; it cannot be replaced by foreign leadership, by guardians however clever, directing them. By their own experiences in fight, in success and adversity, by their own efforts the workers must acquire the capacities to take proper care of their interests.

Thus the two forms of organisation and fight stand in contrast, the old one of trade unions and the regulated strike, the new one of the spontaneous strike and workers' councils. This does not mean that the former at some time will be simply substituted by the latter as the only alternative. Intermediate forms may be conceived, attempts to correct the evils and weakness of trade unionism and preserve its right principles; to avoid the leadership of a bureaucracy of officials, to avoid the separation by narrow craft and trade interests, and to preserve and utilise the experiences of former fights. This might be done by keeping together, after a big strike, a core of the best fighters, in one general union. Wherever a strike breaks out spontaneously this union is present with its skilled propagandists and organisers to assist the inexperienced masses with their advice, to instruct, to organise, to defend them. In this way every fight means a progress of organisation, not in the sense of dues-paying membership, but in the sense of growing class unity.

An example for such a union might be found in the great American union "Industrial Workers of the World" (I.W.W.). At the end of last century in contrast to the conservative trade unions of well-paid skilled labor, united in the "American Federation of Labor," it grew up out of special American conditions. Partly out of the fierce struggles of the miners and lumbermen, independent pioneers in the wilds of the Far West, against big capital that had monopolised and seized the riches of wood and soil. Partly out of the hunger strikes of the miserable masses of immigrants from Eastern and Southern Europe, accumulated and exploited in the factories of the Eastern towns and in the coal mines, despised and neglected by the old unions. The I.W.W. provided them with experienced strike leaders and organisers, who showed them how to stand against police terrorism, who defended them before public opinion and the courts, who taught them the practice of solidarity and unity and opened to them wider views on society, on capitalism and class struggle. In such big fights ten thousands of new members joined the I.W.W., of whom only a small fraction remained. This "one big union" was adapted to the wild growth of American capitalism in the days when it built up its power by subjecting the masses of the independent pioneeers.

Similar forms of fight and organisation may be propagated and may come up elsewhere, when in big strikes the workers stand up, without as yet having the complete self-confidence of taking matters entirely in their own hands. But only as temporary transition forms. There is a fundamental difference between the conditions of future fight in big industry and those of America in the past. There it was the rise, now it will be the downfall of capitalism. There the rugged independence of pioneers or the primitive, egoistic struggle for survival of immigrants were the expression of a middle class individualism that had to be curbed under the yoke of capitalist exploitation. Now masses trained to discipline during a life time by machine and capital, connected by strong technical and spiritual ties to the productive apparatus, organise its utilisation on the new basis of collaboration. These workers are thoroughly proletarian, all obstinacy of middle class individualism having been worn off long ago by the habit of collaborate work. The forces of solidarity and devotion hidden in them only wait for great fights to develop into a dominating life principle. Then even the most suppressed layers of the working class, who only hesitatingly join their comrades, wanting to lean upon their example, will soon feel the new forces of community growing also in themselves. Then they will perceive that the fight for freedom asks not only their adherence but the development of all their powers of self-activity and self-reliance. Thus overcoming all intermediate forms of partial self-determination the progress will definitely go the way of council organisation.

## 3.   Shop Occupation

Under the new conditions of capitalism a new form of fight for better working conditions came up, the shop occupation, mostly called the sit-down strike, the workers ceasing to work but not leaving the factory. It was not invented by theory, it arose spontaneously out of practical needs; theory can do no more than afterwards explain its causes and consequences. In the great world crisis of 1930 unemployment was so universal and lasting that there arose a kind of class antagonism between the privileged number of employed and the unemployed masses. Any regular strike against wage cuttings was made impossible, because the shops after being left by the strikers, immediately would be flooded by the masses outside. So the refusal to work under worse conditions must needs be combined with sticking to the place of work by occupying the shop.

Having sprung up, however, in these special circumstances, the sit-down strike displays some characteristics that make it worth while to consider it more closely as the expression of a further developed fighting form. It manifests the formation of a more solid unity. In the old form of strike the working community of the personnel dissolved when leaving the shop. Dispersed over the streets and homes between other people they were separated into loose individuals. To discuss and decide as one body they had then to assemble in meeting halls, in streets and squares. However often police and authorities tried to hinder or even to forbid this, the workers held fast to their right of using them, through the consciousness that they fought with legitimate means for lawful aims. The legality of trade union practice was generally recognised by public opinion.

When, however, this legality is not recognised, when the increasing power of big capital over State authorities disputes the use of hall and square for assemblies, the workers, if they will fight, have to assert their rights by taking them. In America every great strike was as a rule accompanied by a continuous fight with the police over the use of the streets and rooms for meeting. The sit-down strike releases the workers from this necessity by their taking the right to assemble at the logical place, in the shop. At the same time the strike is made truly efficient by the impossibility of strike-breakers taking their places.

Of course this entails new stiff fighting. The capitalists as owners of the shop consider occupation by the strikers as a violation of their ownership; and on this juridical argument they call for the police to turn the workers out. Indeeed, from the strict juridical viewpoint, shop occupation is in conflict with formal law. Just as striking is in conflict with formal law. And in fact the employer regularly appealed to this formal law as a weapon in the fight, by stigmatising the strikers as contract breakers, thus giving him the right to put new workers in their places. But against this juridical logic strikes have persisted and developed as a form of fight; because they were necessary.

Formal law, indeed, does not represent the inner reality of capitalism, but only its outer forms, to which middle class and juridical opinion cling. Capitalism in reality is not a world of equal and contracting individuals, but a world of fighting classes. When the power of the workers was too small the middle class opinion of formal law prevailed, the strikers as contract breakers were turned out and replaced by others. Where, however, trade union fight had won its place, a new and truer juridical conception asserted itself: a strike is not a break, not a cessation, but a temporary suspending of the labor contract, to settle the dispute over working terms. Lawyers may not accept this point of view in theory, but society does, in practice.

In the same way shop occupation asserted itself as a method in the fight, where it was needed and where the workers were able to take a stand. Capitalists and lawyers might splutter over the violation of property rights. For the workers, however, it was an action that did not attack the property rights but only temporarily suspended their effects. Shop occupation is not shop-expropriation. It is only a momentary suspension of the disposal by the capitalist. After the contest has been settled, he is master and undisputed owner as before.

Yet, at the same time, it is more. In it, as in a flash of lightening at the horizon, a glimpse of future development springs up. By shop occupation the workers, unwittingly, demonstrate that their fight has entered into a new phase. Here their firm interjunction as a shop-organisation appears, a natural unity not to be dissolved into single individuals. Here the workers become conscious of their intimate connection with the shop. To them it is not another man's building where only at his command they come to work for him till he sends them away. To them the shop with its machines is a productive apparatus they handle, an organ that only by their work is made a living part of society. It is nothing foreign to them; they are at home here, much more than the juridical owners, the shareholders who do not even know its whereabouts. In the factory the workers grow conscious of the contents of their life, their productive work, their work-community as a collectivity that makes it a living organism, an element of the totality of society. Here, in shop occupation, a vague feeling arises that they ought to be entirely master of production, that they ought to expel the unworthy outsiders, the commanding capitalists, who abuse it in wasting the riches of mankind and in devastating the earth. And in the heavy fight that will be necessary, the shops again will play a primary role, as the units of organisation, of common action, perhaps as the supports and strongholds, pivots of force and objects of struggle. Compared with the natural connection of workers and shops the command of capital appears as an artificial outside domination, powerful as yet, but hanging in the air; whereas the growing hold of the workers is firmly rooted in the earth. Thus in shop occupation the future can be seen in the growing consciousness that the shops belong with the workers, that together they form a harmonious unity, and that the fight for freedom will be fought over, in, and by means of the shops.

## 4. Political Strikes

Not all the great strikes of the workers in the last century were fought over wages and working conditions. Besides the so-called economic strikes, political strikes occurred. Their object was the promotion or the prevention of a political measure. They were not directed against the employers but against the State government, to induce it to give to the workers more political rights, or to dissuade it from obnoxious acts. Thus it could happen that the employers agreed with the aims and promoted the strike.

A certain amount of social equality and political rights for the working class is necessary in capitalism. Modern industrial production is based upon intricate technics, the product of highly developed knowledge, and demands the careful personal collaboration and capabilities of the workers. The utmost exertion of forces cannot, as in the case of coolies or slaves, be enforced by rough physical compulsion, by whip or outrage; it would be revenged by equally rough mishandling of the tools. The constraint must come from inner motives, from moral means of pressure based upon individual responsibility. The workers must not feel powerless embittered slaves; they must have the means to go against inflicted wrongs. They have to feel themselves free sellers of their labor-power, exerting all their forces, because, formally and apparently, they are determining their own lot in the general competition. To maintain themselves as a working class they need not only the personal liberty and legal equality proclaimed by middle class laws: Special rights and liberties, too, are necessary to secure these possibilities; the right of association, the right of meeting in assembly, the right to form unions, freedom of speech, freedom of press. And all these political rights must be protected by universal suffrage, for the workers to assert their influence over Parliament and law.

Capitalism began by refusing these rights, assisted herein by the inherited despotism and backwardness of existing governments, and tried to make the workers powerless victims of its exploitation. Only gradually, in consequence of fierce struggle against inhuman oppression, some rights were won. Because in its first stage capitalism feared the hostility of the lower classes, the artisans impoverished by its competition, and the workers starved by low wages, the suffrage was kept restricted to the wealthy classes. Only in later times, when capitalism was firmly rooted, when its profits were large and its rule was secured, were the restrictions on the ballot gradually removed, but only under compulsion of strong pressure, often of hard fight from the side of the workers. The fight for democracy fills the history of domestic politics during the 19th century, first in England, and then in all countries where capitalism introduced itself.

In England universal suffrage was one of the main points of the charter of demands put up by the English workers in the Chartist movement, their first and most glorious period of struggle. Their agitation had been a strong inducement to the ruling landowner class to yield to the pressure of the simultaneous Reform movement of the rising industrial capitalists. So through the Reform Act 1832 the industrial employers got their share in political power; but the workers had to go home empty-handed, and to continue their strenuous struggle. Then, at the climax of Chartism, a "holy month" was projected in 1839, when all the work had to rest till the demands were granted. Thus the English workers were the first to proclaim the political strike as a weapon in their fight. But it could not be put into effect; and in an outburst (1842) it had to be broken off without success; it could not curb the greater power of the now combined ruling classes of landowners and factory owners. Not till a generation later, when after a period of unprecedented industrial prosperity and expansion the propaganda was once more taken up, now by the trade unions combined in the "International Workers' Association" (the "First International" of Marx and Engels), public opinion in the middle class was ready to extend, in consecutive steps, the suffrage to the working class.

In France, universal suffrage since 1848, formed part of republican constitution, dependent as such government always was, on the support of the workers. In Germany the foundation of the Empire, in the years 1866-70, product of a feverish capitalist development activating the entire population, entailed universal suffrage as a warrant of continued contact with the masses of the people. But in many other countries the propertied class, often only a privileged part of it, kept fast to its monopoly of political influence. Here the campaign for the ballot, obviously the gate to political power and freedom, roused ever larger parts of the working class to participation, to organisation and to political activity. Conversely, the fear of the propertied classes for political domination of the proletariat stiffened their resistance. Formally the matter looked hopeless for the masses; universal suffrage had to be legally enacted by a Parliament chosen by the privileged minority, and thus invited to destroy its own foundations. This implies that only by extraordinary means, by pressure from outside, finally by political mass strikes the aim could be achieved. How it happens may be learnt from the classical example of the Belgian suffrage strike in 1893.

In Belgium, through a limited census-suffrage, government was perpetually in the hands of a small clique of conservatives of the clerical party. Labor conditions in the coal mines and factories were notoriously among the worst in Europe and led to explosions in frequent strikes. Extension of suffrage as a way to social reform, frequently proposed by some few liberal parliamentarians, always again was defeated by the conservative majority. Then the Workers' Party, agitating, organising and preparing for many years, decided upon a general strike. Such a strike had to exert political pressure during the parliamentary discussion on a new suffrage proposal. It had to demonstrate the intense interest and the grim will of the masses, who abandoned their work to give all attention to this fundamental question. It had to arouse all the indifferent elements among the workers and the small business men to take part in what for all of them was a life interest. It had to show the narrow-minded rulers the social power of the working class, to impress upon them that it refused longer to be kept under tutelage. At first, of course, the parliamentary majority took a stand, refused to be coerced by pressure from outside, wishing to decide after their own will and conscience; so it took the suffrage bill from the rolls and ostensibly began to discuss other matters. But in the meantime the strike went on, extended ever more, and brought production to a standstill; traffic ceased, and even dutiful public services became restive. The governmental apparatus itself was hampered in its functions; and in the business world, with the growing feeling of uncertainty, opinion became loud that to grant the demands was less dangerous than to provoke a catastrophe. So the determination of the parliamentarians began to crumble; they felt that they had to choose between yielding or crushing the strike by military force. But could the soldiers be trusted in such a case? Thus their resistance had to give way; will and conscience had to be revised, and at last they accepted and enacted the proposals. The workers, by means of a political strike, had reached their aim and won their fundamental political right.

After such a success many workers and their spokesmen supposed that this new powerful weapon could be used oftener to win important reforms. But therein they were disappointed; the history of labor movement knows of more failures than successes in political strikes. Such a strike tries to impose the will of the workers upon a government of the capitalist class. It is somewhat of a revolt, a revolution, and calls up in that class the instincts of self-defence and the impulses of suppression. These instincts were repressed when part of the bourgeoisie itself grew annoyed by the backwardness of political institutions and felt the need of fresh reforms. Then the mass action of the workers was an instrument to modernise capitalism. Because the workers were united and full of enthusiasm, whereas the propertied class in any case was divided, the strike succeeded. It could succeed not because of the weakness of the capitalist class, but because of the strength of capitalism. Capitalism is strengthened when its roots, by universal suffrage, securing at least political equality, are driven deeper into the working class. Workers' suffrage belongs to developed capitalism; because the workers need the ballot, as well as trade unions, to maintain themselves in their function in capitalism.

If now, however, in minor points they should suppose themselves able to impose their will against the real interests of the capitalists, they find this class solidly against them. They feel it as by instinct; and not being carried away by a great inspiring aim that dispels all hesitations, they remain uncertain and divided. Every group, seeing that the strike is not general, hesitates in its turn. Volunteers from the other classes offer themselves for the most needed services and traffic; though they are not really able to uphold production, their activity at least discourages the strikers.

Prohibition of assemblies, display of armed forces, martial law may demonstrate still more the power of government and their will to use it. So the strike begins to crumble and must be discontinued, often with considerable losses and disillusionment for the defeated organisations. In experiences like these the workers discovered that by its inner strength capitalism is able to withstand even well organised and massal assaults. But at the same time they felt sure that in mass strikes, if only applied at the right time, they possess a powerful weapon.

This view was confirmed in the first Russian Revolution of 1905. It exhibited an entirely new character in mass-strikes. Russia at that time showed only the beginnings of capitalism: some few large factories in great towns, supported mostly by foreign capital with State subsidies, where starving peasants flocked to work as industrial hands. Trade unions and strikes were forbidden; government was primitive and despotic. The Socialist Party, consisting of intellectuals and workers, had to fight for what middle-class revolutions in Western Europe had already established: the destruction of absolutism and the introduction of constitutional rights and law. Hence the fight of the Russian workers was bound to be spontaneous and chaotic. First as wildcat strikes against miserable working conditions, severely suppressed by Cossacks and police, then acquiring a political character, in demonstrations and the unfolding of red flags in the streets, the struggle manifested itself. When the Japanese war of 1905 had weakened the Czarist government and shown up its inner rottenness, the revolution broke out as a series of wildcat strike movements on a gigantic scale. Now they flamed up, springing like wildfire from one factory, one town to another, bringing the entire industry to a standstill; then they dissolved into minor local strikes, dying away after some concessions from the employers, or smouldered until new outbreaks came. Often there were street demonstrations and fights against police and soldiers. Days of victory came where the delegates of the factories assembled unmolested to discuss the situation, then, joined by deputations of other groups, of rebellious soldiers even, to express their sympathy, whilst the authorities stood passively by. Then again the Government made a move and arrested the entire body of delegates, and the strike ended in apathy. Till at last, in a series of barricade fights in the capital cities the movement was crushed by military force.

In Western Europe political strikes had been carefully premeditated actions for specially indicated aims, directed by the union or the Socialist Party leaders. In Russia the strike movement was the revulsion of heavily abused humanity, uncontrolled, as a storm or a flood forcing its way. It was not the fight of organised workers claiming a long denied right; it was the rise of a down-trodden mass to human consciousness in the only possible form of fighting. Here there could be no question of success or defeat, the fact of an outbreak was already a victory, no more to be undone, the beginning of a new epoch. In outward appearance the movement was crushed and Czarist government again was master. But in reality these strikes had struck a blow at Czarism from which it could not recover. Some reforms were introduced, political, industrial and agrarian. But the whole fabric of the State with its arbitrary despotism of incapable chinowniks could not be modernized, it had to disappear. This revolution prepared the next one, in which old barbarous Russia was to be destroyed.

The first Russian revolution has strongly influenced the ideas of the workers in Central and Western Europe. Here a new development of capitalism had set in that made felt the need of new and more powerful methods of fight, for defence and for attack. Economic prosperity, which began in the nineties and lasted till the First World War, brought an unprecedented increase of production and wealth. Industry expanded, especially iron and steel industry, new markets were opened, railways and factories were built in foreign countries and other continents; now for the first time capitalism spread all over the earth. America and Germany were the scenes of the most rapid industrial development. Wages increased, unemployment nearly disappeared, the trade unions grew into mass organisations. The workers were filled with hopes of continual progress in prosperity and influence, and visions loomed up of a coming age of industrial democracy.

But then, at the other side of society, they saw another image. Big capital concentrated production and finance, wealth and power, in a few hands and built up strong industrial concerns and capitalist associations. Its need for expansion, for the disposal over foreign markets and raw materials, inaugurated the policy of imperialism, a policy of stronger ties to old, and conquest of new colonies, a policy of growing antagonism between the capitalist classes of different countries, and of increasing armaments. The old peaceful freetrade ideals of the "little Englanders" were ridiculed and gave way to new ideals of national greatness and power. Wars broke out in all continents, in the Transvaal, in China, Cuba, and the Phillipines, in the Balkans; England consolidated its Empire, and Germany, claiming its share in world power, prepared for world war. Big capital in its growing power ever more determined the character and opinions of the entire bourgeoisie, filling it with its anti-democratic spirit of violence. Though sometimes it tried to lure the workers by the prospect of a share in the spoils, there was on the whole less inclination than in previous times to make concessions to labour. Every strike for better wages, engaged in order to catch up with rising prices, met with stiffer resistance. Reactionary and aristocratic tendencies got hold of the ruling class; it spoke not of extension but of restriction of popular rights, and threats were heard, especially in continental countries, of suppressing the workers' discontent by violent means.

Thus circumstances had changed and were changing ever more. The power of the working class had increased through its organisation and its political action. But the power of the capitalist class had increased still more. This means that heavier clashes between the two classes might be expected. So the workers had to look for other and stronger methods of fighting. What were they to do if regularly even the most justifiable strikes were met by big lock-outs, or if their parliamentary rights were reduced or circumvented, or if capitalist government made war notwithstanding their urgent protests?

It is easily seen that under such conditions there was among the foremost elements of the working class much thought and discussion on mass action and the political strike, and that the general strike was propagated as a means against the outbreak of war. Studying the examples of such actions as the Belgian and the Russian strikes, they had to consider the conditions, the possibilities, and the consequences of mass-actions and political strikes in the most highly developed capitalist countries with strong governments and powerful capitalist classes. It was clear that strong odds were against them. What could not have happened in Belgium and Russia would be the immediate result here: the annihilation of their organisations. If the combined trade unions, Socialist or Labor Parties should proclaim a general strike, Government, sure of the support of the entire ruling and middle class, doubtless would be able to imprison the leaders, persecute the organisations as endangering the safety of the State, suppress their papers, by a state of siege prevent all mutual contact of the strikers, and by mobilizing military forces, assert its undisputed public power. Against this display of power the workers, isolated, exposed to the threats and calumnies, disheartened by distorted information from the press, would have no chance. Their organisations would be dissolved and would break down. And with the organisations lost, the fruits of years of devoted struggle, all would be lost.

Thus the political and labor leaders asserted. Indeed, to them, with their outlook entirely limited within the confines of present forms of organisation, it must appear so. So they are fundamentally opposed to political strikes. This means that in this form, as premeditated and well decided actions of the existing organisations, directed by their leaders, such political strikes are not possible. As little as a thunderstorm in a placid atmosphere. It may be true that, for special aims entirely within the capitalist system, a political strike can remain entirely within the bounds of legal order, so that after it is over capitalism resumes its ordinary course. But this truth does not prevent the ruling class from being angrily aroused against every display of workers' power, nor political strikes from having consequences far beyond their immediate aims. When social conditions become intolerable for the workers, when social or political crises are threatening them with ruin, it is inevitable that mass-actions and gigantic strikes break forth spontaneously, as the natural form of struggle, notwithstanding all objections and resistance of the existing unions, irresistibly, like thunderstorms out of a heavy electric tension in the atmosphere. And again the workers face the question whether they have any chance against the power of State and capital.

It is not true that with a forcible suppression of their organisations all is lost. These are only the outer form of what in essence lives within. To think that by such Government measures the workers suddenly should change into the selfish, narrow-minded, isolated individuals of olden times! In their hearts all the powers of solidarity, of comradeship, of devotion to the class remain living, are growing even more intense through the adverse conditions; and they will assert themselves in other forms. It these powers are strong enough no force from above can break the unity of the strikers. Where they suffer defeat it is mainly due to discouragement. No government power can compel them to work; it can only prohibit active deeds; it can do no more than threaten and try to intimidate them, try through fear, to dissolve their unity. It depends on the inner strength of the workers, on the spirit of organisation within them, whether that can be successful. Certainly thus the highest demands are made on social and moral qualities; but just for this reason these qualities will be strained to the highest possible pitch and will be hardened as steel in the fire.

This is not the affair of one action, one strike. In every such contest the force of the workers is put to the test, whether their unity is strong enough to resist the attempts of the ruling powers to break it. Every contest arouses new strenuous efforts to strengthen it so as not to be broken. And when, actually, the workers remain steadfast, when notwithstanding all acts of intimidation, of suppression, of isolation, they hold out, when there is no yielding of any group, then it is on the other side that the effects of the strike become manifest. Society is paralysed, production and traffic are stopped, or reduced to a minimum, the functioning of all public life is hampered, the middle classes are alarmed and may begin to advise concessions. The authority of Government, unable to restore the old order, is shaken. Its power always consisted in the solid organisation of all officials and services, directed by unity of purpose embodied in one self-sure will, all of them accustomed by duty and conviction to follow the intentions and instructions of the central authorities. When, however, it stands against the mass of the people, it feels itself ever more what it really is, a ruling minority, inspiring awe only as long as it seemed all-powerful, powerful only as long as it was undisputed, as long as it was the only solidly organised body in an ocean of unorganised individuals. But now the majority also is solidly organised, not in outward forms but in inner unity. Standing before the impossible task of imposing its will upon a rebellious population, Government grows uncertain, divided, nervous, trying different ways. Moreover, the strike impedes the intercommunication of the authorities all over the country, isolates the local ones, and throws them back upon their own resources. Thus the organisation of State power begins to lose its inner strength and solidity. Neither can the use of armed forces help otherwise than by more violent threatening. In the end the army consists either of workers too, in different dress and under the menace of stricter law, but not intended to be used against their comrades; or it is a minority over against the entire people. If put to the strain of being commanded to fire at unarmed citizens and comrades, the imposed discipline in the long run must give way. And then State power, besides its moral authority, loses its strongest material weapon to keep the masses in obendience.

Such considerations of the important consequences of mass strikes, once great social crises stir up the masses to a desperate fight, could mean of course no more than the view of a possible future. For the moment, under the mollifying effects of industrial prosperity, there were no forces strong enough to drive the workers into such actions. Against the threatening war their unions and parties restricted themselves to professing their pacifism and feelings of international class unity, without the will and the daring to call upon the masses for a desperate resistance. So the ruling class could force the workers into its capitalist mass-action, into world war. It was the collapse of the appearances and illusions of self-satisfied power of the working class at the time, now disclosed as inner weakness and insufficiency.

One of the elements of weakness was the lack of a distinct goal. There was not, and could not be, any clear idea of what had to come after successful mass-actions. The effects of mass strikes thus far appeared destructive only, not constructive. This was not true, to be sure; decisive inner qualities, the basis of a new society, develop out of the fights. But the outer forms in which they had to take shape were unknown; nobody in the capitalist world at the time had heard of workers'. councils. Political strikes can only be a temporary form of battle; after the strike constructive labor has to provide for permanency.

## 5.   The Russian Revolution

The Russian revolution was an important episode in the development of the working class movement. First, as already mentioned, it displayed new forms of political strike, instruments of revolution. Moreover, in a higher degree, of self-organisation of the fighting workers, known as soviets, *i.e.,* councils first appeared. In 1905 they were hardly noticed as a special phenomenon and they disappeared with the revolutionary activity itself. In 1917 they reappeared with greater power; now their importance was grasped by the workers of Western Europe, and they played a role here in the class struggles after the First World War.

The soviets, essentially, were simply strike committees, such as always arise in wildcat strikes. Since the strikes in Russia broke out in large factories, and rapidly expanded over towns and districts, the workers had to keep in continual touch. In the shops the workers assembled and discussed regularly at the end of the working day, or in times of tension even continually, the entire day. They sent their delegates to other factories and to the central committees, where information was interchanged, difficulties discussed, decisions taken, and new tasks considered.

But here the tasks proved more encompassing than in ordinary strikes. The workers had to throw off the heavy oppression of Czarism; they felt that by their action Russian society was changing in its foundations. They had to consider not only wages and labor conditions in their shops, but all questions related to society at large. They had to find their own way in these realms and to take decisions on political matters. When the strike flared up, extended over the entire country, stopped all industry and traffic and paralysed the functions of government, the soviets were confronted with new problems. They had to regulate public life, they had to take care of public security and order, they had to provide for the indispensable public utilities and services. They had to perform governmental functions; what they decided was executed by the workers, whereas Government and police stood aloof, conscious of their impotence against their rebellious masses. Then the delegates of other groups, of intellectuals, of peasants, of soldiers, who came to join the central soviets, took part in the discussions and decisions. But all this power was like a flash of lightning, like a meteor passing. When at last the Czarist government mustered its military forces and beat down the movement the soviets disappeared.

Thus it was in 1905. In 1917 the war had weakened the government through the defeats at the front and the hunger in the towns, and now the soldiers, mostly peasants, took part in the action. Besides the workers' councils in the town soldiers' councils were formed in the army; the officers were shot when they did not acquiesce to the soviets taking all power into their hands to prevent entire anarchy. After half a year of vain attempts on the part of politicians and military commanders to impose new governments, the soviets, supported by the socialist parties, were master of society.

Now the soviets stood before a new task. From organs of revolution they had to become organs of reconstruction. The masses were master and of course began to build up production according to their needs and life interests. What they wanted and did was not determined, as always in such cases, by inculcated doctrines, but by their own class character, by their conditions of life. What were these conditions? Russia was a primitive agrarian country with only the beginning of industrial development. The masses of the people were uncivilized and ignorant peasants, spiritually dominated by a gold glittering church, and even the industrial workers were strongly connected with their old villages. The village soviets arising everywhere were self-governing peasant committees. They seized the large estates of the former great landowners and divided them up. The development went in the direction of small freeholders with private property, and presented already the distinctions between larger and smaller properties, between influential wealthy and more humble poor farmers.

In the towns, on the other hand, there could be no development to private capitalist industry because there was no bourgeoisie of any significance. The workers wanted some form of socialist production, the only one possible under these conditions. But their minds and character, only superficially touched by the beginnings of capitalism, were hardly adequate to the task of themselves regulating production. So their foremost and leading elements, the socialists of the Bolshevist Party, organised and hardened by years of devoted fight, their leaders in the revolution became the leaders in the reconstruction. Moreover, were these working class tendencies not to be drowned by the flood of aspirations for private property coming from the land, a strong central government had to be formed, able to restrain the peasants' tendencies. In this heavy task of organising industry, of organising the defensive war against counter-revolutionary attacks, of subduing the resistance of capitalist tendencies among the peasants, and of elucating them to modern scientific ideas instead of their old beliefs, all the capable elements among the workers and intellectuals, supplemented by such of the former officials and officers as were willing to co-operate, had to combine into the Bolshevist Party as the leading body. It formed the new government. The soviets gradually were eliminated as organs of self-rule, and reduced to subordinate organs of the government apparatus. The name of Soviet Republic, however, was preserved as a camouflage, and the ruling party retained the name of Communist Party.

The system of production developed in Russia is State socialism. It is organised production, with the State as universal employer, master of the entire production apparatus. The workers are master of the means of production no more than under Western capitalism. They receive their wages and are exploited by the State as the only mammoth capitalist. So the name State capitalism can be applied with precisely the same meaning. The entirety of the ruling and leading bureaucracy of officials is the actual owner of the factories, the possessing class. Not separately, everyone for a part, but together, collectively, they are possessors of the whole. Theirs the function and the task to do what the bourgeoisie did in Western Europe and America: develop industry and the productivity of labor. They had to change Russia from a primitive barbarous country of peasants into a modern, civilized country of great industry. And before long, in often cruelly waged class war between the peasants and the rulers, State-controlled big agrarian enterprises replaced the backward small farms.

The revolution, therefore, has not, as deceptive propaganda pretends, made Russia a land where the workers are master and communism reigns. Yet it meant progress of enormous significance. It may be compared with the great French revolution: it destroyed the power of monarch and feudal landowners, it began by giving the land to the peasants, and it made the masters of industry rulers of the State. Just as then in France the masses of despised "canaille" became free citizens, recognised even in poverty and economic dependance as personalities with the possibility to rise, so now in Russia the masses rose from unevolving barbarism into the stream of world progress, where they may act as personalities. Political dictatorship as form of government can no more prevent this development once it has started than the military dictatorship of Napoleon hampered it in France. Just as then in France from among the citizens and peasants came up the capitalists and the military commanders, in an upward struggle of mutual competition, by good and by bad means, by energy and talent, by jobbery and deceit—so now in Russia. All the good brains among the workers, and peasants' children rushed into the technical and farming schools, became engineers, officers, technical and military leaders. The future was opened to them and aroused immense tensions of energy; by study and exertion, by cunning and intrigue they worked to assert their places in the new ruling class —ruling, here again, over a miserable exploited class of proletarians. And just as at that time in France a strong nationalism sprang up proclaiming the new freedom to be brought to all Europe, a brief dream of everlasting glory—so now Russia proudly proclaimed its mission, by world revolution to free all peoples from capitalism.

For the working class the significance of the Russian revolution must be looked for in quite different directions. Russia showed to the European and American workers, confined within reformist ideas and practice, first how an industrial working class by a gigantic mass action of wild-cat strikes is able to undermine and destroy an obsolete State power; and second, how in such actions the strike committees develop into workers' councils, organs of fight and of self-management, acquiring political tasks and functions. In order to see the influence of the Russian example upon the ideas and actions of the working class after the First World War, we have to go a step backward.

The outbreak of the war in 1914 meant an unexpected breakdown of the labor movement all over capitalist Europe. The obedient compliance of the workers under the military powers, the eager affiliation, in all countries, of the union and socialist party leaders to their governments, as accomplices in the suppression of the workers, the absence of any significant protest, had brought a deep disappointment to all who before put their hopes of liberation on proletarian socialism. But gradually among the foremost of the workers came the insight that what had broken down was chiefly the illusion of an easy liberation by parliamentary reform. They saw the bleeding and exploited masses growing rebellious under the sufferings of oppression and butchery, and, in alliance with the Russian revolutionaries, they expected the world-revolution to destroy capitalism as an outcome of the chaos of the war. They rejected the disgraced name of socialism and called themselves communists, the old title of working class revolutionaries.

Then as a bright star in the dark sky the Russian revolution flared up and shone over the earth. And everywhere the masses were filled with anticipation and became restive, listening to its call for the finishing of the war, for brotherhood of the workers of all countries, for world revolution against capitalism. Still clinging to their old socialist doctrines and organisations the masses, uncertain under the flood of calumnies in the press, stood waiting, hesitating, whether the tale might still come true. Smaller groups, especially among the young workers, everywhere assembled in a growing communist movement. They were the advance guard in the movements that after the end of the war broke out in all countries, most strongly in defeated and exhausted Central Europe.

It was a new doctrine, a new system of ideas, a new tactic of fight, this communism that with the then new powerful means of government propaganda was propagated from Russia. It referred to Marx's theory of destroying capitalism by means of the workers' class struggle. It was a call for fight against world capital, mainly concentrated in England and America, that exploited all peoples and all continents. It summoned not only the industrial workers of Europe and America, but also the subjected peoples of Asia and Africa to rise in common fight against capitalism. Like every war, this war could only be won by organisation, by concentration of powers, and good discipline. In the communist parties, comprising the most gallant and able fighters, kernel and staff were present already: they have to take the lead, and at their call the masses must rise and attack the capitalist governments. In the political and economic crisis of the world we cannot wait until by patient teaching the masses have all become communists. Nor is this necessary; if they are convinced that only communism is salvation, if they put their trust in the Communist Party, follow its directions, bring it to power, then the Party as the new government will establish the new order. So it did in Russia, and this example must be followed everywhere. But then, in response to the heavy task and the devotion of the leaders, strict obedience and discipline of the masses are imperative, of the masses towards the Party, of the party members towards the leaders. What Marx had called the dictatorship of the proletariat can be realised only as the dictatorship of the Communist Party. In the Party the working class is embodied, the Party is its representative.

In this form of communist doctrine the Russian origin was clearly visible. In Russia, with its small industry and undeveloped working class, only a rotten Asiatic despotism had to be overthrown. In Europe and America a numerous and highly developed working class, trained by a powerful industry, stands over against a powerful capitalist class disposing of all the resources of the world. Hence the doctrine of party dictatorship and blind obedience found strong opposition here. If in Germany the revolutionary movements after the close of the war had led to a victory of the working class and it had joined Russia, then the influence of this class, product of the highest capitalist and industrial development, would soon have outweighed the Russian character. It would have strongly influenced the English and the American workers, and it would have carried away Russia itself along new roads. But in Germany the revolution failed; the masses were kept aloof by their socialist and union leaders, by means of atrocity stories and promises of well-ordered socialist happiness, whilst their advance guards were exterminated and their best spokesmen murdered by the military forces under the protection of the socialist government. So the opposing groups of German communists could not carry weight; they were expelled from the party. In their place discontented socialist groups were induced to join the Moscow International, attracted by its new opportunist policy of parliamentarism, with which it hoped to win power in capitalist countries.

Thus world revolution, from a war cry, became a phrase. The Russian leaders imagined world revolution as a big scale extension and imitation of the Russian revolution. They knew capitalism only in its Russian form, as a foreign exploiting power impoverishing the inhabitants, carrying all the profits out of the country. They did not know capitalism as the great organising power, by its richness producing the basis of a still richer new world. As became clear from their writings, they did not know the enormous power of the bourgeoisie, against which all the capabilities of devoted leaders and a disciplined party are insufficient. They did not know the sources of strength that lie hidden in the modern working class. Hence the primitive forms of noisy propaganda and party terrorism not only spiritual, but also physical, against dissenting views. It was an anachronism that Russia, newly entering the industrial era out of its primitive barbarism, should take command over the working class of Europe and America, that stood before the task of transforming a highly developed industrial capitalism into a still higher form of organisation.

Old Russia essentially, in its economic structure, had been an Asiatic country. All over Asia lived millions of peasants, in primitive small scale agriculture, restricted to their village, under despotic far distant rulers, whom they had no connection with but by the paying of taxes. In modern times these taxes became ever more a heavy tribute to Western capitalism. The Russian revolution, with its repudiation of Czarist debts, was the liberation of the Russian peasants from this form of exploitation by Western capital. So it called upon all the suppressed and exploited Eastern peoples to follow its example, to join the fight and throw off the yoke of their despots, tools of the rapacious world capital. And far and wide, in China and Persia, in India and Africa the call was heard. Communist parties were formed, consisting of radical intellectuals, of peasants revolting against feudal landowners, of hard-pressed urban coolies and artisans, bringing to the hundreds of millions the message of liberation. As in Russia it meant for all these peoples the opening of the road to modern industrial development, sometimes, as in China, in alliance with a modernizing national bourgeoisie. In this way the Moscow International even more than a European became an Asiatic institution. This accentuated its middle class character, and worked to revive in the European followers the old traditions of middle class revolutions, with the preponderance of great leaders, of sounding catchwords, of conspiracies, plots, and military revolts.

The consolidation of State capitalism in Russia itself was the determining basis for the character of the Communist Party. Whilst in its foreign propaganda it continued to speak of communism and world revolution, decried capitalism, called upon the workers to join in the fight for freedom, the workers in Russia were a subjected and exploited class, living mostly in miserable working conditions, under a strong and oppressive dictatorial rule, without freedom of speech, of press, of association, more strongly enslaved than their brethren under Western capitalism. Thus an inherent falsehood must pervade politics and teachings of that party. Though a tool of the Russian government in its foreign politics, it succeeded by its revolutionary talk in taking hold of all the rebellious impulses generated in enthusiastic young people in the crisis-ridden Western world. But only to spill them in abortive sham-actions or in opportunist politics—now against the socialist parties styled as traitors or social fascists, then seeking their alliance in a so-called red front or a people's front—causing its best adherents to leave in disgust. The doctrine it taught under the name of Marxism was not the theory of the overthrow of highly developed capitalism by a highly developed working class, but its caricature, product of a world of barbarous primitivity, where fight against religious superstitions is spiritual, and modernized industrialism is economic progress—with atheism its philosophy, party-rule its aim, obedience to dictatorship its highest commandment. The Communist Party did not intend to make the workers independent fighters capable by their force of insight themselves to build their new world, but to make them obedient followers ready to put the party into power.

So the light darkened that had iluminated the world; the masses that had hailed it were left in blacker night, either in discouragement turning away from the fight, or struggling along to find new and better ways. The Russian revolution first had given a mighty impulse to the fight of the working, class, by its mass direct actions and by its new council forms of organisation—this was expressed in the widespread rise of the communist movement all over the world. But when then the revolution settled into a new order, a new class rule, a new form of government, State capitalism under dictatorship of a new exploiting class, the Communist Party needs must assume an ambiguous character. Thus in the course of ensuing events it became most ruinous to the working class fight, that can only live and grow in the purity of clear thought, plain deeds and fair dealings. By its idle talk of world revolution it hampered the badly needed new orientation of means and aims. By fostering and teaching under the name of discipline the vice of submissiveness, the chief vice the workers must shake off, by suppressing each trace of independent critical thought, it prevented the growth of any real power of the working class. By usurping the name communism for its system of workers' exploitation and its policy of often cruel persecution of adversaries, it made this name, till then expression of lofty ideals, a byword, an object of aversion and hatred even among workers. In Germany, where the political and economic crises had brought the class antagonisms to the highest pitch, it reduced the hard class fight to a puerile skirmish of armed youths against similar nationalist bands. And when then the tide of nationalism ran high and proved strongest, large parts of them, only educated to beat down their leaders' adversaries, simply changed colours. Thus the Communist Party by its theory and practice largely contributed to prepare the victory of fascism.

## 6.   The Workers' Revolution

The revolution by which the working class will win mastery and freedom, is not a single event of limited duration. It is a process of organisation, of self-education, in which the workers gradually, now in progressing rise, then in steps and leaps, develop the force to vanquish the bourgeoisie, to destroy capitalism, and to build up their new system of collective production. This process will fill up an epoch in history of unknown length, on the verge of which we are now standing. Though the details of its course cannot be foreseen, some of its conditions and circumstances may be a subject of discussion now.

This fight cannot be compared with a regular war between similar antagonistic powers. The workers' forces are like an army that assembles during the battle! They must grow by the fight itself, they cannot be ascertained beforehand, and they can only put forward and attain partial aims. Looking back on history we discern a series of actions that as attempts to seize power seem to be so many failures: from Chartism, through 1848, through the Paris Commune, up to the revolutions in Russia and Germany in 1917-1918. But there is a line of progress; every next attempt shows a higher stage of consciousness and force. Looking back on the history of labor we see, moreover, that in the continuous struggle of the working class there are ups and downs, mostly connected with changes in industrial prosperity. In the first rise of industry every crisis brought misery and rebellious movements; the revolution of 1848 on the continent was the sequel of a heavy business depression combined with bad crops. The industrial depression about 1867 brought a revival of political action in England; the long crisis of the 1880's, with its heavy unemployment, excited mass actions, the rise of social-democracy on the continent and the "new unionism" in England. But in the years of industrial prosperity in between, as 1850-70, and 1895-1914, all this spirit of rebellion disappeared. When capitalism flourishes and in feverish activity expands its realm, when there is abundant employment, and trade union action is able to raise the wages, the workers do not think of any change in the social system. The capitalist class growing in wealth and power is full of self-confidence, prevails over the workers and succeeds in imbuing them with its spirit of nationalism. Formally the workers may then stick to the old revolutionary catchwords; but in their subconscious they are content with capitalism, their vision is narrowed; hence, though their numbers are growing, their power declines. Till a new crisis finds them unprepared and has to rouse them anew.

Thus the question poses itself, whether, if previously won fighting power again and again crumbles in the contentment of a new prosperity, society and the working class ever will be ripe for revolution. To answer this question the development of capitalism must be more closely examined.

The alternation of depression and prosperity in industry is not a simple swinging to and fro. Every next swing was accompanied by an expansion. After each breakdown in a crisis capitalism was able to come up again by expanding its realm, its markets, its mass of production and product. As long as capitalism is able to expand farther over the world and to increase its volume, it can give employment to the mass of the population. As long as thus it can meet the first demand of a system of production, to procure a living for its members, it will be able to maintain itself, because no dire necessity compels the workers to make an end of it. If it could go on prospering at its highest stage of extension, revolution would be impossible as well as unnecessary; then there were only the hope that a gradual increase of general culture could reform its deficiencies.

Capitalism, however, is not a normal, in any case not a stable system of production. European, and afterwards American capitalism could increase production so continuously and rapidly, because it was surrounded by a wide non-capitalist outer world of small-scale production, source of raw materials and markets for the products. An artificial state of things, this separation between an active capitalist core and a dependent passive surrounding. But the core ever expanding. The essence of capitalist economy is growth, activity, expansion; every standstill means collapse and crisis. The reason is that profits accumulate continuously into new capital that seeks for investment to bring new profit, thus the mass of capital and the mass of products increase ever more rapidly and markets are sought for feverishly. So capitalism is the great revolutionizing power, subverting old conditions everywhere and changing the aspect of the earth. Ever new millions of people from their secluded, self-sufficient home production that reproduced itself during long centuries without notable change, are drawn into the whirl of world commerce. Capitalism itself, industrial exploitation, is introduced there, and soon from customers they become competitors. In the 19th century from England it progressed over France, Germany, America, Japan, then in the 20th it pervades the large Asiatic territories. And first as competing individuals, then organised in national States the capitalists take up the fight for markets, colonies, world power. So they are driven on, revolutionizing ever wider domains.

But the earth is a globe, of limited extent. The discovery of its finite size accompanied the rise of capitalism four centuries ago, the realization of its finite size now marks the end of capitalism. The population to be subjected is limited. The hundreds of millions crowding the fertile plains of China and India once drawn within the confines of capitalism, its chief work is accomplished. Then no large human masses remain as objects for subjection. Surely there remain vast wild areas to be converted into realms of human culture; but their exploitation demands conscious collaboration of organised humanity; the rough rapine methods of capitalism—the fertility-destroying "rape of the earth"—are of no avail there. Then its further expansion is checked. Not as a sudden impediment, but gradually, as a growing difficulty of selling products and investing capital. Then the pace of development slackens, production slows up, unemployment waxes, a sneaking disease. Then the mutual fight of the capitalists for world domination becomes fiercer, with new world wars impending.

So there can hardly be any doubt that an unlimited expansion of capitalism offering lasting life possibilities for the population, is excluded by its inner economic character. And that the time will come that the evil of depression, the calamities of unemployment, the terrors of war, grow ever stronger. Then the working class, if not yet revolting, must rise and fight. Then the workers must choose between inertly succumbing and actively fighting to win freedom. Then they will have to take up their task of creating a better world out of the chaos of decaying capitalism.

Will they fight? Human history is an endless series of fights; and Clausewitz, the well-known German theorist on war, concluded from history that man is in his inner nature a warlike being. But others, sceptics as well as fiery revolutionists, seeing the timidity, the submissiveness, the indifference of the masses, often despair of the future. So we will have to look somewhat more thoroughly into psychological forces and effects.

The dominant and deepest impulse in man in every living being is his instinct of self-preservation. It compels him to defend his life with all his powers. Fear and submissiveness also are the effect of this instinct, when against powerful masters they afford the best chances for preservation. Among the various dispositions in man those which are most adapted to secure life in the existing circumstances will prevail and develop. In the daily life of capitalism it is unpractical, even dangerous for a worker to nurture his feelings of independence and pride; the more he suppresses them and tacitly obeys, the less difficulty he will encounter in finding and keeping his job. The morals taught by the ministers of the ruling class enhance this disposition. And only few and independent spirits defy these tendencies and are ready to encounter the incumbent difficulties.

When, however, in times of social crisis and danger all this submissivity, this virtuousness, is of no avail to secure life, when only fighting can help, then it gives way to its contrary, to rebelliousness and courage. Then the bold set the example and the timid discover with surprise of what deeds of heroism they are capable. Then self-reliance and high-spiritedness awake in them and grow, because on their growth depend their chances of life and happiness. And at once, by instinct and by experience, they know that only collaboration and union can give strength to their masses. When then they perceive what forces are present in themselves and in their comrades, when they feel the happiness of this awakening of proud self-respect and devoted brother-

hood, when they anticipate a future of victory, when they
see rising before them the image of the new society they
help to build, then enthusiasm and ardour grow to irresistible
power. Then the working class begins to be ripe for revolution. Then capitalism begins to be ripe for collapse.

Thus a new mankind is arising. Historians often wonder
when they see the rapid changes in the character of people
in revolutionary times. It seems a miracle; but it simply
shows how many traits lay hidden in them, suppressed because they were of no use. Now they break forth, perhaps
only temporarily; but if their utility is lasting, they develop into dominant qualities, transforming man, fitting
him for the new circumstances and demands.

The first and paramount change is the growth of community-feeling. Its first traces came up with capitalism itself,
out of the common work and the common fight. It is
strengthened by the consciousness and the experience that,
single, the worker is powerless against capital, and that
only firm solidarity can secure tolerable life conditions.
When the fight grows larger and fiercer, and widens into
a fight for dominance over labor and society, on which life
and future depend, solidarity must grow into indissoluble
all-pervading unity. The new community-feeling, extending
over the entire working class, suppresses the old selfishness
of the capitalist world.

It is not entirely new. In primeval times, in the tribe with
its simple mostly communistic forms of labor the community-
feeling was dominant. Man was completely bound up with
the tribe; separate from it he was nothing; in all his actions
the individual felt as nothing compared with the welfare and
the honour of the community. Inextricably one as he was
with the tribe primitive man had not yet developed into a
personality. When afterwards men separated and became
independent small-scale producers, community-feeling waned
and gave way to individualism, that makes one's own person the centre of all interests and all feelings. In the many
centuries of middle class rising, of commodity production
and capitalism, the individual personality-feeling awoke and
ever more strongly grew into a new character. It is an
acquisition that can no more be lost. To be sure, also in
this time man was a social being; society dominated, and
in critical moments, of revolution and war, the community-
feeling temporarily imposed itself as an unwanted moral

duty. But in ordinary life it lay suppressed under the proud fancy of personal independence.

What is now developing in the working class is not a reverse change, as little as life conditions are a return to bygone forms. It is the coalescence of individualism and community-feeling into a higher unity. It is the conscious subordination of all personal forces in the service of the community. In their management of the mighty productive forces the workers as their mightier masters will develop their personality to a yet higher stage. The consciousness of its intimate connection with society unites personality-feeling with the all-powerful social feeling into a new life-apprehension based on the realisation of society as the source of man's entire being.

Community-feeling from the first is the main force in the progress of revolution. This progress is the growth of the solidarity, of the mutual connections, of the unity of the workers. Their organisation, their new growing power, is a new character acquired through fight, is a change in their inner being, is a new morality. What military authors say about ordinary war, namely, that moral forces therein play a dominant role, is even more true in the war of the classes. Higher issues are at stake here. Wars always were contests of similar competing powers, and the deepest structure of society remained the same, whether one won or the other. Contests of classes are fights for new principles, and the victory of the rising class transfers the society to a higher stage of development. Hence, compared with real war, the moral forces are of a superior kind: voluntary devoted collaboration instead of blind obedience, faith to ideals instead of fidelity to commanders, love for the class companions, for humanity, instead of patriotism. Their essential practice is not armed violence, not killing, but standing steadfast, enduring, persevering, persuading, organising; their aim is not to smash the skulls but to open the brains. Surely, armed action will also play a role in the fight of the classes; the armed violence of the masters cannot be overcome in Tolstoian fashion by patient suffering. It must be beaten down by force; but, by force animated by a deep moral conviction.

There have been wars that showed something of this character. Such wars as were a kind of revolution or formed part of revolutions, in the fight for freedom of the middle class. Where rising burgherdom fought for dominance against the home and the foreign feudal powers of monarchy and landownership,—as in Greece in antiquity, in Italy and Flanders in the Middle Ages, in Holland, England, France in later centuries—idealism and enthusiasm, arising out of deep feelings of the class-necessities, called forth great deeds of heroism and self-sacrifice. These episodes, such as in modern times we meet with in the French revolution, or in Italy's liberation by Garibaldi's followers, count among the most beautiful pages in human history. Historians have glorified and poets have sung them as epochs of greatness, gone for ever. Because the sequel of the liberation, the practice of the new society, the rule of capital, the contrast of impudent luxury and miserable poverty, the avarice and greed of the business men, the job-hunting of officials, all this pageant of low selfishness fell as a chilling disappointment upon the next generation. In middle-class revolutions egotism and ambition in strong personalities play an important role; as a rule the idealists are sacrificed and the base characters come to wealth and power. In the bourgeoisie everybody must try to raise himself by treading down the others. The virtues of community-feeling were a temporary necessity only, to gain dominance for their class; once this aim attained, they give way to the pitiless competitive strife of all against all.

Here we have the fundamental difference between the former middle-class revolutions and the now approaching workers' revolution. For the workers the strong community-feeling arising out of their fight for power and freedom is at the same time the basis of their new society. The virtues of solidarity and devotion, the impulse to common action in firm unity, generated in the social struggle, are the foundations of the new economic system of common labor, and will be perpetuated and intensified by its practice. The fight shapes the new mankind needed for the new labor system. The strong individualism in man now finds a better way of asserting itself than in the craving for personal power over others. In applying its full force to the liberation of the class it will unfold itself more fully and more nobly than in pursuing personal aims.

Community-feeling and organisation do not suffice to defeat capitalism. In keeping the working class in submission, the spiritual dominance of the bourgeoisie has the same importance as has its physical power. Ignorance is an impediment to freedom. Old thoughts and traditions press heavily upon the brains, even when touched already by new ideas. Then the aims are seen at their narrowest, well-sounding catchwords are accepted without criticism, illusions about easy successes, half-hearted measures and false promises lead astray. Thus the importance of intellectual power for the workers is shown. Knowledge and insight are an essential factor in the rise of the working class.

The workers' revolution is not the outcome of rough physical power; it is a victory of the mind. It will be the product of the mass power of the workers, certainly; but this power is spiritual power in the first place. The workers will not win because they have strong fists; fists are easily directed by cunning brains, even against their own cause. Neither will they win because they are the majority; ignorant and unorganised majorities regularly were kept down, powerless, by well-instructed organised minorities. Majority now will win only because strong moral and intellectual forces cause it to rise above the power of their masters. Revolutions in history could succeed because new spiritual forces had been awakened in the masses. Brute stupid physical force can do nothing but destroy. Revolutions, however, are the constructive epochs in the evolution of mankind. And more than any former the revolution that is to render the workers master of the world demands the highest moral and intellectual qualities.

Can the workers respond to these demands? How can they acquire the knowledge needed? Not from the schools, where the children are imbibed with all the false ideas about society which the ruling class wishes them to have. Not from the papers, owned and edited by the capitalists, or by groups striving for leadership. Not from the pulpit that always preaches servility and where John Balls are extremely rare. Not from the radio, where—unlike the public discussions in former times, for the citizens a powerful means of training their minds on public affairs—one-sided pronouncements tend to stultify the passive listeners, and by their never-easing obtrusive noise allow no reposed thinking. Not from the film that—unlike the theatre, in early days for the rising burgher class a means of instruction and sometimes even of fight—appeals only to visual impression, never to thinking or intelligence. They all are powerful instruments of the ruling class to keep the working class in spiritual bondage. With instinctive cunning and conscious deliberation they are all used for the purpose. And the working masses unsuspectingly submit to their influence. They let themselves be fooled by artful words and outside appearances. Even those who know of class and fighting leave the affairs to leaders and statesmen, and applaud them when they speak dear old words of tradition. The masses spend their free time in pursuing puerile pleasures unaware of the great social problems on which their and their children's existence depends. It seems an insolvable problem, how a workers' revolution is ever to come and to succeed, when by the sagaciousness of the rulers and the indifference of the ruled its spiritual conditions remain lacking.

But the forces of capitalism are working in the depths of society, stirring old conditions and pushing people forward even when unwilling. Their inciting effects are suppressed as long as possible, to save the old possibilities of going on living; stored in the subconscious they only intensify the inner strains. Till at last, in crisis, at the highest pitch of necessity they snap and give way in action, in revolt. The action is not the result of deliberate intention; it comes as a spontaneous deed, irresistibly. In such spontaneous action man reveals to himself of what he is capable, a surprise to himself. And because the action is always collective action, it reveals to each that the forces dimly felt in himself, are present in all. Confidence and courage are raised by the discovery of the strong class forces of common will, and they stir and carry away ever wider masses.

Actions break out spontaneously, enforced by capitalism upon the unwilling workers. They are not so much the result as the starting point of their spiritual development. Once the fight is taken up the workers must go on in attack and defence; they must exert all their forces to the utmost. Now falls away the indifference that was only a form of resistance to demands they felt themselves unequal to respond to. Now a time of intense mental exertion sets in. Standing over against the mighty forces of capitalism they see that only by the utmost efforts, by developing all their powers can they hope to win. What in every fight appears in its first traces now broadly unfolds; all the forces hidden in the masses are roused and set in motion. This is the creative work of revolution. Now the necessity of firm unity is hammered into their consciousness, now the necessity of knowledge is felt at every moment. Every kind of ignorance, every illusion about the character and force of the foe, every weakness in resisting his tricks, every incapacity of refuting his arguments and calumnies, is revenged in failure and defeat. Active desire, by strong impulses from within, now incites the workers to use their brains. The new hopes, the new visions of the future inspire the mind, making it a living active power, that shuns no pains to seek for truth, to acquire knowledge.

Where will the workers find the knowledge they need? The sources are abundant; an extensive scientific literature of books and pamphlets, explaining the basic facts and theories of society and labor already exists and more will follow. But they exhibit the greatest diversity of opinion as to what is to be done; and the workers themselves have to choose and to distinguish what is true and right. They have to use their own brains in hard thinking and intent discussions. For they face new problems, ever again, to which the old books can give no solution. These can supply only general knowledge about society and capital, they present principles and theories, comprehending former experience. The application in ever new situations is our own task.

The insight needed can not be obtained as instruction of an ignorant mass by learned teachers, possessors of science, as the pouring of knowledge into passive pupils. It can only be acquired by self-education, by the strenuous self-activity that strains the brain in fell desire to understand the world. It would be very easy for the working class if it had only to accept established truth from those who know it. But the truth they need does not exist anywhere in the world outside them; they must build it up within themselves. Also what is given here does not pretend to be established final truth to be learned by heart. It is a system of ideas won by attentive experience of society and the workers' movement, formulated to induce others to think over and to discuss the problems of work and its organisation. There are hundreds of thinkers to open new viewpoints, there are thousands of intelligent workers who, once they give their attention to them, are able, from their intimate knowledge, to conceive better and in more detail the organisation of their fight and the organisation of their work. What is said here may be the spark that kindles the fire in their minds.

There are groups and parties pretending to be in the

exclusive possession of truth, who try to win the workers by their propaganda under the exclusion of all other opinions. By moral and, where they have the power, also by physical constraint, they try to impose their views upon the masses. It must be clear that one-sided teaching of one system of doctrines can only serve, and indeed should serve, to breed obedient followers, hence to uphold old or prepare new domination. Self-liberation of the working masses implies self-thinking, self-knowing, recognising truth and error by their own mental exertion. Exerting the brains is much more difficult and fatiguing than exerting the muscles; but it must be done, because the brains govern the muscles; if not their own, then foreign brains.

So unlimited freedom of discussion, of expressing opinions is the breathing air of the workers' fight. It is more than a century ago that against a despotic government, Shelley, England's greatest poet of the 19th century, "the friend of the friendless poor," vindicated for everybody the right of free expression of his opinion. "A man has the right to unrestricted liberty of discussion." "A man has not only the right to express his thoughts, but it is his duty to do so" . . . "nor can any acts of legislature destroy that right." Shelley proceeded from philosophy proclaiming the natural rights of man. For us it is owing to its necessity for the liberation of the working class that freedom of speech and press is proclaimed. To restrict the freedom of discussion is to prevent the workers from acquiring the knowledge they need. Every old despotism, every modern dictatorship began by persecuting or forbidding freedom of press; every restriction of this freedom is the first step to bring the workers under the domination of some kind of rulers. Must not, then, the masses be protected against the falsehoods, the misrepresentations, the beguiling propaganda of their enemies? As little as in education can careful withholding of evil influences develop the faculty to resist and vanquish them, just as little can the working class be educated to freedom by spiritual guardianship. Where the enemies present themselves in the guise of friends, and in the diversity of opinions every party is inclined to consider the others as a danger for the class, who shall decide? The workers, certainly; they must fight their way in this realm also. But the workers of to-day might in honest conviction condemn as obnoxious opinions that afterwards prove to be the basis of new progress. Only by standing open to all ideas that the rise of a new world generates in the minds of man, by testing and selecting, by judging and applying them with its own mental capacities, can the working class gain the spiritual superiority needed to suppress the power of capitalism and erect the new society.

Every revolution in history was an epoch of the most fervent spiritual activity. By hundreds and thousands the political pamphlets and papers appeared as the agents of intense self-education of the masses. In the coming proletarian revolution it will not be otherwise. It is an illusion that, once awakened from submissiveness, the masses will be directed by one common clear insight and go their way without hesitation in unanimity of opinion. History shows that in such awakening an abundance of new thoughts in greatest diversity sprouts in man, expressions all of the new world, as a roaming search of mankind in the newly opened land of possibilities, as a blooming richness of spritual life. Only in the mutual struggle of all these ideas will crystallize the guiding principles that are essential for the new tasks. The first great successes, result of spontaneous united action, by destroying previous shackles, do no more than fling open the prison gates; the workers, by their own exertion, must then find the new orientation towards further progress.

This means that those great times will be full of the noise of party strife. Those who have the same ideas form groups to discuss them for their own and to propagate them for their comrades' enlightenment. Such groups of common opinion may be called parties, though their character will be entirely different from the political parties of the previous world. Under parliamentarism these parties were the organs of different and opposite class interests. In the working class movement they were organisations taking the lead of the class, acting as its spokesmen and representatives and aspiring at guidance and dominance. Now their function will be spiritual fight only. The working class for its practical action has no use for them; it has created its new organs for action, the councils. In the shop organisation, the council organisation, it is the entirety of the workers itself that acts, that has to decide what must be done. In the shop assemblies and in the councils the different and opposite opinions are exposed and defended, and out of the contest the decision and the unanimous action has to proceed. Unity of purpose can only be reached by spiritual

contest between the dissenting views. The important function of the parties, then, is to organise opinion, by their
mutual discussion to bring the new growing ideas into
concise forms, to clarify them, to exhibit the arguments in
a comprehensible form, and by their propaganda to bring
them to the notice of all. Only in this way the workers in
their assemblies and councils can judge their truth, their
merits, their practicability in each situation, and take the
decision in clear understanding. Thus the spiritual forces
of new ideas, busting forth in everybody's minds, are organised and shaped so as to be usable instruments of the
class. This is the great task of party strife in the workers'
fight for freedom, far nobler than the endeavour of the
old parties to win dominance for themselves.

The transition of supremacy from one class to another,
which as in all former revolutions is the essence of the
workers' revolution, does not depend on the haphazard
chances of accidental events. Though its details, its ups
and downs depend on the chance of various conditions and
happenings that we cannot foresee, viewed at large there
is a definite progressive course, which may be an object
of consideration in advance. It is the increase of social
power of the rising class, the loss of social power of the
declining class. The rapid visible changes in power form
the essential character of social revolutions. So we have to
consider somewhat more closely the elements, the factors
constituting the power of each of the contending classes.

The power of the capitalist class in the first place consists in the possession of capital. It is master of all the
factories, the machines, the mines, master of the entire
productive apparatus of society; so mankind depends on
that class to work and to live. With its money-power it can
buy not only servants for personal attendance; when threatened it can buy in unlimited number sturdy young men
to defend its domination, it can organise them into well-
armed fighting groups and give them a social standing. It
can buy, by assuring them honourable places and good
salaries, artists, writers and intellectuals, not only to amuse
and to serve the masters, but also to praise them and
glorify their rule, and by cunning and learning to defend
their domination against criticism.

Yet the spiritual power of the capitalist class has deeper
roots than the intellect it can buy. The middle class, out of

which the capitalists rose as its upper layer, always was an enlightened class, self-reliant through its broad world conception, basing itself, its work, its production system, upon culture and knowledge. Its principles of personal ownership and responsibility, of self-help and individual energy pervade the entire society. These ideas the workers have brought with them, from their origin out of impoverished middle-class lawyers; and all the spiritual and physical means available are set to work to preserve and intensify the middle-class ideas in the masses. Thus the domination of the capitalist class is firmly rooted in the thinking and feeling of the dominated majority itself.

The strongest power factor of the capitalist class, however, is its political organisation, State-power. Only by firm organisation can a minority rule over a majority. The unity and continuity of plan and will in the central government, the discipline of the bureaucracy of officials pervading society as the nervous system pervades the body, and animated and directed by one common spirit, the disposal, moreover, when necessary, over an armed force, assure its unquestioned dominance over the population. Just as the strength of the fortress consolidates the physical forces of the garrison into an indomitable power over the country, so State power consolidates the physical and spiritual forces of the ruling class into unassailable strength. The respect paid to the authorities by the citizens, by the feeling of necessity, by custom and education, regularly assure the smooth running of the apparatus. And should discontent make people rebellious, what can they do, unarmed and unorganised, against the firmly organised and disciplined armed forces of the Government? With the development of capitalism, when the power from a numerous middle class ever more concentrated in a smaller number of big capitalists, the State also concentrated its power and through its increasing functions took ever more hold of society.

What has the working class to oppose to these formidable factors of power?

Ever more the working class constitutes the majority, in the most advanced countries the large majority of the population, concentrated here in large and giant industrial enterprises. Not legally but actually it has the machines, the productive apparatus of society in its hands. The capitalists are owners and masters, surely; but they can do no more than command. If the working class disregards their commands they cannot run the machines. The workers can. The workers are the direct actual masters of the machines; however determined, by obedience or by self-will, they can run them and stop them. Theirs is the most important economic function; their labour bears society.

This economical power is a sleeping power as long as the workers are captivated in middle class thinking. It grows into actual power by class consciousness. By the practice of life and labour they discover that they are a special class, exploited by capital, that they have to fight to free themselves from exploitation. Their fight compels them to understand the structure of the economic system, to acquire knowledge of society. Notwithstanding all propaganda to the contrary this new knowledge dispels the inherited middle-class ideas in their heads, because it is based on the truth of daily experienced reality, whereas the old ideas express the past realities of a bygone world.

Economic and spiritual power are made an active power through organisation. It binds all the different wills to unity of purpose and combines the single forces into a mighty unity of action. Its outer forms may differ and change as to circumstances, its essence is its new moral character, the solidarity, the strong community-feeling, the devotion and spirit of sacrifice, the self-imposed discipline. Organisation is the life principle of the working class, the condition of liberation. A minority ruling by its strong organisation can be vanquished only, and certainly will be vanquished, by organisation of the majority.

Thus the elements constituting the power of the contending classes stand over against one another. Those of the bourgeoisie stand great and mighty, as existing and dominating forces, whereas those of the working class must develop, from small beginnings, as new life growing up. Number and economic importance grow automatically by capitalism; but the other factors, insight and organisation, depend on the efforts of the workers themselves. Because they are the conditions of efficient fight they are the results of fight; every setback strains nerves and brains to repair it, every success swells the hearts into new zealous confidence. The awakening of class-consciousness, the growing knowledge of society and its development, means the liberation from spiritual bondage, the awakening from dulness to spiritual force, the ascension of the masses to true humanity. Their uniting for a common fight, fundamentally, means already social liberation; the workers, bound into the servitude of capital resume their liberty of action. It is the awakening from submissiveness to independence, collectively, in organised union challenging the masters. Progress of the working class means progress in these factors of power. What can be won in improvement of working and living conditions depends on the power the workers have acquired; when, either by insufficiency of their actions, by lack of insight or effort, or by inevitable social changes their power, compared with the capitalist power, declines, it will be felt in their working conditions. Here is the criterion for every form of action, for tactics and methods of fight, for forms of organisation; do they enhance the power of the workers? For the present, but, still more essential, for the future, for the supreme goal of annihilating capitalism? In the past trade unionism has given shape to the feeling of solidarity and unity, and strengthened their fighting power by efficient organisation. When, however, in later times it had to suppress the fighting spirit, and it put up the demand of discipline towards leaders against the impulse of class solidarity the growth of power was impeded. Socialist party work in the past contributed greatly to raising the insight and the political interest of the masses; when, however, it tried to restrict their activity within the confines of parliamentarism and the illusions of political democracy it became a source of weakness.

Out of these temporary weaknesses the working class has to lift its power in the actions of the coming times. Though we must expect an epoch of crisis and fight this may be alternated with more quiet times of relapse or consolidation. Then traditions and illusions may act temporarily as weakening influences. But then also, making them times of preparation, the new ideas of self-rule and council organisation by steady propaganda may take a broader hold on the workers. Then, just as now, there is a task for every worker once he is seized by the vision of freedom for his class, to propagate these thoughts among his comrades, to rouse them from indifference, to open their eyes. Such propaganda is essential for the future. Practical realisation of an idea is not possible as long as it has not penetrated the minds of the masses at large.

Fight, however, is always the fresh source of power in a

rising class. We cannot foresee now what forms this fight of the workers for their freedom will assume. At times and places it may take the harsh form of civil war, so common in former revolutions when it had to give the decisions. There heavy odds may seem to be against the workers, since Government and the capitalists, by money and authority, can raise armed forces in unlimited numbers. Indeed the strength of the working class is not situated here, in the bloody contest of massacring and killing. Their real strength rests in the domain of labor, in their productive work, and in their superiority in mind and character. Nevertheless, even in armed contest capitalist superiority is not unquestioned. The production of arms is in the hands of the workers; the armed bands depend on their labor. If restricted in number, such bands, when the entire working class, united and unafraid, stands against them, will be powerless, over-whelmed by sheer numbers. And if numerous, these bands consist of recruited workers too, accessible to the call of class solidarity.

The working class has to find out and to develop the forms of fight adapted to its needs. Fight means that it goes its own way according to its free choice, directed by its class interests, independent of, hence opposed to the former masters. In fight its creative faculties assert themselves in finding ways and means. Just as in the past it devised and practised spontaneously its forms of action: the strike, the ballot, the street demonstration, the mass meeting, the leaflet propaganda, the political strike, so it will do in future. Whatever the forms may be, character, purpose and effect will be the same for all: to raise the own elements of power, to weaken and dissolve the power of the foe. So far as experience goes mass political strikes have the strongest effects; and in future they may be still more powerful. In these strikes, born out of acute crises and strong strains, the impulses are too fierce, the issues go too deep to be directed by unions or parties, committees or boards of officials. They bear the character of direct actions of the masses. The workers do not go into strike individually, but shopwise, as personnel collectively deciding their action. Immediately strike committees are installed, where delegates of all the enterprises meet, assuming already the character of workers' councils. They have to bring unity in action, unity also, as much as possible, in ideas and methods, by continual interaction between the fighting impulses of the shop-assemblies and the discussions in the council meetings. Thus the workers create their own organs opposing the organs of the ruling class.

Such a political strike is a kind of rebellion, though in legal form, against the Government, by paralyzing production and traffic trying to exert such a pressure upon the government that it yields to the demands of the workers. Government, from its side, by means of political measures, by prohibiting meetings, by suspending the freedom of press, by calling up armed forces, hence by transforming its legal authority into arbitrary though actual power, tries to break the determination of the strikes. It is assisted by the ruling class itself, that by its press monopoly dictates public opinion and carries on a strong propaganda of calumny to isolate and discourage the strikers. It supplies volunteers not only for somehow maintaining traffic and services, but also for armed bands to terrorise the workers and to try to convert the strike into a form of civil war, more congenial to the bourgeoisie. Because a strike cannot last indefinitely, one of the parties, with the lesser inner solidarity, must give way.

Mass actions and general strikes are the struggle of two classes, of two organisations, each by its own solidity trying to curb and finally to break the other. This cannot be decided in one action; it demands a series of struggles that constitute an epoch of social revolution. For each of the contending classes disposes of deeper sources of power that allow it to restore itself after defeat. Though the workers at a time may be defeated and discouraged, their organisations destroyed, their rights abolished, yet the stirring forces of capitalism, their own inner forces, and the indestructible will to live, once more puts them on their feet. Neither can capitalism be destroyed at one stroke; when its fortress, State Power, is shattered, demolished, the class itself still disposes of a great deal of its physical and spiritual power. History has instances of how governments, entirely disabled and prostrated by war and revolution, are regenerated by the economic power, the money, the intellectual capacity, the patient skill, the class-consciousness—in the form of ardent national feeling—of the bourgeoisie. But finally the class that forms the majority of the people, that supports society by its labor, that has the direct disposal over the productive apparatus, must win. In such a way that the firm organisation of the majority class dissolves and crumbles

State power, the strongest organisation of the capitalist class.

Where the action of the workers is so powerful that the very organs of Government are paralysed the councils have to fulfil political functions. Now the workers have to provide for public order and security, they have to take care that social life can proceed, and in this the councils are their organs. What is decided in the councils the workers perform. So the councils grow into organs of social revolution; and with the progress of revolution their tasks become ever more all-embracing. At the same time that the classes are struggling for supremacy, each by the solidity of its organisation trying to break that of the other class, society must go on to live. Though in the tension of critical moments it can live on the stores of provisions, production cannot stop for a long time. This is why the workers, if their inner forces of organisation fall short, are compelled by hunger to return under the old yoke. This is why, if strong enough, if they have defied, repelled, shattered State Power, if they have repulsed its violence, if they are master in the shops, they immediately must take care of the production. Mastery in the shops means at the same time organisation of production. The organisation for fight, the councils, is at the same time organisation for reconstruction.

Of the Jews in olden times building the walls of Jerusalem it is said that they fought sword in one, trowel in the other hand. Here, differently, sword and trowel are one. Establishing the organisation of production is the strongest, nay, the only lasting weapon to destroy capitalism. Wherever the workers have fought their way into the shops and taken possession of the machines, they immediately start organising the work. Where capitalist command has disappeared from the shop, disregarded and powerless, the workers build up production on the new basis. In their practical action they establish new right and new Law. They cannot wait till everywhere the fight is over; the new order has to grow from below, from the shops, work and fight at the same time.

Then at the same time the organs of capitalism and Government decline into the role of unessential foreign and superfluous things. They may still be powerful to harm, but they have lost the authority of useful and necessary institutions. Now the roles, more and more manifestly to everybody, are reverted. Now the working class, with its organs, the councils, is the power of order; life and prosperity of the entire people rests on its labor, its organisation. The measures and regulations decided in the councils, executed and followed by the working masses, are acknowledged and respected as legitimate authority. On the other hand the old government bodies dwindle to outside forces that merely try to prevent the stabilisation of the new order. The armed bands of the bourgeoisie, even when still powerful, take on ever more the character of unlawful disturbers of obnoxious destroyers in the rising world of labor. As agents of disorder they will be subdued and dissolved.

This is, in so far as we now can foresee, the way by which State Power will disappear, together with the disappearance of capitalism itself. In past times different ideas about future social revolution prevailed. First the working class had to conquer the political power, by the ballot winning a majority in Parliament, helped eventually by armed contests or political strikes. Then the new Government consisting of the spokesmen, leaders, and politicians, by its acts, by new Law, had to expropriate the capitalist class and to organise production. So the workers themselves had only to do half the work, the less essential part; the real work, the reconstruction of society, the organising of labor, had to be done by the socialist politicians and officials. This conception reflects the weakness of the working class at that time; poor and miserable, without economic power, it had to be led into the promised land of abundance by others, by able leaders, by a benignant Government. And then, of course, to remain subjects; for freedom cannot be given, it can only be conquered. This easy illusion has been dispelled by the growth of capitalist power. The workers now have to realise that only by raising their own power to the highest height can they hope to win liberty; that political dominance, mastery over society must be based upon economic power, mastery over labor.

The conquest of political power by the workers, the abolition of capitalism, the establishment of new Law, the appropriation of the enterprises, the reconstruction of society, the building of a new system of production are not different consecutive occurrences. They are contemporary, concurrent in a process of social events and transformations. Or, more precisely, they are identical. They are the different sides, indicated with different names, of one great social revolution: the organisation of labor by working humanity.

# V. Perspectives

## A Few Reflections

### albert chameau

The problem of violence has always held a veritable fascination for the intellectuals of the developed nations. The word *action* tends to have meaning for them only when coupled with the adjective *violent,* and "violent action" means fighting the police, brutality, etc. In France, after May 1968, when streetfights played a not negligible role in opening things up, many people came to think of violence as an end in itself. Instead of seeing in the brutal violence which goes on today the expression of the need of groups (students, shopkeepers, even workers) to make their voices heard in the system, they see it as pure action against the system.

It is a banality to say that bourgeois society exudes brutal violence from all its pores. Not only does violence appear, exalted or attacked, at all levels of culture, but it can be found in everyday life, where it has become so habitual that it appears normal. The pool of blood is part of the decor of daily life. Car accidents and industrial accidents, veritable assassinations, are naturally assimilated with destiny, meet only with general indifference, and reveal themselves objectively as media for the emergence of a violence which is always there in latent form. Not to speak of past wars, the remembrance of which continues to mark generations, memories—and also perspectives—which vivify the images of massacre and genocide of the present wars. But against this conditioning to bourgeois violence develop, like a byproduct, reactions—individual or collective—opposed to the bourgeois world: terrorism, strikes, wild demonstrations, even insurrections. The multiplicity and diversity of these reactions prove that we are dealing here with inevitable phenomena, and the truth of the slogan: we are right to rebel.

Of all human activities, the most fundamental and the most mutilating is labor: fundamental because labor is the very condition of the reproduction of existence and, at least for an élite, a medium for accomplishment; multilating because it is the very condition of the reproduction of dehumanization and, for the great mass of men, a medium of bondage. Bondage here means subordination to machines and more generally to rules, linked to capitalist production, by which only a small fraction of the ruling classes can pride itself on exercising a limited and most often an illusory power. In exploitative societies—which is to say, at present, in all the countries of the globe—not only is the producer separated from the product of his labor, but he is also reduced to the state of an extension of inert things which modify his behavior without his being able to act on them other than in the prescribed way. For example: the typist dedicated to typing so many letters a day, the worker condemned to tighten the same bolt on an assembly line until the day he retires, the professor giving the same course every year. He is crushed by forces outside him, forces to which he is lead to lend a character both eternal and ineluctable.

The attitude which as a consequence prevails is—passivity. The mental habits formed at the workplace are carried over into life in general. In this latter domain as well, everything tends to reinforce the attitudes of submission and passivity. Just as at work the producer finds himself subjected to preordained systems, so in public life he accepts the domination of institutions and concepts against which he can do nothing, and which strive to mold him and impose modes of conduct on him: nation, government, parties, unions, armies, vacations clubs, culture, etc.

The producer has in fact lost all autonomous life, that is to say, the power to influence, himself, the course of his existence. He compensates for this loss by an exacerbation of what appears to him as his individuality, which in reality is the result of his very conditions of labor: the typist seeks to make herself valuable to her boss, the worker seeks to fulfill his norm, the professor aims at being distinguished, the condition for a successful career.

Thus the division of labor has for corollary the glorification of an individuality false by definition, since a person is the product of the labor of all persons. The individual

high cost of production of the individual engenders, in normal times, a certain respect for the life of first class citizens).

It must be stressed, however, that if traditional political associations and parties have lost, with the essence of their old representative functions, their importance in society, this is not yet true of the various working-class parties and unions, whose role in the return to normalcy is basic. Their function consists in effect in consecrating by law, that is to say in principle in a permanent way, the advantages seized by the struggle and in transforming them into supplementary factors of integration—that work of Sisyphus of which Rosa Luxemburg spoke half a century ago. Products of legality, they present as victories for the masses everything which reinforces legally their control over the masses. In their deepest nature, they are legalists because they know that all suppression of the democratic order entails their disappearance (as in Leninist Russia, Nazi Germany, France, Spain, etc.). But their devotion to the law has not prevented any of the great catastrophes of contemporary history. For it is in the very nature of bourgeois law to profit only individuals or particular groups, to consecrate the division of society into classes, and not to unify the producers and make of them a force which counts for something in society. Thus, in the France of 1968, the legal recognition of the union workplace organization meant that the union delegate will be freed for a certain number of hours from his condition of producer, but does not spell the liberation of his workmates. Thus one sees that these people are not interested in seeing people think and act for themselves and why, as a worker at the Renault plant put it in May, '68, "the CGT is more afraid of one student than of a truckload of riot cops."

The everyday aspects of repression can be neither pinpointed by photography, nor grasped in their infinite variety, because of their apparent insignificance, but they are no less terribly real, and they are the fate, at every moment, of millions of human beings. Police repression is spectacular, and every photo of a cop busy beating a demonstrator's head (or an onlooker's) only flashes a light on the violence inherent in class society, a violence which ordinarily takes shape to begin with in the petty vexations, bullyings, and other abuses directed at an individual by some administrator or foreman.

In its brutality, open and collective oppression breaks down the barriers maintained by false individuality, sectional interests, etc. It lays bare what was hidden, and no longer permits doubt and laziness of soul: it provokes the beginnings of consciousness. In our epoch, social crises have become inescapable and, with them, consciousness of the fact that men are capable of organizing, themselves, their own lives. This at any rate is what was set in motion by the young in France in May–June 1968. This the authorities could not tolerate. They hurled against it their forces of repression. The youth responded by building one night barricades of which they had not dreamed that very morning: the violence of oppressed classes is a reflex of self-defense against the violence of the ruling classes which reveals itself.

Faced with the inevitability of these revolts, the attitude of many comrades is not to investigate things more deeply but to echo Chairman Mao's phrase, "Power flows from the barrel of a gun." Out of this they construct a regular theory of urban guerrilla warfare in the developed countries of which the least one can say is that its foundation is not very sure. This theory only illustrates a romantic attitude to violence. One could say that from this point of view they join the revisionists (the real ones, from pre-1914) who said with Bernstein: the end is nothing, the movement everything.

All of us who are intellectuals admire the well-struck blow, the exhibition of cool in the face of repression, self-sacrifice, etc. The intellectual trades do not predispose to moral courage—quite the contrary. So everyone is attracted to "heavies," and feels ready to accord them a political OK, as if physical courage was in itself a proof of political truth. On this ground one would have to support the Nazis and the Fascists, or the Bolsheviks who were undeniably heavies in the good old days.

It is thus necessary to pose the question, what is revolutionary violence? The way in which we answer this question strongly determines the style of actions which we wish to carry out.

Revolutionary violence is in essence the opposition of the class of producers to the bourgeois class, the class which, individually or collectively,[1] controls the means of production. This violence must culminate in the *dispossession of the bourgeois class and the appropriation of the means of production by the producers themselves.*

From this way of looking at revolutionary violence, control of the pace of work by the workers—as has been attempted in certain cases in Italy—is a hundred times more violent than any fight with the riot squad, quite simply because it transcends bourgeois economic rationality and looks beyond society as it exists to a new social order in which work is organized by the workers for their own wellbeing. In contrast, guerrilla warfare, riots, etc. remain within the bounds of rationality as defined by the system, since they do not attack in any direct way capital's control of the production process.

In general, every attempt, however weak, to organize production *by and for* ourselves is more violent than any destroying a machine or taking a boss prisoner. It is obvious that this organization of production by and for ourselves cannot do without holding bosses captive or eventually armed struggle, but the kind of revolutionary struggle we carry out depends essentially on the aspect—armed struggle or control of production—we wish to emphasize.

If we stress armed struggle, if we see social transformation in terms of a simple "seizure of power," then the old Leninist arguments are irrefutable. The bourgeoisie meets the class of producers in motion with a united front and a unified command, and we must oppose it with our own united front. Faced with the bourgeois strategies we must develop strategies "of the people," and as making war, even guerrilla war, is an operation demanding constant decision-making, we must set up a commanding group which is to decide everything and which is called to account, if at all, only in the course of more or less cultural revolutions.

This short analysis brings out the ultra-leninist character, in its consequences on the plane of organization, of the phrase, "power flows from the barrel of a gun." More, one sees clearly its bourgeois and even quasi-fascist and stalinist character, which leads straight to the cult of the leader, respect for his decisions, obedience *perinde ac cadaver,* even to his thought.

[1] Individually, in part, in Western capitalism, collectively in the state capitalism of the so-called socialist states.

This position, which maintains one of the fundamental distinctions of the bourgeois order, that between leaders and led, is particularly adapted to the backward countries where national capital has yet to be formed. It has shown its efficiency in the Russia of 1917, and in the China 1946. In both cases it made possible the installation of state capitalism, which it prefigured in its division between those who know and think and those who carry out orders. It must, however, be noted that in both cases the ruling system had been shaken by a war with an external enemy (Germany in the case of Russia, Japan in that of China) leading to a collapse of the state apparatus. The other countries in which the gun succeeded in beating the power structure are certain former French colonies and Cuba. But even in these cases, the guerrilla victories cannot be attributed simply to the success of armed struggle. In Cuba Castro's action benefited, at least in an early stage, from the aid or tacit accord of a certain fringe of American capital. In the case of the French colonies, the necessary de-colonization—i.e., change in the mode of exploiting one or another backward country—could not take the form which it took (for example) in the English colonies because of the imbecility of the French bourgeoisie, always loath to lose a little in the short run to gain more in the long. In both Indochina and Algeria the French occupation was torn to bits, faced with insurrection (undeniably more serious and farther developed in the former case), caught between the desire to leave and the desire to crush the revolt at its base like in the good old days. In both cases outside aid (Japanese, American, Nationalist Chinese, then Russian and Communist Chinese for Vietnam, American and Russian for Algeria) was not without its influence on the evolution of these conflicts, which took on the character of rivalries between different capitalist states and economic interests. On the other hand, the OAS (*Organisation Armée Secrète*), a guerrilla movement undeniably "of the people" and like a fish in the water of the European population in North Africa, was bound to lose as soon as the French ruling class, strong and not in a state of collapse, made its choice and decided to impose it.

The theory of "power from the barrel of a gun" works, therefore, at best in the underdeveloped countries because —by its resemblance to the hierarchial system, by the facts that armed struggle allows the formation of the cadres or

administrators of the future society and that guerilla warfare allows the combination of a "democratization" at the
local level with a centralization at the general level—it
is adapted to the transformation of feudal society into state
capitalism, to the replacement of the old ruling classes by
new ones.

These few lines only skim the surface of this subject.
We must return to it at greater length on some other occasion, for the clarification of ideas and the determination of
differences between the Leninist groups and the others necessitates a critique of the Russian, Chinese, and Cuban
regimes.

To return to the developed countries—developed, that
is, from the viewpoint of national capital. If we see in
physical violence and in the eventual armed struggle a
byproduct of the more profound violence which is the
class struggle for the expropriation of the bourgeois class,
we have quite a different position with respect to the immediate and future situation.

We see, to begin with, that *change in the way the producers think* is fundamental and that the role of any revolutionary "organization" is to do everything possible to
aid this change. Without doubt it is essentially in their
struggles that the producers acquire new ways of thinking,
and it is vain to hope to "produce" such a change, especially when the "objective," material conditions are lacking.
Still the role, negative or positive, of ideology in the development of consciousness is not negligible. To spread the
word on the real struggles of the producers, to show in
what way they break with bourgeois tradition, to underline
*that in them which presages a new organization of society*
—this must be the work of a group if it wishes to be really
revolutionary. It is not a matter of constituting oneself as
an avant-guarde in exclusive possession of the truth and
trying to impose it on the producers, but, simply, of becoming an echo of the totality of the thinking and practice of the group's members, thinking and practice which
*themselves also* are part of the class struggle. Spreading
ideas does not mean using only "peaceful" means, or simply
theoretical articles. Sometimes a well-timed action can play
an important role in raising consciousness, even a very important role. What is essential, however, is to keep in mind
that our actions, our positions, are only a little part of the

social process, and for the most part are important only for ourselves. This is why it is essential not to get locked into one type of action, into one organizational form, or into one-upping other groups.

This leads us to the question of "revolutionary action." To deal with this seriously we must distinguish certain characteristics of the producers' movement for the control of social reality, characteristics which depend on the development of the struggle.

In fact—to adopt a "triadic" mode, reasoning in the Maoist style—we can distinguish three phases in the revolutionary process, three phases which cover many years—for the revolution itself, while it is an acceleration and a qualitative transformation of history, cannot be reduced to some great day, even the longest of the year. These three phases correspond to three different levels of development.

(a) In the first phase, the producer understands that he/she is exploited. This consciousness is now reached by everyone. Nearly always the producer sees that he/she is exploited even if the factors of integration push him/her to forget it and if—as is mostly the case—he/she finds this exploitation normal and seeks only to enter the group of exploiters.

(b) In a second phase, the producer understands that he/she is exploited in common with other producers, that is to say, that he/she is part of an exploited class facing an exploiting class. This second phase of consciousness exists at the moment in a latent state. Most often it is masked by trade union and (in France) Stalinist phraseology. It speeds up and becomes manifest in *collective* struggles, strikes, riots, etc., in which the solidarity of the producers in the face of the common enemy begins to assert itself.

(c) Finally, in the third phase, the producer understands that with his/her class he/she can transform society and suppress exploitation. This last phase (which can occur only in the developed countries for simple "objective," material reasons) is by far the most difficult and in fact, historically, has never been reached. At most we have taken part in a few weak steps in this direction. In fact this task is a formidable one, not only in view of the counter-revolution it threatens to unleash, but also and above

all *because capitalist society has reached such a degree of
complexity that it may appear impossible to master it by
and for ourselves.*

It is besides symptomatic and normal that while political groups and political theories exist corresponding to
stages (a) and (b), those corresponding to the last phase
don't exist, or barely do. The theories which we have only
serve up again, with a sauce more or less reheated and
spiced up, the social-democratic ideas left over from the
last century, according to which the transformation of society
will take the form of a "seizure of power" by "workers,"
organizations of the union or party variety. Far from posing the formidable problems raised by the possibility of the
direction of production by "associated, free, and equal producers," by the domination of work by humanity, by the
necessary appropriation of technical skills by the mass of
producers for their own use, by the transmission of knowledge, most of the "thinkers" limit themselves to contemplating or patching up the old fashions. For the most part
they find that the socialist society will be realized as soon
as competent people are in charge, especially if we are careful to make a little cultural revolution from time to time,
which will put the really competent people in their rightful place. A fringe group revives the old myth of the "no-
ble savage," the isolated producer reconciled wth his/her
work and producing for his/her own needs. Others think
in terms of the total abolition of labor, which becomes
unnecessary thanks to the development (by whom?) of an
imaginary automation, an idea which in reality is equivalent to extolling a return to the stone age. Others, finally, are
partisans of the "workers' councils," the content of which
is never made clear, and which is their *Deus ex machina,*
like the party or "democracy" for others.

Without a doubt, as the first historical experiences show,
the "council" form seems to be the one which will insure
production and distribution in the new society, which will
permit the development of the solidarity of all the producers
and the realization of the satisfaction of the egoism of
each in the satisfaction of the egoism of all. But one
cannot escape the problem of how they are to be federated
and coordinated. The only attempt at a theoretical solution
of this problem is the book of the Dutch comrades: *Grundprinzipien Kommunistischer Production und Verteilung,* but

this leaves the theory at an embryonic level, as does Pannekoek's *Workers' Councils.*[2]

Since a solution of this problem—or even a sketch of one—doesn't exist, one cannot be surprised if the most conscious militants, who are unwilling to remain at stages (a) and (b), are caught up in a sort of shit, not knowing what to do. The activity of any revolutionary group demands theoretical reflection. The absence of this reflection matches the weakness of the basic class struggle.

This theoretical work ought to take many forms, because the task to be accomplished is immense and has as many forms as life. It is for this reason that it is essential that there be thousands and thousands of autonomous groups all over the place, dealing seriously with the problems of theoretical and practical work. What we need is as much theory and as many actions as possible—far from the one correct political line dear to all Leninists (real or disguised), which is the spitting image of bourgeois sclerosis and death. This does not imply scattering the struggle—much to the contrary—but an attempt to deal with social realities, and the recognition that the transformation of society will be the work not of some one political group but of the mass of producers themselves, because the basic struggle goes on at the workplace.

There is no need for groups to have a form determined in advance, to copy a specific model, to exist for eternity. Dissolutions, recombinations, reamalgamations, fusions, clusters, etc., ought to go on. All of this is the condition of progress, as is the confrontation of ideas and experience, as is the action of each group or of each individual, as is also the collective actions and reflections of different groups or individuals. This is what went on during the revolutionary periods in Russia, Germany, and Spain (and even in China during certain phases of the cultural revolution), when real social ferment could be seen in the flowering of autonomous groups.

The problem of "political organization" cannot be posed *a priori.* It must take many forms; there is no need to set up guidelines. What is important is not to set up fetishes, to remain modest and to see oneself as a part, *no more and no less* essential than others in the development

2 See Part IV this volume.

of revolutionary society, to be aware that if one transcends bourgeois society on certain points one remains still determined by it on many others, to seek as far as possible for actions which above all try to develop class consciousness and one's own consciousness at the same time, to support the the autonomous action of the masses. By the development of our consciousness we can participate in the development of the struggle at our workplaces with our fellow producers. No place in society is privileged—neither the university nor the factory. The struggle against bourgeois society must go on at all levels.

"We are not lost and we will win if we have not unlearned how to learn."

# Old Left, New Left, What's Left?

## paul mattick, jr.

The American student movement which called itself the New Left came and went with the Sixties. Its disappearance is no doubt denied by individuals and political groups whose feelings of and claims to social significance rest on participation in "the Movement." It is uncontestable, however, that not only the organizations—above all, SDS—of the New Left, but the mass student activity in which they grew, are things of the past. Attitudes which shaped and developed from this activity have remained. I think large numbers of students and young people in general are more cynical about American society than were their counterparts in the Fifties, tend to be antiwar, and don't like the cops. There are students who think of themselves as revolutionaries all over the country; many of whom move around through the small Left organizations. But the last few years have seen a practical conservatism among most students. If large-scale student leftism begins again, it will be in a new social context; the New Left will live again only in a newer Left. By calling itself the New Left, the student movement of the Sixties raised the question of its relation to the radical movements of the past. Its disappearance poses the question of the nature of the New Left also in relation to the social struggles to come.

## 1

The emergence of leftish movements in the Sixties appeared paradoxical. The fifteen years since World War II had been hailed by an American president as "the greatest upsurge of economic well-being in history" for America and for world capitalism as a whole. As a result all social groups were supposed to have a stake in the well-being of the system. Class conflict and with it divisive "ideology" had purportedly come to an end. The continuing presence of racism and poverty in the "affluent" society, the perpetual imperialist warfare making good use of what had become a permanent war economy, and a continuing level of economic difficulty—seen through the economists' glass darkly as the dilemma of high employment versus price stability—appeared as sore spots in a basically healthy organism. Racial discrimination and poverty would no doubt vanish with the continual advance of prosperity, supplemented by government programs. The warfare state forced on the system by the Cold War situation would be controlled as Soviet aggressiveness and/or American paranoia gave way to reason and Realpolitik. The vagaries of the Phillips Curve relating unemployment to inflation merely diagrammed the limiting conditions of a prosperous and growing economy.

From the vantage point of the early Seventies the illusory character of this view is evident. Racism and poverty remain as before, while the real wages of white workers have been sliding downwards. Despite peace agreements war continues in Southeast Asia, and threatens to erupt in Latin America and the Middle East. Simultaneous inflation and high unemployment bear testimony to the end of the postwar economic stability. The problem spots of the Sixties are today more easily identifiable as manifestations of deeper problems whose solutions are not so apparent.

The postwar prosperity might in fact be better characterized as a pseudo-prosperity, from the point of view of the classical capitalist economy. While it has been possible for large enough numbers of workers to achieve levels of real income sufficient to maintain social equilibrium, this has been accomplished since the Twenties only thanks to steadily increasing government interventions into the economy. The private sector of the economy has not grown fast enough to make possible a high level of unemployment under conditions both profitable to capital and bearable to the workers. Thus the program of government-sponsored production begun with the New Deal and World War II had to be continued to "take up the slack."

But only the private sector is the capitalist economy proper (as "right-wing" economists never tire of pointing out). Capitalism developed as that system in which productive activity is organized by owners of capital with the aim of making profits. Employment depends not on the desire to produce goods that people need, but on capitalists' ability to sell at a profit the products made by those they employ. Since goods and services sold to the government are paid for out of funds taxed or borrowed from the private economy, apparent profits made in such transactions in reality represent only the redistribution of profits already made by capital as a whole, to the benefit of those corporations favored with contracts.

Based on the steady expansion of the government sector, the prosperity of the post-Depression "mixed economy" therefore represents not a true capitalist boom, but rather a response to the inability of the economy to generate a rate or profit sufficient for an accelerated rate of growth. Because its role is played outside of, and in lieu of, the investment-profit-expanded investment cycle of the capitalist system, the expanding "public" sector, while successful so far in maintaining social stability, cannot solve the essential problem of declining profitability. Indeed, it even accentuates it, as eventually the expansion of nonmarket, nonproductive (of profit) production must inhibit the growth of a private sector growing at a slower rate, even while it is necessary if the private sector is to be allowed to exist at all.

The limits of economic growth are also limits of social integration.[1] Throughout the nineteenth century the profit-

[1] See Paul Mattick, *Critique of Marcuse*, N.Y.: Herder and Herder, 1973.

ability of capital was high enough to make possible a trend rise in both capital holdings and working-class living standards. The stagnating capitalism of our day, however, threatens a future of deep economic depression, and/or renewed world war. And during the postwar decades it set bounds to the possibilities of social reform. A high and, for a decade or so, rising standard of living was reserved for a minority of workers. The limitations on the expansion of both the "public" and the private sector made full employment out of the question. Blacks and whites pushed out of the South, for instance, found low-paying jobs or no jobs at all in the Northern cities to which they moved. In the suburbs inhabited by "affluent" white workers as well as in the increasingly black and Spanish-speaking central cities, young people without the necessity to look for work or without jobs to look for were offered nothing but regimented boredom in the schools and the commercial culture of a stagnating society outside of school.

Ten years after the war (while the war-established world order cracked and shifted in Eastern Europe and the Third World), the instability of the American social peace made its appearance in various forms. The gang violence and rock 'n' roll music which expressed the frustrations of urban working-class young people; the civil rights movement among Southern blacks; the cultural revolt of beatniks and hipsters and the obsession with folk music among middle-income youth—these were harbingers of a coming "rebirth of ideology."

## 2

Like every group in the population, students experienced capitalism's adjustment to its new conditions of existence in the form of particular changes in their mode of life. These have been due both to the continuation of processes operative throughout the history of capitalist society and to new features particularly related to the mixed economy. The general effect has been that of a simultaneous growth in numbers and deterioration in position of white-collar work, which in turn has affected the nature of higher education.

Changes in technology, if not amounting to a "new industrial revolution," have resulted in a growing proportion of white-collar labor at all levels of industry, from Research and Development to production proper. The concentration and centralization of capital have continued as a main trend of capitalist development, with the attendant elimination of the old petite bourgeoisie, in production and services alike. Multitudes of "independent entrepreneurs" or their sons and daughters came to find themselves in the position of wage-workers, in fact if not in principle (with the notable exceptions of the professions of medicine and law, which have so far staved off their reorganization on industrial lines, though this too is changing). The same concentration and centralization process spawned an enormous financial and industrial bureaucracy as more and more managerial and technical people became salaried employees. Finally, the growth of government interference in the economy and society necessitated a growing state bureaucracy, which has been the main contributor to the increasing white-collar sector of the working class.

All of this brought with it a tremendous expansion of higher education (a continuation of the process whereby the Industrial Revolution brought into being a standardly skilled and socialized manual-labor force). This again swelled the demand for white-collar labor, as the enlargement and multiplication of educational institutions implied an increase in teaching and administrative personnel. The students' experience was shaped both by the futures for which they could see themselves preparing and by the related reorganization of the colleges and their adaptation to new functions.

College became a point of production of the masses of white-collar labor needed by industry, government, and the schools themselves. The lower ranks of the non-manual labor force were processed by the hundred thousand in state and "community" colleges. The élite universities and colleges too were transformed by this process. From "communities" of young gentlemen and their mentors, for the acquisition of the liberal education which as social skills went along with what business skills were taught, they became bureaucratized structures processing ever-larger numbers of students. At the same time, the needs of the economy which gave rise to the "multiversity" led to the addition to its educative functions those of being service centers for both industry and government.

The dominant ideology promulgated by the university remained that of neo-liberalism, the classical political doctrine with some alterations covering the advance of Keynesian economic policies: free enterprise with equal opportunity and reasonable success for all; freedom within the law made by a pluralist-democratic government of, by, and for the people; the ability of the welfare state to mitigate all social problems on the road to their final solution. This ideology jibed with the expectations of the young people who entered the upper level schools in the early Sixties; they assumed that college degrees would open the way to creative, responsible, leadership positions in the construction and administration of the Great Society at the New Frontier. Alas, it was not to be.

Already in 1949 economist Seymour Harris warned on the basis of labor market studies that America was producing more college graduates than could be absorbed into the occupations they would expect to fill. Despite the vast demand for college graduates, this is what happened.[2] The hierarchy of degrees, an extension of grade school certificate and diploma, served as a means of job stratification, as employers systematically restricted classes of jobs to degree holders, despite the "over-qualification" of college graduates for the majority of these jobs discovered by Department of Labor studies.[3] Whatever the (no doubt negligible) value of such studies, the typical college graduate of the 1960s faced a job which required a certain amount of background information and the ability to manipulate concepts, but which was nonetheless largely repetitive and uncreative. As a 1968 conference on the problems of scientific and technical employees and professionals concluded, "as their numbers increase, the uniqueness of the individual and his talents will decrease."[4] What holds for scientific workers holds also for the thousands working in government offices and in the university itself.

Far from shaping the expanding wonder-world of postwar capitalism, students experienced the positions awaiting them as unsatisfying slots into which school channeled them. The social tasks of the university—training and channeling—naturally were reflected in its own functioning. Bureaucratized and limited in its own right, campus life

[2] Cited Ivar Berg, *Education and Jobs: The Great Train Robbery*, Beacon Press, Boston, 1971, p. 30.
[3] See Berg, *op. cit.*, p. 46.
[4] Conference on "Collective Bargaining and Professional Responsibility," reported in AFL–CIO *News*, July 13, 1968, cited in Berg, *op. cit.*, p. 69.

could not meet the desires of those who had been assured that a college education would provide the key to a satisfactory way of living. The conflict between the values inculcated by parents and systematized in the classroom and the realities of modern capitalism could only grow increasingly apparent to students, given by their very position of privilege an opportunity for some degree of critical examination of the world.

## 3

"We are people of this generation," the Port Huron Statement (the founding document of SDS) declared in 1962, "bred in at least modest comfort, housed now in universities, looking uncomfortably to the world we inherit. . . . Atlhough mankind desperately needs revolutionary leadership, America rests in national stalemate, its goals ambiguous and tradition-bound instead of informed and clear, its democratic system apathetic and manipulated rather than 'of, by, and for the people.' " Believing that "the fundamental qualities of life on the campus reflect the habits of society at large," the roots of social stagnation were diagnosed as the apathy of the public, bred by a break in "the vital democratic connection . . . between the mass and the several élites" of business and government, who ruled impersonally and irresponsibly. The response required as the assumption of responsibility for the initiation and organization of social change within the country, which would allow America to play a progressive leadership role in the industrialization of the world.[4]

Students moved "out of apathy" in response to a range of issues: Caryl Chessman's execution; HUAC persecution of leftists; U.S. aggression against Cuba; above all, the threat of thermonuclear destruction and the fact of racism. The anti-bomb movement produced the first national student demonstration, bringing some 7,000 people to Washington, D.C. in 1961. (This was also the first issue to unite students and young people on an international scale.) The threat of future destruction proved to be but the tip of an iceberg of daily catastrophe with the "discovery" of poverty and the spotlight cast on racism by the civil rights movement, which itself was revitalized by the activity of students.

[4] *Port Huron Statement*, SDS: 1962, pp. 1, 8, 9.

The crude material life problem facing the increasing numbers of black students is not hard to grasp: education or no, to white (i.e., most) employers all blacks looked alike, and in a stagnant economy blacks remained the "last hired—first fired." A black with a college degree was likely to do far less well in the world than an educated white and many uneducated whites. The fate of black students was thus objectively tied to the fate of blacks in America generally. At the same time, the industrialization of the South and the migration of the rural population into segregated cities, North and South, was shaking up the system of racist law and order evolved since the Civil War. In the context of the racial ferment of the Fifties, the contradiction between the rising aspirations of black college students and the realities of their position in society emerged in a politicization of black students, especially in the South, where SNCC was formed in 1960.[5]

Hundreds of white students worked with the civil rights movement in Northern cities and in the South. The black movement, in addition, provided a model for attempts of white student activists to organize the Northern urban poor, especially whites, in the Economic Research and Action Project (ERAP) initiated by SDS in 1963. Despite the attacks made by both SNCC and SDS on "the Establishment" in general and the Kennedy regime in particular, the projects of both groups did not transcend the limits of the New Frontier. It is characteristic of the activist spirit of the time, for instance, that the Northern Student Movement (a white civil rights auxiliary) devoted its energy, apart from fund-raising and desegregating projects, to *tutoring* ghetto children—i.e., aiding the black poor to climb the supposed educational ladder to success. Aside from its own good works, the movement was consciously oriented towards the Federal government as the mechanism of change; its aim was to organize social forces which would compel the liberals to keep their promises.

[5] There is an interesting analogy to be drawn with a process which was to occur in the late Sixties among college-educated (mostly white) women: in the context of the student movement, the conflict between equal education and discrimination in access to degree-holder jobs has been an important aspect of the women's liberation movement. Sexist discrimination acquired of course a special impact from being practiced within the radical movement as well as in the society "outside."

With the ERAP program, Richard Rothstein, a participant, explains,

> SDS still believed in the possibility of change within the framework of America's formally representative political institutions. ERAP's goal was to stir these institutions, to . . . reverse the corruption of established liberal and trade union forces.[6]

It was believed that these forces, under pressure from ERAP-organized groups and other "new insurgencies" would demand that resources be transferred from the cold-war arms-race to the creation of a decentralized, democratic, interracial welfare state at home. This program remained in the air breathed by the New Left throughout the Sixties. The orientation towards the allocation of government spending and the legislative energy shows up in the long-term co-existence among the new leftists of the call for "participatory democracy" and radical social change with an attachment to the Democratic Party.

In the South, the initial emphasis on desegregating public facilities gave way to a concentration on voter registration and education, a program oddly hailed by the Port Huron Statement as "perhaps the first major attempt to exercise the conventional instruments of political democracy in the struggle for racial justice." The goal was both the exercise of political power at the local level and pressuring Washington to pass and implement civil rights legislation. (The summer, 1964 voter registration project was even seen by some as a tool to provoke federal military intervention into the South and with it a "New Reconstruction.")

Furthermore, again in the words of the Port Huron Statement,

> Linked with pressure from Northern liberals to expunge the Dixiecrats from the ranks of the Democratic Party, massive Negro voting in the South could destroy the vise-like grip reactionary Southerners have on the Congressional legislative process.[7]

Thus black voter registration was a key to the "redirection

[6] "Evolution of the ERAP Organizers," in P. Long, ed., *The New Left,* Boston: Porter Sargent, 1969; pp. 273-4.
[7] *Op. cit.,* p. 46.

of national priorities" called for by SDS; the political possibilities of the black vote were attested to by the quiet
funding of voter registration projects by Kennedy Democrats. The 1964 registration campaign culminated in the
organization of the Mississippi Freedom Democratic Party,
which was to represent blacks within the national Party.
Despite the rejection of the MFDP by the 1964 convention,
the Democratic Party, as the main organization of "liberal
forces" remained a focus for the New Left. In 1964, for
instance, many members of SDS took the position of "Part
of the Way with LBJ." In 1965 a group of editors of the
journal *Studies on the Left* could write about the irrelevance
of the alternatives of working within the Democratic Party
or independent political action, as "the new movements
which give us hope *are* realigning the Democratic Party
even though they often work outside the Party and their
values go far beyond those of the Democratic leadership."[8]

The concentration of interest on the liberal reform wing of
the Establishment had its counterpart in the moral-human-
ist basis of the ideology of the early New Left. While
SNCC in 1960 sought "a social order of justice permeated
by love"[9] SDS in 1963 expressed the hope for "human
freedom. We care that men everywhere be able to understand, express, and determine their lives in fraternity with
one another. . . . Our quest is for a political and economic
order in which power is used for the widest social benefit
and a community in which men can come to know each
other and themselves as human beings  in the fullest
sense."[10] Or as Carl Oglesby, then president of SDS, put
it in 1965 at an antiwar demonstration, the issue was
changing the corporate system "not in the name of this or
that blueprint or 'ism,' but in the name of simple human
decency and democracy and the vision that brave and
wise men saw in the time of our own Revolution."[11] In
the beginning, then, in accord with the social experience of
those who made up the student left, the destruction wrought
by the capitalist system was experienced through the shroud

[8] "Up From Irrelevance," in M. Teodori, ed., *The New Left:
A Documentary History,* New York: Bobbs-Merrill, 1969, p. 210.
[9] SNCC Founding Statement, in Teodori, *op. cit.,* p. 99.
[10] "America and the New Era," in Teodori, *op. cit.,* pp. 172-3.
[11] "Trapped in a System," Teodori, *op. cit.,* p. 187.

of the liberal ideology, and opposed in the name of the promises—liberty, equality, fraternity—with which that system had begun.

In the confrontation of the system with its own ideology, the latter had slowly to give way. The experience of white volunteers in the voter registration projects in the South was especially powerful. Finding themselves shot at, with some of their comrades killed, they discovered a world of social violence they had not known existed. They were beaten by cops as Federal marshals looked on, then sentenced to jail by Kennedy-appointed judges; they, rather than the KKK, were investigated by the FBI. Nationally, those who supported Johnson against the right-wing and war-prone Goldwater were rewarded with the bombing of North Vietnam and the addition of new thousands of troops to those dispatched by Kennedy to Indochina. The ERAP projects met with frustration after frustration in an economy which could not provide "jobs or income now." The liberal forces did not support the wished-for "interracial movement of the poor" (which anyway was not coming into existence), so that the long-term aim of redistributing federal spending from military to welfare and peaceful employment programs went nowhere. The New Leftists therefore found themselves on their own. They began to conceive the aim of community organizing as political education: the experience of struggle for simple but ungranted needs would lead to radicalization of the people involved. Yet while by the beginning of 1965 "grass-roots organizing" was seen as a radical alternative to working with the liberals, an objective, if not subjective, continuity coexisted with the break. Carl Oglesby expressed the position succinctly in the speeech quoted above:

> We are dealing now with a colossus that does not want to be changed. It will not change itself. It will not cooperate with those who want to change it. Those allies of ours in the government—are they really our allies? If they *are,* then they don't need advice, they need *constituencies;* they don't need study groups, they need a *movement.* And if they are *not,* then all the more reason for building that movement [!] with a most relentless conviction.[12]

Among black activists, the defeat of SNCC's attempt to

[12] "Trapped in a System," in Teodori, *op. cit.,* p. 187.

organize rural blacks and the general failure of the civil
rights movement to get results beyond token desegregation
led to attempts to build political and economic organizations based on the acceptance of segregation. The shift in
the color of the cities' populations required a realignment
of ethnically organized political forces, however reluctantly
this was admitted by local machines; in addition the construction of a Democratic black vote continued on a
national scale. Black nationalist ideology was not only a
response to the failure of the civil rights movement but
facilitated the fudging of class contradictions within the
black population. The result was a certain degree of integration of black "community leaders" into various levels
of the political power structure, while massive rioting was
met with some semblance of Federal aid. "Black power"—
for all its inheritance of the ambiguities and ambivalences
imposed by American capitalism throughout its history on
the struggles of blacks for better conditions of life—had
therefore some practical meaning, ranging from "black
culture" enclaves in the colleges, to local political deals,
to the social-work and/or electorally-oriented activity of
"revoluntionary" groups in several cities.

The white activists, in contrast, had no organic connection with the groups they were trying to organize, and
little of practical importance to offer them. The social
changes needed were more profound than they had seemed
at first, while what they were and so the means to achieve
them were immensely unclear. "By the winter of 1965,"
as Richard Rothstein wrote, "if you asked most ERAP
organizers what they were attempting, they would simply
have answered, 'to build a movement.' "[13] But although
they had come up against a practical impasse, the New
Left organizers had discovered in left politics a realm of
activity in which they seemed to have creative and perhaps
history-making parts to play. This sense of work fit for their
capacities (together with the camaraderie tying together
the small number of militants) was a great deal of what
kept the movement going as it turned from the attempt
to pressure liberals to a vaguely conceived social movement against "corporate liberalism."

With the failure of its original aims, ERAP fell apart
in 1965. At the same time the antiwar movement developed

[13] *Op. cit.*, p. 282.

rapidly in the colleges, spurred by the bombing of Vietnam, the dispatch of large numbers of American troops, and the abolition of student draft deferments. Attempts were made to transfer this movement off campus, by adding agitation around the draft to local issues. Antiwar activists came up against the rigidity of the system in the same way that the SNCC and ERAP organizers had. Beginning with a belief that draft resistance, demonstrations, and/or voting for peace candidates would end the war, the total failure of their efforts forced them to see their activities as important for their educational and "polarizing" effect, and to think in terms of "movement building" for basic social change.

The Port Huron Statement announced the theme of "bringing people out of isolation and into community"; as the enemy came to be seen as not "apathy" (or even the Dixiecrats) but "the system," the community to be organized took shape as a counter-community. For some, this meant the construal of community organizing in terms of concepts adopted from the anti-imperialist ideology of the Third World. Blacks and other ethnic groups were joined by youth, freaks, women, gays as would-be communities. Closer to home, the New Lefts call for "alternative institutions" drew on the same desire for satisfying personal and social relations visible in the various therapeutic, sensitivity-training, etc., businesses frequented by middle- and upper-income people, and in basic themes of the media- and commerce-structured manifestation of disaffiliation called the "youth culture." Rick Margolies spoke for many when he answered the question, "What do we do when we're white and affluent, in a world of starvation and colored revolution?" with a program that began with restructuring personal relationships through communal living:

> As we come together and restructure our relationships, we create the germ cells of a renewed social organism, growing from the ground up, into the institutions which sit heavy on our lives.[14]

Similarly, counter-institutions like "underground" papers could be seen as employing "political guerrilla tactics in the face of mass society" (or, in the jargon of the late Sixties, of "white, male Amerika") "in which enclaves

[14] "On Community Building," in Long, *op. cit.*, pp. 355, 358.

of freedom are created here and there in the midst of the orthodox way of life, to become centers of protest, and examples to others."[15] Weatherman's pitiful attempts at terrorism can be seen as the dead end to which the idea of confrontation of the system from a point outside it was driven in the absence of an oppositional social movement.

An alternate model for the Movement (essentially a revival of the Communist Party Program of the Thirties) was presented by the Progressive Labor Party, a Maoist split from the CP which began a conscious effort to capture SDS in 1965. Despite the difference in style of political pronouncements, the specific focus on "trade union work" among blue-collar workers, and the orientation towards a Marxist-Leninist Party, PL had enough in common with its opponent factions within the SDS national leadership to make possible a long struggle for supremacy within SDS, until the organizational fabric parted under the strain.

What united all factions of the left was the conception of their relationship to actual or fantasized communities as *organizers*—after the example of trade unionists and social workers—rather than as "fellow students" or workers with a particular understanding of a situation shared with others, and ideas of what to do about it. Despite the disagreement over the primary target for organizing—unemployed, blue-collar workers, white-collar workers, dropout youth—in each case the "community" was seen as a potential "constituency" (or, in PL's language, "base"). The radicals saw themselves as professional revolutionaries, a force so to speak outside of society, organizing those inside on their own behalf. Thus the activist played the part reserved in liberal theory for the state, a point not to be neglected in the attempt to understand the drift of the New Left from an orientation to liberal governmental reform to leninist-stalinist concepts of socialism.

### 4

Most bizarre, in rereading position papers of the Sixties, is the reference to students as a constituency to be organized. What this signified was a failure of the New Left, particularly in its later stages, to understand and come to terms

[15] Howard Zinn, "Marxism and the New Left," in Long. *op. cit.,* p. 67.

with its own social roots. Despite the emphasis given in the account above to community organizing, the left was first and foremost a phenomenon born in the groves of academe. Although activists dropped out of school to organize, for periods or for good (though many who left "for good" are returning as the Seventies begin), the base of the movement was the student population. The mass demonstrations were peopled by students and the mass actions of the New Left were student demonstrations.

The Berkeley revolt of 1964 is the exception that proves the rule. This first campus uprising was the only sustained majoritarian one, and the only one squarely on student issues. It originated with civil-rights activists who raised the demand for free speech when forbidden by university administrators to hand out leaflets on campus. Yet, as Mario Savio put it, while the struggle for civil rights provided a "reservoir of outrage at the wrongs done to other people . . . such action usually masks the venting, by a more acceptable channel, of outrage at the wrongs done to oneself." The Free Speech Movement quickly involved masses of students because it expressed not so much the political preoccupations of the radicals as general student dissatisfaction with the nature of the "multiversity." As one commentator put it,

> The students' basic demand is a demand to be . . . taken into account when decisions concerning their education and their life in the university community are being made. When one reviews the history of the Free Speech Movement, one discovers that each new wave of student response to the movement followed directly on some action by the administration which neglected to take the students, as human beings, in to account, and which openly reflected an attitude that the student body was a thing to be dealt with, to be manipulated.[16]

Of course, the problem was not in reality the *attitude* of the administration, but the fact of the new status of students, who are no more simply "human beings" than anyone else but people in a particular social position.

Throughout the Sixties, radicals generally succeeded in maintaining their demands as the apparent focus of university

[16] Jack Weinberg, "The Free Speech Movement and Civil Rights," cited in Teodori, *op. cit.*, p. 31.

activity. But despite the claims of activist leaders to have
"organized" student protests around political issues—racism,
the war—calling for student "service to the people," the
large-scale actions like those at Berkeley, Columbia, Harvard,
S.F. State drew their power from the student frustration
with the institutions through which *they* experienced the
society against whose most flagrant abominations this power
was focused. The growth of campus antiwar feeling attendant
on the abolition of student draft deferments is only an
obvious example, as is the fact that student involvement
typically came in response to the entrance of police on
campus, rather than to the original political issue. (As the
International Werewolf Conspiracy put it in a leaflet at
Berkeley once, *"The issue is not the issue."*) The largest
student action, the national strike of 1970, arose from the
combination of the public expansion of the war into Cambodia with the National Guard shooting of four white
students. (The killings at Jackson State were not much of
a new departure for the forces of law and order.) As a
popular tract of the time put it, white students turned out
to be "niggers" too, if privileged ones. And they didn't like
it.

For the very real reasons mentioned above, black students
could not only feel a moral call to struggle for the under-
privileged, they could feel themselves to be part of the
discriminated against. Thus their political activity with no
strain combined a "black community" orientation with attention to student problems. They fought for issues which
involved a real ameliorization of their position: both by
contesting discrimination and, in the academic version of
black power, by creating in "black studies" an academic
sphere in which simultaneously white racism could be fought
and careers made. (Here again there is a certain parallel
with the on-campus women's movement.) The different
positions of white and black students made sometimes for
odd effects: as at Columbia in 1968 when the blacks negotiated separately and successfully with the administration,
while white students continued the struggle into bloody
fighting against police—over Columbia's racism policies
(among other issues). The fundamental demand of the
whites—to escape proletarianization—could not be met;
black students had practical demands (in addition to the
vaguer ones for "freedom" and "power") which could be.

Aside from the blacks, other minority groups, and, later,

women, university reform was by and large the purlieu of those whom the radicals derogated as liberals, and in fact remained a realm of official committees and other forms of coöptation. For a student movement, the New Left was remarkably uninterested in theoretical work, and shared the low intellectual standards of American university life. Nothing remotely approaching the German "critical university"—the attempt to work out systematically a critique of an alternative to the content of bourgeois education, along with an attack on the official forms of education and structures of student life—developed in the American movement. Even in the brief period of the "student syndicalism" strategy in SDS, campaigning for student power was largely a tactic for getting students involved in confrontations with school and state authorities, which was to lead to student radicalization and transformation into movement militants and organizers.

Thus though the New Left represented the political stirrings of students as a social group in response to its problems in life, the understandings and modes of action developed by the movement's activists bore the most part only unconscious testimony to that fact. "Historical self-consciousness means the attempt to define ourselves as part of a developing social force, to develop concrete explanations about its origins, to project its growth and development, and to demonstrate and articulate its needs and values."[16] Such a self-consciousness was not worked out by the New Left. And, in practice, the growth of opposition to the status quo on the part of white students was expressed through attention to issues removed from their own immediate experience and interests—issues about the interests either of some other group in society or of society as a whole. Insofar as the university was an object of organized attack, it was typically with reference to the academy's direct services to capitalism, and its impact on other groups of social victims, rather than to the situation of the students themselves. This was both a strength and a weakness of the student movement. It encouraged the elaboration of a critique of society as such, dealing with features of the system which do not directly confront students, but which were hardly discussed outside of the student left. But it also obscured the nature

[16] Norman Fruchter, "SDS: In and Out of Context," *Liberation* 16:9 (February, 1972), p. 20.

of the social changes in response to the necessity of which the New Left had arisen, and therefore of the students' potential part in making these changes.

In part the abstract way in which social problems appeared to the student left was due to the circumstance that students are not involved in the production process but are only in training for it. Their problems are not yet the problems of the workers they will be, problems which can reveal the fundamental basis of the unpleasantness of life under capitalism in the social power relation between worker and boss. But there were more fundamental issues involved. It is not without significance that student-left activity in the Sixties was largely centered in the élite colleges, rather than in the junior and "community" institutions into which the lower ranks are channeled. For the latter, until recently at least, college may well have represented a way out of factory labor or Dad's store to white collar and administrative jobs; whereas for the élite students the end of college represented not entrance into a better life but the ending of a relative freedom and enjoyment that had been theirs from birth. Although he states it primarily in the terms in which it was experienced by the students, moral ones, Tom Hayden gave an adequate description of the experience in an article written in 1966: By the early Sixties, "the empty nature of existing vocational alternatives has pushed several hundreds of these students into community organizing. Working in poor communities is a concrete task in which the split between job and values can be healed."[17] It is also a task in which one escapes from being oneself a worker, a part of the larger "poor community."

Student radicals' understanding of their own activity did not simply derive from their own social position. "The ideas of the ruling class are, in every age, the ruling ideas"; they can be challenged by a true appreciation of social affairs only to the extent that class rule is challenged by a social force embodying the principle of a classless society. But the students' rejection of the social positions available to them found no echo in a nonstudent social movement capable of creating a new social system with other options. Since World War II, despite discontent with the limits set to struggle by the unions, and the activities of black caucuses and extra-union groups, proletarian discontent has remained

[17] "The Politics of the Movement," in Teodori, *op. cit.*, p. 207.

localized and thus always susceptible to defeat by employers
and/or union recapture of control. The poor proved to have
no power—with the exception of urban blacks who through
rioting could force some short-term concessions—at any
rate no power that was organizable for a general assault
on the status quo. Above all, the students themselves had no
power. This was of course the secret of their problem, the
essence of their proletarianization, and the basic fact against
which their rebellion was directed all along. But their
powerlessness had to be learned, through their inability to
influence the government or the Democratic Party, to stop
the war, or to organize anyone else to change the world.
In 1970 the student strike involved millions of people
throughout the country. Here the student movement reached
its peak, spreading through "community," junior, and technical colleges, and joined by high-school students across the
country. The impact on the government's activity was nil;
more importantly, perhaps, the strike found little echo
among the population as a whole. The students' plea to
workers for a generalization of the strike, through those
areas of production which really have the power to break
capitalist society and make a new one, went unanswered.
This high point, in terms of numbers, energy, and political
consciousness was also therefore the end of the Movement,
as from that moment dates its steady decline.

## 5

The experience of the New Left, as its desires overflowed the system's channels, led to a conscious rejection
of liberalism. And, despite the important role played by
"red diaper babies," the rejection of many political traits
of the Old Left was as central to the New Left project as
the rejection of liberal anticommunism. But as its understanding of its possibilities as a political movement developed from the goal of left pressure on the lib-lab forces
towards ideas of revolution, its organizational forms and
rhetoric showed a strong tendency to move back towards
those of the Old Left—towards the Party, centralism (democratic and otherwise), leadership as major preoccupation,
ideology, ortho—and heterodoxy, political exclusionism,
factional debate. The remains of the Old Left were waiting
with "theory" and organizational discipline for those who

ascribed the failure of their previous efforts to the lack of these two items.

The strength of the New Left is to be sought in the fact that the liberalism of its beginnings and the Leninism of its later stages represented nodes of failure. Within the history of bourgeois society, measured against the workers' movements and revolutions of the past, the New Left represents a historical phenomenon of minor significance. It is important only as the first politically conscious reaction to the stagnation of postwar capitalism, because it raised again fundamental questions about the nature of revolution, and demonstrated in its own history the relation of liberalism to the "Old Left" and the present-day limits of both.

"Liberalism" denotes neither a simple nor a static form of thought and action. As ever, the course of ideas is formed in the soil of the real social development, and the liberalism of the twentieth century is not that of the eighteenth. In capitalism's period of growth, the doctrine of *laissez-faire* served well in battle against both the traditional ruling groups and the dispossessed peasantry and "laboring poor." With the consolidation of the system, however, and the increasing polarization of classes between capital and labor, liberalism became the project of overcoming social contradictions through state regulation, without the abolition of the class relations which produce them. In the twentieth century this has meant the official recognition and integration of the labor movement with the framework of state interference in economic affairs.[18]

Despite the conflict of ideology, this program had a close affinity to that of the Old Left. Both of the main traditions falling under this rubric—Social Democracy and Bolshevism—failed to challenge the roots of capitalist class relations. The Social Democratic parties and trade unions developed, despite their origins in proletarian opposition to capital, as organs speaking for the working class within the evolving political and economic frameworks of capitalism. The steady

---

[18] A striking example of this development is the difference in their relation to the state, between the pre- and post-Depression unions in America, the AFL and the CIO. The former adopted *laissez-faire* for its own device; in the midst of the Depression its leaders declared their stand against state interference in labor-employer relations. The CIO, in contrast, developed almost as an arm of the New Deal government. The merger of the two unions only marked the triumph of the new principle.

formation, with capitalist development, of a proletarian mass systematically oppressed necessitated the development of forms of integration of this mass—whose interest is essentially opposed to that of their rulers—into the system dominated by those rulers. Political—parliamentary—representation allowed for the large-scale regulation and control of the conditions of exploitation; union organization developed procedures for the handling of grievances and the control of strikes.

Bolshevism represented and represents the adaptation of these forms of organization to the special conditions of backward areas. In Russia, the birthplace and classic example of Bolshevism, economic and social backwardness was tied to political backwardness (Czarist absolutism). Apparent on the horizon was a revolution which while advanced would share the basic character of the French Revolution and the German upheaval of 1848, in which the dynamic of capitalist development would free itself from a *regime* doubly *ancien*, by Europe's standards and Russia's. For the Russian Marxists, the situation was indeed a recapitulation of '48, only with every chance of success in the further evolved world of the 1900s. The socialist movement developing as an aspect of the growth of capitalism in Russia would have a double role to play: first as vanguard in the struggle for bourgeois democracy, then in the proletarian class struggle which would accelerate with the unleashed progress.

While the ultimate model for the organization of the Russian labor movement was the German Social Democracy and its associated trade unions, the bottleneck character of the Russian situation made a mass social democratic organization a practical impossibility. Bourgeois reformism was out of the question when the bourgeois revolution was still to come.

This was part of Lenin's accurate perception of the situation expounded in *What is to be Done?*. The spontaneous class struggle, he held (trade unionist in aims) was not adequate to the tasks imposed by the Russian situation. The accomplishment of revolution—first of all the bourgeois revolution—could not be entrusted to the workers but required an organization of professional revolutionists, able in their isolation from the daily struggle of capital and labor to keep their eyes on the main question: the bourgeois revolution which, by offering the Party a chance to seize power, would open the way to socialism.

The similarities and contrasts between Social Democracy and Bolshevism are equally significant. In the one case, reform, in the other revolution. But they shared the basic idea that Socialism was to be achieved through control of the state by the party which, as the guardian of Marxist theory, was the true representative of the workers (or, as the doctrine had to be expanded under the press of circumstances, the workers and peasants). This idea was fleshed both in the reformist practice of Social Democracy and in the revolutionary activity of Lenin's party. The difference between them stemmed not from varying conceptions of the relation of the proletariat to socialism but from the difference between the socio-political contexts of Russia and the West, which in both cases favored a hierarchical party structure presaging the form of the state-run society to be created. Hence it was natural—despite the gulf which otherwise opened between the two leaders—for Lenin to quote Kautsky with approbation in his attack on "spontaneity." He found "profoundly true and important" Kautsky's opinion that while

> . . . socialist consciousness appears to be a necessary and direct result of the proletarian class struggle . . . this is absolutely untrue. . . . Modern socialist consciousness can arise only on the basis of profound scientific knowledge. . . . The vehicle of science is not the proletariat, but the bourgeois *intelligentsia*.[19]

Lenin summed up in his own memorable words:

> . . . *there could not yet be* social democratic consciousness among the workers. This consciousness could only be brought to them from without. The history of all countries shows that the working class, exclusively by its own efforts, is able to develop only trade union consciousness. . . . The theory of socialism, however, grew out of the . . . theories that were elaborated by the . . . intellectuals.[20]

But whereas in Germany the ideology of the Party as carrier of the consciousness "of" the class suited an organization

---

[19] Cited in *What is to be Done?* in Lenin, *Selected Works,* Vol. I, (International Publishers, 1967), p. 129.
[20] *Ibid*. This, ironically, only two years before the unorganized revolutionary upsurge of 1905, which brought the formation of the first soviets.

which acted in fact as the liberal, progressive force in German capitalism, in Russia the vanguard concept expressed an historical movement towards the very replacement of the bourgeoisie by the Party.

Ideology, because the supposition that revolutionary consciousness is impossible except as incarnated in the controlling leadership of intellectuals organized in the Party, proved false in Germany and Russia alike, as well as in all the areas in which the capitalist crisis of 1913–1920 drove workers to revolt. The German revolution, which, developing in fact in opposition to the Social Democratic Party, created its own form of organization in the workers' councils directing the factory occupations, only destroyed itself when it handed power back to the Party. In Russia, the professional revolutionists of the Bolshevik Party rose to power through *their* support of the *masses'* demands. If the correct Marxist-Leninist line in 1917 was "All power to the soviets!" it was only because the workers and soldiers had already created soviets and factory committees. The Bolshevik seizure of power, in the absence of successful proletarian revolution in the West, was not the completion of the revolutionary process but the beginning of its end. The substitution of a *coup d'état,* even by socialists and even on the basis of workers' support, for the direct seizure and administration of the means of production by the workers themselves, meant inevitably the doom of the effective power of the soviets and the replacement of the dictatorship of by a dictatorship over the proletariat.

That the revolutionary character of the Bolshevik party was due to its situation in a backward area, and not to the strength of the revolutionary will, was shown clearly by the fate of the Communist parties organized in Western Europe under the aegis of the Third International. Their parliamentarism and reformism resulted not only from their subjection to the needs of Soviet foreign policy but also from their adaption to conditions of a revived capitalism—necessary for organizations which want to play a real political role under such conditions.[21] Today, the mass Com-

---

[21] In the case of Germany, where the continuing crisis was resolved only by fascism and the war, the success of this adaptation was not so striking; something forgotten by those who quote Lenin's polemic against *Left-wing Communism, an Infantile Disorder* as the last word on revolutionary strategy.

munist parties and unions in Italy and France have the place of the social democratic organizations of former times; the "mature" tactics of Leninism-for-the-West have been excellently represented by the systematic sabotage of the May, 1968 upheaval by the French CP. The failure of the Old Left organizations to develop in the USA during and after the Great Depression may be traced indeed to the fact that the Democratic government and the trade unions filled the role played in Europe by "socialist" workers' organizations. It is just the latters' place, with modifications stemming from the peculiarities of US history, which was taken by those forces proud to call themselves "liberal."

## 6

In this historical light, the task conceived by those fragments of the New Left who dream of a revival of revolutionary Leninism in the developed countries acquires a clearer (if dismal) character. It is not unrelated to the liberal beginnings of the Movement. The basis for this tendency was to be found all along, in the centrality of the organizer model of left activity. The professional revolutionist is after all only a bureaucrat or social worker for a state apparatus that has yet to come into existence.

The transmutation of "liberals" into Leninist "revolutionaries" is the result of more than the ideological development of some new leftists. The continuing strength of liberalism as a program derives from capitalism's constant tendency to "rationalization." This is an aspect of the nature of capitalist development, which expresses itself both in economic organization (concentration and centralization of capital, search for efficiency within production) and in the necessity of overcoming a tendency towards social instability, in periods when the status quo no longer meets the need imposed on the system by its own logic. The economic and social system built by the Bolsheviks in Russia, in which the Party-State takes the place of the capitalist class as a whole, is the logical endpoint of the trend to concentration of capital and government interference in the economy which define the "mixed economy" of the present-day West. From this point of view the revival of Leninism (and—somewhat surprisingly, though logically enough—of Stalinism) may turn out to represent a chafing at the limitations placed on further evolution towards a state-run system by the representatives of the still fundamental private-property character of the economy. It is thus related to the myth of the technocratic class, whose approach to power is alternatively welcomed (e.g., by J. K. Galbraith) or feared (see N. Chomsky and L. Mumford).

At any rate the bolshevist idea may well appeal to members of a frustrated intelligentsia, hardly approaching power in fact, who see before them the struggles and successes of the intelligentsia of the Third World for whom nationalist movements controlled by Leninist parties are an avenue to power. What left-leaning Harvard graduate student in government could resist the image of the Party cadre, educating the people, organizing them, eventually formulating and overseeing the implementation of the plan which will lead to rapid industrial development, etc? There is a certain parallelism here with Black Power leaders' frequent identification with the masters of emerging African and Asian states. The Black Panther Party, for instance, formed itself not merely after a Bolshevik pattern but directly on the model of a governmental power, with Ministers of Justice, Information, Foreign Affairs, etc., and a military structure of command.[22]

*The identification of the goals* of the American left with those of nationalist and statist movements in the underdeveloped world, itself a reflection of the weakness of the radical movement in the US, revived the Leninist conception of

[22] The attempt of blacks to reproduce in America political forms developed in unindustrialized areas has of course a somewhat different basis than the whites' attempt. Racial discrimination, particularly in the form of the confinement of masses of blacks to the reserve army of the unemployed, seems to be ineradicable within the confines of American capitalism. At the same time, without the activity of a proletarian left cutting across racial lines, no solutions are possible for the blacks except within those confines. Caught on the horns of this dilemma, the black movement has continually swung between integrationist and separatist poles of attraction. In this circumstance is to be found the explanation for the seemingly paradoxical combination, in a group like the Black Panthers, of a reformist social-work practice and a revolutionary Leninist phraseology. Despite the similarities of the blacks' position to that of a colonized "people," the idea of "black national liberation" has no practical significance whatsoever. Black bolshevism can only mean either failure—failure likely to involve systematic and bloody persecution—or else a cover-up for more profitable activities.

the world-wide unity of anti-imperialist forces. Just as in Russia, the theory ran, socialism could be established in an overwhelmingly peasant country due to the control of the state by the Communist Party, representative of the workers, so the anti-colonial movements would combine with the labor movements of the West to make the world revolution, thanks to the unifying guidance exercised by the Russian party-controlled International. The experiences of the last fifty years should have been enough to dispel this myth from leftist minds, national liberation has proved to mean either neocolonialism or else exploitation of the masses of the Third World by state capitalist masters, generally involving in either case the reincorporation (to varying degrees) of the "liberated" countries into new empires, the big powers, East and West, dividing the spoils. Even the most neutralist of the new nations (i.e., those which seek to play the various masters of the world off against each other) have no choice but to adapt themselves to the exigencies of the world market controlled by the industrially advanced countries.

At this point, the prospect of total statification of American capitalism is a dim one. There is no faction of the bourgeoisie with access to political power not dedicated to the preservation of the private corporate system. And the working class has a healthy antipathy to "communism" of the Russian (Chinese, Cuban, etc.) type, which they rightly identify as totalitarian control over the individual's existence (despite the fact that, due to their noncomprehension of the circumstance that individuals are members of classes, their "anticommunism" takes the crazy form of support for the capitalist system). Even among their fellow students, the new Leninists have been unable to attract more than a handful.

The New Left came into existence because what one might call Old Left liberalism is no longer feasible. The program of the Old Left is also scoring no great success. While the full statification of American capital cannot be ruled out as an option which the bourgeoisie might choose at the sacrifice of their private property interests in order to avoid economic collapse and the threat of revolution from below, at the moment the more significant—as well as only real revolutionary—avenue visible in the future of capitalism is that of a truly communist revolution, organized and controlled by the working class itself. The New Left has pointed to a possible renewal of activity by this specter. It is for us now more crucial than ever to get beyond the ideologies of the past, in which the New Left was by and large trapped, to an understanding of what such a revolution will require and mean.

## 7

The uniqueness of capitalism in the history of human society lies in its development of social integration to a point where the overcoming of the opposition of individual (or small group) to social interests becomes possible. The basis of any society is the production (and distribution) of all the goods that satisfy its members' wants—from food and clothing and material means of production themselves to the arts and the systems of ideas with which societies attempt to understand themselves and maintain belief in the worthiness of their ways of life. In precapitalist societies, most of this work was carried out on an individual or narrowly local basis. Though the steady growth of cities as a form of civilized existence made for the development of a division between the labor of the town and that of the country, most people worked directly for themselves, their families, their village communities, or their immediate overlords. Hunters, farmers, artisans made many of their own tools; families provided their own homes, clothes, and nourishment; not only tribute but trade moved the products of specialized labor only for the few.

Capitalism has changed all that. The transformation of peasant or freehold agricultural production into large-scale farming by wage-labor for the market and the development of mass-production industry have bound the producers economically—and so socially—not only to those who hold social power but to each other. This is true for both aspects of the unity of production–distribution. An auto worker labors with thousand of others in the manufacture of a common product; and this product is as little for his own or his colleague's specific use as is the bread they eat produced by them. Common labor at the point of production is but the cell-form of a system of common production by all the workers in society for each other.

At the same time, this social system of production developed historically within a structure of private ownership and control of the means and thereby the results of production. Labor took on the form of wage-labor; people produce for each other only by producing for the capitalists from whom they must then buy back their own products. Thus social production was created in capitalism at the expense of the producers who can work for themselves—each other—only by working for the masters of the process.

The needs of the producers can be met, due to this peculiar system of social production under private control, only within limits set by the mechanism of the market, which includes and is based on their submission to the labor market. The private aspect of the system dominates the communal. Instead of being controlled consciously by the joint producers, production is controlled by the market, and the market by the competitive need of individual capitalist firms to accumulate. Thus arise all the anomalies, ridiculous and tragic, characteristic of this system: from the careful designing of light bulbs that burn out faster to the "overproduction" of food while millions starve. Inevitably, such a system leads to conflicts between the needs of the producers and the capacity of the system to satisfy them, its periods of apparent success resolving only in crises throwing millions out of work or into war.

It is no surprise, then, that, from its origins, opposition to capitalism developed as an integral part of capitalist society. From the beginning this has been a class society in which the interests of the class of producers, production for the "cooperative commonwealth," and those of the class of owners and exploiters, the amassing of profit and the expansion of their individual spheres of power, came constantly (though sometimes more clearly than at others) into opposition to each other. As Marx was perhaps the first to stress, it is this rather than the activities of theoreticians and politicians which accounts for the existence of the working-class movement.

Revolutionary working-class activity has not been the creation of "organizers" either *ex nihilo* or by the infusion of a "good political line" into the workers' "spontaneous" activity. Rather, an examination of past movements reveals a history of radical practice as working-class transcendence of workaday militance in the face of social crisis conditions which transform reformist and integrative movements willy-nilly into revolutionary ones. Reformism is not a doctrine foisted on the workers by bad leaders, but a product of the workers' willingness to be satisfied with the gains obtainable in periods of capitalist prosperity. Similarly, the basis of revolutionary activity is the system's inability to achieve permanent stability, its tendency thus to create situations in which the institutions—unions, political parties —that under "normal" conditions channel and contain working-class dissatisfactions can no longer function. In such situations the producers are forced to find new forms of activity in their struggle against capital.

Just as the origin of proletarian revolt lies in the workers' experience of capitalism's incapacity to meet their desires, the organizational forms of revolt are developed out of social structures of the system. The fact is that the workers are (as we have seen) already and at all times organized: in the factories, offices, schools, neighborhoods, and in the interconnections between all of these established by the capitalist production system itself. From this point of view, the problem of the organization of communist revolution is that of the workers' taking the existing network of social interdependency into their own hands, while re-organising it according to their needs.[23]

To contrast "spontaneity" with organization puts the problem of the forms of revolt in a misleading way. Any attempt of workers to take any degree of social power demands— and has always produced—varying degrees of organization on local and broader levels. What "spontaneity" has been used to refer to is not absence of organization but independence of the control of political groups. In this regard, what is striking if we look at history is the minimal role played by the political groups of the Old Left in the structuring of revolutionary struggle and the extent to which they have served in fact as brakes on the workers' efforts.

Organization is the organization of activity and so grows out of and reflects its needs. Activity pursued within the framework of class society requires for effectiveness the hierarchical structure and business behavior that capitalism calls for; but revolutionary action calls on different principles. Here what is crucial is people's discovery of their power, so systematically denied by the functioning of the system, to control and organize their own activities. On the basis of this principle of workers' "self-organization" the reality of class can develop through action.

---

[23] For an example of what this would mean in practice, see "The Mass Strike in France," this volume.

Tactics can be worked out only in terms of the specific shapes taken on by the struggle in specific situations, and are nothing to be determined by a central committee, although interchange of experiences between people in different areas is so important as to be essential. The same goes for strategy; the cleverest strategies "for the working class" mean nothing if they do not correspond to needs felt by people, arising through their own activity. It should be clear that what is at issue here is not "centralism versus decentralism" but rather the relation between local groups and (various) center(s). What is crucial is, on the one hand, the freedom of the local groups to devise actions responsive to their situations and, of the other, strict control of all supra-local levels of organization by the locals, so that the center is only a means to their coordination and joint action. Such centralism—coordination of local struggles— becomes possible as it becomes necessary, i.e., as the bourg-eoisie is confronted as on a large scale, is confronted as a class. For this means that the various groups of producers in struggle are fighting on a common basis, a situation which calls for the extension of the workers' organization on their workplace to that of several workplaces together, and so on up. It is in this way that the organization of struggle against capitalism can lead to the organization of a new society to replace it.

As the thought of the Party (or its Chairman) is no sub-stitute for the masses' own understanding of the situations they face, neither is its organization a substitute for theirs. While the class of producers derives its revolutionary po-tential from its constitution on the basis of an objectively given shared social function and experience, a political party is (to use Gramsci's words) a voluntary organization, a group of people who share a common program. Groups of revolutionaries, of different persuasions, have their own prob-lems of organization—different ones at different times. Al-though they may be related to the organizational needs of the class as a whole, it is important to recognize the distinction between the class and the political groupings within it (at best). A revolutionary group may feel, as leninists do, that *their* holding of power is crucial to the building of socialism. But it ought to be kept clear that the power of the Party is not the power of the masses them-selves, however representative of the latter the former may be at one time or another. (This was recognized by the

Russian Bolsheviks when they banned all political groupings except their own; for the party voted in could be voted out, while other parties were around.) If the workers are still willing to let some special group monopolize power and make decisions for them, this means that socialism is just not on the agenda.

A group which wishes for the seizure of power by the class of which it is a part has a different problem: that of working within its class—where its members work and live —through propaganda and action to help ensure that no social stratum or political group is allowed to give orders to it. (This involves, obviously, struggle against leninism in all its varieties.) A prime aim for such groups must be education: achievement and propagation of whatever they can understand of the nature of capitalism and the possibilities for socialism in our time; collection and circulation of information about the struggle as it unfolds on local, national, and international levels. But revolutionary theory (like all theory) serves action: radical consciousness means an understanding of capitalism as a system which can be challenged. Overcoming the passivity which allows the perpetuation of our current fate, and which might allow capitalism's replacement by a totalitarian party-state, demands from radicals not "organizing the masses" but participating imaginatively in the development of a sense of autonomous power and activity among those with whom we work and live.

## 8

Student passivity and the attendant collapse of the New Left organizations may be said to express the practical acceptance by students as a group of their place in society. This has happened at a time when the proletarianization of students and college-degree-holders has taken on a particularly grim tone. The need to hustle for grades and degrees has been heightened by the declining proportion of degree-demanding jobs to the numbers of certified. The gradual development of economic crisis conditions has affected students by limiting the number of jobs both in private industry and in the state sector, and by cutting down on funds available to schools for scholarships and research grants.

This situation has raised the specter of "a new kind of student protest," exemplified by the strike at Antioch College

in the spring of 1973. A long strike by cafeteria employees
was followed by a closure of the school for well over a
month as "two hundred to 300 students, many from poor
or working-class families, struck . . . in an attempt to gain
legal guarantees from the college that loans, grants, jobs,
and other financial help would not be cut during their five
years at school."[24] Such phenomena as the formation at
various campuses of unions by graduate student teaching
assistants and junior faculty reflects the same situation as
the discovery by striking Philadelphia public school teachers
that their status as "profesionals" meant less under current
economic conditions than what they share with the other
groups of workers who threatened a general strike in their
support.

Thus the conditions which may be expected to lead to a
rise in working-class activity generally will probably meet
with participation by students and college graduates in whatever left movement develops. In the context of a workers'
movement, the role of students in capitalist society and in
the struggle against it will become clearer. The students
cannot "serve" the workers, who alone by taking over their
workplaces and living areas can liberate themselves. On the
other hand, only a communist movement will give "student
power," or the goal of student/staff control over the school,
any meaning; though this will require the dissolution of the
forms of education which exist and their replacement by
forms—involving, for instance, the end of the distinction
between "worker" and "student"—appropriate to a society
in which "the free development of each is the condition of
the free development of all." Already the student movements of May, 1968 in France and of the last four years
in Italy have pointed to the possibility of the interaction of
workers and workers-to-be in common struggle. This possibility can only be strengthened as the social realities confronting students and workers, and the ties of common
interest between them, continue to be drummed into the
heads of both groups by the pressure of facts. Ultimately
the real significance of the New Left lies in this: in the
extent to which we utilize the experiences of the movement
in the 1960s to make the most revolutionary use possible of
the years of social crisis that lie ahead.

July, 1973

[24] *New York Times,* May 29, 1973.